ROSE ELLIOT'S
Vegetarian
C O O K E R Y

ROSE ELLIOT'S
Vegetarian
C O O K E R Y

TED SMART

A TED SMART Publication 1995
First published in 1988 by
William Collins Sons & Co., Ltd
Reprinted 1991, 1992, 1993 by HarperCollins*Publishers*

ISBN 0 583 32156-9

Typeset in Great Britain by Rowland Phototypesetting Ltd,
Bury St Edmunds, Suffolk
Colour reproduction by Bright Arts, Hong Kong
Printed and bound by New Interlitho S.p.A., Italy

ACKNOWLEDGEMENTS

I would like to express my warmest appreciation to all the people who have helped to create this book. To my agent, Vivienne Schuster, and to Joan Clibbon and Robin Wood of Collins, for giving me the opportunity to write it and for their care and support throughout the project. A very special 'thank you' to my text editor, Helen Dore, for sharing completely my aspirations for the book and helping me to realise them, and for generously sharing many delicious recipe ideas; also to Felicity Jackson, for all her help with the layouts and the practical execution of the book; to Barbara Dixon, my editor, for her hours of hard work on the manuscript and for checking many elusive details; to Janet James, Art Director, for understanding how I wanted the book to look, and all her creative and beautiful ideas, and to Jillian Haines, for her hard work and flair in realising these; to Nick Carman, too, for his creativity and for his superb photographs and for making the photographic sessions such a delight (and a special thank you to Nick's assistant, Edward Allwright, for doing numerous jobs, usually all at once, and for making such excellent coffee); to the home economists, Judy Bugg and Janice Murfitt, for making the food look and taste so good (and special thanks to Judy for hours spent finding unusual and out-of-season foods for the Ingredients section); and my grateful thanks to D. MacLean of Dornock Farm, Crieff, for his help and information for the potatoes section of the book; to my daughters Margaret and Claire for help with recipe testing and to my husband Robert and daughter Katy for understanding and support throughout the project.

Foreword

'Are you writing a coffee-table book or one that people actually use?', a friend asked me when I was describing some of the photography which we had been doing for this book.

I said that I hoped that it would be very much a practical book, but beautiful too; a joy to handle and to look at, but at the same time a practical reference book when identifying ingredients in the market or shop, or following a recipe at the kitchen stove.

A recipe book is written to be used; and I hope that *Vegetarian Cookery* may be the starting-point of many good times both when shopping and cooking, and of memorable meals. I particularly hope that if you're a non-vegetarian, you'll feel welcomed into this book; there's no qualification needed, other than the desire to try something new, and I hope you'll find something you enjoy.

Happy cooking and eating!

Contents

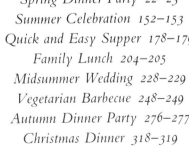

Notes on Measurements

Both metric and Imperial measurements are given throughout this book. As long as you keep to one set of measurements or the other in a recipe you should have no problems.

With liquids I have used fluid ounces as the Imperial equivalent to millilitres, taking 300 ml/10 fl oz as a ½-pint measure, 400 ml/15 fl oz as ¾-pint measure and 600 ml/20 fl oz as 1 pint. Measure liquids with a plastic measuring jug marked in millilitres, pints and fluid ounces.

The eggs used are free-range and always standard, size 3.

Note for Australian/New Zealand users

I should like to take this opportunity to say how pleased I am that this book will be available in Australia and New Zealand, and to extend a warm welcome to all readers in those countries. I believe that you will be able to obtain most of the ingredients without difficulty, and I do hope that you will enjoy the recipes. I think that you should find the measurements straightforward, but please note that British standard tablespoons and teaspoons, 15 ml and 5 ml respectively, have been used in the recipes, and are level unless otherwise stated. The Australian/NZ tablespoon holds 20 ml. A teaspoon is standard to all three countries.

At the time of this book going to press, it has been recommended by the Ministry of Agriculture, Fisheries and Food in the UK that clingfilm should not be used in microwave cooking, as it has been found that some of the plasticiser di-2-ethyhexledipate (DEHA) used to soften clingfilm can migrate into the food during cooking.

Oven Temperature Chart

The oven temperatures given throughout this book are for a conventional oven. Fan assisted (circofan or circotherm) ovens generally require a reduction in temperature and cooking time, and you should refer to the oven handbook.

Temperature	Centigrade (C)	Fahrenheit (F)	Gas Mark
	70	150	
	80	175	
	100	200	
Very cool	110	225	¼
	120	250	½
	140	275	1
Cool	150	300	2
Warm	170	325	3
Moderate	180	350	4
Fairly hot	190	375	5
	200	400	6
Hot	220	425	7
	230	450	8
Very hot	250	500	9

Measurement Equivalents

Metric	Imperial	Metric	Imperial
Grammes (g)	Ounces (oz)	Millilitres (ml)	Fluid Ounces (fl oz)
15	½	25	1
25	1	50	2
40	1½	75	3
50	2	125	4
65	2½	150	5 (¼ pint)
75	3	175	6
100	4 (¼ pound)	200	7
150	5	225	8
175	6	250	9
200	7	300	10 (½ pint)
225	8 (½ pound)	325	11
250	9	350	12
300	10	375	13
325	11	450	15 (¾ pint)
350	12 (¾ pound)	475	16
375	13	500	17
400	14	600	20 (1 pint)
425	15		
450	16 (1 pound)		

Measurement Equivalents for Baking Tins

Millimetres (mm)	Inches
3	⅛
5	¼
Centimetres (cm)	Inches
1	½
2	¾
2.5	1
3	1½
5	2
6	2½
8	3
9	3½
10	4
13	5
15	6
18	7
20	8
22	8½
23	9
24	9½
25	10
28	11
30	12
32	12½
33	13
35	14
37.5	15
40	16

Introduction

This book has grown out of over twenty years of cooking vegetarian food, and originating, testing and also demonstrating vegetarian recipes. During that time I have had the delight of seeing the great increase in interest in this style of cooking, with a dramatic and continuing swing towards vegetarianism, and many people becoming 'demi-veg', if not changing completely.

I like to think that vegetarian cookery has now become a cuisine in its own right. That cuisine embraces non-meat and non-fish dishes from all over the world, as well as wholefood, macrobiotic and its own idiosyncratic recipes. It happily embraces ingredients as different as tofu and wholewheat pasta, tempeh and rice noodles, Indian spices and sea vegetables, pulses and exotic fruits. The only qualification is that fish and other animals are not used. The result is a lively, colourful, eclectic mix which I hope I have represented here.

One of the delights of being involved with cookery is that it is a living art; novel ingredients, new recipes, a dash of herbs here, a sprinkling of spice there, an unfamiliar ingredient, spark off fresh ideas, inspire creativity. . . . Ideas are constantly changing and evolving, as are our shopping and eating habits.

In writing this book, my aim has been to provide the information, recipes and techniques needed in vegetarian cookery, both for those who are new to it, and for more experienced cooks who want to try something different. For those strict vegetarians, vegans, I have also included many recipes and these are marked with a V, together with vegan versions of standard recipes where possible. There is every reason for vegan food to be as exciting and delicious as vegetarian food.

The initial inspiration for the book was, for me, as is so often the case for cooks, the marketplace. Week after week, as I did my shopping, I noticed the increasing range of wonderful, often weird and wonderful, ingredients, particularly fruit, vegetables, nuts, beans, herbs and spices.

These were a godsend to vegetarian cookery, rooted as it is so deeply in the raw ingredients, and dependent on herbs and spices for flavouring. What was needed was information on identifying them, storing, preparing and cooking them. . . . And so the Ingredients section of this book was born. This led on naturally to the Recipe section, with more detailed ways of using the ingredients.

Although I hope this book will be used as a reference book, I decided to put comments, tips and techniques in the margins, by the appropriate recipe, rather than in a separate chapter. This way they have relevance and immediacy, and too much formality is avoided. I do hope you will find the arrangement good to use.

The book begins with information on the nutritional side of vegetarian and vegan cookery, and how to plan meals which are well-balanced, healthy and nourishing, as well as pleasant to eat. This theme of meal-planning is continued throughout the book, both in the Special Menu spreads, which appear at intervals throughout, and in the menus which, taking my publisher at his word, I've frequently included in the margins! I hope you'll enjoy them, and, indeed, the whole book.

Nutrition

In vegetarian eating, meat, fish and poultry are replaced by fresh-tasting meals based on vegetables and herbs, grains and pasta, dried beans and lentils, fresh fruits and nuts, with or without dairy produce. Many people are enjoying the benefits of eating like this some of the time, while continuing to eat meat and fish occasionally: these are the demi-vegetarians. Others are switching completely to vegetarianism, and some are going still further, excluding all dairy produce, and becoming vegans. Any of these ways of eating can supply all the nutrients needed for vibrant good health. In fact many people find their health improves when they become vegetarians. The key lies in planning meals on a good variety of fresh, unprocessed foods.

Eating for health

Studies of people in different parts of the world have shown that those who eat mainly unrefined foods, high in fibre, low in sugar and fat, do not succumb to illnesses like high blood pressure, heart disease, diverticulitis, cancer of the bowel and diabetes. Experts now agree that a healthy diet is one which is high in fibre and low in fat, sugar and salt. This was the kind of food which was commonly eaten in Britain before industrialization and mass food production. Contrary to popular opinion, meat was not eaten in large quantities by the majority of the population for whom cereals and vegetables were staples. Vegetarian eating, with its emphasis on cereals, pulses and vegetables, is not therefore as far removed from what our forebears ate as is sometimes thought, and is naturally high-fibre, low-fat and low-sugar.

Protein

Part of every body cell, protein is essential for healthy growth and repair of cells, for reproduction and protection against infection. Daily requirements are, however, small and there is no problem in getting enough protein on a vegetarian or vegan diet. Main sources of protein for vegetarians are:
- □ *Dairy* cheese, milk and milk products such as yogurt; eggs
- □ *Nuts and seeds* such as almonds, cashew nuts, hazelnuts, brazil nuts, walnuts, pine nuts, pecan nuts and peanuts; sunflower seeds, sesame seeds and pumpkin seeds
- □ *Pulses* dried peas, beans and lentils, including soya beans and products
- □ *Cereals and their products* such as rice, oatmeal, wholewheat flour, pasta

Complementary proteins

Protein consists of about twenty-two parts, called amino-acids. Eight of these are specially important, because they cannot be manufactured by the body. These are called the essential amino-acids. Some foods, such as eggs and oatmeal, contain these in nearly the right proportions for the body to use straight away. Other foods, particularly dried beans and lentils and most cereals, do not have them in such convenient proportions. But this doesn't matter, because during digestion the amino-acids from all the foods eaten at the same meal get mixed up and the body puts them together again in the right proportions. So even if a protein doesn't contain exactly the right amino-acid balance, the chances are that the shortfall will be supplied by something else eaten at the same meal – such as potato, a green vegetable, or milk in a cup of tea or coffee.

Proteins from the four groups listed above complement each other so you can make more protein available to yourself by eating foods from two or more of the groups at the same meal, such as lentil soup with a wholewheat roll. This is not difficult, but even if you don't mix proteins like this, you are not likely to go short of protein unless you are living on a near-starvation diet.

Carbohydrate

Carbohydrates are used in the body for energy. They are found in starches and sugars which are present in grains, flour and products made from these, such as bread, biscuits and cakes; and in sugar, honey, jams and preserves. Potatoes are also a good source, while most vegetables (especially pulses), milk and nuts contain small amounts. Many carbohydrates, in their natural, unrefined state, also contain fibre. This means that the body can draw the sugar out of the fibre gradually, as it passes through the digestive tract, resulting in a steady stream of energy.

Fat facts

Fats and oils have been an essential ingredient throughout history – the Egyptians even extracted oil from radishes. There are two sources of fat: animals and plants. The only animal fats which are used in a vegetarian diet are those found in egg yolks or milk or its products such as cream, butter and cheese. The rest of the fats are of plant origin and include a range of oils and products made from these, namely margarine and hard vegetable fats. Fats can be saturated, unsaturated or polyunsaturated, depending on their chemical structure.

Saturated fats are the ones which are solid at room-temperature. Chemically, all their 'bonds' have been filled with hydrogen atoms. Most animal fats are saturated and are thought more likely to raise the level of fats in the blood. Unsaturated fats are thick, but not solid, at room temperature. These fats have room for a few more hydrogen atoms. Unsaturated fats are thought to have a neutral effect on the level of fat in the blood: they do not lower it, but neither do they raise it. Olive oil is an example of an unsaturated fat, and countries where this is the main fat used, such as Italy and Spain, have a much lower incidence of heart disease than countries where saturated fats are used.

Polyunsaturated fats are completely liquid at room temperature. These could take many more hydrogen atoms. Many vegetable oils, including safflower, sunflower, corn and soya, are polyunsaturated and thought to help to lower the amount of fat in the blood. Polyunsaturated fats can be made more solid, and similar to, but not chemically the same as, saturated fats, by filling up the spare bonds with hydrogen. This process is called hydrogenation and is used in the manufacture of margarines

The sugar question

Refined sugar is an energy food – but that is all it is. It does not supply fibre, to regulate the pace at which the body absorbs it, neither does it contain any vitamins or minerals. It is 'empty calories'. Real barbados sugar – the sticky, molasses type – does contain some minerals, vitamins and trace elements. Honey does not contain fibre, but its sugar is mainly in a form which is slowly absorbed by the body. All forms of sweetening, honey included, are best used with discretion. Make sure that any sugar you eat is through positive choice, such as the occasional favourite pudding, rather than through unquestioned habit, such as sprinkling it unthinkingly into tea or coffee or over breakfast cereal. The majority of the recipes in this book are low in sugar, but some 'sweet indulgences' are included for the occasional treat, which in my opinion does no harm at all – indeed, is to be recommended, so you don't get too rigid and fanatical – if you eat healthily most of the time.

and hard vegetable fats. However, fats which have been hardened in this way may be more harmful to the body than ones which are naturally saturated.

The unsaturated fats are generally considered to be healthiest, although this is a complicated issue, and there are many experts (and I agree with them) who consider that the naturalness of butter makes it preferable to margarine which is a processed food. However, most authorities agree that the important thing is to reduce our total fat intake. Although a small amount of fat is needed for health, most people in developed countries eat too much fat and of the type which the body does not require. Much of this may be in the form of 'hidden fat' in foods like pies, crisps, biscuits, chocolate and cakes. Some foods, such as milk, can be confusing, because although the percentage of fat is low, they are eaten in relatively large quantities, and the fat intake increases. The kind of fat which the body does need is found in cold-pressed unsaturated oils, sunflower seeds and margarines marked 'lineolic-cis'. Apart from these, I think the important thing is to be aware of the amount of fat you're eating and to reduce it where you'll miss it least. Cereal and whole-grain dishes, pasta, pulses, fruit and vegetables are all low in fat, and including generous quantities of these in your meals will automatically reduce the amount of fat you eat.

Fibre

Fibre is found only in fruit and vegetable products; it is the wood, cellulose and gums which make up their structure. Dairy produce does not contain fibre, nor do meat and fish, although they have a chewy texture. Fibre is needed to enable the digestive system to function effectively and is therefore essential for good health. A typical vegetarian diet is naturally high in fibre. Good sources are peas and beans (both dried and fresh), most vegetables, especially cabbage, carrots, jacket potatoes, spinach and sweetcorn; oats and other whole-grain cereals, including products made from them such as wholewheat bread; dried fruits, especially apricots; fresh fruits, especially apples, bananas, blackberries and raspberries. Try to include at least one good source of fibre at every meal.

Minerals and trace elements

Iron

Iron is essential for making red blood cells, and a lack of iron in the diet can lead to anaemia. This is one of the nutrients which needs watching although a properly-balanced vegetarian diet can provide sufficient. Iron is found in all pulses, lentils and soya beans being particularly rich; in whole grains and their products such as wholewheat bread and pasta; nuts and seeds, especially pistachios, pumpkin and sesame seeds; dark green leafy vegetables and dried fruits, of which apricots and prunes (also prune juice) are particularly good sources. Seaweeds are also rich sources, as are brewer's yeast, molasses, wheatgerm and egg yolk.

Zinc

An important trace element, zinc is essential for healthy growth and healing, for sexual maturity and reproduction and the digestion of protein and carbohydrate. A shortage of zinc often manifests as white flecks on the fingernails, and sometimes in skin problems. There also seems to be evidence of a link between a shortage of zinc and the 'slimmers'' diseases anorexia nervosa and bulimia. Whole grains appear to be good sources of zinc, as do pulses, but these all contain a substance called phytic acid which can bind the zinc so that we cannot absorb it all. It is not known to what extent this happens, and there is evidence that the body quickly adapts to the phytic acid when whole grains are eaten regularly. Also,

when bread is made with yeast, the proving process appears to inhibit the phytic acid. Adding some vitamin C to the dough also helps. Best sources of zinc for vegetarians and vegans are wheatgerm, oatmeal, peanuts and brewer's yeast, and, for those eating dairy produce, cheese and skimmed milk. Dried figs are a good source, as are nuts and seeds (especially sesame seeds and pumpkin seeds), sweetcorn and peas. Small but useful amounts are found in most green and yellow fruit and vegetables, such as spinach, asparagus and mango.

Calcium

Calcium is essential for the healthy formation of bones and teeth, and for normal functioning of bones, nerves, muscles and heart. Best sources are cheese, milk and milk products. Other good sources are pulses, especially soya beans and flour; eggs; dried fruit, especially figs; almonds, sesame seeds and spread (tahini), sunflower seeds; most dark green vegetables, especially watercress and broccoli; brewer's yeast, carob and molasses. Seaweeds, especially hiziki, arame and wakame, are particularly rich and Japanese bancha twig tea, from Japanese stores and some health shops, is another useful source. In an area where the water is hard, some calcium is absorbed from this. White bread, biscuits and cakes, and brown (but not wholewheat) bread supply useful amounts of calcium (because the flour is fortified with calcium). Wholewheat flour and bread contains a small amount of calcium but it is not known how well the body can absorb it because of the phytic acid also present.

A balanced vegetarian diet, including some cheese and milk, is unlikely to be short of calcium. Vegans, or vegetarians eating very little dairy produce, need to include plenty of the calcium-rich non-sources mentioned above.

Magnesium

Magnesium is needed for many important roles in the body, including the metabolism of carbohydrates. It is found in a wide range of foods, and is not damaged by heat, though it is soluble, so may be lost if the water in which vegetables have been cooked is thrown away. A deficiency of this mineral alone is rare, except as a result of disease or where there is general malnutrition. Best sources are nuts and seeds, whole grains and products made from them, dried fruits, pulses, especially soya beans, brewer's yeast, fresh fruit and vegetables.

Iodine

A vital trace element, essential for the healthy functioning of the thyroid gland. Most reliable sources of iodine are seaweed and iodised sea salt. Sea salt contains iodine but it disappears during storage. Kelp tablets are a useful source, too.

Vitamins

Vitamin A

Vitamin A is needed for healthy skin, eyesight, hair, nails and mucous membranes, and for resistance to infection. It is found in dairy produce, eggs and margarine, and in all dark green and some yellow vegetables, as carotene, a substance which the body can convert into vitamin A. Carrots are a particularly rich source of carotene, as are apricots (fresh, canned and dried). Prunes, cantaloupe melons, red peppers, spinach, parsley and watercress are also good sources. A normal vegetarian diet, with its emphasis on fresh fruit and vegetables, is unlikely to be deficient in vitamin A.

B Vitamins

The B vitamins are important for the metabolism of other foods, the healthy working of the nervous system, the production of red blood cells and many other vital functions. They are found in wholegrain cereals and products made from them such as wholewheat bread and pasta. Wheatgerm, brewers' yeast and yeast extracts are other excellent sources of B vitamins, as are nuts and seeds, eggs, dried and fresh peas and beans, leafy green vegetables, potatoes, avocados, dried and fresh fruits.

Best sources of B1, thiamin, are dried and fresh peas and beans, especially soya beans and flour, wheatgerm, oranges, dried fruit, sunflower seeds and brazil nuts.

Milk is a major source of vitamin B2, riboflavin, so vegans and vegetarians who are not eating much dairy produce need to make sure that they make frequent use of other foods which are rich in this vitamin: leafy green vegetables, mushrooms, soya beans and flour, nori (p. 81) almonds, prunes and fresh dates.

Levels of B3, nicotinic acid, also need attention by both vegetarians and vegans; this is found in the foods mentioned above, but one of the richest sources of all is mushrooms, and dried peaches, damsons, sesame seeds and sunflower seeds are also particularly good.

The salt question

We all need some sodium, the main ingredient of table salt, but because of the amount of salt added during food processing, cooking and at the table, most of us have two or three times more than is considered healthy. Too much salt can encourage high blood pressure, which, in turn, can make us more vulnerable to heart attacks and strokes. Eating natural high-fibre foods, such as fresh vegetables, pulses and cereals, while using salt sparingly, helps protect against these problems. Personally I like to use sea salt in small quantities rather than one of the salt substitutes or potassium-based salts. Using fresh herbs, spices and lemon juice as seasonings also helps to reduce the need for salt. It is surprising how quickly you get used to the flavour of less salty food.

An adequate supply of B6, pyridoxine, is important for preparation for pregnancy, and studies have found it can also help alleviate pre-menstrual tension. So there's every excuse for eating avocados, as these are a particularly good source, as are bananas, currants, raisins and sultanas, sunflower seeds and soya beans and flour.

Folic acid is another vital B vitamin, especially during pregnancy. In addition to the sources mentioned above, leafy green vegetables are rich in this vitamin, especially endive and lettuce; also avocados, oranges, almonds and walnuts. Up to 50 per cent of folic acid is destroyed by heat, so there is obviously an advantage in eating these foods raw. B12 is found in dairy produce and eggs, yeast extracts, fermented foods, alfalfa sprouts and seaweeds. Some soya milks are also fortified with this vitamin. A B12 supplement may be advisable for vegetarians who are not eating much dairy produce and for vegans, unless they are eating good quantities of the foods mentioned above.

Vitamin C

Vitamin C protects against infection, speeds healing and the growth and repair of tissues and is needed for the absorption of iron. It is found in a wide range of fruit and vegetables and getting sufficient vitamin C is not usually a problem for vegetarians. Particularly good sources are leafy green vegetables, tomatoes, peppers, potatoes, blackcurrants, kiwi fruit, strawberries, pawpaw, cantaloupe and oranges.

Continued on p. 16

MENU
Sunday Brunch

SERVES 8

Gratin Dauphinois
190

*Wild Mushrooms in Cream with
Pastry Leaves*
272

Pipérade
215

Dried Fruit Compote
102

The preparation for this brunch can mainly be done the night before so that you can have a lie in on Sunday morning if you feel like it. Don't forget to put the Gratin Dauphinois into the oven in good time. Move it to the coolest part of the oven (or take it out and keep warm) when you want quickly to bake the pastry leaves for the Wild Mushrooms in Cream with Pastry Leaves; these can be cut out the night before and kept overnight in the fridge. The Dried Fruit Compote can also be kept in the fridge, chilling, until the last minute.

Make the vegetable part of the Pipérade the night before, too. Then all you have to do at the last minute is bake the pastry leaves, heat through the wild mushroom mixture, and finish making the Pipérade after your guests have arrived. To drink, you could serve good spicy Bloody Marys, made by flavouring tomato juice with salt, pepper, lemon juice and a good dash each of Worcester sauce (choose a vegetarian one, without anchovy extract) and Tabasco, then serve in tall wine glasses with ice and vodka. Or, better still, offer Bucks Fizz, made from equal parts of freshly squeezed orange juice and non-vintage champagne, or a fruit juice-based cup using apple or orange juice.

Vitamin D

Vitamin D is necessary for the absorption of calcium, which is needed for strong and healthy bones and teeth. It is not damaged by heat, but is found only in a quite restricted group of foods. The richest sources are margarine, fortified dried, skimmed and evaporated milk, eggs and fortified breakfast cereals. If you are using soya milk, it is a good idea to find one which contains vitamin D: read the label. Seaweeds are the only vegetable source of vitamin D (p. 81).

In white-skinned people, vitamin D is also formed by the action of sunlight on skin, but this does not happen in dark-skinned people, so they can become deficient in this vitamin if they are not getting enough in their diet. Vitamin D supplements are available and some experts recommend these for everyone, particularly children and old people (who are not getting out into the sun very often). Vitamin D is toxic in large doses, so if you take a supplement, do not exceed the recommended dose, and check first whether any multi-vitamin you may be taking contains any vitamin D.

Vitamin E

Vitamin E is needed for the elasticity of tissues, for general vitality and healing, and for the healthy functioning of the heart and arteries. It may also increase fertility and help to avoid high blood pressure.

Vitamin E is found in a wide range of foods and deficiency in this vitamin is rare, especially in a vegetarian diet, which generally contains plentiful amounts. Heat does not damage it significantly, but processing and prolonged storage can. Best sources are cold-pressed corn oil, wheatgerm, nuts and seeds, especially almonds, hazelnuts, peanuts and peanut butter, avocados, blackberries and sweet potatoes. Also valuable are eggs, all whole grains, pulses and leafy green vegetables.

Vitamin K

Vitamin K is needed for the metabolism of proteins and for the clotting of blood. It is made by the intestinal bacteria and is also found in leafy green vegetables, cauliflower, tomatoes, egg yolk, peas and beans, potatoes, carrots, seaweeds and alfalfa. It is not thought to be damaged by cooking processes. A vegetarian diet supplies the requirements of this vitamin, especially if it includes a daily serving of leafy green vegetables.

Vitamin supplements: to take, or not to take?

Opinion is divided between those who say vitamin supplements are a necessary protection in these days of pollution and artificial fertilizers, and those who say that taking concentrated doses of nutrients is unnatural and alien to a pure way of eating. And no one knows how well vitamin supplements are actually assimilated by the body.

Personally I don't take any, although I think that in certain cases they can be useful; if for some reason there is difficulty in eating healthy foods in the quantity needed to give enough vitamins and minerals, for instance (perhaps with faddy children, older people, after illness or during periods of rapid growth).

A vitamin D supplement is recommended for young children and older people who do not see much sun (see left). Yeast tablets are useful if you find it difficult to eat plenty of the B vitamin foods, but you really have to take them by the handful to make any impact. And B12 is a good idea for vegans and vegetarians who are not eating much dairy produce. I have a great deal of faith in the ability of a healthy body to adapt to the foods it is given (provided always that these are natural and unprocessed) and to utilize the nutrients available. I also believe that if you're eating a healthy diet, with plenty of variety, your body will let you know if it is lacking anything vital, by making you fancy certain foods which have the nutrients that you need at that time. So do listen to your body.

Learning to love the soya bean

Soya beans and flour are rich sources of nutrients, but, in my opinion, so difficult to make palatable! However, sprouted soya beans are delicious and make an excellent crunchy addition to salads, stir-fries and sandwiches. They are easy to produce at home (p. 207) so you can always ensure you have a supply of them handy.

Try a vitality salad of soya sprouts, alfalfa sprouts, shredded lettuce, chopped tomatoes, grated raw beetroot and carrot, layered into a bowl and topped with mayonnaise.

Creamy soya milk (p. 106) and tofu (p. 108), which can both be made at home, are other palatable ways to eat soya.

Planning vegetarian meals

When you're changing to vegetarian eating, or trying out some vegetarian meals, it's probably easiest to think of the meal you'd normally eat and then swap the meat or fish with a vegetarian main course: nut or lentil burgers instead of beef burgers; steamed vegetable pudding instead of steak and kidney pudding; savoury nut or lentil loaf instead of meat loaf. Once you've planned the main course, the vegetables and a sauce if needed can be chosen to go with it.

Vegetarian eating can follow the conventional daily pattern of breakfast, one light and one more substantial meal; or it can be based on several light snack meals, or whatever schedule suits you. I do think that for anyone interested in healthy eating, whether they're a meat eater or a vegetarian, it's helpful to think of the fat content of the day's – or even the week's – eating as a whole, balancing a high-fat meal, such as a cheese flan, with a low-fat meal, such as a mixed salad dressed with lemon juice, or a platter of steamed vegetables with chopped fresh herbs. I personally find breakfast an easy meal to make fatless – fresh fruit and weak tea without milk is my favourite – and this allows scope for the rest of the day. Other low-fat breakfasts would be a whole-grain cereal with skimmed or semi-skimmed milk (or soya milk) or wholewheat toast with honey.

Vegetarianism in pregnancy

Ideally, preparation for pregnancy should begin several months before conception, and not only with the prospective mother, but with the father too, as the diet of both determines the health of the baby. During this time of preparation it's a good idea to rely on some form of contraception other than the pill, as this is known to affect the body's ability to metabolize vitamins B6, B2, B12 and folic acid, also zinc and iron. Make sure that your diet contains plentiful sources of these vitamins (see above) and consider taking supplements of vitamins D and B12 if your diet is low in dairy produce. Eat plenty of the foods rich in vitamin E and include sea vegetables or seaweed-based jelling agents whenever you can (see p. 81) for iodine and other trace minerals, or take kelp tablets two or three times a week. It's also advisable to cut out or reduce the amount of alcohol you drink, and to stop smoking.

Nutritional requirements increase dramatically

A typical day of healthy vegetarian eating

Breakfast

*Orange or grapefruit juice
Whole-grain muesli with milk and raisins
Wholewheat toast with honey or marmalade*
or
*Fresh fruits in season
Tea, coffee or herb tea*

Lunch

Salad sandwiches
or
Baked Potato (p. 190) with grated carrot and watercress
or
A vitality salad of shredded lettuce, chopped tomatoes, grated carrot and beetroot, sprouted beans, chopped nuts
or
A bowl of Leek and Potato Soup (p. 134) and wholewheat bread
or
*Hummus (p. 144) with Crudités (p. 143) or pitta bread
Apple
Tea, coffee or herb tea*

Evening meal

*Tagliatelle Verde with Lentil Sauce (p. 252)
Green salad with avocado and fresh herbs
Apricot and Orange Fool (p. 282)
Tea, coffee or herb tea*

Snacks

*Wholewheat bread
Nuts
Fresh and dried fruit*

during pregnancy and lactation. Extra iron, folic acid and other B vitamins, and vitamins A, C, D, and E are needed, as well as about 50 per cent more calcium than normal. You can meet this by having an extra serving of cheese or yogurt, or by taking an extra 450 ml/15 fl oz skimmed milk or calcium-fortified soya milk. Or you could step up the amount of non-dairy sources of calcium in your diet, such as broccoli, kale, dried figs, almonds, sesame seeds, soya beans and flour, arame and hiziki. A couple of glasses a day of the creamy almond milk on p. 238 is another delicious way to take extra calcium as well as plentiful B vitamins, iron and other minerals.

If you don't mind brewer's yeast, a convenient way to boost your intake of the important B vitamins is to take 15 ml (1 tablespoon) brewer's yeast each day. Sprinkle this over your breakfast cereal or stir it into some fruit juice. This will also supply the additional thiamin, riboflavin, nicotinic acid, B6 and folic acid needed during both pregnancy and lactation together with some useful iron, zinc and a little calcium and magnesium, too, while supplying only 46 calories.

A well-balanced vegetarian diet is probably naturally rich enough in vitamins A, C and E to cover the additional requirements for these during pregnancy. However, you could make doubly sure by having a piece of melon, an extra orange or half cup of orange juice, a large banana or an extra serving of green vegetables each day, to supply vitamins A and C, and by using cold-pressed corn oil, for vitamin E, in salad dressings.

Vegetarian babies

For the first six months of life, breast milk supplies all the nutrients a baby needs and ideally solid food should not be introduced before then, although it can be given, with care, when the baby is four months old, if he no longer seems satisfied with breast milk, but certainly not before then. The reason for avoiding the early introduction of solid foods is that because the baby's digestive system is immature an allergic reaction is more likely; also the baby needs the closeness and emotional satisfaction which breast-feeding gives.

Start to introduce the baby to solid food by giving half a teaspoon of a fruit or vegetable purée, either before or after one of the main feeds of the day: lunchtime is often most convenient. Either cooked

---

High-vitality foods

There are certain foods which are particularly rich in a number of nutrients, and worth including in your meals as often as possible. These are:

Pulses *especially soya beans, soya sprouts, soya flour*

Whole grains *especially oatmeal and millet; wholewheat flour and bread; pasta; wheatgerm*

Nuts *especially pistachios, almonds, brazil nuts, hazelnuts and walnuts*

Seeds *sunflower, pumpkin, and sesame seeds and spread*

Fresh fruits *especially apples, bananas, oranges, dates, blackberries, strawberries, cantaloupe, kiwi, mango, paw paw*

Dried fruits *including dried peaches*

Vegetables *especially fresh peas, beans, sweetcorn; mushrooms, avocados, alfalfa sprouts; potatoes, tomatoes, carrots, red pepper and sweet potatoes*

Dark green leafy vegetables *especially broccoli and other brassicas; endive*

Seaweeds *especially hiziki and nori*

Brewer's yeast and yeast extract

Milk and cheese

---

or raw fruit and vegetables can be used; mashed avocado pear, ripe banana, ripe peach or mango; very finely grated raw apple, pear or carrot; or cooked and puréed carrot or mashed potato. These first spoonfuls are really to get the baby used to the texture of solid food; breast milk will still be his main source of nourishment, and he also still needs this for the emotional satisfaction which comes from sucking.

Once the baby is happy with these small quantities of solid food, you can gradually increase the amount so that after a fortnight or so he is having perhaps two tablespoons at a time. Babies of over six months can also have a little bread mashed into the food; remove the crusts and use either a 100 per cent wholewheat bread, or, if this proves to be too laxative (as it can for some babies) try an 81–85 per cent bread, perhaps with added wheatgerm.

Gradually, as the baby takes more solid food, he won't need so much milk, so that when he is about 8 months he will naturally give up one feed completely. Then you can add extra, protein ingredients to the basic fruit and vegetable purées to enrich them. Try adding: mashed cooked beans, mashed drained tofu, cooked and puréed lentils, tahini, peanut butter, low-sodium yeast extract, finely grated nuts and seeds, wheatgerm, brewer's yeast, cottage cheese, low-fat white cheeses such as quark, 'live' natural yogurt, hard cheese, and egg yolk which should be stirred into a hot vegetable purée so that it will cook in the heat.

You can gradually increase the quantities that you give to the baby for this meal of solids, and if you like you can give a savoury course, of, say, puréed lentils or mashed cooked vegetables with some protein added, as suggested above, followed by a 'pudding' course of finely grated fresh fruit, yogurt or egg custard. Once the baby gets used to the texture of solid food, you will probably be able to mash, rather than purée his foods.

Solid foods can be introduced before or after the other main feeds of the day in the same way, so that gradually these, too, can be dropped. When the baby is about 9 months the bedtime feed may be the only one which is left. Let the baby go on enjoying this for as long as possible; it is important for the bonding with you and the emotional satisfaction which sucking gives. The baby will give it up spontaneously when he is ready, sometimes this happens by the time he is around a year old, but often babies need to continue for longer. My daughter Claire had just managed to give it up by her second birthday!

'Finger foods' such as fingers of bread, rusks, raw apple or carrot, can be given from about 9 months, and can be helpful if the baby is teething. Never leave a baby alone with these foods and be ready to hook them out with your little finger or to turn the baby upside down and smack him gently in the small of his back if he starts to choke.

Soon you will find that the baby can eat a little of what you as a family are eating. Make sure that this is not too highly seasoned, either with salt or spices, because of putting too much strain on the baby's kidneys. It may be possible to take a little out for the baby before adding these to the mixture. Other things to avoid are foods which contain preservatives, colouring or other additives, and foods which are high in fat, such as pastry and deep-fried foods. Watch, too, the level of fibre; as a vegetarian diet is naturally high in this, make sure that he has, in addition, some sources of concentrated protein such as egg, cheese, peanut butter or tahini, powdered nuts, yogurt or brewer's yeast.

Vegetarian children

A well-planned vegetarian diet can supply all the nutrients which growing children need. Deficiencies would show up as stunted growth, listlessness, poor appetite, lack of energy, slow healing of cuts and wounds, cracks and sores around the mouth, and mouth ulcers. As long as they are healthy, full of energy and growing well, they are almost certainly getting the nourishment they need. It is, however, important that you watch their diet carefully and make sure it is rich in all the essential nutrients.

Few parents manage to get through the child-rearing process without worrying about their child's diet at some point. One of my daughters was so faddy that I sometimes wondered how she managed to keep going, but we came through this phase and she's bright, happy and healthy. I did get her to take vitamin tablets, and I think that a vitamin tablet, including vitamins B12 and D, is a good idea, for the parents' peace of mind as much as the children's nourishment! In my opinion it's best to let them have the foods that they will eat – provided these are reasonably healthy – rather than to try and make them eat what you think they ought to be eating. There are several good sources of most nutrients, so if they balk at one it's usually possible to find an alternative.

Try to include in their diet as many of the high-vitality foods as you can, keep everything as fresh and unprocessed as possible. Keep a strict eye on the amount of sugar and fat they are eating and make sure there are plenty of wholesome snack foods, such as fruit, wholewheat bread, nuts and dried fruit

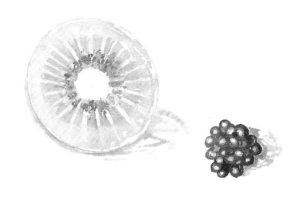

Children's favourites

Children have their own individual tastes, but these are the dishes which I've found to be generally popular with children:

Watercress Soup (p. 130)

Golden Lentil Soup (p. 134)

Leek and Potato Soup (p. 134)

Cheese and Fresh Herb Dip (p. 143)

Red Kidney Bean Salad (p. 157)

Favourite Coleslaw (p. 161)

Baked Potatoes (p. 190)

Stuffed Jacket Potatoes (p. 191)

Potato and Cheese Layer (p. 200)

Savoury Lentil Loaf (p. 213)

Cheese Fondue (p. 217)

Cheese and Parsley Fritters (p. 217)

Pizza (p. 218)

Spaghetti Bolognese Vegetariana (p. 253)

Tagliatelle Verde with Lentil Sauce (p. 252)

Macaroni Cheese (p. 257)

French Onion Flan (p. 261)

Savoury Cheshire Cheese and Onion Pie (p. 265)

Chocolate Mould (p. 279)

Any of the ice creams, but the Chocolate Ice Cream (p. 280) particularly (and it's healthy)

Fresh Fruit Salad (p. 286)

Treacle Tart (p. 294)

Fruit Pie (p. 294)

Steamed Pudding (p. 298)

Pancakes (p. 299)

Any spongey cakes, and particularly Quick Buns (p. 310)

Parkin (p. 308)

available, crudités, cubes of cheese, favourite yogurts, to keep them off the sweets and crisps. Encourage them to drink water or unsweetened fruit juice diluted with water or soda water instead of sweetened canned or bottled drinks. If you have the time, presentation of the food does help; I have found that my youngest daughter, Claire, always eats her food better if I take the time to arrange it attractively on the plate or to bake a mini-savoury in a ramekin dish. She loves a supper platter – small amounts of all her favourite foods arranged on a plate – cubes of cheese, thin slices of apple, some dates stuffed with almonds, a few crisp lettuce leaves, some carrot sticks. Sometimes I've arranged a salad or an open sandwich in the shape of a face, with grated carrot hair, tomato mouth and so on. If you go to this trouble, you have to take care not to over-react if your lovingly arranged offering is rejected, though in my experience it isn't usually.

Vegetarian teenagers

As with younger children, it's most helpful to concentrate on the foods that are liked, rather than to get into a situation of conflict. Some teenagers may wish to experience eating meat and 'junk foods' if they have always had wholesome vegetarian food at home. If they're into junk foods, try and get them to take some kind of vitamin supplement, and have readily available any natural snacks, such as apples, nuts, wholewheat bread or cake, that they will eat. The less intense the emotional atmosphere, the more quickly they will be able to discover what they as individuals really want to eat and make their own responsible decisions.

During this period of rapid growth teenagers, especially boys, may have a big appetite; plenty of wholewheat bread, pasta, rice and potatoes will fill them up, while giving good nourishment. Include as many of the high-vitality foods as possible; soya is a particularly good food if they'll eat it, perhaps in the form of tofu, well-sprinkled with a good-quality, naturally fermented soy sauce. Whole-wheat peanut butter or tahini sandwiches, perhaps with sprouted soya beans, or pitta breads packed with red kidney beans, salad and any other ingredients they particularly like, are quick snacks which I've known to be popular with this age group, as are vegetarian burgers (pp. 210 and 232), or bought Vegeburgers, served with a good supply of burger buns and perhaps some baked beans.

At the opposite end of the scale, slimming is another issue which frequently arises with teenagers, especially with girls. This can be healthily achieved on a vegetarian diet, see below. Include as many iron-rich foods as possible in the diet of teenagers, especially girls. Zinc is also important and shortage of this mineral has been linked with the eating disorders anorexia nervosa and bulimia. Including plentiful amounts of the zinc-rich foods (which are also good sources of iron), such as peanuts, sweetcorn and cheese, makes sound sense.

Slimming on a vegetarian diet

The key to successful slimming lies in finding a diet which suits your life-style and which can become a permanent way of eating for you once you're slim, to prevent the endless fluctuation of weight and constant dieting that leads nowhere. I've known people to have dramatic weight losses when they turned vegetarian. The combination of the additive-free foods and the high fibre just seemed to do the trick for them.

If you base meals on whole grains and pulses, eat more fresh fruit and vegetables and reduce fat and sugar, it is difficult not to lose weight. You could eat exactly the meals suggested in the *Typical day of healthy vegetarian eating* (p. 17), using skimmed milk if you have the muesli or only a scraping of butter on the toast; use yeast extract, mustard or skimmed milk soft cheese to spread the bread for sandwiches, if you have these for lunch, or, if you're making the soup, use the minimum of fat. Top the salad with yogurt or a mixture of yogurt and mayonnaise. Prepare the evening meal with the minimum of fat, and have a large portion of leafy salad with it, dressed with lemon juice. Many of the main courses in this book can be used by slimmers; some which are particularly suitable are shown on the right.

A method of slimming I like is based on the principle of keeping fruit separate from other foods, and not mixing protein foods with carbohydrates. Eat only fruit until noon, and after you have eaten fruit allow an hour to elapse before eating any other foods. For lunch eat fruit (if you want to lose weight fast), or have a large salad, with some bread or a potato if you like. Soup can be included in this meal, or you could have a salad sandwich, but no protein. The evening meal can be built around either protein or carbohydrate, but not both. Fruit can be eaten three hours after other foods.

Continued on p. 24

Main courses for slimmers

These recipes are relatively low in calories. Served with a generous amount of lightly cooked vegetables or salad dressed with lemon juice, they can help you to lose weight:

Corn Chowder (p. 135) made with half the amount of fat

Golden Lentil Soup (p. 134)

Courgettes with Carrot, Ginger and Almond Stuffing (p. 193)

Stuffed Tomatoes (p. 195)

Stuffed Aubergines (p. 192)

Sweet and Sour Vegetable Stir-fry with Almonds (p. 199)

Vegetable Hotpot (p. 200)

Vegetable Curry (p. 202), with brown rice

Lentils and Mushrooms au Gratin (p. 207)

Chilli con Carne Vegetariana (p. 208)

Spicy Lentil Burgers (p. 210)

Lentil Shepherd's Pie (p. 210)

Savoury Lentil Loaf (p. 213)

Pizza (p. 218)

Spanish Omelette (p. 220)

Spinach Roulade (p. 224)

Savoury Cheese Pudding (p. 226)

Cashew Nut Roast (p. 230)

Rice Pilaf (p. 242)

Paella Vegetariana (p. 243)

Millet Pilaf with Nuts and Raisins (p. 245)

Barley Casserole (p. 246)

Couscous (p. 247)

Spaghetti Bolognese Vegetariana (p. 253)

Tagliatelle Verde with Lentil Sauce (p. 252)

Fusille Colbuco with Aubergine and Wine Sauce (p. 255)

MENU
Spring Dinner Party

SERVES 6

Mushroom and Herb Terrine with
Melba Toast
146

Paella Vegetariana with Artichokes
243

Mixed Leaf Salad with
Guacamole Dressing
54 and 144

Glazed Red Fruit Tart
292

This is a relaxed, informal dinner party with fresh flavours. It is also very easy to prepare. Both the Mushroom and Herb Terrine and the Glazed Red Fruit Tart can be made in advance. The Melba Toast can also be made the day before and wrapped in foil to keep it crisp, although it doesn't take long to do on the day. Serve Guacamole as a salad dressing and garnish it with chopped tomato, onion and chilli. The main course of Paella is informal but delicious, and looks attractive served from the pan in which it was cooked (if this is presentable!); otherwise, transfer it to a warmed, shallow dish just before serving.

Choose a wine to reflect the informal nature of the meal; I would be inclined to go Spanish and choose a Rioja, or choose a medium-dry white wine, with enough power to cope with the flavours of the Paella – a Chenin Blanc or a young Riesling, perhaps.

Quick main courses

Pistou (p. 136), using canned beans, with warm rolls and a few Crudités (p. 143)

Cheese and Fresh Herb Dip (p. 143), Hummus (p. 144) or Roquefort Dip (p. 146) with Crudités (p. 143), pitta bread and fruit

Greek Salad (p. 168) with crusty bread and fresh fruit

Spring Vegetable Braise (p. 181), Ratatouille (p. 187) or Peperonata (p. 186) with brown rice (p. 44)

Stuffed Jacket Potatoes (p. 191) with lettuce, tomato, cucumber and grated carrot

Sweet and Sour Vegetable Stir-Fry with Almonds (p. 199) with brown rice (p. 44)

Multicolour Butter Beans (p. 206), buttered noodles or granary bread

Red Kidney Bean Stew (p. 206) with Baked Potatoes (p. 190)

Felafel in Pitta Pockets (p. 208)

Baked Eggs (p. 214), Pipérade (p. 215) or Omelette (p. 220)

Cheese Soufflé (p. 222) with French beans

Savoury Olive Mushroom Cake (p. 226) with a green salad

Quick Savoury Nut Roast (p. 235) with mashed potatoes and frozen peas

Paella Vegetariana (p. 243)

Classic Risotto (p. 244)

Fusilli Verde with Mushrooms and Cream (p. 251)

Tagliatelle with Gorgonzola (p. 250)

Tagliatelle Verde with Lentil Sauce (p. 252)

Macaroni Cheese (p. 257)

Taglione Verde with Tomato Sauce and Aubergines (p. 254)

Summer Linguine (p. 255)

Quick Bread Pizza (p. 334)

Older vegetarians

Unless we are very active, our calorie requirements decrease as we get older. However, our need for nutrients remains as high as ever and it is important to look for foods which provide concentrated sources of these whilst not contributing too many calories. Protein is needed for growth and repair of tissues; vitamins A and C for resistance to infection and general vitality; vitamin D for healthy bones; vitamin E, which has sometimes been called the youth vitamin, for flexibility of joints and tissues, and vitamin B for the nervous system and to combat the effects of stress.

Sometimes it is difficult to eat large enough portions of foods to get the optimum nourishment, and so taking a multi-vitamin pill often makes sense for older vegetarians. It's also helpful to look for foods which are concentrated sources of nutrients, such as nuts and nut butters, cheese, eggs, soya flour, tofu, skimmed milk powder, tahini, brewer's yeast, yeast extract and wheatgerm. Milk is a useful food because it is both easy to eat (or drink) and rich in valuable nutrients, especially calcium and riboflavin. Milk can be fortified further by whisking some dried skimmed milk powder into it. Salads can be difficult to eat, and if you find this to be a problem, fruit and vegetable juices can be useful, but make sure you're getting enough fibre, with foods such as wholewheat bread, soups, baked beans and jacket potatoes.

If you're cooking for one, and have a small deep-freeze, it can be most helpful to make up the full amount of a recipe, divide it into four portions and freeze three of them for later. Many vegetarian dishes freeze well (see p. 26), and if you have a microwave oven as well, which is ideal when you're heating up food for one or two people, see p. 28.

Again, if you're cooking for just one or two people it helps to plan meals for several days at a time. You can often cook extra rice, potatoes, pasta or sauce, for instance, and use them a day or two later, with the addition of some fresh and different ingredients, to create another meal.

Soups make a particularly soothing food and are easy to make. A lentil soup is very nourishing and can be made as thick or thin as you wish. If you serve it with some wholewheat bread and some fresh fruit or vegetable juice, or a little salad, you have a meal which should certainly help to keep you brimming with vitality.

Kitchen Equipment

Equipment needed for vegetarian cookery is modest and likely to be found in most kitchens. Top of the list comes a really good, sharp knife, an essential for any cook. I like traditional Sabatier knives; be sure to get the real thing. There are some cheap substitutes around and these are not satisfactory. The most useful all-purpose size is a knife with a 13 cm/5 inch blade, but a small paring knife is handy, too. You will also need a steel with which to keep them sharp. As well as a good Sabatier knife, I find it useful to have a stainless steel knife with a serrated blade, for cutting delicate fruits like peaches, mangoes and avocados, which can take on a metallic taste when cut with a steel knife.

A good, strong chopping board is another essential. Make sure it is at least 2.5 cm/1 inch thick and measures not less than 40 x 30 cm/16 x 12 inches. This can also double as a pastry board.

It's necessary to have some means of grinding nuts and seeds. You can use a small hand-mill, an electric coffee mill or a liquidizer, but perhaps the best buy for this is a food processor, because it can also be used for so many other jobs. If you're buying a new one, it's worth buying the largest you can.

A pestle and mortar is useful for crushing whole spices. A heavy ceramic one, with a good-sized bowl, is more practical than a wooden one which lacks the weight and tends to absorb and retain flavours.

When choosing saucepans and baking tins, buy the best you can afford because you certainly get what you pay for here. Good ones will last a lifetime and be a joy to use; cheap ones are a source of frustration. I like heavy-gauge stainless steel saucepans; aluminium is not recommended by health experts because it is thought that the traces of aluminium which are absorbed by the food can be detrimental. Cast-iron equipment is pleasant both to look at and to use; the disadvantage is the weight of it, especially when full.

For general frying, a frying pan with a top measurement of 27.5 cm/10¾ inches is best, and for pancakes a shallow frying pan with curved edges, measuring 20 cm/8 inches across. If you make omelettes often it's a good idea to have a frying pan specially for them, although this is a counsel of perfection which I have never managed to achieve. The right size is 13–15 cm/5–6 inches across.

A pressure-cooker saves time and fuel; I find it especially useful for making soups and stews quickly. A stainless steel one is the best from the health point of view, and should last for years.

If you like making stir-fries, a wok is a useful piece of equipment. One with a stand can be used on either gas or electricity, and the most useful size is 35 cm/14 inches in diameter. A wok with wooden handles is easiest to use.

Some of the best baking tins are the ones with a non-stick coating, although I find that they still need lining and greasing in the usual way. Again, look for strong, heavy tins; this applies especially to baking sheets, as cheap, thin ones soon buckle. A spring-clip type is useful for cheesecakes.

When it comes to choosing casserole dishes, the most useful ones are perhaps those which can withstand extremes of temperature, so that you can take them out of the fridge or freezer and put them straight into the oven. Not in this category, but reasonable to buy and attractive and pleasant to use, are French glazed pottery casserole dishes which you can buy in different sizes and lovely muted colours. I also find those round white ceramic pizza plates, measuring 30 cm/12 inches across, very useful for various dishes.

Other useful and time-saving pieces of equipment are a good sturdy metal colander, for draining pasta and vegetables; a sieve with metal mesh and also a nylon one, or a tamis, for sieving delicate fruits and vegetables; a box grater which you can stand on a chopping board and which has a variety of blades of different sizes; some really sharp kitchen scissors; a set of measuring spoons and a 600-ml/1-pint or 1-litre/1¾-pint measuring jug made of glass or transluscent plastic, marked in millilitres, pints and fluid ounces.

Non-essential tools to have include a nylon piping bag with a large plain nozzle and a medium-sized shell nozzle; a melon baller, and an orange zester.

Using the Freezer

The freezer is as much of a boon in vegetarian cookery as it is in conventional cookery and can be used to save both time and money. It is perhaps particularly useful to vegetarians because our main dishes have to be made from scratch. So making a double quantity and freezing half, or freezing some of the components of favourite dishes, such as tomato sauce, pancakes, breadcrumbs for stuffings and toppings, ready-grated cheese and cooked pulses, is really worthwhile. It is also useful to have a supply of favourite commercial frozen foods.

Foods which freeze

- □ *Fresh fruit and vegetables*
- □ *Cooked pulses*
- □ *Dairy produce with a fat content above 40 per cent*
- □ *Soups, savoury bakes and pastries, sauces*
- □ *Cakes, biscuits and breads*

Foods which do not freeze

- □ *Leafy salad vegetables such as lettuce, also raw tomatoes*
- □ *Hardboiled eggs, raw eggs in their shells – store raw egg yolk and white separately to prevent the yolk toughening*
- □ *Dairy products with fat content below 40 per cent*
- □ *Food strongly flavoured with garlic or celery, as garlic may develop 'off' flavours and celery intensifies*
- □ *Dishes containing cooked potato, which toughens, although mashed potato is satisfactory*

Freezer standbys

Commercial frozen foods
Frozen foods which I find particularly useful are orange juice, frozen peas, particularly petits pois and mangetouts; baby haricot beans, sweetcorn, corn on the cob and asparagus. Frozen raspberries and cream are useful for a spur-of-the-moment special meal.

Home-made dishes
The majority of vegetarian dishes freeze well; either make up a double quantity, and freeze one, or have a cooking session to stock up the deep freeze.

Soups, casseroles and stews freeze well, but don't use garlic or celery to flavour soups and savouries. Freeze in a container which allows enough room for expansion. Allow plenty of time for thawing: 6–8 hours for a quantity to serve 4–6 people. Most vegetable and pulse dishes freeze successfully; Red Cabbage Casserole (p. 180) and Ratatouille (p. 187), for instance; also Red Kidney Bean Stew (p. 206) and Lentils and Mushrooms au Gratin (p. 207).

Both savoury and sweet pies and pastries freeze well; I think they are best frozen uncooked; do not make any holes in the top – add these just before cooking. Mushroom Pâté en Croûte (p. 270) is a useful dish to freeze for a special occasion.

Burgers and croquettes freeze exceptionally well. They are best open-frozen. To open-freeze, place on a tray or baking sheet, freeze until solid, then pack. Spicy Lentil Burgers (p. 210), Peanut Burgers (p. 232), Cheese and Parsley Fritters (p. 217) and Felafel (p. 208) are all worth freezing, as are Nut Balls in Tomato Sauce (p. 238).

Spinach Lasagne (p. 256) and Gnocchi alla Romana (p. 227) (frozen before baking) are particularly useful and successful. Nut and lentil roasts are superb cooked until three-quarters done, then cooled and frozen. To use, thaw, then cook for about 30 minutes. Of the puddings, cheesecakes, ices, sorbets, pies and tarts (as mentioned) freeze well, as do cakes, biscuits, scones and breads. Both scones and breads are good par-cooked before frozen, then thawed and cooked before eating.

Ingredients

It's very helpful and time-saving to have some much-used ingredients in the freezer, as well as sauces and other things which are needed for making up dishes.

Stock can be frozen in 300 ml/10 fl oz quantities. Any leftover lemon juice can be poured into ice cube containers and frozen.

There are many uses for spare egg yolks and egg whites. Stir a pinch of sugar or salt into each egg yolk (depending on whether you want to use it for sweet or savoury dishes) to stabilize it. Then freeze yolks and whites separately in ice cube containers.

Basic much-used sauces such as Fresh Tomato (p. 170), Italian Tomato (p. 171), and any others that you particularly like and use often such as Sauce Soubise (p. 173), Béchamel Sauce (p. 175), and Cheese Sauce (p. 175), are also handy to have in the freezer.

Cooked pulses (p. 40) can be packed in 350 g/12 oz portions and frozen, as can cooked crepes. Interleave each crepe with greaseproof paper before freezing so that you can take them out individually as needed.

Pastry flan cases can be baked blind (p. 266) and then frozen. They are handy for filling with vegetables in a creamy sauce or a light egg custard mixture for quick meals.

Chopped parsley, fresh breadcrumbs and grated cheese can all be frozen in polythene bags. Grate up any additional cheese and just add it to the bag.

Secrets of successful freezing

Freeze food which is good quality; if it is hot, cool quickly, package carefully, freeze as rapidly as possible.

Pack foods carefully to protect them and to prevent strongly flavoured foods from tainting others.

Allow room for liquid products to expand.

When sealing polythene bags, make sure that as much air as possible has been extracted.

Label each package with as much information as possible, include contents, date frozen and servings.

Freezer storage times

Biscuits	*3 months*
Bread	*3 months*
Butter: salted	*3 months*
* unsalted*	*6 months*
Cakes, plain or iced with butter icing	*3 months*
Cheese	*6 months*
Cream	*3 months*
Eggs	*6 months*
Fruit prepared with sugar	*9 months*
Fruit without sugar	*3 months*
Ice cream	*3 months*
Margarine	*5–6 months*
Vegetables	*6–9 months*
Vegetarian savoury dishes	*3 months*

Freezing vegetables

For best results, vegetables need to be blanched before freezing. Prepare the vegetables in the usual way. Bring a large saucepan of water to the boil. Put 450 g/1 lb prepared vegetables into a wire basket and plunge this into the boiling water. When the water comes back to the boil start timing the vegetables: 2–3 minutes for leafy vegetables, peas and beans, broccoli, small cauliflower florets, small carrots, Brussels sprouts, courgettes; 7–10 minutes for corn on the cob, depending on size. Remove from the water immediately and put the vegetables under a cold running tap until they are cooled through. Drain well, then package and freeze immediately.

To freeze fresh herbs, see p. 118.

Freezing fruit

Perfect fruit can be frozen raw, or it can be sprinkled with sugar or covered with a syrup made by heating 350 g/12 oz sugar in 600 ml/1 pint water until the sugar has dissolved, then cooling. Less perfect fruit can be stewed in the normal way (p. 84), sweetened with sugar to taste, then frozen; ripe, soft fruits such as strawberries, mangoes and peaches can be puréed raw, sweetened, and frozen. A little lemon juice can be added to prevent the fruit from discolouring. Fruit for making jam or marmalade can be kept in the freezer until you are ready to use it.

Using the Microwave

Another time-saving piece of equipment, the microwave oven can be used to speed preparation of dishes and also to defrost and quickly re-heat prepared dishes. The dishes suggested for freezing can be reheated successfully in the microwave oven if they are frozen in microwave-proof containers.

Microwave power

The power of microwave ovens ranges from 500–700 watt outputs. Many have a variety of settings, ranging from 'warm' 100 watts and 'defrost' 230 watts, to 'full power' 600–700 watts. Personally I do not think there is any advantage in having numerous settings; I find 'defrost' and 'full power' are the only ones needed. I do think, however, that there is a great advantage in having an oven which combines microwave with a conventional oven and grill. These are more expensive to buy, but give excellent results, combining speedy microwave cooking with traditional browning and crisping.

Microwave containers

Choose shallow dishes, preferably round or oval in shape, made from pottery or heatproof glass: dishes sold as suitable for dishwashers are usually suitable for the microwave too. Do not use dishes made of metal or with metallic decorations, and avoid covering food with foil, as these can damage the magnetron.

Cooking in the microwave

Arrange the food around the edges of the dish, with the thickest part of the food towards the outside of the dish; do not pile the food up. Some foods need stirring during cooking time; this helps even distribution of heat. Many dishes need to be allowed to stand (usually for about 5 minutes) after microwaving, to give the heat time to penetrate the food fully. The more food in the microwave oven, the longer the cooking time. When cooking savoury dishes or vegetables, the food cooks more quickly if it is covered; a dinner plate is good for this, and it gets warmed through at the same time, ready to serve the food on.

Vegetables do not cook any more quickly in a microwave oven than by conventional boiling or steaming, but they keep their colour well and the goodness and flavour are conserved because of the small amount of water used. They cook best if cut into fairly small pieces, placed on a large plate and sprinkled with water, allowing about 3 tablespoons water for 450 g/1 lb vegetables.

Pulses can be cooked in a microwave, and although you do not save much time by doing them in this way, they do cook well. Soak the pulses as usual, if necessary (p. 40), then put them into a shallow container. Add boiling water to cover them by about 1 cm/½ inch. Red kidney beans should be soaked and then boiled hard for 10 minutes before you put them into the microwave. Split red lentils and green or brown lentils do not need soaking; just cover them generously with water and cook split red lentils for 10 minutes, and the other types for 20 minutes, in each case followed by 10 minutes standing. It's a good idea to stir the lentils two or three times during the cooking time. Soaked black-eyed beans, cannellini beans or haricot beans take 20–30 minutes, followed by 10 minutes standing; soaked chick peas take 30–40 minutes, plus 10 minutes standing. Red kidney beans, black beans and butter beans, all pre-soaked, and red kidney beans boiled hard for 10 minutes as described, take 45–50 minutes, with 15 minutes standing time after that.

Pasta and rice can be cooked in the microwave, although little time is saved. To cook spaghetti, macaroni or similar pasta shapes, put 225 g/8 oz pasta into a suitable dish and add 600 ml/1 pint boiling water and 1 tablespoon oil. Cook, uncovered, for 12–17 minutes, until *al dente*. For 225 g/8 oz lasagne, use 1 litre/1¾ pints boiling water and 1 tablespoon oil, cook for 10–12 minutes and allow to stand for 2 minutes.

To cook rice, put 225 g/8 oz rice into a deep dish with 600 ml/1 pint boiling water and a knob of butter or vegan margarine; cover and microwave for 12–17 minutes for white long grain rice, 20–25 minutes for brown rice, in both cases followed by 5 minutes standing.

Entertaining and Wine

Creating food which will give pleasure to others, and then enjoying it with them, is, to me, what cooking is all about, and, in this spirit, even a simple meal becomes a celebration. A perfectly planned dinner party can be a delight; but sometimes an impromptu meal, which you've cooked on the spur of the moment while chatting in the kitchen, and washed down with a bottle of *vin ordinaire*, can be even more pleasurable. The kind of meal and the degree of formality with which it is served depend very much on personal taste and the circumstances such as the people involved, the occasion, the venue and the time available.

Throughout this book I have given menu suggestions for different occasions, and there are many more possibilities. The most important thing is to choose food which you like and make well; if you have particular favourites, don't feel shy about repeating them – your friends are probably looking forward to eating them again – at least, I know that's how I feel about my friends' specialities. Choose dishes which will not give you anxiety, then you will be able to enjoy your own dinner party too. A cold first course or pudding – or both – which can be prepared in advance to leave you free to cope with the main course ease the strain. So does serving a simple vegetable accompaniment with the main course, such as French beans or a green salad.

Entertaining has become much more fun now that so many exciting ingredients are available in the shops. Using exotic fruits and vegetables provides a good conversation piece, too. Experiment with a new recipe or ingredients before trying them out on your friends and you will then be able to serve any dish with confidence.

I think everyone feels some degree of nervousness when entertaining others to a meal; will the food be all right – will they like it – have you overlooked something, or made some obvious mistake in the planning? There are various points to look out for, to make sure that everything is as perfect as possible – see the check-list. Then, having prepared everything as carefully as you can, my advice is to relax and enjoy yourself!

Check-list for planning a balanced meal

In planning your meal, check that you have:

☐ *contrasting colours within each course and within the meal as a whole; avoid starting with beetroot soup, for instance, and ending with a compote of red fruits*

☐ *a variety of different dishes; avoid more than one course based on fruit, pastry, nuts, or any other ingredient*

☐ *contrast of textures: crisp crunchy nut roast with a smooth carrot purée, for instance; a creamy soup followed by a crisp main course, such as asparagus in phyllo pastry*

☐ *a good balance of flavours – avoid, for instance, starting with mint-flavoured soup and ending with mint ice cream*

☐ *food of different shapes: don't have a loaf-shaped terrine followed by a loaf-shaped nut roast followed by a chocolate roulade. Plan a balance of round and square, and of dishes which are presented in individual portions and those which are served at the table*

Food presentation

Keep garnishing light, fresh and relevant to the dish. Generally I like to echo in the garnish one of the ingredients which is in the dish, rather than to introduce something new, unless it is witty or relevant in some way. Good food speaks for itself and does not need much garnishing. Instead of garnishing a main course such as lentil burgers or a nut loaf with slices of tomato or lemon, which do nothing for anybody, it can be nicer to serve it with a fresh, light salad, such as Tomato and Basil Salad (p. 73), which gives the colour to the meal and tastes good as well.

Chopped fresh herbs, the same type as used in the dish, can be sprinkled over as a garnish. It's nice to have a herb garden with a good variety of herbs so you always have a plentiful supply, but supermarkets now sell little packs of most fresh herbs.

Wicker baskets and trays, and wooden bowls, are most useful for presenting food attractively. A large round wicker tray, lined with leaves, makes an excellent base for crudités and a dip, and also for carrying a steaming hot casserole of food from the oven to the table, acting as a tray and place-mat in one. Small wicker or wooden bowls, perhaps lined with a coloured paper napkin, make attractive containers not only for warm rolls, but also for 'finger salads', especially for children.

Or try using hollowed out fruit and vegetables as containers for food. Lemons, red, green and yellow peppers, marrows or cucumbers, for example, can all be used imaginatively and give more colour to the meal. Fruits such as pineapples, oranges, grapefruit and melons also make good containers for fruit salad mixtures, ice creams or sorbets, and will add that extra flavour to the food.

Arrange food in clumps of colour, rather than mixing up colours. A pyramid shape is often a most attractive way to present individual items such as Stuffed Vine Leaves (p. 141), Profiteroles (p. 314) or fresh fruit.

Little extras make all the difference: crudités or fruit arranged on fresh (edible) leaves or on crushed ice; ice in a jug of water; a bunch of flowers, simply arranged, on the table, and candles, which immediately give a romantic glow and cover up flaws in the decor and surroundings (which you are probably acutely aware of, but which your friends probably won't even notice). An ice bucket will keep white wine chilled throughout the meal. If you can have matching or harmonizing colours in the table linen, napkins, candles and flowers, this, too, will contribute to the overall atmosphere.

Wine

Wine adds to the pleasure of any meal and gives it a celebratory feeling, while experiencing a meal with food and wines perfectly matched, to enhance each other, is perhaps one of life's greatest pleasures. The way to achieve this is really through experimentation – trying a dish with different wines to see what they do to each other. Try drinking up the last of your main course wine with the pudding, and you'll know what I mean; the sweetness makes a pleasant wine taste overly sharp. Yet that wine would probably taste excellent with a mellow cheese like mild Cheddar or Fontina. (A very good reason for serving the cheese before the pudding whenever possible.) Equally, a sweet, honeyed dessert wine would marry well with the pudding course.

When choosing more than one wine for a meal, it's common sense to start with the younger or less good wine; move from a young, light wine to a medium-bodied wine with some depth, and end with a full-bodied dessert wine. Choosing wine is now much easier and more interesting since some wine shops have introduced a numbering system, grading each wine from 1 to 10 – the dryest being no. 1 and the sweetest no. 10. As a general rule, serve white wine before red, the exception being sweet white dessert wines, which end the meal.

The aim when matching wine with food is to get a balance between the two; light dishes with light wines, sharp, lemon-flavoured dishes, such as a first course, for instance, with a sharp, pointed wine, like a Sauvignon. Mellow, even slightly sweet foods, such as most vegetables, need a more rounded wine, like a Chardonnay or Chenin Blanc; while dishes with many flavours, or a robust, almost 'meaty' taste, need a firm, strong wine which will hold its own beside them, but at the same time is not so good as to be spoilt by the flavourings of the dish: youngish fruity red wines with medium body are ideal.

Some foods do not flatter any wine. Sharply flavoured vinaigrette is an example of this, and it may be better to use a little wine with the olive oil to dress the salad. Strong flavourings of lemon juice, powerful herbs and spices (such as fennel or rosemary, for instance, and curry flavours), artichokes, Brie and Camembert cheese (which make the wine taste strange) and mayonnaise and cream sauces (which coat the palate) are other examples of foods that inhibit the appreciation of a good wine.

Wines with vegetarian food

The choice wine to serve with a special meal begins with the aperitif, which, ideally, should be one which will awaken the palate and prepare it for the meal to follow. My favourite aperitifs to serve (apart from Champagne – the ultimate aperitif, incomparable for putting everyone in a celebratory mood before a special meal!) are light, dry to medium white wines, such as a Chenin blanc, a dry Vouvray or Muscat, or a Sylvaner or Riesling. A dryish Vermouth, such as Chambery, served with plenty of sparkling Perrier or Badoit water and a sliver of lemon is another favourite. Wine connoisseurs say that the best nibble to serve with drinks before a meal is plain biscuits, like water biscuits or other unsweetened cocktail biscuits, though I also like juicy salty black olives.

Many vegetable-based vegetarian dishes are flattered by light-bodied, fruity and not too dry white wines, particularly if the dish also contains nuts, which have a slight sweetness to them. A wine made from the Chenin blanc grape, such as a dry Vouvray, Anjou or, one of the most pleasant, with

an excellent balance of acidity and honeyed fruitiness, a Savennières, is ideal. The Savennières is particularly successful where there are a number of divergent vegetable flavours. An alternative would be an Australian Fumé Blanc.

Chardonnay-based wines also, with their softness and almost appley flavour, work well with nut and vegetable main courses: a Macon, Pouilly Vinzelles or Pouilly Fuissé, for instance, or a White Burgundy or Chablis from Australia; or perhaps an oaky Californian Chardonnay or Australian Wyndham Estate Oak Cask.

Alternatively, light-bodied, young, fruity red wines, perhaps served slightly chilled, can be delightful with these types of main course; wines such as a Saumur Champigny, Côtes-du-Rhône, Gamay de Touraine, St Aubin or Beaujolais-Villages. A

Brouilly, deliciously round and fruity in flavour, would be another possibility. From Australia, suggestions include Rosemount Beaujolais, Wyndham Estate Beaujolais, Merlot or Chardonnay.

For something fuller-bodied, to support strong herby flavourings, or to go with something like a special nut loaf, a Châteauneuf-du-Pape or a Syrah-based wine from the Northern Rhône, such as a Cornas, St-Joseph, Côte Rotie or Crozes Hermitage; or a red from the Loire, such as a Chinon Bourgeuil or St Nicolas de Bourgeuil, with their raspberry-scented bouquet, or a Fleurie. Californian red wines are generally full-bodied and of reliable quality. Among the wines from Australia that have been recommended to me are Wynns Coonawarra Red from South Australia, a Cabernet Sauvignon, Penfolds Bin 389 or a Wolf Blas Yellow Label Shiraz.

For pasta dishes with an Italian orientation, such as Lasagne (p. 256) and Tagliatelle Verde with Lentil Sauce (p. 252) or Fusille Colbuco with Aubergine and Wine Sauce (p. 255), an Italian red wine would be appropriate: a Chianti Classico, Barolo or Barbaresco; or a Côte Rotie from France, or a Cabernet Sauvignon from France or elsewhere.

When it comes to choosing wines for the pudding course, the same principles apply. Sharp-flavoured fruit salads and compotes do not go well with wine, although if they include a flavouring of a fruit liqueur, such as Cointreau, that, well-chilled, can be a good partner for them. Ice creams generally are not good with wine, either, because they numb the palate, though I have enjoyed a good sweet German dessert wine with home-made raspberry ice cream. The wine needs to be sweeter than the dessert so that it does not taste sour when drunk with it.

Hot fruit soufflés, such as Hot Black Cherry Soufflé (p. 290) are complemented by a good sweet wine – as good a quality as you can afford, a German Beerenauslese, Auslese, Sauternes, Barsac or Montbazillac; or, from Australia, a Brown Bros Orange Muscat. One of these sweet wines complements, also, Pashka (p. 288), Apricot and Orange Fool (p. 282) and Compote of Dried Fruit (p. 102), in the latter case especially if it is marinated in a little of the sweet wine – a Sauternes would be especially good. A chilled sweet wine or toning eau-de-vie or liqueur can work with a sorbet; ice-cold Poire Williams eau-de-vie with Pear Sorbet (p. 282) for instance, or, with Champagne Sorbet (p. 283) – champagne!

Ingredients

Good cooking begins with good ingredients, and the aim of this section is to provide a guide both to choosing and getting the best from well-loved basics, and identifying and using some of the more unfamiliar and exotic ingredients. So there are fruits ranging from apples to rhamboutans; vegetables from potatoes to doody; and pulses from familiar haricot beans to black chick peas and urd; plus a worldwide selection of nuts and grains. The sections on mushrooms and truffles, sea vegetables, and cheeses offer further delicacies, and then there's a glorious profusion of pasta, ranging from tiny stelline and convighi piccole to the larger tortellini, cappelletti and ravioli . . . all comprising a feast of vegetarian delights.

◁ *Fresh chestnut*   *Dried chestnut* ▷

Marrons glacés ▽

Chinese water chestnut ▽
The Chinese water chestnut is not actually a nut but a tuber with a crisp texture

Chestnut △
The sweet chestnut has been cultivated for thousands of years in Southern Europe where it is widely used in sweet and savoury dishes

Brazil nut ▽
The seeds of a giant tree which grows wild in the tropical South American jungle, brazil nuts have a creamy texture

Nuts and Seeds

One of our earliest foods, nuts and seeds feature in traditional recipes throughout the world. Many nuts and seeds, such as walnuts, hazelnuts and sesame seeds, are a useful source of oil. They can also be made into butters, such as peanut butter, or ground into flour. Most nuts and seeds are an excellent source of nutrients, especially protein, iron, calcium and B vitamins. Nutrients vary from nut to nut, and by eating a mixture, you can be sure of getting a balanced range in your diet.

△ **Cob nut**
One of the varieties of cultivated hazelnut

Macadamia nut/Queensland nut ▽
A delectable nut, with a melting texture, native to Australia but now also grown in the southern U S A, South Africa, the Caribbean Mediterranean and Hawaii

Cashew nut ▽
Native to Brazil, the cashew nut grows in a kernel, surrounded by toxic oil, at the base of an apple-like fruit

Pistachio nut ▽
The fruit of a small tree native to Asia and grown in Southern Italy, Sicily, the Middle East and in California, Texas and Arizona

Pine nut/Indian nut ▽
The seed of the stone pine, pine nuts were enjoyed by the Romans in Britain and by the Indians of North America

Hazelnut △
The hazelnut grows in Europe, Asia and America and was certainly eaten during the Bronze Age

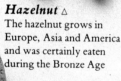

Pecan nut ▽
A relative of the walnut and a native of North America where it is eaten in large quantities as a dessert nut

◁ **Walnut**
The walnut is native to south-eastern Europe and the leading producer is France, but it is found in West and Central Asia, China, Australia, New Zealand, South Africa and South America

Almond △
Native to the Mediterranean, almonds are gastronomically the most important nut world-wide, much used in confectionery and baking

Tahini △
Made from sesame seeds

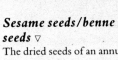

**Sesame seeds/benne
seeds** ▽
The dried seeds of an annual
plant, probably native to
Africa, but cultivated in India
and China since ancient times

Alfalfa seeds ▽
A tiny legume, native
to the Mediterranean

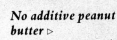

**No additive peanut
butter** ▷
Available either smooth or
crunchy

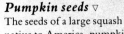

Pumpkin seeds ▽
The seeds of a large squash
native to America, pumpkin
seeds are particularly rich
in minerals

Sunflower seeds ▽
The seeds of the sunflower
plant, native to Peru but now
grown as a crop in many parts
of the world

Poppy seeds △
These vary in colour from
grey-blue to cream

Coconut strands ▽

Peanut/ground nut/monkey nut △
Native to South America, the peanut is
botanically a legume, the outer shell
being the pod

Creamed coconut ▽

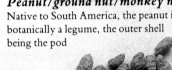

Desiccated coconut △

Tiger nut/chufa nut △
Native to the Mediterranean and Portugal,
tiger nuts are the dried tubers of a sedge

Coconut ▽
The fruit of the coconut palm
which grows throughout
South Eastern Asia, coconut
features in many tropical dishes

Mixed chopped nuts △

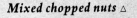

Nuts and Seeds

Choosing and storing

Nuts are at their most delicious when eaten straight from the shell. Because of their high oil content, they go rancid quickly once shelled, so buy them in small quantities from a shop with a quick turnover, and, if possible, keep them in the fridge or freezer; otherwise store nuts in an air-tight jar or tin, and use them up quickly.

Preparation and cooking

Shelled nuts can be used whole, chopped, flaked or ground. The flavour of some, such as hazelnuts and peanuts, is improved by roasting and this also enables the outer skin to be removed. To roast, place the nuts in a single layer on a baking sheet and bake at 180C/350F/Gas Mark 4 for about 20 minutes, until the skins rub off easily and the nuts underneath are golden-brown. Cool, then rub off the skins in a clean cloth (or leave the skins on if you prefer).

The best way to chop nuts is to place them on a sturdy board and chop with a sharp knife, holding the point down and moving the knife round in a semi-circle. To flake nuts such as almonds and brazil nuts, hold the nut down firmly on a board and slice thinly across with a knife. Nuts can be ground in a food processor, blender, electric coffee grinder or food mill, finely (consistency of ground almonds), medium (like medium-ground coffee) or coarsely (about the texture of rolled oats). Coarsely chopped nuts can be bought as MIXED CHOPPED NUTS.

Nuts can be used in sweet and savoury dishes and as a nibble. They can be made into milks, creams, butters, dips and soups; used as a thickener in sauces and casseroles, added to risottos, pilafs, stuffed vegetable mixtures and salads; as a topping for puddings, gratins, cakes and breads. In vegetarian cookery they can form the principal ingredient of many delicious savouries, including burgers, pâtés, pies and loaves.

ALMOND *Prunus dulcis*
Almonds are particularly rich in protein, iron, calcium and vitamin B2. There are two types, sweet and bitter. Bitter almonds are small and contain prussic acid. They are never eaten raw but are made into essence and liqueurs.

Sweet almonds can be bought in the shell, SHELLED, and with the skins removed as whole BLANCHED, FLAKED, NIBBED (not illustrated) and GROUND almonds. For best results, buy almonds in the skin and blanch them at home. Put the almonds into a small saucepan, cover with cold water and boil for 2 minutes. Drain and pop the almonds out of their skins by squeezing them.

Almonds are perhaps best known for their use in sweets and in baking. Almonds are blanched, roasted and salted for serving as nibbles and are delicious in main savoury dishes (p. 238). Almonds can be made into a particularly good milk (p. 238).

BRAZIL NUT
Bertholletia excelsa
Brazil nuts are rich in fat, protein, the B vitamin thiamin and magnesium. They have a creamy texture and a delicate flavour which makes them excellent for eating raw in mueslis and salads or as a stuffing for dates. Although not used widely in traditional cookery, they can be made into tasty vegetarian loaves, crumbles and burgers, as well as making a good addition to a fruit cake.

CASHEW NUT
Anacardium occidentale
Cashew nuts should be white and plump with a slightly sweet, bland flavour. They can be bought whole, both raw and roasted, halved or in pieces, which is cheapest. They are useful in vegetarian cookery for both sweet and savoury dishes. They can be made into a creamy and delicate milk and topping (p. 238).

CHESTNUT *Castanea sativa*
The chestnut contains more starch and less oil and protein than other nuts, although it is rich in B vitamins. Choose chestnuts which are firm with bright, shiny skins.

Chestnuts can be made into soups, added to casseroles, such as Red Cabbage Casserole (p. 180), or pies, used to make a traditional vegetarian Christmas roast (p. 233), or to stuff cabbage leaves, or served with Brussels sprouts. Puréed and sweetened, chestnuts also make the basis of some delicious puddings.

DRIED CHESTNUTS are time-saving, although their texture is less floury than that of fresh chestnuts. Dried chestnuts should be soaked and cooked like pulses (p. 40) and can then be used to replace fresh chestnuts in recipes, allowing 1 part dried chestnuts to 3 parts fresh chestnuts. Canned whole chestnuts and chestnut purée (available either plain or sweetened) are useful store cupboard standbys, while chestnuts preserved whole in sugar or syrup as MARRONS GLACÉS make a sweet treat or garnish.

CHINESE WATER CHESTNUT
Eleocharis tuberosa
This is a tuber which is cultivated in China, Japan and the East Indies. It is used sliced as a vegetable and outside Asia is usually bought canned.

COCONUT *Cocos nucifera*
Coconuts can be bought whole and you should be able to hear the liquid inside when you shake them. Make sure that the 'eyes' look dry, with no smell of rancidity or mould. To open a coconut, pierce two of the eyes with a skewer and drain out the liquid over a jug. Then hold the coconut horizontally in both hands and bang it down on a stone or concrete surface to break it in half. Cut the flesh away from the shell using a sharp knife, and grate or chop the flesh as required. The liquid is delicately flavoured and makes a refreshing, nutritious drink or flavouring for spiced vegetables.

Coconut flesh can be eaten fresh as a snack or in salads, fruit and vegetable mixtures. It can also be bought DRIED (not illustrated), CREAMED, DESICCATED or in FLAKES or STRANDS. Keep these in the fridge or freezer, or store them in an airtight jar and use them up quickly. Desiccated coconut can be added to cakes, biscuits and Crunchy Granola (p. 240), or reconstituted as coconut milk.

HAZELNUT
Corylus avellana, C. maxima, C. colura

Cultivated hazelnuts are derived from the cob, which grows wild in Britain, the filbert, which grows in Southern Europe, and the Turkish hazel which grows in the Middle East. The COB NUT (Kentish Cob), which is grown in Kent, is not really a cob but a filbert, and in Spain hazelnuts are known as Barcelona nuts. It is difficult to tell these types apart, once harvested. They can be bought in the shell, shelled but untreated, and whole but skinned.

Hazelnuts are mainly used in baking and confectionery and are a useful nut in vegetarian cookery, being the lowest in fat, a good source of vitamin E and a tasty addition to stuffings, burger and loaves.

MACADAMIA NUT / QUEENSLAND NUT
Macadamia ternifolia

Usually sold roasted and lightly salted, this has a delicious, delicate flavour. It is expensive and so probably best served simply, as a nibble with drinks, or in a salad, where its flavour and creamy texture can be appreciated.

PEANUT / GROUND NUT / MONKEY NUT
Arachis hypogaea

One of the best sources of protein, iron and niacin in the vegetarian diet, peanuts can be bought in the shell, shelled but raw, roasted unskinned and skinned. They can also be roasted and skinned at home, as described above. Salted and roasted and dry-roasted peanuts are also available, and of course PEANUT BUTTER, either crunchy or smooth.

Peanuts also make an excellent thick sauce for serving with salads or lightly cooked vegetables: reduce roasted peanuts to a purée in a blender or food processor with chilli pepper, garlic and fresh coriander to taste, and enough milk, coconut milk or stock to make a thick sauce.

PECAN NUT *Carya illinoensis*
Pecans can be bought shelled or unshelled and are generally used as a dessert nut and in sweet dishes such as Pecan Pie. In the USA they are also sometimes used as a turkey stuffing and in vegetarian cooking they provide a useful flavouring and delicious mealy texture which is good in salads and hot nut savoury dishes.

PINE NUT / INDIAN NUT
Pinus pinea (Not illustrated)

The most protein-rich of the nuts, pine nuts are always bought shelled and have a fresh, creamy appearance and delicate 'pine' flavour. They can be used as they are or lightly roasted in a moderate oven or under the grill. They are added to omelettes in the pine-clad Landes area of France, but they are more extensively used in Spanish, Italian and Middle Eastern cooking, in pilafs, Stuffed Vine Leaves (p. 141) and Pesto (p. 172), the classic Genoese sauce for pasta. Pine nuts make an excellent garnish for many fruit or vegetable dishes and they can also be made into delicately flavoured nut savouries (p. 237).

PISTACHIO NUT *Pistacia vera*
Pistachio nuts can be bought in the shell or shelled. They can be eaten as a nibble or as a bright garnish for both sweet and savoury dishes. They are rich in iron.

TIGER NUT / CHUFA NUT
Cyperus esculentus sativus

This dried rhizome has a sweet, almond-like flavour. It can be eaten raw, as a nibble, or made into a creamy milk (p. 238). (It is not generally available in Aus./NZ.)

WALNUT *Juglans regia*
Walnuts can be bought in the shell, or shelled, as halves or pieces. Buy fresh walnuts, as older ones can become bitter. Their strong flavour is useful in savoury nut dishes, perhaps combined with other milder nuts, such as cashews. Walnuts are good in salads, with pasta, and in many sweet dishes such as walnut cake or walnut biscuits.

ALFALFA SEEDS
Medicago sativa

Sprinkle alfalfa seeds over bread before baking, or sprout them as on p. 207 and add to salads. Sprouted alfalfa seeds are rich in nutrients including protein, vitamin C and B vitamins.

POPPY SEEDS
Papaver somniferum

Sprinkled over breads, salads or pasta, or added to cakes or savoury dishes, poppy seeds give a pleasant, nutty flavour. In India they are ground and used to thicken curries.

PUMPKIN SEEDS
Cucurbita pepo

Rich in nutrients, particularly protein, iron and zinc, pumpkin seeds can be bought either salted or unsalted and used whole in savoury rice and vegetable dishes and mueslis, sprouted (p. 207) for salads and stir-fries, or ground and added to burgers and savoury loaves.

SESAME SEEDS / BENNE SEEDS
Sesamum indicum

Rich in B3, iron, protein and zinc, sesame seeds are usually white but may be brown, red or black, depending on the variety. They are delicious when lightly roasted and can be added to sweet and savoury crumble toppings, sprinkled over breads, or ground with salt (p. 237). Sesame seeds can also be used in the form of a sticky beige or brown cream, called TAHINI. This is widely used in Middle Eastern cookery, in dips such as Hummus (p. 144) which make delicious additions to vegetarian cuisine. Sesame seeds are also made into the Middle Eastern sweetmeat, halva.

SUNFLOWER SEEDS
Helianthus annuus

These can be bought whole, salted or unsalted, and added to stuffings, salads and savoury bakes, or ground like nuts. Their flavour is improved by roasting lightly. Sunflower seeds can also be sprouted (p. 207). They are a natural source of many nutrients, notably B1, B6 and potassium.

Green split pea ▽

◁ **Yellow split pea**
Split peas – dried peas which have been skinned – can be either green or yellow, and cook quickly without soaking

Pigeon pea △
Originating in Africa, pigeon peas are grown in many warm countries and are an important pulse in Caribbean cooking

Chick pea and flour ▽

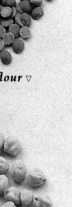

Black chick pea ▽
One of the several varieties of chick pea

Pulses

A staple food throughout the world for thousands of years, pulses are the dried seeds of pod-bearing plants of the Leguminosae family. They are rich in protein, iron, calcium and B vitamins. They are high in fibre but contain virtually no fat, making them the nutritionists' dream food! The word pulse is linked to the Latin word *puls*, porridge, and the Greek *poltos*, poultice. Pulses are an economical food and when well cooked can be delicious.

Dried pea △
Called soup peas in the USA, blue boilers in Aus./NZ, and familiar in the UK as mushy peas, these are soft and sweet-tasting when cooked

Orange/red lentil ▽
Orange/red lentils are brown lentils which have had their outer skin removed

Brown lentil ▽
A tasty lentil which remains whole when cooked but needs careful checking and washing first to remove small pieces of grit

Adzuki bean ▽
The seeds of a bushy annual plant native to China, adzuki beans are a popular ingredient in Chinese and Japanese cookery

Butter bean / Lima bean △
Native to South America and grown extensively in Madagascar and the USA, where it is known as the lima bean

Puy lentil △
Popular in France and considered by some to be the best-flavoured lentil

Split urd ▷
Probably native to India, where they are called urd dal and widely used, urd beans are available both whole and split

△ **Split husked mung bean**

Green lentil △
Green lentils have a savoury flavour and do not break up during cooking

Urd bean △

Black bean △
Native to Mexico and a staple food in Central and Southern America, black beans cook to a delicious mealy texture

Black-eyed bean/cow pea ▽
Native to Africa, black-eyed beans are popular in South America and India. There are around 50 species, some with the black 'eye', others without

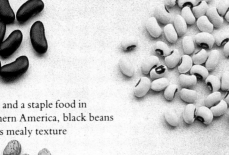

Broad bean △
The original bean, cultivated since the Stone Age; can be pale or mid brown in colour. Popular in the Middle East and Italy where they are known as 'Il carne del povero' – 'the meat of the poor'

Pinto bean △
Also called gunga pea and toor dal, pinto beans are native to India and popular there and in the Caribbean

Butter bean/Lima bean ▷
The dried variety of the butter bean is always flat and kidney-shaped but may be quite small, as here

Ful medames △
Ful Medames beans are native to the Middle East where they are widely eaten

Black haricot bean ▽

Borlotti bean △
Also known as 'rose coco' beans, borlotti are the most popular dried beans in Italy

Flageolet bean △
Delicate in flavour, colour and texture, the flageolet is an immature haricot bean

Haricot bean ▷
Almost certainly native to Guatemala and Southern Mexico, the haricot is popular in Britain as baked beans, and in the USA where it is called the navy bean

Mung bean △
Mung beans are widely cultivated in China and India, where they are known as mung dal. They are the beans which are made into bean sprouts

Soya bean and flour △
Originating in Eastern Asia, and grown for thousands of years in China, where it is known as 'meat without bones', the soya bean is very rich in protein. It is made into many products, including flour

Cannellini bean △
The large creamy white beans popular in Italian cookery

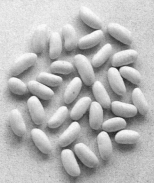

Red kidney bean △
One of the most popular beans, red kidney beans are widely used in South American and Caribbean cookery

Pulses

Choosing and storing

Pulses will keep for many years, but they become drier and harder with time. So buy small quantities of bright, shiny pulses with no hint of dust, damp or mould. Keep them in an airtight container.

Preparation and cooking

Preparation of pulses is simple and involves washing, soaking (some types do not need this) and cooking in plenty of cold water until tender. If you find pulses indigestible – their one disadvantage for some people – careful preparation, as described here, followed by thorough cooking, can help, as can boiling the pulses in an uncovered pan.

1 Washing

Swish the pulses around in a bowl of cold water then drain in a colander. If you're using brown lentils, look out for little lumps of dirt and stones.

2 Soaking

Put the pulses into a deep bowl and cover them with their depth again in water. Leave to soak for about 6–8 hours or overnight. Then drain and rinse again.

Alternatively, put the washed pulses into a roomy saucepan, cover them with water as before and boil for 2 minutes. Then remove from the heat, cover and leave to stand for 1 hour. (This is equivalent to the long, cold soak.) Drain and rinse the beans and cook as follows.

3 Cooking

Tip the pulses into a large saucepan, cover them with their depth again in cold water and bring to the boil. Red kidney beans need to be boiled hard for 10 minutes, to destroy any enzymes which can cause stomach upsets. This isn't necessary for other beans. Then turn the heat down and simmer the pulses, without a lid, until tender (see chart). Sometimes pulses are added to a casserole or made into a soup after soaking but before cooking; just allow them to simmer until tender. It is best to season pulses after they are cooked,

to avoid any possibility of the salt toughening the outside and preventing the inside from cooking properly.

If you are short of time, canned pulses, available in considerable variety, are an excellent buy.

ADZUKI BEAN
Phaseolus angularis
Quick-cooking, with a pleasant, slightly sweet flavour, adzuki beans can be used instead of lentils in any recipe for soups, salads, bakes or burgers. They can also be sprouted (p. 207).

BLACK BEAN *Phaseolus vulgaris*
These tasty beans are used to make American black bean soup, and, with rice, to make the Spanish dish, Moors and Christians. Good in vegetable casseroles, as a moist and tasty filling for Vegetarian Moussaka (p. 212), or in mixed bean salads.

BLACK-EYED BEAN/ COW PEA
Vigna unguiculata
These pretty little beans, often popular with children, have a slightly nutty flavour and are particularly useful because they cook in about 40 minutes, without soaking. Use in stews, soups, salads and casseroles.

BORLOTTI BEAN
Phaseolus vulgaris
Borlotti beans can be used in the same ways as any of the kidney bean family and make a pretty addition to a mixed bean salad.

BROAD BEAN *Vicia faba*
More familiar in their fresh or frozen state, dried broad beans (illustrated) have quite a strong, earthy flavour. They are widely used in the Middle East. I find their tough skin a disadvantage, but if well chopped in a food processor and blended with olive oil, garlic, lemon and parsley, they make a good dip.

BUTTER BEAN/LIMA BEAN
Phaseolus lunatus or P. limensis
Known as the lima bean when it is fresh, and the butter bean when it has been dried. In Australia and the UK the dried form, the butter bean, is more common. It is a tasty bean with a mealy texture which absorbs other flavours well.

A quick way of serving butter beans is in cream with mushrooms: fry 225 g/8 oz sliced button mushrooms in 25 g/1 oz butter or vegan margarine for 3–4 minutes, then add the drained contents of a 425-g/15-oz can of butter beans and heat gently with 300 ml/10 fl oz single cream and 2 tablespoons lemon juice. Season, then serve sprinkled with paprika pepper and chopped parsley.

CANNELLINI BEAN
Phaseolus vulgaris
Cannellini beans combine well with pasta and make a fragrant salad when mixed with a fresh herb vinaigrette. If you want to adapt chicken or fish recipes to vegetarian cooking, cannellini beans make a good replacement, as do any of the white beans.

Soaking and cooking times for pulses

Pulses can be cooked until they are just tender, al dente, or soft, as preferred

All lentils, mung beans and black-eyed beans; split peas	cook without soaking for 25–40 minutes, until tender
Flageolet beans	soak as described, cook for 30–60 minutes
Other beans, including chick peas	soak as described, cook for 1–1½ hours
Soya beans	soak as described, cook for 1½–3 hours

CHICK PEA *Cicer arietinum*

Chick peas are available whole, including a BLACK variety, split, ground into FLOUR and also canned, and have a particularly savoury flavour. Their cooking time is rather variable, ranging from 30 minutes to 3 hours, depending on the type. Chick peas are delicious cooked and then sautéed in garlic butter, or combined with mayonnaise and lightly cooked vegetables, including some artichoke hearts (fresh or canned) to make the Provençal salad, Aigroissade. Chick peas are included in many traditional recipes, including Felafel (p. 208), and Hummus (p. 144) from the Middle East and Couscous from North Africa (p. 247).

FLAGEOLET BEAN
Phaseolus vulgaris

Popular in France. The fresh colour and flavour makes flageolet beans particularly suitable for serving as a vegetable (just boil and serve with butter and freshly ground black pepper) or as a salad.

They are also good in a creamy sauce with mushrooms, as described for butter beans (above).

FUL MEDAMES *Lathyrus sativus*

Although popular in the Middle East, I find ful medames one of the less useful beans because of their tough skin. But like broad beans (see above) they can be made into a good dip, using a food processor. Ful medames are not generally available in Aus./NZ.

HARICOT BEAN
Phaseolus vulgaris

A useful all-purpose bean which absorbs other flavours well. In France haricot beans are used to make the popular and filling Cassoulet and Pistou (p. 136). In the USA haricot beans are also used to make another traditional dish, Boston Baked Beans. To make these, simmer 225 g/8 oz haricot beans as described above until almost tender, then drain and add to 1 quantity of Italian Tomato Sauce, made as described on p. 171 but not boiled after the tomatoes have been added. Stir in 1–2 table-spoons real barbados sugar, then bake at 160 C/325 F/Gas Mark 3 for 2–3 hours, until the sauce is rich and thick and has been well absorbed by the beans. Stir from time to time. Serve with hot crusty bread.

LENTIL *Lens esculenta*

There are several types of lentil, the most common being little BROWN LENTILS, dark greenish-grey PUY LENTILS, larger whole GREEN—sometimes called continental – LENTILS and split ORANGE LENTILS. Lentils can be cooked without soaking, although soaking speeds the cooking time a little. Lentils are used in the Mediterranean and Middle East to make soups, stews, bakes, sauces for pasta (p. 252) and salads (p. 158), and in India, where they are made into spicy dals (p. 209). They make a good replacement for minced meat in recipes such as Shepherd's Pie (p. 210) and Spicy Lentil Burgers (p. 210). Whole lentils can also be sprouted (p. 207), when they become juicy with a slightly spicy flavour.

MUNG BEAN *Phaseolus aureus*

Mung beans are small, round and usually green, although there are some black and yellow varieties. They can also be bought skinned and halved to reveal their golden colour. Whole mung beans make a good salad, dressed with a tangy, lemon vinaigrette. When sprouted (p. 207), they are juicy and good in stir fries and salads.

DRIED PEA *Pisum sativum*

Most familiar in the form of mushy peas, dried peas can also be used in soups and stews. They are known as BLUE BOILERS in Aus./NZ.

PIGEON PEA *Cajanus cajan*

Pigeon peas are widely used in African, Caribbean and Indian dishes, but in my opinion are not as tasty or useful as some of the other pulses, such as chick peas.

PINTO BEAN *Phaseolus vulgaris*

These can be used like red kidney beans and are good in casseroles and to add colour to mixed bean salads such as those on p. 157.

RED KIDNEY BEAN
Phaseolus vulgaris

One of the most useful pulses, red kidney beans are available both dried and canned. They should always be boiled hard for 10 minutes before using. They are used to make the Mexican dish of Refried Beans, in which the cooked beans are fried like a large potato cake; a delicious West Indian stew where they are cooked with carrots, onions, garlic and thyme, with a knob of coconut cream added at the end, to thicken and enrich, and a tasty vegetarian version of Chilli con Carne (p. 208).

SOYA BEAN *Glycine max*

Soya beans have a strong flavour and need powerful flavourings, such as curry, tomato and garlic, to make them taste good. I think they're nicest when sprouted (p. 207), and added to salads and stir-fries.

Many products, such as miso, soy sauce, tempeh, milk and tofu are made from soya beans and described in other sections of this book.

SOYA FLOUR is high in protein and low in starch so cannot be used to make a normal white sauce, although it can be stirred into savoury sauces and gravies to add bulk and nutrients and is sometimes added to flour as a dough improver, in the proportion 8 parts flour to 1 part soya flour.

SPLIT PEAS, YELLOW AND GREEN
Pisum sativum

The split and skinned version of dried peas cook quickly and can be made into a good purée for serving with vegetables, or the two colours may be combined and cooked until just tender, then mixed with a lemon or mint vinaigrette to make an attractive salad. Pease Pudding is a cheap and filling traditional British dish. To make this, see p. 207.

URD BEAN *Phaseolus mungo*

(Not generally available in Aus./NZ.) The split and skinned version of a black bean, about half the size of a pea, this is best cooked without soaking. Urd dal is used to make dosas, the crisp pancakes of Southern India, and also poppadums.

▽ **Brown long-grain rice**
A good all-purpose, healthy rice for savoury dishes

◁ **Brown rice flakes**

Brown short-grain rice △
The variety of brown rice to use for puddings

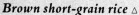
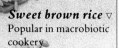

Buckwheat flour △
In Russia, where buckwheat is a staple food, blinis – delicious yeasty pancakes – are traditionally made with buckwheat flour

Sweet brown rice ▽
Popular in macrobiotic cookery

▽ **Basmati rice, brown**

Grains

The seeds of cultivated grasses, grains are the world's most import-ant staple food. They are important in the vegetarian diet, where they are recognized as protein foods and often mixed with other com-plementary proteins, such as seeds, nuts, pulses and dairy products, to make maximum use of their protein (p. 10). As well as protein and carbo-hydrate, grains are a valuable source of iron, zinc, calcium and B vitamins, and, in their natural, unrefined state, are also rich in fibre.

Buckwheat △
Triangular-shaped seeds of a plant belonging to the rhubarb and sorrel family, buckwheat can be bought roasted or unroasted

Pudding rice ▽
Called pearl rice in Aus./NZ, this is a round-grain rice which cooks to a creamy consistency

Millet △
The seeds of a hardy annual grass, millet is eaten as a cereal in Africa and Asia and used as a source of starch in Russia

Millet flakes ▽

Basmati rice, polished ▽
A particularly aromatic long-grain rice with slim, pointed grains

Millet flour △
Millet does not contain gluten, so is useful where there is an allergy to this

American long-grain rice ▷

Wild rice ▽
The seeds of a water grass rather than a grain, wild rice has long black grains which are chewy and nutty-tasting

Brown rice flour ▽
Milled from the whole rice grain, brown rice flour is useful for gluten-free baking

Ground rice ▽
Ground rice is polished rice which has been milled

Italian rice (arborio) △
The rice to use for an authentic Italian risotto

Wholewheat flour (100%) ▽
Milled from the whole grain. No additives (except raising agents) are allowed in 100% wholewheat flour in the U K

▽ **Bran**
The outer husk of the grain, removed during the milling of white flour, and high in fibre

▽ **Rye grains**

△ **Wholewheat flour (85%)**
100% wholewheat flour with some of the bran removed, or may be white flour with some of the germ and bran put back

Rye flakes ▽

Coarse maize meal or polenta ▷
A staple food of northern Italy, where it is used to make polenta, a thick savoury porridge

Rye flour △
Widely used to make dark heavy breads (such as pumpernickel) and crispbread in Germany and Scandinavia

△ **Unbleached white flour**
This consists of 72% of the whole grain

Fine maize meal △
Milled from corn, maize meal is gluten-free and used to make tortillas, tacos and tostadas

Pot barley △
The whole barley grain which can be cooked to make pilafs, or salads

Pearl barley △
Barley which has had most of its outer husk removed (but still contains more fibre than brown rice!)

Corn △
Indigenous to Mexico, corn is one of the world's most important cereals

▽ **Couscous, wholewheat**

Hominy grits △
Corn which has been hulled

Bulgur wheat △
Popular Middle Eastern wheat which has been cracked by boiling, then redried

Barley flour △

Barley flakes ▽

Kibbled wheat △
Wheat grains which have been slightly cracked, good for adding to muesli mixes or sprinkling on top of loaves

Oat grains (groats) △

△ **Wholewheat grains**
Wheat belongs to two main groups: baking wheat and hard wheat

Medium oatmeal ▷
Made by grinding the grain

Couscous, △ **plain**

▽ **Oat flakes or jumbo oats**

Semolina △
Flour made from the hard part of durum wheat. Available wholewheat and white

Wheat flakes △
Made by rolling the whole wheat grains to flatten them and make them easier to eat

Wheatgerm △
The heart of the grain, where germination occurs, wheatgerm is rich in nutrients

Rolled oats △
Oats which have been partially cooked in steam then flattened by rollers

Grains

Choosing and storing

Grains will keep in their natural un-milled form for a year or so, but they do deteriorate and ideally should be bought fresh and used up within 6 months. Cracked and flaked grains, and flours will keep for 3–6 months. Oats – with the exception of rolled oats, where heat has destroyed the enzymes – do not keep well because of their high oil content. Buy in small quantities and use within a few weeks. Oatmeal should smell and taste sweet with no rancid smell or bitterness. Wheatgerm, especially if it is the best unstabilized type, which is free from additives, deteriorates rapidly; keep it in the fridge and use it up within 3–4 weeks. Keep other grains and flours in airtight containers in a cool, dry place.

Preparation and cooking

Wholewheat, oat, barley and rye grains are soaked and cooked like pulses; they can then be tossed in a dressing or mixed with vegetables to make burgers, roasts or stews. Flaked grains, like jumbo oats, and also kibbled wheat, make a pleasantly chewy addition to muesli mix and home-made breads; jumbo oats can be mixed half and half with rolled oats for extra chewy flapjacks.

BARLEY *Hordeum vulgáre*
Barley is available in the form of whole grains, called POT (or WHOLE) BARLEY, as PEARL BARLEY, which is more refined, and as FLAKES and FLOUR. Pearl barley is often added to soups and stews, and makes a tasty casserole (p. 246).

BUCKWHEAT
Fagopyrum esculentum
Buckwheat is gluten-free and a natural source of rutin, which naturopaths use to treat varicose veins and high blood pressure. It can be bought as grains, ROASTED or UN-ROASTED, and FLOUR. Roasted buckwheat is the most useful for cooking, and can be served instead of rice with vegetable dishes. To cook buckwheat, put it into a saucepan with double its volume in water and simmer for about 10 minutes, until the grains are just tender and all the water absorbed. Add butter, or vegan margarine, and seasoning.

BUCKWHEAT FLOUR is used to make pancakes. Try making pancakes as described on p. 299 using a half and half mixture of buckwheat and wheat flour and serving with unsalted butter, Black Olive Pâté (p. 258) and soured cream.

BULGUR WHEAT
Sometimes called burghul, cracked wheat or pourgouri, bulgur wheat is easy to prepare and delicious in pilafs or with lots of chopped fresh parsley

and mint in the popular Middle Eastern salad, Tabbouleh (p. 159). To prepare bulgur wheat, put the grains into a bowl, allowing 50–100 g/2–4 oz per person, cover with plenty of cold water and leave to soak for about 30 minutes. Then drain and put into a saucepan containing a tablespoon of olive oil, or perhaps a chopped onion or other vegetables which have been fried in the oil for about 10 minutes, season with salt and freshly ground black pepper and stir over a gentle heat for about 5 minutes, until the wheat is hot. Or put the wheat into an oiled casserole, cover and bake for 15–20 minutes in a moderate oven (180c/350f/Gas Mark 4) until hot.

CORN *Zea mays*
Corn is available as whole grains – fun for 'popping' – and as COARSE or FINE FLOUR or MAIZEMEAL; also as HOMINY GRITS (not generally available in Aus./NZ), used to make porridge, puddings and breads. Although it is eaten as a staple food in Italy and South America, corn is not ideal for this because of its deficiency in niacin. The flour made from corn is made into spoonbread in the USA and polenta in Italy.

COUSCOUS
Available as PLAIN or WHOLE-WHEAT, this is made by processing semolina into tiny pellets and is another easy grain to prepare: just

---

Cooking perfect rice

There are two methods of cooking rice and each have their devotees. I find both work equally well; it's really a question of which of the methods you find works best for you.

The only rice which needs washing first is basmati, which should be put into a sieve and rinsed under the cold tap until the water runs clear.
Immersion method
Half fill a large saucepan with water, bring to the boil and add 1 teaspoon salt. Throw in the rice, allowing 50 g/2 oz per person if the rice is to be served as an accompaniment, or up to

100 g/4 oz per person if the rice is the main dish, without much else. Simmer, uncovered, until a grain is tender when you bite it. For timings, see table. Drain the rice into a colander and rinse it under the hot tap to remove any starch. Then tip it back into the saucepan and dry the rice off over a low heat for about 5 minutes, stirring it several times with a fork to prevent sticking. Or put the rice into a shallow ovenproof dish and place, uncovered, in a cool oven (170c/325f/Gas Mark 3) for about 10 minutes until it is dry.

Absorption method
For this you need to measure both the rice and the water, and it's handy to use the same container for this – a large mug, or a 300 ml/10 fl oz measure. Put one measure of rice into a saucepan, add two measures of water and a little salt. Bring to the boil, then cover and turn the heat down as low as possible. Leave the rice undisturbed until it's tender and all the water has been absorbed (see table for timings). Then stir gently with a fork. Or, after it has come to the boil, the rice can be cooked in a cool oven (as above).

spread the couscous out on a large plate and sprinkle it with salted water, allowing 600 ml/1 pint water and ½ teaspoon salt to 450 g/1 lb couscous (which is enough to serve 4–5 people). Rub your fingers between the grains to help keep them separate, then leave them for 15–20 minutes, to absorb the water. Put the couscous into a steamer saucepan, metal colander or large metal sieve set over a pan of boiling water, or of spicy stew, as on p. 247, for about 15 minutes, or until heated through.

MILLET *Panicum miliaceum*
Millet contains more protein and iron than any other grain. It can be bought in the form of GRAINS, FLAKES and FLOUR, and is gluten-free. The grains can be made into tasty pilafs (p. 245) and burgers, and the flakes can be cooked to make a creamy porridge – particularly useful for those on gluten-free diets.

OATS *Avena sativa*
Oats contain more of the B vitamin biotin and more fat than wheat; they are also one of the best sources of soluble fibre (p. 12) and are gluten-free. Oats are available as whole GRAINS, called 'whole oat groats', milled to fine, medium or coarse (or 'pinmeal') meal, for making Porridge and Oatcakes (p. 322); as OAT FLAKES, or 'JUMBO OATS', ROLLED OATS, and various pre-cooked 'instant' versions. But even traditional porridge, made from oatmeal, is quick to make. To serve 2 people, bring 600 ml/1 pint water and 1 teaspoon salt to the boil, then gradually whisk in 50 g/2 oz medium oatmeal. Simmer gently for 25–30 minutes, stirring occasionally.

RICE *Oryza sativa*
Although there are many varieties of rice, these can be divided into two basic types: LONG-GRAIN, where the grain is four or five times as long as it is wide, and SHORT-/MEDIUM-GRAIN, where the grain is short and rounded. In long-grain types, which include AMERICAN LONG-GRAIN RICE and BASMATI RICE, with slim pointed grains and a particularly good flavour, the grains are more

separate when cooked, so these are most suitable for pilafs and rice salads, where you want a 'fluffy' texture. The round and medium grains break up more as they cook and cling together. This type includes ITALIAN RICE (ARBORIO), PUDDING (or PEARL) RICE, and SWEET BROWN RICE which is popular in macrobiotic cookery. Many varieties of rice can be bought in a 'BROWN' version, that is, with just the inedible outer husk removed, or 'POLISHED' so that they are completely white (and less nutritious). BROWN RICE FLAKES, GROUND RICE and BROWN RICE FLOUR are also available.

RYE *Secale cereale*
Rye is available in the form of whole GRAINS, FLAKES, FLOUR (white and wholemeal) and kibbled grains for topping loaves. Rye lacks gluten so is usually mixed with wheat flour. Rye is also used to make whiskey.

SEMOLINA
Semolina is the basic ingredient for Gnocchi alla Romana (p. 227) and can also be made into one of the most popular vegetarian dishes, Cheese and Parsley Fritters (p. 217), a variation of gnocchi. Semolina is used to make delectable sweet puddings in India and the Middle East, and can be added to cakes and biscuits.

WHOLEWHEAT
Triticum vulgare, compactum, durum
Wheat is available in a number of forms, including WHOLE GRAINS, KIBBLED WHEAT, WHEAT FLAKES, and flours consisting of various percentages of grain (WHOLEWHEAT FLOUR, 85% and 100%, and WHITE FLOUR, including UNBLEACHED which contains fewer additives than bleached). The parts of the wheat, the GERM and BRAN, removed during the milling of white flour, are also available. Wheat flour is classified as 'strong' or 'soft' depending on its gluten content. Gluten is the protein-rich substance which becomes springy and stretchy when water and heat are applied. Flour made from gluten-rich, hard wheat is generally considered best for making bread and for puff and flaky pastries because it produces a strong, springy dough, although soft wheat produces a better-flavoured bread and is fine for making the one-rise Grant Loaf (p. 328). Soft flour produces light cakes and biscuits.

WILD RICE *Zizania aquatica*
High in protein, and with a slightly smoky flavour, wild rice gives a luxurious touch to a special meal. It can be cooked on its own, using the absorption method described for brown rice, or with brown rice, replacing some of the rice with the same quantity of wild rice (p. 44).

Cooking times for rice (in minutes)

Type	Immersion method	Absorption method Top of Stove	Absorption method Oven (180°C/350°F/ Gas Mark 4)
White Basmati	10–12	15	25
Brown Basmati	12–15	20	30
White long grain/Patna	15	15	35–40
Brown long grain	35	45	50
Italian arborio	15	15	35–40
Japanese glutinous	15	15–25	35–40
Wild rice	35–40	40	50

Fresh fettuccine,
plain and verde ▷

Linguine ▷

Long spaghetti ▽
Best-loved pasta, good with
any sauce – lentil mixtures are
particularly good – or with just
olive oil, garlic and plenty of
freshly ground black pepper

Spaghettini △
Slim pastas, light and
refreshing mixed with
colourful vegetables, cooked
until just tender

Pasta

Pasta means dough in Italian and is
the collective name for all types of
spaghetti, macaroni, ravioli, vermicelli and so on. Although there is a
tradition of pasta making and eating
in other parts of the world such as
China, Spain, Greece and Israel, the
Italians are undoubtedly the world
leaders and have developed hundreds of different pasta shapes. Both
white and wholewheat pasta are
good sources of fibre (wholewheat
more so) and contain useful amounts
of protein, iron and B vitamins.

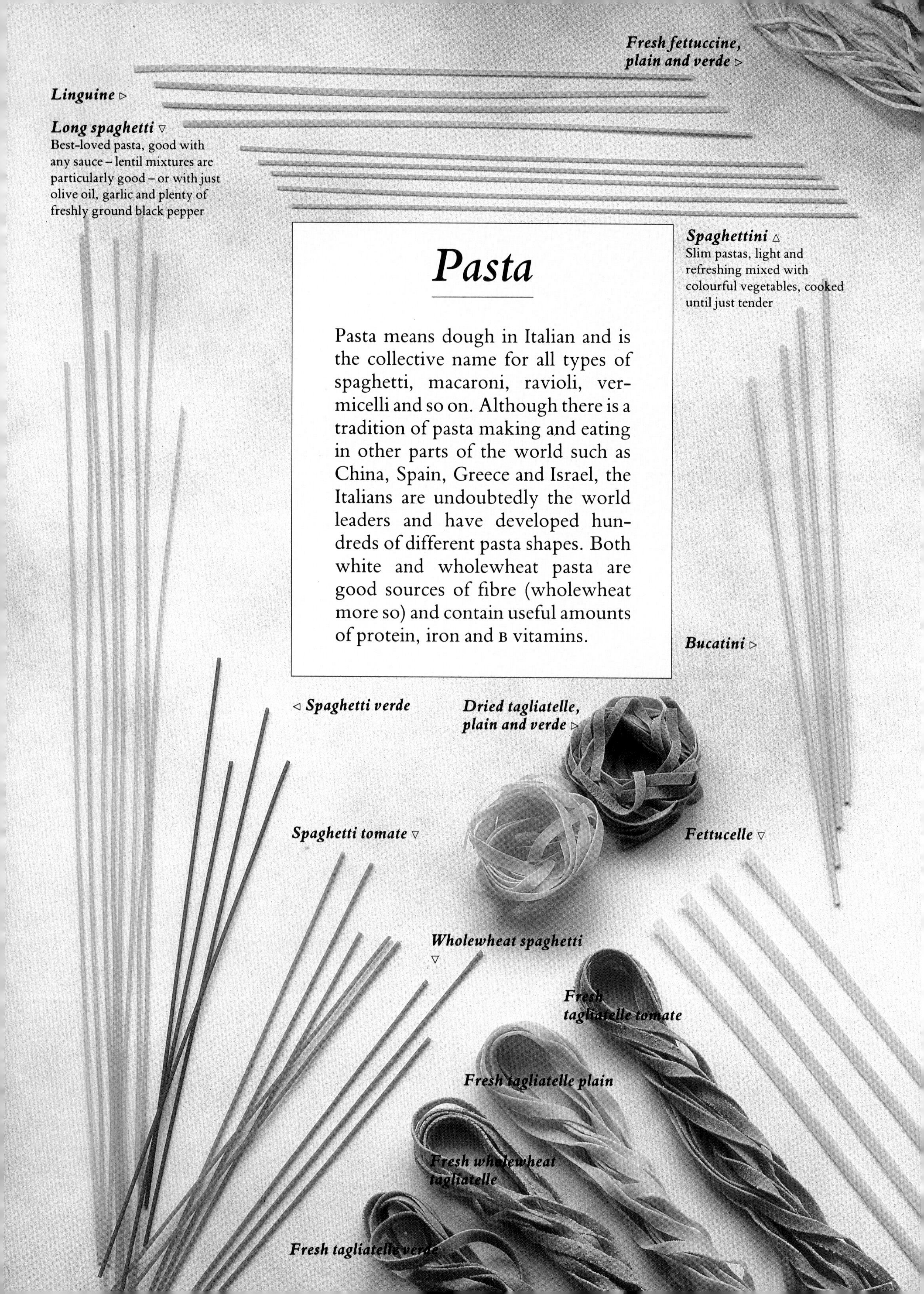

Bucatini ▷

◁ *Spaghetti verde*

Dried tagliatelle,
plain and verde ▷

Spaghetti tomate ▽

Fettucelle ▽

Wholewheat spaghetti
▽

Fresh
tagliatelle tomate

Fresh tagliatelle plain

Fresh wholewheat
tagliatelle

Fresh tagliatelle verde

◁ **Fresh taglioni, plain and verde**

◁ **Rigatoni**
The ridges of this delicious hearty pasta hold sauces well

Macaroni ▽

Coloured rigatoni ▽

◁ **Dried fettuccine verde**

▽ **Penne rigate**

Spiral macaroni ▽

◁ **Penne ziti**
Quill-shaped pasta, available ridged, and plain

Short-cut macaroni,
◁ **wholewheat and plain** ▽

▽ **Elbow macaroni, plain**

△
Elbow macaroni, wholewheat

Ditalini ▽

△ **Quick-cook macaroni**
Macaroni comes in a variety of lengths, widths and shapes. A useful all-purpose pasta

Ditali ▽
Small pasta shapes, for adding to soups and stews

Vermicelli ▽
The thinnest pasta, mixed with chick peas, garlic and olive oil to make a famous dish Tuone e Lampo

Fusilli
Available dried or fresh in several colours ▷

Mezze canneoni △

Fusille colbuco ▽
An attractive pasta which sauces cling to well because of the curls, fusille colbuco is also known as bucati and bucatini spirale

Farfalle ▷
Pasta bows or butterflies, specially good with vegetables, either hot or as a salad
▽

Fiochetti ▽

Farfalline bows ▽
Tiny butterflies/bows, liked by children and pretty in clear soups

Lumache ▽
These 'snails' make good containers for fillings such as ricotta cheese with garlic and fresh herbs, served with tomato sauce

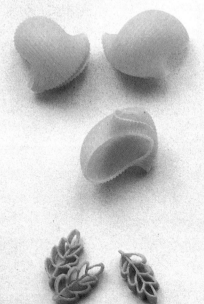

Wheatear wholewheat shapes △
One of the best wholewheat pastas, these can be added to casseroles, served simply with olive oil and seasoning or with a sauce

Pasta may be white or wholewheat, depending on the type of flour used to make it; it can be dyed a variety of colours with vegetable purées and comes in numerous shapes and sizes. Terminology can be confusing, because often the same shape is known by several different names, and in Italy these frequently vary from province to province! Pasta can be bought dried or, increasingly, fresh. Dry pasta may contain eggs – if it does it will say *all'uovo* on the packet; fresh pasta always does. Fresh stuffed pastas, such as ravioli and cappelletti, are increasingly to be found with vegetarian fillings, such as spinach and ricotta.

Frilly lasagne verde ▽

Plain lasagne ▽

Lasagne verde ▽

Easycook wholewheat lasagne ▷
For layering with, or wrapping around, savoury mixtures to make warming bakes

Cannelloni ▽
Large pasta tubes which are usually stuffed, covered with a sauce and baked

Wholewheat conchiglie rigate ▽

Pipe rigate △
Another hearty pasta which sauces cling to well

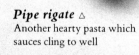

Conchiglie rigate (two sizes) △
Shell pasta, another good shape for serving with a sauce or in a salad with a creamy dressing

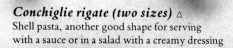

▽ Transparent rice noodles
Delicate pasta, can be soaked for a few
minutes then added to vegetable stir-fries, or
deep-fried until crispy

Dried egg noodles ▷

Fresh egg noodles ▽

**Fresh fine
egg noodles ▷**

**Dried wholewheat
noodles ▷**

Rice noodles ▽

**Fresh oiled
egg noodles △**

**Cappelletti
or 'little hats' ▽**

**Rice ribbon
noodles ▽**

Ravioli ▷
This ravioli is filled
with spinach and
ricotta and
comes in
various
sizes

Conchiglie △
Attractive ridged open shells

Convighi piccole ▽
Tiny pasta, for adding to
soups, come in many
interesting shapes

◁ Tortellini
Another example of a pasta
with a vegetarian filling,
available plain and verde

△ Annelli ▷

◁ Stelline

**Ravioli △
verde**

Pasta

Quick and easy, cheap and delicious, pasta is welcoming, filling and warming. It can be made into many appetizing vegetarian dishes.

Choosing and storing
Good-quality dried pasta should feel hard and silky-smooth and when cooked should have a deliciously wheaty flavour. Store in a cool, dry place. Fresh pasta should smell fresh and look bright and slightly shiny. Store in the refrigerator and use within 24 hours if possible.

How to make pasta
Pasta is easy to make at home and worth doing if you eat a fair amount of it and enjoy cooking. You can roll the pasta out by hand, but better results are obtained by using a pasta machine. The hand-operated ones, consisting of rollers turned by a handle, are perfectly adequate for making family-sized amounts of pasta, or, for large quantities, electric machines are available.

To make 350 g/12 oz pasta – enough for 4 people – put 200 g/7 oz plain strong flour into a bowl with ½ teaspoon salt. Gradually add 2 beaten eggs, to make a pliable dough. Set the rollers of your pasta machine to their widest position. Take a piece of pasta dough about the size of an egg, flatten it roughly with your hands, then feed it through the rollers. Fold the piece of dough in three, then feed it through again. Repeat this process six or seven times, until the dough is smooth and silky, then lay it on one side and repeat the process with the rest of the dough, keeping the pieces in the right order. Next, tighten the rollers a notch and put the pieces of dough through again, once only this time, and without folding. Repeat three times, tightening the rollers a notch each time. Cut the pieces of pasta in half if they become too long to handle, and support them as they come through the machine so that they don't fall in folds and stick together.

If you want to make lasagne, cannelloni or ravioli, feed the pasta through the machine again with the rollers on the tightest setting but one. The pasta can then be cut to the required size and used straight away in savoury bakes, without further drying or cooking. For ravioli, spread half the pieces of pasta out on a flat surface and put small mounds of a savoury mixture (such as 225 g/8 oz curd cheese mixed with 75 g/3 oz grated Cheddar cheese and 25 g/1 oz grated Parmesan cheese) on the pasta about 3 cm/1½ inches apart. Brush around each mound with beaten egg, then cover with the rest of the pasta, pressing down around the edges and trying to exclude as much air as possible. Cut between the mounds with a pastry wheel. Put the ravioli on a lightly floured surface and leave to dry for 30 minutes. Then put the ravioli into a large pan of boiling water and cook for 4–6 minutes. Drain well, put into a hot serving dish and cover with hot tomato sauce.

To make tagliatelle, pass the pieces of pasta through one of the cutting rollers, then spread them out on a clean, lightly-floured cloth, or drape over a piece of dowelling, and leave to dry for about 1 hour. Then cook the pasta as described opposite, allowing 2–3 minutes only.

Preparation and Cooking
Fresh or dried pasta needs no preparation before cooking.

Allow 100–175 g/4–6 oz fresh or dried pasta per person for a main course, less if serving as a first course. For every 100 g/4 oz pasta you will need 1.2 litres (2 pints) water. Bring the water to the boil in a large saucepan. Salt can be added to the water, allowing ½–1 teaspoon for every 100 g/4 oz, but I prefer to add some crunchy flakes of sea salt to the cooked and drained pasta. When the water is boiling vigorously, add the pasta all at once.

To add long straight pasta, such as spaghetti, hold the pasta in your hand like a bunch of flowers, put the ends in the water so that it's standing up, then as the ends soften, gradually bend them, pushing more of the dry pasta into the water. When all the pasta is under water, give it a quick stir, then leave it to boil, half-covered, until tender. This will vary from type to type; smaller types cook more quickly, and fresh pasta is ready in about 5 minutes. The packet will give a guide, but check it before the time is up, as cooking time can vary from batch to batch and even be affected by the weather!

To test whether the pasta is done, bite a piece; it should be tender but still slightly firm, so you can feel it on your teeth, or *al dente* as the Italians say. When this stage is reached, remove from the heat and drain the pasta immediately. The easiest way to do this is to stand a metal colander in the sink and tip the pasta straight into it. Give the colander a good shake to make sure all the water has been dislodged from the pasta, then tip it back into the still-hot pan.

Return to the heat with some olive oil or a knob of butter, a good grinding of black pepper and some sea salt if you didn't add this to the water. Turn the pasta gently with a fork or spoon, so that all of it is coated with butter or oil. Serve immediately on a well-warmed serving dish or individual plates.

Dry lasagne can be cooked as described, then drained and draped over the sides of the colander and saucepan, to prevent it from sticking together, ready for layering into a casserole with a tasty filling and sauce. Or it can be added to the casserole in its dry form. In this case make the filling and sauces with extra liquid for the pasta to absorb during cooking.

Fresh lasagne does not need cooking first, and, again, you should allow extra liquid because it will expand during cooking.

Cooking times for pasta	
very thin pasta, small shapes	5–9 minutes
larger shapes, long tubes	10–20 minutes
fresh pasta	2–3 minutes

Serving pasta

The many varieties of pasta now available provide all sorts of serving possibilities.

The smallest, thinnest types, such as CONVIGHI PICCOLE, FARFALLINE and VERMICELLI, are good to add to soups or lightly fried vegetables as in Pasta Primavera (p. 251), while the ridged and shell-like pastas, such as RIGATONI, PENNE, PIPE and CONCHIGLIE RIGATE, all hold sauces very well. Rigatoni is also very good combined with aubergines in Aubergine and Pasta Charlotte (p. 258) or with olives in Pasta with Black Olives (p. 258).

LASAGNE and MACARONI are used with sauces in baked dishes (p. 256 and p. 257), and many of the smaller pasta shapes, MEZZE CANNEONI or WHEATEAR WHOLE-WHEAT SHAPES, for example, can also be used in bakes such as Whole-wheat Pasta and Mushroom Bake (p. 252).

The large pasta tubes such as CANNELLONI and RIGATONI can be stuffed, with chopped mixed vegetables or just one vegetable such as spinach, and baked in a sauce in the same way as lasagne.

The smaller shapes, such as TORTELLINI, RAVIOLI and CAPPELLETTI, can also be stuffed – cheese and nuts are good – and can be cooked in stock or water, or in a tomato sauce.

Long pastas, SPAGHETTI, SPAGHETTINI, LINGUINE, TAGLIATELLE and FETTUCELLE, are delicious served very simply, with just butter or cream, freshly ground black pepper, some chopped fresh herbs and a grating of Parmesan cheese. Or they can be dressed in numerous sauces; a lentil mixture is a good one to use (p. 252), as is an aubergine and tomato sauce (p. 254). Tagliatelle with Gorgonzola and Walnuts (p. 250) makes a delicious dish for a supper party, while linguine mixed with vegetables and cheese (p. 255) couldn't be simpler for a quick lunch.

Many pastas are now available coloured with vegetables dyes – spinach or tomato, for example. These coloured pastas can make a dish very attractive when served with an appropriately coloured sauce. Children especially enjoy the COLOURED RIGATONI or FUSILLI with a mushroom sauce (p. 251).

There are many varieties of EGG NOODLES available and they are best known for their use in Chinese dishes. They are often sold fresh, coiled in circles or, when dried, in square 'cakes'. They can be used for noodle soups, or stir-fried with vegetable mixtures after they have been boiled.

RICE NOODLES are sold as long strands and are also called rice sticks. TRANSPARENT, or cellophane, RICE NOODLES are lighter in colour. They are both used in soups, stir-fries or can be deep-fried.

Quick serving ideas for pasta

Pasta with fresh herbs
Add 1–2 tablespoons chopped fresh herbs to the cooked pasta with the butter or olive oil. Tarragon and basil are delicious.

Pasta with cream
Stir a little double cream into the hot cooked pasta, allowing 2 tablespoons per person.

Pasta with avocado
Add a small ripe avocado, peeled and chopped, to the hot cooked pasta after draining.

Pasta with nuts
Chopped walnuts go beautifully with hot cooked pasta. They're nicest if you buy them in the shell and crack a few while the pasta cooks. Chop roughly and add to the drained and buttered pasta. A little cream mixed in as well makes this extra good.

Pasta with beans and black olives
While the pasta is cooking, heat through a can of cannellini beans in another saucepan. Drain both the beans and the pasta and mix together with a little crushed garlic, 1–2 tablespoons olive oil and a few whole black olives.

Pasta with chick peas
Add hot cooked and drained chick peas, crushed garlic and a little olive oil to hot drained pasta for a favourite Italian mixture.

Pasta with croûtons
While the pasta is cooking, cut a slice of wholewheat bread per person, remove the crusts, and cut the bread into 5-mm/¼-inch squares. Fry the bread croûtons in olive oil until crisp and golden-brown all over. Drain on kitchen paper. Add the croûtons to each serving of hot pasta.

Pasta with onions
Start this when you put the water for the pasta on to boil, to give the onions time to cook until they're really soft and slightly caramelized. Allow ½–1 large onion per person, peeled and sliced. Heat a knob of butter or vegan margarine in a saucepan or frying pan, add the onion and fry for 10 minutes, then add a sprinkling of salt, pepper and sugar, and continue to fry for a further 5–10 minutes, until the onion is golden-brown but not burnt. Stir the hot, cooked onion into the cooked and drained pasta.

Pasta with Fresh Tomato Sauce
Serve hot spaghetti or pasta spirals with Fresh Tomato Sauce (p. 170); snip plenty of fresh basil on top. Some diced Brie can be mixed with the pasta, to melt deliciously in the heat of the sauce.

Pasta with poppy seeds
Add a good sprinkling of poppy seeds to hot, buttery pasta; they add a nutty flavour and crunchy texture.

Sweet pasta
For a sweet pasta dish, popular in Italy, cook pasta until tender – a bit softer than the usual *al dente*, drain and add (for 350 g/12 oz pasta, which gives 4 servings) 3 tablespoons sugar, 40 g/1½ oz butter and 75 g/3 oz good quality plain chocolate, melted. Mix well and serve immediately.

Feuille de chêne ▷
Also called oak leaf lettuce, referring to the shape of the leaves

Leaf Vegetables

Crisp and refreshing, leaf vegetables whet the appetite and cleanse the palate. Some have been used for centuries – mustard and cress was enjoyed by the Greeks and Romans. Today there is a wide range to choose from and making salads is a particular pleasure. Several of the leaf vegetables, such as watercress, lettuce and spinach, make excellent soups. Leaf vegetables contain vitamin A, calcium, iron, fibre and chlorophyll, which, when eaten raw, protects the body against disease.

Batavia △
A broad-leaf endive with the characteristic slightly bitter flavour

Iceberg lettuce △
Iceberg lettuce has a firm heart and a deliciously crisp texture

Cos lettuce ▷
Cos lettuce has a particularly good flavour and the smaller leaves make good edible scoops for dips

Lamb's lettuce △
Also known as corn salad and mâche, the leaves of a small, hardy plant which grows wild in much of the Northern Hemisphere

Endive ▽
With its curly leaves and slightly bitter flavour, endive makes an attractive contrast with other salad ingredients

◁ Radiccio
A particularly useful salad vegetable because of its red leaves, which lend themselves to all kinds of stunning garnishes and colour schemes

Chard ▽
The thick white stem of chard is delicious cooked with the leaves or cooked and served separately

Sorrel △
A hardy perennial plant often found growing wild in Europe, sorrel has a sharp, almost lemony flavour

Vine leaf ▷
Tender leaves from the vine make a delicious edible wrapping for other foods

Watercress ▷
With its hot, pungent flavour and dark green colour, watercress makes a good contrast to other leaf vegetables in a green salad

Butterhead lettuce
▽

Spinach ▷
One of the most useful of the leaf vegetables, spinach can be used raw in salads, as well as cooked

Cress △
Mild and juicy, cress appeals particularly to children

Leaf Vegetables

Green salad ingredients

- [ ] *lettuce (all kinds)*
- [ ] *curly endive*
- [ ] *chicory*
- [ ] *watercress*
- [ ] *lamb's lettuce (corn salad/mâche)*
- [ ] *tender spinach leaves*
- [ ] *sorrel, rocket and tender nasturtium leaves (they're pungent, so just a few used in the salad will be sufficient)*
- [ ] *spring onions, raw onion rings*
- [ ] *celery, cucumber, fennel, green pepper, avocado pear, thinly sliced*
- [ ] *fresh herbs*
- [ ] *dandelion leaves (pick these carefully from a place unpolluted by dogs, cars or agricultural sprays, taking the tender leaves from near the centre and washing them very thoroughly)*
- [ ] *chopped walnuts or hazelnuts*

Choosing and storing

These vegetables need to be bought as fresh as possible; they should be crisp and slightly damp looking, with no sign of withering or dryness. They are best used as soon as possible but, if bought really fresh, they will keep in the salad compartment of the fridge for two or three days.

Preparation and cooking

Leaf vegetables, especially lettuce, are often sprayed with fungicide, so need thorough but gentle washing in plenty of cold water. Remove any coarse or damaged leaves and tough stems. Tear, rather than cut, delicate leafy vegetables such as lettuce, and if they are going to be eaten raw, dry them carefully in a salad spinner or with a soft absorbent cloth. Many leaf vegetables are tasty when cooked and also make excellent soups.

CRESS / MUSTARD AND CRESS (Not illustrated)

Lepidium sativum and *sinapis alba*
The cress widely available in the shops is not the traditional mixture of mustard and cress but often salad rape. This has a mild flavour which particularly appeals to children. All kinds of mustard and cress make a pleasant addition to a salad bowl and are useful for garnishing.

ENDIVE / BATAVIA / ESCAROLE

Cichorium endivia crispum
There are two main types of endive, curly-leaved and broad-leaved. They all have a refreshing, slightly bitter flavour. Endive is particularly rich in folic acid (see p. 13).

FEUILLE DE CHÊNE

Lactuca sativa
Also called OAK LEAF LETTUCE, this attractive lettuce has a slightly bitter flavour. It makes an excellent addition to a green salad and can also be used on its own. It is particularly good with a walnut dressing and Chèvre cheese (p. 150).

GOOD KING HENRY

Chenopodium Bonus-Henricus
(Not illustrated)
Also called GOOSEFOOT, this is a perennial herb which used to be cultivated and then went out of fashion. It has small, pointed leaves growing either side of a central stem bearing small flowers like those of sorrel.

Both the leaves and the flowers can be eaten. It tastes very similar to spinach and is prepared in the same way.

LAMB'S LETTUCE / CORN SALAD / MÂCHE

Valerianella locusta
Lamb's lettuce has a delicate flavour and makes a useful addition to salads, particularly in winter.

LANDCRESS *Barbarea verna*

(Not illustrated)
This plant looks and tastes rather like watercress, with a similarly pungent flavour, but, as the name implies, it grows on land. It is a useful salad vegetable, and, like watercress, can also be made into soup.

LETTUCE *Lactuca sativa*

Lettuce is an ancient cultivated crop and is probably the number one salad basic. It can be served on its own or mixed with other ingredients; shredded, it makes a good filling for sandwiches or base for other salad ingredients, and large leaves can be rolled around tasty fillings to make an interesting nibble or snack. Firm lettuce hearts can be braised in the same way as fennel (p. 182); outer leaves can be made into an excellent soup (p. 131), or used to impart flavour to peas cooked *à la Française* (p. 183).

There are many different types of lettuce, some of the main ones being:

CABBAGE HEAD

These are round or flat in shape, and can be subdivided into crisp lettuces, such as ICEBERG, and the soft-leaf or BUTTERHEAD varieties.

COS

Tall, well-flavoured lettuces, this group includes cos, DENSITY, and, perhaps the best-flavoured lettuce of all, the hearty 'LITTLE GEM' lettuce.

SALAD BOWL

In this type the leaves do not form a solid heart and the leaves can be picked off individually if required while the plant is growing in the garden. They are usually particularly tender and there are some red, bronze or variegated types available.

RADICCIO *Cichorium intybus*

This red-leaved variety of endive has a slightly bitter flavour; it makes a useful addition to a leafy salad and is a very attractive garnish.

ROCKET *Eruca sativa*
(Not illustrated)

Sometimes classed as a herb, rocket has a hot, almost spicy flavour and a few sprigs make an excellent addition to a green salad.

SORREL *Rumex acetosa*

A few sorrel leaves give interest to a green salad, and a little sorrel cooked with spinach adds sharpness. Puréed sorrel makes a good accompaniment to a nut roast, cutting the richness, and it also makes a refreshing soup. Sorrell used in a Wilted Leaf Salad makes a delicious variation on Green Salad. Put a mixture of green salad ingredients into a bowl, using interesting varieties such as sorrel, rocket, dandelion leaves and spinach. Fry some small cubes of wholewheat bread in butter or olive oil, to make crisp croûtons. Then, just before you want to serve the salad, pour the croûtons and their cooking fat over the salad ingredients, mix quickly and serve at once. Until the eighteenth century sorrel was popular pounded with sugar and vinegar into a green sauce and it is still sometimes served like this in parts of Yorkshire.

Cooked sorrel should not be taken in large quantities too often because of the high level of oxalic acid it contains.

SPINACH *Spinaca oleracea* and SWISS CHARD
Beta vulgaris, var. *Cicla*

Delicious dark green leafy plants which can be shredded raw and added to salads, cooked and served simply as a vegetable accompaniment, or made into substantial main course dishes. The central stem of Swiss chard is particularly good and can be shredded and cooked in a little water for a few minutes before adding the green leaves, or it can be removed, cut into lengths and cooked and served separately.

SEA SPINACH (not illustrated) which can be found growing wild around the coast is a wild form of spinach beet. It can be collected and used just like spinach and has an excellent, naturally salty flavour. NEW ZEALAND SPINACH (*Tetragonia expansa*) (not illustrated) is another green leafy vegetable which is not related to spinach botanically but is similar and prepared in the same way.

Spinach is particularly rich in vitamin A, iron and calcium but, like sorrel, contains oxalic acid, which inhibits the body's ability to absorb some minerals. It's therefore best not to eat cooked spinach more than twice a week, although some natural health experts believe that the oxalic acid in raw spinach does not have the same binding effect.

Spinach is available fresh, frozen – a useful alternative to fresh – and canned, which in my opinion is not worth eating.

In Aus./NZ, if English spinach is unavailable, silver beet makes a good substitute.

VINE LEAF *Vitis vinifera*

Vine leaves are much used as edible wrappings for foods in vine-growing countries, dolmades, or vine leaves filled with a rice stuffing, being perhaps the best-known example. They have a delicious, slightly lemony flavour.

Fresh young vine leaves, when available, need to be blanched in boiling water for a few minutes, to soften them, before being rolled up round a savoury stuffing (p. 141). Vine leaves which have been canned or packed in brine need thorough rinsing in warm water, to wash off the salt, before use.

Cooking perfect spinach

Allow 900 g/2 lb spinach for 4 people. Wash the spinach well by plunging it into a large bowl of water two or three times, until the water is clear. Remove any tough stems; either discard these, or chop them and add to 1 cm/½ inch boiling water in a large saucepan. Boil for 2 minutes, then put the spinach in on top. If you are not using the stems, put the spinach straight into the pan, without any water – the water still clinging to the spinach from the washing will be enough. Push the spinach down into the pan as it cooks. A fish slice is good for this if you hold it so that you can chop down with the slice part. Half cover the pan with a lid and cook for about 7 minutes, chopping the spinach with the fish slice from time to time. Drain the spinach well in a colander, using the back of a spoon to squeeze out the water. Then return it to the still-hot pan and chop it a bit more with the fish slice if necessary; or turn the spinach out on to a board and chop it quickly with a knife. Add a knob of butter or vegan margarine, a good seasoning of sea salt, freshly ground black pepper and perhaps a touch of grated nutmeg. Spinach absorbs a lot of butter, it's up to you how much to use.

WATERCRESS
Nasturtium officinale

Watercress is useful in salads, soups and sauces, and can also be added to stir-fries (p. 181). Although watercress used to be gathered from the wild, it is now specially cultivated, and eating wild watercress is not recommended because of possible contamination.

Watercress should be well washed and will keep in a polythene bag in the salad compartment of the fridge for 2–3 days.

A tangy, bright green Watercress Sauce tastes and looks wonderful with vegetable mousses and terrines, or a white nut roast. To serve 4, fry a small onion, peeled and finely chopped, in 15 g/½ oz butter or vegan margarine for 10 minutes, until soft but not browned. Add 75 ml/3 fl oz dry white wine and 1 tablespoon white wine vinegar and boil until reduced and syrupy. Meanwhile chop 2 bunches of watercress, then add two-thirds of this to the reduced onion mixture, with 600 ml/1 pint Light Vegetable Stock (p. 129). Bubble over a high heat until reduced to about one-third. Add the remaining watercress and purée in a blender or food processor. Stir in 4 tablespoons double or non-dairy cream and reheat gently without boiling. Season to taste with salt and pepper and stir in 15 g/½ oz butter or vegan margarine.

⊲ Brussels sprouts
Said to originate near Brussels
in the thirteenth century

Kale △
Kale means 'non-hearting'

Pak-choi / Mustard greens △
A variety of Chinese cabbage with a crisp,
juicy central stem and pleasantly flavoured
leaves, pak-choi cooks quickly and is ideal
for stir-fries

Brassicas

Brassicas come in a variety of shapes
and sizes, from tiny Brussels sprouts
to big, family-sized cabbages; from
knobbly kohlrabi to beautiful purple
broccoli. They range in colour from
palest greenish-white to deep burgundy red, and they span the seasons. They provide useful quantities
of a range of vitamins and minerals,
including vitamins A, B and C and
useful amounts of iron and calcium.
They also contain enzymes which
are protective and curative when the
vegetables are eaten raw.

Calabrese △
One of the varieties of broccoli,
calabrese is tender, with an
excellent flavour

Kohlrabi ▷
The leaves of kohlrabi can be
eaten, but it is really grown for
its root which is like turnip
with a delicate cabbage flavour

Flowering pak-choi △

Purple cape broccoli △
A type of cauliflower, broccoli
may be in the form of a
compact head, as here, or it
may consist of individual
sprouts

Green cauliflower ▷
This beautiful vegetable is a
variety of cauliflower grown in
Europe

Cauliflower △
Probably originating in the Orient, but not
popular in Britain until the eighteenth
century, cauliflower has a delicate flavour

◁ **Savoy cabbage**
An attractive cabbage with its deeply crenellated leaves, savoy cabbage has an especially good flavour

January King Cabbage ▽

△ *Roundhead cabbage*

Red cabbage △
Particularly useful because it keeps well and is excellent grated as a salad and cooked slowly in a casserole

White salad cabbage△
This firmly packed head grates well and is good for making coleslaw and other raw cabbage mixtures

△ **Spring greens**
Spring greens make a good accompanying vegetable with a clean, refreshing flavour

Chinese leaves/cabbage △
A refreshing, crisp yet juicy vegetable, Chinese leaves make a good salad or stir-fried vegetable

Brassicas

A real kitchen basic, the brassicas provide useful all-year material for soups, salads and main courses, as well as being, if well cooked, second to none as an accompanying vegetable.

Choosing and storing
Select bright, fresh leaves, with no sign of wilting or damp, brownish patches. If there is a heart, as with cauliflower, cabbage and Brussels sprouts, look for one that is firm and tightly packed. Keep in a cool place. Brassicas are best used as soon as possible, although I find that even the more delicate varieties like broccoli, spring greens and cauliflower will keep well if stored in the fridge for several days.

Preparation and cooking
Wash the vegetables in cold water to which some kitchen salt has been added – this acts as a natural disinfectant. Remove hard stems and any tough outer leaves. The way brassicas are cooked makes all the difference to their palatability – and it's so easy. These are the keys to success:

□ cut the leaves up as small as possible so that they cook quickly.
□ put them into just enough fast-boiling water to prevent the greens from sticking: about 1 cm/ ½ inch.
□ cover the pan so that the vegetables above the water will cook in the steam.
□ cook them until they're only just tender – often as little as 4 minutes, or even less for delicate varieties such as pak-choi or Chinese leaves.
□ drain them well and add any seasonings and extra ingredients you like. Personally I like to add some crunchy flakes of sea salt, a grinding of black pepper and, unless the vegetable is going to be served with a dish which is high in fat, a little unsalted butter. For other suggestions, see opposite.

BROCCOLI and CALABRESE
Brassica oleracea
Sometimes described as 'poor man's asparagus', this is one of the most nutritious vegetables. Voted the top by a panel of nutritionists in the USA, it contains large amounts of vitamin A, folic acid and calcium, and is a particularly valuable vegetable for vegans.

When preparing broccoli, remove the toughest part of the stems. Then, unless it is very tender, pare the stems down a little so that they will cook in the same length of time as the more delicate heads. Or remove the stems, cut them into julienne strips (p. 184) and cook them in the water for 1–2 minutes before you put in the heads.

Broccoli is good stir-fried, too, which brings out its vivid green colour. Combined with ginger and almonds, it makes a good accompanying vegetable dish. To make this, wash 700 g/ 1½ lb broccoli, cut the broccoli heads in small pieces and prepare the stems as above. Peel and finely grate a small piece of fresh ginger root. Heat 2 tablespoons olive oil in a large saucepan or wok, add the broccoli, ginger, a little salt and freshly grated black pepper. Stir-fry for 3 minutes until the broccoli has heated through and softened a little. Sprinkle with 25 g/ 1 oz flaked almonds and serve at once.

Broccoli tastes good served simply, with melted butter, or tossed in vinaigrette, cooled and served as a salad. It is luscious with Hollandaise Sauce (p. 176) or with cream and toasted almonds, for a special occasion; or with Fresh Tomato Sauce (p. 170). Broccoli makes a good filling for a flan (p. 262) and goes well with other vegetables in a braise (p. 181).

BRUSSELS SPROUTS
Brassica oleracea
Tiny, firm Brussels sprouts are best; they take longer to prepare, but are worth it. Most people cut a cross about 5 mm/ ¼ inch into the stalk end of sprouts. Personally I prefer to cut them in halves (or even quarters, if they are big) before cooking, a trick I learnt from my mother. This way they cook more quickly and I think they taste better and look more attractive, with their yellow centre showing.

In any case, Brussels sprouts only need the minimum of cooking – 2–4 minutes – in a very little water; take them off the heat before you think they are done, because they will go on cooking in their own heat after draining.

Brussels sprouts are excellent lightly cooked and served simply; or with cream and grated nutmeg, for a special occasion. Cooked chestnuts – fresh or drained whole canned ones – are a pleasant (and, in Britain, traditional) Christmas accompaniment to Brussels sprouts. When they are young and tender, finely shredded Brussels sprouts make a good salad when combined with raisins and chopped apple, or with grated carrots and chopped dates. When they are past their best, they can be made into a delicate, pale green purée. To make this, wash and trim 700 g/ 1½ lb Brussels sprouts and cook them in boiling, salted water for about 10 minutes, or until they are tender. Drain them thoroughly, then purée in a blender or food processor. Put the purée back into the saucepan, add 15 g/½ oz butter, and beat in up to 150 ml/ 5 fl oz single cream until the mixture is soft. Season with salt, freshly ground black pepper and grated nutmeg, then reheat gently and serve.

CABBAGE *Brassica oleracea*
One variety of cabbage or another is available all the year. Early in the year, SPRING GREENS, cut up small and lightly cooked, make a good accompanying vegetable with a clean, refreshing flavour. JANUARY KING, another excellent early cabbage, can be cooked in a similar way, or, if it has a firm heart, makes a particularly good salad when finely shredded and mixed with lemon juice and olive oil, or vinaigrette. ROUNDHEAD CABBAGE is available throughout the year, useful as an accompanying vegetable or shredded to make salads such as Coleslaw (p. 161) or Technicolour Cabbage Salad (p. 162).

WHITE SALAD CABBAGE, a firm variety, good for grating and shredding, is also excellent for salads.

RED CABBAGE is good cooked gently and slowly with onions and butter in a casserole (p. 180) and served as an accompanying vegetable, or, with some cooked chestnuts and perhaps a dash of red wine added, as a main course with jacket potatoes and soured cream. Red cabbage also looks particularly attractive shredded or grated in salads.

SAVOY CABBAGE is good as an accompanying vegetable or main course, hollowed out and filled with stuffing. The individual leaves can also be wrapped round a savoury filling, such as mashed cooked chestnuts and fried onion, or cooked rice with nuts and chopped herbs, packed into a shallow ovenproof dish, covered with a little well-flavoured stock or a sauce (such as Italian Tomato (p. 171) or Savoury Coconut (p. 177)) and baked for about 30 minutes in a moderate oven.

Chopped cooked cabbage is one of the main ingredients of the Russian savoury pastry, Koulibiac. For an easy version of this, mix together 900 g/2 lb finely chopped cooked cabbage, 1 large fried onion, 225 g/ 8 oz sliced and fried mushrooms, 2 chopped hardboiled eggs, 4 tablespoons chopped parsley, the grated rind and juice of ½ lemon, and plenty of salt and freshly ground black pepper. Cover with puff pastry as described on p. 271, bake in a hot oven, 220 C/425 F/Gas Mark 7, for 40 minutes and serve with a Soured Cream and Herb Dressing (p. 156).

CAULIFLOWER / GREEN CAULIFLOWER
Brassica oleracea

Cauliflower has a delicious flavour so long as it is not over-cooked. I think it is best to break the cauliflower into florets and cut these as necessary so that they are all about the same size. Then cook as described above, for only 4–5 minutes, until the cauliflower is just tender but still has some firmness, then drain. Cooked like this, cauliflower hardly needs any accompaniments, though some grated nutmeg, a little grated cheese or a Fresh Tomato Sauce (p. 170) go well with it. One of the tastiest ways to cook cauliflower is in the Indian style, with spices (p. 185).

To make Cauliflower Cheese, a classic vegetarian dish, mix lightly cooked cauliflower florets with a well-seasoned Cheese Sauce (p. 175), sprinkle with breadcrumbs, dot with a little butter and bake or grill until heated through and crisp on top.

Raw cauliflower florets are particularly good for scooping up dips.

CHINESE LEAVES / CABBAGE
Brassica pekinensis

Chinese leaves are tender and, shredded, make a good addition to a leafy salad. Or they can be the main ingredient. A refreshing salad in which they are combined with beansprouts in a sweet and sour dressing can be made as follows. Soak 175 g/6 oz fresh beansprouts in cold water while you prepare the other ingredients. Combine 1 tablespoon clear honey, 3 tablespoons sesame oil or olive oil, 2 tablespoons soy sauce and freshly ground black pepper in a large bowl. Add 2.5 cm/1 inch peeled and finely grated fresh ginger root and mix well. Then add 350 g/12 oz shredded Chinese leaves and 2 coarsely grated carrots and turn them in the dressing. Drain the beansprouts, place in the bowl and mix well.

The best way to serve them as a cooked vegetable is to shred them, then stir-fry for 2–3 minutes, until heated through. Chopped onion, crushed garlic, grated fresh ginger, grated lemon rind and chopped fresh herbs are good flavourings for Chinese leaves, or stir-fry in sesame oil and serve with a dash of soy sauce and a sprinkling of toasted sesame seeds.

KALE *Brassica oleracea*

Kale is a non-hearting type of cabbage. It should be washed well as soil and grit tend to lodge between the stems. Kale is particularly rich in calcium and B vitamins and used to be an important winter vegetable in Britain, though many people find its flavour rather strong. It can be good to eat if it is picked or bought when young, shredded (with any tough stems removed) and cooked until tender, then well drained and served with butter and freshly ground black pepper, or with a creamy sauce, perhaps flavoured with a dash of nutmeg.

KOHLRABI *Brassica oleracea*

Like a cabbage-flavoured turnip, the leaves of kohlrabi can be cooked like kale. The root can be diced or cut into strips and boiled until tender. Kohlrabi is good in a julienne of root vegetables (p. 184), providing an interesting contrast of colour and flavour.

PAK-CHOI / MUSTARD GREENS
Brassica chinensis

This variety of Chinese cabbage is popular in oriental cookery. Prepare and cook it as described for Chinese leaves, above. FLOWERING PAK-CHOI can be cooked in the same way, and also looks pretty in salads and as a garnish. Chinese sauerkraut is made from pak-choi and is available from Chinese shops, as is DRIED PAK-CHOI (not illustrated), which needs to be soaked and can then be added to soups and stews.

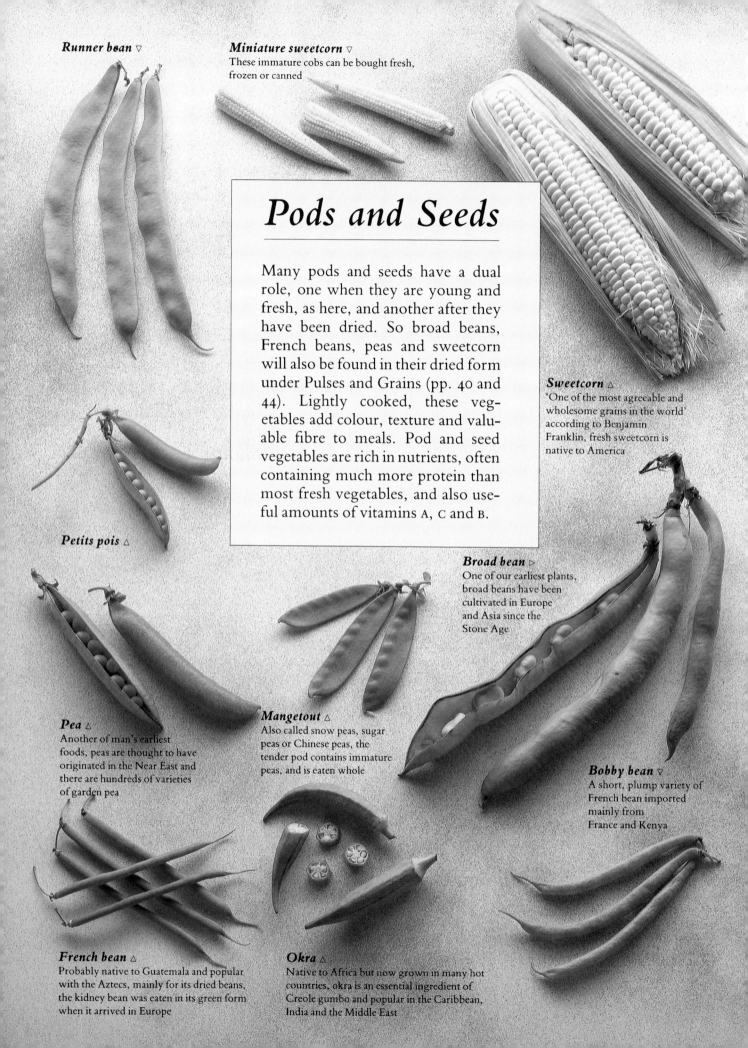

Runner bean ▽

Miniature sweetcorn ▽
These immature cobs can be bought fresh,
frozen or canned

Pods and Seeds

Many pods and seeds have a dual
role, one when they are young and
fresh, as here, and another after they
have been dried. So broad beans,
French beans, peas and sweetcorn
will also be found in their dried form
under Pulses and Grains (pp. 40 and
44). Lightly cooked, these vegetables add colour, texture and valuable fibre to meals. Pod and seed
vegetables are rich in nutrients, often
containing much more protein than
most fresh vegetables, and also useful amounts of vitamins A, C and B.

Sweetcorn △
'One of the most agreeable and
wholesome grains in the world'
according to Benjamin
Franklin, fresh sweetcorn is
native to America

Petits pois △

Broad bean ▷
One of our earliest plants,
broad beans have been
cultivated in Europe
and Asia since the
Stone Age

Pea △
Another of man's earliest
foods, peas are thought to have
originated in the Near East and
there are hundreds of varieties
of garden pea

Mangetout △
Also called snow peas, sugar
peas or Chinese peas, the
tender pod contains immature
peas, and is eaten whole

Bobby bean ▽
A short, plump variety of
French bean imported
mainly from
France and Kenya

French bean △
Probably native to Guatemala and popular
with the Aztecs, mainly for its dried beans,
the kidney bean was eaten in its green form
when it arrived in Europe

Okra △
Native to Africa but now grown in many hot
countries, okra is an essential ingredient of
Creole gumbo and popular in the Caribbean,
India and the Middle East

Pods and Seeds

Choosing and storing

Look for small, crisp pods, bright and fresh-looking. Peas, beans and okra are all best when the pods are small. Sweetcorn needs to be young and tender too; pull back the leaves and look for pale yellow, shiny grains. These vegetables will keep in a cool place for a day or so, or in the fridge for 2–3 days, but they are all at their best when eaten as soon as possible after picking.

Preparation and cooking

See under individual varieties.

BROAD BEAN *Vicia faba*

Broad beans can be prepared in two ways. When they are young and tender, and the pods not much bigger than French beans, they are excellent cooked in the pod; just top and tail, then cut into even-sized lengths and cook in a little fast-boiling water until just tender. Drain and serve with chopped parsley and butter or a creamy sauce.

Later, when the pods become too tough to eat, remove the beans from the pod and cook in boiling water until tender. If the skins of the beans are tough, and you have the time, the beans can be popped out of their skins, revealing the bright green beans inside.

Older broad beans can be made into a good soup. Whizzed in a blender or food processor with olive oil and lemon juice, they also make an excellent pale green dip, good served as a first course on top of large flat mushrooms which have been fried in olive oil then cooled, or in a salad, with lettuce and grated carrot.

FRENCH BEAN
Phaseolus vulgaris

One of the most delicious vegetables, many varieties have been produced including the BOBBY BEAN. Just top and tail and remove any strings from the side, if present (the beans are nicest if they're young enough to have no strings).

The beans can be cooked whole or cut into shorter lengths. Cook in a minimum amount of boiling water (1 cm/½ inch) in a covered pan until just tender (*al dente*). Cooking time will depend on the thickness of the beans: very slender ones take only about 2 minutes, others up to 10 minutes. Drain and serve simply, as they are, or with a little butter and freshly ground black pepper. A squeeze of lemon juice and some toasted almonds are an excellent addition.

Hot French beans mixed with a vinaigrette dressing and chopped fresh herbs, then cooled, make a good first course or salad, or they can be mixed with other vegetables to make Vegetarian Salade Niçoise (p. 169).

MANGETOUTS/SNOW PEAS
Pisum saccaratum

A variety of pea, the pod of which is eaten, mangetouts have a deliciously sweet flavour and, if properly cooked, crunchy texture. To prepare them, choose young, crisp pods, top and tail, then cook in a little boiling water for 1–2 minutes, just to heat through and soften slightly. Drain and serve immediately. Or add them to stir-fries (p. 199). Raw mangetouts make good scoopers for dips.

OKRA *Hibiscus esculentus*

Also known as 'ladies' fingers' and gumbo, okra has an intriguing mucilaginous texture and delicate flavour. Choose small, firm pods and cut off the stalk end. It is delicious prepared as on p. 186 and makes a good addition to vegetable stews, curries and spiced rice dishes.

PEA *Pisum sativum*

Unless you grow your own peas, it is difficult to find fresh peas which taste as good as frozen ones, which are cropped at their peak and frozen within hours of picking. However, cooked fresh peas are a treat if they are young and tender. Simply pop the peas out of the pods and cook in a little boiling water until just tender – about 4 minutes. PETITS POIS, a small, tender, sweet variety, take less time – 1–2 minutes. Drain and serve

with chopped mint and a little butter. They make a colourful addition to many vegetable and rice dishes.

RUNNER BEAN
Phaseolus coccineus

Also called stick beans, because of the way the plants grow up sticks, runner beans originated in South America. They are the most popular green bean in Britain. If you're growing them, do pick them before they get too long; they're delicious when young and tender. Top and tail the beans, and if there are strings, remove these by slicing thinly down each side. Runner beans are usually cut into thin diagonal slices. Cook and serve as for French beans, or prepare in the Greek style and serve warm (p. 186). If you have a glut of runner beans, try making some into chutney or piccalilli.

SWEETCORN *Zea mays*

Sweetcorn has a pleasantly sweet flavour, cheering golden colour and chewy texture. Ideally sweetcorn needs to be picked just before cooking, because once it has been cut, the sugar in the kernels starts to turn into starch, making them tough. When buying fresh sweetcorn pull back the leaves and look for pale yellow, shiny grains. To prepare, strip off the leaves and silky threads, then trim off the stalk end. Cook the sweetcorn in a large saucepan of unsalted water for 3–5 minutes. It is done when a kernel pulls away easily from the cob. Serve with butter and sea salt. If you need the kernels for a recipe, just cut down the cob and they will come away.

Corn on the cob makes a pleasant first course or snack for people with good teeth who don't mind getting messy as they eat. The kernels add a bright dash of colour to salads and vegetable mixtures, and are also good made into fritters (p. 238). Sweetcorn kernels are available fresh, frozen and canned, though canned sweetcorn usually tastes over-sweet because of added sugar.

MINIATURE SWEETCORN, the immature cobs, can be bought fresh, frozen or canned and are pretty in salads and vegetable mixtures, especially stir-fries.

Globe artichoke ▷
When cooked, these giant thistles have an intriguing, subtle flavour and are excellent served either hot or cold

Asparagus △
Asparagus is the cultivated form of a type of lily and has been grown as a delicacy in Europe for over 2,000 years

Shoot Vegetables

This group includes some of the most delectable vegetables, such as asparagus, artichokes, chicory, bamboo shoots and palm hearts, which are wonderful for special occasion cookery, or for using in small quantities to add interest to simple dishes. Alongside these are cheaper basics such as celery and fennel which, with their clean, refreshing flavours and crisp texture, are good either cooked or raw. They all only contain small amounts of vitamins and minerals.

Bamboo shoot △
The tips of various species of bamboo, these are sold fresh in Far Eastern markets, but canned almost everywhere else

◁ **Celery**
There are basically two types of this versatile, crunchy vegetable: green-stemmed and white-stemmed

Fennel ▽
This celery-like shoot with its delicate, feathery leaves and slight aniseed flavour can be used either cooked or raw

Palm heart ▽
The terminal shoots of certain varieties of palm, palm hearts have a delicate flavour

Chicory/Endive/ Witloof ▷
Chicory is a crisp vegetable with a slightly bitter flavour

Shoot Vegetables

Choosing and storing

Choose firm, crisp-looking specimens. With asparagus, avoid any which looks limp or has wet or dry wrinkled ends. Keep in the salad compartment of the fridge, or in a cool place.

Preparation and cooking

See under individual varieties.

ASPARAGUS
Asparagus officinalis

There are three basic types of asparagus, green, white and purple, and experts disagree as to which has the best flavour. Thin spears of green asparagus, called sprue, are a good buy, particularly for inclusion in dishes like Individual Asparagus Tartlets (p. 263), Pine Nut Roulade with Asparagus Hollandaise filling (p. 237), or Asparagus Soup (p. 131).

Allow about 225 g/8 oz asparagus per person. Wash the asparagus carefully, especially around the tips, which can contain grit. Then bend each stem until it snaps – it will break at the point on the stem where it becomes tough and woody. Using a sharp knife or potato peeler, shave right down the stem, from just below the tip to the base, going deeper into the stem as you go down.

Unless you have a special asparagus pan, the best way to cook it is either in a steamer, or to tie it in a bunch and stand this in a saucepan containing 2.5 cm/1 inch boiling water. Arrange a dome of foil over the top, to cover the asparagus tips. Either way, cook for about 10–15 minutes, until just tender. Serve hot with melted butter or Hollandaise Sauce (p. 176), or cold with Vinaigrette (p. 154), or as part of a made-up dish.

Frozen asparagus is useful when fresh is unobtainable, and is best steamed for about 7 minutes; and canned asparagus, while not having the same flavour or texture as fresh, can be used for garnishing or in Asparagus Rolls (p. 334).

BAMBOO SHOOT
Bambusa vulgaris

Even in China and Japan canned bamboo shoots are often used in preference to fresh ones because of their convenience. They also maintain their crispness well, drained and added to stir-fries, or cold in a salad.

CELERY *Apium graveolens*

Celery gives a specially delicious flavour to vegetable casseroles and makes an excellent soup. Break the celery head into individual sticks, trim as necessary, then scrub well under cold water.

Celery can be braised as described on p. 182, or chopped and added raw to salad mixtures. The tender stems are good for serving with dips or for topping with cream cheese or savoury spreads as canapes. Crisp celery sticks are excellent with cheese, especially Stilton.

CHICORY / ENDIVE / WITLOOF
Cichorium intybus

Crisp and slightly bitter-tasting, chicory makes a pleasant addition to a leafy green salad and is also good braised. Allow about 1 head per person if you're serving the chicory in a salad, 2 heads for a cooked dish. Remove any damaged outer leaves. Trim the base, then insert the point of a knife into it and remove the core, which can be bitter. Wash well under cold water, but do not leave chicory soaking in water as this can increase the bitterness. Cook as described for celery on p. 182, or use raw in a salad.

FENNEL *Foeniculum vulgare*

Allow 1 small fennel per person, or a larger one between 2. Trim and wash, then halve, quarter or slice.

To cook, braise as described on p. 182, or add to Spring Vegetable Braise (p. 181) or to casseroles. Steam and serve with Italian Tomato Sauce (p. 171), or cover with cream and a sprinkling of grated cheese and bake until golden-brown. Sliced or chopped fennel is refreshing with grated carrot in a salad (p. 162), in a green salad, mixed with diced cucumber, or replacing the celery in Waldorf Salad (p. 169).

GLOBE ARTICHOKE
Cynara scolymus

Very tender young artichokes can be trimmed, added to a casserole of summer vegetables and cooked gently for 20–30 minutes, until tender.

For most artichokes, however, more preparation is needed. Break off the stalk, removing with it any stringy pieces from the sides. Using a sharp knife or kitchen scissors, snip the points off the scales, then prise them apart until the soft leaves in the centre and the hairy choke are revealed. Scrape the choke out firmly with a teaspoon, then rinse under cold water. Sprinkle the inside of the artichoke with lemon juice, and leave it soaking in acidulated water until you're ready to cook.

Bring a large non-aluminium saucepan of water to the boil, put in the artichokes and cook for 30–40 minutes, until a leaf can be pulled away easily. A tablespoon of lemon juice or white wine vinegar can be added to the water. Drain thoroughly and serve hot, with melted butter and lemon juice, or Hollandaise Sauce (p. 176); or cold, with Vinaigrette (p. 154). It's best not to keep cooked artichokes for more than 24 hours, as they can develop a toxin which can cause stomach upsets.

To prepare just the bottoms or *fonds*, remove the stem and choke as described, to reveal the heart, then cut off all the leaves just above the base, and finally trim round the base. Cook in boiling water until tender. The artichoke bottoms may be topped with a creamy sauce or vegetable mixture, or serve cold with a tasty dip spooned on top.

Artichoke hearts are available in cans and make a useful addition to the store cupboard, for use in vegetable salads, casseroles and risottos.

PALM HEART *Sabal palmetto*

Fresh palm hearts are usually boiled until just tender and eaten hot with melted butter or cold with Mayonnaise (p. 155) or Vinaigrette (p. 154). Canned palm hearts can be served similarly; try slicing them and mixing with diced avocado or sliced button mushrooms and a vinaigrette dressing.

Bulb Vegetables

Valuable in vegetarian cooking for adding flavour, bulb vegetables contain useful though not outstanding amounts of minerals and vitamins (but very little vitamin A). Their main value healthwise lies in their natural antibiotic powers and the way in which, if eaten over a period of time, onions and garlic in particular (both raw and cooked) help lower cholesterol and protect against fatty deposits in blood vessels. Both leeks and shallots have a sweet taste, less pungent than that of onion.

Spanish onion △
These large onions are the mildest in flavour

Spring onion ▽
These are tender young onions, picked before they mature

Pickling onion
These small onions are good used whole as well as for making into pickles

Purple or red onion ▽
Particularly useful for creating pretty colour schemes and garnishes

Shallot △
A variety of onion which produces clusters of bulbs; shallots may be round or oval in shape

◁ **Leek**
Delicately flavoured, with a slightly sweet taste; useful both raw and cooked

Onion △
Second to none as a vegetarian flavouring ingredient, onions are generally included in nut roasts, burgers and all kinds of savouries

Bulb Vegetables

Choosing and storing

Bulb vegetables should look bright and crisp; the bulbs should be firm. Avoid any onions which are sprouting, damp-looking, soft or which smell musty. Leeks and spring onions are best stored in a cool place, preferably the fridge, and used within a day or two. Onions will keep for at least a week if stored in a cool, dry place.

Preparation and cooking

See under individual varieties.

LEEK *Allium porrum*

Leeks need careful washing as they may contain grit. First cut off the roots and trim the green leaves to within about 2.5 cm/1 inch of the top of the white part. Make a slit right down one side of the leek from top to bottom and wash it under the cold tap, gently parting the layers and rinsing between each while keeping the shape of the leek intact. Then keep whole or cut into shorter lengths, or shred into fine rings for serving raw in a salad.

Alternatively, if you want a perfectly whole leek, cut a cross shape about 2.5 cm/1 inch deep in the root end and place the leeks root end down in a deep jug of water for 30–60 minutes. After this any grit will show up as dark patches and you can make a small incision at this point and rinse the grit away under the cold tap.

Leeks are good added to vegetable casseroles and curries, or cooked and served hot as an accompanying vegetable, either whole, sliced or puréed. I think the best way to cook leeks is to steam them or cook them in 2.5 cm/1 inch of water in a covered pan for about 10 minutes, until tender. They can also be cooked until tender in olive oil or butter, or sautéed lightly, then braised in red wine or stock.

I very much like cooked leeks served cold as a first course, tossed in a little well-flavoured vinaigrette while still hot, then served with a sprinkling of chopped parsley. For a more elaborate yet easily prepared presentation, make a leek terrine by packing the cooked and drained leeks, cut to fit, into a 450-g/1-lb loaf tin. Press down firmly, cover with several layers of kitchen paper and weight down. Chill for several hours, then pop the terrine into the freezer for 1 hour before serving, so that it is firm enough to cut easily. Slice and pour vinaigrette over before serving.

ONION *Allium cepa*

There are many varieties of onion, ranging in colour from white and yellow to shades of purple and red, and in size from minute bulbs to large ones weighing around 1 lb/450 g or more. Onions also vary a good deal in strength; some types are mild and sweet, while others are extremely pungent. Even individual varieties can change as the season goes on, changing from mild to strong, or vice versa.

To prepare onions, cut off the root and stalk end, then strip off the outer skins. Wash the onions, then chop or slice as required. If you don't need to use the onions immediately, it's best not to leave them soaking in water; either sauté them in a little oil or butter, or wrap them in clingfilm.

Onions are included in many vegetarian dishes as a flavouring. They are also useful sliced raw in salads, for making a delectable flan (p. 261) and for soup. Large onions can be baked whole in their skins then split open and served with butter, sea salt and freshly ground black pepper as an accompaniment, or stuffed with a nut and breadcrumb mixture and baked to make a warming winter main course.

PICKLING ONIONS can be fiddly to peel, but if you top and tail them, then cover with boiling water and leave for 5 minutes, you should be able to skin them easily.

A quick method of making Pickled Onions which gives an excellent result but is best made in small quantities as the onions do not keep for more than about 4 months, is as follows. Put skinned pickling onions into jars and sprinkle them with pickling spice between the layers, allowing 1 rounded tablespoon spice to a large jar. Then fill the jars with malt vinegar, making sure that the onions are completely covered. Cover with airtight, vinegar-proof lids and store in a cool, dry, dark place for at least 8 weeks before eating with cheese.

SPRING ONIONS (commonly called shallots in Australia) make an attractive garnish and addition to salads or crudités, and are excellent added to a stir-fry or other lightly cooked mixed vegetable dishes. SHALLOTS (*Allium ascalonicum*) can be used wherever a delicate onion flavour is needed and are also excellent for pickling. They can be peeled as described for pickling onions.

The strength of PURPLE or RED ONIONS can vary; some are quite mild, but this is not always the case.

Mild-flavoured SPANISH ONIONS are ideal for slicing and adding to salads as well as for cooking, and are excellent baked with a tasty stuffing. To make stuffed onions for 4 people, rinse, but don't peel, 4 large Spanish onions. Put them into a large saucepan of water and simmer for about 20 minutes until they are tender but not cooked right through. Drain and cool, then remove the root ends and cut the onions in half horizontally. Scoop out the centre of each half, making a cavity for stuffing and leaving three or four layers of onion. Arrange the onion halves in a greased, shallow, ovenproof dish. Set the oven to 180C/350F/Gas Mark 4.

The onions can be stuffed with a Herb Stuffing (p. 239), one of the nut roast mixtures (p. 230), or with an unusual sweet-and-sour mixture. To make this, first chop the onion you scooped out, then crush four macaroons and add to the onion, along with 75 g/3 oz wholewheat breadcrumbs, ¼ teaspoon each ground cinnamon, cloves and nutmeg, 2 beaten eggs, 50 g/2 oz grated Parmesan cheese and 25–50 g/1–2 oz sultanas. Season, then pile the mixture into the onion cavities, dot with butter and bake, uncovered, for 30 minutes. A sharply-flavoured cheese sauce goes well with these.

Daikon ▷
Sometimes called MOOLI, this
is a type of radish popular in
Japanese cookery

Beetroot ▷

◁ **Rose radish**

Radish
There are numerous varieties of
radish; they can be the size of
marbles or grapefruit, round or
long, and range in colour from
white to red and black

Burdock
Popular in
macrobiotic
cooking

Root Vegetables

Nourishing, warming and filling,
root vegetables have long been a
winter mainstay because of their excellent keeping qualities and value
for money. Radishes, carrots and
beetroot add colour to meals, while
parsnips and turnips are delicious
roasted. They contain useful quantities of iron, calcium, protein and B
vitamins, and carrots are one of the
richest sources of vitamin A. Root
vegetables absorb flavours well and
can be made into tasty soups, stews
and casseroles or used in salads.

Carrot ▷
Descended from
the wild carrot

**White
radish** ▷

◁ **Swede and rutabaga**
Called turnips in Scotland and
the USA, swedes and
rutabagas are larger than
turnips and do not have ridges

Turnip △
One of the oldest European
food crops, turnips vary in
shape and size and the skins
may be white, green or tinged
with purple; the flesh is usually
white, juicy and pungent

Scorzonera △
Also called 'vegetable
oyster', because their
flavour is sometimes
considered similar

Parsnip △
A distinctively flavoured, sweet-tasting root
which used to be used in puddings and
sweetmeats in medieval cookery

Celeriac △
A variety of celery with a bulbous root

Root Vegetables

Choosing and storing

Look for bright, firm root vegetables, with no signs of wrinkling.
Store in a cool, dry place; more delicate roots, such as radishes, keep best
in the fridge and I like to store carrots
there, too, if there's room.

Preparation and cooking

Radishes and tender young carrots,
turnips and beetroots only need
scrubbing; older ones need scraping.
Celeriac, turnips, swedes, parsnips
and older beetroot, if used raw, need
peeling quite thickly. Cut into even-
sized pieces, place in a saucepan,
cover with cold water and bring to
the boil, then simmer gently until
tender. Drain, saving the cooking
water for a well-flavoured and nutritious stock, and add seasoning,
butter or vegan margarine, chopped
herbs and perhaps a squeeze of lemon
juice. Salsify, scorzonera and beetroot are cooked in the same way
(beetroot may require 1–2 hours, depending on size, although a pressure
cooker speeds the process) until tender, when the skins will slip off quite
easily.

BEETROOT *Beta vulgaris*

Beetroot is usually red, although
white and golden varieties are also
grown. When preparing beetroot for
cooking, if the leaves are still attached, break these off about 18 cm/
6 inches from the root and do not cut
or pierce the skins, or the colour may
seep out during cooking. The leaves
can also be cooked and taste like
spinach. Cooked beetroot can be
served in salads, dressed with vinaigrette, or mixed with other ingredients such as apple and celery in a
dressing of horseradish, soured
cream, yogurt or mayonnaise. In
Russia and Poland it is made into
Borsch and served with buckwheat
(p. 44) – good, cheap, filling food!
For a lighter version of Beetroot
Soup, see p. 138. Young cooked
beetroots are good served with butter, black pepper and a little orange

juice and grated rind. Beetroot can
also be eaten raw: peel, grate and mix
with an equal quantity of grated
apple and some raisins, or sliced
onion rings and vinaigrette for a very
healthy salad which is said to help
break up fat deposits in the body.

BURDOCK *Arctium lappa*

A tough root vegetable with a distinctive flavour which is an acquired
taste. It should be scrubbed, sliced
thinly and boiled for 30–40 minutes
until tender, or can be added to
vegetable stews.

CARROT *Daucus carota*

One of the most useful and nutritious
vegetables. Delicious either raw or
cooked, carrots are useful in salads,
soups, stews and casseroles, for serving with dips and even for making
into cakes (p. 306). Baby carrots can
be cooked whole, while larger ones
can be cut into rounds or julienne
strips (p. 184), finely or coarsely
grated, shaved lengthways into ribbons with a potato peeler or 'turned'
as shown on p. 182. Simply cooked,
as a side vegetable, carrots are good
with a flavouring of chopped parsley, caraway or anise; or they can be
glazed (p. 182).

CELERIAC
Apium graveolens, var. *rapaceum*

This delicious celery-flavoured root
is good both raw and cooked. To
serve it raw, cut into fine julienne
strips or grate coarsely, then mix
with a well-flavoured vinaigrette
(p. 154). If liked, celeriac can be
blanched for 1 minute in boiling water, then refreshed under cold water
to soften slightly before adding the
dressing. Cooked celeriac mixed
with an equal quantity of potato
makes a delicately-flavoured purée.

DAIKON *Raphanus sativus*

Daikon has a slightly hot taste, like a
cross between a turnip and a radish.
It can be sliced and added to root
vegetable mixtures or stir-fries,
diced or shredded and combined
with salad ingredients, and it can also
be used to make a particularly attractive garnish, see Japanese Flower
Salad (p. 164).

HORSERADISH
Armoracia rusticana
(Not illustrated)
See p. 124.

PARSNIP *Pastinaca sativa*

Parsnips can be roasted like potatoes,
cooked and mashed or puréed, added
to a julienne of mixed root vegetables
(p. 184), made into a winter soup or
added to casseroles and stews.

RADISH *Raphanus sativus*

Thinly sliced radishes make a colourful and pungent addition to salads –
try adding them to cooked, cooled
sweetcorn, along with some chopped
spring onion. Radishes with their
green leaves still attached if possible
make a good addition to a crudités
selection, and radish flowers are easy
to make for garnishing (p. 164).

SCORZONERA
Scorzonera hispanica and
SALSIFY
Tragopogon porrifolius
(Not illustrated)
Cooked and served hot with cream
and Parmesan, or cold mixed with
vinaigrette or mayonnaise, these
delicately flavoured vegetables make
a good first course. Or they can be
dipped in batter or egg and breadcrumbs and fried until crisp, then
served with lemon wedges. Frozen
and canned salsify is available.

SWEDE and RUTABAGA
Brassica napus
Swede and rutabaga have a sweetish
flavour but they also absorb other
flavours well and are good in casseroles, diced as part of a macedoine of
root vegetables or mashed with carrots or potatoes. 'Mashed Neaps' are
traditionally served with haggis at
Burns Night suppers in Scotland.
Raw, swedes make a good salad,
coarsely grated and mixed with
mayonnaise and chopped dates.

TURNIP *Brassica rapa*

Turnips can be served in any of the
ways described for swede, and baby
turnips can be glazed with butter and
sugar (p. 183). The tops, eaten like
spinach, make an extremely nutritious, strongly flavoured, vegetable.

Catriona △

Record △

Wilja △

Tubers

Tuber vegetables (botanically, roots swollen with the plant's winter food supplies) include potatoes (which exceed the world's wheat crop in volume and value), sweet potatoes and yams, which are important throughout the tropics, and delicately flavoured Jerusalem artichokes. As tubers are usually eaten in quite large quantities, they can be an important source of nutrients, including iron, protein and vitamin c and can be made into some particularly economic and delicious dishes.

Cara △

Désirée △

White sweet potato ▽

Arran Victory ▽

Russet Burbank △

Potato
The world's best-known vegetable, the potato, which belongs to the deadly nightshade family, was eaten for centuries in western South America before it gained popularity in other parts of the world

Sweet potato ▷

△
Red sweet potato

Maris bard ▷

Vanessa ▽

◁ *Maris peer*

Estima △

Yam ▷
Probably native to the Orient, and
popular in Chinese, African and
Caribbean cookery, the yam is a
starchy tuber often confused with
the sweet potato

Maris piper △

Pentland Squire ▷

Jerusalem artichoke ▽
Related to the sunflower and
thought to be named after it

Romana △

Diana △

King Edward △

Cyprus new ▷

Italian new △

Ulster sceptre ▷

Tubers

Choosing and storing

Look for firm tubers with no wrinkles or damp patches. Choose firm, even-sized, dry-skinned potatoes (pre-washed potatoes do not keep as well as unwashed ones). When choosing Jerusalem artichokes, look for ones without too many knobbly bits – it makes peeling easier! Store in a cool, dry, dark place.

Preparation and cooking

See under individual varieties.

JERUSALEM ARTICHOKE
Helianthus tuberosus

These can be peeled either before or after cooking. If you peel before, you will need to cut off the smaller knobbles along with the peel. Put the peeled artichokes straight into cold water with a dash of lemon juice added, to help preserve their colour. Alternatively, give them a quick wash, then boil them and slip off their skins, using a small sharp knife, after cooking.

Jerusalem artichokes have a distinctive flavour reminiscent of globe artichokes (hence the 'artichoke' in the name), but not as delicate. They are good mashed to a creamy purée, served cold in a vinaigrette or hot with butter and chopped parsley. They also make a soothing winter soup (p. 128) and go well with Fresh Tomato Sauce. To assemble the dish, first prepare the Fresh Tomato Sauce (p. 170). While it is cooking, peel 700 g/1½ lb Jerusalem artichokes as above and cut into even-sized pieces. Put in a saucepan with 15 g/½ oz butter, 4 tablespoons water and salt. Cover and cook over a gentle heat for about 20 minutes until just tender. Drain the artichokes, pour the Fresh Tomato Sauce over them and serve.

POTATO *Solanum tuberosum*

Nutritious staple vegetables, rich in vitamin C and potassium, and containing useful amounts of particular-ly good quality protein, potatoes are made into some of the most delicious and economical dishes throughout the world.

They are sometimes loosely divided into 'waxy' types, which are moist, even slightly transluscent after cooking, and those which have a dry, fluffy texture, known as 'floury'. Generally speaking, waxy potatoes are best for salads and for frying, because they stay firm, and floury potatoes are best for mashing, boiling and baking in their jackets.

There are, however, many varieties which are good all-rounders. New potatoes, or young potatoes dug early in the season, such as the ITALIAN NEW POTATOES and CYPRUS NEW POTATOES shown, are best when they are from varieties grown specially for this purpose. They are waxy, tender and excellent for boiling and salads, but not for baking, roasting and chipping.

The colour of potato flesh varies from white through to gold. Until fairly recently the yellow-flesh varieties were not popular in Great Britain; however they are now gaining in favour, particularly because of the way they remain intact after cooking.

New varieties of potato are continually being developed. Some, such as DIANA, make a brief appearance and then fade out; others survive to become well-loved favourites. These include WILJA, which is particularly good for boiling and has pale yellow flesh; MARIS PIPER, the most popular white potato in the UK today and a good all-rounder; KING EDWARD, which is making a comeback on account of its popularity with housewives; DÉSIRÉE, the most widely grown red potato in the UK and another excellent all-rounder; MARIS BARD, which has average cooking qualities and needs plenty of flavouring to enliven it; ESTIMA, a Dutch variety, which is growing in popularity; and RECORD, also Dutch, and with very yellow flesh, but a superb potato for making into crisps and indeed for boiling and roasting.

The demand for varieties of potato also varies from area to area. The RUSSET BURBANK, also known as the IDAHO BAKER, is well-known and loved in the USA but virtually unknown in Britain, except to nostalgic ex-patriots who are at present experimenting with the possibility of growing it here. Another type, ARRAN VICTORY, is liked in Scotland and Ireland, but not in England, on account of its blue skin. This potato was bred to celebrate the victory of the 1914–18 war and has very white floury flesh.

Potatoes in Australia are not marketed under variety names, e.g. Désirée, although several varieties are grown. Ask your greengrocer if you are seeking a specific type.

Varieties which are popular with show judges such as the purple-eyed CATRIONA are not always so well-favoured by customers. MARIS PEER, VANESSA (bred from the popular Désirée) and ULSTER SCEPTRE, which have been favoured in the past, are now being replaced by varieties such as ROMANA (also bred from Désirée and with similar qualities). CARA, which was developed in the Republic of Ireland as Oakpark Beauty, and has pink eyes like a King Edward, is growing in popularity and is being widely grown in Cyprus and Egypt.

New potatoes are good just scrubbed and boiled in their skins until just tender, then served hot with butter and chopped herbs, or mixed with vinaigrette and served cold. More mature potatoes can be scrubbed and boiled or baked in their jackets, or peeled before use.

Baked Potatoes, cooked so that their skins are crisp (p. 190), and served with butter, soured cream or a variety of toppings (p. 190), accompanied by a salad, are one of my favourite quick and easy meals. Bircher Potatoes are also popular with children: scrub medium potatoes, cut them in half lengthways and place them cut side down on an oiled baking sheet. Bake in a hot oven, 220 C/425 F/Gas Mark 7, for about 45 minutes, until the tops are soft and the underneath golden-brown and crisp.

Another delicious way with potatoes is to cut well-scrubbed medium ones into 3 mm/⅛ inch slices and arrange overlapping like roof tiles on an oiled baking sheet. Brush the potatoes with olive oil, sprinkle with chopped thyme or rosemary and a little crushed garlic, and bake in a hot oven, 220 C/425 F/Gas Mark 7, until golden-brown and crisp.

Potatoes mashed until very light and creamy, with hot milk, or cream for special occasions, butter or vegan margarine and a good seasoning of salt and freshly ground black pepper, are one of my favourite ways of serving them. Mashed potatoes can be used as a topping for vegetarian shepherd's pie, and any left over can be fried to make crisp potato cakes, a good quick snack for children, especially with some grated nuts added. I start off most soups by frying an onion and one or two potatoes together in butter, then adding the other vegetables: the potato thickens the soup and gives it body. I find children like a plain potato soup, without other vegetables except for a flavouring of onion, whizzed to a smooth creamy purée.

Every national cuisine has its own range of potato dishes: delicious Spiced Potatoes from India (p. 185); Hashed Browns from the USA (p. 191); Rösti from Switzerland (p. 189) and Gratin Dauphinois from France (p. 190), to mention just a few.

Potatoes are available fresh or frozen in the form of the ubiquitous chip, canned and in various dried and powdered forms.

Potato flour makes a lighter, healthier thickening for sauces than flour and butter, and it is also good for making clear fruit soups, such as the Chilled Raspberry or Black Cherry soups on p. 137.

SWEET POTATO
Ipomoea batatas
A member of the convolvulus family, the sweet potato has sweet, mealy flesh. There are two main types, one with yellow flesh and a dryish texture, and the other with particularly sweet white flesh and a

---

How to make perfect roast potatoes and chips

Roast potatoes
Set the oven to 230 C/425 F/Gas Mark 8. Peel even-sized potatoes, allowing about 700 g/1½ lb for 4 people, and cut them into halves or quarters. Parboil the potatoes for 5 minutes.

Meanwhile, pour into a roasting tin just enough oil to cover the base. Don't make it more than 3 mm/⅛ inch deep. Heat the oil in the oven.

Drain the potatoes. Make sure that the potatoes and the oil are both piping hot; a good way of doing this is to put the roasting tin over the gas flame or hotplate while you put the hot potatoes into it, but stand back as the oil will sizzle and splutter.

Turn the potatoes in the oil, then put the tin back into the oven and bake the potatoes for 45–60 minutes, until they are golden and crisp, turning them over after about 30 minutes.

If they are ready before you are, turn the heat of the oven down to 170 C/325 F/Gas Mark 3, but don't cover the potatoes or they will soften. Drain them well on kitchen paper before serving.

Potato chips
There are two ways of making crisp Potato Chips. One is to fry the chips in oil heated to 190 C/375 F until they are soft but not browned, then to reheat the oil to 195 C/390 F and give the chips a final quick dip to brown and crisp them. The other way is to fry them steadily in the oil until they get past the soft stage and become crisp and brown.

Personally I use the first method if I am cooking a large number of chips, because I can get them all partially cooked and then give them their final quick frying in batches just before they're needed; and I use the second method when I'm just making a small quantity which can be cooked in one batch.

Cut potatoes into chips about 1 cm/½ inch wide and 1 cm/½ inch thick and rinse in cold water, then thoroughly dry before frying. After cooking, drain well on crumpled kitchen paper.

Désirée, Maris Piper, King Edward or Majestic are the best potato varieties for chips.

---

more watery texture. The skins vary in colour and may be white, red or purple. Sweet potatoes can be quite large and it is usually possible to buy a piece.

They can be boiled, roasted, fried or mashed and are enhanced by a sprinkling of sweet spice: cinnamon, nutmeg, ground cloves or allspice. Sweet potatoes are also delicious baked like jacket potatoes and served with butter. In the USA, they are boiled and then candied and served as a traditional accompaniment with the Thanksgiving dinner.

Perhaps the nicest way to serve them (but not the most slimming!) is glazed with butter and brown sugar; simply parboil them, then put them into a shallow casserole, dot with butter, and sprinkle with brown sugar. Bake in a fairly hot oven for about 40 minutes until they're golden brown and glazed. Or follow the recipe for Glazed Carrots on p. 182. Cooked in either of these

ways they make an excellent accompaniment to an almond nut roast for a special autumn meal.

YAM
Dioscorea rotundata, D. cayenensis
The yam is a staple food, widely consumed in West Africa and the Caribbean. Yams have brown, woody skins, and their flesh is moist and sweet. They come in a variety of shapes and sizes and are usually cooked in the same way as sweet potatoes. They can be made into casseroles or boiled and served with spicy vegetable mixtures. They absorb other flavours well.

They can also be used instead of ordinary potatoes in potato salad. Peel the yams and quarter them. Boil for about 15 minutes until tender, drain and cool, then dice them. Continue as for any of the other Potato Salad recipes on p. 166.

Yams are also good peeled, sliced and fried like sauté potatoes.

Tomato ▷
An indispensable flavouring, thickening and salad ingredient. Also delicious cooked in a variety of ways

Fruit Vegetables

Originally from tropical or sub-tropical countries, fruit vegetables offer vibrant colours, succulent textures and intense – sometimes hot – flavours. They are nutritious – avocados outstandingly so, being rich in protein, vitamin E and B6 (particularly good for women), while raw sweet peppers are high in vitamin C, green peppers containing twice, and red peppers, four times, the amount in oranges. Fruit vegetables are available all year but are plentiful in summer.

Aubergine △
Originally egg-like both in shape and colour (hence their alternative name 'egg plant') aubergines nowadays are more likely to be shiny, purple-skinned and a good deal larger than eggs

Beefsteak tomato △
These large tomatoes are ideal for stuffing and slicing for salads

Cherry tomato △
Baby cherry tomatoes make a pretty addition to salads and casseroles, or can be hollowed out and stuffed with curd cheese or a dip

Kenyan chilli
▽

Sweet pepper / capsicum △
Peppers start off green, then become yellow or red as they ripen; very dark, almost black, peppers are also available, as well as creamy coloured ones for pickling

Avocado ▷
The fruit of an evergreen tree, avocados range in colour from green with yellow or reddish flecks to almost black, and may be round or pear-shaped

Ancho chilli
▽

Chilli pepper ▷
There are many varieties of chilli pepper, ranging in hotness from mild to very fiery, and in colour from green to yellow or red

Fruit Vegetables

Choosing and storing

Aubergines, sweet peppers and tomatoes should be bright and firm, with no signs of withering or discoloured patches. They vary a good deal in shape and size, so look for ones which are suitable for your purpose; choose squarish peppers, for instance, and medium-sized aubergines, if you plan to stuff them. Store in a cool place – the salad compartment of the fridge is ideal. When choosing an avocado, either choose one which will yield all over to gentle pressure, or buy a hard one and allow up to a week for it to ripen at room temperature. Ripe avocados will keep for 1–2 days in the fridge.

Preparation and cooking

See under individual varieties.

AUBERGINE / EGGPLANT
Solanum melongena, var. esculentum

Aubergines are usually degorged before cooking, to draw out any bitter juices: cut into cubes or slices, then sprinkle with salt and place in a colander for 30 minutes, before rinsing under cold water and drying in kitchen paper ready for use. I must admit I do not always bother to do this and have never come across a bitter aubergine, but degorging does also prevent the aubergine from absorbing too much oil if it is fried.

Aubergines are usually cooked with the skin on, though this can be removed with a potato peeler if you prefer for dishes like Parmigiana (p. 202). Cut aubergines into rounds, short lengths, or cubes or dice. Aubergines for stuffing should be cut in half lengthways, and the cut sides scored diagonally in both directions, without piercing the skin. Salt can then be pressed·into the cuts and the aubergines left to degorge for 30 minutes. The flesh will then have softened and can be scooped out with a small knife and a teaspoon.

Aubergines are excellent stuffed (p. 192), in stews and casseroles, such as Middle Eastern Chick Pea Stew (p. 211), and in dips (p. 145). I also like them peeled and cut into strips, then dipped into a light batter, deep-fried and served with lemon slices and Soured Cream and Herb Dressing (p. 156) as a main or first course.

AVOCADO Persea americana

It's best to use a stainless steel knife to cut avocados as a steel one can leave a metallic taste. Cut the avocado in half lengthways, then hold one side in each hand and twist in opposite directions to separate them, and remove the stone. With their delicate, buttery flesh, avocados are delicious halved and served simply with a good vinaigrette, or stuffed and served either hot or cold. They can be added to salads (p. 163), made into delicious flans (p. 263), or blended into a creamy dip (p. 144) or chilled soup (p. 138).

Avocado flesh discolours after an hour or so, though coating it with lemon juice will help prevent this. If you need to keep a dip for longer, bury the avocado stone in it (remove it before you serve the dip!) and cover with clingfilm: this will preserve the colour. One half of an avocado will also keep its colour if you leave the stone in it, cover with clingfilm and keep in the fridge overnight. Undeveloped baby avocados, without stones, are available; they are attractive sliced into rings as a garnish or in salads.

CHILLI PEPPER
Capsicum annuum

Chillis vary in hotness and a general guide is the smaller the chilli, the hotter. ANCHO CHILLIS are quite sweet and only fairly hot; KENYAN CHILLIS are quite hot and are delicious fried in oil and sprinkled with salt, as a first course. Really HOT CHILLIS need careful handling. One is ample in a dish for 4–6 people. If the recipe requires the chilli to be chopped, cut it and remove the seeds under running water. Be careful not to touch your eyes or skin, as chilli juice can cause irritation, and wash your hands well afterwards. Dried red chillis are used in making chutneys and pickles.

SWEET PEPPER / CAPSICUM
Capsicum annuum

With their bright colours and fresh flavour, sweet peppers are useful both raw, in salads, as part of a crudités selection, and as a garnish, and cooked, in casseroles, stir-fries and vegetable mixtures. Cored and de-seeded peppers make a perfect container for a stuffing. To prepare peppers, cut a thin slice off the stalk end. Remove the seeds, rinsing out any stray ones under the cold tap. Use the peppers as they are, for stuffing, or cut into rings, strips, diamond shapes or dice.

If you want to remove the outer skin, and end up with a semi-cooked pepper, which is good in salads, put the whole peppers under a hot grill and turn them from time to time until the skin is charred, blistered and rubs off easily. Rinse off the skin and also the seeds under the cold tap. Dried peppers can be a good flavouring for casseroles.

TOMATO
Lycopersicon esculentum

There are many varieties of tomato, ranging in size from the baby CHERRY TOMATO to the large BEEFSTEAK variety. PLUM (or EGG) TOMATOES (not illustrated), which are much grown around the Mediterranean, have a particularly intense, sweet flavour and make excellent sauces and salads.

Tomatoes can be used with or without their skin, depending on the recipe and how tender the tomato is. To skin tomatoes, cover with boiling water and leave for 1 minute, then drain and cover with cold water. Use a small sharp knife and your fingers to peel off the skin.

Sometimes recipes suggest de-seeding tomatoes, but I very rarely do this as so much of the tomato is wasted and I find that difficult to do, especially as the jelly around the seeds is a valuable form of soluble fibre. To make tomato salad to serve 4 people, slice 700 g / 1½ lb tomatoes, put into a shallow dish and sprinkle with 1–2 tablespoons of olive oil and salt, freshly ground black pepper and chopped basil to taste. A little sliced raw onion can also be added.

Ridged cucumber ▷
Has a delicious, slightly
lemony flavour,
though can
sometimes
be bitter

Baby cucumber △
Used for making into pickles

**Golden nugget or
onion squash** ▷
One of the winter
squash, with
delicately flavoured
flesh

Cucumbers and Squashes

The name squash originates from the
Red Indian, *askoot-asquash*, and is the
name given to the members of a very
varied family of fruiting vegetables
which includes pumpkins, gourds,
marrows, courgettes and cucumbers. One of the most ancient vegetable families of the world, squashes
are not particularly nutritious,
although the yellow-fleshed varieties
contain useful amounts of vitamin A
and some fibre.

Butternut squash ▽
Has fairly dense, golden flesh
and makes an excellent purée

Cucumber △
Should be firm with a bright
skin; one of the most
refreshing vegetables

Pumpkin △
With its glowing, golden flesh,
this is equally good in sweet
and savoury recipes

Chinese winter melon ▷
This can be used in the same
way as marrow

◁ **Buttercup squash**
Similar to turban squash, and
can be used in the same way.
Also known as yellow
button squash

◁ **Hokido pumpkin**
Can be served as a vegetable or
made into a soup

**Ridge or
acorn squash** ▽
A particularly useful squash as
it can be halved and baked in
the skin

◁ **Doody or
white pumpkin**
Has pale greenish-white flesh
and a delicate flavour

△
Marrow
The more mature version of
courgette, with a delicate
flavour

Courgette/Zucchini ▷
Best when not more than
10–15 cm/4–5 inches long,
delicious lightly cooked

Turban squash ▽
This can be used in the same
way as pumpkin

Spaghetti squash ▷
A type of marrow with fibrous
flesh which looks like spaghetti
when cooked

Cucumbers and Squashes

Cucumbers

CUCUMBER *Cucumis sativus*
One of the first vegetables to be cultivated by man, and one of the most refreshing, cucumbers were a great favourite with the Roman Emperor Tiberius, who demanded a constant supply, even in winter. Various types of cucumber are available, including RIDGED and BABY.

Choosing and storing
Cucumbers should be firm and tender with a bright shiny skin. They need to be stored in a cool place, preferably the fridge, and used within a few days.

Preparation and using
The skin should be scrubbed well before use, or if the cucumbers have been waxed, as in the USA, it should be removed. The cucumber can then be grated, sliced or diced for use in salads: it is particularly good in a sweet and sour dressing using a little vinegar, fresh dill and white mustard seeds, or prepared in the Middle Eastern manner, with yogurt or soured cream and chopped mint (p. 167). Cucumber can also be used as a garnish, formed into cones to hold a savoury filling for a cocktail nibble, or cut into sticks for serving with a savoury dip.

Chilled Cucumber and Yogurt Soup (p. 138) makes a delightful start to a summer meal and, perhaps surprisingly, cucumber also makes one of the most delectable cooked vegetables, gently sautéed in butter with some fennel or dill seeds and a bay leaf, in a covered pan, until the flesh is golden and almost translucent.

Cucumber can also be stuffed and baked; try cutting a good plump cucumber into 20-cm/4-inch lengths, removing the skin, scooping out the seeds and filling the cavity with a mixture of finely chopped walnuts, onions, tomatoes and garlic. Bake in a well-buttered casserole, with a lid, for about 45 minutes in a moderate oven, and serve with Soured Cream and Herb Dressing (p. 156).

Dill pickled cucumbers are widely available and make a piquant addition to salads and sandwiches. Small fresh cucumbers are sometimes available for making your own pickles (p. 342).

Squashes

Squashes come in varied colours, shapes and sizes, but they can be roughly divided into summer and winter types. Summer squash have soft skins – they are said to be too old to eat if you cannot pierce the skin with your fingernail – and watery flesh, while winter squash have hard skins and firmer, more mealy flesh. It was this hard, protective skin developed by the winter squashes which made them such useful vegetables to store for the winter in the days before refrigerators.

Choosing and storing
The more delicate summer squashes should be firm and tender, with a smooth, shiny skin. They need to be stored in a cool place, preferably the fridge, and used within a few days. The more robust winter type should be shiny and hard, with no blemishes. As a rough guide, allow 450 g/1 lb summer squash, or 900 g/2 lb winter squash, for 4 people.

Preparation and cooking
See under individual varieties.

COURGETTE / ZUCCHINI
Cucurbita pepo
These baby marrows, which can be green or gold, reach their peak of perfection when they are no more than 10–15 cm/4–5 inches long. At this point they are tender, with flesh which almost melts in your mouth, and only need topping and tailing. They can then be cooked whole, sliced into rounds or matchsticks, or coarsely grated. Some recipes suggest degorging courgettes, as described for aubergines on p. 73, and this can be helpful if you are planning to sauté the courgettes in butter because it makes them less absorbent. My favourite way of cooking courgettes is to steam them, either in a vegetable steamer or by cooking them in a deep, covered saucepan containing only 1 cm/½ inch of water, so that most of the courgettes are above the water, cooking in the steam. As soon as the courgettes are just tender – 2–4 minutes – drain them and add coarse sea salt, freshly ground black pepper, fresh chopped herbs – parsley, mint, tarragon or basil – and a little butter. Or serve the cooked courgettes with a Fresh Tomato Sauce (p. 170). Courgettes can also be cooked in butter or oil, in a covered pan, over a low heat: this gives a luscious result, but I find it rather too rich and fatty unless the courgettes are served with something very plain.

Courgettes are excellent cooked with onions, garlic, peppers, aubergine and tomatoes, in Ratatouille (p. 187). And Provençal Courgette and Tomato Gratin makes a delicious light supper or lunch dish. Grated courgettes (1 kg/2¼ lb for 4 people) are fried lightly in butter, then layered in a shallow ovenproof dish with Fresh Tomato Sauce (p. 170) and sprinkled with breadcrumbs mixed with grated cheese. They are then baked in a moderate oven for 30–40 minutes.

For another excellent Provençal dish, Rice and Courgette Gratin, cook 250 g/8 oz brown rice. Fry a large onion and 4 diced courgettes in 2 tablespoons of oil until tender, then add to the rice with 50 g/2 oz grated cheese, an egg and seasoning. Spoon into a gratin dish, sprinkle with grated cheese and bake at 180 C/350 F/Gas Mark 4 for 45 minutes.

Larger courgettes make a good base for tasty stuffings, and courgettes always make a pleasant addition to vegetable pilafs and casseroles. They are best added towards the end of cooking time so that they do not overcook.

If you are able to obtain them, COURGETTE FLOWERS make a delicious treat dipped in a light batter and deep-fried, or filled with one of the nut roast mixtures (p. 230) and baked.

MARROW *Cucurbita pepo*

Marrows and larger types of summer squash are nicest when the skin is tender enough to eat; they can then be cut into small dice. If the seeds are very tender, these can be cooked along with the flesh; if not, they should be scooped out. Marrow can be cooked as described for courgettes (the butter/oil method suits marrows especially well, giving a tender, translucent, golden result). A finely chopped shallot or some grated fresh ginger or crushed garlic can be included for extra flavour. Marrow cooked in this way is good served with a crunchy topping of roasted cashew nuts. Béchamel Sauce (p. 175) with chopped herbs complements plainly cooked marrow – steamed until just tender – well.

Marrows with the seeds removed make excellent containers for stuffing, either hollowed out from one end, or halved lengthways, or cut crossways into sections and stood on end. A marrow which has been allowed to mature on the vine can be made into a spicy chutney or that traditional old British favourite, marrow and ginger jam. Warwickshire cottagers used to decorate such marrows with streamers, suspend them from the rafters in the autumn and keep them until Christmas!

Small, individual-size summer squash such as the delectable little PATTYPANS (not illustrated) should be boiled in their skins until tender; the top can then be sliced off, a little butter and seasoning added, and the flesh scooped out with a spoon. The CHINESE WINTER MELON and the DOODY or WHITE PUMPKIN (not generally available in Aus./NZ) can be prepared like marrow, but it may be necessary to remove the skin unless this is tender.

SPAGHETTI SQUASH
Cucurbita pepo

This has fibrous flesh which looks like spaghetti (but tastes like marrow) when cooked. Halve or quarter the marrow without peeling, then boil until the flesh is tender and can be scraped out. Toss the flesh in a little butter or olive oil and season well before serving.

PUMPKIN *Cucurbita pepo*

A pumpkin probably looks more exciting than it tastes, with its rounded shape and golden-orange skin and flesh. Pumpkin can, however, be made into an excellent smooth and creamy soup that is delicious eaten with hot garlic bread on a chilly autumn day. It is of course a traditional ingredient in USA Thanksgiving celebrations in the form of spicy Pumpkin Pie (p. 292), and one of Australia's most popular vegetables. Pumpkin can be served as a vegetable, and I like it best layered in a shallow gratin dish with garlic butter, topped with crumbs and baked in the oven, or cooked with some grated fresh ginger and garlic, then puréed. TURBAN, BUTTERNUT and ACORN SQUASH, HOKIDO PUMPKIN, HUBBARD (not illustrated), GOLDEN NUGGET or ONION SQUASH, and BUTTERCUP (or YELLOW BUTTON) SQUASH can all be prepared in a similar way. (Neither Turban squash nor Hokido pumpkin are generally available in Aus./NZ.)

SNAKE GOURD
Tricosantes cucumerina
(Not illustrated)

This unusual looking, green squash is native to Southeast Asia and Australia, and although sometimes grown in USA and Europe it is not easy to come by. It is much used in Indian vegetarian cookery and has a firm texture and an excellent flavour. It has a white down on the skin, which can be removed by rubbing the gourd all over with coarse salt. It is then cooked without peeling, and is delicious in lightly spiced vegetable dishes and curries. The snake gourd is sometimes confused with the BOTTLE GOURD (not illustrated), a much tougher squash, which is pointed at both ends.

Cooking and serving ideas for winter squashes

□ winter squashes make an excellent purée; steam until tender, then whizz to a cream in a blender or food processor. Season with salt, pepper and garlic. Good with a crisp hazelnut roast or burgers.

□ for a richer version, stew the diced squash gently in butter with a sliced onion, some garlic and grated ginger, until tender, then purée in a blender or food processor.

□ winter squashes, and pumpkin in particular, make an excellent soup, creamy and golden. Allow 1 kg/2¼ lb pumpkin to make a soup for 6 people. Remove the skin and seeds; dice the flesh. Fry 2 large onions in 25 g/1 oz butter for 10 minutes, then add the pumpkin and 2 crushed garlic cloves and fry for a further 5 minutes. Add 1 litre/2¼ pints water and simmer for about 20 minutes, then reduce to a purée in a blender or food processor and add 150 ml/5 fl oz single cream and seasoning to taste. Delicious sprinkled with chopped parsley or crunchy croûtons.

□ all the winter squashes absorb flavours well and are enhanced by the flavour of garlic and warming spices: ginger, curry powder, allspice, chilli, cinnamon, cardamom.

□ pumpkin, or any winter squash, is excellent baked in a casserole. Allow 450 g/1 lb pumpkin (weighed with the skin and seeds) per person, peel and cut into 1-cm/½-inch dice. Toss in seasoned flour, add a generous sprinkling of chopped parsley and crushed garlic, then pack into a well-greased casserole, dot with butter or oil and bake in a cool oven (170 C/325 F/Gas Mark 3) for 2–2½ hours, until the top is crisp and brown and the pumpkin underneath is tender.

□ for an unusual pudding, try pumpkin in orange-flavoured syrup. For 4 people, peel and slice 1.5 kg/3½ lb pumpkin, then cook very gently, for about 10 minutes, in a syrup made from 300 ml/10 fl oz water, 100 g/4 oz sugar and the grated rind of 1 orange. Serve chilled.

Fresh shiitake ▽
These Chinese and Japanese fungi need to be gathered and eaten when young, or they become tough

Cep ▽
One of the most delicious mushrooms, ceps are found in beech and oak woods in the summer and autumn

Oyster mushroom ▽
A fungi which grows on tree clumps and is, increasingly, being cultivated

Champignon de Paris ▽
The first cultivated mushroom, grown in Paris at the turn of the eighteenth century

Mushrooms and Truffles

Wild mushrooms have long been used to add interest and nourishment to meals. Mushrooms, whether wild or cultivated, are among the most useful flavouring ingredients in vegetarian cookery, as well as being filling and substantial if cooked in quantity. Mushrooms are interesting nutritionally, being unusually rich in vitamins B2 and B3 (which vegetarians need to be sure of including in their diet).

Dried shiitake △

Pleurotte ▽
An attractive mushroom with a delicate flavour

Chanterelle or Girolle △
With the colour and aroma of apricots, the chanterelle is found in deciduous woods from summer until mid-winter

Button mushrooms ▽
Tender and delicately flavoured

◁ Black truffle
Black truffles, from the Périgord region of France

Bottled mushrooms
Mushrooms can be bought bottled, but the flavour and texture of most is not good

Champignon marron △
A type of cultivated mushroom with a brownish skin

White truffle △
These are canned and not as white inside as fresh ones

Oyster (bottled) △

Large flat cultivated mushrooms ▽
Excellent for frying, grilling and stuffing

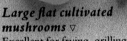

◁ Morel
The morel needs careful washing

Chanterelle (bottled) △

◁ Small open-cup cultivated mushrooms
More strongly flavoured than button mushrooms

Girolle (bottled) △

Cep (bottled) △

Funghi porcini DRIED MUSHROOMS
Available from Italian shops, these are dried ceps

Dried woodear
Used in Chinese dishes, with a gelatinous texture after soaking

Chinese straw mushroom △
A very tasty mushroom and one which survives the bottling process well

Mushrooms and Truffles

Choosing and storing

Wild mushrooms can be found in woods and fields if you're lucky or know where to look; or they can sometimes be bought from specialist greengrocers and markets, but the supply is usually erratic: grab them when you see – or can afford – them! If buying cultivated mushrooms, avoid any that are brownish-looking. Choose mushrooms which smell fragrant and look fresh, almost with a slight bloom on them. Use quickly; they do not keep well, although they can be stored in the fridge for 24–36 hours.

Preparation and cooking

Wild mushrooms should be carefully washed – personally I like to wash cultivated mushrooms, too – and any tough bits should be cut out. Field mushrooms should have the top layer of skin removed.

Most mushrooms are best sliced as necessary and then cooked simply by frying lightly in butter, for about 5 minutes, until cooked through. If mushrooms exude a great deal of liquid during the frying process, you can either pour this off and save it as a flavouring for a soup or sauce, or thicken it by adding a small quantity of cornflour mixed with water. Or – the best way, I think – continue to cook the mushrooms over a high heat until all the liquid has disappeared and you are left with very tasty, tender mushrooms: this may take 20–30 minutes. They are also delicious stuffed, in pâtés, flans and raw in salads.

For Mushrooms in Cream, prepare as described above, allowing 900 g/ 2 lb mushrooms for 4 people. Fry in 25 g/1 oz butter over a high heat for 20–30 minutes until all the liquid has disappeared, then add 150 ml/5 fl oz double cream and season with salt, freshly ground black pepper, a squeeze of lemon juice and a grating of nutmeg.

BLACK TRUFFLE
Tuber melansporum and
WHITE TRUFFLE
T. magnatum
Wildly expensive, black truffles are chopped and added to dishes as a flavouring. White truffles are cut into fine slivers, while raw, over the top of dishes to give them an exquisite fragrance. Canned truffles do not have the aroma and flavour of fresh ones.

CEP *Boletus edulis*
Ceps have tubes under their caps instead of the more usual gills. Ceps are delicious cooked as described above and are also excellent added to casseroles. Italian dried mushrooms, FUNGHI PORCINI, are ceps. They are expensive to buy, but just a few mixed with cultivated mushrooms, or added to a vegetable casserole, give a pronounced flavour. Just rinse, then use as required.

CHANTERELLE or GIROLLE
Cantharellus cibarius
The trumpet-shaped chanterelle is delicious cooked as described above or added to casseroles. It has a slightly peppery flavour and remains chewy however long it is cooked.

CHINESE STRAW MUSHROOM
Volvariella volvacea
Chinese straw mushrooms, available in bottles, make a tasty addition to vegetable stir-fries.

CULTIVATED MUSHROOMS
Agaricus bisporus
These are available at various stages of development. First come the little tight white BUTTON MUSHROOMS, which are excellent in creamy sauces (p. 174), sliced in salads (p. 163), or for using whole in Marinated Mushrooms. The next stage is MEDIUM-SIZED MUSHROOMS and SMALL OPEN MUSHROOMS. These, too, are useful for most purposes, particularly for making into fritters or adding to batter for a mushroomy vegetarian version of toad in the hole, while LARGE FLAT OPEN MUSHROOMS are ideal for stuffing, and for grilling or

frying. CHAMPIGNON MARRON and CHAMPIGNON DE PARIS are other cultivated mushrooms.

FIELD MUSHROOM
Agaricus campestris
(Not illustrated)
These have a wonderful rich mushroomy flavour, much more intense than that of cultivated mushrooms. Delicious fried and served as they are, or made into duxelles, a concentrated mixture of finely chopped mushrooms fried with a finely chopped onion for about 30 minutes, uncovered, until they become a thick purée.

MOREL
Morchella esculenta and
M. vulgaris
This tasty mushroom tends to harbour grit and sometimes insects in its honeycomb cap, so it is best to cut it up first, then wash it in salted water. Fry morels and use in any of the ways suggested above. Dried morels are well worth buying (when you're feeling rich). Soak them in hot water for 30 minutes, then strain, reserving the soaking water for use in cooking. Wash them well, then chop and add to casseroles, soups, sauces for a deliciously intense mushroom flavour.

OYSTER MUSHROOM
Pleurotus ostreatus
With their firm texture these make a useful addition to casseroles, use like cultivated mushrooms.

PLEUROTTE *Pleurotus ostreatus*
This delicately flavoured mushroom can be prepared in a similar way to chanterelles.

SHIITAKE *Lentinus edodes*
Fresh shiitake can be sliced, fried and added to rice dishes, stews and stir-fries; soak the dried ones in boiling water for 30 minutes then drain and chop. Add the soaking water to the dish or keep as stock.

WOODEAR or CLOUDEAR
Auricularia polytricha
Rather tough mushrooms, used in Chinese recipes. Soak in boiling water for 30 minutes before use.

Arame ▽
A delicately flavoured seaweed which grows in the seas around Japan and has a slightly sweet flavour

◁ Dulse
Reddish-purple in colour, dulse has quite a chewy texture

Kombu ▽
From the northern seas of Japan, kombu comes in thick black strips and is useful for flavouring stocks and soups

Sea Vegetables

Seaweeds, or sea vegetables, as they are more appetizingly called, have been an important food for people all over the world since ancient times, many types being cultivated and used. In some poor coastal areas they were eaten as a survival food, but in Japan they are an important part of the national cuisine, many types being cultivated. Seaweeds are high in nutrients, including protein, iron, calcium, potassium, sodium, iodine and are also one of the rare non-animal sources of vitamin B12.

Wakame ▽
A mild-flavoured, useful all-purpose seaweed

Laver ▽
Ranging in colour from pinkish-purple to greenish-brown, laver grows on rocky North European coasts. It can be bought dried, or cooked, as here

Nori ▽
The most popular sea vegetable, and my own favourite, nori is made into sheets in Japan by pressing the seaweed out by hand after drying

▽ Carageen
This pale-coloured, branching seaweed is found on the rocky coasts of Northern Europe, and on the American coast from Maine to North Carolina

Hiziki ▷
Means 'bearer of wealth and beauty' in Japan where it has been used for hundreds of years

Sea Vegetables

Choosing and storing

Seaweeds can be bought dried from health shops and wholefood shops, also shops stocking Japanese ingredients. Keep them in an airtight container in a cool, dry place.

Sea vegetables may not be generally available in Aus./NZ due to import restrictions.

Preparation and using

Most seaweeds (with the exception of nori, see below) need soaking before use. Put the seaweed into a bowl, starting with a small amount, say 15 g/½ oz, if this is the first time you've used it, cover with boiling water and leave for 20 minutes, then drain. The soaking water, which contains useful nutrients, can be used in the recipe or discarded if it is too salty and strongly flavoured. Then put the seaweed into a saucepan, cover with fresh cold water (which can be flavoured with grated fresh ginger or tamari) and simmer gently until tender – generally 20–30 minutes. Alternatively, the seaweed can be added to a vegetable stew or casserole at this point. The cooked seaweed can be added to other cooked vegetables, or cooled and mixed with fresh vegetables and a dressing to make a salad.

Seaweed is naturally gelatinous and some types, notably carageen and AGAR AGAR (not illustrated), can be used to make vegetarian jellies and moulds (see Carageen below).

ARAME *Eisenia bicyclis*

Arame is cut into long thin strips after harvesting. It is a good seaweed to start with if you're unfamiliar with sea vegetables. Arame is pleasant in salads, such as Radish, Cucumber and Arame Salad (p. 164), and in vegetable side dishes. It needs only 5 minutes' soaking followed by 20 minutes' cooking before use.

CARAGEEN *Chondrus crispus*

Carageen can be cooked and served in vegetable dishes or salads. I think it is more useful as a jelling agent, producing a light, delicately flavoured jelly, or blancmange – my mother often made this when I was a child and I loved its curious, delicate flavour. To make Carageen Mould, soak 7 g/¼ oz carageen in warm water for 10 minutes, then drain and put into a saucepan with 900 ml/1½ pints milk and a vanilla pod and simmer for 20 minutes. Strain through a fine sieve, pressing the carageen to extract all the jelly. Add 4 tablespoons clear honey or sugar and an egg yolk; finally fold in the whisked egg white. Pour into moulds to set. This can be made with soya milk and without the egg for a vegan version.

DULSE
Rhodymenia palmata

Dulse never gets very soft even if you cook it for 40–50 minutes, so is not to everyone's taste, though it's a seaweed I particularly like, finely shredded and added to a soup, salad or rice dish.

HIZIKI *Hiziki fusiforme*

Sold coarsely shredded, hiziki has a sweet, delicate flavour rather like that of arame (see above). Hiziki is an outstanding source of iron and calcium, just 15 g/½ oz supplying nearly half the recommended daily requirement for an adult. I think it is most delicious added to salads or rice and vegetable mixtures or stir-fried vegetable side dishes.

KOMBU *Laminaria japonica*

Most often used to flavour stocks, and an essential ingredient of the Japanese stock, dashi, kombu is a strongly flavoured sea vegetable: one strip will flavour 600 ml/1 pint water.

LAVER *Porphyra umbilicalis*

Prepare laver as described above, cooking for 50–60 minutes. Laver can also be bought ready-cooked and canned; it looks like a thick green purée. A purée of laver is mixed with oatmeal to make the Welsh delicacy, laver bread. In my opinion, you have to be either Welsh or a real seaweed devotee to enjoy either laver or laver bread.

NORI *Porphyra tenera*

Another good one to try if you're not familiar with seaweeds, nori is prepared differently from the others. Take a sheet of nori and hold it close to a hotplate or gas flame for a minute or so, moving it slightly until it is toasted and crisp all over. It can then be used to wrap up tasty savoury ingredients to make sushi (p. 142), or you can scrunch it up in your fingers and sprinkle it over the top of salads, soups, stir-fries or vegetable soups.

WAKAME *Undaria pinnatifida*

After soaking the wakame (see above), open up the leaves, cut out the central spine and cook the wakame as described above. Wakame is used to make the classic Miso Soup (p. 133), and is also useful for flavouring soups and stews and adding to salads and vegetable side dishes. For a tangy rice salad, add soaked and shredded wakame to cooked brown rice. Season with salt, pepper, sugar and vinegar, then add shredded fresh vegetables. Garnish with sesame seeds.

Ideas for using sea vegetables

- ☐ Toast nori and crumble over any salad, stir-fry or creamy dip, for a tangy, salty flavour.

- ☐ Soak and shred kombu, flavour with chilli powder, crushed garlic, chopped spring onion, vinegar, sugar, salt and pepper. Serve as a side dish with Japanese-style sweet-vinegared rice (p. 241) and stir-fried vegetables.

- ☐ Soak and shred wakame, mix with diced cucumber, sliced radishes, sugar, vinegar, salt and pepper. Leave for 1–2 hours (or longer) to marinate; serve sprinkled with sesame seeds, as a side dish with Japanese-style rice.

- ☐ For an interesting nibble or side-dish, add soaked and diced wakame to beaten egg; fry on both sides to make a kind of pancake. Cut into pieces. Sprinkle with a few sesame seeds if liked; dip into soy sauce to eat.

◁ **Hothouse grape**

◁ **Muscat grape**

Napoleon red grape △

Seedless grape △

Williams pear ▽

Apples, Pears and Grapes

Apples, pears and table grapes, have been cultivated and enjoyed for centuries. Delicious and refreshing, they are available all year round. They contain a range of useful vitamins and minerals, and apples and pears are rich in particularly valuable fibre. There are many varieties of these fruits, although with apples and pears, in recent years, there has been a tendency to concentrate on a few outstanding ones.

Grape
Grapes are generally classified as being either table grapes, as are the ones shown here, or wine-making grapes

Tientsin ya pear ▽

Chinese pear ▽

Logipont pear ▽

Laxton Fortune apple ▽

Pear
There are around 5000 named varieties of pear, but only about 20–30 are widely cultivated

Crab apple ▽

Ellison's Orange apple ▷

Conference pear ▷

◁ **Comice pear**

Edward VII ▽

◁

Crispin ▽

Spartan ▽

Red Delicious ▽

Granny Smith ▽

Bramley's Seedling△

Jonagold ▽

Yellow/Golden Delicious ▽

◁ Greensleeves

Starking△

Cox's Orange Pippin ▽

Egremont
Russet ▽

James Grieve ▽

Apple
Descended from the crab apple, which grows
wild throughout Europe, apples are
traditionally divided into 'cookers' and 'eaters'

Apples, Pears and Grapes

APPLE *Malus pumila*

Choosing and storing

One of the basics of the store cupboard, one variety or another of apple is available all the year round. Choose bright, firm, sweet-smelling apples with no wrinkles or bruises. They are best stored in a cool, airy place. Only late season apples will store over winter, and if these are wrapped individually in newspaper and put in boxes or shelves in a cool place they will keep for several months.

Preparation and using

Good eating apples are delightful just as they are, or with cheese, such as a piece of mature Cheddar. They can be sliced and added to fruit salads and compotes, or mixed with vegetables in a savoury salad such as the famous Waldorf (p. 169). If you need to keep raw apple for any length of time, either dip the pieces in a light salt and water mixture, or toss them in lemon or orange juice, to preserve the colour. Grated apple forms the basis of the original Bircher muesli (p. 240). Eating apples can also be used for cooking, in fact I prefer them to the sharper cooking apples for some dishes because their natural sweetness means less sugar is needed. Sliced and peeled COX'S ORANGE PIPPIN apples are delightful stewed with raisins, baked in a pie (p. 294) or made into an open tart: follow the recipe on p. 292 but use lightly poached apple slices instead of red fruit, and glaze with sieved and warmed apricot jam.

Another widely cultivated apple is the YELLOW/GOLDEN DELICIOUS, firm, crisp, and some would say tasteless, when young, becoming golden and sweeter when more mature. Like Cox's, Golden Delicious apples can be used for making pies and flans, and are frequently used for this purpose in France. The GRANNY SMITH apple is another variety which you either like or you don't, green in colour, very crisp, with a clean, refreshing flavour. The STARKING apple has a red skin. It is a delicious eating apple, very crisp, with sweet, white flesh. Another popular red-skinned apple is the RED DELICIOUS, a firm, sweet variety developed in the USA. This apple can be eaten raw or baked. The MCINTOSH (not illustrated) is another popular all-purpose American variety. This has a slightly sharp flavour, good for eating raw or baking. SPARTAN apples, developed in Denmark, can be used for both cooking and eating and have a custard-like flavour. Other good eating apples are LAXTON FORTUNE, EDWARD VII and ELLISON'S ORANGE, with a flavour not unlike a Cox apple; the brown-skinned EGREMONT RUSSET with its deliciously mellow flavour; CRISPINS, JAMES GRIEVE, GREENSLEEVES, and JONAGOLD which has a long season, lasting from autumn until the spring.

Cooking apples are best used if a sharp flavour is required; some cooking apples, such as BRAMLEY'S SEEDLINGS, also collapse when cooked, so these are best if you want a soft purée. Large cooking apples are excellent cored, scored round the middle to prevent bursting, stuffed with dried fruit or mincemeat, or honey and chopped nuts, and baked whole for 40–50 minutes in a moderate oven. Or they may be peeled, cored, wrapped in shortcrust pastry and baked to make apple dumplings.

Cooked apple is used as a basis of many excellent puddings: apple crumble and apple meringue, apple fool and apple amber, to mention just a few. I like to make apple purée into ice cream (p. 281), to serve with a Blackberry Coulis (p. 300) or sorbet (p. 282). Cooking apples are also used to make apple sauce, which makes an excellent accompaniment to Savoury Lentil Loaf (p. 213). To make Apple Sauce cook 450 g/1 lb peeled, cored and sliced cooking apples in 25 g/1 oz butter or vegan margarine in a covered pan for about 10 minutes until pulpy. Cooking apples can be used, too, to make herb-flavoured apple jelly, one of the best preserves, and also a sweet and spicy chutney (p. 342).

CRAB APPLES, the original apple, are small, more the size of large cherries than apples as we know them, and very sharp. They range in colour from yellow to red and are mainly useful because they are full of pectin, so they can be made into an excellent ruby-coloured jelly which is delicious for serving with nut roasts (instead of redcurrant or cranberry jelly). They can also be mixed with other wild fruits to make, for very little expense, a delicious sweet/sour Hedgerow Jelly. To make this you need 450 g/1 lb each of crab apples, blackberries and elderberries, and 225 g/8 oz each of sloes, hips, haws and rowan berries. Cook the blackberries and elderberries together in a little water until tender, and, in another pan, cook the rest of the fruits, in water, until tender. Mix the fruit purées, strain. Measure the liquid and return to the pan with 450 g/1 lb sugar for each 600 ml/1 pint, heat gently until the sugar is dissolved, then boil until setting point is reached as described on p. 339.

Stewing fruit

Juicy fruits such as apples (also black and red currants, bilberries, blackberries and rhubarb) are best cooked in the minimum of water, or none at all. Put the fruit into a heavy-based saucepan with 2 tablespoons of water to each 450–700 g/1–1½ lb fruit. Cover the saucepan and then heat gently until the juices run and the fruit is tender – this will probably take around 10 minutes.

Instead of water, butter can be used for stewing apples, and redcurrant jelly for rhubarb. When the fruit is soft, add sugar or honey to taste. Do not put this in sooner or the outside of the fruits may toughen before the inside is properly cooked.

PEAR *Pyrus communis*

Choosing and storing

Pears need choosing carefully, because once perfectly ripe they deteriorate very quickly. It is best to buy them slightly under-ripe and keep them at room temperature for a day or two until they are just right, when they should 'give' slightly at the stalk end. Once this stage is reached, they will keep for a day or two in the fridge, but bring them to room temperature before serving, to draw out all the flavour.

A good dessert pear can be really superlative, with a delicate flavour, natural sweetness and melting flesh.

Preparation and using

Pears like this really need no accompaniment, although they do complement a good ripe cheese, such as a Brie, well and make a delicious first course with a Roquefort Dressing (p. 149), or with a cream and yogurt dressing flavoured with tarragon vinegar to give a hint of sharpness (p. 148).

Perfectly ripe pears can be peeled and served in some of the combinations for which cooked pears are traditionally used, such as Poire Belle Hélène, where they are filled with vanilla ice cream and topped with Hot Chocolate Sauce (p. 300).

Perhaps the most delicious dessert pear is the COMICE, delicately flavoured, juicy and very sweet when at its best. The yellow-skinned WILLIAMS pear is another popular dessert variety. The CONFERENCE pear has a rather tough brownish-green skin, and this, too, has a delicious flavour, especially when fully ripe, but also cooks well (see below) as does the PACKHAM (not illustrated) and indeed many dessert pears, including the LOGIPONT. Poached as described, then drained and chilled, these pears are delicious served with some whipped cream, or in the traditional ways described above. They are also excellent, deeply stained and delicately flavoured, poached in a syrup made with cheap red wine instead of water. Cooking pears can also be pickled or made into chutney.

Poaching fruit

This method is best for pears and other firm fruits such as apricots, peaches and plums. First make a sugar syrup. For 450–700 g / 1–1½ lb fruit you need 300 ml / 10 fl oz water, or other liquid such as wine, cider or fruit juice, and 75 g / 3 oz granulated sugar. Honey can be used instead of sugar but will add its own strong flavour. Put the sugar and water into a heavy-based saucepan and heat gently until dissolved. Then turn up the heat and boil rapidly for 2 minutes. Put in the prepared fruit, bring back to the boil, then simmer gently, half covered, until the fruit feels tender when pierced. It's important to give large fruits like whole or halved peaches or pears time to cook right through to the centre or they may discolour. Allow at least 20–30 minutes for whole pears and 15–20 minutes for the others. Let the fruit cool in the syrup, or remove the fruit with a draining spoon and thicken the syrup by boiling rapidly until reduced in quantity.

It is also possible to buy Asian pears, such as the TIENTSIN YA PEAR and the CHINESE PEAR. These are eaten when they are still firm, and can be used raw, adding a crisp texture to fruit and vegetable salad mixtures, or cooked as described above.

GRAPE *Vitis vinifera*

Choosing and storing

Many varieties of table grape are grown, ranging in colour from white through red, as in the NAPOLEON RED, to deepest purple of which the HOTHOUSE GRAPES are an example. Grapes also vary in sweetness, and the only way to be sure what you are buying is to try one. The green MUSCAT GRAPES are particularly sweet with the characteristic 'MUSCAT' flavour, and SEEDLESS GRAPES, too, are particularly sweet.

Once bought, grapes need to be used quickly, although they will keep for 2–3 days in the refrigerator.

Bring them out and allow them enough time to get back to room temperature before serving.

Preparation and using

A bunch of grapes makes a decorative addition to a fruit bowl or cheese board and, like apples and pears, they are excellent all put together in a salad, with watercress and walnuts too. Grapes make an attractive addition to a fresh fruit salad – choose the colour to complement the other fruits – and can also be made into a delicate jelly, with grape juice set with agar agar (p. 286). Black and white grapes, arranged in alternating circles, make an attractive filling for a flan case or topping for a cheesecake. A white nutmeat made from pine nuts or almonds is good served with a garnish of fresh green grapes, while little bunches of seedless grapes are a mother's best friend as lunch-box fillers and replacements for sugary sweets.

Ideas for using a glut of pears or apples

☐ Spiced pears are easy to make and go well with nut or lentil loaves.

☐ Both pears and apples can be made into excellent ice cream, following the recipe on p. 280. These are good served with a toning sauce or sorbet: pear ice cream with pear sorbet; apple ice cream with blackberry sorbet; pear ice cream with chocolate or raspberry sauce; apple ice cream with blackberry or orange sauce.

☐ If you make wine, both pears and apples can be made into good medium-dry white wine.

☐ Make pear or apple jelly or jam, perhaps flavoured with fresh herbs.

☐ Pear or apple sauce goes well with a savoury lentil loaf.

◁ Peach
Peaches may be white- or yellow-fleshed and free-stone, clingstone or semi-clingstone, depending on how firmly attached the stone is to the flesh

Date ▽
Fresh dates are much more succulent than their dried counterparts (p. 101)

U S A Golden date ▷
A juicy sweet variety

Pitted Fruits

Another group which includes some of the most delectable fruits, many of which delighted the people of China, Greece and Rome thousands of years ago. At the peak of perfection, these fruits all make a fine dessert, served fresh and raw without any adornment. They are health-giving, containing useful amounts of a range of vitamins and minerals. Peaches and apricots are particularly good sources of vitamin A, while dates are rich in B vitamins (especially B2 and B3, and iron).

Nectarine △
This smooth-skinned variety of peach has juicy flesh and a fresh, sweet flavour similar to peaches

Lychee ▽

Golden Cape plum△

Apricot ▽
This fragrant, delicately flavoured fruit originated in China, where it has grown for 4,000 years

Cherry ▽
One of the delights of early summer, ripe, sweet cherries are a delight to eat just as they are

Red ace plum △

Plum
Plums like peaches, are divided into free-stone and clingstone types

Greengage △
A variety of plum and one of the sweetest and best to eat raw

Santa Rosa plum△

△ Prune plum

△ Burbank plum

Damson △
Small plums with an intense, slightly bitter flavour

Switzen plum △

Pitted Fruits

Choosing and storing

Superb when perfectly ripe, these fruits are soon past their best, so need buying and storing carefully. As they are soft, pitted fruits are particularly susceptible to damage during transport, so look for sound fruits without bruises. When buying fresh dates make sure that they really are fresh, with no sign of 'sweating' or flaking. If they have a slightly winey flavour, they are off and, while they won't hurt you, they are certainly not at their best. If you need to keep these fruits, store them in a cool place (or the fridge).

Preparation and cooking

Perfect fruits can be served as they are, or the stones can be removed and the fruit sliced and added to a fruit salad. Peaches can be skinned in the same way as tomatoes (p. 169). Under-ripe peaches, apricots and nectarines can be poached in a sugar syrup (p. 85); plums can be stewed (p. 84), baked into pies and made into crumbles.

APRICOT *Prunus armeniaca*

Perfectly ripe apricots make one of the best dessert fruits; they are also pleasant with cream cheese in a salad or as part of a fruit compote. Less perfect fruits are good poached in vanilla-flavoured syrup and served with thick yogurt or cream, or in a flan or little tartlets. Apricots are used in savoury recipes in the Middle East and go well with chick peas and white beans; an apricot sauce is good served with a savoury nut roast instead of apple sauce, and I also like apricot sauce with Deep-fried Camembert (p. 221) instead of the more usual gooseberry sauce.

Cooked, drained apricots can be topped with an all-in-one cake mixture (p. 304) and a scattering of flaked almonds and baked to make an apricot sponge pudding, and they are included in Danish pastries. They can be pickled or made into jam or chutney. Apricot jam, melted and sieved, makes a useful glaze for fruit dishes and is often used to stick the almond paste on a fruit cake (p. 312). Apricot brandy makes a delicious addition to sweet apricot dishes such as compotes and fools. Apricots are available fresh, dried (p. 102), canned either in syrup or their own juice or made into preserves or chutney (p. 342).

CHERRY *Prunus avium*

Sweet juicy cherries make an easy and refreshing pudding. Ones which are less than perfect, or the sour MORELLO CHERRIES (not illustrated) can be poached to make a compote or jelly, or covered with batter to make a clafoutis, so popular in France. In central Europe cherries are made into chilled soups and they are also excellent made into a tart, or served hot and flambéd with ice cream. The famous Black Forest gâteau, consisting of layers of lightest chocolate sponge, black cherries and cream, with a liberal sprinkling of cherry liqueur, may have been devalued by the popularity of synthetic-tasting versions, but is still a wonderful gâteau when properly made.

Cherry brandy, and Kirsch, an eau-de-vie made from the stones of cherries, are delicious flavourings for any cherry dish, and Kirsch is also traditionally added to Cheese Fondue (p. 217). Cherries are available fresh, frozen, canned and made into preserves: black cherry preserve is one of the most delectable.

DATE / USA GOLDEN DATE *Phoenix dactylifera*

Fresh dates are one of the best sweet-substitutes, either as they are, or with their stones removed and replaced by a freshly cracked brazil nut, a mixture of whipped cream, cream cheese, ground almonds and honey or orange flower water. They make a good addition to a fresh fruit salad, or they can be served with thick Greek yogurt with a topping of a clear honey and, for a really superlative pudding, a little double cream.

LYCHEE *Litchi chinensis*

See p. 92.

NECTARINE
Prunus persica, var. *Nectarina*

Particularly juicy and well-flavoured, nectarines can be used in similar ways to peaches. They are available both fresh and dried.

PEACH *Prunus persica*

A sweet, ripe, juicy peach is a delight and needs no accompaniment. Not-so-perfect peaches can be skinned (as described for tomatoes, p. 169), sliced and added to fruit salads and compotes, or sliced, covered with sweet white wine and chilled.

Peach Brûlée is also good: put sliced peaches into a shallow heat-proof dish, cover with whipped cream and an even layer of brown sugar, chill, then just before serving grill until the sugar caramelizes.

Ripe peaches can be made into an excellent ice cream using the recipe on p. 281. This is good served with Raspberry Sorbet (made as for Blackberry Sorbet, p. 282) or Raspberry Coulis (p. 300). Spiced Peaches (made as for Orange Slices, p. 343) and Peach Chutney (made as for Sweet Spiced Apricot Chutney, p. 342) are other good ways of using less than perfect specimens. Peaches are available fresh, dried (p. 103) and canned in syrup and in fruit juice.

PLUM/GREENGAGE
Prunus domestica, P. institia

Like the other fruits in this group, sweet and tender plums and greengages are excellent eaten *au naturel.* VICTORIA are examples of excellent dessert plums, and when at their peak need no accompaniment. Other good dessert varieties are the SANTA ROSA, RED ACE and GOLDEN CAPE plums. Many varieties, like the SWITZEN, BURBANK and PRUNE PLUM, can be eaten raw when ripe or used for cooking, though sour varieties, like the tiny DAMSON (*Prunus institia*) need to be stewed in a sweetened syrup, perhaps with a touch of cinnamon added (p. 84), made into crumbles (p. 295) or pies (p. 294). Plums are available fresh, dried (in the form of prunes, p. 103) and canned, and also in the form of preserves, crystallized fruits and some liqueurs.

▽ **Cranberry**
Hard, bright red shiny berries with an acidic, slightly spicy flavour

Blackberry ▽
Picking blackberries – and eating them, still warm from the sun – is one of the pleasures of late summer

Raspberry ▷
Exquisitely flavoured, and the most delicate of all the berries

Berries and Soft Fruits

These luscious fruits are also some of the most nutritious. Blackcurrants contain a useful amount of calcium and are one of the best of all sources of vitamin C, and strawberries, too, are unusually rich in this vitamin. Raspberries, blackberries and all the currants contain high levels of fibre. Rhubarb contains calcium but also oxalic acid, preventing its absorption so it is inadvisable to eat rhubarb more than twice a week.

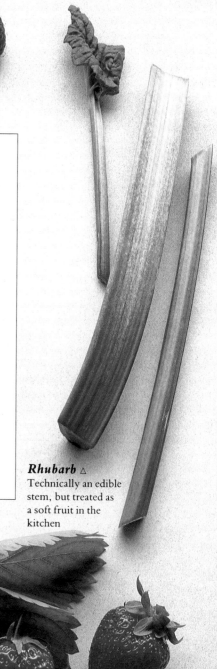

Rhubarb △
Technically an edible stem, but treated as a soft fruit in the kitchen

Blueberry ▽
Related to the BILBERRY, BLAEBERRY or WHORTLEBERRY which grow wild in Europe and Northern Asia, the blueberry is a very popular berry in the USA

Blackcurrant △
Named after dried currants because blackcurrants were thought to resemble them, currants grow wild throughout Europe

Gooseberry ▽
Sharply flavoured fruit of early summer in countries with a fairly cool climate, gooseberries can be yellow, green or red/purple, smooth or hairy

Strawberry △
Sweet and juicy berries of summer

Redcurrant △
Redcurrants have a sharp flavour and a juicy texture

Wild strawberry △
Tiny fruits with perhaps the best flavour of all the strawberries

Berries and Soft Fruits

Choosing and storing

With the exception of cranberries and rhubarb, these fruits are delicate and need gentle handling. Look for bright fruit that is firm but not hard, with no sign of bruising, wetness or mildew. Check the punnets to see if they are stained with juices, and avoid any that are. Rhubarb should be crisp, bright and the sticks not too large (or they could be tough). Use the fruit as soon as possible; if necessary, keep in a cool place, preferably the fridge. Most of these fruits are available frozen, bottled and canned, as well as fresh.

Preparation and cooking

Many people advise against washing soft fruit, but I prefer to do so, to remove dust and any residues of sprays. Pat them dry on kitchen paper. For further preparation, see under the individual fruits. To cook these fruits, put them into a pan over a gentle heat without water for a few minutes until the juices run. A little sugar or honey can then be added to taste, and rhubarb is good cooked with a few tablespoons of redcurrant jelly. This group of fruit is particularly good for preserving.

BLACKBERRY
Rubus macropetalus

Plump juicy berries make a delicious pie, perhaps combined with apples (p. 294). Blackberries can be made into one of the best sorbets (p. 282), or an excellent coulis (p. 300).

BLACKCURRANT and REDCURRANT
Ribes nigrum, R. sativum

Unless they are going to be sieved, currants need to have the stems and flower ends removed. This is easily done with bunches of currants by drawing the prongs of a fork down through the clusters. A few raw currants can be added to a fruit salad or compote, but generally currants are best cooked and can be made into pies, tarts, ice cream and sorbets and the famous Danish red fruit pudding, Rödgröt, where a mixture of red fruits is stewed then puréed, thickened with cornflour, arrowroot or potato flour and allowed to become cool, when it will have a soft, slightly jellied texture. Summer Pudding is another traditional use for currants; stew them with other red fruits, then dip thin crustless slices of bread into the juices and use to line completely the sides and base of a pudding basin. Fill the basin with the drained fruit, then put more juice-soaked bread on top. Put a plate and a weight on top, then leave for several hours. Turn out of the basin and serve with thick yogurt or cream.

BLUEBERRY
Vaccinium corymbosum

Fat, juicy blueberries are delicious served with cream or thick yogurt and a little sugar or honey, or they can be made into pies, crumbles, flans, cheesecake toppings and muffins, or stewed to make a filling for pancakes.

CRANBERRY
Vaccinium macrocarpum

Perhaps best-known in the form of Cranberry Sauce (p. 174). This, by the way, is as delicious with a white, delicately flavoured Christmas nut roast as it is with turkey. Cranberries can also be made into pies and tarts, but they need a lot of sugar to make them palatable.

GOOSEBERRY Ribes uvacrispa

Dessert gooseberries just need topping and tailing before eating. Cooking varieties can be stewed gently with a few tablespoons of water to prevent them sticking to the pan. A few sprigs of elderflowers added to the pan give a delicate muscat flavour. Puréed stewed gooseberries make a good sauce for a brazil nut roast and also for deep-fried Camembert or Brie. Or add to the puréed gooseberries cold custard, yogurt, cream, or a mixture, to make a fool (p. 282). Gooseberries can also be made into excellent pies (p. 294) and crumbles.

LOGANBERRY
Rubus ursinus var. loganobaccus
(Not illustrated)

A natural hybrid between the raspberry and blackberry, first discovered in the garden of Judge J. H. Logan at Santa Cruz in California and named after him. Loganberries have a sharp flavour and can be eaten raw or cooked, in ways similar to blackberries and raspberries. Loganberry ice cream and sorbet are specially good.

RASPBERRY Rubus idaeus

Raspberries are wonderful eaten raw, with sugar and cream, or made into ice cream (p. 281), sorbet or a coulis (p. 300). They do not need initial cooking for these, just rubbing through a sieve (nylon, not metal) to purée and remove the pips.

RHUBARB Rheum rhabarbarum

Rhubarb has a tart flavour and has to be cooked with sugar before it can be eaten. To prepare rhubarb, cut off the leaves (which are poisonous) and trim the base. Peel off any tough skin, then cut the rhubarb into manageable lengths and cook as described above. Rhubarb is complemented by the flavour of cinnamon, ginger or orange and can be made into a creamy fool, an excellent quick crumble (p. 295), or covered with all-in-one sponge mixture (p. 304) and baked to make squashy Rhubarb Upside Down Cake.

STRAWBERRY
Fragaria x ananassa

Strawberries are good simply hulled and served with cream and sugar. They also make an attractive addition to a summer fruit salad or a luscious topping for a cheesecake or little tartlets. The French way of serving them with light, heart-shaped moulds of cream cheese, is also as delectable as it is pretty. Less perfect strawberries can be made into jam, ice cream or fools and mousses. Little WILD STRAWBERRIES (Fragaria vesca) or ALPINE STRAWBERRIES make a pretty decoration to something delicately coloured like a Champagne Sorbet (p. 283), or addition to a compote of summer fruits.

Green banana ▽
Filling and nutritious, the banana is a staple food for poor people in some places where it is grown

Prickly pear ▷
Prickly pears grow around the edges of the large succulent leaves of the prickly pear cactus

Tropical and Exotic Fruits

Often vividly coloured and with intriguing flavours, fragrances and textures, tropical and exotic fruits bring a welcome touch of variety and luxury to the vegetarian table. Some are rather expensive, but many are also rich in valuable nutrients: bananas are an excellent source of magnesium and B6; passion fruit of protein, fibre and B1; kiwi fruit and guavas of vitamin C; and mangoes of vitamin A and zinc.

Golden passion fruit △

Mango ▽
My favourite fruit, the mango has deliciously juicy, deep golden, soft-textured, fragrant flesh

Banana ▷
Botanically a herb rather than a tree, the banana is said to be one of the first fruits to be cultivated

Kiwi ▷
One of the marketing success stories of the 1980s, the kiwi fruit comes mainly from New Zealand

Custard apple ▷
A fruit belonging to the same family as the pawpaw

Japonica △
Fruits of the orange-flowered garden japonica, with an exquisite, heady fragrance which will scent a whole room

Fig ▷
One of the most delicious of fruits, and one of the most ancient

Quince ▷
A small, hard fruit, golden when ripe, with an intense, heady fragrance, like the japonica

◁ **Plantain**
One of the 400 varieties of banana, the starchy plantain is used for cooking in India, South America and the Caribbean

▽ **Passion fruit**
Inside its leathery skin is a fragrantly flavoured greenish pulp containing many seeds

▽ **Pomegranate**
Technically a large, thick-skinned berry, the pomegranate grows on a small tree and is common throughout the Middle East

Pawpaw ▽
Usually a pretty pink inside, though it can be yellow, with sweet, fragrant, slightly melting flesh and shiny black seeds

Persimmon ▽
Native to China, this fruit ripens and becomes deep orange on the tree after the leaves have fallen, a striking sight

◁ **Tamarillo**
The tamarillo can be red or yellow and is related to the kiwi fruit and tomato

Pineapple △
A pineapple is really a cluster of fruits which weld together as they grow

◁ **Guava**
A tart fruit with a strangely exotic flavour and juicy flesh which can be pink, white or yellow

Rhamboutan △
Very similar to the lychee but with a hairy skin

◁ **Lychee**
The fruit of a tree which originated in Thailand and Southern China, the lychee has translucent flesh inside a hard, heavily indented skin (illustrated also on p. 86)

Carambola ▷
Also called Star Fruit, with a delicate fragrance and juicy texture

Tropical and Exotic Fruits

Choosing, storing, preparation and using
See under individual fruits

BANANA *Musa sapientum*
Bananas for exportation are cut when they have reached their full size but are still green, and sometimes they are still slightly green and under-ripe when they reach the shops. Bananas will ripen if left at room temperature for a day or two. As they become riper they become softer and develop brownish spots on the skin; peeled and well-mashed, very ripe bananas are a good early food for babies and can also be made into moist cakes and tea breads (p. 330).

Buy bananas in bunches attached to the stalk, as the skins of loose bananas are easily torn and the flesh will discolour.

In Europe, America and Australia, bananas are mainly used in sweet dishes, although they may be served as a side-dish with a curry. They contrast well with other fruits, so are a popular addition to a fruit salad mixture. More luxuriously, bananas can be split lengthways and served with Vanilla Ice Cream (p. 280) and Chocolate Sauce (p. 300), or flambéd with rum, or made into fritters and served with slices of lime – all rich and fattening ideas, these, although bananas can be a slimmer's friend too, because one or two bananas make a complete, filling, easy, transportable and nutritious meal for around 200 calories.

In India, South America and the Caribbean, GREEN BANANAS are used in savoury dishes. The leaves of the banana plant are also used in Mexico and India, for wrapping food before cooking, as we might use tin foil, with the added advantage that the banana leaf adds a delicate flavour to the dish. The leaves are used to make disposable plates, too. Bananas are available fresh and dried (see p. 102).

CARAMBOLA or STAR FRUIT *Averrhoa carambola*
The carambola looks better than it tastes. Look for plump yellow fruits without blemishes. To use, wash then cut into slices with a sharp, stainless steel knife. The slices will be star-like in shape and make a pretty decoration for a gâteau, cheesecake, sorbet, jelly, or fruit salad.

CUSTARD APPLE *Anonacea squamosa*
Widely used in the tropics, custard apples are ripe when they feel soft to the touch. They have a creamy, custard-like flavour and texture and can be used in compotes or made into fools and ice creams.

FIG *Ficus carica*
The best figs I ever ate were left on our verandah early one morning by the gardener when we were staying in Corfu. We did wonder where he had found them, but they made a fabulous breakfast. There are several types of fig and they vary in colour from golden to red and purple. They need to be completely ripe, when they are fairly soft, but they are highly perishable, so are best used immediately, although they will keep in the fridge for 24–48 hours.

Figs are good to eat at any time of the day, either on their own, or served simply: quartered, for instance, with some cream cheese or thick Greek yogurt and a little clear honey. They are delicious cut almost in half from the pointed end, then almost in half again, gently opened, topped with a little Greek yogurt or whipped cream and served on a Raspberry Coulis (p. 300). In North Africa and other Mediterranean countries, figs are commonly made into a preserve. Figs are available fresh, canned and dried (p. 102).

GUAVA *Psidium guajava*
In my experience fresh guavas can be rather disappointing, because it's not easy to buy one that is sweet and ripe. If you do, use immediately or keep the guava in the fridge briefly. The whole fruit is edible, although guavas are usually peeled, and can be eaten fresh or stewed. They are fre-quently made into jellies and preserves. Guavas are available fresh and canned: I think canned guavas are a safer buy than fresh ones, and their pink colour looks good in a fruit salad.

JAPONICA *Chaenomeles*
These fruits are hard and only suitable for cooking. They are difficult to cut and peel, but only need halving or quartering if you are going to make them into a jelly preserve, the most common way of using them – follow the recipe for Crab Apple Jelly on p. 340. This sweet, scented preserve is good for serving with nut roasts, or for eating on bread.

KIWI *Actinidia sinensis*
These little furry fruits are ripe when they yield to slight pressure. They keep well, either at room temperature, or in the fridge, and should be peeled thinly with a sharp knife before using. The greatest asset of the kiwi fruit is its stunning bright green flesh and attractive central arrangement of seeds which give it a flower-like appearance when sliced. So slices of kiwi fruit make an attractive garnish and decoration for dishes ranging from a tropical fruit salad to a cheesecake, and, of course, the traditional use for kiwi fruits, Pavlova or fruit meringue (p. 285). Kiwis are extremely high in vitamin C and can be a good way of getting children to take this – try slicing the top off a ripe kiwi fruit and letting them scoop the flesh out with a teaspoon, like eating a boiled egg. Kiwi fruits are available fresh and canned.

LYCHEE *Litchi chinensis* and RHAMBOUTAN *Nephelium lappaceum*
Ripe lychees are about the size of a small plum with a red knobbly skin which becomes brown and hard; rhamboutans have spines, reminiscent of a small hedgehog. The skin comes away quite easily if you pull it back with your fingers, like peeling an orange. Inside the flesh is white, juicy and translucent-looking with a distinctive, scented (and very pleasant) flavour, and there is a large shiny brown stone in the middle.

Lychees make a delicious addition to an exotic fruit salad: try a mixture of lychees, ripe segments of orange, with all the skin removed, and slices of kiwi fruit. Available fresh (see illustration on p. 86) and canned (p. 91). Canned lychees lack the crisp texture of fresh ones but make a good sorbet or jelly.

MANGO *Mangifera indica*
Choose a mango which feels just soft all over or buy one when it is hard and let it ripen at room temperature for a few days. I think the rounded, greeny-red variety of mangoes are better than the flatter, more oval yellowy ones. The mango has a large stone in the middle, so it is best to slice it down each side of the stone (see opposite). You can eat the skin, but it is generally peeled off as it is very chewy. Mango is excellent on its own and I like making it into a compote; for this, put slices of mango into a bowl, then liquidize half a cup of chopped mango with enough water to make a thin purée and pour this over the mango slices. Serve chilled, for a special breakfast or brunch. Or allow half a mango for each person and 'turn' the halves as shown above right. Mango makes an excellent fool, sorbet or ice cream (p. 281): the flesh does not need cooking before use. Mango also goes well with other sweet fruits in a salad or compote.

PAWPAW *Carica papaya*
Look for a pawpaw which is slightly soft all over – like a good dessert pear or perfectly ripe avocado. Pawpaw can be served for breakfast or as a first course; cut the pawpaw in half, scoop out the seeds from the centre, and serve with a slice of lime: halved pawpaw is eaten with a spoon, like an avocado. Peeled and sliced, pawpaw, with its pink flesh, makes an attractive addition to fruit salads.

PERSIMMON *Diospyrus kaki*
Persimmons must be very ripe and soft before eating because until then their tannic content makes them unpleasantly acidic. When ripe they are good puréed and made into ice cream, or added to a fruit compote.

PINEAPPLE *Ananas comosus*
Most of the pineapples which are available outside the tropics are poor examples of the fruit, because the sugar which is stored in the stem only enters the fruit when it is ripe, and pineapples for export are picked before this stage. When choosing a pineapple, look for one which has a strong 'pineapple' smell and try pulling out one of the leaves: if it comes out, the pineapple is ripe. To use, cut off the leafy top and peel the pineapple thickly to remove the skin and 'eyes' too. Then slice, removing any hard central core. Pineapple makes a juicy and refreshing addition to sweet and savoury salads and can be made into ices and sorbets. Baby pineapples are pretty halved right through the leaves with the flesh scooped out, diced, mixed with strawberries and liqueur and then piled back into the skins again. A large pineapple, hollowed out, makes an attractive container for a party fruit salad, or for ice cream or sorbet (made from the scooped-out flesh), with the leafy top replaced for serving. Pineapple is available fresh, dried (p. 103), as juice, canned in syrup or its own juice, in slices, cubes, pieces and 'crush'.

PLANTAIN *Musa paradisiaca*
Is widely used in savoury dishes in India, South America and the Caribbean. It is often thinly sliced and fried like potato crisps.

POMEGRANATE
Punica granatum
The pomegranate is full of seeds surrounded by shiny, jewel-bright pulp which is sweet and very juicy and arranged in irregular compartments divided by tough skin. The seeds can be scraped from the skin with a teaspoon or sharp knife and make an attractive topping for puddings or salads. They are widely used in Persian cookery.

PRICKLY PEAR
Opuntia magacanlaa and
O. fiscus-indica
These fruits have prickly skins and you need to wear gloves to handle them. Cut off all the skin, then slice

PREPARING AND TURNING A MANGO

the flesh. Sometimes the flesh is a vivid pink and makes a striking addition to a fruit salad, but it can also be paler and less interesting. The flavour is fairly boring.

PURPLE PASSION FRUIT
Passiflora edulis and
GOLDEN PASSION FRUIT
P. laurifolia
Buy passion fruits when the skin is wrinkled, as this denotes ripeness. Cut the fruits in half and scoop out the pulp and seeds. This passion fruit pulp makes a delectable addition to a fruit salad, which it permeates with its flavour, or sauce for a sorbet or arranged fruit salad, but is at its most delicious, I think, in a sorbet – one of my very favourites (p. 282).

QUINCE *Cydonia oblonga*
Like japonicas, quinces need cooking before use. Peel, quarter and slice them as you would apples, then simmer them in a little water and add sugar to taste. They can be made into compotes, fools and pies and are widely used in Middle Eastern cooking. In the sixteenth and seventeenth centuries they used to be popular in Britain for making into preserves. Quince jelly has a pleasant and distinctive flavour.

TAMARILLO
Cyphomandra betacea
When ripe, the tamarillo feels soft to the touch and can be peeled and sliced and added to fruit salads. The seeds are edible and the fruit has a sweet-sharp flavour.

◁ Honeydew melon
One of the winter melons, the skin can be green, yellow or white, and the flesh greenish-tinged

Gallia ▽
Gallia melons have a rough, bark-like skin which looks as though it has a white net over it, hence the name of 'netted' (or 'musk') melons

Melons

Melons, with their high water content, are one of the most refreshing fruits. They belong to the same family as cucumbers, and there are many different types of varying size, flavour and colouring. They can, however, be divided into three basic groups: winter melons, cantaloupe melons and musk or netted melons. Watermelons belong to a different branch of the family and contain useful minerals. Melons with golden flesh (especially cantaloupes) are exceptionally rich in vitamin A.

Watermelon △
Characterized by their smooth, shiny skin and watery, melting flesh, watermelons are often dark green-skinned with crimson flesh and dark brown seeds, though there are many varieties with other colourings, some with pale seeds or even seedless

Ogen ▷
Named after the kibbutz in Israel where they were developed, these small round melons with greenish-yellow striped and mottled skin and pale green flesh belong to the cantaloupe group

Cantaloupe ▽
This small, orange-fleshed melon, deeply ridged, as if to show where it might be cut into segments, has given its name to the cantaloupe group of melons. In the U S A the melon called a cantaloupe is actually a netted melon

Charentais △
The charentais, with its fragrant, sweet, orange flesh, is the most famous of the cantaloupe melons

Melons

Choosing and storing

Cantaloupe melons, including the CANTALOUPE (or ROCK MELON) itself and the CHARENTAIS and OGEN melons, smell deliciously fragrant when they're ripe, and yield to a little pressure at the stalk end. Netted melons, too, of which the GALLIA (not generally available in Aus./NZ) is one of the best, when ripe, give a little when pressed at the stalk end. CASABA (not illustrated) and HONEYDEW MELONS are ripe when they will yield to a little pressure at the end opposite to the stalk.

It is difficult to tell when a WATERMELON is just right for eating. One way is to look for a matt-skinned (rather than a shiny) melon, and to rap it with your knuckles: it should sound hollow, like a drum; alternatively, you can usually buy cut melon slices, in which case go for bright red flesh without any white streaks or a pale-looking middle. The seeds should look shiny and hard. Never buy cut melon slices from foreign markets because they may be contaminated.

Fully ripe melons should be used as soon as possible; others can be kept for a few days if stored at room temperature.

Preparation and using

Unless you want to marinate melon flesh in a syrup or flavouring liquid, which is useful for melons which are under-ripe or dull-flavoured, it's best to prepare the melon just before you want to eat it.

Large melons can be cut down from the stalk end into sections; smaller melons can be cut in half at right angles to the stem. With very small ones, such as small Ogens, allow a whole one per person, slice the top off, like a boiled egg, and carefully scoop out all the seeds. The melon flesh can also be served without the skin, scooped out into balls using a melon-baller, or simply remove the skin and cut the melon flesh into small dice.

Melons are very low in calories and are therefore an ideal choice if you are trying to lose weight. There are many different ways of serving melon for a low-calorie starter or dessert – see some ideas below.

Watermelon contains less vitamin C than other melons, but is wonderfully refreshing on a hot summer's day. If you are feeding a lot of people, for a summer barbeque, for example, you could buy a small, whole watermelon. Scoop out the flesh and remove the seeds. Mix the chopped flesh with other fruit and serve it in the hollowed-out shell. You can also use the halved and hollowed skins of any of the smaller melons for individual servings filled as suggested below.

Melon is best served chilled, but do not let it get too cold, or the flavour will be dulled. Prepare the melon, then chill it in the fridge for no more than 30 minutes before serving. Or, if the melon has been stored in the fridge, take it out about 30 minutes before you want to serve it, to allow it to 'come to'.

If you have to store cut melon in the fridge, cover it carefully with clingfilm as it easily absorbs the smell and flavour of other foods. Use the melon as quickly as possible as it will soon deteriorate.

Melon seeds are not usually eaten with the melon, although they are in fact a good food and in some parts of the world are dried and used in cooking or as a nibble.

Serving ideas for melon

☐ Marinate diced melon and diced peeled cucumber in a mint and honey vinaigrette for a refreshing starter.

☐ Scoop out the flesh of halved Ogen melons and mix with small strawberries; pile back into the melon shells for a pretty dessert.

☐ Fill halved Charentais melons with ginger ice cream, top with chopped preserved stem ginger and a little of the syrup.

☐ Marinate the diced flesh of winter melons, sliced kiwi fruit, green grapes and slices of green apple in a ginger sugar syrup (1 tablespoon grated fresh ginger added to 300 ml/10 fl oz sugar syrup) for several hours (or overnight) to make green ginger fruit compote.

☐ Cheer up a poorly flavoured melon by topping each portion with some port, ginger wine or chopped stem ginger with a little of the syrup.

☐ A whole melon makes a delightful picnic food, cooling and refreshing on a hot day. Take plenty of kitchen paper and a container to put the seeds in.

☐ Mix balls of bright orange melon flesh (such as Charentais) and pale green melon (such as honeydew or Ogen) for a pretty, simple and low-calorie starter.

☐ For a pretty and refreshing soup, purée two melons, one with green flesh and the other with orange flesh. Put the mixtures into separate jugs, thin with enough water to make a pouring consistency, and sweeten slightly, if necessary. To serve, hold the jugs at either side of a chilled bowl and pour from them at the same time, to create a two-coloured effect. Garnish with fresh mint.

☐ Watermelon mixed with plenty of chopped mint makes a refreshing first course.

☐ Try a red fruit salad made from cubes or balls of watermelon, halved and seeded black grapes, sliced figs and strawberries.

☐ To make Melon Jelly, put cubes of melon into a large bowl or individual bowls. Bring 600 ml/1 pint fruit juice – grape, apple or orange – to the boil and sprinkle in 2 teaspoons agar agar, whisking well until dissolved. Boil for 1 minute. Cool slightly, pour over melon and leave to set.

Navel orange ▷
Navel oranges, so-called because of the navel-like swelling at the flower end, are sweet and juicy

Citrus Fruit

Valued not only for their juicy flesh, but for the oils they contain which are used for making flavourings and scent, and for citric acid, citrus fruits bring tangy flavours to the kitchen and a sharpness which helps to draw out the taste of other ingredients. They are one of the best sources of vitamin C, and oranges are also rich in B1, vitamin A and folic acid, while the bioflavinoids in the white skin and pith of citrus fruit are thought to be particularly helpful to women with menstrual problems.

Valencia sweet orange △
Sweet and very juicy oranges

Jaffa orange △
The shamouti variety, or Jaffa oranges, which originally came from Israel, juicy and slightly sharp-tasting

Clementine △
The clementine is a cross between the tangerine and the orange. It has no pips

Tangerine △
The skin of the tangerine is a deeper colour than mandarines

Satsuma △
Identified by their easily peelable, loose skins and sweet, juicy flesh. Some types are seedless

Lemon △
Together with oranges, the most important citrus fruit and indispensable as a flavouring

Kumquat ▽
Sharp-tasting miniature oranges, useful for garnishing or making into preserves

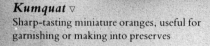

Lime △
Very sour small green citrus fruits with their own almost perfumed taste

Jaffa sweetie ▷
A cross between a grapefruit
and a lime

◁ **Pink grapefruit**
Pink and red grapefruits are
available; the flesh of these
ranges from pale pink to ruby
red and is sweet and juicy

Mineola ▽
A hybrid type of sweet orange
with a deep colour and
smooth skin

Seville orange △
These sour oranges, for making into
preserves, actually reached Europe before
sweet oranges

Pomelo or shaddock ▽
The fruit from which the
grapefruit is descended

△ **Ugli fruit**
Like a big, rather lumpy
grapefruit, this is a cross
between a grapefruit and a
tangerine and tastes like a
particularly juicy, sweet
grapefruit

White grapefruit △
The most widely grown citrus
fruit, sharp and refreshing

Citrus Fruit

Choosing and storing
Citrus fruit should look bright and plump, with no brown patches or shrivelled skin. The fruits, especially grapefruits, should feel heavy, so pick them up before you buy them – it's surprising how they vary.

Preparation and using
Citrus fruits should be scrubbed well if you are going to use the skins, as these are often treated with sprays. Adding a tablespoon of cider vinegar to the washing water is said to help counteract the harmful effect of any chemical residues on the skins.

Left-over citrus juices can be frozen for future use; just put them into ice cube containers, freeze, then transfer to a polythene bag. Slices of lemon, orange and rind also freeze well and can be added straight to drinks, without defrosting. Freeze them until solid on a plate or tray, then put them into a polythene bag or container.

GRAPEFRUIT and
PINK GRAPEFRUIT
Citrus x paradisi
Probably most often served halved as a first course, the skin can be vandyked (see below) and the flesh scooped out and mixed with chopped orange segments and mint, for variety. Or the grapefruit can be halved and the segments loosened (see below) and the top sprinkled with brown sugar then popped under the grill until the sugar has melted and the fruit warmed through. One of my favourite grapefruit dishes is a salad of grapefruit and orange segments, avocado and watercress. Pink grapefruit are particularly sweet and juicy as well as being an attractive colour. Canned grapefruit is available, also grapefruit juice, natural and sweetened.

JAFFA SWEETIE *Citrus* spp
One of the citrus hybrids which have recently been developed, this has a sharp, refreshing flavour.

KUMQUAT *Fortunella margarita*
These are delicious stewed whole in a sugar syrup, or made into a preserve (p. 343), then spooned over home-made Vanilla Ice Cream (p. 280).

LEMON *Citrus limon*
Both the juice and rind of lemons are indispensable in the kitchen for flavouring; lemon juice brings out the flavour of other foods, and the rind gives a subtle tang. A strip of lemon rind added to a bouquet garni is good in soups and vegetable casseroles. Lemon juice can be used to make salad dressings, and I often use it with fruity olive oil instead of wine vinegar. Lemon juice also helps to preserve the colour of other fruits and vegetables which discolour easily; brush the cut surfaces, or dip them in a cupful of water which has had the juice of ½ lemon added. Lemon is used to flavour cakes and puddings – one of the most delicious is traditional Sussex Pond Pudding, in which a whole lemon is surrounded by a suet crust, then steamed, resulting in a delicious lemony syrup filling. Cut into circles, wedges or tiny pieces, lemon makes one of the most refreshing and attractive garnishes.

The candied peel is best bought in whole pieces: it's expensive, but there's no comparison between this and the chopped variety. Bottled lemon juice is a useful store cupboard item, although not as good as fresh.

To make lemon barley water, old-fashioned but soothing, refreshing and easy to make, put 4 tablespoons pearl barley into a saucepan with 600 ml/1 pint water and the pared rind of half a lemon and bring to the boil. Simmer gently, uncovered, for 20 minutes, then strain and cool. Add the juice of ½ lemon and sugar or honey to taste – about 1 tablespoon. Serve chilled, with ice if liked.

LIME *Citrus aurantifolia*
A wonderful flavouring ingredient; try it squeezed over exotic fruit or hot sugary pancakes, or in Guacamole (p. 144). It has many uses in sweet dishes, including Key Lime Pie and as a flavouring for ice cream, parfaits and cheesecake.

ORANGE *Citrus sinensis*
There are a number of types of dessert oranges, including NAVEL ORANGES which are deliciously sweet and have the characteristic navel at the flower end; the juicy

VANDYKING A GRAPEFRUIT

PREPARING HALVED GRAPEFRUIT FOR SERVING

JAFFA (or SHAMOUTI) and the VALENCIA. Oranges are good to eat just as they are, cut into segments, with all the skin and pith removed. Sprinkled with orange flower water and a little orange blossom honey, and chilled, they make one of the most refreshing desserts which is good served with an almond or cashew nut cream (p. 238), rather than dairy cream. Alternatively the sliced oranges can be sprinkled with crushed caramel for a sweet crunchy topping. Oranges also make an excellent addition to a fresh fruit salad and their juice helps pale fruits, such as apples and pears, to keep their colour. Whole oranges can be simmered in sugar syrup then cooled and served with shreds of the peel, blanched and drained.

Orange peel is included in chopped mixed peel, but the best way to buy it is in whole pieces. Various types of orange juice are available: read the packet or carton to make sure it is real juice you are getting.

BLOOD ORANGES (not illustrated) are small oranges shot with red; the juice and a little shredded peel is added to Hollandaise Sauce (p. 176) to make Maltese sauce, traditionally served with asparagus.

POMELO or SHADDOCK
Citrus grandis
Probably the fruit from which the grapefruit evolved, it has a sour, slightly bitter flavour. (Not generally available in Aus./NZ.)

SEVILLE ORANGE
Citrus aurantium
These are unsuitable for eating raw but are used in marmalade and to make liqueurs and orange flower water. The grated rind and juice can also be used as a flavouring.

TANGERINE, MANDARINE, MINEOLA, CLEMENTINE, SATSUMA *Citrus reticulata*
These members of the citrus family are all very easily peeled, and their flesh separates readily into segments. Clementines are the smallest, have a good flavour and, like Satsumas, have no pips. They all have a more delicate flavour than oranges. Mandarine segments can be bought canned, either whole or in pieces. Delicious for eating just as they are and a popular way of making sure children get their daily requirement of vitamin C, these are also good in fruit salads. (Mineolas are not generally available in Aus./NZ.)

UGLI *Citrus* spp
A cross between a tangerine and a grapefruit, the ugli is native to the East Indies. It tastes like a superb grapefruit, and can be prepared in the same ways. In fact an ugli can be a better choice than grapefruit if you want sweet, juicy segments for a breakfast compote or salad.

Its lumpy mottled skin peels easily and the flesh can be segmented very quickly. It is very juicy and has few pips. (Not generally available in Aus./NZ.)

How to make candied peel

Home-made candied peel, for use in cakes and puddings, can be made at home using grapefruit, orange or lemon skins. You will need the skins of 6 oranges or lemons, or 4–5 grapefruits, or an equivalent amount of more than one type.

Scrub the fruit thoroughly, halve and remove the pulp, or use the (well-scrubbed) skins of fruits after you have squeezed the juice from them.

Put the skin halves into a saucepan, cover with cold water, bring to the boil and simmer until tender. This takes 1–2 hours, and it's a good idea to change the water 3 times, to remove any trace of bitterness, especially with grapefruits.

Drain the skins thoroughly, reserving the liquid. Make the liquid up to 300 ml/10 fl oz with water if necessary, then pour into a saucepan and add 225 g/8 oz sugar. Heat gently until the sugar has dissolved, then bring up to the boil. Add the peel, remove from the heat and leave for 2 days.

Remove the peel from the syrup with a perforated spoon; add another 100 g/4 oz sugar to the syrup, heat gently until dissolved, then add the peel and simmer gently until transluscent.

Leave the peel to soak in this syrup for 2 weeks, then remove peel with a perforated spoon and place on a wire rack to drain and dry. Once the peel is dry, it can be stored in an airtight jar.

PEELING AN ORANGE

SEGMENTING AN ORANGE

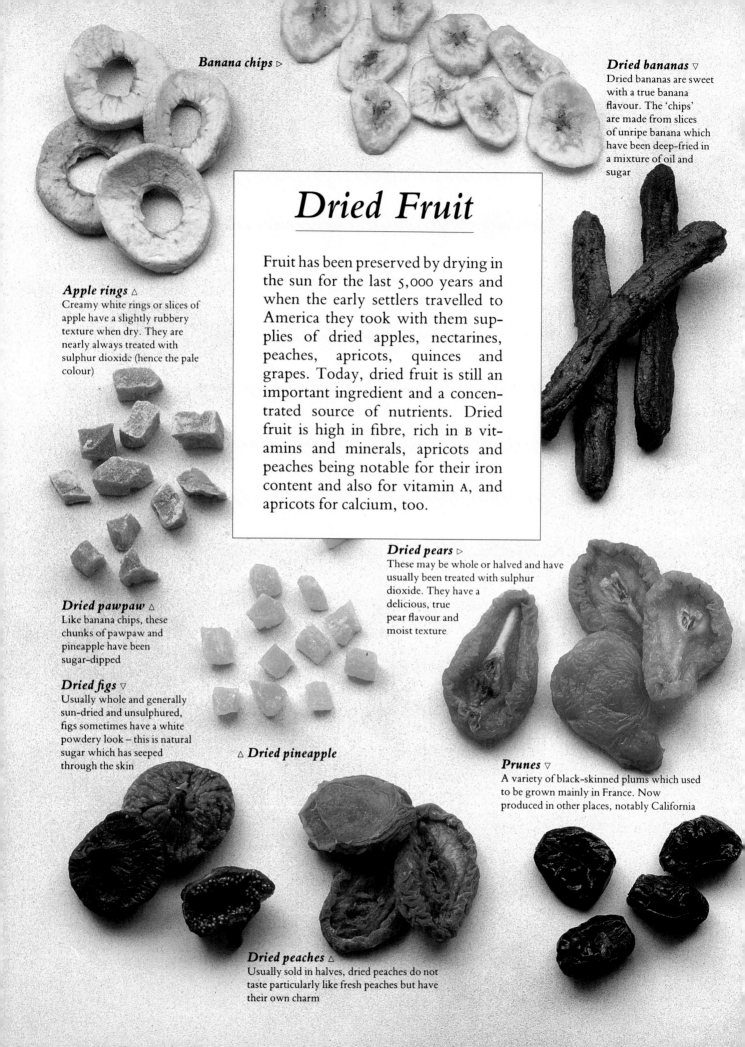

Banana chips ▷

Dried bananas ▽
Dried bananas are sweet with a true banana flavour. The 'chips' are made from slices of unripe banana which have been deep-fried in a mixture of oil and sugar

Apple rings △
Creamy white rings or slices of apple have a slightly rubbery texture when dry. They are nearly always treated with sulphur dioxide (hence the pale colour)

Dried Fruit

Fruit has been preserved by drying in the sun for the last 5,000 years and when the early settlers travelled to America they took with them supplies of dried apples, nectarines, peaches, apricots, quinces and grapes. Today, dried fruit is still an important ingredient and a concentrated source of nutrients. Dried fruit is high in fibre, rich in B vitamins and minerals, apricots and peaches being notable for their iron content and also for vitamin A, and apricots for calcium, too.

Dried pawpaw △
Like banana chips, these chunks of pawpaw and pineapple have been sugar-dipped

Dried pears ▷
These may be whole or halved and have usually been treated with sulphur dioxide. They have a delicious, true pear flavour and moist texture

Dried figs ▽
Usually whole and generally sun-dried and unsulphured, figs sometimes have a white powdery look – this is natural sugar which has seeped through the skin

△ **Dried pineapple**

Prunes ▽
A variety of black-skinned plums which used to be grown mainly in France. Now produced in other places, notably California

Dried peaches △
Usually sold in halves, dried peaches do not taste particularly like fresh peaches but have their own charm

◁ Muscatel raisins
These are the original raisin, muscatel grapes, purplish-black in colour, dried in the sun and with a delicious muscat flavour

Lexia raisins ▽
Another delicious raisin, the Lexia type comes from Australia; it is sold seeded and is particularly juicy and sweet

Sun-dried raisins ▷
The smaller, more common 'seedless raisin' does not have the flavour or the moist texture of the other two types, but is widely available and a useful all-purpose raisin

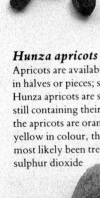

Hunza apricots ▽
Apricots are available whole or in halves or pieces; small dried Hunza apricots are sold whole still containing their kernels. If the apricots are orange or yellow in colour, they have most likely been treated with sulphur dioxide

◁ Dried apricots

▽ Sun-dried apricots

Dates ▽
Very sweet and nutritious, dates can be bought whole, pitted and unpitted, or pressed into a block for use in cooking

Currants ▽
Originally grown around Corinth, these are small sweet grapes which are dried and packaged without the addition of sulphur dioxide

Sultanas △
These are dried seedless white grapes, similar to small seedless raisins. They originated from Izmir (later called Smyrna) in Turkey and are now widely grown in other places, notably Australia

Dried Fruit

Choosing, storing and preparation

Fruit is either dried in the sun or in dehydration chambers where the moisture is evaporated by hot air. Dried fruit may be treated with sulphur dioxide gas during the drying process to prevent it from becoming too dark in colour. Sulphur dioxide interferes with the body's ability to absorb vitamin B1 and has been linked with digestive upsets and possibly genetic mutations. So look for unsulphured fruits if possible. The effect of the sulphur dioxide can be reduced if you first wash the fruit well in warm water, then cover it with cold water and bring to the boil. Allow the fruit to simmer without a lid for 5 minutes, then drain off the water and rinse the fruit again. It can then be used, or soaked in cold water, or covered with fresh water and simmered gently until tender.

Many fruits are also coated with mineral oil in order to prevent them from sticking together. This, too, is an additive which is not recommended as it can interfere with the body's ability to absorb some minerals. It can be removed by washing the fruit in several changes of warm water, or can be avoided altogether by looking for fruit which has been packaged without oil, or with vegetable oil rather than mineral oil (although I still prefer to wash this off before using the fruit). Drain the rinsed fruit in a colander then spread it out on a tray lined with absorbent kitchen paper and leave it in a warm place overnight to dry off.

When buying dried fruit, check the date stamp on the packets, buy in fairly small quantities and keep the fruit in an airtight jar.

APPLE RINGS

They can be eaten as they are, or chopped and added to cakes and puddings. They are often included as part of a dried fruit salad mix and make a pleasant addition to fruit compotes.

APRICOTS

Dried apricots can be eaten as they are or soaked (and cooked until tender, if liked) and served simply with yogurt or cream, or made into purées, fools (p. 282) and other desserts. Sun-dried HUNZA APRICOTS have a particularly good flavour and make a wonderful compote, just soaked and simmered gently until tender if necessary. Dried apricots can be made into an excellent jam all the year round. To make about 2.3 kg/5 lb, put 450 g/1 lb dried apricots into a bowl, cover with 2.4 litres/4 pints of water and leave to soak overnight. Next day, put the apricots and their water into a preserving pan, add the juice of a lemon and simmer until the apricots are really tender – about 50–60 minutes. Then remove from the heat and add 1.4 kg/3 lb of granulated sugar and 50 g/2 oz blanched almonds, roughly chopped. Heat gently until the sugar has dissolved, then boil for 20–25 minutes, stirring often. Test for a set (p. 339) and when this is reached, remove from the heat and add a knob of butter. Let the mixture cool slightly, then spoon into warm, sterilized jars.

BANANAS

Ordinary DRIED BANANAS, which look like slim (or flattened) dark brown versions of fresh bananas, make a pleasant nibble or addition to home-made dried fruit bars and bonbons. They can be reconstituted by soaking in water, but the texture is rather soggy and not particularly pleasant. Soaked and puréed dried banana could be used to make a tea bread (p. 330) instead of mashed fresh banana. BANANA CHIPS, slices of banana prepared with a crisp sugar coating, are also available and make a relatively healthy sweet-treat which children like.

CURRANTS

A very useful ingredient, currants are used extensively in baking, for instance in currant buns, Eccles cakes, fruit cakes (p. 310) and Christmas pudding (p. 296); they are also often added to savoury pilafs and stuffings in Middle Eastern cookery.

Mixed with almonds and spice, they make sweet crisp biscuits. Sift 100 g/4 oz plain wholewheat flour, ½ teaspoon baking powder and ½ teaspoon allspice into a large bowl. Tip the bran from the sieve into the bowl and add 50 g/2 oz butter, 15 g/½ oz ground almonds, and 50 g/2 oz currants. Mix well, then stir in 1 tablespoon water to make a dough. On a lightly-floured board, roll dough out to about 5 mm/¼ inch thick, then stamp into rounds of 5 cm/2 inches. Prick each round, place on floured baking sheets and bake for 10 minutes at 200 C/400 F/Gas Mark 6.

DATES

Dates make a pleasant sweet treat or nibble, either as they are, or with the stone replaced with an almond or brazil nut, some almond paste or cream cheese.

Dates can be added to cakes and puddings and made into very good biscuits (p. 321). If you're buying cooking dates, check that they're not 'sugar-rolled', an unnecessary treatment in view of the intense sweetness of dates. Pitted dates need looking over before use, because the odd stone or hard stalk end does creep in.

FIGS

Often sold squashed in blocks, figs are high in fibre. They can be eaten as they are, soaked as part of a fruit compote, or made into wholesome sweetmeats and cookies. Steamed fig pudding with rum sauce is a warming winter pudding.

DRIED FRUIT SALAD
(Not illustrated)

This is a mixture of a number of fruits shown overleaf; usually prunes, apple rings, apricots and perhaps peaches and pears. You can buy it ready-made or make it up yourself from your favourite varieties.

Dried fruit salad mix can be made into an excellent compote. To do this, cover the mixture with boiling water and leave to soak overnight. Allow 350 g–450 g/12 oz–1 lb to serve 4 people. Next day, simmer gently, half-covered, until the fruit is tender and all the liquid reduced to a glossy syrup. Serve hot or chilled. If you are serving it cold, some fresh fruits can be added for contrasting flavour and texture. It's a pleasant dish for serving at breakfast as well as for a pudding. A friend of mine makes an alcoholic version with brandy added, which is excellent, though perhaps not for breakfast.

PAWPAW
This is perhaps not as healthy as naturally dried fruit, because of the added sugar, but is still a pleasant and relatively healthy sweet treat.

PEACHES
You can eat dried peaches as they are, but I prefer them lightly soaked, or soaked and simmered until tender. They make a pleasant addition to savoury dishes such as pilafs as well as being delicious in cakes, puddings and compotes.

PEARS
Pears can be eaten raw, or soaked and cooked; chopped, they make an unusual and delicious addition to a fruit cake and are one of the ingredients in the famous Swiss Christmas fruit pastry, Birnbrot.

To make Birnbrot, make up a half quantity of dough as described for Quick Rolls on p. 328. While the dough is rising for the first time, make the filling. Chop 225 g/8 oz dried pears and 100 g/4 oz dried stoned prunes and put them into a saucepan with 50 g/2 oz seedless raisins and 300 ml/10 fl oz water. Bring to the boil, then simmer gently until the mixture is thick and dry. Sieve or purée in a blender or food processor, then add the grated rind and juice of half a lemon, 50 g/2 oz soft brown sugar and a little ground cinnamon and grated nutmeg.

Knead the risen dough, then roll it out to a square about 38 × 38 cm/15 × 15 inches and not more than 6 mm/¼ inch thick. Spread the pear mixture to within about 2.5 cm/1 inch of the edges. Fold the edges over to enclose the filling, then roll it up firmly, like a Swiss roll and put it on to a baking sheet. Prick the roll all over, then cover it with a clean cloth and put it into a warm place for 30 minutes, to rise.

Heat the oven to 180 C/350 F/Gas Mark 4. Brush the bread all over with beaten egg and bake it in the centre of the oven, for about 35 minutes, until golden brown and crisp. Serve warm. It's an excellent pastry for serving with coffee, or as a pudding after something rich like Fondue.

PINEAPPLE
Crunchy cubes of pineapple preserved in sugar syrup make a delicious addition to rich fruit cake mixtures, tutti frutti ice cream or a platter of bonbons to serve with after-dinner coffee.

PRUNES
Prunes are not usually treated with sulphur dioxide but may have undergone other processes to 'tenderize' them or soften the skins, and they are often coated with mineral oil, so wash them carefully. They are one of those things which you either like or you don't; if you still have unfortunate childhood memories of them, do try them as part of a boozy compote, extra light Christmas pudding or ice cream – you may have a pleasant surprise! Prune mousse is surprisingly good, as is the classic French Prune Tart. Prune juice is available and is extremely rich in iron, one of the best sources, if you're feeling run down.

RAISINS
Any of the types of raisins shown overleaf are excellent for eating with nuts as a snack or for adding to mueslis or fruit or vegetable salads. Raisins are also indispensable in baking, for fruit cakes, puddings and cookies.

SULTANAS
Some sultanas are treated with sulphur dioxide, others are not: check the packet. They are useful in baking for cakes, Christmas pudding (p. 296) and mince pies (p. 297), as well as in salads, puddings and mueslis.

Drying fruit and vegetables

Drying fruit and vegetables is one of the most natural and ancient methods of food preservation. It involves drying out the natural moisture present in all fruit and vegetables so that the enzymes which cause decay are inhibited. The drying process can be done in the sun or in an oven. Oven-drying can be done over several days, perhaps in the residual heat of the oven after it has been used for something else. The drying temperature needs to be between 50–70 C/120–150 F and it is best to leave the oven door ajar to allow moisture to escape.

Fruit and vegetables to be dried in the sun need to be spread out on clean mesh or trellis trays, slats of wood or wire trays. Raise them off the ground and turn the produce over twice a day so that it dries evenly. Cover the produce with clean muslin to keep off flies and dust. Bring the fruit in at night time because the increased moisture in the air then will affect the drying process. Alternatively, fruits and vegetables can be threaded onto string and hung up to dry.

Preserve the colour of fruits such as apples and pears by plunging them into a bowl containing 10 g/¼ oz citric acid to every 1 litre/1¾ pints of water; drain and pat dry, then dry in the oven or in the sun as described.

Vegetables such as mushrooms, onions, garlic and peppers can be dried as they are; others, such as runner or French beans, need blanching for 2 minutes in boiling water before being patted dry with a cloth and then dried as described above.

Store dried fruit and vegetables in an airtight jar or tin. They will keep for a year. Dried fruit can be used as it is; dried vegetables should be soaked for a few hours first, then cooked in the soaking water, or they can be added to stews and casseroles without pre-soaking.

Aromatic dried tofu △
A well-flavoured dried tofu; a plain
version is also available

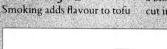

Smoked tofu △
Smoking adds flavour to tofu

Firm tofu △
Firm tofu comes in a block (like
a block of cheese) and can be
cut into cubes or slices and fried

Soft tofu △
Made by cooking and
curdling soya milk,
tofu is a white
curd product

Dried deep-fried tofu △
One of a number of varieties of dried tofu

Seitan △
This original 'textured vegetable protein'
can be bought as pâtés and pastes
(below)

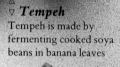

▽ **Tempeh**
Tempeh is made by
fermenting cooked soya
beans in banana leaves

△
Textured vegetable protein
Chunks and 'mince', made from soya

Dairy
and Non-Dairy
Ingredients

These foods enrich and fortify
vegetarian cooking. Some are concentrated and high in fat so are
generally used in small quantities.
They include dairy and non-dairy
products as well as a range of high
protein foods, some of which have
been used in countries in the East for
thousands of years but are relatively
new to the West.

◁ **Cow's milk**
Another basic food which has
been used for centuries, milk is
a useful source of protein,
calcium and the B vitamin
riboflavin in the
lacto-vegetarian diet

Soya milk △
This liquid is made
from soya beans

Dried skimmed milk ▽
A useful store cupboard standby

Goat's milk △
Considered by some health experts to be
more digestible and healthy than cow's milk

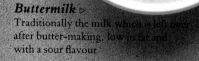

Buttermilk ▷
Traditionally the milk which is left over
after butter-making, low in fat and
with a sour flavour

Single cream ▽
Single cream will not whip

Double cream ▷
Has a high fat content and whips up to a thick consistency

△
Clotted cream
Thick cream, being the fat skimmed from rich Devon milk after it has been heated and cooled rapidly

◁ **Whipping cream**
This cream whips to a light consistency

Non-dairy cream ▽
Made from water and vegetable oil, the flavour varies from brand to brand

Soured cream ▽
Has a similar fat content to single cream, a thick texture (although it will not whip) and a soured flavour

◁ **Soya cream**
May be sold as soya cream or you can use a concentrated type of soya milk without diluting it

Greek yogurt ▽
Available strained (left) and unstrained, this is made from ewe's milk

Quail's egg ▽
An attractive ingredient, makes a delightful garnish

Smetana ▷
In Russia a mixture of soured cream and double cream; here it is usually made from single cream and skimmed milk

◁ **Hen's egg**
A nutritious ingredient in the lacto-vegetarian larder. Free-range eggs do not involve cruelty

Parev ▷
A cream replacement made from water, vegetable oil, sugar and flavourings, available from Jewish shops

Duck's egg △
As nutritious as hen's eggs, and, some say, with a finer flavour

Live yogurt △
A soured milk product made by culturing milk with a bacterium called *lactobacillus bulgaricus*

Dairy and Non-Dairy Ingredients

MILK

MILK is a basic ingredient, containing a balanced range of nutrients including protein, calcium, riboflavin and vitamins A, D and B12, and is available in various forms. Most milk is pasteurized, which means it has been heated to 71C/160F for 15 seconds, to destroy bacteria. Milk is available with all the cream remaining, with some removed, or semi- or fully skimmed. DRIED SKIMMED MILK is also available in tins and is useful for adding to drinks and other dishes to increase their nutritional value; I prefer the powder (from health shops and not to be confused with milk powder with added fat) to the granules. Skimmed milk may have been fortified with the fat-soluble vitamins, A, D and E which are lost when the fat is removed. GOAT'S MILK, thought by some experts to be healthier and more digestible than cow's, is also available in both liquid and powdered form.

HOMOGENIZED MILK has been mechanically treated so that the cream does not separate from the milk and rise to the surface, while UHT MILK has been heated to 132C/270F for 1–2 seconds, then rapidly cooled and packed in sterile conditions.

EVAPORATED MILK, a useful store cupboard item, has been homogenized and had half its water removed by evaporation. It is then sterilized and canned. CONDENSED MILK is whole or skimmed milk which has been boiled down to about a third of its original volume and then, usually, sweetened with sugar and canned. It's useful for making fudge (p. 345) and a wonderful ice cream (p. 280), as well as being the binding ingredient in the traditional Bircher Muesli (p. 240). If you boil a can for 4 hours, then cool the can,

beat lightly and pour into a crumb-crust or pastry flan case and chill, you have Gypsy Tart. It's also useful for making Toffee Shortcake: boil the contents of a small can of condensed milk with 100 g/4 oz each of sugar and butter and 2 tablespoons golden syrup for 5 minutes, then pour on top of a shortbread baked in a tin (p. 320). When it's cool, spread 175–225 g/6–8 oz melted chocolate on top! Wicked, but delicious.

BUTTERMILK is mainly useful in making certain breads and cakes, as in Soda Bread (p. 330), where it helps the bread to rise. The SMETANA sold outside Russia is like a low-fat soured cream and can replace soured cream in recipes. Various brands of SOYA MILK are available. The nutritional content of most is not the same as that of cow's milk although the taste is similar; if the milk is for babies, children or old people, I recommend buying a soya milk which has been fortified with vitamins so that it has the same nutritional value as cow's milk. Check the labels; you may need to go to a health shop.

YOGURT

Look for 'live' YOGURT cultured from *lactobacillus bulgaricus*. Avoid those which contain thickeners or which have been pasteurized after culturing. Although the bacterium does not survive in the gut, yogurt is more digestible than milk. Good yogurt should be sweet and thick, not thin and sour. GREEK EWE'S MILK YOGURT, both the normal version and the thicker, strained type, are excellent. If you think you don't like yogurt, try these before finally writing it off! NON-DAIRY SOYA YOGURT, suitable for vegans, is available from health shops, and can also be made at home from soya milk (p. 280).

Yogurt is easy to make at home, in a wide-necked Thermos which will hold 600 ml/1 pint. Bring 600 ml/1 pint milk to the boil, then remove from the heat and leave to stand until you can comfortably dip your little finger into it. Whisk in the skin on the top of the milk together with 4 tablespoons skimmed milk powder or granules and 1 teaspoon real live

yogurt. Pour into the scalded Thermos, screw on the lid and leave overnight or for 10–12 hours, until thick and creamy. Store in the refrigerator, where it will thicken further, and save a teaspoonful for starting off your next batch.

You can make yogurt from any kind of milk – 'untreated' gives the creamiest result, but use skimmed milk if you want to reduce the calories. When you leave the mixture to stand, make sure you put the Thermos in a place where it won't get touched, and don't open it for 10 hours or so, because for some reason knocks and rough movements can upset the fermentation process. You may find you need to buy a new tub of real live starter yogurt from time to time, if the finished mixture does not get as thick as usual.

For fruit yogurt, make the yogurt as described. When it is ready, simply add chopped fresh fruit, cooked fruit purée or good-quality jam and sugar or honey to taste. Reduced sugar jams are excellent stirred into yogurt.

For gloriously thick, Greek-style yogurt, line a large sieve or colander with muslin or gauze. Scald the gauze by pouring a kettleful of boiling water through it. Set the sieve or colander over a bowl, pour the yogurt into the sieve or colander and leave to drip overnight.

CREAM

CREAM, a concentration of the fatty part of the milk, comes in various concentrations. HALF CREAM (not illustrated) is the lowest in fat, containing around 12 per cent; SINGLE CREAM and SOURED CREAM contain 18 per cent fat, while CANNED CREAM (not illustrated) has around 23 per cent. WHIPPING CREAM contains 35 per cent fat, DOUBLE CREAM 48 per cent and CLOTTED CREAM 55 per cent. Obviously, in view of its relatively high fat content cream needs to be used with discretion, but is useful for adding richness to soups and sauces, making a quick sauce for pasta, and in special puddings such as ice cream and parfait. CRÈME FRAÎCHE is a sharp-tasting cream, the flavour somewhere between double cream and soured cream. It goes particularly well with sweet fruits, such as strawberries, and it makes a good alternative to SOURED CREAM (though higher in calories) when a dish is going to be cooked, as it doesn't separate. You can make crème fraîche by whipping together equal quantities of double and soured cream, then leaving at room temperature for 24 hours. Refrigerate after this, which will make the cream thicker. Crème fraîche will keep in a covered container in the fridge for 2 weeks. SOYA CREAM, with the consistency of single cream, and various non-dairy whipping creams, including the kosher PAREV, are available and can replace dairy cream in recipes. All fresh dairy products need to be kept in a cool place, preferably in the fridge, as do canned and packaged milks once opened. Use within 1–3 days.

EGGS

When buying hen's eggs, look for genuine free-range eggs, which are becoming easier to find – many supermarkets now supply them. All the recipes in this book assume the use of free-range eggs. Store in the fridge or in a cool place for 7–14 days. Always bring eggs to room temperature before use. DUCK'S EGGS should be well cooked before eating because shells are porous, and ducks are not always choosy about where they lay their eggs! Tiny QUAIL'S EGGS can be hardboiled (for 4 minutes), then shelled (which needs patience!) and either used whole or sliced for a pretty, luxury garnish to starters, salads and savouries. They look charming set into a clear jelly (made from 300 ml/ 10 fl oz boiling Dark Vegetable Stock (p. 132), with 1 teaspoon agar agar (p. 286) whisked into it and boiled for 1 minute). Add a few sprigs of leafy tarragon and any small lightly cooked vegetables you fancy.

In the UK, eggs are graded by size according to weight. Size 1, for example, is over 70 g/2¾ oz, while size 7, the smallest, is below 45 g/1¾ oz. Size 3, 60–65 g/2¼–2½ oz, is used in most recipes.

VEGETARIAN PROTEIN FOODS

SEITAN is a chewy, high protein food made from protein-rich wheat gluten. It is available frozen and in cans, jars and vacuum packs; various types of SEITAN PÂTÉ and spreads are also available. (Seitan is not generally available in Aus./NZ.) It is also easy (but rather messy) to make seitan at home by making dough out of a high-gluten flour and water, soaking it under water for 1 hour, then rinsing it under cold water until all the white starch has come out and you're left with an elastic-like, thread-like mass. This is then simmered in seasoned stock to which some tamari (p. 184) has been added. The resulting seitan is a brownish colour because of the tamari. It can be cut into cubes or slices, marinated in more tamari and other tasty ingredients such as garlic and fresh grated ginger, then fried or used to make kebabs. Or it can be grated and used as meat-eaters would use minced meat, for shepherd's pies, burgers and savoury loaves.

TEMPEH is another nutritious, high protein food and has antibiotic properties. It is much liked by some wholefood cooks, but not by me: I find the flavour of soya beans too strong and the texture too stodgy. It needs to be soaked in, or served with,

---

Four simple ways to cook an egg

Boiling an egg
For foolproof boiling, it helps to prick the rounded end of the egg to allow the air to escape and prevent bursting. You can buy a special egg-pricker for this purpose, or pierce the rounded end of the egg with a needle. Then, three-quarters fill a small saucepan with water and bring to the boil. Put the egg into the water and start timing the egg, keeping the water at a steady simmer. Remove the egg with a slotted spoon.

Timings for boiled eggs
These timings are for medium-sized eggs at room temperature:

For a runny yolk	4 minutes
For a slightly runny yolk	6 minutes
For a lightly hardboiled egg	8 minutes
For a dry yolk and set white	10 minutes

When hardboiling an egg, plunge the egg straight into cold water once the time is up; this will prevent over-cooking and the formation of a grey mark between the egg yolk and the white.

Frying an egg
Pour enough oil into a non-stick frying pan to lightly cover the base, then heat it until it sizzles. Break an egg and slip it into the oil. As the egg cooks, spoon over some of the hot oil, to cook the top. As soon as the white in the centre of the egg, around the yolk, is set, slip a fish slice under the egg, lift the egg out and hold it over the frying pan for a moment or two to drain off excess oil. Put the egg straight on to a warmed plate.

Poaching an egg
Fill a wide, shallow pan, such as a deep frying pan, with water. Add 1 tablespoon vinegar and bring to the boil. Break an egg into a cup, then slip it into the water. Immediately turn up the heat so that the water boils vigorously and the bubbles help draw the white around the yolk, then lower the heat and poach gently until set – 2–3 more minutes. Remove the egg with a slotted spoon, and trim the edges to neaten if you wish.

Scrambling eggs for 2
Beat 4 eggs, and, for perfection, pass them through a strainer to remove threads. Season with salt and pepper. Melt 20 g/¾ oz butter in a medium heavy-based saucepan. When it sizzles, add the eggs. Cook over a low heat, stirring. For creamy scrambled eggs, remove from the heat just before the eggs set. They will cook a little more in the heat of the pan. If you want firmer scrambled eggs, cook for a moment or two longer, until no longer runny. But don't overcook: remember they'll go on cooking in their own heat. Serve immediately on warmed plates.

a good strong marinade of crushed garlic, grated ginger and soy sauce, maybe some Dijon mustard, too. It is usually cut into cubes or slices and shallow-fried in oil.

FIRM TOFU can be treated in any of the ways described for seitan and tempeh; it should be kept covered with water in a bowl in the fridge before use. SOFT TOFU, in a vacuum pack, can be kept outside the fridge until opened. It can be beaten to a smooth consistency for dips, dressings, flan fillings and fools. Various other types of tofu such as SMOKED TOFU, AROMATIC DRIED TOFU and DRIED, DEEP FRIED TOFU can sometimes be obtained, and make an interesting addition to stir-fries.

Tofu absorbs flavours well and benefits from being soaked in a marinade before use. Wine, herbs, spices, garlic, oil, citrus rinds and juice, mustard, soy sauce and strongly-flavoured stock can all be used.

A stock made by simmering a sea vegetable such as wakame in water, until the water has reduced well, then straining it, makes a very pleasant marinade when you feel like giving tofu a taste of the sea.

TEXTURED VEGETABLE PROTEIN is available in various meat flavours as well as natural, and comes in assorted shapes and sizes. It is easily rehydrated in hot water according to packet instructions, but has more flavour if left to soak in stock overnight. Many vegetarians find this a useful product when they are making the changeover from meat-eating, or if they have to cook for a meat-eater too. Non-vegetarians can eke out mince and make it healthier by adding or replacing one-third to one-half with reconstituted textured vegetable protein. Reconstituted textured vegetable protein can be added to nut and lentil dishes, such as roasts, savoury loaves, burgers and shepherd's pies, to add bulk, nourishment and flavour. It is useful for this because it adds moisture and also a chewy texture, which can be pleasant and is also particularly valuable in vegetarian cookery where a lot of the ingredients lack this.

How to make tofu

This is best when made from the super soya milk (p. 280). You also need nigari, a white powder which, when added to the soya milk, makes it separate into curds and whey.

You can buy nigari at some health shops. If you cannot get it, Epsom salts can be used, but the result is not as good.

Put 600 ml/1 pint super soya milk (p. 280) into a saucepan and bring to the boil. Dissolve ½ teaspoon nigari (or Epsom salts) in about 4 tablespoons hot water and add to the milk. Leave for 5 minutes for the mixture to curdle. Line a sieve with a piece of muslin, then pour the curdled mixture through, separating the curds from the liquid. The liquid will not be needed. Fold the muslin over to cover the curds and place a weight on top. Leave for at least 1 hour, then remove the curds – which are now tofu – from the muslin and store in cold water in the fridge.

Ideas for using tofu and vegetarian protein foods

☐ Make vegetarian toad-in-the-hole: set the oven to 220 C/425 F/Gas Mark 7. Put 2 tablespoons of oil into a 20 × 20 cm/8 × 8 inch roasting tin and heat in the oven until smoking hot. Put 100 g/4 oz plain 85% wholewheat flour into a bowl with ½ teaspoon salt and 2 eggs. Gradually mix in 300 ml/10 fl oz milk, to make a batter. Have ready 225 g/8 oz seitan or tempeh, cut into cubes, or reconstituted textured vegetable protein cubes. Quickly pour the batter into the tin containing the hot oil, add the cubes of seitan, tempeh or vegetable protein and return to the oven. Bake for about 35 minutes, until puffed up and golden brown. Serve with a vegetarian gravy and cooked vegetables.

☐ Thread cubes of firm tofu, seitan, tempeh or textured vegetable protein on to skewers with mushrooms, tomatoes and onions.

Marinate in a mixture of 1 tablespoon each of soy sauce, brown sugar, mustard and wine vinegar, then brush with oil and grill to make tasty kebabs.

☐ Whizz tofu with strawberries and honey to make a smooth, dairy-free fruit fool.

☐ Dip slices of firm tofu, tempeh or seitan in flour which has been seasoned and flavoured with a crushed garlic clove, shallow-fry in olive oil until crisp on both sides and serve with wedges of lemon.

☐ Any of these protein foods can be mashed then mixed with fried onion, garlic, herbs and spices, formed into burgers, coated in flour, or egg and breadcrumbs, and fried in oil, or baked on an oiled baking sheet.

☐ Simmer textured vegetable protein in red wine with a bay leaf then drain, reserving the liquid. Fry a chopped onion, crushed garlic clove and some button mushrooms in butter or vegan margarine for 10 minutes, then add the protein chunks and stir over the heat until they are heated through. Add a very little flour, to take up any excess fat, then add the reserved cooking liquid and simmer for 10 minutes. Add a small carton of soured cream and cook over a gentle heat until the cream is hot (but don't let it boil). Season and serve.

☐ For a vegetarian-style mixed grill, fry chunks of seitan, textured vegetable protein or tempeh in oil and serve with grilled tomatoes, fried potatoes, onions and mushrooms.

☐ For a tasty dressing, whizz together some tofu with fresh herbs such as basil or coriander, lemon juice and seasoning.

◁ Farmhouse Cheddar
Cheddar cheese made in the traditional way and allowed to mature naturally, with a strong, distinctive flavour

Parmesan ▷
One of Italy's most famous cheeses, a hard cheese with a granular texture, used for grating and cooking

Gjetost ▷
A Norwegian cheese with a fudge-like consistency and slightly sweet flavour

Cheese

Cheese was first made by herdsmen as a convenient way to carry milk, and contains all the nutrients present in milk in a more concentrated form. Cheese was made by the Sumerians 6,000 years ago, then by the Ancient Greeks and by the Romans, who brought their cheese-making skills to the UK. Delicious to eat as it is or to use in cooking, cheese is a very nutritious food, being one of the best vegetarian sources of protein, calcium, vitamins A, B (including B12), D and E, and zinc.

△ Vegetarian Cheddar
Cheddar cheese made with vegetarian rennet

Pecorino △
Can be used as a grating or table cheese

Tilsit ▷
A strongly flavoured, semi-hard cheese made in Germany

Provolone △
A smoked Italian cheese

▽ White Stilton
This is a traditional Stilton before the mould has been allowed to develop

Raclette △
A semi-hard cow's milk cheese from Switzerland with a sweet, mild flavour

Gruyère △
Cow's milk semi-hard cheese from Switzerland with a nut-like flavour

◁ Monterey Jack
A variety of American Monterey cheese with a high moisture content and creamy flavour

Fontina △
Has a slightly smoky flavour

Emmenthal △
Fairly sweet, nutty-flavoured semi-hard cheese from Switzerland

Cantal △
Semi-hard cheese, good for cooking, the French equivalent of our cooking Cheddar

Edam ▷
Famous semi-hard Dutch cheese made in a ball shape with distinctive red wax covering

Gouda ▷
Semi-hard Dutch cheese which can be eaten fresh or matured

Petit Suisse ▷
This unripened cream cheese is good with fresh or poached fruit

Mozzarella ▷
Originally made from buffalo's milk, Mozzarella is an unripened Italian cheese with a soft, moist consistency and a mild, creamy flavour; buy genuine Italian Mozzarella

Boursin △
An unripened cream cheese which comes with various flavourings added; this one is flavoured with herbs and garlic

Fresh, unripened cheeses are for eating shortly after they are made. Soft cheeses, which have been matured for a short period of time so contain less moisture than fresh cheeses, are firmer but still spreadable. Blue cheeses are ripened by the growth of mould from within them, giving them their characteristic sharp, tangy flavour and dappled blue-green appearance. The fat content of these cheeses, which is usually given on the packet or wrapping in the form of a percentage of the whole cheese, varies from very low to high, depending on the type of milk or cream they are made from.

Chèvre △
Goat's cheese from France, which comes in a range of shapes and sizes

Fromage blanc △
This smooth low-fat cheese from France has a light texture almost the consistency of whipped cream

Quark ▷
Smooth unripened cheese from Germany. Different types are available with varying fat contents

Chèvre Lezay ▷
Mild, larger log shape with edible rind

Chèvre ▷
Small soft goat's cheese coated in various herbs and spices

Ricotta cheese △
Unripened Italian cheese, made in the classic pudding basin shape

Cream cheese △
A soft, unripened cheese with a high fat content

Cottage cheese △
A low-fat white cheese with a lumpy texture and creamy flavour

◁ **Skimmed soft cheese**
A smooth, rather bland cheese with the minimum of fat

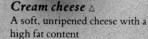
◁ **Curd cheese (or Baker's cheese)**
This name covers all soft unripened cheeses, but is also used specifically for a low–medium fat soft cheese with a pleasantly tangy flavour

◁ Stilton
A relative newcomer to the blue cheese scene, Stilton first became known in the eighteenth century and is said to have originated in Leicestershire, in England

Feta ▽
A fresh soft Greek cheese, made from ewe's milk, with a crumbly texture and a sharp, tangy flavour

Dolcelatte ▷
Made in Italy from cow's milk, similar to Gorgonzola, and good with pasta

Danish Blue △
Made in rounds, from homogenized cow's milk, with a good, sharp, tangy flavour.

Camembert ▽
Similar to Brie, although often stronger-flavoured, Camembert, also from France, is made in small, deep rounds and sold in halves and portions, as well as whole

Roquefort △

Brie ▷
A French fresh soft cheese, made in a large flat round, with a soft, almost 'runny' texture, an edible rind and a mild, creamy flavour

Gorgonzola △
Probably the world's most famous cheese and certainly one of the best, Gorgonzola has been made in Italy since the ninth century. It is made in large cylinder shapes

Cheese

Choosing and storing

All cheese is best bought at its peak and used as soon as possible, within twelve hours, if practicable. This applies especially to unripened and fresh soft cheeses, though semi-hard and hard cheeses will keep for longer.

A cold larder is said to be the best place to store cheese, lightly covered. I keep mine, in small quantities, in a polythene container in the fridge for up to a week. If stored in the fridge, the cheese should be removed and allowed to 'come to' at room temperature for an hour or so before serving.

Hard, semi-hard and fresh soft cheeses which contain over 45 per cent fat, such as full fat and cream cheeses, can be wrapped in polythene and kept for up to 3 months in the deep freeze. Grated Cheddar or Parmesan keeps well in a container in the freezer and can be used from frozen. I grate up left-over pieces of cheese and add them to the container, to save waste and ensure a supply of grated cheese when I need it. Unripened cheese with a high fat content will freeze, but the low-fat ones like cottage cheese, fromage blanc and quark will not.

In order to separate milk into curds and whey, cheesemaking rennet is added to milk in the proportions 1 part rennet to 5000 parts milk. The rennet most commonly used is a digestive juice taken from the stomachs of calves. This means that many cheeses are not totally vegetarian. However, now that vegetarian rennet is available (and gives cheesemakers more reliable results than traditional rennet) it is possible to buy vegetarian versions of a number of cheeses, and the range is increasing. However, cheese made with vegetarian rennet is not always labelled as such, so it's well worth making enquiries.

Cooking and using

See under individual sections.

UNRIPENED CHEESES

Delicious to eat just as they are, with vegetable or fruit salads or as fillings for cherry tomatoes, pitted apricot halves or juicy fresh dates; beaten with fresh herbs and garlic, coarsely crushed black peppercorns or paprika pepper as a dip or topping for crisp crackers, or shaped into small balls or corks and coated with crushed roasted nuts as a cocktail nibble.

The low-fat cheeses such as QUARK, FROMAGE BLANC and SKIMMED SOFT CHEESE are particularly useful as cream substitutes to reduce the fat in traditional dishes such as fools, flan fillings and uncooked cheesecakes. They can be diluted to a creamy consistency with skimmed milk, flavoured with a dash of honey and vanilla, and served with puddings instead of cream. For cooked cheesecake, CURD CHEESE or RICOTTA give just the right moist texture, while ricotta is also excellent with pasta, as a filling for ravioli or layered into a lasagne bake (p. 256).

COTTAGE or CREAM CHEESE and BOURSIN are good in salads; cream cheese with pineapple is a classic salad mixture, served on a base of crisp lettuce, with tomato and cress. Boursin makes a particularly pleasant addition to a cheeseboard and is available with different flavourings. MOZZARELLA, too, is particularly good in salads; with avocado and tomato, in the famous Italian Tricolour Salad, for instance, and it is the best cheese to use as a topping for pizza (p. 218) or Parmigiana (p. 202), because it melts to a delectable soft, creamy consistency. PETIT SUISSE, served as it is, or with fresh fruit, makes a pleasant and easy pudding course.

SOFT CHEESES

These cheeses make an excellent addition to a cheeseboard, and, like the unripened cheeses, are good in salads; the mixture of cubes of FETA cheese with tomato, cucumber, onions and black olives in a Greek salad is a classic. Hot BRIE or Deep-fried CAMEMBERT are a favourite first course or light main course (p. 221).

A whole Brie baked in phyllo pastry makes a spectacular (and easy) dish for a supper party. Either Camembert or Brie can be mashed with walnuts and cream to make a dip or a filling for open mushrooms which are then baked. CHÈVRE, or goat's cheese, comes in a range of shapes and sizes, and may be mild or strong, creamy or firm. CHÈVRE LEZAY is a mild variety of the larger log-shaped Chèvre; CHÈVRE BOUCHERON (not illustrated) is more strongly flavoured. Small logs of Chèvre sliced into little circles just ask to be made into pretty salads. Slices of large Chèvre logs are excellent just melted under the grill; try grilling them on top of tomato slices and serving on a base of crisp lettuce and watercress for supper.

BLUE CHEESES

Blue cheeses, such as STILTON, ROQUEFORT, DANISH BLUE, GORGONZOLA and DOLCELATTE (not generally available in Aus./NZ), are ripened by the growth of green moulds which develop inside them, giving the characteristic flavour and colour. These cheeses are excellent eaten with crispbread or fruit – they have a special affinity with pears. They are also useful in dips, dressings, salads, soups and sauces for pasta. In this way blue cheeses are invaluable in vegetarian cooking because they are one of few very strongly flavoured ingredients.

Making soft cheese

You can make your own curd cheese from milk which has turned sour, or from milk which you have soured yourself by adding lemon juice and boiling for 10–15 minutes, using 2 tablespoons lemon juice to 1 litre/1¾ pints of milk.

Pour the soured milk through a metal sieve or colander lined with a double layer of muslin. Leave the sieve over a bowl until it stops dripping – this should take an hour or so. The residue in the sieve is your curd cheese; add salt and flavourings, such as chopped fresh herbs or crushed garlic, to taste.

SEMI-HARD AND HARD CHEESES

Semi-hard and hard cheeses contain less moisture than soft cheeses; they cut easily but do not spread. They have been ripened by the action of enzymes and bacteria within over a period of months. Most can be used either for grating and cooking or as dessert cheese. CHEDDAR, Britain's best-known cheese, is an example of this adaptability. A fine Cheddar is one of the best cheeses to serve for dessert, but is also one of the best cooking cheeses, because it melts well and has a good flavour. Cheddar is available in various strengths, mild as well as strong and well-matured. A piece of mature FARMHOUSE CHEDDAR, some crusty bread and pickled onions (p. 65), washed down with a glass of beer, makes a traditional Ploughman's Lunch. TILSIT, GOUDA, the famous Dutch cheeses, and MONTEREY JACK, from the USA, are other cheeses which are particularly good eaten with crusty bread, crisp crackers or salad.

For another quick snack meal, try putting a round slice of PROVOLONE on top of a lightly fried large, open mushroom, or a thick slice of large beefsteak tomato, grilled until the cheese has melted, then serve with salad and French bread.

EDAM, with its red skin, is another popular cheese, particularly with slimmers, because it is lower in fat than many cheeses. I find Edam a good cheese for making fondue, although EMMENTHAL is the classic for this. GRUYÈRE, another Swiss cheese which is also made in France, has a nutty flavour and smooth, uniform texture containing some holes, much smaller than those in Emmenthal. Gruyère, too, is used for fondue and is a useful cheese for cooking, because of its fine flavour and good melting qualities.

Other cheeses which melt well are CANTAL, the French cheese quite similar to Cheddar, and FONTINA which is used to make, among other things, an Italian version of cheese fondue with eggs and truffles. RACLETTE (not generally available in Aus./NZ) is an interesting cheese. It is melted to make a Swiss dish which is eaten with potatoes and accompanied by gherkins.

PARMESAN cheese is an important cheese for cooking because of its strong, sharp flavour. It can be bought ready-grated, but for the best flavour, buy a piece of Parmesan, if possible, and grate it yourself as needed. PECORINO is another excellent hard cheese from Italy, suitable both for cooking and eating as it is. One of the more unusual cheeses is GJETOST from Norway. This looks like fudge and has a slightly sweet, floury taste. It can be eaten with bread or made into savouries, starters and desserts.

Selecting a cheeseboard

When choosing cheeses for a cheeseboard, I prefer to concentrate on one or two perfect pieces of cheese, rather than offer a great variety. An excellent, generously sized piece of matured Cheddar, for instance, really needs no accompaniment except some crisp crackers or crusty bread and perhaps some fresh celery. A 'white' cheeseboard made up of just three or four Chèvre cheeses is another favourite of mine, especially if it is served before the pudding and there is some dry white wine to be finished up with the cheese.

Alternatively, try making up a cheeseboard of a complementary pair of cheeses, one soft and creamy, such as Brie or a creamy Chèvre, and one hard or semi-hard – perhaps a red one, like DOUBLE GLOUCESTER or LEICESTER, or, a superb piece of STILTON, or, another of my favourites, WENSLEYDALE.

If you have a large gathering of cheese-lovers at Christmas, it's fun to offer them a whole Stilton, but make sure everyone slices it across and no one wrecks the cheese by pouring port into the middle!

Quick serving ideas for cheese

Cheese is one of the most useful convenience foods; here are some ideas for using it:

□ Form low-fat soft cheese into a log shape; roll log in a mixture of sesame seeds and chopped parsley.

□ Alternatively, roll low-fat cheese into balls the size of walnuts and roll in chopped herbs, sesame seeds or ground nuts.

□ Make raw kebabs: spear cubes of firm cheese on to skewers with wedges of tomato, cubes of cucumber or pineapple, spring onions, radishes, baby button mushrooms, gherkins, stoned olives, or any other fruit or vegetable you fancy. The skewers can be coated with a vinaigrette marinade before serving if you like.

□ Slice the top off green peppers and scoop out seeds and core, then pack peppers with a mixture of curd cheese and sultanas or chopped spring onion, press down firmly and chill until required, then cut into slices and serve as part of a salad.

□ Make cheese spread for sandwiches by mixing very finely grated Cheddar or Cheshire cheese with milk to make a soft paste. Flavour with chopped chives or spring onion, curry powder or a pinch of chilli powder.

□ For a sweet and sour salad with a crunchy texture, mix 350 g/12 oz shredded cabbage with 225 g/3 oz diced cheese and 100 g/4 oz each of chopped dates and roasted peanuts. Dress with natural yogurt.

□ For Cheese Curry, melt 25 g/1 oz butter in a saucepan and fry a chopped onion for 10 minutes. Then stir in 25 g/1 oz flour and 2–3 teaspoons curry powder. Add 300 ml/10 fl oz water, stirring over the heat until the sauce thickens. Simmer gently for 10 minutes, then add 225 g/8 oz cubed cheese and 25 g/1 oz sultanas. Serve immediately, with hot cooked rice.

Herbs

Herbs have been used for centuries, both for flavouring and for healing. Some, like parsley, which is rich in iron, potassium, calcium and vit-amin C, are unusually high in nutrients, others have medicinal and curative properties. Thyme and rosemary (which is an excellent hair tonic) are natural disinfectants; dill is sleep-inducing, fennel is helpful for nursing mothers, mint aids diges-tion, and sage not only makes a good hair rinse but is said to promote a healthy old age.

*◁ **Summer savory***
More delicate in flavour than winter savory, summer savory goes well with fresh beans

Lemon balm △
Delicately flavoured with lemon, and soothing to the digestion, lemon balm is good in tea and added to fruit cups

Winter savory △
Winter savory is known as 'the bean herb' in Germany, because its spicy, peppery flavour complements them so well

Feverfew △
Hot and peppery, a few leaves of feverfew, eaten each day in a sandwich, has been found to be helpful to migraine sufferers

Borage ▽
An unusual herb in that the flowers are used, giving a cucumber flavour and attractive colour to salads and summer punches

Camomile △
A popular herb for making into tea, camomile is soothing and sleep-inducing

*◁ **Sweet cecily***
A sprig of sweet cecily added to stewed fruit reduces the need for sugar

Salad burnet ▷
With a cucumber fragrance when crushed, salad burnet is a popular salad herb in Southern European countries

Hyssop ▷
A warm, aromatic herb which grows wild in Southern Europe and is used in liqueurs such as Chartreuse

Lovage △
A delicious herb, which tastes like spicy, lemony celery and deserves to be more widely used

▽ **Comfrey**
Comfrey leaves have healing properties and used to be used to treat wounds

Angelica △
Best-known in its crystallized form, angelica has a musky scent and can be used fresh in salads and vegetable dishes

Curry plant ▽
The leaves of this herb smell and taste of curry and are widely used in Indian, Malaysian and Indonesian cooking

Fenugreek △
A spicy, rather bitter-tasting herb, popular in Indian cookery

Coriander △
A most popular herb worldwide, with a strange but addictive flavour, widely used in South America, China and Japan, South East Asia and India, and the Middle East

Chervil △
Chervil has a fresh, delicate flavour and is one of the herbs (along with parsley and chives) which make up the classic *fines herbes* mixture

Flat-leaved (or Italian) parsley △
Flat-leaved parsley is considered to have a superior flavour to the curly type

Curly parsley △
The most widely used herb, there are various varieties of parsley

Chives ▽
Chives have a delicate onion flavour and are at their best in raw or very lightly cooked dishes

Tarragon ▷
One of the most important herbs, tarragon comes in two varieties; choose French tarragon rather than Russian, as it has a finer flavour

Basil ▽
Favourite of many cooks, chopped fresh basil brings a taste of summer sunshine and is the classic flavouring for tomatoes and Pesto Sauce

◁ **Apple mint**
A delicately flavoured mint, for flavouring apple dishes, adding to fruit cups, making into teas

Sage ▽
A popular herb in traditional British cookery, sage has a strong, camphor-like flavour and makes a good tea

◁ **Spearmint**
The best all-purpose mint, along with round-leaved Bowles Mint (*M. rotundifolia* var. Bowles) (not illustrated)

◁ **Ginger mint**
One of the many interesting varieties of mint

◁ Fennel
Golden-flowered,
anise-flavoured fennel is a
classic flavouring for fish but
useful for vegetarians too,
especially combined with
lemon and olive oil

Dill △
Although native to Southern
Europe, by adoption dill is
Scandinavian, in which cuisine
it is widely used

Oregano ▽
Widely used in Italy, oregano
has an intense, savoury flavour

Rosemary △
Widely used in the Mediterranean, rosemary
has a delicious pine-like flavour that can
enhance both sweet and savoury dishes

Bay △
One of the bouquet garni
herbs, the intense flavour of
bay gives depth to casseroles,
stocks and soups

◁ Thyme
A fragrant herb, one of the ingredients of a
classic bouquet garni

Sweet marjoram ▷
Related to oregano, marjoram
has a sweet, slightly spicy
flavour, making it a useful
all-purpose herb.

Lemon thyme ▷

Herbs

Choosing and storing

The best way to experience herbs is freshly picked. Once picked, they should be kept in a jar of water or loosely wrapped in a polythene bag in the fridge for a day or so. Dried herbs lack the aroma of fresh herbs, but are useful when fresh ones are unavailable, and bay leaves actually taste better when dried. Keep dried herbs in small air-tight bottles, in a dark place if possible.

Preparation and cooking

Fresh herbs should be lightly washed, then patted dry before use. Handle them gently to preserve their fragrant oils. Then use them whole, or chop them, according to the recipe. To chop herbs, remove any coarse stems, then put the herbs on a board and chop with a sharp knife, holding the point of the blade down with one hand and pivoting the knife from the point in a quarter-circle. Herbs can also be chopped in a food processor; this is excellent for chopping large quantities.

As dried herbs are more strongly flavoured than fresh ones, a smaller quantity is needed: only a quarter to a third of the amount of fresh herbs. Dried herbs can be added to a dish at the beginning of cooking, as can a bouquet garni and the robust fresh herbs such as bay, rosemary, thyme, but the fresh delicate green herbs are better added towards the end of the cooking, to make the most of their flavour and colour.

To make a bouquet garni, tie a sprig of parsley, thyme and a bay leaf together. Sometimes I like to include a strip or two of lemon peel too, for a fresh, citrus flavour. Alternatively, one of the best ways to make a bouquet garni is to slit a trimmed, washed leek down one side, pop the herbs inside the leek and tie it to hold the herbs in place.

Chopped fresh herbs make an excellent flavouring for butter or vegan margarine; just mix finely chopped herbs into soft butter or margarine, together with a few drops of lemon juice, if you like. Keep in the fridge for a day or two; or freeze for several weeks. Add to hot cooked vegetables, use to make herb bread or swirl into hot cooked pasta.

Drying and preserving

Pick herbs for preserving at the height of their season, before they flower, on a sunny day after the dew has dried. Cut them with long stems and hang up in bunches in a cool, dark place to dry naturally. Keep different herbs apart so that the flavours do not merge. When the herbs are completely dry and brittle, store them in dark, airtight containers.

Alternatively, herbs can be deep-frozen. Cut them as described, then blanch them by dipping them briefly into a deep pan of boiling water. Refresh immediately in cold water, pat dry, then freeze on open trays. When frozen, pack in polythene bags. Or chop the herbs, put into ice cube containers, top up with water and freeze. When frozen, transfer to a polythene bag, keeping individual types together.

One of the best ways of preserving the flavour of basil is to chop the leaves, then put them into a jar in layers, sprinkling each layer with salt. Cover with olive oil and keep the jar in the fridge. Although the leaves darken, the flavour remains.

Or make basil-flavoured oil, to bring a summer taste to winter salads. Put several sprigs into a bottle and fill up with olive oil; the oil will be impregnated with the flavour after several weeks. Herb-flavoured vinegars can be made in a similar way.

ANGELICA
Angelica archangelica

Best-known in its crystallized form, angelica has a musky scent and can be used fresh in salads and vegetable dishes.

BASIL *Ocimum basilicum*

Best known as a flavouring for tomatoes and the classic Italian sauce, Pesto (p. 172), basil is good in any salad mixture or chopped over lightly cooked vegetables. It is the flavouring for Pistou soup (p. 136).

BAY *Laurus nobilis*

Bay can be used either dried or fresh. It is usually included in a bouquet garni and is good in vegetable casseroles, soups and stews, and to flavour the milk used to make sauces, such as Bread Sauce (p. 175). A bay leaf is an old-fashioned flavouring for rice pudding. Fresh bay leaves make an attractive garnish or base for serving fresh cheeses or sorbet in fresh orange skins.

BORAGE *Borago officinalis*

An unusual herb in that the flowers are used, giving a cucumber flavour and attractive colour to salads and summer punches. Try adding the flowers to ice cubes.

CAMOMILE *Anthemis nobilis*

A popular herb for making into tea, camomile is soothing and sleep-inducing.

CHERVIL *Anthriscus cerefolium*

Chervil has a fresh, delicate flavour and can be used lavishly in salads and over lightly cooked vegetables. As part of the traditional *fines herbes* mixture, it is a delicious flavouring for an omelette.

CHIVES *Allium schoenoprasum*

Very useful wherever you need a subtle onion flavour, chives are also one of the most useful garnishing herbs; just snip them over the top of pale coloured soups, dips and salads. Chives are a particularly good flavouring for egg and cheese dishes and are added to some cheeses.

COMFREY *Symphytum officinale*

Cucumber-flavoured, like borage, comfrey can be chopped into salads or dipped in batter and fried as a nibble. The flowers can be used in fruit cups.

CORIANDER
Coriandrum sativum

Similar in appearance to flat-leaved parsley, this is the world's most popular herb, with a strange but addictive flavour, widely used in South America, China and Japan, South East Asia and India, and the Middle East.

CURRY PLANT
Murraya koenigii
The leaves of this herb smell and taste of curry and are widely used in Indian, Malay and Indonesian cooking.

DILL *Anethum graveolens*
A pretty, feathery herb, attractive as a garnish as well as a flavouring, dill goes particularly well with any cucumber dish; I like it chopped into soured cream as a sauce or topping for jacket potatoes; it's also particularly good in Potato Salad (p. 166).

FENNEL *Foeniculum vulgare*
This herb, with its aniseed flavour, helps to cut the oiliness of foods; sprinkle it over fried potatoes or aubergines, add a little to nut burgers (p. 232), or mix it with yogurt and serve with a nut roast made from an oily nut, like brazil nuts (p. 236). Fennel is also good in a green salad dressed with fresh lemon and fruity olive oil.

FENUGREEK
Trigonella foenum-graecum
A spicy, rather bitter-tasting herb, popular in Indian cookery.

FEVERFEW
Chrysanthemum parthenium
Most useful, as some people have found, as a cure for migraine. Eat a few leaves each day in a sandwich.

HYSSOP
Hyssopus officinalis
A warm, aromatic herb which grows wild in southern Europe and is used in liqueurs such as Chartreuse.

LEMON BALM
Melissa officinalis
Delicately flavoured with lemon, and soothing to the digestion, lemon balm is good in tea and added to fruit cups, or used to flavour a cake by sprinkling on the lining paper before putting in the cake mixture.

LOVAGE *Levisticum officinale*
An unusual but delicious herb, particularly good in a lettuce or cabbage salad, or added to celery soup to intensify the flavour. Lovage is powerful; a little goes a long way.

SWEET MARJORAM
Origanum marjorana
A useful herb which is best added towards the end of cooking time, to preserve its sweet flavour. Excellent in nut and pulse roasts (pp. 239, 213) and savoury bakes, in stuffings and burgers.

MINT *Mentha*
One of the most important and widely used flavourings, there are many varieties of mint including APPLE MINT, SPEARMINT and GINGER MINT. It is a traditional flavouring for peas and new potatoes and is chopped to make fresh Indian chutneys and Mint Sauce which is good, in a vegetarian meal, as an accompaniment to a lentil roast. To make Mint Sauce, mix 4 tablespoons chopped mint with 1 tablespoon caster sugar, 1 tablespoon boiling water and 2 tablespoons wine vinegar.

OREGANO *Origanum vulgare*
This is one herb which retains its flavour well when dried. It is useful in any dish where you want quite an intense taste, and is widely used in Italian cookery, in sauces to serve with pasta, lasagne bakes, and sprinkled on top of pizza (p. 218). Oregano is also pleasant in a nut or lentil roast or burgers.

PARSLEY *Petroselinum crispum*
The most commonly used herb in European and American cooking, parsley comes in CURLY and FLAT LEAF (or ITALIAN) varieties. Parsley has a fresh, mild flavour, and can be used lavishly, added to sauces and stuffings, sprinkled over cooked vegetables and pasta, included in salads. It is used almost like a vegetable in the Middle Eastern salad, Tabbouleh (p. 159). Parsley stalks make an excellent flavouring; tie them together and add to any soup or casserole.

ROSEMARY
Rosmarinus officinalis
This fragrant herb, with pine and camphor notes, is good in pilafs and nut dishes; as a natural 'skewer' for kebabs and as a flavouring for bread, egg custards and ice creams.

SAGE *Salvia officinalis*
A strongly flavoured herb, traditionally used with onions to make a stuffing (which can be baked between layers of a cashew nut roast or used to fill a marrow). Sage complements split peas and split orange lentils, and is a good flavouring for savoury apple jelly; it is found in cheeses and is a good addition to home-made cheese dips.

SALAD BURNET
Poterium sanguisorba
With a cucumber fragrance when crushed, salad burnet is a popular salad herb in many southern European countries.

SUMMER and WINTER
SAVORY
Satureja hortensis and *S. Montana*
These peppery herbs go well in any savoury dish, particularly any which include split peas or lentils. Try adding winter savory to lentil soups; chop summer savory over tender young broad beans or add to a haricot bean salad.

SWEET CECILY *Myrrhis odorata*
A sprig of sweet cecily added to stewed fruit reduces the need for sugar.

TARRAGON
Artemisia dracunculus
Tarragon is good in omelettes, or any delicate egg dish. Try adding it to a savoury jelly, delicately flavoured flan filling, omelette or mildly flavoured cheese soufflé. Or add some chopped tarragon to the filling for stuffed eggs, then serve them on a base of fresh tarragon leaves. It's also good chopped into salads, including rice salad, and added to butter for serving with fresh summer vegetables or pasta.

THYME and LEMON THYME
Thymus vulgaris and *T. serpyllum*
Excellent for adding to any long-cooking casserole or stew, and one of the components of bouquet garni. Thyme is one of the herbs which survives the drying process well. It makes an excellent addition to almost any savoury mixture.

Caraway seeds ▽
Caraway has a sweet, slightly aniseed flavour

Aniseed △
Fragrant seeds of an umbelliferous plant

Cardamom △
Pods of a perennial plant of the ginger family, and the second most expensive spice in the world, cardamom has a eucalyptus-like scent and flavour

Allspice △
The dried berries of an evergreen tree native to the West Indies

Spices

Spices are the dried buds, flowers, fruits, leaves and barks of aromatic plants, mainly from tropical countries. They have been used for centuries, highly revered for their rarity and use in the preservation of food and the making of medicines and scents. For hundreds of years spices were a precious trading commodity. Today they are an essential ingredient in good cooking and especially in vegetarian cooking because of the strong flavours they provide for so many dishes.

Cayenne pepper △
A powder made from dried small hot red chilli peppers from Central America

Celery seeds △
The dried seeds of the celery plant, native to Italy

Chinese five-spice △
This is made from equal parts of finely ground fennel, cloves, cinnamon (or cassia), star-anise and anise, and is subtly aniseed-flavoured

Chilli △
The dried fruit of a hot and spicy pepper from South America

Cloves ▷
Cloves have antiseptic and preservative properties and can be bought whole or ground

Coriander seeds △
These dried seeds are the world's most-used spice

Cumin seeds △
The dried seeds of a plant related to the parsley family have a slightly bitter flavour

Cinnamon △
The dried bark of an aromatic evergreen of the laurel family

Dill seeds △
Have a slightly sweet flavour

Fennel seeds △
Aniseed-flavoured seeds of the fennel plant

Fenugreek △
Rectangular yellowish-brown seeds

Garam masala △
Blend of roasted and ground spices

△
Curry powder
A blend of several spices, in varying strengths

Garlic ▷
The bulb of a perennial plant native to Asia

Ginger △
Has a fresh, citrus-like smell

◁ Horseradish
The root of a plant native to South Eastern Europe, horseradish has a hot, pungent flavour

Mace ▽
Mace can be bought whole, as 'blade' mace, or ground

Mixed spice ▽
Usually consists of four parts each ground nutmeg and cinnamon, two parts ginger and one part ground cloves

Juniper berries ▷
The berries of a small prickly shrub which grows wild in many parts of the northern hemisphere, including Britain

Nutmeg ▽
The dried kernel of an apricot-like fruit: see mace. Nutmeg is available whole and ground and has a slightly sweet aromatic flavour

Paprika ▽
A sweet mild powder made from a variety of peppers

◁ Black mustard seeds
Hottest of the mustard seeds

◁ Wholegrain mustard
Contains whole brown mustard seeds

△ White mustard seeds

◁ Dijon mustard
A hot, made-up mustard from France

Dried green peppercorns ▽

◁ Brown mustard seeds

Fresh green peppercorns ▽

▽ Black peppercorns
The sun-ripened berries of the pepper vine

Pink peppercorns ▽

Pickled green peppercorns ▽

△ Green peppercorns
The unripened berries of the pepper, available dried, pickled and sometimes fresh, with a sharp, hot flavour

◁ White peppercorns
Peppercorns which have been ripened then skinned

Pickling spice ▽
A mixture of spices for chutneys and pickles

Star anise △
Dried fruit of an evergreen tree

Tamarind ▽
Tamarind has a sharp flavour, rather like lemon juice

Poppy seeds △
The seeds of the opium poppy, native to the Middle East

Saffron △
Saffron is the dried golden stamens of a crocus-type flower

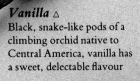

Turmeric △
A rhizome belonging to the ginger family, but with a different flavour

Vanilla △
Black, snake-like pods of a climbing orchid native to Central America, vanilla has a sweet, delectable flavour

Spices

Choosing and storing

Buy spices in small quantities – enough to be able to use it up within six months – from a shop with a rapid turnover. Keep the spices in airtight jars. Strictly speaking, they should be kept away from the light, or stored in dark jars, but I like the decorative look of them on an open shelf and find I experiment with them more if I have them in front of me. Prices vary, and although it's worth spending extra for high quality spices, make sure that you're not really paying for fancy packaging. Indian and Middle Eastern food shops often sell excellent spices, simply packaged and reasonably priced.

There's no doubt that many spices are best bought whole so that you can grind them as you need them. This is easy and practical with some of the spices, such as black and white peppercorns, which can be kept in separate grinders, and also whole coriander, which you can grate through a pepper mill, too. Nutmeg is easy to grate as you need it, either on a special nutmeg grater (which may have a handy compartment for keeping the pieces of half-grated nutmeg) or on the finest blade of a box grater. Most other spices can be pounded in a mortar with a pestle, or – easier – whizzed to a powder in an electric coffee grinder.

Using

Spices are used to flavour both sweet and savoury dishes, and some can also be added in large quantities to thicken sauces. The basic spices are black peppercorns and fresh nutmeg; others can be added as you need them for individual recipes. One way of getting to know spices is to cook a new spicy recipe every week or so and buy the spices needed for it, then see how they taste added to other dishes, too.

Spices can also be used as flavourings for ice creams, hot and cold milk, and as toppings and garnishes.

ALLSPICE
Pimenta diocia

Allspice can be bought whole, or ground and tastes like a mixture of cinnamon, nutmeg and cloves. It is useful in baking, instead of mixed spice (of which it is often an ingredient), or a few whole berries make an interesting addition to stews and casseroles.

ANISEED *Pimpinella anisum*

Available whole or ground, but most useful whole, when it can be added to cooked vegetables (it goes particularly well with carrots). Aniseed can also be used in baking, to flavour cakes, pastries and biscuits. It is also a flavouring used in ouzo, Ricard and pastis.

CARAWAY SEEDS *Carum carvi*

Curved seeds of a plant native to Europe and Asia, caraway is popular in German and Austrian cookery. It is famous in England for its use in seed cake, which was popular in Victorian times. Caraway can be used to sprinkle on top of bread or savoury pastries, included in coleslaw and sprinkled over cooked cabbage. It is used in goulash and in liptauer cheese, a flavoured cheese dip from Hungary. Some cheeses contain caraway seed, and caraway is used to make certain liqueurs, such as Kümmel, made in Germany, Denmark and Holland.

CARDAMOM
Elettaria cardamomum

Cardamom pods can range in colour from white or pale green to almost black (which are an inferior type). Cardamom is available whole or ground and is a fragrant spice, one of my favourites. It can be used to flavour spiced vegetable dishes and pilafs, or the small black seeds can be taken out of the pods and crushed. Cardamom also makes a pungent and unusual flavouring for sweet dishes such as the Indian ice cream Kulfi, and the Middle Eastern sweetmeat, Halva.

Ground cardamom is available, but it is better to buy it in the pod and crush the seeds to a powder yourself in a mortar with a pestle.

CAYENNE PEPPER
Capsicum annuum

Useful for giving a kick to bland dishes such as an avocado dip or cream cheese dip; good in cheese dishes.

CELERY SEEDS
Apium graveolens

Used whole or in the form of celery salt and can be added to any dishes requiring a celery flavour: soups, savouries, casseroles, on top of loaves, even in a salad dressing; but use with discretion as too many can taste bitter.

CHILLI *Capsicum annuum*

Chilli can be bought whole, flaked or ground. The pungency of ground chilli varies from mild to very hot, depending on the blend. Use in vegetarian chilli con carne and other Mexican dishes; like cayenne pepper, chilli can be used to give a kick to mild dishes.

CHINESE FIVE-SPICE

This slightly aniseed-tasting flavouring is used in Chinese dishes; try adding a pinch to vegetable stir-fries.

CINNAMON
Cinnamomum zeylanicum

Cinnamon can be bought as pieces of bark, 'quills' made from the inner bark, and powder. This warm, fragrant flavouring is good in both sweet and savoury dishes. The bark and quills can be used to flavour pilafs and spiced vegetable dishes; the quills are also useful for flavouring poached fruits and fruit compotes. Cinnamon is difficult to grind at home, so it's useful to buy it ready ground too for adding to cakes and biscuits. A cinnamon stick can be kept in a jar of caster sugar, to flavour it; this sugar, or sugar mixed with cinnamon, is good for cheering up a bland melon; and sprinkled on top of hot buttered toast makes cinnamon toast.

CLOVES *Syzygium aromaticum* and *Eugenia aromatica*

Cloves are the dried flower buds of a tall aromatic evergreen of the myrtle family native to South Eastern Asia.

It is useful to have both whole and ground cloves, since cloves are difficult to grind at home, and ground cloves are useful in fruit cakes and in some bean dishes. Whole cloves make a delicious flavouring for apple pie, whole baked onions, bread sauce and cheese fritters.

Cloves also have natural antiseptic and preservative properties, as I discovered for myself recently when my young daughter had half made a pomander: the half of the orange studded with cloves was still dry and perfectly preserved, while the other side was rotten.

CORIANDER SEEDS
Coriandrum sativum
Coriander seeds have a slight burnt-orange flavour and are available whole and ground. I find it useful to keep both. Coriander complements many vegetable, grain and bean dishes. The whole seeds can be roasted in a dry saucepan then lightly crushed or finely ground before use; or you can keep a pepper mill full of coriander, or it can be bought ready ground.

Ground coriander is used to flavour spicy Pakoras from India. They can be served as a first course or as a side dish. To make pakoras, put 100 g/4 oz chick pea flour into a bowl with 1 teaspoon each salt and grated fresh ginger, ½ teaspoon each chilli powder and ground coriander, ¼ teaspoon turmeric, and enough water to mix to a thin batter – about 200 ml/7 fl oz. Leave the batter to stand for about 30 minutes. Meanwhile, peel and slice into rings 2 large onions. Dip the onion rings into the batter, then fry in deep or shallow fat until crisp – deep fat gives the crisper result. Drain the onion rings on kitchen paper and serve immediately.

As it is mild, coriander is often used in quite large quantities to thicken as well as flavour Indian or Middle Eastern vegetable dishes. Mushrooms or vegetables can be flavoured with coriander to make a delicious first course (p. 150). Coriander is also an essential ingredient of curry powder and garam masala (see below).

CUMIN SEEDS
Cuminum cyminum
The whole seeds are best if roasted in a saucepan before use to mellow the flavour. Along with coriander, cumin is frequently used in curries and spiced vegetable dishes. I find it useful to have both the whole seeds and ground cumin on my kitchen shelf.

CURRY POWDER
A popular flavouring in the West, but not much used in India, curry powder consists of a blend of spices, usually including coriander, turmeric, fenugreek, cumin and chilli. It can be bought in varying strengths from mild to hot. I find it quite useful for perking up some bland mixtures such as the filling for devilled eggs, or to flavour mayonnaise, but not for making curries – for these a mixture of coriander, cumin, fresh ginger, chilli, garlic and other spices gives a much better flavour.

DILL SEEDS *Anethum graveolens*
Probably best known as the flavouring in dill pickled cucumbers, dill seeds have a refreshing flavour. They are a popular flavouring in Scandinavian cooking, and dill is excellent in any cucumber dish, such as cucumber soups and salads, as well as with cabbage, carrots and any of the root vegetables.

FENNEL SEEDS
Foeniculum vulgare
Fennel seeds are much used in Indian cookery and when added to pulse dishes are said to counteract any indigestibility, though I have never had any proof of such effectiveness. Nice lightly roasted in a dry pan before use.

FENUGREEK
Trigonella foenum-graceum
Fenugreek is an ingredient in curries and Indian dishes, but you do not need much as it has quite a harsh flavour. I think the whole seeds are best to use, and they should be lightly roasted in a saucepan before use. The seeds can also be sprouted (p. 207) but watch your teeth when you eat them.

GARAM MASALA
Garam masala can be bought ready-blended, although in India cooks make up their own mixture, often to old family recipes. The mixtures usually include coriander, cumin, cloves, cinnamon and black pepper. Add to curries at the end of the cooking, to flavour and thicken.

GARLIC *Allium sativum*
Garlic is indispensable for subtly enhancing the taste of other ingredients or giving its own wonderful flavour to savoury dishes. It can be used in a whole range of savoury dishes, from soups and salads – rub a salad bowl with a cut clove of garlic, for a delicate flavour – to casseroles, bakes, accompaniments such as hot buttery garlic bread and dips and sauces such as the famous aïoli of Provence.

Garlic Potatoes are delicious. Peel and cut potatoes into even-sized chunks and boil for about 15 minutes until just tender. Drain and spread the potatoes in a shallow, ovenproof dish. Crush one or two garlic cloves with some butter and dot over the surface of the potatoes. Season and cook in a fairly hot oven for about 40 minutes, turning the potatoes from time to time to coat them in the garlic butter.

Garlic can be bought fresh, as a paste in a tube, as flakes, powder or as a salt. Fresh garlic is by far the best, and worth the small effort involved in peeling and crushing the individual cloves from the bulb.

A bulb of garlic will keep well for several weeks in a dry kitchen; when I can I like to buy a string of garlic – it looks attractive hanging up in the kitchen and means there's always plenty available. Choose firm bulbs with no sign of powderiness and look for nice big fat ones made up of fat individual cloves – they're so much easier to peel and crush. To crush garlic, either use a good-quality, sturdy garlic press with nice large holes, or crush with the side of a knife on a small board, adding a little salt to help grind it into a paste.

Garlic is a natural antiseptic, excellent for cleansing heavy metals from the body and keeping colds (and, alas, probably one's friends) at bay.

GINGER *Zingiber officinale*
The rhizome of a flowering plant which is native to South East Asia but has been grown in China for thousands of years. It can be bought fresh, dried and ground. FRESH GINGER has a deliciously fresh, citrus-like smell and flavour, along with the characteristic 'hotness', and is used in Chinese, Caribbean and Indian dishes. It transforms a dish of simple root vegetables into a gourmet feast and can give a wonderful lift to a winter compote of dried fruit. DRIED GINGER ROOT is useful when making preserves and chutneys, and POWDERED GINGER is a popular flavouring for cakes (such as gingerbread, Parkin (p. 308) and fruit cakes), biscuits and cookies – Gingerbread Men are a perennial children's favourite.

To make about 12, set the oven to 180C/350F/Gas Mark 4. Melt 25 g/1 oz butter or vegan margarine, 40 g/1½ oz barbados sugar, 1 tablespoon black treacle and 2 tablespoons golden syrup gently in a saucepan, then cool until you can put your hand against the saucepan. Sift in 100 g/4 oz fine 100% wholewheat flour and ½ teaspoon each bicarbonate of soda and ground ginger. Mix to a pliable dough. If the dough is too soft to roll, chill in the fridge for about 20 minutes, otherwise roll it out about 5 mm/¼ inch thick and cut into gingerbread men shapes. Put the gingerbread men on the baking tray and bake for about 10 minutes, until firm and beginning to darken round the edges. Cool on a wire rack.

Ginger is available preserved in syrup and crystallized, both excellent for adding to ice cream, cakes, fruit salads, a compote of dried fruits.

HORSERADISH
Armoracia rusticana
Finely grated horseradish can be added to mayonnaise or cream to make horseradish sauce. Or it can be made into a dressing for sliced tomato salad. To make this, combine in a bowl 125 g/4 oz curd cheese, 2 tablespoons natural yogurt, 2 teaspoons olive oil, ½ teaspoon wine vinegar and 1 teaspoon grated horseradish. Mix until creamy then pour over sliced tomatoes and garnish with chopped fresh herbs. It is pungent and can make your eyes water as you grate it. I think a jar of preserved grated horseradish or creamed horseradish is a better bet.

JUNIPER BERRIES
Juniperus communis
Juniper berries take three years to ripen, so the bushes carry berries at different stages of development. Juniper berries can be used fresh or dried, and a few berries added to casseroles and vegetable dishes give an intriguing flavour. Juniper is used to make gin, and in Germany juniper is added to sauerkraut and preserves.

MACE *Myristica fragrans*
Mace is the lacy covering surrounding the kernel inside the apricot-like fruit of an evergreen tree of the myrtle family. A BLADE of mace is useful for flavouring Béchamel Sauce (p. 175) and delicate soups; while a pinch of GROUND MACE enhances many savoury mixtures and is specially good in delicate nut roasts made from white nuts (p. 239).

MIXED SPICE
The flavour of different makes of mixed spice varies, so it's worth experimenting to find your favourite. A useful flavouring for cakes, biscuits and fruit mixtures such as mincemeat.

MUSTARD SEEDS
Brassica hirta and *B. nigra*
WHITE, BLACK and BROWN mustard seeds are used in curries and Indian dishes and the white ones make a delicious addition to cucumber and dill salad, cucumber pickle and chutneys. MUSTARD POWDER (not illustrated) is a mixture of varieties together with wheat flour and turmeric. A pinch or so brings out the flavour of cheese dishes: it should be blended with cold water for the best flavour. Many types of prepared mustard are available, often with intriguing additions like fresh herbs and green peppercorns. They are interesting to try, but the best basics to have in the store cupboard, in my opinion, are DIJON MUS-TARD, which is delicious in salad dressings, and a whole-grain mustard, especially MOUTARDE DE MEAUX which, as well as being a useful ingredient, is a good accompaniment to many cold savoury dishes.

NUTMEG *Myristica fragrans*
Traditionally, nutmeg was used for sweet dishes, such as milk puddings, egg custards and custard tarts, while mace was used in savoury dishes. However, nutmeg is equally at home with vegetables such as mushrooms, spinach and cabbage, and in dishes such as onions in cream sauce. The flavour of freshly grated nutmeg is much better than that of ready-ground nutmeg.

PAPRIKA *Capsicum tetragonum*
Makes a cheering garnish to a plate of creamy-coloured Hummus (p. 144), Cheese and Fresh Herb Dip (p. 143), Guacamole (p. 144) or mashed potato. Paprika is useful for its subtle, peppery taste as well as its colour, and is an essential ingredient in many Hungarian recipes, where it is used to thicken, as well as flavour. The best paprika is Hungarian noble sweet, followed by semi-sweet, rose, strong and commercial, in descending order of quality.

PEPPERCORNS *Piper nigrum*
GREEN PEPPERCORNS are included in some special dishes, for their colour as much as their flavour. BLACK PEPPERCORNS have a mellow flavour and, when freshly ground, give an appetizing piquancy to food. WHITE PEPPERCORNS have a sharper, more astringent flavour, which is useful at times, and some cooks prefer to use white pepper for seasoning pale mixtures which would be discoloured by flecks of black pepper. MIG-NONETTE (not illustrated) is a mixture of white and black peppercorns and is widely used in France. You can make up your own mignonette mixture by putting both white and black peppercorns in a pepper mill. This gives a pleasant flavouring, worth trying. The other flavouring which is based on either black or white pepper

and popular in France (where it can be bought at any supermarket) is Quatre Epices, a mixture of ground peppercorns, cloves, nutmeg and cinnamon – a pleasant mixture to experiment with. PINK PEPPER-CORNS (*Schinus molle*), also known as Baie rose and false pepper of America, are the fruits of a small ornamental tree of the cashew family. They can be used to make an attractive garnish because of their pretty colour.

PICKLING SPICE
An essential ingredient in chutneys and pickles, a little pickling spice can also be added to a casserole or ground in a mortar with a pestle and used to add piquancy to a nut roast.

POPPY SEEDS
Papaver somniferum
Widely used in Indian and Jewish cookery, poppy seeds have a nutty flavour and crunchy texture and make a pleasant addition to curries, hot vegetable dishes and salads, and sprinkled over hot buttery pasta. They are also used as a topping for breads (p. 329) and as an ingredient in the famous Jewish poppyseed cake.

SAFFRON *Crocus sativus*
The world's most expensive spice, saffron has an aromatic flavour and will colour pale ingredients (such as rice) soft yellow. Classically it is used in Paella (p. 243) and in Cornish saffron cake. Buy the dried stamens (rather than 'powdered saffron' which is almost always a dye) and soak a few in a couple of tablespoons of boiling water for 15 minutes before use, then add to the dish, together with the soaking water.

STAR ANISE *Illicium verum*
This star-shaped fruit is a pod which contains shiny golden-brown seeds. It is added whole to casseroles and stir-fries and has a delicate aniseed flavour. It is used particularly in China where it is believed to have a beneficial effect on the digestive system.

TAMARIND *Tamarindus indica*
The dried fruit of the tamarind tree, native to East Africa and known as 'Indian dates' because of its sticky, fibrous appearance, tamarind can be added to curries and Indian dishes to give sharpness. To use, soak a small piece in water until pulpy, then press through a sieve and use the liquid and pulp which comes through.

TURMERIC *Curcuma longa*
Turmeric is a rhyzome. It is sometimes available fresh, when it looks rather like fresh ginger, but it is normally bought either whole or ground, when it is bright gold. Ground turmeric is useful for adding flavour and a vivid golden colour to rice and vegetable dishes and is much used in Indian cookery. It is also used in some chutneys and pickles.

A traditional British use for turmeric is in piccalilli, piquant pickle for serving with cold nut or lentil savouries. To make piccalilli, prepare 450 g/1 lb each of pickling onions, cucumber, cauliflower florets and runner beans, cutting them into bite-sized pieces. Put the vegetables into a large dish or on to a plastic tray, sprinkle with 225 g/8 oz kitchen salt and leave for 24 hours. Meanwhile, put 1.2 litres/2 pints white vinegar into a saucepan with 4 dried chillis, 4 cloves, 25 g/1 oz dried ginger, bruised with a rolling pin, and

175 g/6 oz granulated sugar. Heat gently until the sugar has dissolved, then bring to the boil. Remove from the heat, cool and strain. Rinse and drain the vegetables. Put 75 g/3 oz flour into a bowl with 25 g/1 oz mustard powder, 15 g/½ oz turmeric and 2 crushed garlic cloves. Add enough cooled vinegar to make a smooth paste. Bring the rest of the vinegar to the boil, add some of this to the flour mixture and stir, then add the flour mixture to the vinegar in the pan and stir well until thickened. Add the vegetables to the pan. Cook for 5 minutes. Spoon the mixture into warm, sterilized jars. Cover with vinegar-proof tops. Keep for 3 months before using. Makes 2.5–3 kg/5–6 lb.

VANILLA *Vanilla planifolia*
Vanilla pods are expensive, but they can be used over and over again. Break a vanilla pod in half and bury the pieces in a jar of caster sugar to make a delicate vanilla-flavoured sugar for using in ice cream, delicate fruit dishes and egg custards. Or simmer a whole pod in a sugar syrup or milk which you're going to use to make egg custard. The vanilla pod can later be extracted, rinsed in warm water, patted dry on kitchen paper and left to dry on an airy shelf in the kitchen before storing in an airtight jar. A more extravagant use is to grind the whole vanilla pod up with cashew nuts, carob powder and honey to make rather superior healthy sweet treats (p. 344). Vanilla extract, made by extracting the vanilla flavouring from the pods with alcohol, is available but expensive. Cheaper vanilla essence is made from a synthetic vanillin, made from eugenol, which is found in clove oil.

Recipes

In choosing recipes for this section, I've aimed for a balance between the essential basics, such as Nut Roast, Lentil Soup, Cheese Flan and Soufflé, to more unusual recipes such as Two-Colour Soup, Roasted Cashew Nut Roulade with Wild Mushroom Filling, and Aubergine and Pasta Charlotte. I have also borne in mind both the dictates of healthy eating and of the palate, which are not by any means always contradictory, as is demonstrated in the majority of the recipes. However, some indulgences have crept in, like Profiteroles and Summer Fruit Meringue, as have some particularly health-conscious recipes, including Sugarless Dundee Cake and Reduced-Sugar Jam. None of the recipes are unduly difficult or time-consuming to make; I hope you will enjoy both making and eating them.

Soups

Thick, warming and filling, thin and elegant, or ice-cold and refreshing, soup is one of the most versatile dishes. It is also economical and quick and easy to make. Vegetarian soups are flavoured with vegetable stocks, herbs, spices, and, for more intensity, miso (p. 133) or yeast extract (p. 232). Using home-made stock produces an excellent soup, but if you haven't any, don't let this deter you; use ordinary water and season carefully, for a delicate soup which lets the flavour of the vegetables sing out.

Making Stock for Soup

Many recipes for soup call for stock, and for vegetarians this of course means a vegetable stock. Whilst some good vegetable stock powders and cubes are available, if you use these regularly, all your soups tend to have a similar flavour. On the other hand, home-made vegetable stock has a delicate flavour which varies from batch to batch and is easy to make.

V JERUSALEM ARTICHOKE SOUP WITH V ROASTED PINE NUTS

The flavour of the pine nuts goes particularly well with the artichokes, but toasted hazelnuts or flaked almonds are also good.

SERVES 6

2 tablespoons lemon juice
700 g/1½ lb Jerusalem artichokes
1 onion, peeled and chopped
15 g/½ oz butter or vegan margarine
600 ml/1 pint Light Vegetable Stock
   (p. 129) or water
600 ml/1 pint milk or soya milk
freshly grated nutmeg
salt and freshly ground black pepper
25 g/1 oz pine nuts, toasted under the grill

1 Add the lemon juice to a bowl of cold water. Peel the artichokes, cut them into even-sized pieces and put them into the acidulated water, to prevent them from discolouring.

2 Fry the onion in the butter or vegan margarine in a large saucepan, covered, for 5 minutes, without allowing the onion to brown.

3 Drain the artichokes. Add to the pan, cover again and cook gently for a further 5–10 minutes. Stir from time to time during the cooking, and don't let the vegetables brown.

4 Stir in the stock or water and milk. Cover the pan and leave the soup to simmer for 20–30 minutes, until the artichokes are tender. Test by piercing them with a fork.

5 Purée the soup in a blender or food processor, then sieve for a really velvety texture. Season to taste with nutmeg, salt and pepper. Reheat gently without allowing it to boil.

6 Serve the soup in warmed bowls, each portion sprinkled with a few pine nuts in the centre.

V   CARROT AND GINGER SOUP   V

A delicately flavoured soup with a beautiful colour.

SERVES 4

1 onion, peeled and chopped
15 g/½ oz butter or vegan margarine
700 g/1½ lb carrots, scraped and sliced
1 teaspoon grated fresh ginger
salt and freshly ground black pepper
900 ml/1½ pints Light Vegetable Stock
    (p. 129) or water
TO GARNISH (OPTIONAL)
4 tablespoons single or non-dairy cream

1 Fry the onion gently in the butter or vegan margarine in a large saucepan, covered, for 5 minutes, without browning, then add the carrots, ginger and a sprinkling of salt. Cover and fry for a further 10 minutes, stir from time to time and do not allow the vegetables to brown.
2 Add the stock or water and bring to the boil, then simmer gently for about 15 minutes, until the carrots are tender. Purée the soup in a blender or food processor, then sieve.
3 Return the soup to the rinsed-out pan, reheat gently and season to taste with salt and pepper. Serve in warmed bowls, each topped with a spoonful of cream, if liked.

Variations

CARROT, APPLE AND GINGER SOUP

Make as described, adding 450 g/1 lb peeled, cored and chopped dessert apples with the carrots, increasing the amount of water to 1 litre/1¾ pints and adding 3 tablespoons sherry with the water. Serves 4–6.

CARROT, ORANGE AND CORIANDER SOUP

Add 1 tablespoon coarsely crushed coriander seeds and the thinly pared rind of 1 orange with the carrots. Flavour the puréed and sieved soup to taste with 2–3 tablespoons orange juice. This looks pretty with each portion of soup garnished with a scattering of shreds of pared orange rind.

SPICED PARSNIP SOUP

Use parsnips instead of carrots and add 1 tablespoon curry powder to the onions when you fry them. A swirl of single or non-dairy cream is good on top of this version, and add some crisp croûtons for extra flavour.

Light Vegetable Stock

Put an onion, a couple of garlic cloves, a celery stick, a carrot and a bouquet garni into a saucepan. Cover generously with water and bring to the boil. Simmer, half-covered, for about 1 hour, then strain.

Other vegetables and flavourings, such as leeks, thinly-pared lemon rind and allspice berries, can be added. Peelings from well-scrubbed potatoes also give a particularly pleasant flavour to vegetable stock.

Clockwise from right: Carrot and Ginger Soup; Corn Chowder (p. 135); Watercress Soup (p. 130)

V ## TOMATO SOUP WITH BASIL V

Made with fresh tomatoes and basil, this is one of the most
delicious soups, wonderful for supper in
the cool of a summer evening.

SERVES 4

Garnishes for Soup

□ Fresh parsley or chives, snipped,
on top of a bowl of soup, looks
attractive, tastes good and goes well
with most soups

□ Snip fresh basil over tomato soup,
mint over pea soup, dill or fennel
over cucumber soup

□ A swirl of single or soured cream
looks good on a dark soup such as
ruby-red beetroot soup, or on carrot
and ginger soup, or chilled avocado
soup

□ A few roughly chopped walnuts
or toasted flaked almonds or pine
nuts go well with creamy soups such
as cauliflower or Jerusalem artichoke

□ Wholewheat croûtons add a
pleasant crunch to vegetable soup.
Make these by frying 6 mm/¼ inch
dice of wholewheat bread in a little
oil until golden brown and crisp all
over; drain on kitchen paper

□ Top mushroom soup with a few
slices of fried mushroom, and
asparagus soup with one or two
asparagus tips, cooked at the
beginning of the soup-making
process and reserved

1 onion, peeled and chopped
15 g/½ oz butter or vegan margarine
350 g/12 oz potatoes, peeled and diced
450 g/1 lb tomatoes, skinned and sliced, or
    1 × 400-g/14-oz can tomatoes
900 ml/1½ pints Light Vegetable Stock
    (p. 129) or water
salt and freshly ground black pepper
TO GARNISH
basil sprigs

1 Fry the onion in the butter or vegan
margarine in a large saucepan, covered,
for 5 minutes, without browning.
2 Add the potatoes, cover again and
cook gently for a further 5–10 minutes,
then add the tomatoes and cook for a
further 4–5 minutes. Stir from time to
time and do not allow the vegetables to
brown.
3 Add the stock or water, cover the pan
and leave the soup to simmer for 15–20
minutes, until the potatoes are tender.
4 Purée the soup in a blender or food
processor and if you want it really
smooth, sieve it to remove the tomato
seeds – this isn't essential. Reheat the
soup gently without boiling.
5 Serve in warmed bowls, garnished
with basil sprigs.

V ## WATERCRESS SOUP V

The all-time most popular soup in my family, and very quick and
easy to make. I like to add the watercress at the end of cooking, as
this gives the soup a better flavour and colour. Most watercress
seems to come, stalks removed, in a packet; if you are using a
bunch of watercress with stems, separate the stems from the leafy
tops and cook the stems with the potatoes. Watercress soup, with
all its variations, is excellent served chilled, as well as hot.

SERVES 4

1 onion, peeled and chopped
15 g/½ oz butter or vegan margarine
700 g/1½ lb potatoes, peeled and diced
900 ml/1½ pints Light Vegetable Stock
    (p. 129) or water
1 bunch or packet of watercress
salt and freshly ground black pepper
3–4 tablespoons double or non-dairy cream,
    optional

1 Fry the onion in the butter or vegan
margarine in a large saucepan, covered,
for 5 minutes, without browning.
2 Add the potatoes, cover again and
cook gently for a further 5–10 minutes.
Stir from time to time and do not allow
the vegetables to brown.
3 Stir in the stock or water, cover the pan
and leave the soup to simmer for about 20
minutes, until the potatoes are tender.
4 Reserve 4 small watercress sprigs for
garnishing if liked, then liquidize the
soup with the rest of the watercress.
Season to taste with salt and pepper,
reheat without boiling and serve in
warmed bowls, each topped with a
swirl of double or non-dairy cream and a
watercress sprig if liked.

Variations

LETTUCE SOUP

For this delicious summer variation, omit the watercress, and cook 450 g/1 lb chopped outside lettuce leaves along with the potatoes. Some fresh chopped mint or parsley stirred in at the end of cooking is pleasant, and a little single or non-dairy cream swirled on top is even better.

SPINACH SOUP

Omit the watercress and cook 450 g/1 lb chopped spinach leaves with the potatoes. Flavour the soup with a little freshly grated nutmeg.

SORREL SOUP

A sharp, refreshing variation, made by substituting the watercress for 75 g/3 oz chopped sorrel leaves which are added with the potatoes. Season with plenty of salt, freshly ground black pepper and freshly grated nutmeg. A swirl of single, non-dairy or soured cream on top of each bowl makes this soup extra good.

FRESH HERB SOUP

For this fragrant variation, liquidize the soup with a small bunch of herbs instead of the watercress. Parsley, tarragon or chives are particularly good.

V ASPARAGUS SOUP V

This is a very good way of making full use of all the asparagus; the tips can be used as a luxurious garnish, or served at another meal in a dish such as Asparagus Tartlets (p. 263). Asparagus soup is also very good chilled.

SERVES 6

700 g/1½ lb asparagus, well-washed
2 onions, peeled and chopped
25 g/1 oz butter or vegan margarine
1.4 litres/2½ pints Light Vegetable Stock
(p. 129) or water
150 ml/5 fl oz single or non-dairy cream
salt and freshly ground black pepper

1 Cut the tips from the asparagus, then simmer these in 2.5 cm/1 inch boiling water for about 4 minutes, until tender.

2 Set the asparagus tips aside (in the pan) for garnishing, or drain and keep for another use. Cut the asparagus stalks into even-sized pieces.

3 Fry the onion in the butter or vegan margarine in a large saucepan, covered, for 5 minutes, without browning. Add the asparagus pieces and cook gently for a further 5–10 minutes.

4 Stir in the stock or water, cover the pan and leave the soup to simmer for about 30 minutes, until the asparagus pieces are very tender.

5 Liquidize the soup, then sieve. Return to the rinsed-out pan, add the cream, reheat without boiling and season to taste with salt and pepper. Reheat the asparagus tips, if used, then drain. Ladle the soup into warmed bowls and place the asparagus tips on top dividing them equally between the bowls.

CELERY AND STILTON SOUP

SERVES 4–6

1 head celery, tough outer stalks removed
1 onion, peeled and chopped
15 g / ½ oz butter
900 ml / 1 ½ pints Light Vegetable Stock
   (p. 129) or water
100 g / 4 oz Stilton cheese, grated
salt and freshly ground black pepper

1 Wash and chop the celery. Discard most of the leaves, reserving a few.
2 Fry the onion in the butter in a large saucepan, covered, for 5 minutes, without browning. Add the celery, cover again and cook gently for a further 5–10 minutes. Stir from time to time and do not allow the vegetables to brown.
3 Add the stock or water. Cover the pan and leave the soup to simmer for 30 minutes, until the celery is very tender.
4 Purée the soup, together with the cheese, in a blender or food processor, until smooth. Season to taste, return to the rinsed-out pan and reheat gently.
5 Serve the soup in warmed bowls and snip the reserved celery leaves on top.

Variations
CELERY AND CHESTNUT SOUP
For this vegan version, add 225 g / 8 oz fresh peeled chestnuts (p. 233) or the drained contents of a 400-g / 14-oz can of chestnuts to the onion with the celery. Use 1.2 litres / 2 pints liquid for this recipe.

CELERY AND PEAR SOUP WITH TARRAGON
Another vegan version which sounds strange but tastes good. Add 450 g / 1 lb pears, peeled, cored and diced, with the celery. Use 1.2 litres / 2 pints stock or water. Snip some fresh tarragon on top of the soup before serving.

CAULIFLOWER SOUP WITH CHEDDAR CHEESE
Use a medium–large cauliflower instead of the celery, and grated Cheddar cheese instead of the Stilton. A few chopped walnuts make a pleasant garnish.

MENU

A Japanese Meal

Miso Soup with Bean Curd

Vegetable Tempura with Dipping Sauce
198
Sweet Vinegared Rice
241
Stir-fried Carrots with Watercress and Sesame Seeds
181

Tangerine and Lychee Fruit Salad
286

V   # FRENCH ONION SOUP   V

This soup is very filling, and makes a good main course, followed by fruit or a light pudding.

SERVES 4–6

Dark Vegetable Stock

Wipe and chop 225 g / 8 oz mushrooms, then put them into a saucepan with a sliced onion, a bouquet garni and 1.2 litres / 2 pints water. Bring to the boil, then cover and simmer gently for 1 hour. Cool, then leave overnight before straining. This makes just under 900 ml / 1 ½ pints.

The water which vegetables have been cooked in makes good stock and contains useful nutrients. Strain it into an old jug, cool and keep in the fridge for 2–3 days.

900 g / 2 lb onions, peeled and thinly sliced
2 tablespoons oil
4 teaspoons sugar
salt and freshly ground black pepper
1.8 litres / 3 pints Dark Vegetable Stock
   (left)
2 garlic cloves, crushed
a few drops of lemon juice
TO GARNISH
chopped parsley or chives

1 Fry the onions in the oil in a large saucepan for 10 minutes until soft. Add the sugar and salt and pepper to taste and fry for a further 15–20 minutes, until the onions are a deep golden-brown, but don't let them burn.
2 Add the stock, garlic, and lemon juice. Bring the soup to the boil and let it simmer for about 10 minutes. Check the seasoning and serve in warmed bowls, sprinkled with parsley or chives.

Variations
GOLDEN ONION SOUP
Make as described, adding 3 tablespoons sherry and 2–3 tablespoons Dijon mustard along with the stock.

FRENCH ONION SOUP GRATINÉE

Ladle the soup into a warmed heatproof tureen (or large casserole dish) or individual bowls for this non-vegan version.

Top with a slice of French bread for each person sprinkled with about 25 g / 1 oz grated cheese per person. Place under a hot grill until the cheese is melted and golden-brown.

V

MISO SOUP WITH BEAN CURD

V

This Japanese soup is light but sustaining, and has a savoury flavour. It is particularly good as part of a Japanese menu, perhaps followed by Vegetable Tempura with Dipping Sauce (p. 198) and Sweet Vinegared Rice (p. 241).

SERVES 4

300 g / 10 oz firm bean curd (tofu, p. 108)
2 spring onions, trimmed and finely chopped
900 ml / 1½ pints Light Vegetable Stock
(p. 129)
4 tablespoons miso (right)
1 teaspoon soy sauce

1 Cut the bean curd into 16 equal cubes and divide between warmed soup bowls. Divide the spring onion between the bowls, too.
2 Heat the stock in a saucepan, then take out a little and blend with the miso, to soften it and give a creamy consistency. Tip this back into the saucepan with the rest of the stock.
3 Bring the soup almost to the boil, but do not let it boil, or valuable enzymes in the miso will be destroyed. Add the soy sauce, then pour the soup into the bowls on top of the bean curd and spring onion. Serve immediately.

Variation
MISO SOUP WITH BEAN CURD AND WAKAME

This is made exactly as described, except that wakame seaweed (p. 81) is added to the bowls. Soak 4 pieces of wakame in cold water for 10 minutes, then cut out the spine and any hard pieces and snip the wakame into rough pieces with kitchen scissors. Put into the bowls along with the bean curd and spring onion. Serve the soup immediately.

Miso

Miso is a thick brown paste made by fermenting soya beans, barley or rice under pressure for up to 2 years, then adding a little salt. Miso is rich in nutrients, including protein and B vitamins. There are various types: light coloured miso has a more delicate flavour than darker ones, but they all have a deliciously savoury taste and are useful in soups, casseroles, sauces and gravies. Miso should be added at the end of cooking time to conserve the vitamins.

Miso Soup with Bean Curd; Vegetable Tempura with Dipping Sauce (p. 198), Sweet Vinegared Rice (p. 241)

V LEEK AND POTATO SOUP V
_____

This makes a thick soup, a real meal in itself on a cold day. For a
lighter result, add enough extra stock or water to give the
consistency you want. For real luxury, add an extra spoonful or
two of cream and top with some snipped chives.

SERVES 4–6

Main Course Soup

Some soups make warming and satisfying main courses, especially welcome for a winter lunch or Sunday supper round the fire. The thick bean and lentil soups, and those which contain cheese, such as Celery and Stilton (p. 132) and Cauliflower and Cheddar (p. 132), make a filling meal with just some warm crusty bread or rolls, or (especially with lentil soup) Garlic Bread (p. 137). I like French onion soup with a small side salad or some crudités; grated cheese is good on top of tomato soup or thick leek and potato soup, and for a really hearty meal, add tasty wholewheat dumplings to vegetable soup.

Lentil Soup Ideas

Lentil soup lends itself to experimentation. Here are some ideas:

Fry 1–2 teaspoons curry powder with the onions when making the soup; purée the soup with 25 g/1 oz coconut cream.

Fry an onion and some garlic, and perhaps a teaspoon of ground cumin, in a little butter or vegan margarine and add to the soup after puréeing.

Garnish with plenty of chopped parsley or some croûtons made as described on p. 130 and tossed in a little curry powder or crushed garlic.

3 leeks, washed and sliced
700 g/1½ lb potatoes, peeled and diced
25 g/1 oz butter or vegan margarine
1 litre/1¾ pints Light Vegetable Stock
*   (p. 129) or water*
3–4 tablespoons double cream or non-dairy
*   cream (optional)*
salt and freshly ground black pepper
TO GARNISH (OPTIONAL)
chopped parsley

1 Fry the leeks and potatoes very gently in the butter or vegan margarine in a large saucepan, covered, for 10 minutes, stirring often.

2 Cook gently, without browning, still covered, for a further 10 minutes, stirring from time to time to prevent vegetables sticking to the pan.

3 Add the stock or water, stir, then simmer for 5–10 minutes, until the vegetables are tender.

4 Purée, in a blender or food processor, adding the cream if using. Season to taste with salt and pepper, stir, and serve in warmed bowls, sprinkled with a little chopped parsley, if used.

Variation
VICHYSSOISE
For this creamy, chilled version of Leek and Potato Soup, purée the mixture, adding 300 ml/10 fl oz milk or soya milk and 300 ml/10 fl oz single or non-dairy cream. Sieve, then chill the soup. Season carefully with salt, pepper and grated nutmeg. Serve in chilled bowls, sprinkled with snipped chives. Serves 8.

V GOLDEN LENTIL SOUP V
_____

A satisfying, comforting soup which makes an excellent cheap,
filling main course with crusty wholewheat rolls or garlic bread. If
you have a pressure-cooker, you can make it in about 10 minutes.

SERVES 4

1 large onion, peeled and chopped
15 g/½ oz butter or vegan margarine
225 g/8 oz split red lentils
1 litre/1¾ pints Light Vegetable Stock
*   (p. 129) or water*
1–2 teaspoons lemon juice
salt and freshly ground black pepper
TO DECORATE
lemon butterflies

1 Fry the onion in the butter or vegan margarine in a saucepan or pressure-cooker pan, for 10 minutes, until it is soft

but has not browned.
2 Add the lentils and stir for 1–2 minutes, then add the stock or water. Bring to the boil, then half cover the pan and leave the soup to simmer gently for 20 minutes, until the lentils are very tender and pale-coloured. Or cook in a pressure-cooker for 5 minutes.
3 Beat the soup with a spoon to break up the lentils and make it smoother, or purée in a blender or food processor. Add the lemon juice and salt and pepper to taste. Decorate with lemon butterflies to serve.

ROASTED HAZELNUT SOUP

V   V

SERVES 4

1 onion, peeled and chopped
25 g/1 oz butter or vegan margarine
450 g/1 lb potatoes, peeled and diced
1 garlic clove, crushed
salt and freshly ground black pepper
900 ml/1½ pints Light Vegetable Stock
 (p. 129) or water
90 g/3½ oz roasted, skinned hazelnuts
 (p. 37), finely ground
1 tablespoon lemon juice
TO GARNISH
a few chopped, roasted hazelnuts
chopped chives

1 Fry the onion in the butter or vegan margarine for 5 minutes, until lightly browned, then add the potato, garlic and a little salt and pepper. Cook gently, covered, for a further 5–10 minutes.

2 Add the stock or water, bring to the boil, then leave to simmer gently for 15–20 minutes, until the potatoes and onion are tender. Purée the soup in a blender or food processor and stir in the ground hazelnuts, lemon juice and salt and pepper to taste.

3 Serve the soup in warmed bowls, each topped with a sprinkling of chopped hazelnuts and chives.

Variation

ALMOND SOUP
Use ground almonds instead of hazelnuts.

Dumplings for Soup

Put 175 g/6 oz plain wholewheat flour into a mixing bowl with 1½ teaspoons baking powder, ½ teaspoon salt and 65 g/2½ oz grated hard butter. Mix well. Dissolve 1 teaspoon yeast extract in 2 tablespoons water and add to the flour mixture, then add more water, just enough to make a soft dough. Form the mixture into 8 dumplings, then drop them into half a panful of gently simmering water for 20 minutes, until puffed up. Remove with a slotted spoon and serve them in a vegetable soup.

CORN CHOWDER

V   V

This thick and filling soup is most delicious when made with fresh sweetcorn, cut from the husk with a sharp knife (one husk will yield about 100 g/4 oz corn), but frozen sweetcorn kernels are a very good alternative. The chowder can be made just with stock or water, which is my preference, or with half milk (or soya milk) and water.

SERVES 4

1 onion, peeled and sliced
700 g/1½ lb potatoes, peeled and diced
25 g/1 oz butter or vegan margarine
salt and freshly ground black pepper
900 ml/1½ pints Light Vegetable Stock
 (p. 129) or water
350 g/12 oz sweetcorn kernels, fresh or
 frozen

1 Fry the onion and potatoes very gently in the butter or vegan margarine in a large saucepan, covered, for 10 minutes, stirring often.

2 Season to taste with salt and pepper, stir, then cook gently, still covered, for 10 minutes, stirring often. It doesn't matter if the vegetables brown slightly, but don't let them get too brown.

3 Add the stock or water, stir, then simmer for 5–10 minutes, until the potatoes are almost tender. Add the sweetcorn and cook for a further 5 minutes. Check the seasoning and adjust if necessary.

4 Serve the chowder as it is, in warmed bowls, or purée 1–2 cupfuls in a blender or food processor, then add to the rest of the chowder. This thickens the liquid and gives a pleasantly creamy texture.

Left to right: Golden Lentil Soup (p. 134); Pistou; Roasted Hazelnut Soup (p. 135)

V

PISTOU

V

A wonderful, easy-to-make and very filling vegetable soup from southern France. Serve it with crusty bread for a complete main course. If you're using dried beans, you need to soak and cook them first. This soup reheats well and tastes even better the next day.

SERVES 4

1 onion, peeled and chopped
2 tablespoons olive oil
100 g/4 oz haricot beans, soaked and cooked, or 1 × 425-g/15-oz can cannellini beans, drained
2 carrots, scraped and diced
2 potatoes, peeled and diced
3 leeks or courgettes, washed and sliced
1 × 425-g/15-oz can tomatoes
2 garlic cloves, crushed
1–2 tablespoons chopped fresh basil or 1 teaspoon dried basil
salt and freshly ground black pepper
1 litre/1¾ pints Light Vegetable Stock (p. 129) or water
50 g/2 oz thin pasta or pasta shapes

1 Fry the onion in the oil in a large saucepan for 5 minutes, then add the drained haricot beans, all the vegetables, the garlic, the dried basil, if used, and salt and pepper to taste, and cook for a further 5 minutes.

2 Add the stock or water, cover and simmer for 20–30 minutes, then add the pasta and cook for a further 10 minutes. If you're using fresh basil, add this now and check the seasoning. Serve the soup in warmed bowls.

Variations
VEGETABLE AND LENTIL SOUP
Use continental lentils instead of dried beans. Omit the pasta, or not, depending on how hearty you want the soup to be.

SIMPLE VEGETABLE SOUP
For this lighter version (which makes a good basis for dumplings, p. 135) make as described, but omit the haricot or cannellini beans and pasta.

V   CREAM OF MUSHROOM SOUP   V

A few dried Italian mushrooms intensify the flavour of this soup and make it extra good for a special occasion. They are horribly expensive to buy, but they keep well and a few of them go a long way. Soak about 25 g/1 oz in 600 ml/1 pint boiling water for about 30 minutes, then remove and chop the mushrooms and add to the fresh mushrooms. Use the soaking water as part of the water or stock.

SERVES 4

1 onion, peeled and finely chopped
25 g/1 oz butter or vegan margarine
350 g/12 oz mushrooms, washed and finely chopped
1 tablespoon plain flour
600 ml/1 pint Dark Vegetable Stock (p. 132) or water
300 ml/10 fl oz milk or soya milk
salt and freshly ground black pepper
freshly grated nutmeg
dash of lemon juice
2–3 perfect button mushrooms, thinly sliced and fried in butter or vegan margarine

1 Fry the onion in the butter or vegan margarine in a large saucepan, covered, for 5 minutes, without browning.
2 Add the mushrooms, cover again and cook gently for a further 5 minutes. Stir in the flour and cook for 1–2 minutes.
3 Stir in the stock or water and the milk, cover the pan and leave the soup to simmer for 15–20 minutes.
4 Check the seasoning, adding grated nutmeg to taste and a dash of lemon juice. Serve in warmed bowls, with a few slices of fried mushroom on top of each.

Garlic Bread

Crisp, hot garlic bread goes well with many soups and also with salads, and it's easy to make. Make slices in a French stick 2.5 cm/1 inch apart, cutting almost through so that the slices are still joined at the base. Beat 2–3 crushed garlic cloves into 100 g/4 oz butter or vegan margarine and spread this on both sides of the slices of bread. Push the slices together to re-form the loaf, then wrap it in foil. Place on a baking tray and bake for about 20 minutes at 200 C/400 F/Gas Mark 6 for about 20 minutes, until the bread has heated through and the butter melted. Serve immediately.

V   CHILLED RASPBERRY SOUP   V

Fruit soups, such as this, are popular in Europe and Scandinavia, and make an attractive and refreshing start to a summer meal.

SERVES 4

750 g/1½ lb fresh or frozen raspberries
100 g/4 oz sugar
450 ml/16 fl oz water
6 teaspoons potato flour or cornflour
3 tablespoons port
3 tablespoons fresh orange juice
TO GARNISH
4 tablespoons soured or non-dairy cream

1 Put the raspberries into a saucepan with the sugar and water. Heat gently until the sugar has dissolved, then cook over a gentle heat for 5–10 minutes, until the raspberries are very soft.
2 Purée the soup in a blender or food processor, then return to the rinsed-out pan and reheat gently.
3 Blend the potato flour or cornflour to a smooth paste with the port and orange juice, then pour the mixture into the soup, stirring all the time. Stir over a gentle heat until thickened, then remove from the heat and allow to cool.
4 Taste and add more sugar if necessary, then pour into a bowl, cover and chill.
5 Serve the soup in chilled bowls, each topped with a swirl of cream.

Variation
CHILLED BLACK CHERRY SOUP
Use 3 × 425-g/15-oz cans black cherries. Remove the stones from the cherries, then put them into a saucepan with their liquid and 50 g/2 oz sugar and bring to the boil. Blend the potato flour or cornflour with the port and orange juice and continue as described.

Serving Chilled Soup

For a dramatic presentation, ideal for a special summer dinner, stand each bowl of chilled soup in an outer bowl of crushed ice.

V ICED BEETROOT SOUP V
WITH DILL

Although it's wonderful cold, this soup, incidentally, is also very
good served hot. Use cooked beetroot without vinegar (see p. 67
for cooking beetroot). Serve with hot Herb and Onion Bread (p. 328).

SERVES 4–6

1 onion, peeled and chopped
1 tablespoon oil
225 g/8 oz potatoes, peeled and diced
450 g/1 lb cooked beetroot, peeled and diced
1.2 litres/2 pints Light Vegetable Stock
  (p. 129) or water
grated rind of ½ lemon
1 tablespoon lemon juice
salt and freshly ground black pepper
TO GARNISH
3 tablespoons single or non-dairy cream
dill sprigs

1 Fry the onion in the oil in a large
saucepan, covered, for 5 minutes, without browning. Add the potatoes, cover
again and cook gently for a further 5–10
minutes.
2 Add the beetroot and stock or water.
Bring to the boil, then cover the pan and
leave the soup to simmer for about 20
minutes, until the potatoes are tender.
3 Purée the soup in a blender or food
processor, then add the lemon rind and
juice, and salt and pepper to taste. Allow
to cool, then pour into a bowl, cover and
chill until ice-cold.
4 Serve the soup in chilled bowls, each
topped with a swirl of cream and a small
sprig of dill.

V CHILLED AVOCADO SOUP V

One of the easiest soups to make, with a beautiful colour. It's best
to make it no more than 1 hour in advance, in case it discolours.

SERVES 6

2 large ripe avocado pears
1 small onion, peeled and roughly chopped
1 garlic clove, crushed
2 tablespoons lemon juice
900 ml/1½ pints Light Vegetable Stock
  (p. 129) or water
1 tablespoon red wine vinegar
salt and freshly ground black pepper
TO GARNISH (OPTIONAL)
6 tablespoons soured or non-dairy cream
1–2 tablespoons snipped chives

1 Halve the avocado pears and remove
the stones and skin. Cut the flesh into
chunks and purée in a blender or food
processor with the onion, garlic, lemon
juice and about a third of the stock or
water.
2 Add the rest of the stock or water and
blend again until very smooth.
3 Add the vinegar and season carefully to
taste with salt and pepper, then pour into
a bowl and cover. Allow to cool, then
chill.
4 Check the seasoning, then serve in
chilled bowls, each topped with a swirl of
soured or non-dairy cream and/or
chives, if liked.

Variation
CHILLED CUCUMBER AND
YOGURT SOUP
Make as described, using a peeled and
cubed cucumber instead of the avocado
and 450 g/16 oz plain live or vegan
yogurt and 2–3 tablespoons double or
non-dairy cream instead of the stock.
Garnish with chopped fresh mint.

Chilled Two-colour Soup

V   CHILLED TWO-COLOUR SOUP   V

This stunning vegetable soup is made from leeks, carrots and
potatoes. Make it well in advance, so it is thoroughly chilled, and
pour into bowls just before serving.

SERVES 8

350 g/12 oz sliced leeks, white part only
450 g/1 lb carrots, scraped and diced
1 onion, peeled and chopped
350 g/12 oz potato, peeled and diced
1.2 litres/2 pints water
50 g/2 oz butter or vegan margarine
2 tablespoons double or non-dairy cream
salt and freshly ground black pepper
TO GARNISH
8 small mint sprigs

1 Put the leeks into one large saucepan
and the carrots into another. Divide the
onion, potato and water between the
saucepans, cover and simmer until
tender.
2 Purée each mixture separately, adding
half the butter or vegan margarine to
each. Add the cream to the leek mixture.
3 Season both mixtures, then put each
soup into a separate jug and chill.

4 To serve, pour the soup into chilled
bowls, holding one jug at each side of the
bowl, and pouring from both at the same
time, so that there is one colour in each
half of the bowl, as illustrated. Top each
bowl with a mint sprig.

Variation

CHILLED TWO-COLOUR BEETROOT AND POTATO SOUP

For this colourful variation, omit the carrots and use instead 450 g/1 lb cooked,
skinned beetroot. Purée the cooked beetroot as above, then flavour the beetroot
mixture with a little lemon juice. Continue with the other ingredients as above.
Chill the jugs of soup, then serve as
above, carefully pouring from each jug.
Decorate each bowl of soup with some
fresh dill sprigs just before serving.

POURING TWO-COLOUR
SOUP

Pour the soups into the bowl from
jugs at either side of the bowl,
pouring from both at the same time,
to create a two-colour effect with
one colour in each half of the bowl.

First Course Dishes

First courses are rewarding to make because they can be perfect little works of art, with plenty of scope for imaginative use of colour, flavourings and garnishes. This chapter contains a range of possibilities for both first courses and nibbles. You'll also find recipes in other sections (particularly Salads (pp. 154–169), Accompanying Vegetables (pp. 180–191), Main Vegetable Dishes (pp. 192–203), and Pasta (pp. 250–259) which, served in small portions, make equally tempting first courses. Similarly, many of the first courses in this section make good light main courses, if served with suitable accompaniments such as warm bread or rolls.

STUFFING VINE LEAVES

1 Place a vine leaf on a flat surface, shiny side down

2 Place a spoonful of filling close to its base

3 Fold the lowest pair of leaf sections over the filling, then fold in the middle sections and roll up the leaf

THREE-COLOUR LAYERED OMELETTE

This is easy to make and very effective, either sliced into bite-sized pieces as a nibble, or into larger pieces and served with a sauce as a first course. It can be made in advance.

SERVES 6–8 AS A FIRST COURSE, 12 AS A NIBBLE

1 tomato, skinned and chopped
1 small red pepper, de-seeded and chopped
50 g/2 oz butter
175 g/6 oz mushrooms, wiped and finely chopped
225 g/8 oz frozen chopped spinach, thawed
6 eggs
salt and freshly ground black pepper

1 Fry the tomato and pepper gently in 15 g/½ oz of the butter in a small saucepan for about 5 minutes, until tender, then purée in a blender or food processor.
2 Fry the mushrooms in another 15 g/½ oz of the butter for 2–3 minutes, until they are just tender.
3 Squeeze all excess water out of the spinach.
4 Have three bowls ready and break 2 eggs into each. Beat, then add the spinach to one, the mushrooms to another, and the red pepper mixture to the third. Season all three mixtures to taste with salt and pepper.
5 Melt one-third of the remaining butter in a small frying pan (p. 25). When it's hot, pour in the spinach-flavoured mixture.
6 Cook until it's set on the bottom, then reduce the heat, cover and cook until the top is set – about 5 minutes.
7 Lift the omelette out with a spatula and put it, moist side uppermost, on to a large plate.
8 Make an omelette with the red pepper mixture in the same way, then turn it out on top of the spinach omelette, moist side down.
9 Repeat the process with the mushroom mixture, then press the layered omelette down lightly all over and leave to cool completely – about 1 hour.
10 Cut the omelette into bite-sized or larger slices as required and place them sideways on a plate to show off the coloured stripes.

V   STUFFED VINE LEAVES WITH   V
YOGURT DIP

These make a light and refreshing first course or nibble with drinks:
serve the vine leaves on a large plate or in a flat basket, with
the yogurt dip in the middle.

MAKES ABOUT 36

36 fresh vine leaves or a package of preserved
   vine leaves
225 g/8 oz long-grain brown rice
1 large onion, peeled and chopped
2 tablespoons chopped parsley
2 tomatoes, skinned and chopped
50 g/2 oz pine nuts
50 g/2 oz raisins
½ teaspoon ground cinnamon or allspice
2 garlic cloves, crushed
salt and freshly ground black pepper
6 tablespoons olive oil
150 ml/5 fl oz water
juice of 1–2 lemons
TO SERVE
Yogurt and Mint Dressing (p. 156)
lemon slices

1 If you're using preserved vine leaves,
drain them and rinse under the cold tap,
then drain again.

2 For fresh vine leaves, half fill a large
saucepan with water and bring it to the
boil. Trim the stems off the leaves, then
put into the boiling water, cover and
simmer for 2 minutes. Drain and refresh
under the cold tap and drain again.

3 Half fill a large saucepan with water,
add the rice and boil for 10 minutes, then
drain and mix with the onion, parsley,
tomatoes, pine nuts, raisins, cinnamon or
allspice, garlic and salt and pepper to
taste.

4 Place a heaped teaspoon of the filling
on each leaf, fold the edges over and place
the little bundles side by side in a frying
pan with a lid. If there are some leaves left
over, use them to fill in any gaps.

5 Mix together the oil and water and
pour over the vine leaves. Sprinkle a little
lemon juice on top.

6 Cook, covered, over a very gentle heat
for 2–2½ hours until the rice and leaves
are tender. Keep an eye on the water
level, and add a little more from time to
time if necessary. Cool, then chill.

7 Arrange the stuffed vine leaves on a
large plate or in a shallow basket with the
bowl of Yogurt and Mint Dressing in the
middle to dip the stuffed vine leaves into.
Garnish with lemon slices.

Stuffed Vine Leaves with Yogurt Dip;
Soured Cream Dressing (p. 156); Flaky
Spinach and Fennel Pastries (p. 151)

V   # SUSHI   V

Creamy-coloured rice with a deep purple wrapping of nori makes piquant, intriguing-looking morsels to have with drinks, or they can be served as part of a Japanese meal. Serve them arranged around the dipping sauce, on a small tray or flat plate.

MAKES ABOUT 20

Umeboshi Plums

A popular ingredient in Japanese and macrobiotic cooking, umeboshi plums are plums which have been pickled for at least two years. During this time they develop lactic acid which makes them a particularly healthy ingredient, cleansing the gut and aiding digestion. They have a sharp, pungent, salty flavour and can be added to dishes – particularly grain dishes – or served alongside.

2 sheets of nori (p. 81)
½ quantity Sweet Vinegared Rice (p. 241)
100 g/4 oz cooked spinach, fresh or frozen, drained and chopped
1 umeboshi plum (left), stone removed, flesh chopped
FOR THE DIP
2 teaspoons Dijon mustard
6 tablespoons shoyu (p. 184)
TO GARNISH
radish flowers (p. 164)

1 Toast the nori sheets on both sides by holding them above a gas flame or electric hot plate until they become crisp.
2 Put one of the nori sheets on a Japanese mat or double layer of kitchen paper and spread with half the rice, taking it to within 1 cm/½ inch of the top of the nori. Place the spinach on top of the rice in a horizontal strip about 1 cm/½ inch from the bottom of the nori.

3 Starting from the bottom, carefully roll up the nori so that the spinach is enclosed and the rice and nori rolled round, like a Swiss roll.
4 Press the roll firmly together and bang each end on the work surface to firm them up. Leave the roll for 20 minutes (or longer) to settle.
5 Using a sharp knife, carefully cut the roll crossways into 1-cm/½-inch slices.
6 Repeat the process with the second piece of nori and the rest of the rice, using the chopped umeboshi plum instead of the spinach.
7 To make the dip, put the mustard into a bowl and gradually blend in the shoyu, to give a smooth consistency. Put the mixture into a small bowl, place in the centre of a small tray or large plate and arrange the sushi around, alternating the 2 types of filling. Garnish with a radish flower.

MAKING SUSHI

1 Lay the nori on a raffia mat, place the filling on top

2 Roll up, using the mat to help make a good shape

3 Cut into 1-cm/½-inch slices and place on a serving plate

Sushi; Three-colour Layered Omelette (p. 140)

CHEESE AND FRESH HERB DIP

This is a simple dip which is popular with children. We sometimes eat it with crudités (right) for a weekend lunch, with perhaps a vegetable soup as a first course.

SERVES 4

40 g / 1½ oz soft butter
150 g / 5 oz vegetarian Cheddar cheese, grated
6 tablespoons milk
3–4 drops Tabasco sauce
salt and freshly ground black pepper
1 tablespoon chopped fresh herbs, such as chives, chervil or parsley
TO GARNISH
1 chervil sprig

1 Cream the butter, then gradually add the cheese and milk, beating until smooth and soft; or blend in a blender or food processor.
2 Add the Tabasco sauce and salt and pepper to taste. Stir in the chopped fresh herbs and mix well. Transfer the dip to a small bowl, smooth the surface slightly with a fork or the back of a spoon and serve, garnished with chervil.

Cheese and Fresh Herb Dip

LITTLE ASPARAGUS TIMBALES WITH FRESH TOMATO SAUCE

An attractive first course, pretty to look at, easy to make, light yet filling to eat. If you have some Fresh Tomato Sauce in the freezer, the dish can be assembled very quickly.

SERVES 4

200-g / 7-oz packet frozen asparagus
150 ml / 5 fl oz single cream
2 eggs
salt and freshly ground black pepper
grated nutmeg
butter for greasing
TO SERVE
1 quantity Fresh Tomato Sauce (p. 170)

1 Preheat the oven to 170 C / 325 F / Gas Mark 3. Grease four 100-ml / 4-fl oz dariole moulds thoroughly with a little butter.
2 Cook the asparagus as described on the packet; drain thoroughly.
3 Remove the four best asparagus tips, cutting them to fit into the base of the dariole moulds. Reserve.
4 Purée the stems, and the rest of the asparagus, with the cream and eggs, in a blender or food processor.

5 Season the purée with salt, freshly ground black pepper and a little grated nutmeg.
6 Pour the asparagus purée into the dariole moulds. Cover the top of each mould with foil.
7 Put the darioles into a roasting tin; pour boiling water into the tin so that it comes halfway up the moulds. Place the tin in the oven.
8 Bake the timbales for about 40 minutes, until they are firm in the centre and a knife comes out clean.
9 While the timbales are cooking, heat the sauce.
10 Slip a knife round the edges of the timbales to loosen, then turn them out on to warmed plates and pour a little of the sauce round. Place one of the reserved asparagus tips on top of each mould. Serve at once.

Crudités

Crudités are popular with most people and served with a piquant dip make a refreshing and easy-going starter, and are useful for serving with drinks. Choose really crisp, fresh vegetables in contrasting colours and flavours. Have at least three different types, arranged in little heaps on a leaf-lined plate or tray, or pile them up in a small basket with the dips arranged around the outside. The basic preparation of the vegetables can be done several hours in advance and the vegetables kept in a polythene bag in the salad compartment of the fridge until needed, but it is best to cut vegetables into matchsticks just before you want to serve them. Some possibilities are:

□ Ruby-red radishes, with the root trimmed but the leaves left on
□ Spring onions, trimmed
□ Matchsticks of scraped carrot
□ Matchsticks of crisp celery
□ Matchsticks of red, green or yellow pepper, or cucumber
□ Sprigs of cauliflower – especially good for scooping up dips
□ Crisp chicory leaves
□ Large juicy black olives
□ Cherry tomatoes
□ Baby button mushrooms

V   # HUMMUS   V

Served with warm wholewheat pitta bread or some raw salad
items, such as raw cauliflower florets, celery, carrot and spring
onion, for dipping in the mixture, this delectable creamy dip makes
a filling main meal for two.

SERVES 4

*225 g/8 oz dried chick peas, soaked and
    cooked, or 1 × 425-g/15-oz can chick peas*
½ garlic clove, crushed
1 tablespoon light sesame cream (tahini)
3 tablespoons olive oil
2 tablespoons lemon juice
salt and freshly ground black pepper
TO GARNISH
olive oil
paprika pepper (optional)
black olives
lemon wedges

1 Drain the chick peas, reserving the
liquid. Put the chick peas into a blender
or food processor with all the other
ingredients and blend until the mixture is
smooth.
2 Alternatively, mash the chick peas as
smoothly as possible and then beat in the
other ingredients to make a smoothish
mixture. Add enough of the reserved
cooking liquid to give a light, soft consistency like softly whipped cream.
3 Spoon the hummus on to a plate and
level it with a knife so that it is about
1 cm/½ inch deep. Pour a little olive oil
over the top, then sprinkle with paprika,
if using, and garnish with lemon wedges
and olives.

V   # GUACAMOLE   V

The chilli pepper in this smooth green dip gives it quite a kick;
leave it out for a less hot version. As well as being a delicious starter
or dip for serving with drinks, Guacamole makes an excellent
vegan alternative to mayonnaise.

SERVES 6–8 AS A FIRST COURSE

*2 ripe avocado pears, halved, peeled and
    stones removed*
2 tablespoons lemon or fresh lime juice
1 small onion, peeled
2 tomatoes, skinned and de-seeded
1 garlic clove
1 small green chilli pepper, de-seeded
a few coriander or parsley sprigs
salt and freshly ground black pepper
TO GARNISH
mild paprika pepper (optional)
parsley sprig

1 Mash the avocado with the lemon or
lime juice, then finely chop the rest of the

ingredients and add, mixing well.
2 Check the seasoning, then spoon into a
small bowl, smooth the top and sprinkle
with paprika, if wished. Garnish with a
parsley sprig.

Variation
AVOCADO CREAM
For this mild, creamy, non-vegan variation, omit the onion, tomatoes and chilli
pepper. Add 225 g/8 oz curd cheese to
the mashed avocado and other ingredients. Mix well until smooth and light.
Garnish with coriander, parsley or
chopped chives.

V *Guacamole (p. 144); Aubergine Dip; Hummus (p. 144)*

V

AUBERGINE DIP

Aubergines make an excellent dip, moist yet with body, and there are a number of classic versions. Here is the simplest of these. Some crisp Melba Toast (p. 146) goes well with this dip.

SERVES 6–8

2 aubergines, total weight about 450 g / 1 lb, washed
4 tablespoons lemon juice
4 tablespoons olive oil
4 tablespoons chopped parsley
1–2 garlic cloves, crushed
salt and freshly ground black pepper
TO GARNISH
chopped parsley
lemon wedges (optional)
extra olive oil
TO SERVE
Melba Toast (p. 146) or Crudités (p. 143)

1 Preheat the oven to 200 C / 400 F / Gas Mark 6. Put the aubergines on a baking sheet and bake for about 40 minutes, until soft. Remove from the oven and leave until completely cold.

2 Remove the stalks from the aubergines (use a cloth or gloves to avoid getting the little prickles in your hands – they can be extraordinarily difficult to get out).

3 Purée the aubergine in a blender or food processor with the lemon juice, oil, parsley and garlic (or chop the aubergine very finely by hand, then mash and mix in the other ingredients). Season to taste with salt and pepper.

4 Serve the dip on individual plates, garnished with parsley, lemon wedges, if wished, and olive oil. Or spoon it into a small bowl and garnish before serving with Melba Toast.

Aubergine Dip Ideas

Aubergine dip has a delicate flavour which can be intensified in various ways.

Try adding a tablespoon of tahini to the dip before puréeing; garnish with toasted sesame seeds.

For a smoky, 'mock caviar' version, grill the aubergine for 20–30 minutes until charred all over. Scrape off the charred skin, rinse the aubergine, then continue as described in the recipe.

V   RED PEPPER AND ALMOND DIP   V

SERVES 6

Serving Dips

Serve small quantities of 3 or more contrasting dips, say beige-cream Hummus (p. 144), Red Pepper and Almond Dip (right), pale green Guacamole (p. 144) and golden Cheese Dip (p. 143), on individual plates, or in bowls on a wicker tray, surrounded by an equally colourful selection of crudités and some big juicy black olives and lemon wedges.

Any of these dips make excellent fillings or toppings for skinned and hollowed-out tomatoes, lightly fried cup mushrooms (with the stalks removed) or artichoke hearts. A selection of quickly made (or bought) dips, together with a couple of different cheeses, a basket of warm, assorted rolls and a simple fresh crisp salad – say lettuce, tomato wedges, cucumber and onion rings – with fresh fruit to follow, and good coffee, makes a delicious spur-of-the-moment lunch.

2 large red peppers, total weight about 300 g/ 10 oz
4 garlic cloves
50 g/2 oz ground almonds
3 tablespoons oil
salt and freshly ground black pepper
TO GARNISH
extra ground almonds
red pepper strips

1 Put the whole peppers and garlic cloves into a saucepan and half cover with cold water. Bring to the boil, then simmer for 15–20 minutes until very tender. Drain and remove the pepper stems and seeds. Pop the garlic cloves out of their skins.

2 Purée the peppers and garlic in a blender or food processor, together with the ground almonds and oil, to make a smooth cream. Season to taste with salt and pepper. Turn into a small bowl and garnish with ground almonds sprinkled around the edge and in 3 lines across the dip, and with red pepper strips placed at one side.

ROQUEFORT DIP

SERVES 4

100 g/4 oz Roquefort cheese
150 ml/5 fl oz soured cream
freshly ground black pepper
TO SERVE
Crudités (p. 143)

1 Mash the cheese in a small bowl, then gradually stir in the soured cream. Add a grinding or two of black pepper, to taste.

2 Serve in a small bowl, with fresh crisp Crudités for dipping.

V   MUSHROOM AND HERB TERRINE   V

SERVES 6

Melba Toast

This thin, crisp toast goes well with many dips. It can be made a few hours in advance and kept in an airtight tin until needed. It's easiest to make using bread from a sliced loaf. Toast the bread on both sides, then with a sharp knife cut through the bread to split each slice in half, making each into two thin slices. Place the bread slices, untoasted side up, on a grill pan and grill until crisp and browned: the edges will curl up. Transfer to a wire rack and leave to cool completely.

700 g/1½ lb small firm button mushrooms, washed
50 g/2 oz butter or vegan margarine
1 tablespoon chopped fresh herbs, such as chives, parsley or chervil
salt and freshly ground black pepper
TO GARNISH
rosemary sprigs
tiny lemon wedges

1 Remove one or two perfect mushrooms and slice; set aside for garnishing. Grate the rest of the mushrooms in a food processor, or finely chop them by hand.

2 Heat the butter or vegan margarine in a large saucepan and quickly fry the reserved sliced mushrooms for about 2 minutes, then remove from the pan and set aside.

3 Fry the rest of the mushrooms over a moderate heat for about 15 minutes, until all the liquid has evaporated. Add the herbs and salt and pepper to taste.

4 Press into an oiled and base-lined 450-g/1-lb loaf tin, cover with greaseproof paper, top with a weight and leave until completely cold. Turn out and slice carefully. Garnish with the reserved mushroom slices, rosemary and lemon wedges.

STRIPY VEGETABLE TERRINE

This pretty terrine, with its delicate texture and flavour, makes a
perfect first course. It is also an excellent dish for a buffet table,
turned out on a large plate, with the sauce served separately; it
works very well made in larger quantities, particularly if you have a
long, rather narrow tin.

SERVES 6

*225 g/8 oz carrots, scraped and cut into even-
     sized pieces*
*225 g/8 oz shelled broad beans, or peas, fresh
     or frozen*
225 g/8 oz frozen chopped spinach, thawed
3 egg yolks
3 tablespoons single cream
salt and freshly ground black pepper
freshly grated nutmeg
butter for greasing
TO SERVE
1 quantity Sweet Pepper Sauce (p. 172)
carrot slices
dill sprigs

1 Preheat the oven to 170C/325F/Gas
Mark 3. Grease a 450-g/1-lb loaf tin with
butter and line with a strip of greased
greaseproof paper to cover the base of the
tin and extend up the narrow sides.
2 Cook the carrots and broad beans, or
peas, in separate saucepans in a little boiling water until tender. Cook the spinach
in a dry saucepan for 3–4 minutes.
3 Drain the vegetables thoroughly, then
purée each separately in a blender or food
processor, adding one of the egg yolks to
each mixture.
4 Add the cream to the puréed broad
beans or peas to make a smooth, creamy
purée. Season the three mixtures to taste
with salt and pepper, and add a little
nutmeg to the spinach purée.
5 Spoon the carrot purée into the bottom
of the prepared tin, levelling with a spoon
to make a smooth layer. Then carefully
spoon the broad bean or pea purée in an
even layer on top, and the spinach purée
on top of that.
6 Cover with foil and bake for 1 hour,
removing the foil after about 45 minutes.
The terrine should be firm in the centre
when touched lightly. Leave to cool in
the tin, then chill.

7 To serve, spoon a little Sweet Pepper
Sauce on to the centre of 6 small flat
plates. Slip a knife round the sides of the
terrine to loosen, then turn out of the tin
and strip off the greaseproof paper.
8 Cut the terrine into slices 1 cm/½ inch
thick and place a slice on top of the sauce.
Garnish with carrot and dill.

Red Pepper and Almond Dip (p. 146);
Stripy Vegetable Terrine

Vegan Variation
VEGETABLE TERRINE
This version does not need baking in the
oven. Return the vegetable purées to
separate saucepans with 4 tablespoons of
the cooking liquid, bring to the boil and
sprinkle ½ teaspoon agar powder over
each, mixing well. Boil for 1 minute.
Spoon the mixtures into the tin in layers
as described, then leave to cool and set.

V AVOCADO ON A RASPBERRY COULIS V

A pretty, summery first course which is simple to make but needs
assembling at the last minute so that the avocados do not discolour.

SERVES 4

HALVING AN AVOCADO

1 Using a stainless steel knife, cut
the avocado lengthways, cutting as
far in as the large central stone

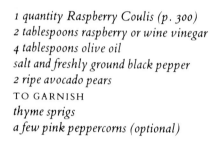

2 Holding the avocado in both
hands, twist the two cut halves of
the avocado in opposite directions to
part them

3 Ease out the stone using your
fingers, or a knife point

4 Take off the skin with the help of
a sharp knife. Sometimes this strips
off easily, other times you may have
to peel it off thinly with the knife

1 quantity Raspberry Coulis (p. 300)
2 tablespoons raspberry or wine vinegar
4 tablespoons olive oil
salt and freshly ground black pepper
2 ripe avocado pears
TO GARNISH
thyme sprigs
a few pink peppercorns (optional)

1 Make a vinaigrette by mixing together
the Raspberry Coulis, vinegar and oil.
Season to taste with salt and pepper.
2 Pour a pool of this coulis on to 4
individual serving plates.
3 Halve the avocado pears and carefully
remove the skin and stones. Place half an
avocado cut-side down on a palette knife,
then cut it across into fairly thin slices.
4 Slide the sliced avocado off the palette
knife into the centre of the plate on top of
the Raspberry Coulis, so that the avocado
half keeps its shape.
5 Repeat this process with all the avocado halves. Garnish with thyme sprigs
and a scattering of pink peppercorns.
Serve immediately.

Variation
AVOCADO ON TWO PEPPER
SAUCES
Make two sauces as described on p. 172,
using a large green and a large yellow
pepper. Add 1 tablespoon olive oil to
each, with wine vinegar to taste. Cool,
then put the sauces into two jugs. Holding one jug in each hand, pour from them
both at once on to the serving plates, to
create a 2-colour effect. Arrange each
avocado half on the plate where the
2 sauces meet.

V PEARS WITH PIQUANT CREAM DRESSING V

The pears for this recipe need to be perfectly ripe, so that they slice
like butter. If they are a bit on the hard side when you buy them,
they will ripen up if left in a fruit bowl for a day or two.

SERVES 4

150 ml/5 fl oz whipping or non-dairy cream
4 tablespoons plain or vegan yogurt
1–2 teaspoons tarragon or wine vinegar
a little sugar
salt and freshly ground black pepper
2 Comice pears
lemon juice
TO GARNISH
pink peppercorns
6 tarragon sprigs
TO SERVE
tender lettuce leaves

1 Whisk the whipping or non-dairy
cream until thick, then add the yogurt
and 1 teaspoon vinegar and whisk again.
2 Add a little sugar, salt and pepper to
taste, and the remaining teaspoon of
vinegar if liked.
3 Give the mixture a final whisking, so
that it holds its shape.
4 Halve the pears, then carefully remove
the cores and peel. Brush the pears all
over with lemon juice.
5 Put a lettuce leaf on each serving plate,
then place a pear half on top, cut-side
down. Spoon the piquant cream mixture
on top and garnish each with a few pink
peppercorns and a tarragon sprig. Serve
immediately.

Variations

CUCUMBER WITH PIQUANT CREAM

For this delicious version, replace the pear with 1 cucumber, peeled and thinly sliced. Place the cucumber slices in a colander, sprinkle with salt and leave for 30 minutes, then rinse and drain well. Sprinkle with sugar, wine vinegar and salt (if necessary). Divide the cucumber between the serving plates just before serving. Top with the cream and garnish.

PEARS WITH ROQUEFORT CREAM

Use the Roquefort Dip mixture (p. 146), instead of the piquant cream for an excellent (but non-vegan) version.

SLICING AN AVOCADO

1 Put the skinned avocado half on a palette knife and slice

2 Lift the slices on the knife and slide on to a plate

Linguine with Tomatoes, Basil and Cream

V V

LINGUINE WITH TOMATOES, BASIL AND CREAM

A delicious and easy first course, excellent before a main course of summer vegetables.

SERVES 4

225 g/8 oz green linguine
1 bunch spring onions, trimmed and chopped
25 g/1 oz butter or vegan margarine
450 g/1 lb firm tomatoes, skinned, de-seeded and chopped
150 ml/5 fl oz single or non-dairy cream
salt and freshly ground black pepper
TO GARNISH
1–2 tablespoons chopped fresh basil

1 Cook the linguine in a large saucepan as described on p. 50, until *al dente*. Drain the pasta in a colander immediately.

2 Meanwhile fry the spring onion gently in the butter or vegan margarine in a large saucepan for 2–3 minutes, then add the tomatoes and cook for a further 1–2 minutes. Stir in the cream, remove from the heat and keep warm.

3 Add the pasta to the tomato and cream mixture. Season to taste with salt and pepper, then serve in heated deep plates, each portion sprinkled with a little chopped fresh basil.

SALAD OF FEUILLE DE CHÊNE, CHÈVRE CHEESE AND WALNUTS WITH WALNUT VINAIGRETTE

This is very quick to make and delicious before a main course of pasta, for a quick supper.

SERVES 4

MENU

Quick Autumn Supper

Salad of Feuille de Chêne, Chèvre Cheese and Walnuts with Walnut Vinaigrette

Taglioni Verde with Tomato Sauce and Aubergines
254
Crusty Bread

Fresh Fruit Bowl

Coffee

1 head feuille de chêne
1 medium firm Chèvre cheese, about 2.5 cm/ 1 inch in diameter, sliced into circles, or soft goat's cheese, cut into cubes
1 quantity Walnut Vinaigrette (p. 154)
4 tablespoons chopped walnuts
TO GARNISH
lovage sprigs

1 Wash the feuille de chêne and shake, pat or spin dry. Divide among 4 individual serving plates, tearing the leaves in half if necessary to fit, and putting a few curly pieces in the centre. Place the Chèvre cheese circles or goat's cheese cubes on top of the feuille de chêne.
2 Just before serving drizzle a little of the Walnut Vinaigrette over the top and sprinkle with the chopped walnuts and garnish with lovage.

Variation
SALADE TIÈDE
Arrange the feuille de chêne and walnuts on the plates as described. Just before serving, grill the Chèvre cheese, on a lightly-oiled baking sheet, until melting, and add to the feuille de chêne and walnuts. Serve the vinaigrette separately at the table.

V   # MARINATED VEGETABLES   V

This fragrantly spiced dish makes an excellent first course, or it can be served as a light lunch. Some warm crusty bread goes well with it.

SERVES 6

2 tablespoons olive oil
1 large onion, peeled and chopped
2 large garlic cloves, crushed
1 medium cauliflower, trimmed, washed and broken into florets
350 g/12 oz French beans, trimmed and cut into 2.5-cm/1-inch pieces
225 g/8 oz button mushrooms, washed and cut into even-sized pieces
1 tablespoon coriander seeds, crushed
1–2 tablespoons lemon juice
salt and freshly ground black pepper
TO GARNISH
chopped parsley
black olives

1 Heat the oil in a large saucepan, then add the onion and fry gently for 5 minutes, without browning.
2 Add the garlic, cauliflower and French beans and fry gently for a further 2–3 minutes, stirring often, then add the mushrooms and coriander seeds and fry for a further 2 minutes.
3 Remove from the heat, stir in the lemon juice, and salt and pepper to taste. Cool, then chill. Serve garnished with parsley and olives.

Variation
MARINATED MUSHROOMS
Make as above, just using 700 g/1½ lb baby button mushrooms.

V FLAKY SPINACH AND FENNEL V
PASTRIES

Crisp golden triangles of phyllo pastry enclosing a tasty filling.
Serve them with Soured Cream Dressing (p. 156).

MAKES 20

8 sheets phyllo pastry
75 g / 3 oz butter or vegan margarine, melted
FOR THE FILLING
1 onion, peeled and finely chopped
1 tablespoon olive oil
225 g / 8 oz cooked fresh spinach, well-drained
   and chopped, or frozen spinach, thawed
   and squeezed as dry as possible
2 tablespoons chopped parsley
1 teaspoon fennel seed
salt and freshly ground black pepper
TO GARNISH
parsley sprigs

1 First make the filling. Fry the onion in the olive oil in a large saucepan until soft but not browned, then add the cooked spinach, chopped parsley and fennel seed. Mix well, then season the mixture to taste with salt and pepper.

2 Preheat the oven to 190 C / 375 F / Gas Mark 5.

3 Unroll the sheets of phyllo pastry and spread them out flat in a pile with a damp cloth over them.

4 Take 1 phyllo pastry sheet, spread it out on a board and brush the top surface all over with the melted butter or vegan margarine. Lay another phyllo pastry sheet on top, and brush with more butter or vegan margarine, then make 4 equally-spaced cuts from one short end of the phyllo to the other so that you end up with 5 long strips.

5 Place a teaspoon of the filling about 2.5 cm / 1 inch from the top of one of the strips and fold one of the top corners over it, making a triangular shape. Then fold the triangle down from the base, and then at an angle again, and continue in this way until you end up with a neat layered triangle. Place on a baking sheet.

6 Continue with the rest of the phyllo and filling in this way, until they are all used up, then brush the triangles all over with butter or vegan margarine. Bake for about 15 minutes, until the pastry is golden-brown and crisp, and the filling piping hot. Serve immediately, garnished with parsley sprigs.

SHAPING THE PASTRIES

1 Place filling on the pastry strip

2 Fold one of the top corners over to cover filling

3 Fold over triangle again, and continue in this way to make a triangular pastry

Phyllo Pastry

Fresh phyllo pastry can be bought from Greek or Middle Eastern shops; frozen phyllo pastry, which works just as well, can also be bought from ethnic shops and many large supermarkets. Frozen phyllo usually comes in 400-g / 14-oz packets, containing around 16 sheets pastry. Allow the frozen phyllo to thaw in its packet in the fridge for up to 2 days.

Salad of Feuille de Chêne, Chèvre Cheese and Walnuts with Walnut Vinaigrette (p. 150); Marinated Vegetables (p. 150)

MENU

Summer Celebration

SERVES 6

Iced Beetroot Soup with Dill
138

Warm Herb and Onion Bread
328

Pine Nut Roulade with Asparagus Hollandaise Filling
237

Courgettes with Herbs
New Potatoes
Bitter Leaf Salad
54

Champagne Sorbet with Wild Strawberries
283

This is a delectable meal, but not too difficult to cope with, because the Iced Beetroot Soup with Dill and the Champagne Sorbet can both be made in advance. The Pine Nut Roulade does need some last-minute attention; get it all ready (except for garnishing) before you sit down to the meal so that it can be heating through in the oven while you eat your soup.

The wine served with the roulade needs to be strong enough to support the flavour of the asparagus; perhaps a mature Graves or a medium-dry wine with a honeyed flavour such as a Savennières or Chenin Blanc. Finish this off with a cheeseboard if you are serving one, then end the meal with a flourish by serving chilled champagne with the sorbet.

Salads

Another versatile category, salads can be as light and refreshing or as substantial and filling as you choose; they can be first courses, accompaniments or, if they are substantial enough, and perhaps served with bread, potatoes or rice, the main course itself. They are particularly healthy and slimming, too, if you use a light dressing or a richer one in moderation. This section contains a variety of salads for different occasions, as well as a selection of useful and easy dressings. When making salads, you will get excellent results if you use the freshest ingredients you can find and aim for a good contrast in colours, textures and flavours.

Walnut Oil

A delectable oil for use in salad dressings, walnut oil is high in polyunsaturates and has a rich, nutty flavour. Hazelnut oil is equally delectable – and expensive! – but both are wonderful for making the occasional extravagant salad dressing, or for tossing freshly-cooked pasta in. These oils make lovely presents for keen cooks.

V VINAIGRETTE V

Exact proportions for this basic French dressing are very flexible. If you use good ingredients and are generous with the oil and fairly mean with the vinegar you can't go wrong!

MAKES ABOUT 60 ml/2–3 fl oz

1 teaspoon salt
2 teaspoons red wine vinegar
freshly ground black pepper
3 tablespoons olive oil

Whisk all the ingredients together until thoroughly blended.

Variations
WALNUT VINAIGRETTE
Make as described, using 3–4 table-spoons walnut oil.

GARLIC VINAIGRETTE
Add a crushed garlic clove to the mixture, blending well.

MUSTARD VINAIGRETTE
Start by mixing 2–3 teaspoons Dijon mustard with the salt and vinegar, then gradually mix in the oil, for this thick and tangy version.

HERB VINAIGRETTE
Add 1–2 teaspoons chopped fresh herbs.

V AVOCADO DRESSING V

A delicious vegan dressing for salads. It can be diluted with a little water to make a thinner dressing.

MAKES ABOUT 200 ml/7 fl oz

1 ripe avocado, halved, peeled and stone removed
1 tablespoon lemon juice
1 tablespoon white wine vinegar
1 teaspoon Dijon mustard
salt and freshly ground black pepper
dash of Tabasco sauce

1 Put the avocado into a blender or food processor with the lemon juice, wine vinegar and Dijon mustard and blend to a smooth cream.
2 Season to taste with salt, pepper, and a drop or two of Tabasco. Taste and add more Tabasco if wished.

MAYONNAISE

Home-made mayonnaise is a delicious treat, is not difficult to make
and will keep for at least a week in a covered container in the fridge
(but it won't freeze).

MAKES ABOUT 225 ml/8 fl oz

2 large egg yolks
¼ teaspoon salt
¼ teaspoon mustard powder
2–3 grindings black pepper
2 teaspoons white wine vinegar
2 teaspoons lemon juice
200 ml/7 fl oz cold-pressed sunflower oil

1 Put the egg yolks, salt, mustard, pepper, vinegar and lemon juice into a bowl and whisk lightly until combined.
2 Add the oil, a drop at a time, whisking well after each addition.
3 When you have added about half the oil, the mixture will emulsify and start to look like mayonnaise. At this point you can add the oil a little more quickly, still whisking well.
4 Continue until the mixture is really thick, then taste the mixture and adjust the seasoning if necessary.
5 If the mayonnaise seems a bit on the thick side, you can thin it by beating in a teaspoon or two of boiling water.

Variations

BLENDER METHOD

Mayonnaise can be speedily made in a blender or food processor. Put in the egg yolks, seasonings, vinegar and lemon juice and then blend for 1 minute. Then gradually add the oil, drop by drop, through the top of the goblet. When you have added about half the oil and the mixture has thickened, you can add the rest more quickly, in a thin stream.

AÏOLI

For this very delectable garlic-flavoured mayonnaise, blend 6–8 peeled garlic cloves in the blender or food processor, then proceed exactly as for mayonnaise. Makes a wonderful dip for crudités.

MAYONNAISE WITH GREEN PEPPERCORNS

Add 1 tablespoon drained and rinsed pickled green peppercorns to the finished mayonnaise for a pungent, green-flecked version. Makes an excellent sauce for slices of cold Quick Savoury Nut Loaf (p. 235), or Savoury Lentil Loaf (p. 213).

MAYONNAISE WITH GREEN HERBS

Add 2–4 tablespoons finely chopped fresh herbs to the mayonnaise. You can use a mixture of herbs, such as parsley, chives and another herb such as basil, tarragon, coriander or mint. Or use just one herb (and only 2 tablespoons), to complement the dish you're going to serve with the mayonnaise. Fresh coriander mayonnaise goes well with grain and lentil salads, and basil mayonnaise with a tomato-based mixture.

MANGO CHUTNEY MAYONNAISE

A good variation for serving with cold lentil loaf or nut burgers. Stir 2–4 tablespoons mango chutney into the mayonnaise, first chopping up mango.

Dressing Tips

☐ A quick and easy way to make a vinaigrette-type dressing is to put all the ingredients into a screwtop jar and shake until emulsified. If you only need a little of the dressing, the jar makes a convenient storage container for the fridge. Let the dressing 'come to' at room temperature for 30 minutes or so before use, then give it a shake to re-emulsify the ingredients.

☐ Although you can make dressing in bulk and store in the fridge, it only takes a moment to make, and I think it's better made fresh when you need it. If you are making the salad in a bowl, it saves time and washing up to make the dressing straight into the bowl. If it's a delicate, leafy salad, and you are not planning to serve it straight away, put a pair of crossed salad servers in the bowl, then put the salad in on top. The salad servers will keep the salad above the dressing until you are ready to toss and serve the salad, preventing it from getting soggy.

V   CREAM AND MUSTARD DRESSING   V

This makes an excellent alternative to mayonnaise, especially for vegans if non-dairy cream is used.

MAKES 200 ml/7 fl oz

1 tablespoon Dijon mustard
2 tablespoons white wine vinegar
150 ml/5 fl oz whipping or non-dairy cream
salt and freshly ground black pepper

1 Mix the mustard and vinegar together in a small bowl, then add the whipping or non-dairy cream.
2 Whisk until thick, then season to taste with salt and pepper.

SOURED CREAM DRESSING

MAKES 150 ml/5 fl oz

Pulse Salads

Pulses – peas, beans and lentils – make excellent salads, filling and full of flavour. Particularly good are all members of the kidney bean family, including of course the red and black varieties; butter beans; continental, brown and puy lentils, and the always-delicious chick peas. A mixture of different colours, shapes and sizes gives a particularly attractive result, great for a buffet party.

Put the dressing on these salads – a vinaigrette is delicious – when the beans are freshly cooked, drained, but still hot. Add flavouring ingredients such as raw onion rings, chopped spring onions, fresh chopped herbs, grated fresh ginger, garlic, black olives – the possibilities are wide. Leave to get cold, stirring the salad gently from time to time. The beans will absorb the full flavour of the dressing and any flavouring ingredients, resulting in a moist, shiny salad, full of flavour.

150 ml/5 fl oz soured cream
salt and freshly ground black pepper

1 Just stir the soured cream and season to taste with salt and pepper, for a simple yet delicious dressing.

Variations
SOURED CREAM AND CHIVE DRESSING
Add 2 tablespoons snipped chives to the soured cream.

SOURED CREAM OR YOGURT AND HERB DRESSING
Add 2 tablespoons chopped fresh green herbs – mint, parsley, tarragon or basil, or a mixture of them all – to the soured cream or yogurt.

VEGAN YOGURT AND MINT DRESSING
Use vegan yogurt instead of soured cream and add 2 tablespoons chopped mint. Mix well.

V   SWEET PEPPER DRESSING   V

This light, translucent dressing is another one which makes an excellent vegan alternative to mayonnaise.

MAKES ABOUT 200 ml/7 fl oz

1 large red pepper, about 175 g/6 oz
50–75 ml/2–3 fl oz olive oil
2 teaspoons wine vinegar or raspberry vinegar
salt and freshly ground black pepper

1 Put the whole pepper into a saucepan and half cover with water. Bring to the boil, then simmer for 15–20 minutes,

until the pepper is very tender. Test by piercing it with a fork.
2 Drain the pepper and remove the stalk and seeds. Purée the pepper in a blender or food processor, then add the oil and blend again. You should have a thickish scarlet emulsion, like a mayonnaise. Gently stir in the vinegar and salt and pepper to taste.

V # RED KIDNEY BEAN SALAD V

A bean salad looks colourful and attractive and contrasts well with other salads if you're serving a selection. It is filling and, served simply, with warm rolls or wholewheat pitta bread and a little lettuce or watercress, makes an excellent quick meal.

SERVES 4

225 g/8 oz red kidney beans, soaked, cooked
  and drained (p. 40), or 2 × 425-g/15-oz
  cans red kidney beans, drained
2 tablespoons finely chopped onion
2 tablespoons tomato purée
1 quantity Vinaigrette (p. 154)
salt and freshly ground black pepper
a pinch of sugar
1 tablespoon chopped parsley

1 Put the red kidney beans into a bowl with the onion. Add the tomato purée and vinaigrette and mix well.
2 Season the beans with salt, pepper and sugar. Mix again, then leave for 2–3 hours for the beans to absorb the flavours. Sprinkle with chopped parsley.

Variations

RED KIDNEY BEAN AND
SWEETCORN SALAD
Make the salad as described, adding 100 g/4 oz cooked fresh or frozen sweetcorn kernels, for a pretty colour contrast.

RED KIDNEY BEAN AND
WALNUT SALAD
Make the salad as described, using either the basic vinaigrette or the walnut version, and adding 1 large coarsely grated carrot, 2 sliced celery sticks and 100 g/4 oz roughly chopped walnuts.

MULTICOLOUR BEAN SALAD
For this vibrantly coloured version, which is lovely for a party, use a mixture of beans in contrasting colours: red kidney beans, butter beans, cannellini beans, flageolet beans, black beans, black-eyed beans. Cook them separately, until tender, and make the salad as described above, but omit the tomato purée. Garnish with chopped parsley and coriander sprigs.

RED KIDNEY BEAN,
HARICOT BEAN AND BLACK
OLIVE SALAD
Use 100 g/4 oz red kidney beans and 100 g/4 oz haricot beans, soaked, cooked and drained, or a 425-g/15-oz can of red kidney beans and one of cannellini beans, drained. Omit the tomato purée and add 100 g/4 oz black olives to the mixture.

Multicolour Bean Salad; Rice Salad Ring (p. 159)

UNMOULDING A RICE SALAD

1 Slip a knife between the rice salad and the sides of the mould, to loosen

2 Invert your serving dish on top of the rice mould

3 Turn the mould and the serving dish over together, giving the mould a shake to help the rice to slide out

4 Lift off the mould

Making a Round Rice Salad Mould

If you haven't a ring mould, make a round rice salad mould instead, using a cake tin or soufflé dish, lined with well-oiled foil. This mould looks pretty if you fry 6–7 small flat open mushrooms in oil and arrange these attractively in the base of the mould before putting in the rice. Add the rice gently, to keep the pattern intact.

Any rice salad mixture can be moulded in this way. Make sure your serving plate is large enough, because the salad tends to crumble once it is cut.

V CONTINENTAL LENTIL AND WALNUT SALAD V

This makes an excellent winter salad, filling and satisfying.

SERVES 4

225 g/8 oz continental lentils, cooked and drained (p. 40)
50 g/2 oz walnuts, chopped
1 garlic clove, crushed
1 bunch spring onions, trimmed and chopped
1 quantity Walnut Vinaigrette (p. 154)
salt and freshly ground black pepper
TO GARNISH
1–2 tablespoons chopped parsley

1 Put the lentils into a bowl with the walnuts, garlic, onions and vinaigrette. Mix well, season with salt and pepper, then leave to marinate for several hours.
2 Put the salad into a serving bowl, then chill until needed. Sprinkle the parsley on top just before you serve the salad.

Variations
LENTIL, MUSHROOM AND WALNUT SALAD
Add 175–225 g/6–8 oz very fresh button mushrooms, washed, thinly sliced and sprinkled with 1–2 tablespoons lemon juice, to the mixture.

CONTINENTAL LENTIL, CARROT AND WALNUT SALAD
Add 1–2 coarsely grated carrots to the mixture for a good contrast of colour.

CONTINENTAL LENTIL, WALNUT AND ONION SALAD
Add a mild raw onion, peeled and sliced.

CONTINENTAL LENTIL, WALNUT AND EGG SALAD
For this excellent (but non-vegan) version, make the salad as described, put into a shallow bowl and surround with 2–4 hardboiled eggs cut into wedges.

V RICE AND VEGETABLE SALAD V

This is one of my favourite rice salads, and is especially effective if you make it in a ring (see opposite).

SERVES 6 AS A MAIN COURSE SALAD, 10–12 AS PART OF A MEAL WITH OTHER SALADS

225 g/8 oz long-grain brown rice
600 ml/1 pint water
1 garlic clove, crushed
1 onion, peeled and chopped
225 g/8 oz aubergine, washed and diced
1 small red pepper, de-seeded and chopped
2 tablespoons olive oil
1 large tomato, skinned and chopped
a few drops of Tabasco sauce
salt and freshly ground black pepper
TO GARNISH
chopped parsley

1 Cook the rice in a heavy-based saucepan as described on p. 44, then drain.
2 Meanwhile, fry the garlic, onion, aubergine and pepper in the oil for 10 minutes. Add the tomato and cook for a further 5 minutes.
3 Add the cooked rice to the vegetable mixture, together with a drop or two of Tabasco and season to taste with salt and pepper.
4 Cool, then sprinkle with parsley before serving.

Variations

RICE SALAD RING

For this attractive moulded version, make the salad as described. Fry 6 flat or button mushrooms and place these gills side down in a 2–2.4 litre/3½–4-pint ring mould. Spoon the rice salad into the mould and press down. Leave until cold, then turn out and garnish with sprigs of watercress and flat or button mushrooms. Fill the centre with water-cress, mayonnaise, sliced tomatoes, diced avocado, cold ratatouille, or any colourful mixture of salad ingredients that you fancy, if desired.

RICE SALAD WITH BEANSPROUTS AND WILD RICE

For this particularly good version, cook 50 g/2 oz wild rice with the long-grain rice, using 750 ml/1¼ pints water. Omit the aubergine and tomato. Fry the onion with the garlic and pepper, then add to the rice, together with 350 g/12 oz beansprouts.

Continental Lentil and Walnut Salad (p. 158); Tabbouleh

V   # TABBOULEH   V

This is a Middle Eastern salad based on bulgur wheat. Although it's substantial, the herbs and lemon juice give it a light, refreshing flavour and it's a good hot-weather salad.

SERVES 4–6

225 g/8 oz bulgur wheat
600 ml/1 pint boiling water
4 tablespoons lemon juice
2 tablespoons olive oil
8 tablespoons chopped parsley
8 tablespoons chopped spring onion
a 10-cm/4-inch piece of cucumber, diced
4 tablespoons chopped fresh mint
4 tomatoes, skinned and finely chopped
salt and freshly ground black pepper
TO GARNISH
lemon slices
tomato slices
black olives
mint sprig

1 Put the bulgur wheat into a bowl and cover with boiling water; leave for 10–15 minutes, until the water is absorbed.
2 Add the lemon juice, oil, parsley, spring onion, cucumber, mint and toma-to. Mix well and season to taste with salt and pepper. Spoon the mixture into a large, shallow serving dish. Garnish the salad with lemon and tomato slices, black olives and mint.

Variation

TABBOULEH RING

To make a moulded ring, like the Rice Salad Ring (above), press the mixture into a 2–2.4-litre/3½–4-pint ring mould, press down firmly, and leave until cold. Then turn out and fill the centre with some watercress, black olives, or thinly sliced tomatoes.

Rice Salad Ideas

Rice salad is easy to make: just add the ingredients to the rice. The more contrast you can get in the ingredients you add, the better.

Choose from chopped raw onion or spring onion, small cubes of cucumber, chopped red or green pepper, sweetcorn kernels, cooked peas, small cubes of cooked carrot or coarsely grated raw carrot, finely chopped celery, raisins or sultanas, finely chopped dried apricots, chopped nuts, chopped skinned tomato, cooked beans, black olives, chopped fresh herbs.

Moisten the mixture with a little vinaigrette dressing or mayonnaise thinned with some milk.

LUMACHE WITH SPRING ONIONS, FENNEL AND MAYONNAISE

Served on individual bowls or plates, this salad makes a light,
refreshing first course.

SERVES 4–6

225 g/8 oz lumache
8 tablespoons Mayonnaise (p. 155)
8 tablespoons plain yogurt
1 bunch spring onions, trimmed and finely
    chopped
salt and freshly ground black pepper
TO GARNISH
2 tablespoons chopped fennel herb

1 Cook the lumache in a large saucepan
as described on p. 50, until *al dente*. Drain
immediately.
2 Add the mayonnaise, yogurt, spring
onion and salt and pepper to taste. Mix
well and leave to cool completely.
3 Transfer to a serving bowl or individual plates and sprinkle with the fennel.

PASTA BOW SALAD

This is a filling, main course salad, good with some crusty bread.

Pasta Bow Salad

SERVES 4

225 g/8 oz pasta bows
1 quantity Vinaigrette (p. 154)
1 red pepper, de-seeded and chopped
½ cucumber, washed and diced
50 g/2 oz black olives
175 g/6 oz red Leicester or red Cheshire
    cheese, diced
TO GARNISH (OPTIONAL)
½ bunch watercress

1 Cook the pasta in a large saucepan as
described on p. 50, until *al dente*. Drain
thoroughly and put into a bowl. Add the
vinaigrette, pepper, cucumber and olives
and mix well. Leave until the pasta is
cold, then mix in the red Leicester or red
Cheshire cheese.
2 Put the salad into a serving bowl and
garnish with the watercress divided into
sprigs, if liked.

Variation
VEGAN PASTA SALAD
Use 1 large scraped, grated carrot and
100 g/4 oz roasted cashew nuts, peanuts
or chopped walnuts or pecan nuts instead
of the diced cheese.

V

CHICORY, WATERCRESS AND WALNUT SALAD

V

An example of one of the many varieties of green salad; this is particularly good with cheese dishes. Other leafy salad ingredients can be used as available: endive, laitue frisée, dandelion and spinach leaves and lamb's lettuce.

SERVES 4

2 heads chicory, washed
1 bunch watercress, washed
1 quantity Vinaigrette or Walnut Vinaigrette
    (p. 154)
50 g/2 oz chopped walnuts

1 See that the chicory and watercress leaves do not have any excess water clinging to them. If there's time, wash and dry them in advance and put them into a polythene bag in the salad compartment of the fridge, to chill and crisp.
2 Put the dressing into a salad bowl, cross the salad servers on top, then put in the chicory, watercress and walnuts. Turn the leaves in the dressing at the last minute, just before serving.

Variation
CHICORY,
WATERCRESS AND
ORANGE SALAD
Make as described, substituting 2 large oranges, peeled and cut into segments, for the radiccio. Hold the oranges over a bowl as you cut them, to catch the juice. Use some of this to make the vinaigrette dressing for the salad, instead of the vinegar.

This is a particularly good accompaniment to hot pulse and nut dishes; or, topped with a blue cheese dressing, and served with a warm wholewheat roll, it makes a good light lunch or supper dish on its own.

Dressing a Salad

Some salads, such as pulse and grain salads and those made from cooked vegetables and firm vegetables, such as cabbage, are ideal if dressed in advance and left for the flavours to blend. Others, especially delicate leafy mixtures, are best dressed at the last minute, even at the table, just before serving.

For a really good salad, leafy ingredients need to be dried of excess water. This can be done by putting them in a salad shaker or drier, or by patting them gently in a clean, absorbent cloth or kitchen paper. I find a salad drier, consisting of a perforated basket which spins the salad inside a container, so removing the water, most useful. If there is time, wash and dry the leaves, then put them into a polythene bag and chill them in the fridge for 30–60 minutes to crisp.

FAVOURITE COLESLAW

This traditional favourite is a useful salad because it can be made ahead of time. It goes particularly well with crisp nut burgers.

SERVES 4

225 g/8 oz white cabbage, finely shredded
100 g/4 oz carrots, scraped and coarsely
    grated
1 tablespoon chopped chives
1 small green pepper, de-seeded and chopped
2 tablespoons plain yogurt or water
2 tablespoons Mayonnaise (p. 155)
salt and freshly ground black pepper
TO GARNISH
chive tassels

1 Put the cabbage, carrot, chives and green pepper into a large bowl. Add the yogurt or water, mayonnaise and salt and pepper to taste. Garnish with chives.

Variation
CARAWAY COLESLAW
Make as described, adding 1 teaspoon caraway seeds, for a mid-European flavour to the salad.

*Low-calorie Salad
Dressings*

☐ Sprinkle vegetables with lemon juice or rice vinegar, seasoning and chopped fresh herbs or finely chopped onion

☐ Use fresh orange juice to dress root vegetable salads: grated carrot and grated raw beetroot are particularly good with orange

☐ Lemon or lime juice makes a good dressing for grated cabbage salad, perked up with herbs, seasoning and perhaps a dash of Dijon mustard

☐ Plain yogurt, or the Yogurt and Herb Dressing on p. 156

☐ For a low(er)-calorie mayonnaise, mix mayonnaise (home-made or bought) with an equal (or even double) quantity of plain yogurt

V SWEET CARROT AND FENNEL SALAD V

SERVES 4

Fennel Tip

If you find the flavour of fennel rather strong, plunge the bulbs into boiling water for 2 minutes before slicing.

2 bulbs fennel
450 g/1 lb carrots, scraped and coarsely grated
½ quantity Vinaigrette (p. 154)
salt and freshly ground black pepper
a little sugar
TO GARNISH
fennel leaves

1 Remove any tough outer leaves from the fennel. Cut off and reserve any feathery green leaves. Slice the fennel and put it into a bowl with the grated carrot.
2 Add the vinaigrette and mix well.

Season to taste with salt and pepper, then add a little sugar to taste, if liked. I think this touch of sweetness enhances the flavour of the carrot and fennel pleasantly. Garnish with fennel.

Variation

SWEET CARROT, FENNEL AND
RED PEPPER SALAD

Make as described, adding a small, red pepper, de-seeded and chopped, to the ingredients. This is a good salad for serving with a creamy pasta dish.

V TECHNICOLOUR CABBAGE SALAD V

SERVES 4–6

Cold-pressed Oils

Oils are extracted from nuts, seeds, pulses and (in the case of olive oil) from fruits by pressing them. This is usually done several times, at first by using pressure alone and later, to extract the maximum oil, by using heat too. Cold-pressed oil is oil obtained by the early pressings and is the richest in flavour and nutrients (some of which are damaged when heat is used). Other chemicals may also be used in the later pressings and anti-oxidants may be added to increase the keeping qualities. Cold-pressed oil is the best both for flavour and health. It is more expensive, and should be bought in small quantities (that can be used up within about a month) and kept in the fridge. If the oil goes a bit cloudy or solid, don't worry; it will return to normal if you take it out of the fridge and leave it at room temperature.

350 g/12 oz white cabbage, finely shredded
2 large carrots, scraped and coarsely grated
1 medium red pepper, de-seeded and chopped
1 onion, peeled and finely chopped
2 tablespoons chopped parsley
50 g/2 oz raisins or black olives
1 quantity Vinaigrette (p. 154)
50 g/2 oz roasted peanuts or sunflower seeds

1 Put the shredded white cabbage into a bowl with the grated carrots and the chopped pepper, onion and parsley. Stir in the raisins or black olives.
2 Add the vinaigrette and stir well to coat all the ingredients.
3 Add the nuts or sunflower seeds just before serving.

V SCANDINAVIAN-STYLE V
CUCUMBER SALAD

Serve with rich dishes, or as a contrast to creamy salads in a buffet selection.

SERVES 4–6

1 large cucumber, peeled and sliced
salt
1 onion, peeled and thinly sliced
2 tablespoons white wine vinegar
1 teaspoon sugar
1 tablespoon white mustard seeds
2 tablespoons chopped fresh dill
freshly ground black pepper
TO GARNISH
1–2 dill sprigs

1 Put the cucumber slices into a sieve or colander and sprinkle with salt. Set a weight on top and leave for 30 minutes, to draw out the excess liquid. Then squeeze and pat dry on kitchen paper.
2 Put the cucumber into a bowl and add the onion, vinegar, sugar, mustard seeds, dill and pepper. Stir well.
3 Leave to marinate for at least 2 hours. Garnish with dill before serving.

V   AVOCADO AND MUSHROOM SALAD   V

*Sweet Carrot and Fennel Salad
(p. 162); Scandinavian-style Cucumber
Salad (p. 162)*

A useful salad for serving with hot pasta or jacket potatoes, to turn
them into a meal – quick, simple and good.

SERVES 4

*2 avocado pears, halved, peeled, stones
   removed and diced*
2 tablespoons lemon juice
*450 g/1 lb small white button mushrooms,
   washed and sliced*
1 quantity Garlic Vinaigrette (p. 154)
2 tablespoons snipped chives
salt and freshly ground black pepper

1 Put the avocado into a large bowl and
sprinkle with the lemon juice. Add the
mushrooms, together with the vinaigrette and the chives.
2 Check the seasoning and add more –
especially pepper – if needed.

Variation
AVOCADO, LETTUCE AND TOMATO SALAD

Make as described, replacing the
mushrooms with a small round lettuce,
torn into pieces, and 4 skinned and
chopped tomatoes. Mix well with the
vinaigrette and the chives.

AVOCADO AND PALM HEART SALAD

Make the salad as described, then drain a
425-g/15-oz can of palm hearts, slice
them into thin circles and mix them into
the salad.

MAKING RADISH FLOWERS

1 Cut a thin petal of skin from the tip of the radish to the stem. Repeat, making 5 petals

2 To make a rose, cut a slice off the root end, then make 3 small cuts round that before making the petals

3 Drop radishes into iced water for the petals to open

MENU

Quick Late-night Supper for Two

Guacamole
Illustrated on p. 145
144

Cheese Fondue with
French Bread
217
Japanese Flower Salad

Passion Fruit Sorbet
Illustrated on p. 283
282

Opposite page, clockwise from top: Pink Potato Salad (p. 166); Radish, Cucumber and Arame Salad; Japanese Flower Salad

V

RADISH, CUCUMBER AND ARAME SALAD

V

Don't be put off by the seaweed – arame – in this recipe. With a sweet and sour dressing, it makes a very good salad, full of nutrients, and looks pretty with the cucumber and radishes. Excellent for serving with Japanese-style rice dishes.

SERVES 4

15 g/½ oz arame
½ cucumber, peeled and diced
1 bunch radishes, trimmed and sliced
1 teaspoon sea salt
1 teaspoon sugar
2 tablespoons rice vinegar

1 Rinse the arame under the cold tap, then soak in cold water for 5 minutes. Drain the arame, place in a saucepan, cover with water, bring to the boil, and simmer gently for 10 minutes. Drain and leave the arame to cool.

2 Add the cucumber, radishes, sea salt, sugar and rice vinegar to the cooled arame and mix well to combine all the ingredients.

Variation

RADISH, CUCUMBER AND
HIZIKI SEAWEED
SALAD

Make this in the same way, using hiziki, another kind of seaweed, instead of the arame. Prepare the hiziki as described on p. 81.

V

JAPANESE FLOWER SALAD

V

This pretty salad makes an excellent accompaniment to a rich main course such as Cheese Soufflé (p. 222), Cheese Fondue (p. 217) or a creamy flan. Serve Vinaigrette (p. 154) separately. If you have the time to cut the vegetables as suggested (p. 166), it adds to the charm of this salad.

SERVES 4

1 medium head laitue frissée, leaves separated, washed and broken into even-sized pieces
1 medium head radiccio, leaves separated, washed and broken into even-sized pieces
12 radishes, cut into roses (above left)
12 cherry tomatoes, skinned
2 large carrots, scraped and cut into 8 chrysanthemums (p. 166)
a 10-cm/4-inch piece of daikon (mooli), scraped and cut into 8 chrysanthemums (p. 166), or 8 cauliflower florets
8 spring onions, trimmed and curled
a few parsley sprigs

1 On 4 individual plates, or in 4 small shallow baskets lined with coloured napkins, make a base of mixed laitue frissée and radiccio.
2 Arrange the radishes, tomatoes, carrot and daikon flowers, or cauliflower florets, attractively amongst the mixed leaves on the plates.
3 Garnish with the spring onions and parsley sprigs.

Variation

Other vegetables of your choice can be used in this salad, as well as edible flowers, such as nasturtiums and borage. Garnish with parsley sprigs or flowers.

MAKING CARROT AND DAIKON FLOWERS

1 Cut carrot or daikon into 2.5-cm/1-inch rectangles. Round off the corners slightly

2 Hold the rectangle between two chopsticks and cut across first one way then the other, cutting down as far as the chopsticks

3 Sprinkle salt into the cuts and leave for 30 minutes, then rinse

4 Gently open up the cuts with your fingers

Root Salads

Root vegetables – carrots, swedes, celeriac and raw beetroot – make good, substantial salads. They can be made several hours in advance if convenient, as they will not spoil. The effect can be varied according to how coarsely you grate the roots, and the dressing used. Little heaps of different coloured root vegetables on a base of lettuce, with perhaps a creamy dip or dressing in the centre, and some parsley sprigs or black olives to decorate, make a colourful and vitamin-rich lunch. Or the roots can be served separately, as part of a mixed salad selection. Here are some good combinations:

☐ grated raw beetroot and apple, dressed with orange juice or Herb Vinaigrette (p. 154)

☐ grated raw beetroot and sliced raw onion rings, with Vinaigrette (p. 154)

☐ grated swede with chopped dates, dressed with a mixture of yogurt and Mayonnaise (p. 155)

☐ celeriac, cut into julienne strips, dressed with Mustard Vinaigrette (p. 154) or Soured Cream Dressing (p. 156)

☐ young turnips, coarsely grated, mixed with Vinaigrette (p. 154) and raisins or chopped parsley

☐ coarsely grated raw carrot with apple and celery, dressed with orange juice

POTATO SALAD

New potatoes, cooked in their skins, as described, are specially good for this salad, though I make it all the year round and find it works well with old potatoes: the secret is to undercook them slightly, so that they still have a bit of bite to them and hold together well. And if you can get hold of an interesting, well flavoured variety, they will make this salad extra good.

SERVES 4

450 g/1 lb small even-sized potatoes, scrubbed
3 tablespoons Mayonnaise (p. 155)
3 tablespoons plain yogurt or soured cream
salt and freshly ground black pepper
2 tablespoons snipped chives, chopped spring onion or parsley

1 Cook the potatoes in boiling water to cover, until they are just tender when pierced with a knife – about 15 minutes, depending on the size of the potatoes.

2 Drain the potatoes immediately they are done and, if you wish, slip off the skins with a sharp knife. (Usually I prefer to leave the skins on.)

3 Dice the potatoes if necessary and put them into a bowl with the mayonnaise and yogurt or soured cream. It's fine – indeed, best – to do this while they are still hot.

4 Leave to get completely cold, then check the seasoning and serve, sprinkled with the chives, spring onion or parsley.

Variations

PINK POTATO SALAD

Make as described, adding 1–2 tablespoons cooked and diced beetroot to the mixture. This will turn the whole salad a pretty pink, making this a good salad for serving with a pale dish, such as French Onion Flan (p. 261).

POTATO SALAD WITH VINAIGRETTE DRESSING

A good vegan version. Use ½–1 quantity of Vinaigrette (p. 154) instead of the mayonnaise. A bunch of radishes, trimmed and sliced, or a little chopped red pepper, are good added to this, for extra colour.

V GREEN-BEAN SALAD WITH RADICCIO V

This is a light salad, made from fresh rather than dried beans, and the different shades of green look pretty against the red of the radiccio leaves. This salad goes excellently with Cheese Soufflé (p. 222) for a nourishing lunch or supper.

SERVES 4–6

225 g/8 oz frozen broad beans
225 g/8 oz fresh or frozen French beans, trimmed and cut into 2.5-cm/1-inch lengths
½ quantity Vinaigrette (p. 154)
salt and freshly ground black pepper
2 tablespoons chopped summer savory or other fresh herbs (such as chives or mint)
1 medium head radiccio, leaves washed and separated

1 Cook the broad and French beans together in a little boiling water for 5–10 minutes, until just tender and still crisp. Drain well.
2 Put the hot beans into a bowl with the vinaigrette, salt, pepper and herbs. Mix well, then leave until cool.
3 Just before serving, add the radiccio to the beans and stir gently to mix all the ingredients.

V TSATSIKI V

This Middle Eastern salad is a good accompaniment to cooked grain dishes. It also makes a refreshing starter, served on small plates and eaten with strips of warmed pitta bread.

SERVES 4–6 AS A SIDE SALAD, 6–8 AS A FIRST COURSE

Tsatsiki

1 large cucumber, peeled and cut into small dice
salt
225 g/8 oz thick plain yogurt, preferably Greek, or vegan yogurt
4 tablespoons chopped fresh mint
2 garlic cloves, crushed
freshly ground black pepper
TO GARNISH
mild paprika pepper
mint leaves

1 Put the cucumber into a sieve or colander and sprinkle with salt. Set a weight on top and leave for 30 minutes, to draw out excess liquid which would dilute the dressing too much. Then squeeze and pat dry on kitchen paper.
2 Put the cucumber into a bowl and add the yogurt, mint, garlic and a grinding of pepper. Stir well, taste and add more salt and pepper if necessary. Put into a shallow serving dish, sprinkle with paprika and garnish with mint leaves.

Waldorf Salad (p. 169); Greek Salad

GREEK SALAD

Instant nostalgia for anyone with happy memories of Greece, this
makes a substantial salad for 4 people or a side salad for 8. A
generous portion of Greek salad, accompanied by warm
wholewheat pitta bread or rolls, makes a delicious
light lunch or supper.

SERVES 4 AS A MAIN COURSE, 8 AS A SIDE SALAD

1 large, mild onion, peeled and thinly sliced
1 quantity Vinaigrette (p. 154)
450 g/1 lb tomatoes, skinned if necessary, and
   sliced
1 cucumber, diced
100 g/4 oz black olives (optional)
225 g/8 oz feta cheese or other white,
   crumbly cheese such as Wensleydale or
   Cheshire, diced
TO GARNISH (OPTIONAL)
chopped parsley

1 Put the onion into a bowl with the
vinaigrette; mix well, then leave to
stand for 30–60 minutes, to allow the
onion to soften in the dressing. Stir
occasionally.
2 Add the tomatoes, cucumber, olives,
if used, and cheese, stirring gently to
distribute all the ingredients. Divide the
salad among the individual serving plates
and sprinkle each portion with chopped
parsley, if wished.

WALDORF SALAD

This classic salad goes well with cheese dishes, as well as
slices of cold nut or lentil loaf.

SERVES 4

3 red-skinned apples, cored and diced
2 tablespoons lemon juice
3 celery stalks, chopped
¼ cup Mayonnaise (p. 155)
¼ cup plain yogurt
½ cup walnuts, chopped
salt and freshly ground black pepper

1 Put the apple into a bowl, sprinkle
with the lemon juice and mix well. Add
the celery, mayonnaise, yogurt, walnuts
and seasoning to taste.

2 Serve immediately; or, if the salad has
to wait for any length of time, leave out
the walnuts until just before serving.

Variation
GRAPE, CELERY, PEAR AND ALMOND SALAD
Replace the apples with 2 cups mixed
black or red and green grapes, halved and
seeded, and 2 ripe pears, peeled, cored
and diced. Use ½ cup toasted slivered
almonds instead of the walnuts.

VEGETARIAN SALADE NIÇOISE

Served with crusty French bread, this makes an excellent light
lunch or, in smaller portions, a refreshing first course.

SERVES 4 AS A MAIN COURSE, 6–8 AS A STARTER

1 large head of lettuce, washed, torn into
*   pieces and shaken dry*
1 medium onion, peeled and sliced into rings
1 pound firm tomatoes, washed and sliced
5 hard-boiled eggs, quartered
1 pound green beans, cooked and cut into
*   1-inch lengths*
12 black olives
2 tablespoons chopped parsley
1 quantity Vinaigrette (p. 154)

1 Line a large serving plate with the lettuce, then arrange all the ingredients, except the vinaigrette, on top, not too neatly.
2 Spoon a little of the vinaigrette over
the salad just before serving. Serve the
rest of the vinaigrette separately in a small
pitcher.

Variation
VEGAN SALADE NIÇOISE
Use the drained contents of one 15-ounce
can of lima beans, or ⅔ cup dried lima
beans, soaked, cooked and drained, instead of the hard-boiled eggs cut into
quarters.

Onion Tip
If you want to include raw onion in a
salad but find it too strong, blanch
the onion first by covering with
boiling water, leaving for 2 minutes,
then draining.

PEELING A TOMATO

1 Put the tomato into a bowl and cover with
boiling water. Leave for 1 minute

2 Drain. Slip off the skin with a sharp, pointed
knife

Sauces

Sauces can add the final, delicious touch to a dish, often contributing colour as well as moisture; they also form an integral part of some vegetarian dishes such as Aubergine and Pasta Charlotte (p. 258) and Stuffed Cabbage Rolls in Coconut Sauce (p. 196). A good sauce, such as Fresh Tomato (below), Pesto (p. 172) or Cheese Sauce (p. 175) can turn plain freshly cooked pasta or vegetables into a quick and tasty meal. When making your favourite sauces, it's worth cooking extra portions which can be frozen. The sauces in this chapter are the ones which I consider the most useful both as components of recipes and for serving with other dishes.

V   FRESH TOMATO SAUCE   V

I find this fresh, lightly cooked tomato sauce one of the most useful. Its flavour and bright colour go well with many savoury dishes, and it's excellent with pasta and many cooked vegetables, especially pale ones like cauliflower. Another advantage is that, unlike many sauces, it is very low in calories. This sauce is definitely best when made with fresh tomatoes: canned tomatoes just don't give the same result. If you have to use these, make Italian Tomato Sauce (p. 171) instead.

SERVES 6

Keeping Sauces Warm

It is often convenient to make sauces in advance, to avoid feeling pressured at the last minute. Both the Tomato Sauces (pp. 170 and 171), Vegetarian Gravy (p. 172), Cranberry Sauce (p. 174), Curry Sauce (p. 177) and Savoury Coconut Sauce (p. 177) can be reheated gently in a saucepan. Béchamel Sauce (p. 175), and its variations, can also be reheated, but keep the heat low and stir, or use a double saucepan. A double saucepan is also best for Bread Sauce (p. 175) and Sauce Soubise (p. 173) and these can be kept warm in a bain marie (or a saucepan standing in a roasting tin half filled with boiling water, with foil over all). Hollandaise Sauce (p. 176) can be kept warm in a bain marie, too; take care that this sauce does not get too hot, or it may start to curdle. (If this happens, quickly add an ice cube – or start again, adding the curdled sauce gradually to a fresh egg yolk.)

1 onion, peeled and finely chopped
1 tablespoon olive oil
900 g/2 lb tomatoes, skinned and roughly chopped
salt and freshly ground black pepper

1 Fry the onion in the oil in a large saucepan for 10 minutes, until softened but not browned.
2 Add the tomatoes and cook for a further 10 minutes, until the tomatoes are soft but still bright in colour and fresh in flavour.
3 Purée the tomato mixture in a blender or food processor. Season to taste with salt and pepper.

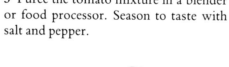

Variations

FRESH TOMATO AND BASIL SAUCE
For this summery version, make as described, adding 1 tablespoon chopped fresh basil just before serving.

FRESH TOMATO AND GARLIC SAUCE
Add 1–2 crushed garlic cloves to the onion with the tomatoes.

FRESH TOMATO AND MUSHROOM SAUCE
While the tomatoes are cooking, fry 100 g/4 oz finely chopped button mushrooms in 1 tablespoon olive oil in a pan, until tender. Stir into puréed sauce.

FRESH TOMATO AND CHILLI SAUCE
Add 1 green chilli, de-seeded and finely chopped, to the onion with the tomatoes.

V   ITALIAN TOMATO SAUCE   V

A well-flavoured sauce which goes well with many vegetarian
savoury dishes.

SERVES 4

1 onion, peeled and chopped
1 celery stick, finely chopped
1 carrot, scraped and finely chopped
2 tablespoons olive oil
2 garlic cloves, crushed
2 × 400-g/14-oz cans tomatoes
½ teaspoon each basil and oregano
1 bay leaf
*150 ml/5 fl oz red wine, Dark Vegetable
Stock (p. 132) or water*
salt and freshly ground black pepper

1 Fry the onion, celery and carrot in the
oil in a medium saucepan for 10 minutes,
until soft but not browned. Add the garlic, tomatoes, basil, oregano, bay leaf,
and the red wine, Dark Vegetable Stock
or water.

2 Cook gently for 20 minutes, stirring
from time to time, until the tomatoes
have almost reduced to a purée.

3 Remove the bay leaf, then purée the
sauce in a blender or food processor.
Season to taste with salt and pepper. A
little extra liquid can be added at this
point for a thinner sauce, if wished. Add
either more red wine, Dark Vegetable
Stock or water.

*Pesto (p. 172); Fresh Tomato Sauce
(p. 170)*

V   # VEGETARIAN GRAVY   V

This is a tasty gravy, quite like a conventional meat gravy.
The soy sauce both flavours and colours it.

MAKES JUST OVER 450 ml/15 fl oz

Gravy Tip

Gravy freezes well, and it is very useful to have a supply in the freezer. Make a double batch and freeze in ice cube trays; when solid remove gravy cubes and store in a polythene bag to use as required. This is particularly useful if you only need small quantities of gravy at a time.

1 onion, peeled and chopped
2 tablespoons oil
2 tablespoons plain flour
1 garlic clove, crushed
450 ml/15 fl oz Dark Vegetable Stock
   (p. 132) or water
1 teaspoon yeast extract
1–2 tablespoons soy sauce
salt and freshly ground black pepper

1 Fry the onion in the oil in a medium saucepan for 5 minutes, then add the flour, and cook for a further 5–10 minutes, until the flour and the onion are nut-brown and the onion is soft and slightly pulpy.
2 Add the garlic, cook for 1–2 minutes, then gradually stir in the Dark Vegetable Stock. Bring to the boil, then simmer for 10 minutes.
3 Strain the gravy into a clean saucepan and add the yeast extract, soy sauce and salt and pepper to taste. Stir well to mix, then serve.

PESTO

This popular Italian sauce for pasta can also be added to vegetable soups.

SERVES 4–6

MENU

Speedy Supper

Pasta with Pesto

Quick Savoury Nut Roast
235
Stir-fried Carrots with
Watercress and Sesame Seeds
181
Potato Purée
Illustrated on p. 276
189

Black and Green Grapes

2 garlic cloves, crushed
6 tablespoons finely chopped fresh
   basil
4 tablespoons chopped parsley
50 g/2 oz pine nuts or cashew nuts
50 g/2 oz grated Parmesan cheese
150 ml/5 fl oz olive oil
freshly ground black pepper

1 Put all the ingredients into a blender or food processor and blend until smooth.

Variation

PARSLEY PESTO
Instead of fresh basil, use an extra 4–6 tablespoons chopped parsley and a teaspoon of dried basil.

V   # SWEET PEPPER SAUCE   V

Like tomato sauce, this scarlet sauce is low in calories and excellent with many savouries. For non-vegans, it may be enriched by adding 15–25 g/½–1 oz butter just before serving.

SERVES 4

2 large red peppers
4 garlic cloves, peeled
salt and freshly ground black pepper

1 Put the peppers into a saucepan with enough water to almost cover. Bring to the boil, then simmer until tender.
2 Remove the peppers from the water, discard the stems and seeds. Chop and place in a blender or food processor.
3 Add the garlic to the peppers, together with 300 ml/10 fl oz of the cooking water, and blend to a purée.
4 Transfer the sauce to a clean saucepan. Season to taste with salt and pepper and reheat gently without boiling.

V

SAUCE SOUBISE

V *Sauce Soubise; Sweet Pepper Sauce*
(p. 172); Hollandaise Sauce (p. 176)

One of my personal favourites, this delicately flavoured, thick
onion sauce is excellent with crisp nut loaves, such as the one on
p. 235, and nut burgers. If there's any left it's excellent poured over
hardboiled eggs, heated through in the oven and served with
fingers of hot wholewheat toast. You do need to use white rice for
this recipe because of its starchiness, which thickens the sauce.

SERVES 4

25 g/1 oz white long-grain rice
225 g/8 oz onions, peeled and coarsely
    chopped
15 g/½ oz butter or vegan margarine
75 ml/3 fl oz water
a few parsley sprigs
1 thyme sprig
1 small bay leaf
2 tablespoons double or non-dairy cream
salt and freshly ground black pepper
freshly grated nutmeg
a pinch of sugar

1 Parboil the rice in plenty of boiling
water for about 5 minutes, then drain.
2 Meanwhile, fry the chopped onions in
the butter or vegan margarine in a
medium saucepan for 10 minutes. Add
the drained rice, water and herbs.
3 Cover the pan and cook over a gentle
heat for 20–25 minutes, or until the
onions are very soft.
4 Remove from the heat and discard
the parsley, thyme and bay leaf. Purée
the onion mixture in a blender or food
processor.
5 Reheat the sauce gently in a double
saucepan or heatproof bowl set over a
saucepan of simmering water.
6 Just before serving, add the cream, and
season carefully with salt, pepper, nutmeg and sugar.

Gravy Alternatives

Don't get stuck in a gravy rut! There
are many other delicious sauces
which go excellently with vegetarian
savouries. Both the tomato sauces
on pp. 170 and 171 make excellent
alternatives to gravy and are
delicious with many vegetarian
dishes. Other good sauces to use in
place of gravy are:

Mushroom Sauce (p. 174)

Wine Sauce (p. 174)

Sweet Pepper Sauce (p. 172)

Sauce Soubise (left)

V MUSHROOM SAUCE V

SERVES 4

Making Quick Meals from Sauces

It's useful to have some sauce in the fridge or freezer, because it can make the basis of good quick meals. Try:

Fresh Tomato Sauce (p. 170) – over hot cooked pasta or with lightly steamed root vegetables or winter squash, served with cooked brown rice and roasted sunflower seeds; or parboil halved and de-seeded green peppers, fill with a mixture of cooked brown rice, fried onion, mushrooms and nuts, place in a casserole, pour tomato sauce round the peppers and bake

Italian Tomato Sauce (p. 171) – layered with lasagne, grated Mozzarella cheese and fried mushrooms or aubergines, or puréed spinach

Vegetarian Gravy (p. 172) – with fried onion and cubed left-over nut roast or bought canned nut savoury

Sauce Soubise (p. 173), Béchamel (p. 175) or Cheese Sauce (p. 175) – over cooked leeks, cauliflower or diced mixed root vegetables, or over hardboiled eggs

Egg Sauce (p. 175) – over any steamed vegetables; particularly good with fennel or courgettes

Curry Sauce (p. 177) or Savoury Coconut Sauce (p. 177) – over hardboiled eggs, drained canned chick peas or butter beans, or lightly steamed cauliflower

100 g/4 oz button mushrooms, washed and chopped
15 g/½ oz butter or vegan margarine
1 teaspoon cornflour
150 ml/5 fl oz milk, soya milk or single cream
salt and freshly ground black pepper
a few drops of lemon juice
freshly grated nutmeg

1 Fry the mushrooms in the butter or vegan margarine in a small saucepan for 4–5 minutes, until just tender, then stir in the cornflour.
2 Cook for 1–2 minutes, then add the milk, soya milk or cream, stirring all the time. Boil for 1 minute, then remove from the heat.
3 Season the Mushroom Sauce to taste with salt and pepper, a little lemon juice and freshly grated nutmeg.

Variation
WILD MUSHROOM SAUCE
A good way of using just a few precious wild mushrooms, delicious with a special nut roast or as a filling for vol au vents. Replace all, or some, of the button mushrooms with wild mushrooms, well-washed and chopped.

V WINE SAUCE V

Serve this rich sauce on individual plates, with nut burgers or roasts.

SERVES 4

1 onion, peeled and finely chopped
50 g/2 oz mushrooms, finely chopped
2 tablespoons olive oil
300 ml/10 fl oz red or white wine
25 g/1 oz butter or vegan margarine
salt and freshly ground black pepper
a little sugar

1 Fry the onion and mushrooms in the oil in a small saucepan for 10 minutes, until lightly browned.
2 Add the wine and let the mixture bubble away over the heat for a few minutes, uncovered, until the liquid has reduced by about half.
3 Cut the butter or vegan margarine into pieces, then add them to the sauce. Stir gently. Season to taste with salt, pepper and a little sugar. Serve the Wine Sauce immediately.

V CRANBERRY SAUCE V

For me, cranberry sauce, made from fresh cranberries, is an essential part of Christmas dinner.

SERVES 8

175 g/6 oz cranberries, washed
4 tablespoons water
75 g/3 oz sugar
1 tablespoon port or fresh orange juice

1 Put the cranberries into a saucepan with the water. Bring to the boil, then simmer for about 10 minutes, until the berries are tender.
2 Add the sugar and cook gently until it has dissolved. Remove the pan from the heat and add the port or fresh orange juice. Stir well, then serve the Cranberry Sauce at once.

V

BÉCHAMEL SAUCE

V

This sauce will keep, well covered, in the fridge, for a few days.

MAKES 450 ml/15 fl oz

25 g/1 oz butter or vegan margarine
25 g/1 oz plain flour
600 ml/1 pint milk or soya milk
a piece each of onion, celery and scraped
  carrot
1 bay leaf
6 black peppercorns
1 thyme sprig
1–2 mace blades
salt and freshly ground black pepper
freshly grated nutmeg

1 Melt the butter or vegan margarine in a medium saucepan. Add the flour, stir over the heat for 1–2 minutes, then add the milk, a quarter at a time, mixing well between each addition.
2 Add the onion, celery, carrot, bay leaf, peppercorns, thyme and mace, then leave the sauce to simmer gently for 10–15 minutes.
3 Strain the sauce through a sieve into a clean saucepan. Season to taste with salt, pepper and nutmeg.

Variations

PARSLEY SAUCE
Add 2–4 tablespoons chopped parsley and a few drops of lemon juice to the sauce after straining.

MORNAY OR CHEESE SAUCE
A non-vegan variation. Make as described. Add 1 teaspoon Dijon mustard and 50–100 g/2–4 oz grated Cheddar or Gruyère cheese to the sauce after straining. Reheat gently but do not allow to boil after adding the cheese or it may become stringy.

EGG SAUCE
Stir 2 finely chopped hardboiled eggs into the sauce after straining for another non-vegan variation.

V

BREAD SAUCE

V

Serve with a nut roast such as White Nut Roast (p. 239) as part of a traditional vegetarian Christmas dinner.

SERVES 4–6

3 cloves
1 onion, peeled
300 ml/10 fl oz milk or soya milk
1 bay leaf
50 g/2 oz white bread, crusts removed
15 g/1/2 oz butter or vegan margarine
2 tablespoons single or non-dairy cream
salt and freshly ground black pepper
freshly grated nutmeg

1 Stick the cloves into the onion, then put the onion into a saucepan with the milk and bay leaf.

2 Bring to the boil, then remove from the heat, add the bread, cover and set aside for 15–30 minutes, to allow the flavours to infuse.
3 Remove the onion and the bay leaf. Beat the mixture to break up the bread, and stir in the butter or vegan margarine, cream and salt, pepper and nutmeg to taste. Sprinkle nutmeg on top.

HOLLANDAISE SAUCE

Wonderfully rich, horribly fattening, but great for a special treat,
such as with the first asparagus of summer, or as a
filling for globe artichokes.

SERVES 6

Blender Hollandaise or Béarnaise Sauce

A blender or food processor can be used for no-fuss labour-saving versions of these sauces. Have the butter melted and cooled. Put the egg yolks into a blender or food processor with the lemon juice and water (for Hollandaise Sauce) or the strained reduced vinegar (for Béarnaise Sauce). Whizz until combined and thickened a little. Then add the melted butter through the top of the blender or food processor, a little at a time. The mixture will thicken. Add the lemon juice and seasoning to taste.

2 egg yolks
1 tablespoon water
1–2 teaspoons lemon juice
100 g / 4 oz unsalted butter
salt and freshly ground black pepper

1 Put the egg yolks, water and 1 teaspoon lemon juice into the top of a double saucepan, or into a heatproof bowl set over a saucepan of gently simmering water (with the base of the bowl above the level of the water).
2 Whisk the mixture until the egg yolks begin to thicken slightly.
3 Add the butter, about a teaspoon at a time, whisking well after each addition.

The sauce will thicken and become creamy.
4 Add the rest of the lemon juice, and salt and pepper to taste. Serve warm.

Variations
LIGHT HOLLANDAISE SAUCE
For a lighter version, whisk 2 egg whites until stiff and fold into the sauce before serving.

SAUCE MOUSSELINE
For this richer variation, lightly whip 75 ml / 3 fl oz whipping cream and gently fold into the sauce.

BÉARNAISE SAUCE

Another rich sauce, though a little goes a long way. It's wonderful
with crisp nut or lentil burgers. For a quick and easy
blender version, see left.

SERVES 6

MENU

Summer Supper for Two

Asparagus with Hollandaise Sauce

Summer Linguine
Illustrated on p. 254
255

Blackcurrant Sorbet
Illustrated on p. 283
282

½ small onion, peeled and chopped
1 bay leaf
6 black peppercorns
4 tablespoons white wine vinegar
1 tarragon sprig, or a pinch of dried tarragon
2 egg yolks
100 g / 4 oz unsalted butter
salt and freshly ground black pepper

1 Simmer the onion, bay leaf, peppercorns, vinegar and tarragon in a small saucepan until the liquid has reduced to 1 tablespoon.
2 Put the egg yolks into the top of a double saucepan, or into a heatproof bowl set over a saucepan of gently simmering water (with the base of the bowl above the level of the water).
3 Strain the reduced vinegar liquid over the egg yolks, pressing against the sieve to extract as much as possible.
4 Whisk the mixture until the egg yolks begin to thicken slightly.
5 Add the butter, about a teaspoon at a time, whisking well after each addition. The sauce will thicken and become creamy. Season to taste with salt and pepper. Serve warm.

V   # CURRY SAUCE   V

A useful sauce for turning a few vegetables into a meal, or for
serving with a spiced rice dish. The quantities of the spices can be
adjusted according to taste.

SERVES 4

4 tablespoons olive oil
1 garlic clove, crushed
1 onion, peeled and chopped
1 teaspoon grated fresh ginger
2½ teaspoons ground coriander
2½ teaspoons ground cumin
½ teaspoon curry powder
½ teaspoon turmeric
½ teaspoon white mustard seed (optional)
1 bay leaf
1 × 225-g/8-oz can tomatoes
450 ml/15 fl oz Dark Vegetable Stock
  (p. 132) or water
1 teaspoon garam masala
salt and freshly ground black pepper
TO GARNISH
1 lime slice
mustard seeds
1 bay leaf

1 Heat the oil in a medium saucepan and add the garlic, onion and ginger. Fry gently for 10 minutes, until the onion is soft but not brown.
2 Add all the spices except the garam masala, together with the bay leaf, and cook for a further 2 minutes, then add the tomatoes, Dark Vegetable Stock or water and simmer gently for 15 minutes, uncovered.
3 Stir in the garam masala and season to taste with salt and pepper and mix well together.
4 Remove the bay leaf. Serve the sauce as it is, or blend in a blender or food processor for a smoother texture. Transfer the sauce to a small bowl and garnish with the lime slice, mustard seeds and bay leaf.

Curry Sauce

V   # SAVOURY COCONUT SAUCE   V

A delicately flavoured, golden sauce. Serve it with steamed
vegetables and brown rice, for a simple meal, or heat halved
hardboiled eggs through in it for a delicious egg curry.

SERVES 4

100 g/4 oz desiccated coconut
600 ml/1 pint water
1 onion, peeled and chopped
25 g/1 oz butter or vegan margarine
1 teaspoon turmeric
1 teaspoon grated fresh ginger
1 garlic clove, crushed
½ cinnamon stick or a pinch of ground
  cinnamon
salt and freshly ground black pepper
a little sugar
a few drops of lemon juice (optional)

1 Put the coconut into a saucepan with the water. Bring to the boil, then remove from the heat, cover and leave to stand in

the saucepan for 10 minutes.
2 Meanwhile, fry the onion in the butter or vegan margarine in a medium saucepan for 5 minutes. Add the turmeric, ginger, garlic and cinnamon, and fry gently for a further 5 minutes.
3 Strain the coconut mixture into the onion mixture, pressing as much liquid through as you can. Discard the coconut in the sieve.
4 Remove the cinnamon stick, then purée the mixture in a blender or food processor. Return the sauce to the rinsed-out pan, season to taste with salt, pepper and a little sugar, and add the lemon juice to sharpen if necessary.

MENU

Quick and Easy Supper

SERVES 4

Fusille Colbuco with Aubergine and Wine Sauce
255

Parmesan Cheese
Chicory, Watercress and Walnut Salad
161

Quick Cherry and Lime Cheesecake
288

This is a meal which you can whizz up on the spur of the moment, assuming you have some fresh salad vegetables in the fridge and the ingredients for the Quick Cherry and Lime Cheesecake. Otherwise, serve the pasta with some frozen vegetables which, hopefully, you have in the freezer, and offer fresh fruit or biscuits and cheese instead of a pudding, if you have them available.

First make the cheesecake, then while that is chilling prepare the Aubergine and Wine Sauce. While that cooks, wash the salad, make a dressing and, when the sauce is almost done, cook the pasta. Serve with whatever drink you happen to have in the kitchen: a chilled lager, or a wine with some body, to support all the flavours of the sauce, perhaps an Italian red, a Chianti, Barolo or Barbaresco, or a good value Cabernet Sauvignon from anywhere.

Accompanying Vegetables

These recipes for accompanying vegetable dishes are the ones which I find the most practical and useful. Some, such as Red Cabbage Casserole (below), are labour-saving because they can be cooked slowly and add moisture to a main dish, eliminating the need for a separate sauce. Many also add a bright splash of colour, enhancing the look of the meal. Sometimes a simply cooked accompanying vegetable is best, especially if the main course is vegetable-based, and you will find some recipes for these in this section, and further ideas in the Ingredients section (p. 32), under individual vegetables.

V   ## STEAMED AND MARINATED AUBERGINE   V

A very simple yet delicious way of preparing aubergine without any oil. This is especially good with Chinese and Japanese dishes.

SERVES 4

Quantities for Vegetables

It's difficult to give exact quantities, because these depend on what else you're serving at the meal – whether there's another vegetable, for instance, and the type of main dish – and how much you like vegetables! As a general rule, allow 175–225 g/ 6–8 oz per person. I'm quite greedy with vegetables, because my favourite way of staying slim is to have lots of vegetables and just a small amount of the main course.

2 medium aubergines, total weight about
   450 g/1 lb
2 tablespoons soy sauce
1 teaspoon sugar
2 teaspoons vinegar
salt and freshly ground black pepper

1 Remove the stems from the aubergines and cut the flesh into large dice.
2 Steam the aubergine until tender – 5–10 minutes. Transfer to a shallow dish and sprinkle with the rest of the ingredients.
3 Serve hot, warm or cold.

V   ## RED CABBAGE CASSEROLE   V

A useful dish, because it can cook away gently, and the result is moist enough to stand in for both a vegetable and a sauce.

SERVES 4–6

1 red cabbage, about 1 kg/2¼ lb, cored and
   shredded
1 large onion, peeled and chopped
2 tablespoons oil
2 tablespoons lemon juice
salt and freshly ground black pepper
a little sugar

1 Put the cabbage into a large saucepan, cover with water and bring to the boil, then drain thoroughly.
2 Meanwhile, fry the onion in the oil in a large saucepan for 5 minutes, then add the cabbage, cover and cook very gently for 45–60 minutes, until the cabbage is very tender, stirring occasionally.
3 Add the lemon juice and salt, pepper and sugar to taste.

V   # SPRING VEGETABLE BRAISE   V

This is a particularly good way to cook a colourful selection of
tender young vegetables, but this method can be used throughout
the year for different mixtures, according to what is in season.

SERVES 4

6 tablespoons olive oil
6 tablespoons water
pared rind of ½ lemon
a good sprig each of parsley and thyme
450 g/1 lb tender young carrots, scraped and
   halved or quartered if large
450 g/1 lb tender young turnips, scrubbed and
   halved or quartered if necessary
225 g/8 oz mangetouts, topped and tailed
225 g/8 oz broad beans (shelled weight)
salt and freshly ground black pepper
2–3 tablespoons chopped parsley

1 Put the oil into a large saucepan with
the water, lemon rind, parsley and thyme
and bring to the boil.
2 Add the carrots and turnips; cover and
simmer gently for 5–10 minutes, until
just tender.
3 Meanwhile, blanch the mangetouts by
plunging them into a saucepan of boiling
water, bringing back to the boil and boiling for 1 minute. Drain and refresh under
the cold tap, to preserve the colour.
4 Add the beans and mangetouts to the

carrot mixture and cook for a further 2–3
minutes, until heated through.
5 Season with salt and pepper. Serve
sprinkled with parsley.

Spring Vegetable Braise

V   # STIR-FRIED CARROTS WITH   V
WATERCRESS AND SESAME SEEDS

A quick vegetable dish, excellent with Japanese or Chinese meals.

SERVES 2–4

2 teaspoons oil
4 spring onions, trimmed and sliced
350 g/12 oz carrots, scraped and cut into
   matchsticks
1 bunch watercress, tough stems removed
1 tablespoon soy sauce
salt
TO GARNISH
1–2 tablespoons sesame seeds

1 Heat the oil in a wok or saucepan, then
add the onions and carrots and stir-fry for
2 minutes.
2 Add the watercress, stir-fry for 1–2
minutes, then cook gently for a further
3–4 minutes, stirring from time to time.
3 Stir in the soy sauce and a little salt,
then sprinkle the vegetables with sesame
seeds and serve immediately.

BRAISED CELERY HEARTS

V   V

Braised vegetables are cooked slowly with a little liquid and flavouring ingredients. Sometimes the vegetables are lightly browned in fat before the liquid is added. Braising suits bulb vegetables such as celery, leeks and fennel particularly well.

SERVES 4

TURNING CARROTS

1 Cut carrots into rectangles about 5 cm/2 inches long

2 Round off the corners with a sharp knife, to make a barrel shape

4 celery hearts, trimmed to about 12–15 cm/ 5–6 inches
1 onion, peeled and chopped
2 carrots, scraped and diced
1 bouquet garni, including a piece of lemon peel
salt and freshly ground black pepper
TO GARNISH
chopped parsley

1 Wash the celery thoroughly, using a bottle brush, if necessary, to clean the inside.
2 Put the celery into a large saucepan, cover with water, bring to the boil, then boil for 10 minutes. Drain well, saving the water.
3 Cover the base of a large, heavy saucepan with the onion and carrot, then place the celery on top. Add the bouquet garni, season to taste with salt and pepper, then pour in enough of the reserved cooking water to cover.

4 Bring to the boil, then simmer, with a lid on the pan, until the celery is very tender – 45–60 minutes.
5 Remove the celery from the saucepan with a slotted spoon and put it into a warmed shallow serving dish.
6 If the liquid has reduced to a sauce-like consistency, strain this over the celery. If not, boil it vigorously for a minute or two to reduce it, then strain it over the celery.
7 Sprinkle the celery with parsley and serve immediately.

Variation
BRAISED FENNEL
Make this in the same way, but cut the bulbs in half and instead of par-boiling the fennel, fry it in a little olive oil, for about 10 minutes, in a covered pan. Turn the fennel pieces from time to time during the cooking, allowing them to brown evenly on all sides.

GLAZED CARROTS

V   V

For a special effect and a professional finish, the carrots can be 'turned'; I do this sometimes when I feel like being impressive, but normally I cut them into rings or sticks. They are particularly delicious with nut savouries.

SERVES 4

900 g/2 lb carrots, peeled or scraped and sliced into sticks or rings
25 g/1 oz butter or vegan margarine
salt and freshly ground black pepper
2 tablespoons caster or soft light brown sugar
TO GARNISH
2 tablespoons chopped parsley

1 Put the prepared carrots into a large saucepan, cover them with cold water

and bring the water to the boil.
2 Half cover the saucepan, and leave the carrots to simmer gently until just tender – 8–15 minutes.
3 Drain the carrots, then return them to the pan with the butter or vegan margarine, salt and pepper. Cook over a gentle heat until the butter or vegan margarine has melted, shaking the pan to coat all the carrots in butter or margarine.

Glazed Carrots (p. 182); Peas Cooked in the French Style

4 Sprinkle on the sugar, mixing gently over the heat until all the sugar has melted and the carrots are shining with glaze. Sprinkle the chopped parsley over the top and serve immediately.

Variation

GLAZED TURNIPS

Cook as described, using whole baby turnips if you can get them, otherwise use sliced or 'turned' turnips.

V PEAS COOKED IN THE FRENCH STYLE V

This is a wonderful way to make frozen peas (or fresh peas, when you can get young, tender ones) taste really good.

SERVES 4

1 small bunch spring onions, trimmed and chopped
25 g/1 oz butter or vegan margarine
outer leaves from 1 lettuce, washed and roughly shredded
450 g/1 lb frozen peas or shelled fresh peas
½ teaspoon sugar
salt and freshly ground black pepper
2–3 mint sprigs when available

1 Fry the spring onions in half the butter or vegan margarine in a medium sauce-pan for 2–3 minutes on medium heat.
2 Add the lettuce and peas. Sprinkle with the sugar and salt and pepper to taste.
3 Dot with the remaining butter or vegan margarine, pop the sprigs of mint, if used, on top, then cover.
4 Cook over a gentle heat for 10–15 minutes, until the peas are tender.
5 Check the seasoning and remove the mint. Serve the cooked peas immediately, with (my preference) or without the shredded lettuce.

V JULIENNE OF ROOT VEGETABLES V

This mixture of orange carrots, yellow swede and white turnip works well, but you could use just two of these vegetables, or different vegetables. Some kohlrabi makes a pleasant addition.

SERVES 4

CUTTING JULIENNE SLICES

1 Cut rounded edges off root vegetables so that they are rectangular in shape

2 Cut into thin slices one way, then the other way, to make matchsticks

300 g/10 oz carrots, scrapea
300 g/10 oz turnips, peeled
300 g/10 oz swede, peeled
15 g/½ oz butter or vegan margarine
salt and freshly ground black pepper
TO GARNISH
1–2 tablespoons chopped parsley

1 Cut the vegetables into julienne strips, then put them into a saucepan, cover with cold water and bring to the boil.
2 Half cover the pan and cook gently until the vegetables are just tender – about 10 minutes, depending on how thinly you cut them.
3 Drain, saving the water which makes particularly good stock, then return the vegetables to the pan and add the butter or vegan margarine. Season to taste with the salt and pepper, sprinkle with the chopped parsley and serve.

Variations

JULIENNE BUNDLES
Keep the vegetables separate during cooking. Soften a chive or thin strip of leek by dipping in boiling water for 1–2 minutes. Serve the vegetables in bundles tied with the blanched chive or leek strip.

JULIENNE OF CARROTS
This is very good made with carrots alone, especially when you want to bring a splash of bright colour to a meal. A pinch or two of aniseed, caraway or dill gives a pleasant, unusual flavour to this vegetable dish.

Soy Sauce

This is a richly flavoured, slightly sweet flavouring liquid which has been used in China and Japan for centuries and is useful for adding both flavour and colour to stews, casseroles, sauces and marinades, as well as for flavouring stir-fries, and as a dip for tempura. Choose a naturally fermented soy sauce without added caramel. Tamari has the strongest flavour and the darkest colour; shoyu is lighter; the difference between these in cooking terms can be compared to that between red and white wine, though they can really be used interchangeably in most recipes.

V CHINESE-STYLE MUSHROOMS V

This simple dish is pleasant with Chinese dishes such as Chinese-Style Fried Rice (p. 243).

SERVES 4

225 g/8 oz small button mushrooms, wiped
1 tablespoon olive oil
1 teaspoon cornflour
3 tablespoons soy sauce
TO GARNISH (OPTIONAL)
spring onion curls

1 Fry the mushrooms quickly in the olive oil in a small saucepan for 2–3 minutes, over high heat, until just tender.
2 Blend the cornflour and soy sauce. Add to the mushrooms, and stir for 1–2 minutes, until thickened. Garnish with the spring onion curls, if using, and serve immediately.

V   GOLDEN SPICED CAULIFLOWER   V

A beautiful golden dish, one of my favourite ways of preparing cauliflower. Some chopped fresh coriander (or parsley) is the perfect finishing touch, but it's also very good without.

SERVES 4

1 onion, peeled and chopped
2 tablespoons oil
1 garlic clove, crushed
½ teaspoon turmeric
1 teaspoon ground coriander
2 cardamom pods
1 small cauliflower, divided into florets
150 ml/5 fl oz water
salt and freshly ground black pepper
TO GARNISH
sprig of mint

1 Fry the onion in the oil in a medium saucepan for 8 minutes, then add the garlic, turmeric, coriander and cardamom. Stir over the heat for a further 2–3 minutes.

2 Add the cauliflower, turning it gently with a spoon to coat with the onion and spice mixture, then add the water and some salt and pepper. Bring the mixture to the boil.

3 Cover and leave to cook gently for about 15 minutes, until the cauliflower is just tender. Shake the pan from time to time to prevent sticking and ensure even cooking.

4 Check the seasoning, then garnish with a sprig of mint and serve the cauliflower immediately.

Variations

SPICED POTATOES

For this excellent variation, use 900 g/ 2 lb peeled potatoes, cut into 1-cm/ ½-inch dice. Make exactly as described, but do cook it gently and keep an eye on the pan, to prevent sticking. Most of the liquid should have been absorbed by the time the potatoes are cooked – 8–10 minutes – leaving them bathed in just a little golden, spicy sauce. The chopped fresh coriander is particularly good with potatoes cooked this way but parsley can be used if coriander is unavailable.

SPICED ROOT VEGETABLES

A delicious winter variation. Use 900 g/ 2 lb peeled root vegetables cut into 1-cm/ ½-inch dice. A mixture of root vegetables can be used: swedes, carrots, turnips, parsnips as well as sliced onions and celery, as available. Make as described for the Spiced Potatoes variation. This makes a good accompaniment to a mild-flavoured dish and goes well with nut or lentil burgers.

Okra with Cumin and Coriander (p. 186); Golden Spiced Cauliflower

PEPERONATA

V   V

For this delicious Italian pepper stew, you can use all red peppers,
or a mixture of red, yellow and green peppers, which gives a
particularly attractive result.

SERVES 4

1 large onion, peeled and chopped
15 g / ½ oz butter or vegan margarine
1 tablespoon olive oil
2 large red peppers
2 large yellow peppers
2 large green peppers
1 large garlic clove, crushed
450 g / 1 lb tomatoes, skinned and chopped
salt and freshly ground black pepper
TO GARNISH
1–2 tablespoons chopped parsley

1 Fry the onion in the butter or vegan margarine and the oil in a large saucepan for 10 minutes, allowing the onion to brown lightly.
2 Meanwhile, de-seed the peppers and cut them into strips, them add them to the onion. Cover and cook gently for 10–15 minutes.
3 Add the garlic and tomatoes, then cover and cook for a further 40 minutes or so, until the peppers are very tender and soft.
4 Season to taste with salt and pepper, sprinkle with chopped parsley and serve. Peperonata reheats well, or is excellent served cold.

V OKRA WITH CUMIN AND CORIANDER V

This lightly spiced dish can be made in advance and then reheated.

SERVES 2, OR 4, WITH OTHER DISHES, AS PART OF A CURRY MEAL

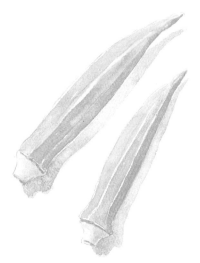

1 onion, peeled and chopped
2 tablespoons oil
225 g / 8 oz okra, washed and trimmed
1 teaspoon salt
1 teaspoon whole cumin seeds
1 tablespoon ground coriander
200 ml / 7 fl oz water
2 tomatoes, chopped
salt and freshly ground black pepper
TO GARNISH
1–2 tablespoons chopped coriander

1 Fry the onion in the oil in a medium saucepan for 5 minutes, then add the okra, salt, cumin and coriander. Mix well, then cook gently, uncovered, for 5 minutes.
2 Add the water, then simmer, un-covered, for 20 minutes, until the okra is tender and most of the water has been absorbed. Shake the pan, or stir, from time to time to prevent sticking.

3 Add the tomatoes, check the season-ing, and sprinkle with the chopped coriander. Serve hot or warm. (It's also pleasant cold, garnished with a slice of lemon and chopped parsley.)

Variations
SPICED RUNNER BEANS
This is also a good way to serve runner beans, especially if you grow them and are getting tired of them while they're still producing prolifically! Top, tail and slice the beans in the usual way (p. 61), then cook as described.

SPICED AUBERGINE
Another variation which works well and makes a useful side dish for serving with curries. Dice and degorge (p. 73) a medium-sized aubergine and fry with the onion for 10 minutes before adding the tomatoes.

V # RATATOUILLE V

This delicious Provençale vegetable mixture is good with cooked
brown rice or crusty bread and a crisp salad. If you're serving it with rice,
put this on to cook before you start making the Ratatouille.

SERVES 4

3 tablespoons olive oil
2 large onions, peeled and chopped
3 large red peppers, de-seeded and sliced
3 garlic cloves, crushed
450 g / 1 lb courgettes, cut into even-sized
*   pieces*
450 g / 1 lb aubergines, diced
700 g / 1½ lb tomatoes, skinned and chopped
salt and freshly ground black pepper
TO GARNISH
chopped parsley

1 Heat the oil in a large saucepan and
fry the onions and peppers gently for
5 minutes.
2 Add the garlic, courgettes and the
aubergines. Stir gently, then cover and
cook over a low heat for about 25 minutes, until all the vegetables are tender.
3 Add the tomatoes, stir gently and
cook, uncovered, for about 5 minutes, to
heat through. Season to taste with salt
and pepper and sprinkle with parsley.
Serve hot or cold.

*Flavouring Vegetarian
Dishes*

You can introduce strong, almost
'meaty' flavours by using yeast
extracts and soy preparations such as
miso and soy sauces. Or – and I
must admit that this is my own
preference – you can concentrate on
the assets of the vegetarian diet,
which are the fresh flavours of the
vegetables, nuts and grains, and
accent these by joyous use of fresh
herbs, chopped and in bouquets
garnis; citrus rinds and juices; good-
quality salt and freshly ground black
pepper; the judicious – and
sometimes generous – use of spices;
the use of wine.

V # LEEK AND PEAR PURÉE V

This is particularly good with pulse and nut savouries.

SERVES 4–6

450 g / 1 lb leeks, trimmed, cleaned and sliced
450 g / 1 lb pears, peeled, cored and sliced
300 ml / 10 fl oz water
4 garlic cloves
25 g / 1 oz soft butter or vegan margarine
salt and freshly ground black pepper

1 Put the leeks and pears into a large
saucepan with the water and whole garlic
cloves. Boil for about 15 minutes, until
tender.
2 Remove the garlic cloves and pop
them out of their skins; put them into a
blender or food processor with the leeks,
pears and cooking liquid, and blend until
smooth.
3 Reheat the mixture gently and stir in
the butter or vegan margarine. Season to
taste with salt and pepper.

Variations
CARROT, APPLE AND
CORIANDER PUREE
Make as described, using carrots instead
of leeks and dessert apples instead of

pears, and a medium onion, peeled and
sliced. Add 1 tablespoon crushed coriander seeds, tied in a small piece of muslin,
to the mixture. Remove this, squeezing it
well to extract all the flavour, before
puréeing. Garnish with fresh chopped
coriander, if available, or chopped
parsley.

PUMPKIN AND GINGER
PURÉE
Replace the leeks and pears with 900 g /
2 lb pumpkin or winter squash (weighed
without skin and pips). Cook the squash
with the water as described and a walnut-
sized piece of ginger, grated.

CARROT AND SWEDE
PURÉE
Replace the apples with swede, peeled
and cut into even-sized pieces. Some
freshly grated nutmeg and a pinch of a
warm spice such as cinnamon, allspice or
ground cloves are good with this, or 2–3
tablespoons chopped parsley.

Potato and Almond Croquettes; Carrot Purée (p. 189)

V POTATO AND ALMOND CROQUETTES V

These croquettes make a good vegetarian cooked breakfast, served with grilled tomatoes and mushrooms. For a light meal, serve them with Sweet Carrot and Fennel Salad (p. 162); or with Mushrooms in Cream (p. 79) and a green vegetable.

SERVES 4

4 large potatoes, peeled and cut into even-sized pieces
15 g / ½ oz butter or vegan margarine
2–3 tablespoons milk or soya milk
100 g / 4 oz flaked or chopped almonds
3 tablespoons chopped parsley
salt and freshly ground black pepper
wholewheat flour or ground almonds for coating
oil for shallow-frying
TO GARNISH
lovage sprig

1 Boil the potatoes in water to cover until they are tender – about 20 minutes.

2 Drain the potatoes, then dry them in the pan over a low heat for 1–2 minutes.
3 Mash the potatoes with the butter or vegan margarine and enough milk or soya milk to give a creamy consistency.
4 Stir in the chopped almonds and parsley, and season with salt and pepper.
5 Form into 8 croquettes, then coat in wholewheat flour or ground almonds.
6 Shallow-fry in a little hot oil in a frying pan until the undersides are crisp, then turn the croquettes and fry on the other side until crisp.
7 Drain on kitchen paper. Serve immediately, garnished with lovage.

V   POTATO PURÉE   V

This is really a way of saying very light, smooth, mashed potatoes, perhaps made a bit moister than you normally would. It's one of my favourite ways of serving potatoes, very useful because not only is it delicious, but it adds some moisture to the meal, often eliminating the need for extra sauces.

SERVES 4

700 g / 1½ lb potatoes, peeled and cut into
   even-sized pieces
150 ml / 5 fl oz milk or soya milk
salt and freshly ground black pepper
15–25 g / ½–1 oz butter or vegan margarine
TO GARNISH
chopped parsley

1 Put the potatoes into a large saucepan, cover with cold water and bring to the boil. Boil, half-covered, for about 15 minutes, until just tender.
2 Drain the potatoes, and either return to the pan and mash very thoroughly with a potato masher, or, for best results, pass the potatoes through a vegetable mill.
3 Put the puréed potato back into the saucepan. Heat the milk or soya milk in another saucepan and, when it comes to the boil, add it gradually to the potatoes, beating all the time. The potatoes will become fluffy and whiter and should be the consistency of whipped cream.
4 Season to taste with salt and pepper. If you are serving the potatoes straight away, beat in the butter or vegan margarine; if not, keep the potatoes warm by standing the saucepan in an outer pan of boiling water; or transfer the potatoes to another container standing in a saucepan of water. Then beat in the butter or vegan margarine just before serving. Sprinkle with chopped parsley, to serve.

Variations

POTATO PURÉE WITH GARLIC
Add 1–2 crushed garlic cloves to the mixture after puréeing the potatoes.

POTATO AND CELERIAC PURÉE WITH PISTACHIOS
Replace 225 g / 8 oz of the potatoes with celeriac, peeled, cut into even-sized pieces and cooked with the potatoes. Garnish with a scattering of chopped shelled pistachio nuts.

CARROT PURÉE
Replace the potatoes with the same amount of carrots. Cook until tender, then drain. Use some of the cooking water instead of some of the milk, if wished. Garnish with chopped parsley.

V   RÖSTI   V

This delicious crisp golden potato cake from Switzerland is quick and easy to make.

SERVES 4

4 tablespoons oil
450 g / 1 lb potatoes, scrubbed or peeled, then
   coarsely grated
salt

1 Heat the oil in a large frying pan with a lid, add the potatoes and salt. Press down.
2 Cook the potatoes gently, covered, until they are browned on the bottom.
3 Turn the rösti over, either with a fish slice, or by turning it out on to a plate then sliding it back into the frying pan.
4 Cook until the second side is browned and crisp. Serve immediately.

MENU
Winter Brunch for Four

Rösti
Illustrated on p. 191

Scrambled Eggs
107
Warm Quick Wholewheat Rolls
328
Grilled Tomatoes

Fresh Fruit Salad
286

MENU
Winter Brunch for Eight

Millet Pilaf with Nuts and Raisins
245
Rösti
Illustrated on p. 191

Scrambled Eggs
107

Waffles with Clear Honey
298
Dried Fruit Compote
Illustrated on p. 14
102

V BAKED POTATOES V

Baked potatoes make one of the easiest and most economical dishes. Simply scrub one or two large potatoes per person, prick and bake at 230C/450F/Gas Mark 8 for 1–1½ hours, until the potatoes feel soft when squeezed and the skins are crisp. Then split open and serve with butter and grated cheese, or some cottage cheese or soured cream or plain yogurt, or with one of the following toppings:

Accompanying Vegetables as Main Courses

Some accompanying vegetables make excellent main courses if served with extras such as cooked brown rice, warm rolls, garlic bread, hot cooked pasta or a potato dish. Some suggestions are:

Spring Vegetable Braise (p. 181) with wedges of hardboiled egg and new potatoes, or with warm crusty bread

Red Cabbage Casserole (p. 180) with Baked Potatoes (right) and soured cream, or with Gratin Dauphinois (below right)

Stir-Fried Carrots with Watercress and Sesame Seeds (p. 181) with Chinese-Style Mushrooms (p. 184) and Sweet Vinegared Rice (p. 241)

Toppings for Baked Potatoes

CREAMY MUSHROOMS
Top the potatoes with Mushroom Sauce (p. 174).

CREAMY SWEETCORN
Heat 100 g/4 oz frozen sweetcorn kernels in 4 tablespoons cream, dairy or vegan, stirring, until the sweetcorn is hot, then season to taste with salt and pepper.

CHILLI-TOMATO-CHEESE
A non-vegan topping. Fry a small, finely chopped onion in 15 g/½ oz butter for about 10 minutes, until soft but not browned. Then add a 225-g/8-oz can tomatoes, mashing them a bit as you put

them in, and a pinch of chilli powder and 100 g/4 oz grated cheese. Stir gently over the heat until the cheese has melted and the mixture is hot.

GUACAMOLE
Spoon Guacamole (p. 144) over the hot potatoes.

SOURED CREAM AND CHIVES
Add 2 tablespoons snipped chives to 150 ml/5 fl oz soured cream for this excellent non-vegan topping. Mix the chives and cream together gently, season to taste with salt and pepper, and spoon over the hot potatoes.

Braised Celery Hearts (p. 182) with Cheese Sauce (p. 175) and crusty bread

Ratatouille (p. 187) with hot cooked brown rice and a lettuce and fresh herb salad

Baked Potatoes (above right) with Technicolour Cabbage Salad (p. 162)

Stuffed Jacket Potatoes (p. 191) with Favourite Coleslaw (p. 161)

Rösti (p. 189) or Hashed Brown Potatoes (p. 191) with Apple Sauce (p. 84) and Carrot, Fennel and Red Pepper Salad (p. 162)

GRATIN DAUPHINOIS

A delectable dish for a special occasion. Keep the other vegetables in the meal fairly simple.

SERVES 6

40 g/1½ oz butter
700 g/1½ lb potatoes, peeled and sliced as thinly as possible
salt and freshly ground black pepper
freshly grated nutmeg (optional)
1 large garlic clove, crushed
150 ml/5 fl oz double cream

1 Preheat the oven to 170C/325F/Gas Mark 3. Use half the butter to grease a shallow ovenproof dish generously.
2 Put the potato slices into a colander and

rinse well under the cold tap; drain and dry on kitchen paper.
3 Layer the potato slices in the prepared dish, seasoning with salt, pepper and nutmeg, if using, and a smear of crushed garlic between each layer.
4 Pour the cream evenly over the top of the potatoes and dot with the rest of the butter.
5 Bake, uncovered, for 1½–2 hours, until the potatoes feel tender when pierced with the point of a knife.

V   # HASHED BROWN POTATOES   V

This American way with fried potatoes gives a particularly
savoury result.

SERVES 2–4

4 tablespoons oil
450 g / 1 lb potatoes, scrubbed or peeled and
   diced, cooked or uncooked
1 small onion, finely chopped (optional)
salt and freshly ground black pepper

1 Heat the oil in a large frying pan with a
lid, then add the potatoes with the onion,
if used, and press down with a spatula.
2 If the potatoes are raw, cook them over
a gentle heat, covered, until they are tender, then turn up the heat to brown them.
3 Fry cooked potatoes over a moderate
heat until golden-brown underneath.
Press them down into the oil several
times with a spatula.
4 Divide the potatoes in the middle and
turn each half over. When they are
golden brown and crisp, drain on kitchen
paper. Season and serve immediately.

V   # STUFFED JACKET POTATOES   V

*Clockwise from top: Hashed Brown
Potatoes; Rösti (p. 189); Gratin
Dauphinois (p. 190)*

Serve these with some salad, such as Technicolour Cabbage Salad
(p. 162) or Sweet Carrot and Fennel Salad (p. 162).

1–2 large potatoes per person
a little butter and milk per person
25–50 g / 1–2 oz grated cheese per person
salt and freshly ground black pepper
2–3 tablespoons chopped fresh herbs

1 Scrub and prick the potatoes, then
bake them at 230 C / 450 F / Gas Mark 8 for
1–1½ hours until the skins are crisp and
the potatoes feel tender inside when
squeezed.
2 Halve the potatoes and scoop out the
insides. Place the skins on a baking sheet.
Mash the scooped-out potato with a little

butter and milk and half the cheese.
Season to taste with salt and pepper.
3 Pile the mixture back into the potato
skins, sprinkle with the remaining cheese
and return the potatoes to the oven for
about 20 minutes, until golden-brown
and crisp.

Vegan Variation
HERBY STUFFED JACKET
POTATOES
Omit the cheese, replace the butter with
vegan margarine and use plenty of herbs.
Season well with salt and pepper.

Main Vegetable Dishes

Vegetables can be made into some filling and tempting main courses, ranging from simple homely dishes like Vegetable Hotpot (p. 200), to exquisite stuffed vegetables, one of my favourite main courses for a special meal. Other particularly popular dishes include vegetable kebabs and vegetable tempura which, served with rice, make main courses that appeal – especially to non-vegetarians. Although some of the stuffed vegetables are a little fiddly to make, other recipes in this section, such as the Sweet and Sour Vegetable Stir-Fry (p. 199) and the Potato and Cheese Layer (p. 200), are particularly easy, good for mid-week and family cooking, when time presses.

V STUFFED AUBERGINES À LA PROVENÇALE V

Served on a bed of cooked rice, potato purée or cooked noodles, and accompanied by a green salad, these stuffed aubergines make a delicious main course.

SERVES 4

2 aubergines, total weight about 450 g/1 lb
salt
olive oil
1 large onion, peeled and chopped
4 tomatoes, skinned and chopped
2 garlic cloves, crushed
2 tablespoons chopped parsley
freshly ground black pepper
4 tablespoons fresh wholewheat breadcrumbs
a little butter or vegan margarine

1 Remove the stalks from the aubergines and cut them in half lengthways. Make cuts across the flesh, without piercing the skin, then degorge as described on p. 73.
2 Scoop the flesh out of the skins, chop the flesh.
3 Preheat the oven to 200 C/400 F/Gas Mark 6.
4 Heat a little oil in a large saucepan and fry the aubergine skins for about 3 minutes on both sides. Remove from the pan, place in a shallow ovenproof dish and set aside.
5 Next fry the onion and aubergine flesh for 7 minutes, adding a little more oil if necessary. Add the tomatoes and garlic and fry for a further 3 minutes, then mix in the parsley and season to taste with salt and pepper.
6 Spoon the mixture into the aubergine skins, sprinkle with the crumbs, dot with butter or vegan margarine and bake for 20–30 minutes, until the aubergine skins are tender and the filling mixture is browned on top.

SCOOPING OUT AN AUBERGINE

Cut around the edge of the aubergine, and make criss-cross cuts over the surface. Degorge (p. 73), then scoop out the flesh

V COURGETTES WITH CARROT, GINGER V
AND ALMOND STUFFING

Light and delicately spiced, these courgettes are good with a green
salad and a Vegan Yogurt and Herb Dressing (p. 156).

SERVES 4

1 large onion, peeled and chopped
2 tablespoons olive oil
4 medium courgettes, total weight about
  750 g / 1½ lb
1 garlic clove, crushed
350 g / 12 oz carrots, scraped and finely diced
¾ teaspoon grated fresh ginger
75 g / 3 oz flaked almonds
salt and freshly ground black pepper

1 Preheat the oven to 190 C / 375 F / Gas
Mark 5.
2 Fry the onion in the oil in a medium
saucepan for 5 minutes.
3 Meanwhile, halve the courgettes
lengthways and scoop out as much of the
centres as you can, to make a good cavity
for stuffing.
4 Chop the scooped-out courgette and
add it to the onion along with the garlic,
carrot and ginger. Cover and fry gently
for about 10 minutes, until the vegetables
are soft.

5 Remove from the heat and add the
almonds and salt and pepper to taste.
6 Place the courgette skins in a greased
shallow casserole and fill them with the
carrot mixture. (If the courgettes are
long, they can be cut in halves or
thirds.)
7 Cover with foil and bake for about 40
minutes, until the courgettes are tender.
Serve immediately.

Variation
COURGETTES WITH
CURD CHEESE AND ALMOND
STUFFING
For this variation, which is good served
on a base of stir-fried shredded Chinese
leaves, replace the carrots with 350 g/
12 oz curd cheese. Flavour with fresh ginger as suggested, or with 1–2 teaspoons
grated lemon rind and a few drops of
lemon juice. 1–2 tablespoons chopped
parsley or chives can also be added.

PREPARING A
COURGETTE FOR
STUFFING

Cut in half lengthways and scoop
out the seeds and pulp to leave a
cavity for stuffing

Baked Stuffed Avocado (p. 196);
Stuffed Peppers (p. 194), Courgettes
with Carrot, Ginger and Almond
Stuffing

V Marrow with Hazelnut Stuffing V
and Apple Sauce

This is a pleasant blend of flavours. Serve as a main course with crisp roast potatoes and one or two cooked vegetables, such as French beans and carrots. A Vegetarian Gravy (p. 172) can be served with it as well as the apple sauce.

SERVES 4–6

1 medium marrow, weighing about 1 kg/
   2¼ lb
2 large onions, peeled and chopped
50 g/2 oz butter or vegan margarine
100 g/4 oz hazelnuts, roasted, skinned and
   grated
100 g/4 oz fresh wholewheat breadcrumbs
2–3 tablespoons chopped fresh sage
salt and freshly ground black pepper
a little extra butter or vegan margarine for
   greasing
1 quantity Apple Sauce (p. 84)

1 Preheat the oven to 200 C/400 F/Gas Mark 6.
2 Cut the stalk off the marrow, then peel the marrow, keeping it whole. Cut a slice off one end, and, using a spoon, scoop out the seeds, to leave a cavity for stuffing.
3 Fry the onions in the butter or vegan margarine for 10 minutes, until soft, then add the hazelnuts, breadcrumbs, sage and salt and pepper to taste. Push the mixture into the marrow, then replace the sliced-off end.
4 Grease a large piece of greaseproof paper with butter or vegan margarine and wrap the marrow completely in this. Place in a baking tin.
5 Bake for about 1 hour, until the marrow is tender when pierced with a skewer. Remove the greaseproof paper and serve cut into slices with Apple Sauce.

SCOOPING OUT A MARROW

Cut a thin slice off the stalk end, then scoop out the seeds and pulp; replace the slice after stuffing

DE-SEEDING A PEPPER

Halve the pepper, cut out the white membranes, then rinse away the seeds

V   Stuffed Peppers   V

Red, green or yellow peppers can be used for this, either 6 of one type, or a mixture, for a multicoloured dish. I think a puréed vegetable, particularly potatoes, or buttered noodles with poppy seeds, and a simple green salad of cucumber or lettuce goes well with this dish.

SERVES 6

SCOOPING OUT A TOMATO

Slice the top off the tomato and scoop out the flesh with a teaspoon

1 large onion, peeled and finely chopped
4 tablespoons olive oil
2 garlic cloves, crushed
2 large tomatoes, skinned and chopped
225 g/8 oz long-grain brown rice
1 teaspoon dried oregano
600 ml/1 pint water
salt
6 peppers with a good, squarish shape
freshly ground black pepper
2 tablespoons chopped parsley
a little extra oil, for greasing

1 Fry the onion in the oil in a medium heavy-based saucepan, then add the garlic, tomato and rice, and cook gently, stirring often, for a further 3–4 minutes until the onion is soft.
2 Add the oregano, water and a teaspoon of salt. Bring up to the boil, then cover tightly and leave to cook very gently for 45 minutes.
3 Meanwhile, cut the peppers in half lengthways and scoop out the seeds. Parboil the peppers in 2.5 cm/1 inch water

for 5 minutes, then drain and dry on kitchen paper.

4 Preheat the oven to 180 C/350 F/Gas Mark 4. Season the rice mixture with pepper and more salt if necessary, and stir in the parsley, then spoon this mixture into the peppers.

5 Stand the peppers in a lightly oiled casserole. Bake for 25–30 minutes, until the peppers feel tender when pierced with a skewer.

Variations

The stuffing mixture can be varied in many ways. Try adding small quantities of tasty vegetables such as finely chopped mushrooms or celery; add grated cheese for non-vegan versions. For a Middle Eastern flavour, replace the oregano with 1 teaspoon ground cinnamon or allspice and add 50 g/2 oz each of chopped dried apricots, currants and pine nuts or cashew nuts to the mixture.

V TOMATOES WITH SPICY STUFFING V

Beefsteak tomatoes lend themselves to many different stuffings. One of my favourites is this spicy potato mixture. Serve these tomatoes with plain or spiced brown rice (p. 241), and, if you've time, Curry Sauce (p. 177) or a moist side dish, such as Okra with Cumin and Coriander (p. 186)

SERVES 4

Tomatoes with Courgette and Sweetcorn Stuffing

4 large beefsteak tomatoes
salt and freshly ground black pepper
1 large onion, peeled and chopped
4 tablespoons oil
450 g/1 lb potatoes, peeled and cut into 5-mm/¼-inch dice
2 garlic cloves, crushed
2 teaspoons cumin seeds
½ teaspoon turmeric
2 tablespoons roughly chopped coriander
salt and freshly ground black pepper
butter for greasing
TO GARNISH
coriander sprigs

1 Cut off and reserve the tops of the tomatoes, then scoop out the pulp. Chop the pulp, season with salt and pepper, then put it in the base of a lightly greased shallow ovenproof dish large enough to hold all the tomatoes.

2 Sprinkle the inside of each tomato with salt, then turn them upside down to drain. Preheat the oven to 200 C/400 F/Gas Mark 6.

3 Next, make the stuffing. Fry the onion in the oil in a frying pan for 5 minutes, then add the potato and garlic.

4 Cook gently for 10 minutes, then add the spices and coriander. Cook for a further 4–5 minutes, until the potato is just tender. Season to taste with salt and pepper.

5 Spoon the potato mixture into the tomatoes. Stand the tomatoes in the dish on top of the tomato pulp, replace their sliced-off tops, and bake for 15–20 minutes, until the tomatoes are just tender. Garnish with the coriander sprigs and serve immediately.

Variations

TOMATOES WITH HERB STUFFING

This variation has a Provençal flavour. Prepare the tomatoes as described. For the filling, use the Herb Stuffing mixture on p. 239. Bake as described. These tomatoes are good served on a base of potato purée, accompanied by a lightly cooked vegetable, such as French beans, or a green salad.

TOMATOES WITH COURGETTE AND SWEETCORN STUFFING

Replace the potatoes with 225 g/8 oz courgettes, cut into 6-mm/¼-inch dice, and 225 g/8 oz frozen sweetcorn. Omit spices and add 2 tablespoons roughly chopped parsley and a pinch of chilli powder, if wished.

MENU

Meal with a Mexican Flavour

Guacamole with Tortilla Chips
Illustrated on p. 145
144

Tomatoes with Courgette and Sweetcorn Stuffing

Boiled Potatoes with Butter and Parsley
70

Chocolate Pots
279

BAKED STUFFED AVOCADO

A hot stuffed avocado makes an easy and luxurious meal. Serve with Sauce Soubise (p. 173) and lemony carrots, or on a base of cooked rice or puréed carrot or potato.

SERVES 4

1 onion, peeled and chopped
15 g/½ oz butter or vegan margarine
2 large ripe avocado pears, halved and stones removed
100 g/4 oz brazil nuts, chopped
100 g/4 oz Gruyère cheese, diced
4 tablespoons grated Parmesan cheese
2 tablespoons chopped parsley
2 tablespoons sherry
salt and freshly ground black pepper

1 Preheat the oven to 200 C/400 F/Gas Mark 6.
2 Fry the onion in the butter or vegan margarine for 10 minutes, until soft but not browned.
3 Meanwhile, scoop the flesh out of the avocado skins with a teaspoon, taking care not to damage the skins. Dice the flesh.
4 Add the fried onion to the avocado flesh, together with the brazil nuts, cheeses, parsley and sherry. Season to taste with salt and pepper.
5 Pile the mixture back into the avocado skins, place them in a shallow ovenproof dish and bake for 10–15 minutes. Serve immediately.

Stuffed Vegetable Platter

A selection of 3 or 4 different types of stuffed vegetables arranged on a base of saffron rice makes a stunning centre-piece for a special meal. Choose small vegetables, so that everyone can have several types, and arrange them attractively on a base of saffron rice on two large, flat serving dishes. This is a slightly fiddly meal to make, but the work can be done well in advance, and a cold sauce or dip, such as Guacamole (p. 144), or Yogurt and Herb Dressing (p. 156), and a green salad, are all the accompaniments needed. This selection would serve 6:

- 3 small Stuffed Aubergines à la Provencale (p. 192), using ½ stuffing ingredients
- 2 Courgettes with Carrot, Ginger and Almond Stuffing (p. 193), using ½ stuffing ingredients, and halved to give 8 portions
- 6 large (but not 'beefsteak') tomatoes filled with 1 quantity Herb Stuffing (p. 239)
- 6 flat mushrooms stuffed with Broad Bean Dip as described on p. 61
- Double quantity Saffron Rice (p. 241)

Fillings for Crepes

Golden Spiced Cauliflower (p. 185)
Red Cabbage Casserole (p. 180)
Ratatouille (p. 187)
Peperonata (p. 186)
Multicolour Butter Beans (p. 206)
Brown Lentil Bake mixture (p. 211)
Mushrooms – or Wild Mushrooms – in Cream (p. 79)
Glazed Carrots (p. 182)
Okra with Cumin and Coriander (p. 186)
Spring Vegetable Braise (p. 181)

V V

STUFFED CABBAGE ROLLS IN COCONUT SAUCE

In this recipe cabbage leaves are rolled around a simple rice stuffing and baked in a lightly spiced Savoury Coconut Sauce (p. 177). I think a crunchy salad, such as Sweet Carrot and Fennel (p. 162), or Chicory, Watercress and Walnut Salad (p. 161), goes well with it, or lightly cooked French beans (p. 61).

SERVES 4

1 onion, peeled and chopped
1 tablespoon oil
175 g/6 oz long-grain brown rice
450 ml/15 fl oz water
salt
8 outer cabbage leaves
50 g/2 oz cashew nuts, chopped
50 g/2 oz raisins
freshly ground black pepper
double quantity Savoury Coconut Sauce (p. 177)

1 Fry the onion in the oil in a large saucepan for 10 minutes. Add the rice, stir for a moment or two over the heat, then add the water and a teaspoon of salt.
2 Bring to the boil, then reduce the heat, cover and cook for 45 minutes.
3 Meanwhile, blanch the cabbage leaves by adding them to half a pan of boiling water and simmering for 2 minutes. Drain and refresh under the cold tap, then drain again.
4 Preheat the oven to 190 C/375 F/Gas Mark 5.
5 Add the nuts and raisins to the rice and check the seasoning.
6 Divide the rice mixture between the cabbage leaves, rolling each one around the filling to make a fat parcel.
7 Place the rolls in a shallow ovenproof dish and pour the sauce on top of them.
8 Bake, uncovered, for about 40 minutes, until heated through.

CREPES STUFFED WITH ASPARAGUS AND CREAM CHEESE

Serve this summery main course with baby carrots and new potatoes. Begin the meal with a chilled soup.

SERVES 4–6

Crepes Stuffed with Asparagus and Cream Cheese

750 g/1½ lb fresh asparagus, trimmed, washed and cooked as described on p. 63, or 450 g/1 lb frozen asparagus, cooked
450 g/1 lb curd cheese
finely grated rind of 1 lemon
salt and freshly ground black pepper
FOR THE BATTER
100 g/4 oz plain flour
½ teaspoon salt
2 eggs
1 tablespoon olive oil or melted butter
150 ml/5 fl oz milk
150 ml/5 fl oz water
TO FINISH
300 ml/10 fl oz single cream
TO GARNISH
lemon twists
asparagus spears

1 First make the filling: cut the asparagus into 2.5-cm/1-inch lengths, then mix with the curd cheese and lemon rind and season to taste with salt and pepper.
2 Next make the pancake batter: either put all the ingredients into a blender or food processor and whizz until smooth, or put the flour into a bowl with the salt, make a well in the centre and add the eggs, oil and a little of the liquid. Beat until smooth, then gradually add the rest of the liquid.
3 Preheat the oven to 180 C/350 F/Gas Mark 4.
4 Use the pancake batter to make about 12 thin pancakes as described on p. 299.
5 Roll each pancake around a little of the asparagus mixture, dividing it between them. Place them side by side in a shallow casserole.
6 Pour the cream over the top of the pancakes. Cover with foil and bake for 20–30 minutes, until heated through. Remove the foil and garnish the pancakes with lemon twists and asparagus spears.

Variations

VEGAN CREPES

For vegan pancakes, mix 100 g/4 oz chick pea flour (p. 41) with 350 ml/12 fl oz cold water and ½ teaspoon salt. Fry as described, using enough oil to prevent the pancakes from sticking; these pancakes need more fat than egg-based pancakes, but are excellent. Use Sauce Soubise (p. 173) instead of the curd cheese, and non-dairy cream instead of the single cream.

CREPES WITH CREAM CHEESE AND MUSHROOMS

Use 450 g/1 lb sliced button mushrooms instead of the asparagus. Fry in 25 g/1 oz butter for 2–3 minutes, until just tender. Mix the mushrooms with the curd cheese, omitting the lemon rind.

Coloured Crepes

The basic crepe batter can be coloured with saffron, turmeric, or vegetable purées, and, served with contrasting fillings, some attractive colour effects can be created.

For pale green crepes, add 2 tablespoons spinach purée to the batter; try this with a vivid red filling such as Ratatouille (p. 187) or Peperonata (p. 186).

To make pale yellow crepes, soak a few strands of saffron in the milk before making the batter, or add ½–1 teaspoon turmeric. The turmeric version is good with a spicy vegetable filling such as Okra with Cumin and Coriander (p. 186).

VEGETABLE TEMPURA WITH DIPPING SAUCE

SERVES 4

Serving Ideas for Vegetable Tempura

A basket of these crisp mixed vegetable fritters looks appetizing and makes a delicious meal. Serve them with Sweet Vinegared Rice (p. 241), and follow with fresh lychees, for a meal with a Japanese flavour. All the main preparation can be done in advance, leaving only the frying to be completed just before eating.

225 g/8 oz aubergine, cut into 1-cm/½-inch cubes
2 large carrots, scraped and cut into strips
8 medium flat mushrooms, wiped
1 green pepper, de-seeded and cut into strips
½ cauliflower, broken into florets, larger ones halved or quartered
FOR THE DIPPING SAUCE
4 tablespoons mirin (p. 308)
150 ml/5 fl oz soy sauce
1 teaspoon grated fresh ginger
FOR THE BATTER
2 large eggs
300 ml/10 fl oz water
225 g/8 oz plain flour
1 teaspoon salt
oil for deep-frying
TO GARNISH
julienne strips of carrot, fresh ginger and pepper

1 First make the dipping sauce. Bring the mirin to the boil in a small saucepan.
2 Remove from the heat and add the soy sauce and ginger. Pour the dipping sauce into 4 small bowls.
3 Make the batter: break the eggs into a bowl and beat gently until just broken up but not foamy.
4 Mix in the water, then sift in the flour and salt; mix lightly until combined. Don't worry if there are one or two lumps.
5 Have all the vegetables prepared and in separate piles ready for coating in batter.
6 Heat a deep-fryer, half-filled with vegetable oil, to 180C/350F, or when bubbles form on a chopstick dipped into the hot oil.
7 Dip the aubergine into the batter, then put into the hot oil. Do not put in more than a single layer at a time.
8 After about 2 minutes turn the pieces over and fry the other side for a further 2 minutes, until light golden-brown.
9 Remove from the oil on to kitchen paper. Keep the aubergine fritters warm while you fry the rest of the vegetables in the same way.
10 As soon as all the vegetables are done, serve them on 4 heated plates or in baskets lined with paper napkins, garnished with strips of carrot, ginger and pepper. Serve with the bowls of sauce.

V   AUBERGINE FRITTERS IN CHICK   V
PEA BATTER

Serve these fritters with potatoes and a green vegetable, and follow with a substantial pudding, such as Rose Cheesecake (p. 289).

SERVES 4

2 medium-sized aubergines
oil for shallow frying
FOR THE BATTER
100 g/4 oz chick pea flour
½ teaspoon salt
350 ml/12 fl oz cold water
TO SERVE
lemon slices

Soured Cream, or Yogurt, and Herb Dressing (p. 156)

1 Cut the aubergines lengthways into 5-mm/¼-inch slices, place in a colander, and degorge, as described on p. 73.
2 Rinse the aubergine slices under cold water; pat dry on kitchen paper.

3 To make the batter, mix the chick pea flour and salt with the water until the mixture is completely smooth and thick.
4 Dip the aubergine slices in the batter, then fry on both sides in hot shallow oil.

5 Drain on kitchen paper. Keep the first batch warm while you fry the rest, then serve at once, garnished with lemon slices and accompanied by Soured Cream and Herb Dressing.

V

SWEET AND SOUR VEGETABLE STIR-FRY WITH ALMONDS

A delicious mixture of sweet and sour flavours with the crunch and nourishment of almonds. If you are planning to serve this with cooked brown rice (which goes very well with it), put the rice on to cook well in advance, as the stir-fry is very quick to make, and the rice takes 45 minutes. It's also very good cold, as a salad or first course.

SERVES 4

225 g/8 oz red pepper, de-seeded
225 g/8 oz green pepper, de-seeded
225 g/8 oz courgettes
225 g/8 oz celery
225 g/8 oz spring onions
225 g/8 oz button mushrooms, wiped
4 tablespoons olive oil
100 g/4 oz blanched almonds
FOR THE SWEET AND SOUR DRESSING
2 garlic cloves, crushed
15 g/½ oz fresh ginger, grated
4 tablespoons soy sauce
4 tablespoons lemon juice
1 tablespoon wine vinegar
2 tablespoons clear honey

1 Cut the peppers, courgettes and celery into 5-cm/2-inch matchsticks. Trim the spring onions so that there is about 2 cm/ 1 inch of the green part left. Slice the mushrooms.
2 Next make the sweet and sour dressing: blend all the ingredients in a blender or food processor, or mix them in a bowl.
3 Make the stir-fry just before you want to eat: it only takes a few minutes to cook. Heat the oil in a wok or large saucepan, then put in the vegetables and stir-fry for 2 minutes, until they are beginning to soften.
4 Add the almonds and the sweet and sour mixture and stir-fry for a further 1–2 minutes, to heat through.

V

MENU

Slimmers' Lunch

Carrot and Ginger Soup
129

**Sweet and Sour Vegetable
Stir-Fry with Almonds**

Apricot Fool
282

Sweet and Sour Vegetable Stir-Fry with Almonds

Quick Main Courses

Multicolour Butter Beans (p. 206) and Red Kidney Bean Stew (p. 206) are both quick to make if you use canned beans; Lentil Dal (p. 209) is also speedy and good served with Spiced Potatoes (p. 185) or Golden Spiced Cauliflower (p. 185). The Spicy Peanut Sauce, in the Ingredients Section (p. 37), makes an excellent quick meal if served over hot cooked potatoes. Many egg and cheese dishes are quick, especially Baked Eggs (p. 214), Pipérade (p. 215), Cheese Fondue (p. 217) and any of the omelettes (pp. 220 and 221).

Quick Savoury Nut Roast (p. 235), Peanut Burgers (p. 232), Risotto (p. 244), Rice Pilaf with Apricots, Raisins and Pine Nuts (p. 242) and Millet Pilaf with Nuts and Raisins (p. 245) are fast to make, too, as are many pasta dishes, especially Fusille Verde with Mushrooms and Cream (p. 251), Tagliatelle with Gorgonzola and Walnuts (p. 250), Tagliatelle Verde with Lentil Sauce (p. 252) and Summer Linguine (p. 255).

Quick Spring Onion and Fresh Herb Flan (p. 266) is a speedy pastry dish, and Sweet and Sour Vegetable Stir-Fry with Almonds (p. 199) is a particularly quick vegetable mixture.

POTATO AND CHEESE LAYER

This is very quick and easy to make and popular with children; you need to allow time for it to cook slowly in a cool oven. It's nice with a plainly cooked green vegetable or some watercress.

SERVES 2–4 AS A MAIN COURSE

25 g/1 oz butter
2 large potatoes, peeled and thinly sliced
2 onions, peeled and thinly sliced
100 g/4 oz Cheddar cheese, grated
salt and freshly ground black pepper
4 tablespoons milk or soya milk
TO GARNISH
parsley sprigs
tomato slices

1 Preheat the oven to 170C/325F/Gas Mark 3. Grease a shallow casserole with half the butter.

2 Put a layer of potatoes in the bottom of the dish, then a thin layer of onion slices, a little grated cheese, then season with salt and pepper.

3 Continue in layers like this until all the ingredients are used, ending with a layer of potato slices. Pour the milk over the top and dot the remaining butter over the top.

4 Bake for about 1½ hours, until the potato feels tender when pierced with a sharp knife or skewer. Garnish with parsley and tomato slices.

V

VEGETABLE HOTPOT

V

Serve this family dish with lightly cooked broccoli and perhaps Vegetarian Gravy (p. 172).

SERVES 4

1 × 400-g/14-oz can chopped tomatoes
100 g/4 oz walnuts, chopped
1 tablespoon dried oregano
salt and freshly ground black pepper
4 large potatoes, peeled, cut into 5-mm/¼-inch slices, parboiled for 4 minutes, then drained
2 green peppers, de-seeded and sliced
2 onions, peeled and sliced
1 tablespoon olive oil
butter for greasing
TO GARNISH
parsley sprigs

1 Preheat the oven to 200C/400F/Gas Mark 6. Grease a deep casserole with a little butter.

2 Mix together the tomatoes, walnuts and oregano. Season with salt and pepper.

3 Put a layer of potato slices in the casserole, followed by a layer of pepper, a layer of onion and then some of the tomato and walnut mixture.

4 Continue in this way until all the ingredients are used, ending with potato. Drizzle the olive oil on top.

5 Cover with foil and bake for 1 hour, removing the foil for the last 20 minutes, to brown the top. Garnish with parsley.

Variation

CHEESY VEGETABLE HOTPOT
For a richer, non-vegan version, add 225 g/8 oz grated cheese, layering it with the rest of the ingredients.

V VEGETABLE KEBABS WITH ROSEMARY V

Marinating the vegetables for several hours allows them to absorb the flavours. Serve with Rice Pilaf with Apricots, Raisins and Pine Nuts (p. 242).

SERVES 6

12 small button mushrooms, wiped

225 g/8 oz firm tofu, cut into 1 cm/½ inch cubes

1 small red pepper, de-seeded and cut into strips about 2.5 cm/1 inch long and 1 cm/½ inch wide

12 miniature sweetcorn

3 small courgettes, total weight about 350 g/12 oz, cut into slices 1 cm/½ inch thick

12 cherry tomatoes

6 × 20–25-cm/8–10-inch rosemary sprigs, leaves scraped off the lower part, or 6 kebab skewers

FOR THE MARINADE

1 teaspoon mustard powder

1 garlic clove, crushed

2 tablespoons clear honey

2 tablespoons soy sauce

2 tablespoons olive oil

1 teaspoon salt

freshly ground black pepper

1 Thread the vegetables and tofu on to the rosemary sprigs or skewers, putting on first a mushroom, then a piece of tofu followed by some red pepper, sweetcorn, courgette and a cherry tomato.

2 Continue in this way until all the rosemary sprigs or skewers are full.

3 To make the marinade, mix together the mustard, garlic and honey, then gradually stir in the other ingredients.

4 Lay the kebabs on a non-metal tray, polythene container, large plate or casserole big enough for them to lie flat.

5 Spoon the marinade over them, turning them to make sure that all the vegetables are coated.

6 Let the kebabs marinate for at least 1 hour, preferably for several hours, spooning the marinade over them occasionally.

7 Cook the kebabs under a hot grill or on the grid of a barbecue for 10–15 minutes, until the vegetables are tender, turning the skewers so that the vegetables cook evenly.

8 Pour the remaining marinade into a small jug and serve separately.

Variation

All kinds of vegetables, cut into suitably-sized pieces, can be used for Vegetable Kebabs, and the tofu can be replaced by the same amount of seitan, or cubes of bought or home-made nut or lentil loaf.

Vegetable Hotpot (p. 200); Spinach Gnocchi (p. 203)

Side Dishes for Curries

Any of these, served in small wooden bowls or ramekins, make attractive accompaniments to curries and spiced rice dishes:

Roasted peanuts or cashew nuts

Macadamia nuts

Sliced tomatoes

Mango chutney or pickle

Sweet Spiced Apricot Chutney (p. 342)

Lime pickle

Sliced banana

Desiccated coconut

Sliced cucumber in plain yogurt

Nuts and raisins

Chopped celery and red pepper

Diced apple

V   # VEGETABLE CURRY   V

This curry is easy to make and has a good balance of spices. Serve it with plain or spiced rice and whatever accompaniments you fancy.

SERVES 4

1 onion, peeled and chopped
40 g/1½ oz butter or vegan margarine
2 teaspoons each turmeric, ground cumin and
*   ground coriander*
¼ teaspoon chilli powder
2 bay leaves
100 g/4 oz cabbage, shredded
450 g/1 lb potatoes, peeled and quartered
600 ml/1 pint water
salt and freshly ground black pepper
100 g/4 oz frozen peas or green beans
TO GARNISH
coriander sprig
lemon twist

1 Fry the onion in the butter or vegan margarine in a large saucepan for 7 minutes, until beginning to soften.
2 Stir in the spices and bay leaves, and cook for a further 2–3 minutes.
3 Add the cabbage, potatoes, water and some salt and pepper. Bring to the boil, then simmer, uncovered, for 15–20 minutes, until the potatoes are nearly tender and the liquid well reduced.
4 Add the peas or beans and cook for a further 5 minutes. Check the seasoning and serve, garnished with a coriander sprig and a lemon twist.

Olive Oil

Perhaps the most delicious oil, made by pressing ripe olives. The oil is extracted by centrifugal force to give pure, pale green-gold 'first pressing', cold pressed oil. The pulp is then pressed again, under heat, to yield more virgin oil. 'Virgin' on the label means that the oil has not been chemically treated to keep its natural acidity at a safe level. There are several permitted categories of 'virgin' oil:

EXTRA VIRGIN   Must be under 1 per cent acidity

SOPRANO OR 'EXTRA FINE VIRGIN'   Can be up to 1.5 per cent acidity

FINE VIRGIN   Can have less than 3 per cent acidity

VIRGIN   Can have up to 4 per cent acidity

These categories are often grouped into just two: extra virgin, below 1 per cent acidity, and virgin, below 4 per cent acidity.

PARMIGIANA

This makes an excellent supper, especially when washed down with some red wine. Serve it with a green salad and some crusty bread, and follow with fresh fruit or a basket of home-made biscuits.

SERVES 4

900 g/2 lb aubergines
salt
olive oil, for frying
2 large onions, peeled and finely chopped
2 garlic cloves, crushed
1 × 400-g/14-oz can chopped tomatoes
225 g/8 oz cheese, preferably Mozzarella,
*   thinly sliced*
6 tablespoons grated Parmesan cheese
freshly ground black pepper

1 Cut the aubergines into 5-mm/¼-inch circles. Salt, drain and rinse the aubergine slices as described on p. 73.
2 Preheat the oven to 200C/400F/Gas

Mark 6. Heat a little oil in a large saucepan and fry the onion and garlic for 10 minutes.
3 Remove the onion mixture with a draining spoon to a plate, add the aubergine circles to the pan and fry until crisp and lightly browned, adding more oil if necessary.
4 Layer the aubergines, onion, tomatoes and sliced cheese in an ovenproof dish, sprinkling some Parmesan cheese and salt and pepper between the layers and ending with a layer of aubergines.
5 Bake, uncovered, for 40–60 minutes, until the aubergines are tender.

SPINACH GNOCCHI

Clockwise from top right: Lentil Dal (p. 209), Vegetable Curry (p. 202); Sweet Spiced Apricot Chutney (p. 342); sliced tomatoes and onions

Serve the gnocchi with buttered pasta and a colourful salad with an Italian flavour for a light main course.

SERVES 4

700 g/1½ lb fresh spinach, cooked, drained and chopped, or 450 g/1 lb frozen chopped spinach, thawed
225 g/8 oz skimmed milk soft white cheese
175 g/6 oz curd cheese
50 g/2 oz Parmesan cheese, grated
2 egg yolks
salt and freshly ground black pepper
freshly grated nutmeg
wheatgerm or flour for coating
a little butter
TO SERVE
grated Parmesan cheese

1 Make sure the spinach is well drained, then purée it in a blender or food processor. Put the purée into a saucepan and dry off over the heat for a minute or two. Remove from the heat.

2 In a bowl, mix together the skimmed milk cheese, curd cheese, Parmesan cheese, egg yolks, and spinach. Season with salt, pepper and nutmeg. If the mixture is very soft, put it into the fridge to firm up for about 30 minutes.

3 Roll heaped teaspoons of the mixture in wheatgerm or flour. (All this can be done in advance.)

4 To cook the gnocchi, first heat the oven to low, to keep the gnocchi warm as they're ready. Half fill a large saucepan with lightly salted water and bring just to the boil.

5 Drop 6–8 gnocchi into the water and let them simmer very gently for about 4–5 minutes, until they float to the surface.

6 Make sure the water does not get beyond a bare simmer, and remove the gnocchi as soon as they are ready, or they may fall apart.

7 Drain the gnocchi well, then put them into a warmed serving dish, dot with a little butter and keep them warm while you cook another batch.

8 When all the gnocchi are done, sprinkle with grated Parmesan cheese and serve immediately.

MENU
Family Lunch

SERVES 4–6

Tomato Soup with Basil
130

Garlic Bread
137

*Cheese and Parsley Fritters
with Parsley Sauce*
217 and 175

Healthy Chips
71

Green Beans

Fresh Fruit Salad
286

This is a warming lunch for a chilly winter Saturday, when everyone needs cheering up! Most children, in my experience, like this home-made Tomato Soup and they usually adore Garlic Bread, too. (If some don't like garlic, leave this out when you butter one end of the loaf.) The Cheese and Parsley Fritters are another winner, but get organized in advance for this, as the mixture has to get completely cold, before cutting; make it the evening before, or first thing in the morning. Since this is a day for spoiling the family, I've suggested chips and green beans to go with the fritters, with Fresh Fruit Salad for dessert, to balance the richness.

To drink, I suggest a sparkling fruit cup made from mixed apple and orange juices and soda water; or, if you feel like something alcoholic for the grown ups, I'd go Italian, with either a chilled white Soave or a red wine, a Chianti, perhaps.

Pulse Dishes

I know that some people are put off using pulses because of the need to soak and cook them in advance. All the recipes in this section can either be made from quick-cooking pulses which do not need soaking first, or from canned ones, which I find excellent. However, the most economical way is to buy dried pulses and soak and cook them yourself, and all the information about this is to be found in the Ingredients section of the book (p. 40) along with more ideas for using the various types of pulse. Once cooked, pulses can be made into a range of excellent main dishes, ranging from colourful casseroles to savoury bakes, loaves and burgers.

MENU

Family Sunday Lunch

Pease Pudding
207
Yorkshire Pudding

Vegetarian Gravy
172
Mint Sauce
119
Buttered Brussel Sprouts
58
Roast Potatoes
71

Country Apple Pie or
294
Rhubarb Crumble
295

V MULTICOLOUR BUTTER BEANS V

SERVES 4

3 celery sticks, cut into 5-mm/¼-inch dice
1 small red pepper, de-seeded and cut into 5-mm/¼-inch dice
1 tablespoon oil
2 teaspoons curry powder
225 g/8 oz frozen sweetcorn kernels
225 g/8 oz butter beans, soaked, cooked and drained, or 2 × 425-g/15-oz cans butter beans, drained
salt and freshly ground black pepper
TO GARNISH
chopped parsley

1 Fry the celery and red pepper in the oil in a large saucepan for 10 minutes, until soft but not browned.
2 Stir in the curry powder, then add the sweetcorn and butter beans. Cook over a gentle heat for 4–5 minutes, until heated through. Season to taste with salt and pepper, sprinkle with parsley and serve.

V RED KIDNEY BEAN STEW V

SERVES 4

1 tablespoon olive oil
1 large onion, sliced
1 large red pepper, de-seeded and chopped
2 carrots, scraped and diced
2 leeks or medium courgettes, sliced
2 celery sticks, sliced
175 g/6 oz mushrooms, washed and sliced
4 tomatoes, skinned and quartered
100 g/4 oz red kidney beans, soaked, cooked and drained (p. 40), or 1 × 425-g/15-oz can, rinsed and drained
½ teaspoon paprika pepper
salt and freshly ground black pepper

1 Heat the oil in a large saucepan and add the onion, red pepper, carrots, leeks or courgettes and celery.
2 Cook gently for 10 minutes, covered, then add the mushrooms, tomatoes, kidney beans, paprika and salt and pepper to taste.
3 Continue to cook, covered, for a further 10–15 minutes. Check the seasoning and serve.

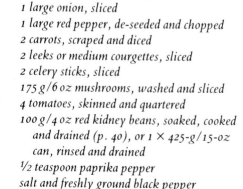

LENTILS AND MUSHROOMS
AU GRATIN

In this recipe, lentils are made into a thick sauce, poured over mushrooms, topped with crumbs and cheese and baked until crisp and browned. Serve with a lightly cooked green vegetable such as cabbage or broccoli.

SERVES 4

175 g/6 oz split red lentils
600 ml/1 pint water
1 large onion, peeled and finely chopped
50 g/2 oz butter
finely grated rind and juice of ½ lemon
1 teaspoon yeast extract
salt and freshly ground black pepper
100 g/4 oz mushrooms, washed and sliced
50 g/2 oz fresh wholewheat breadcrumbs
50 g/2 oz Cheddar cheese, grated

1 Put the lentils and water into a medium saucepan and simmer very gently, uncovered, until the lentils are tender and all the liquid absorbed – about 20 minutes.
2 Preheat the oven to 180C/350F/Gas Mark 4.
3 Fry the onion in half the butter for 10 minutes until soft and lightly browned.
4 Add the onion to the lentils, together with the lemon rind and juice, yeast extract and salt and pepper to taste. Purée in a blender or food processor, or beat well with a wooden spoon, to make a thick purée.
5 Fry the mushrooms in the remaining butter for 2–3 minutes, then put them into a shallow ovenproof dish and pour the lentil mixture on top. Sprinkle with the breadcrumbs and the grated cheese.
6 Bake for 40–45 minutes, until golden and crisp on top, and hot and bubbly underneath.

Variation
LEEKS AND LENTILS
AU GRATIN
Make the lentil sauce exactly as described. Replace the mushrooms with 1 kg/2¼ lb leeks, cleaned, cut into 2.5-cm/1-inch lengths, boiled until tender, then drained.

PEASE PUDDING

This is traditionally served as an accompaniment to meat.

SERVES 4

450 g/1 lb yellow split peas
2 large onions, peeled and chopped
50 g/2 oz butter
2 teaspoons fennel seeds
2 eggs (optional)
salt and freshly ground black pepper

1 Put the split peas into a saucepan, cover with water and cook gently until soft – this takes about 30 minutes or so. Drain.
2 Preheat oven to 180C/350F/Gas Mark 4. (Or, if you're roasting potatoes at a higher temperature, put the pease pudding on a low shelf – the temperature isn't crucial.)
3 Fry the onions in the butter for 8 minutes, then add the fennel seeds, stir for 1–2 minutes, then add the split peas and the eggs, if you're using these. Season with salt and pepper.
4 Spoon the mixture into a lightly-greased fairly shallow ovenproof dish and bake for 50–60 minutes, until browned on top.

Sprouting Pulses

Most whole pulses, with the exception of red kidney beans, can be sprouted, and make a delicious, crunchy and highly nutritious addition to salads and stir-fries.

To sprout pulses, put 2 heaped tablespoons of your chosen variety into a jar – a large empty coffee jar is ideal. Cover pulses with cold water and leave overnight. Next day fix a piece of gauze over the top, securing with an elastic band. Pour the soaking water out through the gauze, then, again without removing the gauze, fill the jar with cold water, shake, and pour it out. Leave the jar on its side for 2–4 days until the pulses have sprouted, repeating the rinsing at least twice a day. Once sprouted, the pulses can be stored in a polythene bag in the fridge.

V CHILLI CON CARNE VEGETARIANA V

A tasty, substantial dish which has been responsible for more than one male convert to vegetarianism. Serve with hot brown rice or jacket potatoes with soured cream and chives, and a green salad.

SERVES 4

1 tablespoon olive oil
1 onion, peeled and chopped
1 red pepper, de-seeded and chopped
1 garlic clove, crushed
1 × 400-g/14-oz can tomatoes
225 g/8 oz red kidney beans, soaked, cooked and drained (p. 40), or 2 × 425-g/15-oz cans red kidney beans
100 g/4 oz whole green lentils, simmered in plenty of water for 40–45 minutes, until tender
1 teaspoon mild paprika pepper
1/2–1 teaspoon chilli powder
salt and freshly ground black pepper
a little sugar
TO GARNISH
coriander sprig

1 Heat the oil in a large saucepan and fry the onion and pepper for 10 minutes, then add the garlic and tomatoes.
2 Drain the red kidney beans and lentils, reserving the liquid. Add the beans and lentils to the tomato mixture, together with the paprika and chilli powder.
3 Simmer for about 15 minutes, then season with salt, pepper and sugar, and serve, garnished with coriander.

FELAFEL IN PITTA POCKETS

SERVES 4

These crisp, tasty little savoury balls make a filling and delicious snack, served in a pocket of pitta bread with salads and any spicy relishes you fancy. Or the felafel are good served with a salad and a Yogurt and Herb Dressing (p. 156). If you're using canned chick peas, which are usually softer than home-cooked ones, you may need to add a few fresh breadcrumbs to the mixture to make it firm enough to shape. The parsley is important for the flavour.

225 g/8 oz chick peas, soaked, cooked and drained, or 2 × 425-g/15-oz cans, drained
1 egg, beaten
1 large onion, finely chopped
2 tablespoons chopped parsley
1 garlic clove, crushed
1 teaspoon ground coriander
1 teaspoon ground cumin
a pinch of chilli powder
salt and freshly ground black pepper
plain flour for coating
oil for shallow frying
TO SERVE
4 wholewheat pitta breads
2 tomatoes, sliced
1/2 cucumber, sliced
lemon wedges
fennel sprigs

1 Mash the chick peas thoroughly, then add the egg, onion, parsley, garlic and spices. Mix well; season to taste with salt and pepper.
2 Shape the mixture into balls about the size of chestnuts, then coat in flour.
3 Put the pitta bread to warm under the grill or in a moderate oven.
4 Pour enough oil into a frying pan to cover the base thinly, and when it is hot fry the felafel for 3 minutes on each side, until golden-brown. Drain well on kitchen paper.
5 Cut each pitta bread in half across the centre, then fill each with felafel, sliced tomato and cucumber and garnish with lemon and fennel.

Variation
VEGAN FELAFEL
Use 2 tablespoons chick pea flour to bind the felafel mixture instead of the beaten egg. Mix it in well.

V

LENTIL DAL

V *Chilli con Carne Vegetariana (p. 208);*
Felafel in Pitta Pockets (p. 208)

Dal is usually served as an accompaniment to curries or spiced rice
dishes, spooned or poured over the top, adding extra flavour.

SERVES 4

225 g/8 oz split red lentils
1 onion, peeled and chopped
1 large garlic clove, crushed
1 bay leaf
1 whole fresh green chilli
2.5-cm/1-inch piece fresh ginger, peeled and
  grated
½ teaspoon turmeric
2 teaspoons each ground cumin and ground
  coriander
1–2 teaspoons salt
25 g/1 oz coconut cream
1 tablespoon lemon juice
TO GARNISH
bay leaves

1 Put the lentils into a saucepan with
enough cold water to come 1 cm/½ inch
above them, and add the chopped onion,

garlic, bay leaf, whole chilli, ginger and
turmeric.
2 Cook gently, half-covered, for about
20 minutes, until the lentils are soft, stirring occasionally and adding a little more
water if necessary to prevent the lentils
from sticking. The final mixture should
be quite runny, like a purée, but not
watery.
3 Stir in the cumin, coriander and salt to
taste. If possible, leave to stand, covered,
for 20–30 minutes, to allow the flavours
to blend.
4 Discard the bay leaf and chilli, and stir
in the coconut cream. Reheat gently, stirring, until the coconut has melted. Add
the lemon juice, check the seasoning and
serve the lentil dal, garnished with a few
bay leaves.

Serving Ideas for
Lentil Dal

I also like dal as a main dish, poured
over lightly cooked vegetables and
served with mango chutney and
lime pickle, or with some plain
boiled rice and some wedges of
hardboiled egg. It's also good served
with the Spiced Potatoes on p. 185,
with a side dish of tomato and onion
salad. It depends how hungry you're
feeling!

V   # SPICY LENTIL BURGERS   V

Lightly spiced, moist and delicious, these burgers can be
served in soft wholewheat burger buns, with salad and a yogurt
and herb sauce or mayonnaise, or with cooked vegetables and a
savoury sauce. The burgers freeze well and can
be cooked from frozen.

SERVES 4

Oils for Cooking

CORN OIL   Made from the
kernels of maize, this is a bland oil,
high in polyunsaturates and suitable
for general purposes and for cakes
and pastry

GRAPESEED OIL   Made from
the seeds of grapes, this is a light
oil, high in polyunsaturates and with
a high flash point, so good for
deep-frying

GROUND NUT OIL   Another
useful all-round oil, fairly low
in polyunsaturates but stable
when heated, so a healthy oil for
deep-frying

SAFFLOWER OIL   Made from
the seeds of the safflower (a
relative of the sunflower), this is one
of the most nutritious oils, rich in
polyunsaturates, and cold-pressed
safflower oil can be mixed with olive
oil to increase the polyunsaturates.
Safflower oil has rather a strong
flavour which limits its uses

SESAME OIL   An oil which
keeps well and is fairly high in
polyunsaturates, sesame oil is made
from roasted sesame seeds and has a
strong, distinctive flavour. It is
much used in Chinese and Indian
cooking

SOYA OIL   A good, mild-
flavoured oil made from the soya
bean and rich in polyunsaturates.
Reasonably priced and useful for all
general purpose cooking, including
cakes and pastries

SUNFLOWER OIL   High in
the valuable linoleic acid, and in
polyunsaturates generally,
sunflower oil has a delicate flavour
and is another useful general-
purpose oil

2 large onions, peeled and finely chopped
2 carrots, scraped and finely chopped
1 celery stick, finely chopped
2 tablespoons olive oil
1 large garlic clove, crushed
225 g/8 oz green or brown lentils, cooked
*   until tender and well drained (p. 40)*
1/2 teaspoon ground cumin
1/2 teaspoon ground coriander
6 tablespoons chopped parsley
1 tablespoon lemon juice
salt and freshly ground black pepper
plain flour for coating
oil for shallow frying
TO GARNISH
watercress
tomato slices

1 Fry the onion, carrot and celery in the
oil in a large saucepan for 10 minutes until
soft and lightly browned, stirring from
time to time.
2 Add the garlic, lentils, cumin, coriander, parsley and lemon juice. Mash by
hand, or purée roughly in a food processor or blender, until the mixture holds
together. Season with salt and pepper.
3 With floured hands, shape the mixture
into 10–12 flat burgers, using a palette
knife. Coat the burgers with flour.
4 Fry the burgers in a little oil until crisp
and browned, turning them over carefully to fry the second side.
5 Drain on kitchen paper and serve garnished with watercress and tomato.

V   # LENTIL SHEPHERD'S PIE   V

This can be prepared in advance, ready for cooking, and only
needs a quickly cooked vegetable, such as sprouts or
carrots, to go with it.

SERVES 4

225 g/8 oz green or brown lentils
50 g/2 oz butter or vegan margarine
2 large onions, peeled and thinly sliced
1 garlic clove, crushed
1 teaspoon dried mixed herbs
1 × 425-g/15-oz can tomatoes, chopped
2 tablespoons soy sauce
2–3 tablespoons chopped parsley
salt and freshly ground black pepper
700 g/1 1/2 lb potatoes, cooked and mashed
a little extra butter or vegan margarine

1 Put the lentils into a large saucepan,
cover with water and boil gently until
tender – about 45 minutes. Drain.
2 Preheat the oven to 200 C/400 F/Gas

Mark 6. Use half the butter or vegan
margarine to grease a shallow ovenproof
dish.
3 Fry the onions in the remaining butter
or vegan margarine in a large saucepan
for 10 minutes.
4 Add the garlic, mixed herbs, tomatoes, soy sauce, lentils, parsley and salt
and pepper to taste.
5 Spoon the mixture into the dish.
Spread the mashed potatoes evenly over
the top, draw the prongs of the fork over
the surface to make ridges and dot with a
little butter or vegan margarine.
6 Bake the pie for 45 minutes, until the
potato is golden-brown.

V MIDDLE EASTERN CHICK PEA STEW V

SERVES 4

900 g/2 lb aubergines
salt
2 large onions, peeled and chopped
4 tablespoons olive oil
2 garlic cloves, crushed
1 × 425-g/15-oz can tomatoes
100 g/4 oz chick peas, soaked, cooked and
*   drained, or 1 × 425-g/15-oz can chick*
*   peas, drained*
freshly ground black pepper
TO GARNISH
bay leaves

1 Cut the aubergines into 1-cm/½-inch dice, sprinkle with salt, place in a colander, put a weight on top and leave for 30 minutes.
2 Rinse the aubergines and gently squeeze out as much liquid as you can.
3 Preheat the oven to 200C/400F/Gas Mark 6.
4 Fry the onion in half the oil in a large saucepan for 10 minutes. Remove with a slotted spoon, and fry the aubergine pieces in the remaining oil until crisp and lightly browned. Drain on kitchen paper.

5 Put the aubergine and onion into an ovenproof dish, with garlic, tomatoes, chick peas and salt and pepper. Cover and bake for 40–60 minutes. Garnish.

Middle Eastern Chick Pea Stew

V BROWN LENTIL BAKE WITH V
PINEAPPLE

SERVES 4

2 large onions, peeled and finely chopped
2 tablespoons olive oil
1 large garlic clove, crushed
225 g/8 oz green or brown lentils, cooked
*   until tender and well drained (p. 40)*
2 tablespoons chopped parsley
1 teaspoon mixed herbs
2 tablespoons soy sauce
salt and freshly ground black pepper
25–50 g/1–2 oz wholewheat breadcrumbs
1 × 225-g/8-oz can pineapple rings, drained

1 Preheat the oven to 180C/350F/Gas Mark 4.

2 Fry the onion in the oil in a large saucepan for 10 minutes until soft and lightly browned, stirring occasionally.
3 Add the garlic, lentils, parsley, mixed herbs and soy sauce. Mash by hand, or purée roughly in a blender or food processor, until the mixture holds together. Season to taste with salt and pepper.
4 Transfer to a shallow ovenproof dish. Sprinkle with the crumbs.
5 Bake for 20 minutes, then remove from the oven, carefully place the pineapple rings on top and bake for a further 10–15 minutes, until the pineapple is hot.

Fruit with Pulses

The flavour of fruit complements pulses well and a number of traditional recipes, especially in Germany, Scandinavia and Russia, feature this.

Try the Brown Lentil Bake with Pineapple (left) and the Savoury Lentil Loaf (p. 213) with Cranberry or Apple Sauce; and the Spicy Lentil Burgers (p. 210) with sliced pineapple or mango.

VEGETARIAN MOUSSAKA

This is excellent with a crisp green salad and some full-bodied but inexpensive red wine. For a complete meal with a Greek flavour, start with Tsatsiki (p. 167) and warm pitta bread and finish with an Arranged Fruit Salad (p. 287) or dates with yogurt, cream and honey. The Moussaka freezes well, either fully cooked (for simply heating through when required) or uncooked, in which case the topping is best added just before baking.

Vegetarian Moussaka

SERVES 6

450 g / 1 lb aubergines, thinly sliced
salt
2 large onions, peeled and chopped
4 tablespoons olive oil
1 garlic clove, crushed
225 g / 8 oz black beans, soaked and cooked
    until tender, or 2 × 425-g / 15-oz cans red
    kidney beans
1 × 225-g / 8-oz can chopped tomatoes
¼ teaspoon ground allspice or cinnamon
freshly ground black pepper
a little sugar
150 ml / 5 fl oz soured cream or plain yogurt
1 egg
freshly grated nutmeg
4 tablespoons grated Parmesan cheese
butter for greasing

1 Salt, drain and rinse the aubergine slices, as described on p. 73.
2 Meanwhile, fry the onion in 2 table-spoons of the oil for 10 minutes. Add the garlic, drained beans, tomatoes and allspice or cinnamon.
3 Mix well, mashing the beans to make a rough purée. Season with salt, pepper and a pinch of sugar if necessary.
4 Preheat the oven to 180 C / 350 F / Gas Mark 4. Grease a large shallow oven-proof dish.
5 Fry the aubergine slices in the rest of the olive oil for 2–3 minutes on each side, until tender. Drain on kitchen paper.
6 Put a layer of aubergine slices in the base of the ovenproof dish; cover with half the bean mixture. Repeat the layers, then finish with a final layer of aubergine.
7 Whisk the soured cream or yogurt with the egg. Season with salt, pepper and nutmeg. Pour over the moussaka.
8 Sprinkle with Parmesan cheese and bake for 40–45 minutes, until golden.

V   SAVOURY BROWN LENTIL STEW   V

SERVES 4

1 large onion, thinly sliced
4 tablespoons oil
900 g/2 lb potatoes, cut into even-sized
    chunks
450 g/1 lb carrots, scraped and diced
4 celery sticks, sliced
225 g/8 oz mushrooms, wiped and sliced
100 g/4 oz brown or green lentils, or split
    orange lentils
2 tablespoons plain flour
2 teaspoons dried mixed herbs
1.2 litres/2 pints Dark Vegetable Stock
    (p. 132) or water
4 tablespoons soy sauce
salt and freshly ground black pepper
TO GARNISH
chopped parsley

1 Fry the onion in the oil in a large saucepan over a moderate heat for 3–4 minutes, stirring occasionally until soft, but not brown.
2 Add the potatoes, carrots, celery, mushrooms and lentils; stir, then sprinkle in the flour and herbs and stir again.
3 Add the stock or water, soy sauce and salt and pepper to taste. Bring to the boil, stir well, then cover and simmer gently until the lentils are tender – 20–30 minutes for split lentils, 40–50 minutes for whole green or brown. Stir the stew occasionally.
4 Check the seasoning, then sprinkle a little chopped parsley over the top and serve immediately.

SAVOURY LENTIL LOAF

Serve this loaf with roast potatoes, green vegetables and
Apple Sauce (p. 84).

SERVES 6–8

350 g/12 oz split red lentils
475 ml/16 fl oz water
1 bay leaf
225 g/8 oz Cheddar cheese, grated
1 large onion, peeled and finely chopped
50 g/2 oz button mushrooms, washed and
    finely chopped
75 g/3 oz fresh wholewheat breadcrumbs
1 tablespoon chopped parsley
1 tablespoon lemon juice
2 eggs, lightly beaten
salt and freshly ground black pepper
butter and dried breadcrumbs for coating

1 Line a 900 g/2 lb loaf tin with a long, narrow strip of greased greaseproof or non-stick paper on the base and up the narrow sides. Grease well with butter and sprinkle generously with dried crumbs.
2 Put the lentils, water and bay leaf into a medium saucepan, cover and simmer very gently, until the lentils are tender and all the liquid absorbed – about 20 minutes. Remove the bay leaf.
3 Preheat the oven to 190 C/375 F/Gas Mark 5.
4 Add the cheese to the lentils, together with the onion, mushrooms, breadcrumbs, parsley, lemon juice and egg. Mix well and season to taste with salt and pepper, then spoon the mixture into the tin and level the top.
5 Bake, uncovered, for 1–1½ hours, until firm and golden-brown on top. Slip a knife around the edges of the loaf to loosen, then carefully turn out.

Variation
VEGAN LENTIL LOAF
Omit the egg and cheese and beat in 75 g/3 oz vegan margarine. Form into a roll. Coat in crumbs and bake in a little oil on a baking sheet instead of in the loaf tin.

MENU
*A Simple Winter
Supper*

Carrot and Ginger Soup
129

Savoury Brown Lentil Stew

Baked Potatoes
190
Technicolour Cabbage
Salad
162

Egg and Cheese Dishes

Eggs and cheese are useful protein foods for lacto-vegetarians and can be made into some particularly pleasant dishes such as fondues (p. 217), soufflés (p. 222), roulades (p. 224) and gnocchi (p. 227). Served with lightly cooked vegetables or a fresh salad, there is no reason why cheese and egg dishes, although relatively high in fat, should not feature in the main meals of a healthy diet. Aim to achieve a good balance by serving pulse, pasta, cereal or nut dishes frequently on other days, and by keeping your other meals of the day low in fat. Then you can enjoy these tasty and time-saving dishes with a clear conscience!

Reducing the Calories in Cheese

If you want to cut down on the calories in a cheese dish, try using small quantities of a strongly-flavoured cheese such as a mature farmhouse Cheddar or Parmesan. Personally I prefer following this course of action to using the reduced-fat cheeses which are now available. I would rather have half or two-thirds the quantity of a traditionally produced cheese with a really good flavour and texture.

EGGS FLORENTINE

SERVES 4

15 g/½ oz butter
900 g/2 lb fresh spinach, or 450 g/1 lb frozen spinach, cooked, drained and chopped
salt and freshly ground black pepper
freshly grated nutmeg
4 eggs
300 ml/10 fl oz Cheese Sauce (p. 175)
25 g/1 oz Gruyère or Cheddar cheese, grated

1 Add the butter to the spinach and mix well. Season to taste with salt, pepper and nutmeg and put it into a shallow oven-proof dish.
2 Heat the grill. Poach the eggs as described on p. 107.
3 Carefully place the eggs on top of the spinach, pour the Cheese Sauce on top and sprinkle with the grated Gruyère or Cheddar cheese.
4 Place the dish under the grill until the cheese is golden and melted. Serve immediately.

MENU

Quick Easy Supper for Two

Charentais Melon Halves

Eggs Florentine

Crusty Wholewheat Stick
Tomato Salad

73

Assorted Yogurts

BAKED EGGS

A quick and easy supper dish, baked eggs can be varied according to the ingredients available. Serve with hot wholewheat toast or warm rolls.

SERVES 1

1 egg
a little butter
2 tablespoons cooked vegetables (onion, sweet pepper, tomato, asparagus, ratatouille, etc.)
salt and freshly ground black pepper

1 Preheat the oven to 180C/350F/Gas Mark 4. Using a little butter, grease a small ramekin dish.
2 Have ready a roasting tin and a kettle of boiling water.
3 Put the cooked vegetables into the ramekin, making a well in the centre.
4 Break in an egg, season with salt and pepper and dot with a little butter.
5 Place the ramekin in the roasting tin and pour in boiling water to come half-way up the sides of the ramekin. Cover the top of the ramekin with foil.

6 Bake for 10–12 minutes, until the egg is lightly set. Serve immediately with toast or rolls.

Variation
BAKED EGGS IN TOMATO CUPS

Use a medium beefsteak tomato for each person. Cut off the top and reserve this for a lid. Scoop out enough of the tomato pulp to make room for the egg (keep this pulp for another use). Season the inside of the tomato with salt and freshly ground black pepper, and scatter with a little chopped fresh basil if available. Break an egg into each tomato, season, dot with butter, replace the tomato top, place in a lightly greased shallow casserole dish and bake for about 20 minutes, until the egg is set and the tomato tender. Serve with hot buttered toast or noodles for a complete light meal.

PIPÉRADE

This French version of scrambled eggs with vegetables makes a delicious and economical supper dish in the late summer when tomatoes and peppers are cheap. It's an excellent dish for one person: just halve the ingredients.

SERVES 2

Eggs Florentine (p. 214); Baked Eggs (p. 214)

1 large onion, peeled and chopped
25 g / 1 oz butter
1 large green pepper, de-seeded and chopped
450 g / 1 lb tomatoes, skinned and chopped
1–2 garlic cloves, crushed
4 eggs, beaten
salt and freshly ground black pepper
TO GARNISH
lovage sprig
TO SERVE
hot, crusty rolls or fingers of hot wholewheat toast

1 Fry the onion in the butter for 10 minutes, until soft but not browned.
2 Add the green pepper, tomatoes and garlic and cook gently, uncovered, for a further 15–20 minutes, until the vegetables are soft but not mushy, stirring from time to time.
3 Strain in the beaten eggs and stir gently until they begin to set. Remove from the heat (the eggs will continue to cook in their own heat).
4 Season with salt and pepper, garnish with lovage and serve with the crusty rolls or fingers of toast.

STUFFED EGGS

Lightly flavoured with curry, these make a tasty first course
or snack. In my experience, they're particularly popular
with children.

SERVES 4 AS A STARTER, 2 AS A LIGHT MEAL

Basic Egg Cookery

For simple, basic ways of cooking
eggs – boiling, scrambling,
poaching and frying – see the
Ingredients section (p. 107).

Hardboiled Eggs

The best egg for hardboiling is
several days old. A newly laid egg is
difficult to peel because the white
sticks so firmly to the shell.

4 hardboiled eggs, shelled
¼ teaspoon curry powder
50 g / 2 oz Cheddar cheese, finely grated
4 tablespoons milk
salt and freshly ground black pepper
TO GARNISH
a few lettuce leaves
chopped chives

1 Cut the eggs in half lengthways and
scoop the yolks into a bowl without
breaking the whites.
2 Mash the yolks with the curry powder,

cheese and milk and mix until smooth.
3 Season with salt and pepper.
4 Spoon the mixture back into the egg
whites and place on a base of lettuce
leaves on a serving plate. Sprinkle with
chopped chives.

Variation
STUFFED EGGS WITH BLACK
OLIVE PÂTÉ
Omit the curry powder and chives. Top
each stuffed egg with ½ teaspoon Black
Olive Pâté (p. 258).

SCOTCH EGGS VEGETARIAN-STYLE

The colour of the eggs against the dark brown lentils looks
particularly attractive when these eggs are cut, and the
flavours combine excellently. Serve with salad.

SERVES 4

Scotch Eggs Vegetarian-Style

4 hardboiled eggs, shelled
1 egg, beaten
½ quantity Brown Lentil Bake mixture
(p. 211)
salt and freshly ground black pepper
wholewheat flour and fresh wholewheat
breadcrumbs for coating
vegetable oil for deep-frying

1 Dip each egg into beaten egg, then coat
with a quarter of the lentil mixture,
pressing it round smoothly and firmly.
2 Coat the eggs first in the remaining
beaten egg, then in seasoned flour; then
repeat egg and breadcrumbing.
3 Heat the oil in a deep-fryer to 160 C /
325 F, or when a small cube of stale bread
browns in 1 minute. Put the Scotch eggs
into the oil and fry gently until golden.
4 Remove the Scotch eggs with a slotted
spoon and drain on kitchen paper. Cut
the eggs in half and serve hot or cold.

SWISS CHEESE FONDUE

Cheese fondue makes an excellent, cosy supper for 2–4 people. It's best made in a heavy-based saucepan or casserole which can be brought to the table and set on a fondue burner.

SERVES 4

1 garlic clove, halved
300 ml / 10 fl oz dry white wine or cider
400 g / 14 oz Gruyère or Edam cheese, grated
1 tablespoon cornflour
2 tablespoons Kirsch or gin (optional)
2 teaspoons lemon juice
salt and freshly ground black pepper
freshly grated nutmeg
TO SERVE
2 French sticks, 1 white and 1 wholewheat, cut into bite-sized pieces and warmed in the oven

1 Rub the garlic around the inside of a medium saucepan, then discard.
2 Put all but 4 tablespoons of the wine or cider into the saucepan and bring just to the boil, then add the cheese and stir over a gentle heat until melted.
3 Mix the cornflour with the remaining wine or cider and the Kirsch or gin, if using. Pour this into the cheese mixture, stirring until slightly thickened.
4 Remove from the heat and add the lemon juice. Season to taste with salt, pepper and nutmeg. Put the warmed bread cubes into 2 baskets, mixing up the 2 types.
5 Place the pan of fondue in the centre of the table, and use long forks to spear pieces of warm French bread and dip them into the cheese fondue.

Oils for Cooking

Some oils and fats are chemically more stable than others (and therefore better for health) when heated and so are better for cooking. These include butter, clarified butter and ghee, and of the oils, olive and ground nut oil.

Almost-instant Cheese Fondue

Cheese fondue is an excellent emergency meal. Keep a bag of grated cheese and a couple of French sticks in the freezer, and a bottle of dry cider or white wine in the cupboard, and you can whizz up a cheese fondue in minutes.

CHEESE AND PARSLEY FRITTERS

Children love these served with Parsley Sauce (p. 175), chips (if allowed!), and a lightly cooked vegetable.

SERVES 4

600 ml / 1 pint milk
1 small onion, peeled and stuck with 1 clove
1 bay leaf
100 g / 4 oz semolina
100 g / 4 oz Cheddar cheese, grated
1–2 tablespoons chopped parsley
good pinch cayenne pepper
salt and freshly ground black pepper
1 large egg, beaten with 1 tablespoon water
dried breadcrumbs for coating
oil for shallow-frying
TO GARNISH
lemon slices
parsley sprigs

1 Bring the milk, onion and bay leaf to the boil in a large saucepan.
2 Remove from the heat, cover and leave to infuse for 10–15 minutes.
3 Remove and discard the onion and bay leaf. Return the milk to the boil, then gradually sprinkle the semolina over the top, stirring all the time.
4 Simmer for about 5 minutes, stirring often, to cook the semolina, then remove from the heat and beat in the cheese, parsley, cayenne pepper and salt and pepper.
5 Spread the mixture out to a depth of about 1 cm / ½ inch on an oiled plate or baking sheet. Smooth the surface and allow to cool completely.
6 Cut the mixture into squares or triangles. Dip first into beaten egg, then dried breadcrumbs, to coat thoroughly. Shallow-fry in hot oil until crisp on both sides, then drain the fritters well on kitchen paper.
7 Garnish with lemon slices and parsley sprigs and serve immediately.

Cooking Cheese

Certain cheeses, mainly the hard and semi-hard types, are best for cooking, because they melt well without becoming tough or stringy. Sometimes a particular type is best, in which case I have suggested this in the recipe; where no type is specified, use a normal, reasonably-priced Cheddar or Cheddar-type cheese.

YEAST PIZZA

SERVES 4

450 g/1 lb plain 85% wholewheat flour
1 sachet instant dried yeast
½ teaspoon salt
about 175 ml/6 fl oz warm water
2 tablespoons oil
FOR THE TOPPING
2 large onions, peeled and chopped
oil
4 tablespoons tomato purée
1 garlic clove, crushed
salt and freshly ground black pepper
100 g/4 oz mushrooms, washed and sliced or
*   1 green pepper, de-seeded and sliced*
100 g/4 oz Mozzarella cheese, sliced
a few black olives
a little dried oregano

Yeast

Dried yeast, easy-blend yeast (which you add straight to the flour without mixing with water) and fresh yeast are all interchangeable.

Allow 25 g/1 oz fresh yeast or 15 g/½ oz (1 tablespoon) dried yeast to 1.5 kg/3½ lb flour. For easy-blend yeast, follow packet directions.

It is essential that the yeast, whether fresh or dried, is in good condition. Buy from a shop with a quick turnover and store carefully.

Fresh yeast will keep in a screwtop jar in a cool place for up to a week. It should be pale beige in colour with no dark specks and look moist but not damp; it should feel cool to the touch and break cleanly and easily when crumbled. It should have a sweet, fresh smell. Dried yeast does not last for ever. If it smells 'winey' and does not froth up vigorously when mixed with water and sugar, it is not working properly – throw it away; if you use it you will only waste your time and ingredients.

Although yeast likes warmth, too much heat kills it. So don't let it get too hot at any stage.

Opposite page: Fancy Pizza

1 First make the dough. Put the flour, yeast, salt, water and oil into a large mixing bowl and mix to a dough.
2 Turn the dough out onto a lightly floured work surface and knead for 5 minutes until smooth and silky.
3 Put the dough into a large bowl, cover with a damp cloth and leave until doubled in size.
4 Punch down the dough, divide it between two well-greased 20-cm/8-inch flan tins or one 30-cm/12-inch one, or press it into a 30-cm/12-inch circle on a baking sheet. Leave in a warm place while you make the filling.
5 To make the topping, fry the onion in 2 tablespoons oil for 10 minutes, until soft and lightly coloured, then stir in the tomato purée and garlic and season to taste with salt and pepper.
6 Preheat the oven to 250 C/500 F/Gas Mark 9.
7 Flatten the dough with your hands, pressing it well into the tins and up the sides a little, or raising the edge of the dough circle slightly.
8 Spread the tomato mixture on top of the dough, then arrange the mushrooms or green pepper, cheese slices and olives on top.
9 Drizzle a little oil over the top and sprinkle with oregano. Leave in a warm place for 15–20 minutes, for the dough to prove, then bake for 15–20 minutes, until the pizza is puffed up and golden-brown on top.

Variations
QUICK SCONE PIZZA
Make the scone mixture (p. 326), adding 40 g/1½ oz grated cheese before putting in the liquid. Use 150 ml/5 fl oz milk or soya milk and omit the egg. Roll out the dough and make the topping as described above. Bake the pizza immediately, at 220 C/425 F/Gas Mark 7, for 20–25 minutes until golden-brown.

KALEIDOSCOPE PIZZA
Using a knife, gently score the top of the pizza into six sections. Fill each section with a different coloured topping, for instance, cooked and drained sweetcorn kernels, sliced tomatoes, lightly-fried onion rings, lightly-fried green pepper, sliced and fried mushrooms, lightly-steamed sliced courgettes. Sprinkle with a little grated cheese and oil, then bake as described.

PEPPER PIZZA
Divide the pizza as described above, making six or eight sections. Fill the sections with different coloured peppers, de-seeded, chopped and lightly fried. Use as many different colours as you can find: green, red, yellow and black, frying them separately to keep the colours clear. Sprinkle with cheese and bake as described.

FANCY PIZZA
For this pretty variation, arrange pepper slices in the centre, then a circle of sliced button mushrooms, a circle alternating sliced cooked corn on the cob and black olives and an outer circle of sliced Mozzarella cheese. Cover the pizza with foil. Bake for 10 minutes, then uncover for the remaining baking time. Garnish the pizza with bay leaves.

OMELETTE

SERVES 1

Making Omelette Rolls

These make a pleasant savoury nibble and look attractive as part of a canapés selection. Make a 1-egg omelette, keeping it flat. Spread thinly with a coloured filling such as spinach or tomato purée, Black Olive Pâté (p. 258) or Mushroom and Herb Terrine (p. 146), roll up like a Swiss roll, then cut into 6-mm/¼-inch slices.

Omelette Fillings

Allow about 2 heaped tablespoons filling for an omelette to serve 1 person. Have the filling warmed and ready when you start to make the omelette. Here are some ideas for fillings:

- Fines herbes: chopped fresh parsley, chives and chervil
- Skinned, de-seeded (if you like), chopped tomato, heated through – a little chopped fresh basil is good with this
- Cooked, chopped asparagus; reserve an asparagus tip to garnish
- Sliced button mushrooms fried in butter
- Black Olive Pâté, spooned thinly (p. 258)
- Finely chopped spring onion, lightly fried in butter first, or used raw
- Watercress, lightly fried in butter to soften
- 4–6 tablespoons very finely grated cheese, half added to the eggs before cooking, then the remainder sprinkled on top before rolling the omelette

2–3 eggs
salt and freshly ground black pepper
10 g/¼ oz butter

1 Crack the eggs into a bowl, season with salt and pepper, and beat lightly, just to combine.
2 Put a 12–15-cm/5–6-inch non-stick frying pan over a moderate to high heat and add the butter. When it has melted and the froth has subsided, pour in the eggs.
3 Stir the eggs gently with a fork, and as the bottom begins to set draw it back with a spatula and tip the pan to allow the

unset egg to run on to the hot pan.
4 When the omelette is almost set – remember it will go on cooking in its own heat – arrange your chosen filling on top of it.
5 To fold the omelette and turn it out of the frying pan in one movement, hold the frying pan up by its handle at right-angles to a warmed plate.
6 Using the spatula, roll the top third of the omelette down, and at the same time tip the frying pan over the plate, so that the omelette rolls and comes out of the pan on to the plate, fold-side down, at the same time. Serve immediately.

ROLLING AN OMELETTE

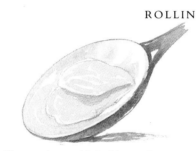

1 Flip over the top third of the omelette

2 Holding the handle of the pan uppermost, tip the omelette on to a warmed plate, allowing it to roll over itself as it comes out of the pan

SPANISH OMELETTE

These quantities can be halved to serve one person.

SERVES 2

2 tablespoons olive oil
1 onion, peeled and chopped
1 carrot, scraped and coarsely grated
1 small green pepper, de-seeded and chopped
225 g/8 oz courgettes, diced
1–2 garlic cloves, crushed
2 tablespoons chopped parsley
4 eggs, beaten
salt and freshly ground black pepper

1 Heat the oil in a large non-stick frying pan and fry the onion, carrot and pepper,

uncovered, for 5 minutes, then add the courgette and cook for a further 5 minutes. Heat the grill.
2 Add the garlic, parsley and eggs to the vegetables and season with salt and pepper. Stir gently until the omelette starts to set.
3 When the omelette is set underneath, put it under the grill to set the top, but don't let it get too firm or it will be rubbery. Cut the omelette in half and serve immediately.

Variation

KOOKOO

For this thick, Middle Eastern version of a Spanish omelette, fry 450 g/1 lb sliced courgettes or cauliflower florets, 3 garlic cloves and a bunch of chopped spring onions in butter in a frying pan with a lid for 2–3 minutes. Season with salt and pepper, then pour in 6 beaten eggs. Cover and cook for about 20 minutes, until browned on the underside, then turn the kookoo over and cook the other side until set and flecked with brown. Cut into thick wedges, like a cake, and serve with a tomato salad and some crisp French bread.

SOUFFLÉ OMELETTE

A soufflé omelette can be savoury or sweet. Serve a savoury one with a simple salad, such as watercress, for a quick main course, and a sweet one with Apricot Jam Sauce, or one of the other suggestions on the right.

SERVES 1

2 eggs, separated
2 tablespoons cold water
salt and freshly ground black pepper, for a savoury omelette
15 g/½ oz butter

1 Heat the grill.
2 Put the egg yolks into a fairly large bowl with the water. Season lightly with salt and pepper, for a savoury omelette.
3 In another bowl, whisk the egg whites until they form soft peaks.
4 Gently fold the egg whites into the egg yolk and water mixture.

5 Heat the butter in a small non-stick frying pan, swirling the pan so that the butter coats the sides as well as the base. Then pour in the egg mixture. Cook over a moderate heat until the omelette is golden-brown underneath.
6 Put the pan under the grill to cook and brown the top of the omelette, but don't let it get too firm.
7 Cut across the surface of the omelette at right angles to the frying pan handle and insert the filling, if using, then fold the omelette in half and lift it gently on to a serving plate.

Separating Eggs

Crack the egg by tapping it smartly against the edge of a bowl or other hard surface, then, holding the egg over a bowl, carefully prise apart the two halves. Tip the white from the half of the shell which does not contain the yolk into a bowl, then tip the yolk into this empty half shell, allowing the white surrounding it to drip into the bowl. Transfer the egg yolk between the two shells until it is separated from as much of the egg white as possible.

Sweet Fillings for Soufflé Omelettes

☐ 2 tablespoons raisins, soaked in rum for 30 minutes
☐ Canned black cherries, heated through, with a little Kirsch added
☐ Apricot jam, warmed with a little water, a few flaked almonds, a dash of Grand Marnier
☐ Any good reduced-sugar preserve, warmed through
☐ A little preserved ginger in syrup

DEEP-FRIED CAMEMBERT

The crisp coating makes a delightful contrast with the hot, runny cheese inside. Serve with a fresh salad and mango or apricot chutney.

SERVES 2–3

1 box of Camembert, containing 6 individual triangles, chilled in the fridge
1 egg, beaten with 1 tablespoon water
dried breadcrumbs or wheatgerm for coating
oil for deep-frying

1 Dip the Camembert triangles, with the rind, into the egg, then into the crumbs or wheatgerm, to coat well. Chill in the refrigerator while you heat the oil for deep-frying.

2 Pour oil into a deep-fryer so that it fills not more than one-third of the pan. Heat the oil to 190C/375F, or when a small cube of stale bread sizzles immediately it's dropped in and becomes golden-brown in 30 seconds.
3 Put in the pieces of Camembert and fry for 4–5 minutes, until crisp and golden-brown. Remove them with a slotted spoon and drain on kitchen paper. Serve immediately.

Deep-frying

Use a deep, heavy pan, so that by the time the food has been put in the oil will not come further than half way up the pan. The fat is hot enough if a small cube of bread sizzles and rises immediately it is dropped into it.

Make sure the food is dry before putting it into the oil, to avoid spluttering; after frying, drain well on crumpled kitchen paper.

CHEESE SOUFFLÉ

In spite of its reputation, a soufflé is very easy to make, and an excellent dish if you have to rustle up something good on the spur of the moment. This soufflé is light but filling and serves 4 people generously. Serve with a green salad and perhaps a tomato salad too.

SERVES 4

*Moulded Layered Soufflé (p. 223);
Spanish Omelette (p. 220)*

50 g / 2 oz butter
50 g / 2 oz plain flour
225 ml / 8 fl oz milk
*150 g / 5 oz cheese, including some Gruyère if
available, grated*
4 eggs, separated
salt and freshly ground black pepper
extra butter for greasing
buttered breadcrumbs for coating

1 Preheat the oven to 190 C / 375 F / Gas Mark 5.
2 Grease a 1-litre / 1¾-pint soufflé dish or straight-sided casserole generously with butter and press breadcrumbs into it, to give the finished soufflé a crisp coating.
3 Melt the butter in a medium saucepan and stir in the flour. Cook for 2–3 minutes, until frothy, then add the milk and stir over the heat until thickened.
4 Remove from the heat and beat in the cheese. Leave to cool until you can put your hand against the pan, then beat in the egg yolks and salt and pepper.
5 Whisk the whites until they form stiff peaks. Stir a couple of tablespoons of egg white into the cheese mixture to lighten it. Using a metal spoon, gently fold in the rest of the egg whites, until none is visible.
6 Turn the mixture into the prepared dish. Bake for about 40 minutes, until the soufflé is puffed-up, doesn't wobble when shaken slightly, and a skewer inserted into the centre comes out clean. Serve immediately.

Variations
COURGETTE SOUFFLÉ

For this pretty, green-flecked version, stir 225 g/8 oz raw grated courgette into the soufflé mixture before beating in the egg yolks.

ASPARAGUS SOUFFLÉ

Mix 225 g/8 oz cooked asparagus, cut into 2.5-cm/1-inch lengths, into the mixture before adding the egg whites.

LEEK SOUFFLÉ

Use either 225 g/8 oz finely shredded raw leek (including some of the green), or 225 g/8 oz cooked thin leeks, cut into 2.5-cm/1 inch-lengths. Add after the egg yolks.

MUSHROOM SOUFFLÉ

Add 225 g/8 oz mushrooms, sliced and fried until no liquid remains, to the mixture after adding the egg yolks.

MOULDED LAYERED SOUFFLÉ

SERVES 4

50 g/2 oz butter
50 g/2 oz plain flour
225 ml/8 fl oz milk
150 g/5 oz cheese, including some Gruyère if available, grated
4 eggs, separated
salt and freshly ground black pepper
150 g/5 oz cooked and puréed carrots
150 g/5 oz cooked and puréed peas or spinach
extra butter for greasing
TO GARNISH
pieces of cooked carrot, baby sweetcorn, mangetouts and sliced courgettes

1 Preheat the oven to 180C/350F/Gas Mark 4.

2 Grease a 1.4-litre/2½-pint pudding basin, mould or cake or bread tin generously with butter and line the base with well-greased non-stick paper.

3 Melt the butter in a medium saucepan and stir in the flour. Cook for 2–3 minutes, until frothy, then add the milk and stir over the heat until thickened.

4 Remove from the heat and beat in the cheese. Leave to cool until you can put your hand against the pan, then beat in the egg yolks and salt and pepper.

5 Remove half the mixture from the pan and put equal amounts of this into 2 bowls. Add the carrot purée to one bowl and the pea or spinach purée to the other. Mix each well.

6 Whisk the whites until they form stiff peaks. Divide this into 3 equal parts, adding one part to the mixture in the saucepan and one part to each of the bowls containing purée.

7 When adding the egg white, stir in one tablespoon first, to loosen the mixture, then gently but thoroughly fold in the rest until well mixed.

8 Spoon the carrot mixture into the base of the prepared basin, mould or tin, smoothing the surface level. Put the green mixture on top, then the plain mixture on top of that, and smooth the surface level.

9 Stand the container in a roasting tin and pour sufficient boiling water around it, to come halfway up the sides of the container.

10 Bake for 50 minutes, until browned and set.

11 Remove from the oven and leave the soufflé to stand for 4–5 minutes, to settle, then turn it out on to a warmed serving plate. Garnish the soufflé with pieces of cooked carrot, baby sweetcorn, mangetouts and sliced courgettes and serve immediately.

Variation
CREAMY LAYERED SOUFFLÉ

Turn the mould out on to an ovenproof plate, coat it all over, thinly, with lightly whipped cream, then sprinkle with grated Parmesan cheese. Return the mould to the oven and bake for 20 minutes, until slightly puffed up and golden-brown.

Small Soufflés

You can make individual soufflés, an excellent first course or light lunch, by baking the mixture in 4 ramekins for 15–20 minutes.

For soufflé tomatoes, bake the mixture in 4 hollowed-out and seasoned 'beefsteak' tomatoes.

The basic quantities can be halved to make a soufflé for 2 people, and the soufflé will take about 30 minutes to cook.

To make a soufflé for 1 person, follow the method given, using a quarter of all the ingredients and baking for 15–20 minutes.

Soufflé Tips

A soufflé can be completely prepared for baking, covered in clingfilm and kept in the refrigerator for several hours before cooking. Let it stand at room temperature for 30 minutes or so before putting it into the oven.

If the soufflé is ready before you are, leave it in the oven with the heat turned off: it will stay risen for several minutes, though it's best eaten immediately it's done.

ROLLING A ROULADE

GRUYÈRE ROULADE

This is a soufflé baked flat, then spread with a filling and rolled up.

SERVES 6

1 Place the cooked roulade on a piece of greaseproof paper on top of a tea-towel; remove backing paper and trim edges

2 Spread the filling on top of the roulade and roll up like a Swiss roll, removing the paper as you do so

1 quantity Cheese Soufflé mixture (p. 222)
1 quantity Peperonata (p. 186) or double
*   quantity Mushroom Sauce (p. 174)*
butter for greasing
4–6 tablespoons grated Parmesan cheese for
*   coating*
TO GARNISH (OPTIONAL)
avocado slices
lime slices
fennel sprigs

1 Preheat the oven to 190C/375F/Gas Mark 5.
2 Line a 24 × 33-cm/9½ × 13-inch Swiss roll tin with non-stick paper, grease generously with butter and sprinkle with half the Parmesan cheese.
3 Spoon the soufflé mixture into the tin, easing it into the corners, and level gently with the back of the spoon.
4 Bake for 15–20 minutes, until puffed up, golden-brown and set in the middle.
5 Have ready a damp tea-cloth spread with a large piece of greaseproof paper

sprinkled with the rest of the Parmesan.
6 Turn the roulade out on to the paper and carefully strip off the lining paper.
7 Trim the edges, then spread the roulade with your chosen filling. Gently roll up the roulade, from one of the long edges.
8 Carefully lift the roulade on to a flat ovenproof dish and put into the oven for 5–10 minutes to heat through. Garnish, if wished, and serve immediately, cut into slices.

Variation
GRUYÈRE ROULADE WITH
AVOCADO FILLING
For this cold version, turn the roulade out on to the greaseproof paper, strip off the lining paper and allow the roulade to get completely cold. Then spread it with Guacamole (p. 144); carefully roll up. Salad fillings, such as mayonnaise and chopped lettuce, tomato and avocado can also be used.

SPINACH ROULADE WITH CURD CHEESE AND PINK PEPPERCORNS

SERVES 4–6

900 g/2 lb fresh spinach, or 450 g/1 lb frozen
*   spinach, cooked and drained*
25 g/1 oz butter
4 eggs, separated
salt and freshly ground black pepper
freshly grated nutmeg
225 g/8 oz curd cheese
1–2 tablespoons pink peppercorns
extra butter for greasing
4–6 tablespoons grated Parmesan cheese
TO GARNISH
radiccio
endive
pink peppercorns

1 Preheat the oven to 190C/375F/Gas Mark 5.
2 Line a 24 × 33-cm/9½ × 13-inch Swiss roll tin with non-stick paper, grease generously with butter and sprinkle with half the Parmesan cheese.
3 Using your hands, squeeze as much water as you can from the cooked and drained fresh or frozen spinach, then chop it.
4 Put the spinach in a saucepan with the butter and cook gently until heated through. Remove the saucepan from the heat and add the egg yolks, mixing them in thoroughly.

Spinach Roulade with Curd Cheese and Pink Peppercorns (p. 224)

5 Whisk the egg whites until stiff but not dry and fold them into the spinach. Season with salt, pepper and nutmeg.

6 Spoon the soufflé mixture into the tin, easing it into the corners, and level gently with the back of the spoon.

7 Bake for about 15–20 minutes, until the roulade is puffed up, golden-brown and set in the middle.

8 Have ready a damp tea-cloth spread with a large piece of greaseproof paper sprinkled with the rest of the Parmesan cheese.

9 Turn the roulade out on to the paper and carefully strip the lining paper off the roulade. Allow to cool completely if you're serving the roulade cold.

10 Beat the curd cheese to soften it, then spread it evenly over the roulade and sprinkle with the peppercorns.

11 Gently roll up the roulade, from one of the long edges. Trim the ends with a sharp serrated knife.

12 If serving the roulade cold, put it on to a serving plate. If serving hot, lift the roulade on to a flat ovenproof dish and put into the oven for 5–10 minutes to heat it through. Serve immediately garnished with radiccio, endive and a few pink peppercorns.

SAVOURY OLIVE MUSHROOM CAKE

This recipe was given to me by a French friend and I love the combination of flavours. If you haven't any left-over white wine, water will do, but the wine gives a subtle, fruity flavour. Serve cut into thick wedges, like a cake, with a green salad dressed with walnut oil, and a glass of full-bodied white wine, such as a Chablis or robust Chardonnay.

SERVES 4

300 g/10 oz self-raising 85% wholewheat flour
a pinch of salt
4 eggs
150 ml/5 fl oz white wine
4 tablespoons olive oil
225 g/8 oz pitted green olives, sliced
175 g/6 oz mushrooms, sliced
175 g/6 oz cheese, grated
butter for greasing
TO GARNISH
chicory
watercress

1 Preheat the oven to 250 C/500 F/Gas Mark 9. Grease a 20-cm/8-inch cake tin or 900-g/2-lb loaf tin.
2 Put the flour and salt into a mixing bowl and break in the eggs. Add the wine and oil. Mix until smooth, then stir in the olives, mushrooms and cheese.
3 Spoon the mixture into the prepared tin. Bake for 10 minutes, then turn down the oven to 190 C/375 F/Gas Mark 5 and bake for a further 40–50 minutes, until firm, golden-brown and shrunk from the sides of the tin. Garnish with chicory and watercress and serve immediately.

SAVOURY CHEESE PUDDING

This cheese pudding is enlivened with green pepper, tomatoes, onion, parsley and a dash of Tabasco. Serve it for an economical supper, with crisp celery, chicory or watercress.

SERVES 4

Tabasco

This is a hot flavouring liquid made from the tabasco variety of chilli pepper. It is very useful for perking up all kinds of mixtures from avocado dip to cheese sauce. It is very hot, so you only need a drop or two. Do get the original type: the imitations are not as good.

1 large onion, peeled and chopped
1 green pepper, de-seeded and chopped
25 g/1 oz butter
100 g/4 oz fresh wholewheat breadcrumbs
1 × 225-g/8-oz can tomatoes
2 tablespoons chopped parsley
100 g/4 oz Cheddar cheese, grated
1 egg
a few drops of Tabasco sauce
salt and freshly ground black pepper
a little milk (optional)
butter for greasing

1 Preheat the oven to 190 C/375 F/Gas Mark 5.
2 Fry the onion and pepper in the butter for 10 minutes, until softened but not browned. Add the breadcrumbs, tomatoes with their juice, parsley, cheese, egg and Tabasco. Season to taste with salt and pepper.
3 Stir a little milk or water into the mixture if necessary to make a soft consistency.
4 Spoon the mixture into a shallow greased dish and bake for 30 minutes until golden-brown. Serve the pudding cut into slices, with crisp celery, chicory or watercress.

Opposite page:
Gnocchi alla Romana; Savoury Olive Mushroom Cake (p. 226)

GNOCCHI ALLA ROMANA

This is a little bit more trouble than some of the dishes in this book, but it can be made in stages and is cheap and delicious. Serve this with a simple tomato and basil salad, or with Italian Tomato Sauce (p. 171) and Red Kidney Bean, Haricot Bean and Black Olive Salad (p. 157), or Chicory, Watercress and Walnut Salad (p. 161).

SERVES 4

600 ml / 1 pint milk
100 g / 4 oz semolina
1 small egg
75 g / 3 oz Parmesan cheese, grated
salt and freshly ground black pepper
freshly grated nutmeg
15 g / 1/2 oz butter
a little oil
TO GARNISH
dill sprig

1 Put the milk into a large saucepan and bring to the boil.
2 Gradually sprinkle the semolina over the top of the hot milk, whisking well.
3 When all the semolina has been added, allow the mixture to simmer gently for 5 minutes.

4 Remove from the heat and beat in the egg and two-thirds of the Parmesan cheese. Season the mixture with salt, pepper and nutmeg.
5 Spread the mixture out to a depth of about 8 mm / 1/3 inch in a lightly oiled shallow tin or on an oiled plate. Leave to get completely cold.
6 Heat the grill to high. Lightly oil a shallow ovenproof dish or pizza plate.
7 Cut the gnocchi into circles using a 6-cm / 2 1/2-inch pastry cutter. First put the trimmings into the dish, then arrange the circles on top.
8 Dot with the butter, sprinkle with the remaining Parmesan and put under the grill until golden-brown and heated through. Garnish with dill.

MENU
Midsummer Wedding

SERVES 30

Pink Potato Salad
166

Asparagus Boats
263

Gruyère Roulade with Avocado Filling
224

Green Salad
54

Technicolour Cabbage Salad
162

Profiteroles
314

All the main preparation for this wedding buffet, with its pink theme, can be done in advance. Make the pastry cases (as thin as you can!) for the Asparagus Boats up to 4 weeks in advance and freeze. Fill them the day before the wedding, then warm them in the oven before serving.

Fill the roulade, assemble the salads and finish the profiteroles on the morning of the wedding. If you are a member of the bridal party, you will need a reliable friend to take over from you on the day, and mastermind the operation, together with someone to see to all the drinks and others to 'waitress'.

Phone round local catering hire firms well in advance to hire linen, plates, flat serving dishes, cups and saucers, cutlery. Book glasses for wine and champagne from the shop where you order these. Drink champagne throughout the wedding if your budget can stand it, otherwise welcome guests with a medium-dry white wine, such as a Vouvray which you can then drink throughout the meal, then, for the toast, pink champagne!

Nut Dishes

Nuts are one of the most nutritious ingredients and can also be one of the most tasty, forming the basis of some excellent recipes. I particularly like both a good nut roast and the 'dreaded nut cutlet', which can be moist, full of flavour and a real pleasure to eat. They are good served with some of the sauces and accompaniments generally reserved for meat: tasty Vegetarian Gravy (p. 172), for instance, or Apple or Gooseberry Sauce (p. 84), Horseradish Sauce (p. 124) or, for that Christmas pièce de résistance, Bread Sauce (p. 175) and Cranberry Sauce (p. 174).

LINING A TIN

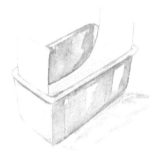

Line the tin with a long strip of greased greaseproof or non-stick paper to cover the base and extend up the narrow sides

CASHEW NUT ROAST

This is a tasty nut roast which slices well both hot and cold. It's excellent served hot, with a tasty sauce and vegetables, or cold, when it slices very thinly, and is good with chutney and pickles, or a yogurt and fresh herb dressing, and salad.

SERVES 6–8

1 medium onion, peeled and chopped
25 g/1 oz butter
1 large tomato, skinned and chopped
2 medium mushrooms, washed and chopped
1½ teaspoons plain flour
150 ml/5 fl oz Light Vegetable Stock (p. 125)
1½ teaspoons yeast extract
1 teaspoon dried mixed herbs
50 g/2 oz ground almonds
100 g/4 oz cashew nuts, finely ground
100 g/4 oz fresh wholewheat breadcrumbs
1 egg
salt and freshly ground black pepper
a little butter for greasing
2–3 tablespoons dried breadcrumbs for coating
TO GARNISH
2–3 mushrooms, sliced and lightly fried in butter
a few roasted cashew nuts
1 tomato, sliced (optional)

1 Preheat the oven to 190 C/375 F/Gas Mark 5. Grease a 450-g/1-lb loaf tin with butter and line with a strip of buttered greaseproof paper to cover the base of the tin and extend up the narrow sides.

Sprinkle the base and sides with dried breadcrumbs.

2 Fry the onion in the butter for 10 minutes until soft, then add the tomato and mushrooms and fry for 2–3 minutes.

3 Stir in the flour, cook for a minute or two, then add the stock and stir until thickened. Remove from the heat and add the rest of the ingredients. Season.

4 Spoon the mixture into the prepared tin, level the top and cover with a piece of greased foil. Bake for 45 minutes, until firm in the centre. (Remove the foil for the last 15 minutes cooking time to allow the top to brown.)

5 Let the loaf stand for 4–5 minutes, then slip a knife around the edges and invert it on to a warmed serving dish.

6 Decorate with the mushrooms, roasted nuts and tomato, if wished.

Variations

BROWN ALMOND NUT ROAST
Make as described, using whole almonds, ground, instead of the cashew nuts. For a darker, savoury nut roast, add 1–2 tablespoons soy sauce.

BRAZIL NUT RINGS WITH PEPERONATA

Small ring moulds, measuring 11 cm/4½ inches in diameter, and holding about 75 ml/3 fl oz, or 10-cm/4-inch flan tins with a round pastry cutter in the centre, are used for these rings. They make an attractive main course, either served on a large dish, or arranged on individual plates with a selection of colourful vegetables.

SERVES 6

1 quantity Cashew Nut Roast mixture (p. 230), using brazil nuts instead of cashew nuts
1 quantity Peperonata (p. 186)
a little butter for greasing
dried breadcrumbs for coating
TO GARNISH
thyme sprigs

1 Preheat the oven to 190 C/375 F/Gas Mark 5.
2 Grease six individual ring moulds, or flan tins (see above), generously with butter and sprinkle with dried crumbs, tapping out the excess.
3 Spoon the nut mixture into the rings, smoothing the tops. Bake, uncovered, for 20 minutes, until firm.
4 While the rings are baking, make the Peperonata filling, as described on p. 186.
5 Slip a knife around sides of the rings, then turn out the nut rings, tapping them firmly if necessary.
6 Put a heaped tablespoon of the Peperonata into the centre of each and garnish with a few thyme sprigs. Serve the rings at once.

Variations

VEGAN BRAZIL NUT RINGS
Use the Quick Savoury Nut Roast mixture (p. 235) instead of the Cashew Nut Roast Mixture, and vegan margarine to grease the tins.

LITTLE BRAZIL NUT RINGS WITH ASPARAGUS HOLLANDAISE FILLING
Make the rings as described. For the filling, mix the stems of six chopped asparagus spears with 1 quantity Hollandaise Sauce (p. 176), spoon into the centre of the rings, and top each with an asparagus tip.

LITTLE BRAZIL NUT RINGS WITH MUSHROOM AND CHESTNUT FILLING
Fill the centre of the rings with a mixture of 100 g/4 oz sliced fried button mushrooms and 100 g/4 oz hot cooked chestnuts. Sprinkle with chopped parsley.

Brazil Nut Rings with Peperonata; Cashew Nut Roast (p. 230)

Peanut Burgers; Nut Balls in Tomato Sauce (p. 238)

V## PEANUT BURGERS ##V

These burgers freeze well and can be fried from frozen.

MAKES 6

Yeast Extract

A sticky dark brown paste made from brewers' yeast, and often fortified by other vitamins (such as B12), yeast extracts are highly nutritious and are useful for giving a savoury flavour to casseroles, sauces, nut roasts and other dishes, and also as a spread for bread. Use with a light touch; add a little at a time.

50 g/2 oz butter or vegan margarine
1 onion, peeled and chopped
1 celery stick, finely chopped
1 teaspoon dried mixed herbs
1 tablespoon wholewheat flour
150 ml/5 fl oz Light Vegetable Stock
  (p. 129)
1 tablespoon soy sauce
1 teaspoon yeast extract
175 g/6 oz roasted, unsalted peanuts, fairly
  finely ground
50 g/2 oz cashew nuts, fairly finely ground
100 g/4 oz fresh wholewheat breadcrumbs
salt and freshly ground black pepper
dried breadcrumbs for coating
oil for shallow-frying
TO GARNISH
lettuce leaves
tomato slices
cucumber slices

1 Melt the butter or vegan margarine in a large saucepan and fry the onion and celery for 10 minutes. Stir in the herbs and flour and cook for a further 1–2 minutes.

2 Add the stock and stir until thickened, then add the soy sauce, yeast extract, nuts, breadcrumbs and salt and pepper.

3 Leave the mixture to cool, then form into 6 flat burgers about 1 cm/½ inch thick, and coat with dried breadcrumbs.

4 Fry the burgers in a very little oil – the frying pan should be 'greased' rather than oily – for about 3 minutes on each side, until browned and crisp. Drain on kitchen paper. Garnish and serve.

Variation

MACADAMIA BURGERS
Using macadamia nuts instead of the peanuts makes these burgers special. Serve with Béarnaise Sauce (p. 176).

CHESTNUT ROAST

A pleasant roast for a chilly winter day, and a traditional Christmas
main course for many vegetarians.

SERVES 4–6

25 g/1 oz butter
1 large onion, peeled and chopped
2 celery sticks, finely chopped
900 g/2 lb chestnuts, peeled and cooked
 (yields about 750 g/1½ lb), or 3 × 425-g/
 15-oz cans whole chestnuts, or about
 250 g/8 oz dried chestnuts, soaked and
 cooked
2 tablespoons chopped parsley
2 tablespoons lemon juice
1 garlic clove, crushed
a few fresh wholewheat breadcrumbs
 (optional)
salt and freshly ground black pepper
4 tablespoons oil
dried breadcrumbs for coating

1 Melt the butter and fry the onion and
celery for 10 minutes until soft but not
brown. Transfer to a large bowl. Drain
the chestnuts and add to the bowl. Mix
these ingredients together well.
2 Mash the chestnuts, onion and celery,
then mix into the bowl the chopped
parsley, lemon juice and garlic.
3 The mixture should be soft but firm
enough to form into a roll, so add a few
wholewheat breadcrumbs, if necessary,
especially if you're using canned chestnuts. Season the mixture with salt and
pepper to taste.
4 Preheat the oven to 200 C/400 F/Gas
Mark 6. Pour a little oil into a roasting tin
and put into the oven to heat.
5 Form the chestnut mixture into a roll
about 20 cm/8 inches long, pressing it
together well, then coat with the dried
crumbs.
6 Put the chestnut roll into the roasting
tin and carefully turn it so that it is coated
with hot oil.
7 Bake for 45 minutes, until it is crisp on
the outside, spooning a little of the oil
over the roll from time to time during the
cooking. Serve the Chestnut Roast cut
into slices.

MENU

Christmas Menu

Chilled Two-Colour Soup
139

Chestnut Roast

Sauce Soubise
173
Red Cabbage Casserole
180
Braised Celery Hearts
182

Traditional Trifle
285

PEELING CHESTNUTS

1 Place chestnut flat-side down
on a board and make a cut in the
pointed end

2 Boil or bake the chestnuts in a
hot oven for 10–20 minutes until the cuts open

3 Strip the skins off the chestnuts using a small, sharp,
pointed knife

SHAPING NUT OR LENTIL BURGERS

1 Flatten burgers and give them a professional look
by tapping them firmly on top and around the sides
with a palette knife

2 Press them together firmly, which will help the
nut or lentil burgers to remain intact when you fry
them

Making Breadcrumbs

Bread which is a day or two old is
best for these. Cut off the crusts and
crumble the bread between your
fingers, or pop chunks of bread into
a food processor or blender and
whizz for a moment or two. If you
have a freezer, it's worth making
any left-over pieces of bread into
crumbs and freezing in a polythene
bag. The breadcrumbs can be used
straight from the freezer.

Alternatively, you can dry out
slices of bread in the bottom of the
oven while something else is
cooking, or in a microwave (they
only take about 5 minutes). Then
crush them with a rolling pin. It's
useful to have both fresh and dried
breadcrumbs available.

CROUSTADE OF MUSHROOMS

This is an up-dated version of my most popular recipe, which I invented for one of my first dinner parties, and which first appeared in my second book, *Not Just a Load of Old Lentils*.

SERVES 4–6

75 g / 3 oz flaked almonds, or other nuts, flaked in a food processor
75 g / 3 oz fresh wholewheat breadcrumbs
75 g / 3 oz ground almonds or other finely ground nuts
1 small onion, peeled and grated
1 garlic clove, crushed
90 g / 3½ oz softened butter
salt and freshly ground black pepper
450 g / 1 lb mushrooms, washed and sliced
300 ml / 10 fl oz soured cream
freshly grated nutmeg
paprika pepper

1 Preheat the oven to 180 c / 350 f / Gas Mark 4.
2 Reserve a few of the flaked almonds for garnishing. Mix together the breadcrumbs, ground and remaining flaked almonds, or other nuts, onion, garlic and 75 g / 3 oz of the butter. Season well with salt and pepper. The mixture should hold together like a crumbly pastry.
3 Press the mixture into the base of a 20-cm / 8-inch loose-bottomed flan tin. Bake for 20 minutes, until golden-brown and crisp.
4 Meanwhile, fry the mushrooms in the remaining butter for 15–20 minutes, until all the liquid has evaporated. Season with salt and pepper.
5 Spoon the mushrooms on top of the croustade. Stir the soured cream with a fork, season with salt, pepper and nutmeg, then swirl about half the soured cream on top of the mushrooms, so that some show through the cream. Sprinkle with paprika.
6 Return the croustade to the oven for 10–15 minutes, to heat through, then remove from the tin and serve on a warmed plate. Scatter reserved flaked almonds over the top. Serve the rest of the soured cream separately, in a small bowl or jug.

Variations
VEGAN CROUSTADE OF MUSHROOMS
Use vegan margarine instead of butter, and non-dairy cream or yogurt instead of soured cream.

CROUSTADE OF LEEKS
Replace the mushrooms with 450 g / 1 lb cleaned and sliced leeks. Cook the leeks in a little fast-boiling lightly-salted water for about 10 minutes, then drain well and add the soured cream and seasoning.

Croustade of Mushrooms

HAZELNUT AND VEGETABLE CRUMBLE

V   V

Simple and good, an excellent way of turning vegetables into a main course. Serve with a lightly cooked green vegetable, potato purée and Vegetarian Gravy (p. 172) for a family winter meal.

SERVES 4

900 g/2 lb peeled and diced vegetables:
  carrots, swedes, turnips, onions, celery
100 g/4 oz butter or vegan margarine
salt and freshly ground black pepper
75 g/3 oz rolled oats
75 g/3 oz hazelnuts, finely ground
75 g/3 oz hazelnuts, chopped or flaked
1 small onion, peeled and grated
1 garlic clove, crushed
½ teaspoon dried thyme or mixed herbs

1 Preheat the oven to 180 C/350 F/Gas Mark 4.
2 Boil the vegetables in water to cover for 15–20 minutes, or until tender. Drain, reserving the water.
3 Blend about one-third of the vegetables with 25 g/1 oz of the butter or vegan margarine and enough of the reserved water to make a purée in a food processor or blender.
4 Add this purée to the rest of the vegetables. Season to taste with salt and pepper. Spoon the mixture into a shallow ovenproof casserole.
5 To make the crumble topping, put the oats into a bowl with all the nuts, the onion, garlic, herbs and salt and pepper. Add the rest of the butter or vegan margarine, and mix with a fork until the topping mixture resembles coarse breadcrumbs.
6 Sprinkle the crumble mixture evenly over the top of the vegetables. Bake for 30–40 minutes, until the topping is crisp and lightly browned.

MENU

Warming Family Supper

Hazelnut and Vegetable Crumble

Baked Potatoes
190
Steamed Broccoli
Vegetarian Gravy
172
or Italian Tomato Sauce
171

Fresh Fruit
or
Pancakes with Lemon and Honey
299

QUICK SAVOURY NUT ROAST

V   V

This easy-to-make roast is good served hot or cold.

SERVES 4

50 g/2 oz butter or vegan margarine
2 large onions, peeled and finely chopped
1 teaspoon dried thyme
1 tablespoon wholewheat flour
150 ml/5 fl oz water
100 g/4 oz cashew nuts, fairly finely ground
100 g/4 oz hazelnuts, fairly finely ground
100 g/4 oz dried wholewheat breadcrumbs
1 tablespoon lemon juice
salt and freshly ground black pepper
dried crumbs for coating
8 tablespoons oil for roasting

1 Preheat the oven to 200 C/400 F/Gas Mark 6.
2 Melt the butter or vegan margarine in a large saucepan and fry the onions gently for 10 minutes, until tender.
3 Add the thyme and flour; stir for 1–2 minutes, then add the water and stir until thickened.
4 Remove from the heat, add the nuts, breadcrumbs, lemon juice and salt and pepper to taste. Mix well. Form into a loaf shape and coat in dried crumbs. Heat the oil in a small roasting tin in the oven until smoking hot. Put the nut roast into the tin and baste with the oil.
5 Bake for 35–40 minutes.
6 Remove from the tin. Serve immediately, cut into thick slices or leave to cool if serving cold.

Serving Nut or Lentil Roast

It's useful to make enough nut or lentil roast for one serving hot, and one cold. Sliced cold nut roast is delicious with salad and any of the following

Mayonnaise with Green Peppercorns (p. 155)
Mango Chutney Mayonnaise (p. 155) or Cranberry Sauce (p. 174)
Sliced Fresh Mango
Yogurt and Herb Dressing (p. 156)

V   BRAZIL NUT ROAST EN CROÛTE   V

Salts

Salt, or sodium chloride, has been used as a flavouring and food-preservative since Neolithic times. It is available in various forms.

SEA SALT Sometimes called 'gros sel', is evaporated naturally in bays and enclosures or from salt marshes. It contains traces of minerals, including iodine. Most cooks agree that there is nothing to touch sea salt from the point of view of flavour. Sea salt is available as coarse granules, for use in a grinder, or as fine grains or flakes.

ROCK SALT The kind that is mined from the deposits made by ancient seas. It is sold in various degrees of coarseness.

TABLE SALT, BLOCK SALT and KITCHEN SALT are produced from rock salt. Iodine is sometimes added to table salt, to make iodized salt. This is a useful way of adding essential iodine to the diet in parts of the country where it is not present in the soil (and thus in the vegetables). Flavoured salts, such as onion salt, garlic salt and celery salt, are made from table salt with dried and powdered onion, garlic or celery seed added.

SERVES 8

1 quantity Flaky Pastry made with white flour (p. 268) or 450 g/1 lb frozen puff pastry
beaten egg to glaze (optional)
FOR THE NUT ROAST
2 large onions, peeled and chopped
50 g/2 oz butter or vegan margarine
450 g/1 lb brazil nuts, finely ground
225 g/8 oz fresh fine breadcrumbs
½ teaspoon dried thyme
3 tablespoons lemon juice
2 eggs (optional)
a good pinch each of grated nutmeg, ground cloves and ground cinnamon
salt and freshly ground black pepper
FOR THE STUFFING
225 g/8 oz fresh fine white breadcrumbs
25 g/1 oz chopped parsley
grated rind of 1 lemon
1 tablespoon lemon juice
1 teaspoon each dried thyme and marjoram
1 tablespoon grated onion
75 g/3 oz butter or vegan margarine
TO GARNISH
8 clementine halves filled with cranberries
thyme sprigs

1 Preheat the oven to 200 C/400 F/Gas Mark 6.
2 To make the nut roast, fry the onion in the butter or vegan margarine for 10 minutes, until soft but not browned.
3 Remove from the heat and add the rest of the nut roast ingredients. Season.
4 Make the stuffing by mixing all the ingredients together to make a soft mixture which holds together. Season.
5 Roll out the pastry on a floured board to a 30 × 35-cm/12 × 14-inch rectangle.
6 Form the stuffing into a sausage about 25 cm/10 inches long and place down the middle of the pastry. Pile the nut roast mixture all over the stuffing, covering it.
7 Fold the ends of the pastry up to enclose the nut mixture completely. Tuck in the ends, then place on a damp baking sheet, join side down. Mark a lattice design on the top.
8 Make one or two steam-holes, decorate with pastry trimmings and brush with beaten egg, if using. Bake for 30 minutes, until crisp. Garnish with clementine halves filled with cranberries and thyme sprigs.

PREPARING NUT ROAST EN CROÛTE

1 Put the stuffing in the centre of the pastry

2 Cover the stuffing with the nut mixture

3 Fold up the sides of the pastry, to enclose the nut mixture

4 Place on a baking sheet, seam-side down

PINE NUT ROULADE WITH ASPARAGUS HOLLANDAISE FILLING

This dish, which I've developed from a recipe invented by Michael Smith, is very rich, wonderful for a celebration summer meal. It can be made a few hours in advance and reheated just before serving. Serve with new potatoes, mangetouts and baby carrots.

SERVES 6

4 large eggs
salt and freshly ground black pepper
225 g/8 oz pine nuts, lightly crushed
a little butter and oil for greasing
FOR THE FILLING
1 quantity Hollandaise Sauce, light version
  (p. 176)
450 g (1 lb) fresh young asparagus, lightly
  cooked, tips only
12 quails' eggs, hardboiled, shelled and
  halved
2 tablespoons snipped chives

1 Preheat the oven to 200 C/400 F/Gas Mark 6. Line a 33 × 23-cm/13 × 9-inch Swiss roll tin with buttered greaseproof paper, letting it extend 5 cm/2 inches above the edge of the tin and snipping diagonally into the corners (p. 230).
2 Whisk the eggs with salt and pepper until thick, fold in half the pine nuts and pour into the tin, spreading the mixture evenly into the corners.
3 Bake near the top of the oven for 6–8 minutes, until firm in the middle.
4 Put a clean tea-towel, wrung out in cold water, on to a flat surface. Cover with a piece of greaseproof paper spread evenly with the remaining pine nuts. Invert the roulade on to the pine nuts and remove the lining paper.
5 Spread the roulade with all but 2 tablespoons of the Hollandaise Sauce. Arrange the asparagus tips (reserving 6 for the garnish), quail's eggs (reserving 3 halves) and chives on top.
6 Carefully roll up the roulade by folding one long side into the centre and the other on top. Place a large oiled piece of foil on top and turn the roulade upside down. Slide a baking sheet underneath, and remove the cloth.

7 Reheat, either immediately, or when required, still wrapped in foil, at 190 C/375 F/Gas Mark 5, for 15–20 minutes.
8 Remove the foil and transfer the roulade to a heated oval or oblong serving plate. Spoon the reserved sauce down the centre and arrange the reserved asparagus tips and quails' eggs on top. Serve immediately.

Variations

ROASTED CASHEW NUT ROULADE WITH WILD MUSHROOM FILLING

Make as described, using roasted cashew nuts instead of pine nuts, and Wild Mushrooms in Cream (p. 272) for the filling, instead of the asparagus and Hollandaise Sauce. Use the quails' eggs, or not, as you like, and garnish with fried mushrooms and roasted cashew nuts.

PECAN NUT ROULADE WITH RATATOUILLE FILLING

A less rich, but still very tasty version. Use pecan nuts instead of pine nuts, and replace the asparagus and Hollandaise Sauce with Ratatouille (p. 187). Use the quails' eggs, or not, as you like, and garnish with parsley and pepper rings.

HAZELNUT ROULADE WITH LEEK FILLING

Use roasted hazelnuts (p. 37) instead of the pine nuts, 450 g/1 lb cleaned and sliced leeks, cooked in a little fast-boiling water until tender, and well-drained, instead of the asparagus, and 300 ml/10 fl oz soured cream instead of the Hollandaise Sauce.

Salt Substitutes

Various substitutes for salt are available, some based on potassium chloride instead of sodium chloride, others consisting of mixtures of herbs and other seasonings. These are certainly worth a try, though none of them are very satisfactory, in my opinion – personally I'd rather use just a little sea salt with other flavourings such as fresh herbs, sea vegetables and lemon juice, than one of the substitutes. If you have a heart condition, or are on a potassium-restricted diet, you should get your doctor's advice before using a potassium-based salt.

Gomasio

A savoury mixture of roasted sesame seeds and salt, much used in Japan. To make gomasio, put ten parts sesame seeds and one part sea salt into a frying pan and heat gently, stirring, for a few minutes, until the sesame seeds smell roasted, turn a darker.brown and one or two start to 'pop'. Then remove from the heat and grind to a fairly fine powder in a coffee grinder. Store in an airtight jar. Use in cooking or at the table instead of salt. This is a useful way of reducing salt intake as well as adding a savoury flavour.

Nut Milk made with Blanched Almonds

Making Nut Milks

You can make some delicious milks from nuts, far superior in flavour, I think, to cow's milk. All you do is whizz up a few cashew nuts or freshly blanched almonds with some water in a liquidizer or blender. You can make the mixture thick, like cream, or thin and delicate. I find 25 g/1 oz blanched almonds (about 30 nuts) to a tumbler of water makes a good consistency for drinking. You can drink as it is, or strain it.

For a fruit and nut drink, which makes a reviving and sustaining lunch or evening meal when you don't feel like eating anything else, try whizzing up a peeled banana or a few strawberries or raspberries with the almonds and water. This is especially good – like a thick milk shake – when made with a fruit which you've popped into the freezer for a few hours beforehand.

NUT BALLS IN TOMATO SAUCE

Serve these with buttered spaghetti and a crisp green salad.

SERVES 4

1 onion
1 tablespoon oil
100 g/4 oz brown nuts, such as unblanched almonds or roasted hazelnuts, finely ground
50 g/2 oz fresh wholewheat breadcrumbs
50 g/2 oz Cheddar cheese, finely grated
2 teaspoons tomato purée
1 egg yolk
1/2 teaspoon dried thyme
salt and freshly ground black pepper
butter for greasing
1 quantity Italian Tomato Sauce (p. 171)
TO GARNISH
thyme sprigs

1 Preheat the oven to 180 C/350 F/Gas Mark 4.
2 Fry the onion in the oil for 10 minutes, until softened, then remove from the heat and mix in all the rest of the ingredients except the Italian Tomato Sauce.
3 Form the mixture into 8 balls. Place in a shallow ovenproof dish.
4 Pour the tomato sauce over the nut balls. Bake for 25–30 minutes. Garnish with thyme and serve hot.

Variations
NUT BALLS BAKED IN RATATOUILLE
Make as described, but instead of baking the nut balls in tomato sauce, add them to a shallow casserole of Ratatouille (p. 187).

VEGAN NUT BALLS
Use 2 tablespoons peanut butter instead of the cheese and egg. You may find you need less salt.

SWEETCORN FRITTERS

These fritters make a good light breakfast or supper dish, perhaps accompanied by some grilled tomatoes and lightly fried mushrooms. Or they can be served as an accompaniment to a nut roast with Potato Purée (p. 189) and Cranberry Sauce (p. 174).

SERVES 2–3 AS A MAIN COURSE, 4–6 AS AN ACCOMPANIMENT

225 g/8 oz frozen sweetcorn kernels, or fresh ones scraped from the cob, lightly cooked and drained
50 g/2 oz chopped almonds
1 egg, separated
25 g/1 oz wholewheat flour
salt and freshly ground black pepper
oil for shallow frying

1 Put the cooked sweetcorn into a bowl with the chopped almonds, egg yolk and flour. Mix well and season to taste with salt and pepper.
2 Whisk the egg white until it stands in stiff peaks, then gently fold into the sweetcorn mixture.
3 Heat a little oil in a frying pan, then drop tablespoons of the sweetcorn mixture into the oil and fry them on both sides until crisp.
4 Drain the fritters on kitchen paper. Keep the first batch warm in a low oven while you fry the rest, then serve them immediately.

Variation
VEGAN FRITTERS
Make the batter using 225 g/8 oz chick pea flour, 1/2 teaspoon salt and 200–250 ml/7–8 fl oz water. Put the flour and salt into a bowl and mix in water to make a coating batter. Stir in the sweetcorn.

WHITE NUT ROAST WITH HERB STUFFING

I like to serve this at Christmas with all the traditional accompaniments including Bread Sauce (p. 175), Cranberry Sauce (p. 174) and Vegetarian Gravy (p. 172).

SERVES 8–10

1 large onion, peeled and chopped
50 g/2 oz butter
1 teaspoon dried thyme
1 tablespoon plain flour
300 ml/10 fl oz milk
225 g/8 oz mixed white nuts, finely ground:
  use cashew nuts, blanched almonds and
  pine nuts
100 g/4 oz fresh white breadcrumbs
salt and freshly ground black pepper
freshly grated nutmeg
2 egg whites
a little extra butter for greasing
3–4 tablespoons dried breadcrumbs for coating
FOR THE HERB STUFFING
175 g/6 oz fresh white breadcrumbs
100 g/4 oz butter
4 tablespoons chopped parsley
grated rind of ½ lemon
2 tablespoons grated onion
1 teaspoon each dried marjoram and thyme
2 egg yolks
TO GARNISH
lemon slices
parsley sprigs

1 Preheat the oven to 190 C/375 F/Gas Mark 5.

2 Grease a 900-g/2-lb loaf tin with butter and line with a strip of buttered grease-proof paper to cover the base of the tin and extend up the narrow sides. Sprinkle with dried breadcrumbs.

3 Fry the onion in the butter for 10 minutes until soft. Add the thyme and flour and cook for a minute or two, then add the milk and stir until thickened.

4 Remove from the heat and add the nuts and breadcrumbs. Season generously with salt, pepper and nutmeg.

5 Whisk the egg whites until stiff but not dry, then fold in.

6 Make the stuffing by thoroughly mixing all the ingredients together and sea-soning to taste with salt and pepper.

7 Spoon half the nut mixture into the prepared tin in an even layer.

8 With your hands, form the stuffing into a flat layer which will fit over the top of the nut mixture; put into the tin on top of the layer of nut mixture.

9 Cover the stuffing with the rest of the nut mixture.

White Nut Roast with Herb Stuffing

10 Level the top, cover with buttered foil, and bake for 1–1¼ hours, until firm in the centre. (Remove the foil for the last 15 minutes of cooking time to allow the top to brown.)

11 Let the loaf stand for 4–5 minutes, then slip a knife around the edges and invert it on to a warmed serving dish. Garnish with the parsley sprigs and lemon slices.

Grain Dishes

Nutritious, high-fibre protein food, grains can be made into some particularly healthy dishes, excellent for alternating with richer ones, perhaps those based on cheese and eggs, for creating a balanced diet. Most grain dishes are also quick and easy to make, thus being excellent mid-week standbys; in addition, left-overs can often be made into croquettes or used to stuff peppers or large tomatoes, saving time another day. It's worth experimenting with some of the more unusual grains; you'll find full details of basic cooking in the Ingredients section (p. 44).

Bircher Muesli

This is the original muesli invented by Dr Bircher-Benner for the patients in his famous natural health clinic in Zurich. He used condensed milk because that was the only kind which was safe when he was practising at the end of the last century. You can replace this with ordinary milk or plain yogurt if you like, though the condensed milk gives a pleasant, almost jellied texture which ordinary milk and yogurt do not. Dr Bircher-Benner served his muesli to his patients for their evening meal, with thinly sliced wholemeal bread, honey and herb tea.

BIRCHER MUESLI

This muesli makes a nourishing snack at any time of day.

SERVES 1

2 tablespoons rolled oats
1 tablespoon sweetened condensed milk
3 tablespoons cold water
a little grated lemon rind
1 tablespoon lemon juice
100 g/4 oz grated apple or 200 g/7 oz soft fruit in season
1 tablespoon grated hazelnuts

1 Put the oats, condensed milk, water, lemon rind and juice into a bowl and mix to a creamy consistency.
2 Add the fruit. According to Dr Bircher-Benner, the whole apple should be used, skin, core and pips!
3 Spoon the mixture into a serving bowl. Sprinkle with the grated nuts.

V   ## CRUNCHY GRANOLA   V

MAKES 1.25 kg/2¾ lb

300 ml/10 fl oz boiling water
200 ml/7 fl oz sunflower or corn oil
300 ml/10 fl oz clear honey
1 teaspoon vanilla extract
450 g/1 lb rolled oats
75 g/3 oz sesame seeds
50 g/2 oz wheatgerm
100 g/4 oz shredded coconut
100 g/4 oz sunflower seeds
175 g/6 oz raisins
100 g/4 oz hazelnuts

1 Preheat the oven to 180 C/350 F/Gas Mark 4.
2 In a large jug mix together the boiling water, oil, honey and vanilla.

3 Put the oats, sesame seeds, wheatgerm and coconut into a large baking tin.
4 Gradually add the honey mixture, stirring all the time, so that all the dry ingredients get coated. (I find it easiest to use my hands for this, rather like rubbing fat into flour.)
5 Bake for 15 minutes, stirring the mixture a couple of times. Then reduce the oven setting to 140 C/275 F/Gas Mark 1 and bake for 1½–2 hours, stirring every 15 minutes or so, until the granola is crisp and golden-brown.
6 Cool, then mix in the sunflower seeds, raisins and nuts. Store the granola in an airtight container.

Simple Muesli

A simple muesli base can be made by mixing 225 g/8 oz rolled oats with 100 g/4 oz each of raisins and nuts. Other whole grains and dried fruits and nuts can be added to taste.

V   # SAFFRON RICE   V

SERVES 4

225 g/8 oz long-grain brown rice
600 ml/1 pint water
1 teaspoon salt
good pinch of saffron strands

1 Wash the rice, drain and dry on kitchen paper.
2 Put the rice into a heavy-based saucepan with the water, salt and saffron.
3 Bring to the boil, then cover and turn the heat down as low as possible.
4 Cook the rice for 40–45 minutes, until it is tender and all the water absorbed.
5 The rice will improve if you can allow it to stand off the heat, but still covered, for a further 15 minutes. Fluff the rice by stirring gently with a fork.

Variations

SWEET VINEGARED RICE
Sweet Vinegared Rice is used to make Sushi (p. 142) and I like to serve it with Japanese vegetable dishes too. Make rice as described, above, using short-grain rice. Put a piece of kombu (wiped with a damp cloth), if available, in the saucepan with the rice and water. When the water comes to the boil, remove the kombu. This flavours the rice delicately. When the rice is cooked, add 2 teaspoons sugar which have been dissolved in 4 tablespoons rice vinegar. Mix gently.

RICE WITH WILD RICE
Wild rice is very expensive, but the addition of a little to brown rice makes it extra special. The dark brown grains of wild rice look attractive against the paler brown rice. Make as described, adding 50 g/2 oz wild rice and increasing the amount of water to 750 ml/1¼ pints.

V   # SPICED RICE   V

This delicately flavoured golden rice is a good accompaniment for curries, spiced vegetable mixtures and stuffed vegetables.

SERVES 4

225 g/8 oz brown rice
1½ tablespoons oil
¾ teaspoon turmeric powder
3 cloves
1 bay leaf
600 ml/1 pint water
salt and freshly ground black pepper

1 Wash the rice, drain and dry on kitchen paper. Heat the oil in a medium-sized saucepan, then add the rice, and fry without browning, stirring, for 3–4 minutes.
2 Stir in the turmeric, cloves and bay leaf. Cook for a few seconds longer, then pour in the water and add some salt and pepper.
3 Bring to the boil, then put a lid on the saucepan and turn the heat down as low as possible. Cook the rice undisturbed for about 40–45 minutes, until the grains are tender and all the water has been absorbed.
4 Fluff the rice by stirring gently with a fork to separate the grains.

Vinegar

One of the earliest flavouring ingredients of all, vinegar is made by souring wine, beer or cider and generally contains 4%–6% acetic acid.

MALT VINEGAR Dark brown in colour and made from beer, it has a strong flavour which is too harsh for most cooking purposes, though it is good for some chutneys and pickles.

WINE VINEGAR Made from both red and white wine, by the slow Orléans method, it has a delicate flavour and makes a delicious dressing. Look for the word 'Orléans' on the bottle.

RICE VINEGAR Made from rice wine and used widely in the Far East.

CIDER VINEGAR Made from cider, has many health-giving properties associated with it. It can be used for salad dressings and complements fruity mixtures, though I personally do not much like the flavour.

DISTILLED VINEGAR Malt vinegar which has been distilled so it is clear and contains up to 12% acetic acid. It is used for pickling. Many different kinds of flavoured vinegar can be bought, such as tarragon, raspberry, garlic, chilli, rose and violet. these are fun to experiment with, and you can quite easily make them yourself by adding flavouring ingredients – such as sprigs of tarragon – to a bottle of wine vinegar.

Rice Pilaf with Apricots, Raisins and Pine Nuts

V   RICE PILAF WITH   V
APRICOTS, RAISINS AND PINE NUTS

SERVES 6

4 tablespoons olive oil
300 g / 10 oz long-grain brown rice
good pinch of saffron strands (optional)
50 g / 2 oz dried apricots, snipped into slivers
½ cinnamon stick
8 cloves
4 black peppercorns
4 cardamom pods, lightly crushed
salt and freshly ground black pepper
750 ml / 1¼ pints water
2 onions, peeled and sliced
50 g / 2 oz raisins
50 g / 2 oz pine nuts or slivered almonds
TO GARNISH
mint sprig

1 Heat half the oil in a heavy-based saucepan. Add the rice and fry for 5 minutes, stirring gently.
2 Add the saffron, if using, the apricots, spices, 1 teaspoon salt and the water.
3 Bring to the boil, then cover tightly and leave to cook over a very gentle heat for 45 minutes. Then turn off the heat and leave covered.
4 Fry the onion in the remaining oil for 10 minutes, until softened and lightly browned. Add to the rice, together with the raisins and nuts. Check the seasoning and stir lightly with a fork. Garnish with a mint sprig to serve.

V # PAELLA VEGETARIANA V

In this vegetarian version of Spanish paella, the traditional fish is replaced by leeks and black olives, with red pepper, peas and chopped parsley, and a good flavouring of saffron, onion and garlic. It's one of my favourite vegetarian dishes. Nuts – blanched almonds, flaked brazil nuts or whole cashew nuts – can be served with this, separately, in a bowl, for people to help themselves if liked. I prefer it without. A wide shallow pan, such as a wok, large frying pan or, best of all, a special paella pan, if you have one, is ideal for this, as it is roomy enough to show off the pattern of the vegetables.

SERVES 4

4 tablespoons olive oil
225 g/8 oz long-grain brown rice
1 large onion, peeled and sliced
2 large garlic cloves, crushed
good pinch of saffron strands
750 ml/1¼ pints Light Vegetable Stock
*   (p. 129) or water*
thinly pared rind of ½ lemon, cut into thin
*   shreds*
salt and freshly ground black pepper
450 g/1 lb washed and trimmed leeks, cut
*   into 2.5-cm/1-inch lengths*
100 g/4 oz frozen peas
50–100 g/2–4 oz black olives
TO GARNISH
chopped parsley

1 Heat the oil in a large, deep pan. Add the long-grain brown rice and onion slices and stir until the rice is coated and begins to turn opaque.

2 Add the garlic, saffron, stock or water, lemon rind and salt and pepper. Mix well, then bring up to the boil. Mix again, to distribute the saffron colouring.
3 Arrange the vegetables and olives attractively on top of the rice
4 Bring to the boil. Cover with a lid or foil and simmer for 45 minutes.
5 Sprinkle with parsley and serve straight from the pan.

Variation
PAELLA VEGETARIANA WITH ARTICHOKES
Use 4–6 globe artichokes instead of the leeks. Very tender baby artichokes can simply be quartered; otherwise cut the leaves and choke from the artichokes as described on p. 63, then halve or quarter the artichoke bottoms. Garnish with bay leaves and artichoke leaves.

Tips for Cooking Rice

The test of perfect long-grain rice is for all the grains to be separate when you pick up a small handful of the cooked rice. This does not apply to rice for serving with Chinese or Japanese meals. For these, a more glutinous type of rice (p. 45) should be used, so that it clings together when cooked, making it easy to eat with chopsticks.

V # CHINESE-STYLE FRIED RICE V

SERVES 4

300 g/10 oz long-grain brown rice
2 tablespoons olive oil
100 g/4 oz mushrooms, chopped
100 g/4 oz frozen sweetcorn kernels
8 spring onions, trimmed and chopped
1–2 tablespoons soy sauce

1 Fill a large saucepan two-thirds full of lightly-salted water, and bring to the boil, then put in the rice and return to the

boil. Cover the pan and leave to boil for about 20 minutes until the rice is tender, then drain.
2 Heat the olive oil in another saucepan. Fry the mushrooms for 1–2 minutes, and add the rice, sweetcorn and spring onions. Stir-fry for 3–4 minutes, until heated through.
3 Add soy sauce to taste and check the seasoning.

MENU
Chinese-style Vegetarian Meal

Chinese-Style Fried Rice

Chinese-style Mushrooms
184
Stir-fried Carrots
181

Lychees and Mandarin
Orange Segments

BIRIANI

V   V

Serve this tasty dish with a Curry Sauce (p. 177) and some Indian breads, such as chapatti or poppadums. I like to serve several side dishes as well, such as a cucumber salad, tomato and onion salad and some chutneys and pickles.

SERVES 6

1 large aubergine, cut into 1-cm/½-inch dice
salt
350 g/12 oz long-grain brown rice
900 ml/1½ pints water
2½ teaspoons turmeric
50 g/2 oz butter or vegetable ghee
1 teaspoon poppy seeds
1½ teaspoons white mustard seeds
1 teaspoon garam masala
½ teaspoon ground coriander
pinch of cayenne pepper
freshly ground black pepper
1 red pepper, de-seeded and sliced
1 onion, peeled and sliced
2 garlic cloves, crushed
butter for greasing

1 Sprinkle the aubergine with salt and leave for 30 minutes, to draw out any bitter juices. Rinse and pat dry.
2 Put the rice into a heavy-based saucepan with the water, 1 teaspoon salt and 2 teaspoons of the turmeric. Bring to the boil, then cover and cook very gently for 45 minutes.
3 Preheat the oven to 180 C/350 F/Gas Mark 4. Grease a deep casserole.
4 Heat the butter or ghee in a saucepan, then add the poppy seeds and mustard seeds.
5 Stir for 1–2 minutes, then add the rest of the turmeric, the garam masala, coriander, cayenne and a generous grinding of black pepper. Cook for 1–2 minutes, stirring.
6 Add the aubergine, red pepper and onion. Cook gently, covered, for 7–8 minutes, then add the garlic and cook for a further 2 minutes. Taste the mixture and add more seasoning, if necessary.
7 Put one-third of the rice in a layer in the casserole. Top with half the vegetable mixture. Repeat the layers, ending with a final layer of rice.
8 Cover and bake for 30 minutes. Serve straight from the casserole.

MENU

Winter Brunch for Six

Classic Risotto

Scrambled Eggs
107
Mushrooms in Cream
79

Muffins or
327
Warm Croissants with
Assorted Preserves
Black Grapes

Coffee and Tea

CLASSIC RISOTTO

SERVES 6

100 g/4 oz butter
1 onion, peeled and chopped
1 whole garlic clove
2 tablespoons finely chopped parsley
650 g/1¼ lb Italian arborio rice
2 litres/3½ pints boiling Light Vegetable Stock (p. 129)
salt and freshly ground black pepper
4–6 tablespoons grated Parmesan cheese
TO SERVE
extra grated Parmesan cheese

1 Melt half the butter in a large, heavy-based saucepan and sauté the onion and garlic. When the onion is soft and golden, add the parsley.
2 Cook over a moderate heat for a few minutes, then discard the garlic and add the rice.
3 Fry the rice for a few minutes, stirring constantly, then add 250 ml/8 fl oz of the boiling stock and cook gently until absorbed.
4 Continue cooking gently, adding stock 250 ml/8 fl oz at a time, and stirring occasionally, for 20–30 minutes, or until the rice is tender and all the liquid absorbed.

5 Season to taste with salt and pepper, stir in the remaining butter and the Parmesan cheese, and leave the risotto over a low heat for a few minutes before serving.

6 Serve with plenty of extra grated Parmesan cheese handed separately.

Variations

ARTICHOKE RISOTTO

Cut the leaves and hairy choke from 3 globe artichokes. Slice the bases and fry them with the onion and garlic, then discard the garlic, add the rice and continue as described.

MUSHROOM RISOTTO

Make as described, frying 225 g/8 oz sliced button mushrooms with the parsley.

COURGETTE RISOTTO

Add 225 g/8 oz sliced courgettes with the parsley.

V MILLET PILAF WITH NUTS V
AND RAISINS

Millet cooks quickly and makes a good pilaf which is a pleasant change from rice. It is the richest grain in both protein and iron. Serve this pilaf as a main course accompanied by a juicy tomato salad, Sweet Carrot and Fennel Salad (p. 162) or Green-bean Salad with Radiccio (p. 167).

SERVES 4

300 g/10 oz millet
2 tablespoons oil
1 large onion, peeled and chopped
2 carrots, scraped and diced
1 garlic clove, crushed
1 walnut-sized piece of fresh ginger, grated
2.5 cm/1 inch cinnamon stick
750 ml/1¼ pints water
salt and freshly ground black pepper
50 g/2 oz raisins (optional)
50 g/2 oz flaked almonds (optional)

1 First toast the millet by putting it into a large saucepan and stirring over a moderate heat for 3–4 minutes, until it begins to smell roasted and some of the grains start to 'pop'. Remove from the heat and tip the millet on to a plate.

2 Heat the oil in the saucepan and fry the onion for 5 minutes, then add the carrots, garlic, ginger and cinnamon, and cook for a further 5 minutes.

3 Add the toasted millet to the onion and carrot mixture. Pour in the water and season to taste with salt and pepper.

4 Bring to the boil, then cover, turn down the heat and cook very gently for 15–20 minutes, until all the water has been absorbed and the millet is tender.

5 Check the seasoning, then add the raisins and flaked almonds, if using, mixing them in lightly with a fork.

Millet Pilaf with Nuts and Raisins

Couscous with Spicy Chick Pea Stew (p. 247)

V

BARLEY CASSEROLE

V

This is a pleasantly simple, wholesome dish, good for a family meal
on a chilly autumn or winter day. Serve it on its own, followed by
a warming, homely pudding like Treacle Tart (p. 294), baked
apples or, for real indulgence and nostalgia, steamed jam sponge.

SERVES 4

Using Barley

Barley makes a pleasant change from
rice and is just as easy to cook. Other
vegetables can be used in Barley
Casserole; try making it with green
and red peppers, plenty of onions
and garlic, tomatoes and button
mushrooms.

2 onions, peeled and chopped
50 g/2 oz butter or vegan margarine
900 g/2 lb leeks, cleaned, trimmed and sliced
*   into 2.5-cm/1-inch lengths*
225 g/8 oz carrots, scraped and diced
2 celery sticks, chopped
300 g/10 oz pearl barley
750 ml/1¼ pints Light Vegetable Stock
*   (p. 129)*
salt and freshly ground black pepper
700 g/1½ lb potatoes, peeled and cut into
*   even-sized chunks*
TO GARNISH
4 tablespoons chopped parsley

1 Fry the onion in the butter or vegan
margarine for 5 minutes in a large,
heavy-based saucepan. Add the leeks,
carrots and celery, mixing gently to coat
with the butter.
2 Cover the pan and cook gently for 5
minutes.
3 Add the barley, mix well, then add the
stock together with a good teaspoon salt
and plenty of freshly ground black
pepper.
4 Cover and cook over a gentle heat for
40 minutes, then add the potatoes, putting them into the top of the casserole.
5 Cook for a further 20 minutes,
covered, or until the potatoes and barley
are tender and all the water has been
absorbed.
6 Check the seasoning: more salt will
probably be needed. Sprinkle with the
parsley and serve.

V   COUSCOUS WITH SPICY   V
CHICK PEA STEW

Couscous is quick and easy to prepare because, being pre-cooked,
it only needs soaking briefly before being heated through. The best
way to do this is to put the couscous into a steamer saucepan, metal
colander or sieve on top of the saucepan in which the stew is
cooking; it can then absorb the flavour of the stew.

SERVES 4–5

450 g / 1 lb couscous
½ teaspoon salt dissolved in 600 ml / 1 pint
   warm water
4 tablespoons olive oil
2 onions, peeled and chopped
225 g / 8 oz carrots, scraped and sliced
2 teaspoons each ground cinnamon, ground
   cumin and ground coriander
100 g / 4 oz sweetcorn
225 g / 8 oz courgettes, diced
225 g / 8 oz dried chick peas, soaked, cooked
   until tender, then drained, or
   2 × 400-g / 14-oz cans chick peas, drained,
   or 450 g / 1 lb frozen broad beans
900 ml / 1½ pints water
4 tablespoons tomato purée
salt and freshly ground black pepper
TO GARNISH
coriander sprig

1 Spread the couscous out on a large
deep plate and pour the salt water evenly
over it, then rub the couscous lightly
with fingers to separate the grains. Set the
plate of couscous aside.
2 Heat half the oil in a large saucepan or
saucepan part of a steamer, add the onion
and carrots and fry gently for 10 minutes.
Stir in the spices and cook for a further
2–3 minutes, stirring.
3 Stir in the sweetcorn, courgettes and
the chick peas or broad beans, then add
the water and tomato purée. Bring to the
boil, then turn the heat down so that the
chick pea stew simmers.
4 By now the couscous will have
absorbed the water. Put it into the
steamer saucepan, metal colander or
sieve, breaking it up a bit with your
fingers again as you do so. (If your container has large holes, you may like to line
it with a piece of cloth, to prevent the
grains falling through, but I've never
found this necessary.)
5 Put the steamer, colander or sieve
over the vegetable stew, cover with a lid
or plate, and cook gently for 25–30
minutes.
6 Season to taste with salt and pepper.
Stir the remaining olive oil into the couscous, then put the couscous and the chick
pea stew on to a large, warmed serving
dish, garnish with the coriander and
serve immediately.

MENU

Easy Summer Supper

Avocado Vinaigrette
154

**Couscous with Spicy Chick
Pea Stew**

Green Salad
54
Tomato Salad
73

Strawberries with Cream or
thick Greek Yogurt

MENU
Vegetarian Barbecue

SERVES 6

Spicy Lentil Burgers
210

Vegetable Kebabs with Rosemary
201

Saffron Rice
241

Favourite Coleslaw
161

Baked Apples in Foil
84

Carrot Cake
306

Get the barbecue lit in good time, so that it is at the white ash stage by the time you want to cook. I suggest that you cook the Saffron Rice beforehand, then keep it warm. Both the kebabs and burgers can be made in advance.

Brush the barbecue grill with oil and cook the kebabs on this for about 10–15 minutes, until the vegetables are tender, basting with the marinade. Fry the burgers for 10–15 minutes on an oiled baking sheet placed on the barbecue grill; turn them over once during cooking.

Prepare the baked apples as described on p. 84, filling them with dried fruit sprinkled with a little sherry or brandy and left overnight to marinate. Sprinkle them with a little brown sugar, dot some butter over and wrap in a double layer of kitchen foil. Cook on the barbecue grill for about 50 minutes, until tender.

Serve soft drinks as well as chilled beer, lager, or a white or rosé vin ordinaire, well chilled. Alternatively, sangria would be pleasant. Make this by mixing together a bottle of Spanish red wine and a bottle of lemonade, then adding a glass each of brandy and port, plenty of ice and a thinly sliced orange and lemon.

Pasta Dishes

Another really healthy food, pasta is popular with most people and is quick, economical and very filling. It is interesting to try different types of pasta, as I have suggested in the recipes, although you can always substitute your personal favourite or fall back on good old spaghetti if the more unusual ones are not available. A number of different pastas are identified in the Ingredients section (pp. 46–9), along with basic cooking instructions. Most of the pasta recipes in this section also make excellent first courses, if served in smaller portions, perhaps before a vegetable main course.

TAGLIATELLE WITH GORGONZOLA AND WALNUTS

Serve this quickly made, rich and delicious dish with a green salad.
If you can't get Gorgonzola, other blue cheeses such as
Roquefort can be used.

SERVES 4

MENU

Spur of the Moment Supper for Two

Avocado Vinaigrette or
154
Cannellini Bean Salad with
Fresh Herbs, served with
Warm Wholewheat Rolls
328

**Tagliatelle with
Gorgonzola and Walnuts**

Green Salad
54

Fresh Figs, or
Honeyed Poached Pears with
Poire Williams Liqueur

Coffee

450 g/1 lb tagliatelle
½ oz butter
salt and freshly ground black pepper
100 g/4 oz walnuts, roughly chopped
300 ml/10 fl oz double cream
1 garlic clove, crushed
100 g/4 oz Gorgonzola cheese, crumbled

1 Cook the tagliatelle in a large saucepan as described on p. 50, until *al dente*.
2 Drain immediately, then return to the still-warm pan with the butter, salt, pepper and walnuts.
3 While the tagliatelle is cooking, make the sauce. Put the cream into a small, heavy-based saucepan; add the garlic and Gorgonzola and heat gently, stirring occasionally, until the cheese has melted. Season with salt and pepper.
4 Turn the pasta on to a large warmed serving dish, or individual plates, and pour the sauce into the centre. Serve immediately.

V   FUSILLI VERDE WITH MUSHROOMS V
AND CREAM

SERVES 4

450 g/1 lb fusilli verde
FOR THE SAUCE
1 onion, peeled and chopped
40 g/1½ oz butter or vegan margarine
1 garlic clove, crushed
450 g/1 lb button mushrooms, wiped and
   sliced
150 ml/5 fl oz double or non-dairy cream
salt and freshly ground black pepper
freshly grated nutmeg

1 To make the sauce, fry the onion gently in 25 g/1 oz of the butter or vegan margarine for 10 minutes, until softened.

2 Add the garlic and mushrooms and cook for 15–20 minutes, until all the liquid has evaporated.

3 Add the cream. Season with salt, pepper and nutmeg. Remove from the heat.

4 Cook the fusilli in a large saucepan as described on p. 50, until *al dente*.

5 Drain the pasta immediately, then return to the still-warm pan with the remaining butter, salt and pepper.

6 Quickly reheat the sauce, then tip the fusilli into a warmed serving dish, pour the sauce over the top and serve.

V   PASTA PRIMAVERA V

SERVES 4

Pasta Primavera

25 g/1 oz butter or vegan margarine
1 onion, peeled and finely chopped
225 g/8 oz young carrots, scraped and diced
225 g/8 oz courgettes, sliced
225 g/8 oz fresh shelled peas or mangetouts
350 g/12 oz vermicelli
2 tablespoons chopped mint
salt and freshly ground black pepper
TO GARNISH
mint sprig

1 Melt the butter or vegan margarine in a large saucepan, then cover and fry the onion without browning for 5 minutes.

2 Add the carrots and cook for 10 minutes, then put in the courgettes and cook for a further 5 minutes. Add the peas or mangetouts and cook for 2–3 minutes.

3 Just before the vegetables are ready, cook the vermicelli in a large saucepan as described on p. 50, until *al dente*. Drain immediately, then return to the pan.

4 Add the vegetables to the vermicelli, together with the mint, salt and pepper. Mix, then serve garnished with mint.

WHOLEWHEAT PASTA AND MUSHROOM BAKE

This is another tasty, homely dish, and like many pasta bakes, freezes well. Frozen peas go well with it, or fresh watercress.

SERVES 4

100 g/4 oz small wholewheat pasta shapes such as leaves or rings
2 onions, peeled and chopped
1 tablespoon oil
100 g/4 oz mushrooms, washed and chopped
225 g/8 oz tomatoes, skinned and chopped
1 egg, beaten
100 g/4 oz grated Cheddar cheese
freshly ground black pepper
butter for greasing
a few wholewheat breadcrumbs mixed with chopped parsley for topping

1 Preheat the oven to 190 C/375 F/Gas Mark 5. Grease an ovenproof dish.

2 Cook the pasta in a large saucepan as described on p. 50, until *al dente*. Drain.
3 While the pasta is cooking, fry the onions in the oil for 7 minutes, then add the mushrooms and tomatoes and cook for a further 3 minutes.
4 Stir in the egg and stir over the heat for a moment or two longer until the egg begins to set. Remove from the heat and add the drained pasta, two-thirds of the cheese and salt and pepper to taste.
5 Spoon the mixture into the dish and sprinkle crumbs and remaining cheese over the top. Bake for 25–30 minutes, until crisp and golden-brown.

V # TAGLIATELLE VERDE WITH LENTIL SAUCE V

This is a useful dish to make when you have to rustle up a meal for a crowd unexpectedly, because it uses store cupboard ingredients.

SERVES 4

Tagliatelle Verde with Lentil Sauce

225–350 g/8–12 oz tagliatelle verde
15 g/½ oz butter or vegan margarine
FOR THE SAUCE
2 tablespoons olive oil
2 onions, peeled and chopped
2 garlic cloves, crushed
½ teaspoon ground cinnamon
225 g/8 oz red lentils, washed
1 × 425-g/15-oz can tomatoes
450 ml/15 fl oz water
salt and freshly ground black pepper
TO SERVE (OPTIONAL)
coriander sprig
grated Parmesan cheese

1 To make the sauce, heat the olive oil in a large pan and fry the onion for 10 minutes, then add the garlic, cinnamon,

lentils, tomatoes and water. Bring to the boil.

2 Reduce the heat and let the mixture simmer gently for about 20 minutes, until the lentils are tender; season to taste with salt and pepper.

3 Meanwhile, cook the tagliatelle in a large saucepan as described on p. 50, until *al dente*.

4 Drain immediately, then return to the still-warm pan with the butter or vegan margarine. Season with salt and pepper.

5 Turn the tagliatelle on to a large warmed serving dish, or individual plates, and pour the sauce into the centre. Garnish with coriander and serve immediately, with grated Parmesan cheese handed separately, if liked.

Variation

TAGLIATELLE VERDE WITH LENTIL AND RED WINE SAUCE

Make as described, replacing a little of the water with red wine, say 75–150 ml/3–5 fl oz – as much as you can spare! This makes an excellent supper, accompanied by a good green salad and the rest of the wine used to make the sauce.

V SPAGHETTI BOLOGNESE V

VEGETARIANA

This is popular with my student daughter and her friends, because it's quick to make, cheap, filling and tasty. The sauce freezes well.

SERVES 4

350 g/12 oz spaghetti
½ oz butter or vegan margarine
FOR THE SAUCE
175 g/6 oz whole green lentils cooked in plenty of water for 45–50 minutes, until tender, or 2 × 400-g/14-oz cans lentils
1 large onion, peeled and sliced
2 tablespoons oil
1 garlic clove, crushed
100 g/4 oz carrot, diced
2 tablespoons tomato purée
2 tablespoons chopped parsley
salt and freshly ground black pepper
TO SERVE (OPTIONAL)
grated Parmesan or Cheddar cheese

1 To make the sauce, drain the lentils, reserving the liquid.

2 Fry the onion in the oil in a medium saucepan for 5 minutes, allowing it to brown lightly, then add the garlic and carrot.

3 Cover the pan and cook gently for about 15 minutes, until the vegetables are tender.

4 Stir in the lentils, tomato purée, parsley, salt and pepper and a little of the reserved lentil liquid, to give a thick but moist consistency.

5 About 10 minutes before the lentil sauce is cooked, cook the spaghetti in a large saucepan as described on p. 50, until *al dente*.

6 Drain well, then return the spaghetti to the still-warm pan with the butter or vegan margarine and black pepper.

7 Check that the spaghetti and the sauce are really hot, then turn the spaghetti into a large warmed serving dish and pour the sauce on top. Offer grated cheese separately, if liked.

Tomato Purée

This can be bought in a can, tube or jar, and is useful for adding extra flavouring and natural thickening to tomato dishes or other savoury mixtures which would be complemented by a tomato flavour. Use discreetly, as too much can give rather an acid flavour, and I find tomato purée in a tube the most useful as a little can be used at a time and the rest stored in the fridge where it will keep for several weeks.

V # TAGLIONI VERDE WITH V
TOMATO SAUCE AND AUBERGINES

The green of the taglioni against the orange-red tomato sauce and
the purple tones of the aubergine give this dish a warming,
appetizing look, ideal for a quick supper on a chilly autumn day. I
like to serve it on its own, followed by a leafy salad, then a
cheeseboard, and, finally, perhaps a refreshing sorbet,
such as pear or blackberry.

SERVES 4

*Summer Linguine (p. 255), with an
avocado and mushroom salad*

2 medium aubergines, total weight about
    450 g/1 lb
salt
8 tablespoons olive oil
1 onion, peeled and chopped
750 g/1½ lb tomatoes, skinned and chopped
freshly ground black pepper
350 g/12 oz taglioni verde
TO SERVE (OPTIONAL)
basil sprig
grated Parmesan cheese

1 Slice the aubergines thinly lengthways, then cut into strips about 5 cm/2
inches long and 2.5 cm/1 inch wide. Salt,
rinse and drain the aubergine strips as
described on p. 73.

2 Fry the aubergine strips in 6 tablespoons of the olive oil in a medium saucepan until crisp and brown on both sides.
Remove from the pan and drain on
kitchen paper. Then fry the onion in the
olive oil left in the pan for 10 minutes,
without browning. Add the tomatoes
and cook gently for 5 minutes.

3 Purée in a blender or food processor,
return to the pan and season with salt and
pepper.

4 Cook the taglioni in a large saucepan as
described on p. 50, until *al dente*.

5 Drain the pasta immediately, then return to the pan and add the remaining
olive oil and salt and pepper to taste.

6 Turn the taglioni on to a warmed
shallow serving dish. Pour the sauce
on top, then put the aubergine strips
on top of that. Garnish with the basil
sprig. Serve the pasta immediately, with
some grated Parmesan cheese handed
separately, if liked.

V FUSILLE COLBUCO WITH AUBERGINE V
AND WINE SAUCE

Fusille colbuco, a long spiral pasta, is particularly attractive in this
dish, but any other long type of pasta, including
spaghetti, would be good.

SERVES 4

350 g/12 oz fusille colbuco
FOR THE SAUCE
2 medium aubergines, total weight about
   450 g/1 lb
salt
1 onion, peeled and chopped
4 tablespoons olive oil
1 garlic clove, crushed
1 green pepper, de-seeded and chopped
225 g/8 oz tomatoes, skinned and chopped
1 tablespoon chopped fresh basil or 1 teaspoon
   dried basil
4 tablespoons red or white wine
freshly ground black pepper
TO GARNISH
basil sprigs
TO SERVE (OPTIONAL)
grated Parmesan cheese

1 Dice the aubergines, then salt, drain and rinse as described on p. 73.

2 Fry the onion in half the olive oil in a medium saucepan for 5 minutes, without browning, then add the aubergine, garlic, green pepper, tomatoes, basil and wine and cook gently for 25 minutes, until the vegetables are soft. Season with salt and pepper.

3 Just before the sauce is ready, cook the fusille colbuco in a large saucepan as described on p. 50, until al dente.

4 Drain immediately, then return to the still-warm pan with the remaining olive oil, salt and pepper.

5 Turn the pasta on to a warmed large serving dish, or individual plates, and pour the wine sauce on top. Garnish with the basil sprigs and serve immediately, with some grated Parmesan cheese handed separately, if liked.

MENU
*Easy Autumn Supper
for Six*

**Taglioni Verde with
Tomato Sauce and
Aubergines**
254
Chicory, Watercress and
Walnut Salad with Walnut
Vinaigrette
Illustrated on p. 179
161 and 154

Selection of White Cheeses,
(including a cream one and
one or two goat's cheeses)
Assorted Breads and
Crackers

Pear or Blackberry Sorbet
Illustrated on p. 283
282

Espresso, Filter or
Capuccino Coffee

SUMMER LINGUINE

A perfect dish for a lazy summer's lunch in the garden, hot linguine
(or any other long slim pasta) is served here with summer
vegetables and soft melting cheese.

SERVES 4

450 g/1 lb tomatoes, skinned and sliced
1 bunch spring onions, trimmed and chopped
2 garlic cloves, crushed
2–3 tablespoons fresh basil leaves
225 g/8 oz Mozzarella or Brie cheese, cubed
salt and freshly ground black pepper
450 g/1 lb linguine or other long, thin pasta
2 tablespoons olive oil

1 Put the tomatoes, onions, garlic, basil and cheese into a serving bowl which is large enough to hold the cooked pasta as well. Season with salt and pepper.

2 Cook the linguine in a large saucepan as described on p. 50, until al dente. Drain immediately, then return to the still-warm pan with the olive oil, salt and pepper.

3 Mix well, then add the linguine to the vegetables in the bowl and stir to distribute all the ingredients. Serve immediately.

*Spinach Lasagne; Wholewheat Pasta
and Mushroom Bake (p. 252)*

SPINACH LASAGNE

This makes a big dish of particularly tasty lasagne, great for feeding
a crowd, especially if accompanied by some robust red wine. A
crisp green salad with fresh herbs goes well with it.

SERVES 6

1 large onion, peeled and chopped
2 tablespoons olive oil
2 garlic cloves, crushed
900 g / 2 lb cooked, fresh spinach, chopped, or
  frozen chopped spinach, thawed
900 g / 2 lb skimmed milk soft cheese
salt and freshly ground black pepper
1 quantity Italian Tomato Sauce (p. 171)
225 g / 8 oz oven-ready lasagne or 350 g / 12 oz
  fresh lasagne
225 g / 8 oz Mozzarella cheese
butter for greasing

1 Preheat the oven to 200 C/400 F/Gas
Mark 6. Grease a large, shallow ovenproof dish.

2 Fry the onion in the olive oil in a large
saucepan for 10 minutes, until soft but
not browned. Add the garlic, cook for a
minute or two longer, then remove from
the heat.

3 Squeeze any excess liquid out of the
spinach, then add to the onion mixture,
together with the skimmed milk soft
cheese, salt and plenty of pepper.

4 Cover the base of the dish with a thin layer of the tomato sauce, then put a layer of lasagne on top, followed by a layer of the spinach mixture. Thinly slice 175 g/ 6 oz of the Mozzarella cheese. Next make a layer of Mozzarella cheese slices, then of tomato sauce.

5 Continue like this until all the ingredients are used up, ending with a layer of sauce. Grate the remaining cheese and arrange in 3 lines on the top.

6 Bake for 1 hour, covering the dish with foil after 40–45 minutes if the top begins to get too brown.

Variation

MIXED VEGETABLE LASAGNE
Make as described, but instead of the spinach and cheese filling use a vegetable mixture. To make this, fry the onion in oil as described, then add the garlic and 700 g/1½ lb each of diced carrots and sliced leeks, 450 g/1 lb of diced courgettes and 1 chopped and de-seeded green pepper. Cover and fry for about 15 minutes until tender. Layer this mixture with the lasagne, Mozzarella cheese and tomato sauce.

LENTIL LASAGNE
Use a double quantity lentil Bolognese mixture (p. 253), layered with Italian Tomato Sauce.

MACARONI CHEESE

An ever-popular old favourite, with a tangy sauce. My young daughter always asks for this when she has a friend to a meal, and they certainly eat it up enthusiastically. But I sometimes wonder what their parents think when they hear that their daughters have had such an apparently uninspired vegetarian dish in the home of someone who is supposed to be an expert!

SERVES 4

225 g/8 oz quick-cook macaroni
50 g/2 oz butter or vegan margarine
2 rounded tablespoons plain flour
600 ml/1 pint milk
2 teaspoons Dijon mustard
175 g/6 oz cheese, grated
salt and freshly ground black pepper
100 g/4 oz fresh wholewheat breadcrumbs
a little extra butter or vegan margarine for greasing

1 Heat the grill, or preheat the oven to 200 C/400 F/Gas Mark 6. Grease a shallow flameproof dish which will fit under the grill, if using this method for browning the macaroni cheese.

2 Cook the macaroni in a large saucepan as described on p. 50, until *al dente*. Drain well.

3 Meanwhile, make the sauce. Melt the butter or vegan margarine in a saucepan, then add the flour; stir for 1–2 minutes over the heat, then stir in the milk, a quarter at a time, stirring well and allowing the sauce to thicken between each addition.

4 Leave the sauce to simmer gently over the heat for 5 minutes, then remove from the heat and add the mustard, two-thirds of the grated cheese and salt and pepper to taste.

5 Mix together the cooked macaroni and the cheese sauce. Check the seasoning, then spoon the mixture into the dish and level the surface. Sprinkle the breadcrumbs and the remaining cheese over the top.

6 Place the dish under the preheated grill for 5–10 minutes, or heat through in the oven for about 20 minutes, until the mararoni cheese is hot inside and golden-brown and crisp on top.

MENU
Freezer Supper for Six

Flaky Roquefort or Spinach and Fennel Pastries
Illustrated on p. 141
151

Mixed Vegetable Lasagne

Green Salad
54

Orange Parfait or
284
Vanilla Ice Cream with
Illustrated on p. 281
280
Raspberry Coulis
300

AUBERGINE AND PASTA CHARLOTTE

Here is pasta dressed up for a special occasion, a tasty mixture of rigatoni with tomato sauce and cheese, encased in slices of aubergine in a round mould and turned out like a cake. It's easy to do, yet always impresses. Eat as a main course, with one or two simply cooked vegetables, like French beans and baby carrots.

SERVES 6 AS A MAIN COURSE, 8 AS A STARTER

Olives

The fruit of a tree native to the Mediterranean, olives are gathered and preserved in oil or brine at various stages of development. The ones which are picked and pickled early become green olives, while the later, more mature olives become black olives. Green and black olives differ in flavour and both have their uses; green olives are also available stoned and stuffed with pimiento. They make a delicious nibble, garnish and addition to salads and savoury dishes. The best way to buy olives is loose at a good delicatessen. They will keep for a couple of weeks or so in the fridge.

A delicious Olive Pâté can be bought in a jar or made by stoning and puréeing black olives in a blender or food processor. I think of this as the vegetarian answer to caviar and find it an attractive and piquant garnish for canapés, salads, hardboiled and scrambled eggs; it's also excellent thinly spread on Melba Toast (p. 146) or with crusty bread.

2 medium aubergines, total weight about 450 g/1 lb
salt
olive oil
400 g/14 oz rigatoni
1 quantity Italian Tomato Sauce (p. 171)
75 g/3 oz butter
225 g/8 oz Mozzarella cheese, grated
4 tablespoons grated Parmesan cheese
4 tablespoons grated mature Cheddar cheese
1 tablespoon dried oregano
freshly ground black pepper
2 tablespoons dried breadcrumbs

1 Slice the aubergines diagonally into 5-mm/¼-inch slices. Salt, rinse and drain the aubergine slices as described on p. 73. Pat dry on kitchen paper.
2 Fry the aubergine slices in a little olive oil for 2–3 minutes on each side, until soft and lightly browned. Drain well on kitchen paper.
3 Preheat the oven to 190 C/375 F/Gas Mark 5. Brush a 20-cm/8-inch round springform tin with olive oil.

4 Cook the rigatoni in a large saucepan as described on p. 50 until almost done: it should be a bit undercooked. Drain well, then return to the pan with 2 tablespoons of the tomato sauce. Mix well.
5 Melt the butter in the remaining tomato sauce; pour over the rigatoni and mix, together with the Mozzarella, Parmesan and Cheddar cheeses. Add the oregano, and season with plenty of salt and pepper.
6 Arrange the aubergine slices over the base and sides of the prepared tin. Make sure that the slices in the base of the tin radiate attractively from the centre, and that all gaps are filled.
7 Spoon the pasta mixture into the tin, press down lightly and sprinkle with the breadcrumbs. Bake for 20 minutes.
8 Allow the charlotte to stand for 15 minutes to settle, and for the flavours to develop, then slip a knife round the edges of the tin and turn the charlotte out on to a warmed serving dish.
9 Press any fallen aubergine slices back in place, and serve immediately.

V PASTA WITH BLACK OLIVES V

SERVES 4

350 g/12 oz rigatoni
2 tablespoons olive oil
salt and freshly ground black pepper
1 quantity Sweet Pepper Sauce (p. 172)
50 g/2 oz black olives, stoned and roughly chopped

Opposite page:
Aubergine and Pasta Charlotte

1 Cook the rigatoni in a large saucepan as described on p. 50, until *al dente*.

2 Drain immediately and return the rigatoni to the still-warm pan with the olive oil; season the pasta to taste with salt and black pepper.
3 While the pasta is cooking make the sauce.
4 Serve the pasta on warmed plates, pour the sauce on top and sprinkle with the chopped olives.

Pastry Dishes

Favourites with most people, pastry dishes are useful for many occasions
ranging from picnics and hearty family meals to dinner parties and
celebrations. I use wholewheat flour for all pastry-making except puff, for
which I use unbleached white flour, when I make it, although for this pastry
I do often take a short cut and use a good quality frozen pastry, made without
animal fat (check the label). Keep the high-fat pastries, such as puff,
rough-puff and flaky, for specials, and serve any pastry dish with low-fat
accompaniments such as steamed vegetables or a lightly dressed
salad, for healthy, well-balanced eating.

Fats for Pastry

Traditional fats for pastries are butter and lard. Vegetarians can use a vegetable lard, or solid white fat. I use this for some pastries, such as flaky. Otherwise I use butter which I prefer to manufactured fats such as margarine and solid vegetable fat.

Polyunsaturated vegan margarine can be used in place of butter to make pastry. Some people use vegetable oil for shortcrust pastry, but I have never, myself, been able to make a really good, light pastry with this.

V BASIC SHORTCRUST PASTRY V

MAKES 225 g/8 oz

225 g/8 oz plain 100% or 85% wholewheat
* flour*
½ teaspoon salt
100 g/4 oz butter or vegan margarine, diced
3 tablespoons ice-cold water

1 Put the flour into a mixing bowl with the salt and butter or vegan margarine.
2 Using your fingertips, rub the fat into the flour until the mixture resembles fine breadcrumbs.
3 Add the water and gently press the mixture together to form a dough.
4 Turn the dough on to a lightly floured board and knead lightly, pressing it into a round, square or oblong, as required, then roll it out, using a floured rolling pin and short strokes, and making sure that the pastry does not stick to the board. Use as required.

5 If you do not need the pastry immediately, wrap it in clingfilm and leave it in the fridge for up to 24 hours.

Variations
CHEESE SHORTCRUST
Add 50–100 g/2–4 oz finely grated Cheddar cheese before you add the water for this non-vegan variation.

NUT SHORTCRUST
Mix in 25 g/1 oz grated or finely chopped nuts – almonds, walnuts, brazil nuts or hazelnuts – before adding the water.

RICH SHORTCRUST
For this light, melt-in-the-mouth pastry, use self-raising flour and increase the fat to 150 g/5 oz. You won't need any water because the extra fat will bind the dough.

Pastry Weights

By convention, the weight of pastry needed for a recipe is always given as the weight of the flour used to make it. So 225 g/8 oz pastry means pastry made from 225 g/8 oz flour. However, the weight stated on a packet of frozen pastry is the weight of the whole amount.

LINING A FLAN TIN WITH PASTRY

1 Hold the pastry board at an angle of 45° at the far edge of the flan tin

2 Gently slide the pastry off the board and on to the tin, moving the pastry board back towards you as you do so

FRENCH ONION FLAN

This rich and delicious classic French flan makes a wonderful main course with a tomato and basil salad or a crisp green salad; or it can be served cut into thin slices, as a first course.

SERVES 4–6 AS A MAIN COURSE, 6–8 AS A STARTER

½ quantity Basic Shortcrust Pastry (p. 260)
FOR THE FILLING
450 g / 1 lb onions, peeled and sliced
25 g / 1 oz butter
150 ml / 5 fl oz single cream
1 whole egg or 2 egg yolks
salt and freshly ground black pepper
freshly grated nutmeg
butter for greasing
TO GARNISH
chopped parsley

1 Preheat the oven to 200 C / 400 F / Gas Mark 6. Heat a baking sheet. Lightly grease a 20-cm / 8-inch flan tin or ring.
2 Roll out the pastry as thinly as possible and use to line the tin or ring. Bake blind as described on p. 266. Turn down the oven to 180 C / 350 F / Gas Mark 4.
3 Meanwhile, make the filling. Fry the onions gently in the butter for 25–30 minutes, until very soft. Remove from the heat and add the cream, and egg or egg yolks, with salt, pepper and nutmeg to taste.
4 Pour the onion mixture into the flan case, then return the flan to the oven on the baking sheet and bake for 30–35 minutes, until the filling is set.
5 Serve warm or cold, sprinkled with a little parsley.

Variations
RATATOUILLE FLAN
Make as described, using a good, thick, tasty Ratatouille mixture (p. 187) instead of the onions.

SPINACH, CHEESE AND ALMOND FLAN
Use 450 g / 1 lb fresh spinach, cooked (225 g / 8 oz frozen spinach), 75 g / 3 oz grated cheese and 100 g / 4 oz toasted flaked almonds; mix with 1 egg and omit the cream or milk.

MUSTARD, TOMATO AND MOZZARELLA FLAN
Spread the base of the flan case with 2 tablespoons Dijon mustard, cover with 450 g / 1 lb skinned and sliced tomatoes. Arrange 100 g / 4 oz sliced Mozzarella cheese on top, season, then carefully pour in the egg and cream mixture.

CAULIFLOWER, CHEDDAR CHEESE AND WALNUT FLAN
Use cooked florets from a small cauliflower, 100 g / 4 oz grated Cheddar cheese and 100 g / 4 oz chopped walnuts, instead of the onion.

WATERCRESS AND STILTON CHEESE FLAN
For this tangy version, use 2 eggs, 300 ml / 10 fl oz cream or milk, a bunch of watercress, chopped, and 100 g / 4 oz grated Stilton cheese.

MUSHROOM FLAN
Fry just 1 small chopped onion for 7 minutes, then add 350 g / 12 oz sliced mushrooms and a crushed garlic clove and fry for about 15 minutes until all the liquid has disappeared. Add 1 tablespoon chopped parsley to the egg mixture.

LEEK AND BLACK OLIVE FLAN
Use 700 g / 1½ lb leeks, cooked, 2 tablespoons chopped parsley and 50–100 g / 2–4 oz black olives.

Filling a Flan Case
If you're worried about spills, put the flan into the oven first, then fill with the egg mixture, using a jug.

Serving Flans

Flans are adaptable, can be light and elegant, with thin, crisp pastry, or hearty and rustic, with thick pastry and a deep filling. They can be party-sized or individual.

Eminently portable and ideal for picnics or lunch boxes, a flan can also be eaten with pleasure at any meal from brunch to late night supper, as a starter or main course.

V # BROCCOLI, RED PEPPER AND ALMOND FLAN V

In this flan, bright green broccoli is covered with a light-textured sauce of red peppers and almonds and finished with a topping of roasted flaked almonds.

SERVES 4–6 AS A MAIN COURSE, 6–8 AS A STARTER

Vegan Flan Fillings

Many combinations of cooked vegetables, vegetable purées and dips can be used to make colourful and delicious non-dairy fillings. Here are some possibilities:

- Ratatouille (p. 187), made fairly thick
- Cooked leeks topped with Hummus (p. 144), thin circles of red pepper and black olives
- Golden Spiced Cauliflower (p. 185)
- Mushroom and Herb Terrine (p. 146) topped with thin slices of mushroom brushed with oil
- A thick, well-flavoured purée of carrots or celeriac (p. 189), topped with lightly-fried circles of courgette

½ quantity Basic Shortcrust Pastry (p. 260)
450 g/1 lb broccoli, divided into even-sized florets, stalks removed
1 tablespoon oil
salt and freshly ground black pepper
1 quantity Red Pepper and Almond Dip (p. 146)
25 g/1 oz flaked almonds
butter for greasing

1 Preheat the oven to 200 C/400 F/Gas Mark 6. Put a baking sheet into the centre of the oven, to heat up. Lightly grease a 20-cm/8-inch flan tin or ring.
2 Roll out the pastry as thinly as possible and use to line the tin or ring; trim the edges. Bake blind as described on p. 266.
3 Meanwhile, cook the broccoli in 2.5 cm/1 inch boiling water for 4–5 minutes, or until just tender. Drain and return to the pan with the oil and salt and pepper.
4 Half-fill the flan case with the Red Pepper and Almond Dip, then arrange the broccoli on top, pressing the florets into the dip to secure them.

5 Spoon the remaining Red Pepper and Almond Dip evenly over the top, making sure that it runs down between the broccoli florets. Leave a few florets peeping out, for colour contrast. Sprinkle with the flaked almonds.
6 Return the flan to the oven on the baking sheet and bake for 25–30 minutes, until the almonds are lightly browned and the filling heated through and 'set'-looking. Serve hot, warm or cold.

Variations
MUSHROOM, RED PEPPER AND ALMOND FLAN

For this tasty variation, replace the broccoli with 450 g/1 lb button mushrooms, sliced and fried until all the liquid has evaporated.

SPICY VEGETABLE AND LENTIL FLAN

Use 225 g/8 oz cooked mixed vegetables such as carrots, potatoes and peas, and 1 quantity Lentil Dal (p. 209). Top with flaked or desiccated coconut.

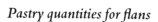

Pastry quantities for flans

Flan size	Weight of flour for pastry
10 cm/4 inch	50 g/2 oz
15 cm/6 inch	100 g/4 oz
18 cm/7 inch	150 g/5 oz
20 cm/8 inch	175 g/6 oz
23 cm/9 inch	200 g/7 oz
25 cm/10 inch	225 g/8 oz
30 cm/12 inch (shallow)	300 g/10 oz

Broccoli, Red Pepper and Almond Flan
(p. 262); Individual Asparagus Tartlets

ASPARAGUS TARTLETS

These tartlets – made in 10-cm/4-inch flan tins – are perfect for a summer garden lunch. The little Asparagus Boats are ideal for a buffet party.

MAKES 6

1 ½ quantity Basic Shortcrust Pastry
(p. 260)
1 bunch asparagus, trimmed and cooked as
described on p. 63, or 450 g/1 lb frozen
asparagus, cooked and drained
300 ml/10 fl oz single cream
2 egg yolks
salt and freshly ground black pepper
freshly grated nutmeg

1 Preheat the oven to 200 C/400 F/Gas Mark 6. Put a baking sheet into the centre of the oven, to heat up. Lightly grease 6 × 10-cm/4-inch flan tins.
2 Divide the pastry into 6 equal pieces. Roll out each piece as thinly as possible and use to line the tins; trim the edges. Bake blind as described on p. 266.
3 Turn the oven down to 180 C/350 F/Gas Mark 4.
4 Remove the tips from the asparagus and chop the tender part of the stalks. Divide the chopped asparagus and the tips among the tartlets.
5 Whisk the cream and egg yolks together; season to taste with salt, pepper and grated nutmeg. Divide this mixture between the tartlets, then put them back into the oven on the baking sheet and bake for about 15 minutes, until the filling is set. Serve hot or warm.

Variations

INDIVIDUAL AVOCADO FLANS

Use the diced flesh from 3 small ripe avocado pears, skinned, a crushed garlic clove and 2 tablespoons lemon juice instead of the asparagus. Make as described. These need to be cooked just before eating, and it's important not to over-heat the avocado which gives it a bitter taste.

ASPARAGUS BOATS

The ingredients given above make 30 boats. Roll out the pastry, line boat-shaped tins and bake as above. Cut the asparagus spears into lengths to fit each boat shape; divide amongst the boats, pour in the egg mixture and bake for 8–10 minutes. Garnish each serving with a slice of lemon and parsley sprig.

Preparing Flans in Advance

Filled flans do not freeze well – they emerge with soggy bottoms. It's best to bake the flan cases (and be sure to give them the hot-oil treatment (p. 266) for superb results), then freeze. Pack carefully. Ideally, fill and bake just before eating, though if you've a lot to do, they can be cooked the night before, then kept in a cool, airy place until required.

V　POTATO AND MUSHROOM PASTIES　V

These pasties are good either hot or cold and are popular for picnics and lunch boxes. Serve with a mixed salad.

MAKES 4

SHAPING A PASTY

Potato and Mushroom Pasties

1 quantity Basic Shortcrust Pastry, Plain or
　　Cheese (p. 260)
beaten egg to glaze (optional)
FOR THE FILLING
1 onion, peeled and chopped
2 tablespoons oil
225 g/8 oz potato, peeled and cut into
　　5-mm/¼-inch dice
1 garlic clove, crushed
225 g/8 oz mushrooms, washed and chopped
1 tablespoon chopped parsley
salt and freshly ground black pepper

1 First make the filling. Fry the onion in the oil for 5 minutes, then add the potato and garlic.
2 Cook gently for 10 minutes. Add the mushrooms and cook for a further 4–5 minutes, until the vegetables are just tender. Add the parsley and season with salt and pepper. Cool.
3 Preheat the oven to 200 C/400 F/Gas Mark 6. Divide the pastry into 4 equal pieces; roll each into a circle 15 cm/ 6 inches in diameter.
4 Spoon a quarter of the potato mixture on to each circle. Fold over the pastry and press the edges together.
5 Make a couple of small steam-holes in each pasty, brush the pasties with beaten egg, if used, then place them on a baking sheet and bake for 20–25 minutes, until golden-brown.

Variations
SPICED CHICK PEA AND POTATO PASTIES
Make these in the same way, adding 1 tablespoon ground coriander and 1 teaspoon ground cumin to the onion, and replacing the mushrooms with 100 g/ 4 oz chick peas, soaked, cooked and drained, or 1 × 425-g/15-oz can chick peas, drained.

VEGETABLE PASTIES
Replace the mushrooms with 100 g/4 oz scraped and diced carrots and 100 g/4 oz shredded leeks and a chopped skinned tomato, added to the pan with the potatoes and fried until tender. Flavour with ½ teaspoon each dried oregano and basil. Other combinations of cooked vegetables can be used and different flavourings such as rosemary or thyme. Drained cooked chick peas, red kidney beans or cannellini beans can be added to the mixture, or some chopped nuts, such as hazelnuts or almonds.

SAVOURY CHESHIRE CHEESE AND ONION PIE

Simple and good, a vegetarian family favourite.

SERVES 4

1 quantity Basic Shortcrust Pastry (p. 260)
FOR THE FILLING
700 g / 1½ lb onions, peeled and sliced
175 g / 6 oz Cheshire cheese, grated
salt and freshly ground black pepper
freshly grated nutmeg

1 Preheat the oven to 220 C / 425 F / Gas Mark 7. Put a baking sheet into the centre of the oven, to heat up.
2 Parboil the onions in 2.5 cm / 1 inch lightly-salted water for 5 minutes, then drain and cool.
3 Roll out just under half the pastry to fit a 20–23-cm / 8–9-inch pie plate.
4 Add the cheese to the onions; mix together and season with salt, pepper and nutmeg, then spoon on top of the pastry.
5 Roll out the remaining pastry to fit the top; press the edges together and trim. Bake for 30 minutes, until golden-brown. Serve hot.

Variations

BUTTER BEAN, CHEESE AND PICKLE PIE

Make this in the same way, using 100 g / 4 oz butter beans, soaked, cooked and drained, or 1 × 425-g / 15-oz can butter beans, drained, in place of one of the onions, and reducing the amount of cheese to 50 g / 2 oz. Add 3 tablespoons pickle or chutney to the mixture before spooning on top of the pastry.

LEEK PIE

Wash 900 g / 2 lb leeks and cut them into pieces about 2.5 cm / 1 inch long. Cook them in 2.5 cm / 1 inch boiling water for about 10 minutes, until just tender. Drain them very well, then mix them with 300 ml / 10 fl oz soured cream or Béchamel Sauce (p. 175). Season.

MUSHROOM AND CHESTNUT PIE

Fry 1 large chopped onion and 2 chopped celery sticks in 25 g / 1 oz butter for 10 minutes, then add 225 g / 8 oz washed and sliced mushrooms and cook for a further 2–3 minutes, or until the mushrooms are tender. Remove from the heat and add 350–450 g / 12 oz–1 lb cooked chestnuts (you can use fresh cooked chestnuts, or canned whole chestnuts, or dried ones which have been soaked and cooked as described on p. 36). Add 1 tablespoon soy sauce and salt and pepper to taste.

MUSHROOM FLAN

SERVES 6 AS A MAIN COURSE

double quantity Basic Shortcrust Pastry
  (p. 260)
double quantity Mushrooms in Cream
  (p. 79)
butter for greasing
TO GARNISH
chopped parsley

1 Preheat the oven to 200 C / 400 F / Gas Mark 6. Put a baking sheet into the centre of the oven, to heat up. Lightly grease a 30-cm / 12-inch flan tin.
2 Roll out the pastry and use to line the tin; trim the edges. Bake blind as described on p. 266.
3 Spoon the Mushrooms in Cream into the flan case and smooth the top. Return the flan to the oven on the baking sheet for 10–15 minutes to heat through. Sprinkle with parsley. Serve hot or cold.

A Quiche by Any Other Name . . .

Strictly speaking, 'quiche' refers to a light, creamy French flan, and in particular, Quiche Lorraine (which contains cream, bacon, onion and Gruyère cheese). 'Flan' is the English term (which I prefer) and 'tart' generally refers to a pastry case with a sweet filling.

When you're handling wholewheat pastry, which tends to be more crumbly than pastry made with white flour, it helps to roll the pastry out on a lightly floured board, then you can tip it straight from the board into your tin or dish, avoiding any breakages.

MENU

Autumn Meal for Six

Pumpkin Soup
77

Mushroom Flan

Red Cabbage Casserole
180
Potato Purée
189

Poached Pears with
Cinnamon Cream
85

QUICK SPRING ONION AND FRESH HERB FLAN

This is a light and melting flan, rather than a crisp one. It is quick and makes a delicious lunch or supper, with a crisp, leafy salad, such as radiccio, watercress and walnut.

SERVES 4

MAKING A REALLY CRISP FLAN CASE

I find this method of 'baking blind' better than the conventional one, where the flan base is weighed down with greaseproof paper and dried beans, because it's less trouble and gives a crisper result. Have a look at the flan after 5 minutes to see if the base is rising up; if so, simply press it down gently with the back of a fork.

1 Heat the oven to 200 C/400 F/Gas Mark 6. Put a baking sheet into the centre of the oven, to heat up. Lightly grease a flan tin or flan ring set on baking sheet.

2 Roll out the pastry and ease it into the tin or ring. Press down, trim edges.

3 Prick the pastry base all over. Bake for 12–20 minutes, depending on the size and thickness of the pastry, until firm to a light touch and lightly browned.

4 When the flan comes out of the oven, have ready 2–3 tablespoons sizzling hot oil and pour this into the pastry case. This will ensure that the base of your flan will be wonderfully crisp.

5 Next brush a little beaten egg over the base of the flan to seal any holes and return the flan to the oven for 3–4 minutes, until the beaten egg glaze is thoroughly set.

½ quantity Rich Shortcrust Pastry (p. 260)
butter for greasing
FOR THE FILLING
150 ml/5 fl oz milk or single cream
2 eggs
3 tablespoons chopped fresh herbs
salt and freshly ground black pepper
freshly grated nutmeg
1 bunch spring onions, washed, trimmed and chopped

1 Preheat the oven to 190 C/375 F/Gas Mark 5. Put a baking sheet into the centre of the oven, to heat up. Lightly grease a 20-cm/8-inch flan tin or ring.

2 Roll out the pastry and use to line the tin or ring; trim the edges. Chill in the fridge for a few minutes while you make the filling.

3 Whisk together the milk or cream and the eggs. Add the herbs and salt, pepper and nutmeg to taste. Put the spring onion into the base of the flan, then pour the egg mixture on top.

4 Place the flan case on the baking sheet and bake for 35–40 minutes, until the filling is set and lightly browned. Serve hot or warm.

Variations

QUICK MUSHROOM FLAN

Use 100 g/4 oz button mushrooms, thinly sliced, instead of the onions, and a crushed garlic clove instead of the chopped fresh herbs.

QUICK SWEETCORN FLAN

Use 100 g/4 oz frozen sweetcorn kernels instead of the onions and parsley.

QUICK CHEESE AND TOMATO FLAN

Add 50–100 g/2–4 oz grated Gruyère cheese and 1 thinly sliced tomato.

QUICK MINT AND PEA FLAN

Use 2 tablespoons finely chopped mint and 100 g/4 oz frozen peas. This mixture is good with or without the onion.

QUICK BEAN FLAN

Add ½ teaspoon made mustard to the egg mixture and put the well-drained contents of ½ × 425-g/15-oz can butter beans, chick peas or cannellini beans on the flan base before pouring on the milk and egg mixture. Omit the onion and parsley, or keep them, as liked. A crushed garlic clove mixed in with the eggs is also nice in this, and so are a few juicy black olives.

V   STEAMED VEGETABLE PUDDING   V

This is a vegetarian version of a steamed steak and kidney pudding, with vegetable suet or butter used for the pastry and vegetables in a savoury sauce instead of the steak and kidney.

SERVES 4

175 g/6 oz self-raising wholewheat flour
½ teaspoon salt
75 g/3 oz butter or vegan margarine
2–3 tablespoons cold water
butter for greasing
FOR THE FILLING
1 onion, peeled and chopped
1 tablespoon oil
1 potato, peeled and cut into 1-cm/½-inch
   dice
2 carrots, scraped and thinly sliced
225 g/8 oz mushrooms
2 tablespoons soy sauce
2 tablespoons water
salt and freshly ground black pepper
TO GARNISH
parsley sprigs

1 Grease a 900-ml/1½-pint pudding basin thoroughly with butter or vegan margarine.

2 Fry the onion in the oil for 5 minutes, then add the potato, carrots and mushrooms, cover and cook gently for 10–15 minutes. Add soy sauce, water and season with salt and pepper.

3 While the vegetables are cooking put the flour into a mixing bowl with the salt, then rub in the butter or vegan margarine with your fingertips, until the mixture looks like fine breadcrumbs. Add enough water to make a dough.

4 Turn the dough on to a floured board and knead lightly, then roll out two-thirds of it to fit the pudding basin. Use to line the basin and press down well.

5 Spoon the vegetable mixture into the basin.

6 Roll out the rest of the dough to fit the top of the pudding. Press down firmly and trim the edges.

7 Prick the top of the pudding several times with a fork, then cover with a piece of pleated greased greaseproof paper and a piece of foil and tie down.

8 Stand the basin in a large saucepan and pour in boiling water to come halfway up the sides of the basin. Return to the boil, then simmer gently for 1½ hours. Keep the water level topped up with boiling water as necessary.

9 To serve the pudding, remove the paper coverings, slip a palette knife around the sides of the basin to loosen the pudding, then turn it out on to a warmed serving plate. Serve immediately, garnished with parsley sprigs.

LIFTING A STEAMED PUDDING OUT OF THE PAN

Steamed Vegetable Pudding

Making Palmiers

These crunchy biscuits are an excellent way to use up left-over pieces of puff pastry. Push the pieces of pastry roughly together, and roll out into a rectangle about 3 mm/⅛ inch thick. Sprinkle thickly with demerara sugar.

Fold each of the 2 long sides to the centre, so they meet. Then fold the long edges to the middle again. Finally fold one of these rolled edges on top of the other and press down gently.

Cut into slices about 3 mm/⅛ inch thick and place on a baking sheet. Bake at 230 C/450 F/Gas Mark 8 for 7–8 minutes, until golden-brown. Cool on a wire rack.

Flaky Pastry

There are three types of flaky pastry:

ROUGH PUFF PASTRY The quickest and easiest of the flaky pastries to make, rises in flaky layers but does not get as high and light as puff pastry.

FLAKY PASTRY Almost as quick to make as rough puff, this rises higher and looks better. It is also possible to get a good result using 100% wholewheat flour.

PUFF PASTRY The richest pastry of all, rising in glorious golden flaky layers. It's wonderful for special occasion cookery, feuilletés, fleurons, bouchées and vol au vents. Making your own puff pastry is satisfying and rewarding, though you can also buy excellent frozen puff pastry: look for a brand which does not contain animal fat. Puff pastry made with 100% wholewheat flour is not very successful; it does not rise any higher than flaky pastry made with 100% wholewheat flour.

V   # ROUGH PUFF PASTRY   V

MAKES 225 g/8 oz

225 g/8 oz fine wholewheat flour
1 teaspoon salt
175 g/6 oz chilled butter or block vegan margarine
4 teaspoons lemon juice
about 8 tablespoons ice-cold water

1 Put the flour and salt into a mixing bowl and grate in the butter or vegan margarine. Add the lemon juice and water, then mix quickly to a fairly soft dough.
2 Gather the dough into a ball, wrap in clingfilm and chill in the fridge for at least 1 hour.
3 Take the dough out of the fridge. If it's very cold, leave it for 10 minutes to soften a bit, then roll it into a rectangle on a lightly floured board.
4 Mark the oblong lightly into 3 equal sections, then fold the bottom third up and the top third down, to make 3 layers.
5 Seal the edges by pressing them lightly with your rolling pin (to keep the air in), then give the pastry a quarter turn.
6 Repeat the rolling, folding and turning 4 times. The pastry is then ready to be used, or can be wrapped in clingfilm and put back into the fridge until needed.
7 Roll the pastry out about 5 mm/¼ inch thick and bake at 220 C/425 F/Gas Mark 7.

MAKING ROUGH-PUFF PASTRY

1 Grate the butter into the flour

2 Roll the dough into a rectangle, then fold the bottom third up and the top third down

3 Seal the edges by pressing them lightly with a rolling pin

FLAKY PASTRY

MAKES 225 g/8 oz

225 g/8 oz unbleached white flour
pinch of salt
75 g/3 oz butter
150 ml/5 fl oz ice-cold water
75 g/3 oz white vegetable fat

1 Sift the flour and salt into a mixing bowl. Rub in half the butter. Add enough water to make a dough.
2 Turn the dough on to a lightly floured board and knead until smooth. Shape the dough into a rectangle shape.
3 Roll the dough into a 12 × 25-cm/5 × 10-inch rectangle. Make sure you have the edges of the pastry straight and the ends square.
4 Cut half the vegetable fat into small pieces and place them in rows over the top two-thirds of the pastry, well clear of the edges of the pastry rectangle.
5 Fold the bottom of the dough (without the fat on it) up and the top third down.

Seal the edges by pressing them lightly with a rolling pin. Give the dough a quarter turn, so that the folds are at the sides.

6 Roll and fold the pastry once more, without adding any fat.

7 Repeat steps 4, 5 and 6, using the rest of the butter.

8 Repeat steps 4 and 5, using the rest of the vegetable fat.

9 Wrap the dough in clingfilm and chill in the fridge for 15–30 minutes, then roll and fold again without adding any fat. The pastry is now ready for use. Roll out as required and bake at 230 C/450 F/Gas Mark 8.

V PUFF PASTRY V

Puff pastry is quite time-consuming but not difficult to make and is very rewarding. Most of the time the dough is resting in the fridge between rollings.

MAKES A 250 g/9 oz QUANTITY, WEIGHING 450 g/1 lb (EQUIVALENT TO A 450 g/1 lb PACKET OF FROZEN PUFF PASTRY)

225 g/8 oz strong unbleached plain white flour
225 g/8 oz chilled butter or block vegan margarine
½ teaspoon salt
150 ml/5 fl oz ice-cold water
1½ teaspoons lemon juice

1 Put the flour into a mixing bowl with 25 g/1 oz of the fat, and rub it into the flour until the mixture looks like coarse breadcrumbs.

2 Dissolve the salt in the water and add to the flour mixture, with the lemon juice. Mix to a dough.

3 Place the dough on a lightly floured surface, knead lightly and shape into a square. Wrap in clingfilm and chill in the fridge for 1 hour. (Have the remaining butter or vegan margarine chilling at the same time.)

4 Put the chilled butter or vegan margarine into a roomy polythene bag and beat with a rolling pin to soften it slightly. Then put it on to a floured board and roll it into a square about 15 cm/6 inches.

5 Next, roll out the dough on a lightly floured work surface, to make a 25-cm/10-inch square.

6 Put the square of butter or vegan margarine diagonally on the square of dough and fold the corners of the dough over, overlapping them a little, to make a pack-age which completely encloses the fat.

7 Put this package of dough on a lightly floured work surface and roll it out, using short, sharp, firm forwards and backwards strokes, to a rectangle 1 cm/½ inch thick.

8 Mark the dough into thirds. Fold the bottom third up and the top third down. Seal the edges by pressing them lightly with the rolling pin.

9 Now give the dough a quarter turn so that the folds are at the sides, and roll it out again so that it is about 5 mm/¼ inch thick and three times as long as it is wide. Fold the dough in 3 again.

10 The dough has now had 2 foldings, so mark it by pressing 2 fingers into the dough, then put it into a polythene bag and chill it in the fridge for 1 hour (or longer, if this is more convenient).

11 Remove the dough from the fridge and unwrap it. If it is very cold, let it rest for 10 minutes before you roll it. Then roll and fold the dough twice as before, and mark it with 4 fingers. Wrap and chill the dough for 1 hour or more as before.

12 Repeat step 11. The dough is then ready for use, or it can be kept in the fridge for several days, or frozen for several weeks. When you have rolled out the pastry, chill it again for about 30 minutes before baking at 230 C/450 F/Gas Mark 8.

V MAKING PUFF PASTRY

1 Roll the dough into a 25-cm/10-inch square. Place the square of butter diagonally on the square and fold the corners of the dough over

2 Roll the dough out to a rectangle 1 cm/½ inch thick. Fold the bottom third up and the top third down

3 Seal the edges with a rolling pin

4 Give the pastry a quarter turn and repeat rolling and folding. Chill. Repeat the whole process twice more

*Mushroom Pâté en Croûte; Flaky
Vegetable Pie (p. 271)*

V　　MUSHROOM PÂTÉ　　V
EN CROÛTE

A favourite recipe, this makes a delicious main course served with a
Soured Cream and Herb Dressing (p. 156) with cooked vegetables
to accompany.

SERVES 6

1 quantity Flaky Pastry (p. 268), or
　450 g/1 lb frozen puff pastry, thawed
a little raw egg yolk
FOR THE FILLING
1 onion, peeled and chopped
25 g/1 oz butter
900 g/2 lb mushrooms, washed and finely
　chopped
2 garlic cloves, crushed
2 tablespoons chopped parsley
100 g/4 oz dried wholewheat breadcrumbs
2 tablespoons lemon juice
salt and freshly ground black pepper

1 Preheat the oven to 220 C/425 F/Gas
Mark 7.
2 Fry the onion in the butter in a large
saucepan for 10 minutes. Add the
mushrooms and fry for 20–30 minutes,
until all the liquid has evaporated.

3 Remove from the heat and add the
garlic, parsley, breadcrumbs, lemon
juice and salt and pepper to taste. Allow
the mixture to cool.
4 Roll one third of the pastry into a
15 × 30-cm/6 × 12-inch rectangle. Place
on a baking sheet, spoon the mushroom
mixture on top, brush the edges with
water.
5 Roll out the remaining pastry to a 23 ×
30-cm/9 × 12-inch rectangle.
6 Fold the pastry in half lengthways and
make diagonal cuts to give a fancy finish,
if you like. Ease the pastry on top of the
mushroom mixture.
7 Press the edges together and trim.
Make a few steam-holes, decorate with
pastry trimmings and brush with egg
yolk. Bake for 30 minutes, until golden-
brown. Serve hot or warm.

V # FLAKY VEGETABLE PIE V

SHAPING MUSHROOM PÂTÉ EN CROÛTE

SERVES 4–6

½ quantity Rough Puff or Flaky Pastry
 (p. 268), or 225 g/8 oz frozen puff pastry,
 thawed
beaten egg to glaze
FOR THE FILLING
1 onion, peeled and chopped
2 tablespoons oil
2 garlic cloves, crushed
350 g/12 oz carrots, scraped and diced
350 g/12 oz courgettes, trimmed and diced
450 g/1 lb leeks, trimmed, washed and
 sliced
2 tomatoes, skinned and chopped
2 tablespoons dried breadcrumbs
2 tablespoons chopped parsley
½ teaspoon each dried basil and oregano
salt
100 g/4 oz haricot beans, soaked, cooked and
 drained, or 1 × 425-g/15-oz can cannellini
 beans, drained
freshly ground black pepper

1 Preheat oven to 220 C/425 F/Gas
Mark 7.

2 First make the filling. Fry the onion in
the oil in a large saucepan for 5 minutes,
then add the garlic, carrot, courgette,
leek, tomato, breadcrumbs and herbs.
3 Season with a little salt, then cook for
10–15 minutes, covered, until the vegetables are tender, stirring occasionally.
Add the beans and check the seasoning.
4 Put the vegetable mixture in a 1.1-
litre/2-pint pie dish and leave to cool.
5 Roll the pastry out 2.5 cm/1 inch
larger all round than the pie dish. Cut off
a strip from all round the pastry. Place the
strip round the rim of the pie dish and
brush with cold water, then place the rest
of the pastry on top.
6 Trim the edges of the pastry and press
together firmly to seal, then knock up
and flute. Make a steam-hole in the
centre. Decorate with pastry trimmings,
sticking them on with cold water.
7 Brush the pie with beaten egg, if used,
then bake for 30 minutes, until puffed up
and golden-brown. Serve hot.

1 Spread out the smaller piece of
pastry on a baking sheet and top
with the mushroom mixture,
heaping it up well

2 Fold the larger piece in half and
make diagonal cuts with scissors to
within 1 cm/½ inch of the centre

CHOUX PASTRY

Choux pastry works well with either unbleached white or
wholewheat flour, but sometimes with wholewheat flour the
mixture will only take about ¾ of the egg; more and it would
become sloppy, so stop adding it at this point.

MAKES ENOUGH FOR 8 ÉCLAIRS OR 12 PROFITEROLES

50 g/2 oz butter or block margarine
150 ml/5 fl oz water
65 g/2½ oz plain or strong flour
2 eggs, lightly beaten

1 Preheat the oven to 200 C/400 F/Gas
Mark 6.
2 Put the fat and water into a saucepan
and heat gently until the fat has melted,
then bring to the boil.
3 Remove from the heat and add the
flour all at once, beating well with a
wooden spoon.

4 Return the pan to the heat and stir with
the wooden spoon for 1 minute until the
dough leaves the sides of the pan. Tip the
dough into a clean bowl.
5 Add about a quarter of the egg, beating
vigorously until the dough has absorbed
it and become glossy again, then add
another quarter of the egg in exactly the
same way.
6 Repeat until all the egg has been used
and the mixture is glossy and soft, but
not sloppy. Cover with a plate until
needed.

3 Open out and carefully place over
the mushroom mixture, being
careful to maintain the shape of the
mushroom mixture

4 Press the edges together and trim

VEGETABLE GOUGÈRE

An impressive and delicious dish, a big puffed-up ring of golden choux pastry, the centre filled with colourful vegetables.

SERVES 6

double quantity Choux Pastry (p. 271)
a good pinch of cayenne pepper
175 g/6 oz Cheddar cheese, finely grated
1 quantity Peperonata (p. 186), or Spring Vegetable Braise (p. 181), or 1 quantity Mushrooms in Cream (p. 79)

1 Preheat the oven to 220 C/425 F/Gas Mark 7.
2 Make the choux pastry as described on p. 271. Add the cayenne and 100 g/4 oz of the grated cheese.
3 Spoon or pipe the choux pastry round the edge of a 30-cm/12-inch pizza plate or large shallow ovenproof dish.
4 Sprinkle with the rest of the cheese and bake for about 40 minutes, until the gougère is puffed up and golden-brown.
5 Reheat the Peperonata or other chosen filling and spoon this into the centre of the gougère when you remove it from the oven. (If there is any filling over, serve this separately.)

WILD MUSHROOMS IN CREAM WITH PASTRY LEAVES

As the puff pastry is such an important part of this dish, it is best when made with home-made puff pastry, which has a buttery flavour lacking in most bought puff pastry. It makes a beautiful autumn main course, served with Potato Purée (p. 189) and followed by a Chicory, Watercress and Walnut Salad (p. 161).

SERVES 6

1 quantity Puff Pastry (p. 269) or 450 g/1 lb frozen puff pastry, thawed
beaten egg to glaze
double quantity Wild Mushrooms in Cream (p. 79)
TO GARNISH
fennel sprigs
thyme sprigs

1 Roll out the pastry 5 mm/¼ inch thick and cut into 6 leaf-shaped ovals about 10 × 5 cm/4 × 2 inches. Chill for 1 hour.
2 Preheat the oven to 230 C/450 F/Gas Mark 8.
3 Moisten the surface of a baking sheet and place the pastry leaves on it. Make leaf markings on the top. Brush the pastry leaves with beaten egg.
4 Bake the leaves for 10 minutes, then turn down the oven to 190 C/375 F/Gas Mark 5 and bake for a further 10–15 minutes, until the pastry is baked crisply through.
5 Gently reheat the wild mushroom mixture. Slit the pastry leaves in half horizontally, using a sharp knife. Place the bases on a warmed serving dish, or individual dishes.
6 Spoon the mushroom mixture on top of the bases, letting it flow over the edges of the pastry. Then cover with the tops of the pastry leaves. Garnish with fennel and thyme sprigs and serve immediately.

V

VOL AU VENTS WITH ARTICHOKE HEART FILLING

V

Light, crisp vol au vent cases are filled with a creamy mixture of artichoke hearts. They make a good main course, with Potato Purée (p. 189) and green beans. It's best to make the vol au vent cases in advance, then reheat and fill them just before serving.

MAKES 12, SERVES 4–6

1 Cut circles of pastry using a round pastry cutter

1 quantity Puff Pastry (p. 269), or 450 g/1 lb frozen puff pastry, thawed, or 12 frozen uncooked vol au vent cases

FOR THE FILLING
100 g/4 oz spring onions, peeled and finely chopped
15 g/½ oz butter or vegan margarine
2 teaspoons cornflour
300 ml/10 fl oz single or non-dairy cream
1 × 400-g/14-oz can artichoke hearts
salt and freshly ground black pepper
paprika
TO GARNISH
fennel sprigs
onion tassels
artichoke heart slices

2 Make another circular cut with a smaller pastry cutter inside each circle, being very careful not to cut right through the pastry

1 Preheat the oven to 230 C/450 F/Gas Mark 8.
2 Roll out home-made pastry 5 mm/¼ inch thick, bought puff pastry a little thinner.
3 Cut into circles or ovals using a 7.5-cm/3-inch cutter, then cut into the centre of each one, but not right through, with a 5-cm/2-inch cutter. (This will form the lid when the vol au vent has risen.)
4 Put the vol au vents on to a baking sheet and bake for about 5 minutes, until risen and golden-brown. Cool on a wire rack, then remove the lids and some of the pastry from inside the vol au vents.
5 To make the filling, fry the onions gently in the butter or vegan margarine in a saucepan for 10 minutes, until soft but not browned. Stir in the cornflour, cook for a minute or two, then add the cream. Stir over the heat until thickened. Remove from heat.
6 Drain the artichoke hearts and chop roughly. Add to the onion mixture and season with salt, pepper and paprika.

7 Before serving, reheat the vol au vent cases at 180 C/350 F/Gas Mark 4 for 15 minutes. Have the filling hot and spoon this into the vol au vents as soon as they come out of the oven. Replace the lids, garnish and serve immediately.

Variation

MUSHROOM VOL AU VENTS
Replace the artichoke hearts with 350 g/12 oz sliced mushrooms, fried in 15 g/½ oz butter or vegan margarine for 15 minutes, until the liquid has evaporated. Fill the vol au vents as above.

Vol au Vents with Artichoke Heart Filling

SPANIKOPITA

This Greek pie is equally good as a starter or main course. It's good served with a Yogurt and Mint Dressing (p. 156).

SERVES 6 AS A MAIN COURSE, 8 AS A FIRST COURSE

10 sheets phyllo pastry
150–175 g/5–6 oz butter, melted
900 g/2 lb fresh spinach or 450 g/1 lb frozen
    spinach, cooked, drained and cooled
1 bunch spring onions, trimmed and chopped
100 g/4 oz feta cheese, crumbled
salt and freshly ground black pepper
butter for greasing

1 Preheat the oven to 200 C/400 F/Gas Mark 6.
2 Grease a deep pie dish, then place a sheet of phyllo pastry in it, allowing the edges to hang over the sides of the dish.
3 Brush with melted butter, then place another sheet of phyllo pastry on top. Continue in this way, using 5 sheets of phyllo pastry. (Keep the rest covered with a damp cloth, see p. 151.)

4 Chop the spinach and mix with the spring onions, cheese and salt and pepper to taste. Spoon on top of the pastry.
5 Cover with the rest of the phyllo pastry sheets, brushing each one with melted butter as before, and finishing with melted butter. Neaten the sides; prick and decorate the top with leaves cut from pastry trimmings.
6 Bake for 40–45 minutes. Serve hot or warm.

Variation
VEGAN SPANIKOPITA
Make in the same way, but replace the cheese with mashed tofu or 100 g/4 oz pine nuts or flaked almonds. Use vegan margarine or olive oil for brushing the pastry instead of butter.

SHAPING A SAMOSA

1 Form a semi-circle of pastry into a cone, pressing the edges together well

2 Fill with vegetable mixture

3 Fold over the top edge, pressing down well

V   # SAMOSAS   V

These crisp, spicy little savouries are delicious as an accompaniment to curries, or as a snack, with some mango chutney or thick plain yogurt to dip them into.

MAKES 32

FOR THE PASTRY
300 g/10 oz plain wholewheat flour
1 teaspoon salt
2 teaspoons baking powder
4 tablespoons oil
150–200 ml/5–7 fl oz ice-cold water
oil for deep-frying
FOR THE FILLING
1 large onion, peeled and chopped
2 tablespoons olive oil
1 large garlic clove, crushed
2 teaspoons each mustard seed, grated fresh
    ginger, ground cumin and ground coriander
700 g/1½ lb potatoes, cooked and diced
225 g/8 oz frozen peas, thawed
salt and freshly ground black pepper

1 First make the filling. Fry the onion in the oil for 8 minutes, until soft but not browned, then add the garlic, mustard seed, ginger, cumin and coriander and cook for a further 2 minutes.
2 Remove from the heat and add the potato and peas, mix well. Season with salt and pepper, then cool.
3 Meanwhile, make the pastry. Put the flour, salt and baking powder into a bowl, then add the oil and water. Mix to a soft but not sticky dough.
4 Knead the dough for 5 minutes, then divide into 16 equal pieces. Roll each into a circle about 15 cm/6 inches in diameter, then cut each circle in half, using a sharp

knife, to make 32 half-circles.

5 Take one of the half circles of pastry and brush the cut edges with water, then fold it in half and press the moistened cut edges firmly together to form a cone.

6 Fill the cone with about 2 heaped tea-spoons of the filling, then moisten the top edges and fold them over to enclose the filling. Fill the rest of the samosas.

7 Heat the oil in a deep-fryer to 180 C/ 350 F, then fry the samosas in batches until golden-brown and crispy. Drain on kitchen paper and keep the samosas warm in a low oven until all are ready.

V ASPARAGUS STRUDEL V

SERVES 6

2 large onions, peeled and finely chopped
175 g/6 oz butter or vegan margarine
100 g/4 oz fine fresh breadcrumbs
8 sheets phyllo pastry (p. 151)
700 g/1½ lb trimmed asparagus, washed,
 chopped and cooked until tender (p. 63)
4 tablespoons finely chopped parsley
TO GARNISH
chervil sprigs
lemon slices
asparagus tips
TO SERVE
1 quantity vegan Yogurt and Herb Dressing
 (p. 156)

1 Preheat the oven to 200 C/400 F/Gas Mark 6.

2 Fry the onions in 25 g/1 oz of the but-ter or vegan margarine for 10 minutes, until soft but not browned.

3 In another pan, heat 50 g/2 oz of the butter or vegan margarine and fry the crumbs until crisp. Melt the remaining butter or vegan margarine in a small saucepan.

4 Spread one phyllo pastry sheet out on a large board and brush with melted butter or vegan margarine. Put another pastry sheet on top, and brush with more butter or vegan margarine. Repeat until all the sheets have been used.

5 Spread the onion evenly on top of the pastry, keeping the edges clear.

6 Put the asparagus over the top of the onion and sprinkle with three-quarters of the crumbs and the parsley.

7 Fold over 5 cm/2 inches all round the pastry, then fold the long edges over, to make a roll.

8 Place the roll, seam-side down, on a

Asparagus Strudel

baking sheet and bend it round into a horse-shoe shape.

9 Brush with the remaining melted butter or vegan margarine and sprinkle with the remaining crumbs.

10 Bake for 40 minutes, until golden and crisp. Garnish with chervil sprigs, lemon slices and asparagus tips. Serve with the Yogurt and Herb dressing.

MENU

Autumn Dinner Party

SERVES 6

Salade Tiède
150

Vegetable Gougère with Peperonata Filling
272 and 186

Potato Purée
189

Buttered Spinach
55

Apple Ice Cream with Blackberry Sauce
281

This is a warming dinner party full of fruity, autumn flavours. The salad can be mainly prepared in advance, ready for the hot Chèvre or goat's cheese to be added to the plates at the last minute. Both the Apple Ice Cream and the Blackberry Sauce can be made well in advance. Make the Peperonata for the Vegetable Gougère the night before, ready for reheating in the saucepan just before serving. The Gougère mixture can be put on to a shallow ovenproof serving dish and chilled in the fridge ready for popping into the oven 40 minutes before you want to serve it. Then just spoon the Peperonata into the centre. The potatoes can be sieved before you start the meal; add butter, cream and seasoning, but don't mix; cover the pan or bowl in a bain-marie, and keep warm, then mix the potatoes just before serving.

A sharp, flinty wine would go well with the salad – a Sancerre or a Pouilly Fumé would be ideal – and you could follow this with a medium-dry wine which goes well with vegetables, such as a Savennières, Vouvray or Macon Blanc, or you could serve a red Burgundy.

Puddings

A pudding rounds off a meal perfectly, and even if, like me, you eat them rarely, it is good to have the occasional indulgence. This chapter opens with cold desserts, including cheesecake and sorbets, and progresses to hot puddings, amongst which you will find pies, tarts, a hot soufflé, and Christmas pudding. Finally, there are some sweet sauces to serve with fresh and poached fruit, ice cream, pancakes and other puddings. Lots more pudding ideas feature on the fruit pages in the Ingredients section (pp. 84–103), and you will also find a number of cakes, in the next chapter, to finish a meal in style.

Types of Coffee

A cup of coffee goes particularly well with the richness of puddings such as the Little Baked Custards and Chocolate Pots. There are many varieties to choose from; it is interesting to experiment with different ones, and to blend two or more. Some of the best are:

BLUE MOUNTAIN Very rare and expensive; the best, full-bodied, with a fine, sweet flavour

BRAZILIAN Smooth and mild

COLOMBIAN Strong, rich flavour

CONTINENTAL Dark roasted with a strong flavour

JAVA A good after-dinner coffee with a mellow flavour

KENYA Mild. Has a slightly sharp flavour: another good after-dinner one

MOCHA Strong but with a subtle flavour

MYSORE Rich and flavoursome, one of my favourites

VIENNA Smooth and strong

LITTLE BAKED CUSTARDS

These smooth, velvety custards can be served warm or chilled;
I like them best chilled.

SERVES 6

3 eggs
3 egg yolks
50 g / 2 oz caster sugar
450 ml / 15 fl oz milk or single cream
1 vanilla pod or 1 teaspoon vanilla extract
TO DECORATE (OPTIONAL)
whipped cream

1 Preheat the oven to 170 C / 325 F / Gas Mark 3.

2 Put the eggs, egg yolks and sugar into a bowl and whisk until well combined.

3 Heat the milk or cream with the vanilla pod or extract to just below boiling point. Remove the vanilla pod if used (rinse, dry and keep for future use).

4 Add the hot milk or cream to the eggs, whisking gently.

5 Strain the custard mixture into a jug, then pour into 6 ramekins.

6 Put the ramekins into a baking tin and pour boiling water around them to come about two-thirds of the way up the sides of the ramekins.

7 Bake the custards for 40–45 minutes, until set. Remove from the oven, leave to cool, then chill before serving. Decorate the custards with piped whipped cream if liked.

Variation

LITTLE COFFEE CUSTARDS
For this delicious variation add 2–3 teaspoons continental or espresso instant coffee, dissolved in a little boiling water, to the milk or cream.

CHOCOLATE POTS

This is a versatile recipe, because it can be served chilled or the mixture can be baked, to make Little Chocolate Soufflés (see variation). Both versions are equally good.

SERVES 6

75 g/3 oz plain chocolate
150 ml/5 fl oz double cream
3 egg yolks
1 teaspoon continental or espresso instant coffee
4 egg whites
pinch of cream of tartar
25 g/1 oz caster sugar
TO DECORATE
whipped cream
chocolate coffee beans

1 Break the chocolate into pieces and put into a heavy-based saucepan with the cream. Heat over a gentle heat until melted.
2 Remove from the heat and beat in the egg yolks and coffee.
3 Whisk the egg whites with the cream of tartar until stiff, then whisk in the sugar.

4 Lightly but thoroughly fold the egg white mixture into the chocolate mixture until all the egg white is distributed.
5 Pour the mixture into 6 ramekins. Chill until set. Decorate each pot with a whirl of cream and a chocolate coffee bean.

Variation

LITTLE CHOCOLATE SOUFFLÉS

Fill ramekins to within 1 cm/½ inch of the tops and place on baking sheets. (This can be done several hours in advance and the mixture covered and refrigerated if convenient. Remove from the fridge at least 30 minutes before baking.) Bake at 220 C/425 F/Gas Mark 7 for 10 minutes, until risen. Sift icing sugar on top. Serve immediately, with whipped cream handed separately if liked.

Chocolate for Cooking

As with most ingredients, you get what you pay for with cooking chocolate. The large bars of chocolate sold as 'cooking chocolate' are not a good buy because they have a synthetic flavour and fatty consistency. The chocolate which gives the best results is a good quality plain or dessert chocolate or *chocolat menier.*

Chocolate Caraque

These chocolate curls make an attractive garnish for chocolate puddings and cakes and are easy to make. Pour 100 g/4 oz melted chocolate in a thin layer on to a baking tray and leave until it is firm enough not to stick to your hand when you touch it lightly. Then, holding a knife in both hands so that the blade is straight, draw it across the chocolate, like a comb, to draw off the chocolate in long curls. Another way to make curls, is to 'shave' a block of chocolate with a potato peeler.

Chocolate Shapes and Leaves

Chocolate shapes can be made by cutting a sheet of chocolate, made as described above, with tiny pastry cutters.

For chocolate leaves, dip one side of clean, dry, non-poisonous leaves, such as rose leaves or small fresh bay leaves, in chocolate. Leave until the chocolate has set, then gently peel away the leaf.

V # CHOCOLATE MOULD V

This pudding is easy to make, healthy and, in my experience, always popular with children. If preferred, it can be made in one large bowl.

SERVES 4–5

2 tablespoons cocoa or carob powder
50 g/2 oz soft light brown or caster sugar
600 ml/1 pint milk or soya milk
2 teaspoons agar agar
1 teaspoon vanilla extract
TO DECORATE
2 tablespoons flaked almonds, or grated chocolate or carob bar
TO SERVE (OPTIONAL)
single or non-dairy cream

1 Put the cocoa or carob powder into a medium saucepan with the sugar.

2 Gradually add the milk, stirring all the time. Heat to boiling point.
3 Over a low heat, gradually sprinkle the agar agar over the surface of the milk, whisking all the time. Boil the mixture for 1 minute.
4 Remove from the heat and add the vanilla.
5 Pour into 4 serving glasses. Cool, then chill.
6 Decorate with the flaked almonds or grated chocolate or carob. Serve with the cream, if liked.

VANILLA ICE CREAM

How to make Soya Milk

The soya milk used in the vegan version of ice cream is widely available. However, it is also possible to make a delicious soya milk at home. This is a bit fiddly, but it works out cheaper than bought soya milk, and tastes delicious.

To make soya milk, soak 225 g/8 oz soya beans in plenty of water for 2 days, changing the water twice a day. Then liquidize the beans with 1.4 litres/2½ pints fresh water. Line a sieve with a piece of clean muslin, then scald it by pouring boiling water through. Put the sieve over a large saucepan and pour the soya mixture through the sieve, squeezing through as much liquid as possible. Add a vanilla pod, or 1–2 teaspoons vanilla extract. Heat the milk to boiling point, then remove the vanilla pod (wash, dry and re-use). Then put the milk into a blender or food processor with 1 tablespoon cold-pressed sunflower oil and a little sugar or honey to taste, and whizz. Strain through muslin again, and it's ready.

3 egg yolks
75 g/3 oz caster sugar
100 ml/4 fl oz water
450 ml/15 fl oz whipping cream
1 teaspoon vanilla extract

1 Whisk the egg yolks until thick and pale.
2 Put the sugar into a heavy-based saucepan with the water. Heat gently until the sugar has dissolved, then bring to the boil and boil for 5 minutes.

3 Add the hot sugar syrup to the egg yolks in a steady stream, whisking all the time. (Keep the syrup away from the whisk or it may solidify on this.)
4 Whisk until the mixture is thick, pale and mousse-like. Allow the mixture to cool completely.
5 Whip the cream with the vanilla until thick, then fold into the egg yolk mixture. Pour into a polythene container.
6 Freeze until half solid, then beat again and return to the freezer until firm.

QUICK VANILLA ICE CREAM

A simple ice cream, but always popular, especially with children.
Serve with Almond Tuiles (p. 325)

SERVES 8

600 ml/1 pint whipping cream
1 × 400-g/14-oz can condensed skimmed milk
1 teaspoon vanilla extract

1 Whip the cream until thick, then add the condensed milk and vanilla and whip again until thoroughly blended.
2 Pour the mixture into a polythene container and freeze until firm.

CHOCOLATE ICE CREAM

SERVES 6–8

Vegan Ice Cream

To make a vegan version of Chocolate Ice Cream, use soya milk (see above) instead of dairy milk and replace the evaporated milk or single cream with concentrated soya milk or a non-dairy cream such as parev.

900 ml/1½ pints milk
100 g/4 oz plain chocolate or carob bar, broken into pieces
40 g/1½ oz sugar
1 tablespoon custard powder
1 × 410-g/14½-oz can evaporated milk or 300 ml/10 fl oz single cream
TO DECORATE
grated chocolate

1 Put all but 4 tablespoons of the milk into a saucepan with the chocolate or carob pieces and sugar and bring gently to the boil.
2 Mix the custard powder to a paste with the rest of the milk in a bowl.
3 Add a little of the boiling milk mixture

to the custard mixture, blend, then pour the custard mixture into the saucepan of hot milk.
4 Stir over a moderate heat for 2–3 minutes, until the mixture has thickened a little. Remove from the heat and cool slightly, then add the evaporated milk or single cream and whizz in a blender or food processor, to give a smooth consistency.
5 Pour into a polythene container and allow to cool completely. Freeze until half solid, then beat again and return to the freezer until firm. This ice cream freezes hard; remove from the freezer to room temperature 30–40 minutes before eating. Decorate with grated chocolate.

V   RASPBERRY ICE CREAM   V

Fruit ice creams are among the simplest to make, because all you do is fold a sweetened fruit purée into whipped cream, then freeze. Many different types of fruit are suitable; soft fruits only need puréeing (and sieving if necessary to remove pips), other types should be stewed gently with the sugar first.

SERVES 8–10

Vanilla Ice Cream (p. 280) with Almond Tuiles (p. 325); Raspberry Ice Cream

*450 g/1 lb fresh raspberries, washed, or
  frozen raspberries, thawed*
225 g/8 oz caster sugar
600 ml/1 pint whipping or non-dairy cream
TO SERVE (OPTIONAL)
raspberry leaves
1 quantity Raspberry Coulis (p. 300)

1 Reserve 16 raspberries for decoration. Purée the remainder in a blender or food processor, then sieve to remove the pips. Stir in the sugar.
2 Whip the cream until thick, then gently fold in the raspberry purée.
3 Pour the mixture into a polythene container. Freeze until half solid, then beat well and return to the freezer until firm.
4 Transfer the ice cream from the freezer to the fridge 30–40 minutes before you want to serve it. Serve in individual bowls decorated with the reserved raspberries and raspberry leaves, if available. Hand the Raspberry Coulis separately in a jug, if liked.

Variations
APPLE ICE CREAM WITH BLACKBERRY SAUCE
Use 450 g/1 lb cooking or dessert apples, peeled, cored and stewed with the sugar and 2 tablespoons water. Drain if necessary, then purée and cool before folding into the cream. Taste and add more sugar if liked. I like to colour this ice cream pale green with a little vegetable colouring. Serve with a Blackberry Coulis (p. 300) or Sorbet (p. 282) for a pleasant blend of autumn flavours.

MANGO ICE CREAM
Remove the stones and peel from 2 large mangoes. Purée the flesh in a blender or food processor, then fold into the cream.

APRICOT AND ORANGE FOOL

SERVES 4

Making Fruit Fools

Any soft, puréed fresh fruit, or firmer fruit, stewed, then mashed, or puréed, is suitable for making into a fool. Yogurt can be used, or chilled egg custard, or cream, or a mixture of these.

For a richer, special-occasion version of Apricot Fool fold in 150 ml/5 fl oz whipping cream, whipped, and 2–3 tablespoons apricot brandy or Cointreau before folding in the egg whites.

Try using 450 g/1 lb drained, stewed gooseberries. Purée, then sieve if you like, although puréed but unsieved gooseberries produce a fool with a pleasant texture.

Or use 450 g/1 lb drained, stewed rhubarb. Mash or purée. This is pleasant with a delicate flavouring of ginger (up to ½ teaspoon added to the rhubarb when stewing it).

225 g/8 oz dried apricots, covered with boiling water, soaked overnight, then simmered in the soaking liquid for 20–30 minutes until tender
240 g/8½ oz strained Greek yogurt
clear honey or sugar to taste
2 egg whites
grated rind of 1 orange

1 Purée the apricots in a blender or food processor, or mash them very well.

2 Mix the apricot purée with the yogurt to make a thick, creamy mixture. Add honey or sugar to taste.
3 Whisk the egg whites until they form stiff peaks. Fold a tablespoon of egg white into the apricot mixture, to loosen, then gently fold in the rest, together with half the orange rind.
4 Spoon the apricot mixture into individual glasses and chill. Sprinkle with the remaining rind before serving.

V   PASSION FRUIT SORBET   V

SERVES 6

Vegan Sorbet

Egg whites give a sorbet a particularly light texture, but thorough beating can also achieve this, so they are not essential. Sorbets therefore make a delightful vegan dessert.

175 g/6 oz caster sugar
300 ml/10 fl oz water
16–18 passion fruits
1 tablespoon lemon juice
2 egg whites (optional)

1 Dissolve the sugar in the water over a low heat, then bring to the boil and boil for 3–4 minutes to make a sugar syrup. Remove from the heat and cool.
2 Scoop all the pulp and seeds out of the passion fruits and add to the cooled sugar syrup, through a nylon sieve if you like.
3 Add the lemon juice. Pour the mixture into a polythene container and freeze, uncovered, until half solid.
4 Mash the mixture well to break up the icy particles and return to the freezer until solid. Or whisk the egg whites, if used, until they form stiff peaks, then gradually add the mashed frozen mixture, whisking all the time. Return to the freezer until solid.
5 Remove the sorbet from the freezer to room temperature 10 minutes before you want to serve it.
6 Mash the sorbet well with a fork to break it up, then spoon it into serving glasses, or mould it as shown on p. 283 and serve on a flat plate.

Variations
BLACKCURRANT SORBET
Cook 750 g/1½ lb blackcurrants without water in a covered saucepan until soft – about 10 minutes. Purée in a blender or food processor, then sieve. Use in place of the passion fruit pulp. 1–2 tablespoons cassis is excellent in this: add before the first freezing. Decorate the sorbet with a few blackcurrants and blackcurrant leaves, if available.

BLACKBERRY SORBET
Make as described for Blackcurrant Sorbet, using blackberries instead of blackcurrants and adding 1–2 tablespoons orange liqueur, or port, instead of the cassis.

PEAR SORBET
Stew 750 g/1½ lb ripe dessert pears, peeled, in enough water just to cover. Remove the pears from the water; boil the water rapidly to reduce to 300 ml/10 fl oz, then add the sugar and proceed with the recipe, using the pear purée instead of the passion fruit pulp. 1–2 tablespoons Poire Williams liqueur stirred into the mixture makes a wonderful addition for a special occasion.

V CHAMPAGNE SORBET WITH WILD STRAWBERRIES

V *Passion Fruit, Pear and Blackcurrant Sorbets (p. 282)*

Bringing the champagne to the boil removes the alcohol which could otherwise prevent the sorbet from freezing properly, but does not spoil the flavour. This, however, is unnecessary if you're making the sorbet in a sorbetière. Pink champagne makes the sorbet especially pretty.

SERVES 6

600 ml / 1 pint champagne
350 g / 12 oz granulated sugar
450 ml / 15 fl water
4 tablespoons lemon juice
4 tablespoons orange juice
100 g / 4 oz wild strawberries or strawberry slices

1 Put three-quarters of the champagne into a saucepan and bring to the boil. Remove from the heat and cool.
2 Heat the sugar and water gently until all the sugar has dissolved, then boil the mixture hard for about 20 minutes, until it becomes syrupy and forms a short thread when you pull a little between your finger and thumb. Remove from the heat immediately.
3 Add the champagne and fruit juices to the sugar syrup and leave to cool.
4 Pour the mixture into a polythene container and freeze until icy. This will take several hours: I leave it overnight.
5 Turn the frozen mixture into a chilled bowl, or the bowl of an electric mixer, and whisk until smooth and creamy.
6 Return the mixture to the freezer until firm. When you are ready to serve the sorbet, scoop on to chilled plates or glasses and quickly decorate with the wild strawberries or strawberry slices. Serve immediately.

SHAPING SORBET FOR SERVING

1 Fill a dessert spoon with sorbet, heaping it up. Cup another dessert spoon on top of the sorbet and press down, to mould the sorbet, scraping off excess

2 Repeat this once or twice, moving the sorbet between the two spoons, until you have a smooth oval shape, then place on a plate

Notes on Liqueurs

A dash of liqueur adds a delicious flavour to many sweet dishes. Some of the most popular and useful liqueurs are:

AMARETTO DI SARONNO Almond flavour

ANISETTE Aniseed liqueur

BAILEY'S IRISH CREAM Chocolate, double cream and whiskey liqueur

CALVADOS An apple brandy

CHARTREUSE Herb-flavoured liqueur

COINTREAU Orange curaçao

EAUX-DE-VIE Delicious fruit brandies, including Kirsch (cherry), framboise (raspberry), Poire Williams (pear) and fraise (strawberry)

MARASCHINO Cherry liqueur

TIA MARIA Jamaican liqueur made from coffee, rum and spices

ORANGE PARFAIT WITH
GRAND MARNIER AND STRAWBERRIES

A parfait is an extra rich ice cream which is useful because it can be kept in the freezer until the beginning of the meal, then turned out and served with a flourish.

SERVES 8–10

6 egg yolks
175 g/6 oz caster sugar
finely grated rind of 1 large, well-scrubbed orange
600 ml/1 pint whipping cream
1 tablespoon lemon juice
3 tablespoons Grand Marnier
TO DECORATE
100 g/4 oz small sweet strawberries, plus leaves
thinly pared rind of 1 orange, cut into strips
orange segments

Summer Fruit Meringue (p. 285); Orange Parfait with Grand Marnier and Strawberries

1 Whisk the egg yolks with the sugar and grated orange rind until thick and pale, then stand the bowl over a saucepan of steaming water off the heat (don't let the bowl touch the water) and continue to whisk until the mixture is tepid.

2 Remove the bowl from the heat and whisk until the mixture is cold.

3 Whisk the cream until standing in soft peaks. Fold into the egg yolk mixture with the lemon juice and Grand Marnier.

4 Pour the mixture into a 1.1-litre/2-pint mould, pudding basin or cake tin. Freeze until solid.

5 Transfer the parfait from the freezer to the fridge 30–40 minutes before you want to serve it.

6 Loosen the sides of the parfait by slipping a knife round the edge.

7 Invert the mould over a serving plate; if it does not come out with a slight shake, hold the mould under the hot tap for a second or two; dry the edges of the plate with kitchen paper. The parfait should slide out easily.

8 Arrange the strawberries, strips of orange rind and orange segments on top of the parfait and serve at once.

Variations
CHOCOLATE AND ORANGE PARFAIT

Stir 100 g/4 oz coarsely grated plain chocolate into the parfait before freezing. Decorate with chocolate curls, pared orange rind – and strawberries, too, if liked.

CHRISTMAS PARFAIT

For this delectable alternative to Christmas pudding, omit the Grand Marnier and grated orange rind. Sprinkle 175 g/6 oz mixed crystallized fruits (including a little ginger, if you like this) with 4–5 tablespoons brandy (or fruit juice or the syrup from the ginger, if children are sharing this). Make the parfait as described, folding the crystallized fruits (and any syrup) into the egg yolks before adding the cream. 50 g/2 oz toasted flaked almonds or hazelnuts can be added, too. Freeze in a pudding basin.

TRADITIONAL TRIFLE

Traditional English trifle, properly made, is a delicious treat, and the preparation can be done in stages, fitted in when convenient.

SERVES 6

½ quantity Whisked Sponge Cake (p. 302), unfilled, or 8 trifle sponges
100–175 g/4–6 oz raspberry jam
100 g/4 oz macaroons, lightly crushed
100 ml/4 fl oz medium sherry or sweet white wine
double quantity Pouring Egg Custard (p. 301), cooled
150 ml/5 fl oz whipping cream
50 g/2 oz flaked almonds, toasted

1 Spread the cake or trifle sponges with the jam, cut into pieces and place in a 2-litre/3½-pint glass serving bowl with the macaroons.
2 Sprinkle the sherry or wine over the top and leave to soak for about 2 hours.
3 Pour the custard on top of the cake mixture. Whip the cream, then spread over the custard, and top with the flaked almonds. Chill until needed.

SUMMER FRUIT MERINGUE

This version of the classic Pavlova makes a stunning centrepiece to any table, and when served with a selection of other puddings at a party, is always the first one to go.

SERVES 8

4 egg whites
a pinch of cream of tartar
225 g/8 oz caster or demerara sugar
2 teaspoons vinegar
4 teaspoons cornflour
½ teaspoon vanilla extract
FOR THE FILLING
300 ml/10 fl oz whipping cream, whipped
2 kiwi fruits, peeled and sliced into thin rounds plus leaves, or greengages, stoned and sliced
2 nectarines or peaches, skinned, halved and thinly sliced
100 g/4 oz strawberries, hulled and halved, or raspberries or blackberries

1 Preheat the oven to 140C/275F/Gas Mark 1. Line a baking sheet with non-stick baking parchment.
2 In a clean, grease-free bowl, whisk the egg whites and cream of tartar until the egg whites are so stiff that you can turn the bowl upside down without the egg whites falling out.
3 Add a quarter of the sugar to the whisked egg whites and whisk well. Then add another quarter. Continue in this way until all the sugar has been added.
4 Mix in the vinegar, cornflour and vanilla. Pipe or spoon the mixture into a large circle on the prepared baking sheet.
5 Bake the meringue in the coolest part of the oven for 1¼ hours, until crisp. Remove from oven and cool on a wire tray.
6 Just before you are ready to serve, place the meringue on a flat plate and spread most of the cream on top. Arrange circles of kiwi fruit and nectarines or peaches in the centre of the meringue. Pipe the remaining cream in rosettes around the edge and arrange the strawberry slices on top. Place a strawberry slice and leaves in the centre.

MENU
Vegetarian Christmas Dinner
Celery and Stilton Soup
132

White Nut Roast with Herb Stuffing
239
Cranberry Sauce
174
Vegetarian Gravy
172
Bread Sauce
175
Roast Potatoes
71
Baby Brussels Sprouts
58
Glazed Carrots
Illustrated on p. 183
182

Christmas Pudding or
Illustrated on p. 319
296
Christmas Parfait

V

PINEAPPLE JELLY

V

A useful pudding for children. Skimmed Milk Topping (p. 301)
or Nut Cream (p. 238) go particularly well with it.

SERVES 6

1 × 425-g/15-oz can pineapple pieces in
   pineapple juice
just under 600 ml/1 pint unsweetened
   pineapple juice
1½ teaspoons agar agar
a little caster sugar or clear honey (optional)
TO DECORATE
mint sprigs

1 Drain the pineapple, reserving juice.
2 Divide the pineapple between 6 individual serving dishes or glasses.
3 Measure the reserved juice and make up to 600 ml/1 pint with the extra pineapple juice.
4 Put the 600 ml/1 pint pineapple juice into a medium saucepan and bring to the boil. Sprinkle on the agar agar, a little at a time, whisking constantly.
5 When all the agar agar has been added, boil for 1 minute. Then remove from the heat. Taste and sweeten with sugar or honey if necessary. Cool slightly if using glass dishes.
6 Pour the mixture over the pineapple pieces. Cool, then chill until set. Decorate with mint sprigs.

Variation
RASPBERRY JELLY
Use 225 g/8 oz fresh or thawed frozen raspberries instead of the pineapple, and a red fruit juice, such as redcurrant, instead of the pineapple juice; sweeten to taste.

Fruit Jellies

Other combinations of fruits and juices can be used; try orange juice with orange segments or strawberries; or halved and de-seeded grapes with non-sparkling grape juice.

Agar Agar

Agar agar is a vegetarian gelatine made from a number of seaweeds and can be obtained in the form of powder, flakes, strips and strands, which are dissolved in boiling water (2 teaspoons powder, 1 tablespoon flakes, to 600 ml/1 pint liquid, to give a firm jelly).

V

FRESH FRUIT SALAD

V

An attractive mixture of colours.

SERVES 4

2 large oranges, peeled and segmented
   (p. 99)
175 g/6 oz black grapes, halved and
   de-seeded
2 kiwi fruits, peeled and sliced into rounds
2 apples, cored and sliced, unpeeled if skin is
   good
150 ml/5 fl oz orange or apple juice
TO DECORATE
mint sprig

1 Put all the fruit into a large bowl. Add the orange or apple juice. Mix well.
2 Transfer to a large serving bowl or divide between 4 individual dishes. Chill before serving.

Variations
GREEN FRUIT SALAD
Replace the oranges with a small melon with green flesh: dice the flesh or use a melon baller to scoop it out of the skin. Use green grapes instead of black.

ORANGE AND KIWI FRUIT SALAD
Use 4 large oranges and 4 kiwi fruits and omit the apples and grapes. Either segment the oranges, or cut them into thin rings, arranging them alternately with the kiwi fruit in circles on a flat plate, on top of the orange juice.

TANGERINE AND LYCHEE FRUIT
SALAD
A refreshing mixture to serve after a Chinese or Japanese style meal. Omit the apples, kiwi fruit and grapes. Use 6–8 tangerines, instead of the oranges, skinned and sliced into thin rounds, and the white flesh of 10–12 lychees. One star fruit, sliced, makes an attractive decoration to this salad.

Making Fruit Salads and Compotes

For best effect aim either for a real multi-colour look, combining five or six colours, or keep it simple and bold, with just one or two colours. For the liquid, you can use a fruit juice such as orange or apricot, or a sugar syrup (p. 85) made from water or wine. Soft fruits will produce their own juice if sprinkled with a little sugar, and treated this way make a delicious red fruit compote.

An Arranged Fruit Salad, of prepared pieces of fruit arranged attractively on a coulis of raspberries or blackberries, can look jewel-bright and stunning.

Top to bottom: Pashka (p. 288); Pineapple Jelly (p. 286); Fresh Fruit Salad (p. 286)

PASHKA

This traditional Russian Easter dish makes a luscious dessert.
Unless you have a special wooden Russian Pashka mould, you'll
need a 15-cm/6-inch clay flower-pot, scrubbed and baked in a hot
oven for 30 minutes or so, or a 1-kg/2 lb-2 oz yogurt pot with
some holes pierced in the bottom.

SERVES 6

Flower Waters

A little orange or rose water makes a delectable flavouring for Pashka; add 1–2 tablespoons to the mixture.

When choosing flower waters, look for the 'triple distilled' type; you can buy these from specialist food shops, shops specializing in Middle Eastern foods, and some chemists.

Rose water is delicious in many creamy puddings, fillings, toppings and icings, and can be used to flavour a delectable jam (p. 338). Orange flower water can be used similarly, but is particularly good, I think, as a flavouring for a fresh orange salad, together with a little orange blossom honey.

2 egg yolks
75 g/3 oz vanilla sugar, or caster sugar and a few drops of vanilla extract
4 tablespoons single cream or creamy milk
100 g/4 oz unsalted butter, softened
700 g/1½ lb curd cheese
50 g/2 oz whole candied peel, chopped
50 g/2 oz chopped blanched almonds
TO DECORATE
crystallized fruits

1 Beat the egg yolks in a bowl with the sugar until pale and foamy. Heat the cream or milk in a saucepan to just below boiling point, then add to the egg yolks. Stir well.
2 Return the mixture to the saucepan and stir until thickened. This only takes a moment, so watch it carefully: the mixture must not boil, or it will curdle. Remove from the heat and set aside to cool.

3 Beat the butter until light and creamy, then gradually beat in the egg yolk mixture.
4 Continuing to beat, add the curd cheese, a little at a time, then add the chopped peel and almonds.
5 Line the flower-pot or yogurt carton with a double layer of kitchen paper, to extend over the top.
6 Spoon the pashka mixture into the lined mould and smooth the surface, then fold the ends of the kitchen paper over the top.
7 Put a small plate on top and weight down. Stand the pashka on a plate to catch any moisture which seeps out of the base. Refrigerate for 6–8 hours or overnight.
8 To serve, invert the container on to a serving 'dish, turn out the pashka and remove the kitchen paper. Decorate with crystallized fruits.

QUICK CHERRY AND LIME CHEESECAKE

SERVES 6

175 g/6 oz semi-sweet wholewheat biscuits, crushed
75 g/3 oz butter, melted
225 g/8 oz curd cheese
150 ml/5 fl oz double cream
50 g/2 oz caster sugar
grated rind and juice of 2 limes or 1 lemon
284 g/9½ oz drained canned cherries, pitted
TO GLAZE
2–3 tablespoons strawberry jam or redcurrant jelly, melted
TO DECORATE
lime twists

1 Mix the biscuit crumbs with the butter. Press the mixture firmly into the base of a 20-cm/8-inch spring-form cake tin or other suitable shallow dish, using the base of a clean jam jar.
2 Put the curd cheese, cream, sugar and lime, or lemon, rind and juice into a bowl and whisk together until smooth and thick. Spoon the mixture on top of the biscuit mixture and level the surface.
3 Arrange the cherries on top. Pour the jam or jelly over the cherries. Chill well. Decorate with lime twists to serve.

ROSE CHEESECAKE

This is an exquisite cheesecake. Rose Petal Jam (p. 338) can be made
from fragrant roses in the summer, or bought at a shop specializing
in Middle Eastern produce.

SERVES 8–12

*175 g/6 oz semi-sweet wholewheat biscuits,
    crushed*
50 g/2 oz butter, melted
325 g/11 oz rose petal jam
225 g/8 oz curd cheese
150 ml/5 fl oz soured cream
*75 g/3 oz vanilla sugar or caster sugar with a
    few drops of vanilla extract*
1 tablespoon cornflour
1 tablespoon lemon juice
2 large eggs, separated
a pinch of cream of tartar
a little extra butter for greasing
TO DECORATE
crystallized rose petals
pistachio kernels

1 Preheat the oven to 170 C/325 F/Gas
Mark 3. Grease a 20-cm/8-inch spring-
form cake tin.
2 First make the crumb crust. Mix
together the biscuit crumbs and melted
butter. Spoon this mixture into the bottom of the tin. Press down firmly, using
the base of a clean jam jar.
3 Spread the rose petal jam evenly on top
of the crumbs. Chill.
4 Next make the filling. Put the curd
cheese into a bowl with the soured
cream, sugar, cornflour, lemon juice and
egg yolks. Beat until smooth.
5 Whisk the egg whites in a clean bowl
with the cream of tartar until stiff but not
dry. Fold into the curd cheese mixture.
6 Pour the mixture into the tin on top of
the crumb crust. Bake the cheesecake for
1–1½ hours, until firm in the centre.
7 Turn off the oven and leave the cheesecake to cool in the still-warm oven for
15–20 minutes, When cool, chill.
8 To serve, decorate with the crystallized rose petals and pistachios.

Cooling Baked Cheesecakes

A cheesecake cracks if it is cooled
too quickly; that is the reason for
allowing it to cool gently in the
turned-off oven.

Freezing Baked Cheesecakes

Baked cheesecakes freeze
excellently. Cool the cheesecake
thoroughly as described, then
remove from the tin. Place on a plate
and freeze until solid, then remove
from the plate, pack carefully, label
and store in the freezer. To use,
remove wrappings, place on a wire
rack for about 3 hours to thaw, then
transfer to a serving plate.

Rose Cheesecake

HOW TO GET
A TOP HAT EFFECT

Make a deep groove in the top of the soufflé with the handle of a teaspoon so that it cooks with a 'top hat' effect

Hot Black Cherry Soufflé

HOT BLACK CHERRY SOUFFLÉ

A hot soufflé makes an impressive and delicious ending to a meal, yet is very easy to make. The uncooked soufflé will keep perfectly in the freezer, so you can do all the preparation a day (or more) in advance, but use a container which can withstand the extremes of temperature.

SERVES 4

350 g/12 oz drained canned black cherries, pitted
3 tablespoons Kirsch
5 egg whites
50 g/2 oz caster sugar
a little oil
TO DECORATE (OPTIONAL)
icing sugar
TO SERVE
whipped cream

1 Prepare an 18-cm/7-inch soufflé dish by tying a double layer of greaseproof paper round it, to extend it by about one-third. Brush the dish and paper with oil, then dust with caster sugar. Secure the top of the paper with a paper clip.
2 Preheat the oven to 190 C/375 F/Gas Mark 5.
3 Purée the cherries in a blender or food processor and add the Kirsch.
4 Whisk the egg whites until they form stiff peaks, then whisk in the sugar until stiff and glossy.
5 Fold the cherry purée into the egg whites.
6 Pour the mixture into the soufflé dish, level the top, then draw a teaspoon round about 1 cm/½ inch from the edge, to make a deep groove.
7 Bake for 30–35 minutes, until the soufflé is firm and doesn't wobble when shaken.
8 Remove the greaseproof paper, sift a little icing sugar over the soufflé, if liked, and serve with whipped cream.

Variations
RASPBERRY SOUFFLÉ
Make as described, using 350 g/12 oz puréed and sieved fresh or thawed frozen raspberries. Flavour with a little Kirsch or framboise.

APRICOT SOUFFLÉ
Use 350 g/12 oz stewed and puréed apricots and 50 g/2 oz sugar. Use Cointreau or Grand Marnier instead of Kirsch.

BLACKCURRANT SOUFFLÉ
For this excellent variation, use 350 g/12 oz stewed, puréed and sieved blackcurrants and 100 g/4 oz sugar. Use kir instead of Kirsch.

LEMON SURPRISE PUDDING

Another old favourite, this mixture separates as it cooks, ending up
as a light sponge on top of a lemon flavoured sauce.

SERVES 4

25 g / 1 oz butter
100 g / 4 oz caster sugar
grated rind and juice of 1 lemon
2 eggs, separated
150 ml / 5 fl oz milk
25 g / 1 oz plain flour
a little extra butter for greasing

1 Preheat the oven to 190 C / 375 F / Gas
Mark 5. Lightly grease a 600-ml / 1-pint
ovenproof dish. Have ready a roasting tin
which is large enough to hold the ovenproof dish.

2 Cream the butter with 25 g / 1 oz of the
sugar, then beat in the lemon rind and
juice, egg yolks, milk, flour and the
remaining sugar.
3 Whisk the egg whites until stiff, then
fold into the lemon mixture.
4 Pour the mixture into the prepared
dish. Stand the dish in the roasting tin and
pour 2.5 cm / 1 inch boiling water into the
tin.
5 Bake for about 40 minutes, until risen
and golden-brown. Serve the pudding
immediately.

LEMON MERINGUE PIE

A traditional family favourite.

SERVES 4

2/3 quantity Basic Shortcrust Pastry (p. 260)
FOR THE FILLING
4 tablespoons cornflour
300 ml / 10 fl oz water
175 g / 6 oz sugar
grated rind and juice of 2 small lemons
25 g / 1 oz butter
2 eggs, separated

1 Preheat the oven to 200 C / 400 F / Gas
Mark 6. Roll out the pastry and line a
20-cm / 8-inch flan dish; prick the base
and bake for 20 minutes (p. 266).
2 Meanwhile, put the cornflour into a
bowl and blend to a paste with a little of
the water.
3 Bring the rest of the water to the boil
with 50 g / 2 oz of the sugar. Stir into the

cornflour paste, then return the mixture
to the pan, add the lemon juice and rind,
and stir over the heat until the mixture
has thickened.
4 Remove from the heat and stir in the
butter and egg yolks. Pour into the flan
case and allow to cool.
5 Turn down the oven to 170 C / 325 F /
Gas Mark 3. Whisk the egg whites until
stiff and dry, then whisk in the remaining
sugar.
6 Spread the meringue over the top of
the lemon mixture, being sure to take it
right to the edges, to prevent the
meringue from going soggy.
7 Bake for 40–45 minutes, until lightly
browned and crisp on the outside. Serve
warm or cold.

Thickening Agents

The lemon layer of the lemon
meringue pie is thickened with
cornflour, which is starch
extracted from maize. This is just
one of the thickening agents
available; others are:

ARROWROOT A fine white
powder originally made from the *aru*
root of the Aruac Indians. Less
refined than cornflour so preferred
by wholefood cooks for small
thickening jobs, but arrowroot loses
its thickening powers if cooked for
more than 1–2 minutes. Excellent
for thickening fruit juice for a clear
glaze for fruit flans. The proportions
are 1 rounded teaspoon to
150 ml / 5 fl oz liquid.

POTATO FLOUR The gluten-free
starch from potato; can be used in
the same way as arrowroot and
cornflour, but as it has a slight
potato flavour it is best in savoury
dishes.

KUZU Made from the roots of a
mountain plant in Japan, and
gluten-free, kuzu is used in similar
ways to the above and in Japan is
used to prevent colds and as a
general digestive tonic.

Rice Pudding

To make traditional British Rice
Pudding, put 25 g / 1 oz short-
grain pudding rice into a shallow
buttered ovenproof dish. Stir in
600 ml / 1 pint milk and 2
tablespoons soft light brown
sugar. Add a vanilla pod or a few
drops of real vanilla extract and
dot the top with a little butter.
Bake for 2½–3 hours at
170 C / 325 F / Gas Mark 3, stirring in
the skin after about 30 minutes,
and again about an hour later.

HOW TO MAKE PÂTE SUCRÉE

1 Sift 250 g/9 oz plain 85% wholewheat flour on to a clean work surface

2 Make a well in the centre and into this put 150 g/5 oz caster sugar, 150 g/5 oz soft butter and 4 egg yolks

3 Work these ingredients together with one hand while you push the ingredients to the centre with the other hand, to make a dough

4 Knead firmly until smooth, then wrap in clingfilm and chill for at least 1 hour before use

5 Roll out as required, and bake at 190 C/375 F/Gas Mark 5

PUMPKIN PIE

SERVES 6

1 egg
75 g/3 oz soft light brown sugar
225 g/8 oz cooked and puréed pumpkin
1 teaspoon ground cinnamon
1/2 teaspoon each ground ginger, cloves and
    allspice
a pinch of ground cardamom (optional)
a pinch of salt
3 tablespoons double cream
2/3 quantity Basic Shortcrust Pastry (p. 260)
TO DECORATE
50 g/2 oz pecan or walnut halves

1 Preheat the oven to 230 C/450 F/Gas Mark 8.
2 Whisk the egg with the sugar until pale and light, then stir in the pumpkin purée, cinnamon, ginger, cloves, allspice, cardamom, salt and cream.
3 Roll out the pastry and use to line a 20-cm/8-inch flan tin. Trim the edges. Pour in the filling.
4 Bake for 7 minutes, then turn down the oven to 170 C/325 F/Gas Mark 3 and bake for a further 35–40 minutes, until a skewer inserted in the centre comes out clean.
5 Remove the flan from the oven and arrange pecan or walnut halves decoratively around the edge, pressing them lightly into the warm filling. Put 2 more pecans or walnuts in the centre. Allow the pie to cool completely before cutting into slices.

V GLAZED RED FRUIT TART V

A luscious, shiny red tart is one of the best things to make from summer strawberries or other red fruit, such as redcurrants, glazed with a toning jam or jelly. I like to use a 30-cm/12-inch diameter round flan tin; for a 20-cm/8-inch tin, halve all the ingredients. This flan is delicious served with some crème fraîche, soured cream or plain (or vegan) yogurt.

SERVES 8

1 quantity Basic Shortcrust Pastry (p. 260)
    or Pâte Sucrée (left)
700–900 g/1 1/2–2 lb strawberries or a
    mixture of strawberries, redcurrants and
    raspberries
450 g/1 lb redcurrant jelly
butter for greasing
TO DECORATE
strawberry leaves

1 Preheat the oven to 190 C/375 F/Gas Mark 5. Lightly grease a 30-cm/12-inch flan tin.
2 Roll out the pastry to fit the flan tin. Place in the tin and trim the edges. Prick the base and bake blind for 20 minutes (p. 266), until pale brown. Cool.
3 Prepare the fruit. Slice any large strawberries. Arrange in the pastry case.
4 Melt the jelly gently in a small saucepan and pour over the fruit. Allow to cool and set. Decorate with strawberry leaves before serving.

Variation
JEWELLED FRUIT FLAN
For this very pretty variation, a variety of ripe fruits replace the red fruits. Choose contrasting colours, such as 175 g/6 oz each of strawberries or raspberries, sliced peaches or oranges, kiwi fruit, black grapes, banana or pear. Arrange as shown on p. 23; use sieved apricot jam to glaze instead of redcurrant jelly.

LINZERTORTE

V   V

I'm particularly fond of the combination of flavours in this Austrian tart. It is especially good after a vegetable main course.

SERVES 6

175 g/6 oz plain wholewheat flour
1 teaspoon ground cinnamon
a pinch of ground cloves
175 g/6 oz ground almonds
grated rind of 1 lemon
40 g/1½ oz soft light brown sugar
175 g/6 oz soft butter
1 egg yolk, optional
225 g/8 oz raspberry, black cherry or
    blackcurrant preserve
butter for greasing
TO FINISH
icing sugar

1 In a mixing bowl, combine the flour, cinnamon, cloves, ground almonds, lemon rind, sugar, butter and egg yolk, if used, to make a dough.

2 Knead lightly, then wrap in clingfilm and chill for 30 minutes.
3 Preheat the oven to 200 C/400 F/Gas Mark 6. Lightly grease a 20-23-cm/8-9-inch flan dish or loose-based flan tin.
4 Roll out three-quarters of the dough, fairly thickly, to fit the flan dish or tin. Ease into the dish or tin and trim the edges.
5 Spoon the jam evenly over the pastry.
6 Roll out the remaining pastry, again fairly thickly, and cut into long strips. Arrange these in a lattice pattern on top of the jam.
7 Bake for 25–30 minutes, until the tart is slightly risen and golden-brown. Dredge with sifted icing sugar. Serve hot, warm or cold.

MENU
Bonfire Party

Warming food to come back to!

Leek and Potato Soup
134
Warm Wholewheat Rolls
Illustrated on p. 331
328

Parmigiana
202
Crisp Green Salad

Linzertorte

PITHIVIERS

This delicious almond tart, which originated in the town of Pithivier, in northern France, is easy to make and delicious served with crème fraîche, whipped cream or thick Greek yogurt.

SERVES 6

25 g/1 oz butter
50 g/2 oz caster sugar
2 egg yolks
100 g/4 oz ground almonds
2 tablespoons rum
1 quantity Puff Pastry (p. 269) or 450 g/1 lb
    bought puff pastry
beaten egg
icing sugar

1 Preheat the oven to 230 C/450 F/Gas Mark 8.
2 Cream together the butter and sugar, then add the egg yolks and beat until creamy. Fold in the ground almonds and rum.
3 Divide the puff pastry into two pieces, one slightly larger than the other. Cut the smaller one into a 20-cm/8-inch circle. Place on a baking sheet.
4 Spread the almond filling on top of the pastry circle to within 1 cm/½ inch of the edges.
5 Roll out the second piece of pastry to go on top. Ease into place, trim and decorate the edges. Make a hole in the middle.
6 Brush with beaten egg and bake for 10 minutes. Turn down the oven to 200 C/400 F/Gas Mark 6 and bake for a further 35 minutes.
7 About 10 minutes before the end of the baking time, remove the tart from the oven and dredge with icing sugar; return it to the oven to melt the icing sugar to a glaze. Serve warm.

Note on Pithiviers

This is a particularly useful pudding to serve when you're entertaining, because it can be completely prepared, except for cooking, the night before. You can then put it into the oven either when you start your main course, or, if you're serving cheese first, when you start the cheese course, and it will be ready, all puffed-up, flaky and golden, 25 minutes later. Serve it with single cream.

V   OLD-FASHIONED TREACLE TART   V

Top favourite pudding with many of the men I know, treacle tart is
easy to make if you follow the tip I learnt from Prue Leith and pour
the syrup straight into the pastry case on top of the crumbs,
without attempting to mix.

SERVES 4

⅔ quantity Basic Shortcrust Pastry (p. 260)
100 g/4 oz fine wholewheat breadcrumbs
1 teaspoon lemon juice
350 g/12 oz golden syrup

1 Preheat the oven to 190 C/375 F/Gas
Mark 5.
2 Roll out the pastry and use to line a
20-cm/8-inch flan dish. Trim the edges.
3 Put the crumbs evenly into the pastry
case without pressing them down.

Sprinkle with the lemon juice.
4 Pour the golden syrup on top of the
crumbs (you can do this straight from the
jar or tin) so that they are all evenly
covered. Don't try to mix; the crumbs
will soak up the syrup as the tart cooks.
5 Roll out the pastry trimmings and cut
into strips. Arrange the pastry strips in a
lattice pattern on top of the tart.
6 Bake for 25 minutes, until the pastry is
crisp and lightly browned. Serve warm.

V   COUNTRY APPLE PIE   V

SERVES 4

⅔ quantity Basic Shortcrust Pastry (p. 260)
*700 g/1½ lb cooking apples, peeled, cored
    and sliced*
75 g/3 oz soft light brown sugar
3–4 cloves (optional)
TO GLAZE
milk or soya milk
caster sugar

1 Preheat the oven to 220 C/425 F/Gas
Mark 7.
2 Roll out the pastry so that it is about
2.5 cm/1 inch bigger all round than a
900-ml/1½-pint pie dish. Cut a 2.5-cm/
1-inch wide strip from the pastry.
3 Brush the rim of the pie dish with
water and press the pastry strip on to it.
Put the apples into the pie dish, sprinkle
with the sugar and add the cloves if used.
4 Brush the pastry strip with water, then
put the large piece of pastry on top, pressing it down round the edges. Trim,
knock up and flute or fork the edges.
Make a steam-hole in centre of pastry.
5 Cut decorations from the pastry trim-

mings, if you like, and stick these on to
the pie with water.
6 Brush the pastry with milk or soya
milk and sprinkle with a little caster
sugar. Bake for 10 minutes, then turn
down the oven to 180 C/350 F/Gas Mark
4 and bake for a further 35–40 minutes.
7 Sprinkle with more caster sugar and
serve hot or cold.

Variations

PLUM PIE
Make as described, using plums instead
of apples, and omitting the cloves. Halve
and stone large plums (small types, such
as damsons, can be left whole). Unless
the plums are very sweet, increase the
amount of sugar to 100–150 g/4–5 oz.

GOOSEBERRY PIE
Make as described, using gooseberries
instead of the apples and omitting the
cloves. Increase the amount of sugar to
150–175 g/5–6 oz, depending on how
sharp the gooseberries are.

V DOUBLE-CRUST BLACKCURRANT PIE V

SERVES 4

650–700 g/1¼–1½ lb fresh or thawed frozen
    blackcurrants, topped and tailed
150 g/5 oz soft light brown or caster sugar
1 quantity Basic Shortcrust Pastry (p. 260)
butter or vegan margarine for greasing
TO GLAZE
milk or soya milk
caster sugar

1 Preheat the oven to 200 C/400 F/Gas
Mark 6. Grease a 24-cm/9½-inch pie
plate.
2 Put the blackcurrants into a heavy-
based saucepan and cook gently for 4–5
minutes, until the juices run. Drain the
fruit, to remove excess juice (which can
be used for another pudding, such as a
jelly).
3 Stir the sugar into the blackcurrants.
Set aside to cool.
4 Roll out just over half the pastry to a
round which will fit the pie plate. Transfer this to the pie plate, using a board to
help (p. 260).

5 Put the fruit into the pastry-lined plate
to within 1 cm/½ inch of the edge.
Dampen the edge with water.
6 Roll out the remaining pastry and place
on top of the fruit. Press the edges
together, trim, knock up and flute or fork
the edges. Make a steam-hole in the centre of the pastry.
7 Cut decorations from the pastry trimmings, if you like, and stick these on to
the pie with water.
8 Brush with milk or soya milk, sprinkle
with caster sugar, and bake for 30 minutes. Serve hot or cold.

Variations

SUMMER FRUIT PIE

Make as described, but use a mixture of
fresh or frozen raspberries, redcurrants
and blackcurrants.

APPLE PIE

Use 700 g/1½ lb apples, stewed as
described on p. 84.

DECORATING A
FRUIT PIE

V RHUBARB CRUMBLE V

I use a shallow French glazed pottery ovenproof dish measuring
25 × 32 cm/10 × 12½ inches, which seems a large quantity for 4,
but in my experience there's never any problem with leftovers!

SERVES 4–6

900 g/2 lb rhubarb cut into 2.5-cm/1-inch
    lengths
75 g/3 oz sugar
butter or vegan margarine for greasing
FOR THE CRUMBLE
250 g/9 oz self-raising 85% wholewheat
    flour
175 g/6 oz butter or vegan margarine
175 g/6 oz demerara sugar

1 Preheat the oven to 200 C/400 F/Gas
Mark 6.
2 Put the fruit into a lightly greased large
shallow ovenproof dish. Mix in the

sugar; make sure the fruit is in an even
layer.
3 Put the flour into a mixing bowl and
rub in the butter or vegan margarine with
your fingertips until the mixture looks
like fine breadcrumbs and there are no
lumps of fat showing.
4 Add the sugar and mix gently. Spoon
the crumble topping over the fruit in an
even layer, covering all the fruit.
5 Bake for 30–40 minutes, until the
crumble is crisp and lightly browned and
the fruit feels tender when pierced with a
skewer. Serve hot.

TRADITIONAL CHRISTMAS PUDDING

In this pudding, soft butter or margarine replaces the traditional beef suet. The pudding tastes just as good, and has a deliciously spicy flavour. It can be made up to 2 months in advance and will keep well (and mature) in a cool, dry place.

SERVES 8

Flaming a Christmas Pudding

Flaming a Christmas pudding with brandy just before serving gives it a wonderful flavour. The important thing is to warm the brandy first. Put 4 tablespoons brandy into a metal ladle and warm by holding over a gas flame or electric ring, then quickly light the brandy and pour over and round the pudding.

Vegetarian Suet

A vegetarian suet is available from health shops and can replace animal suet in recipes such as Christmas pudding, mincemeat and suet pudding.

225 g/8 oz soft butter or vegan margarine
175 g/6 oz real barbados sugar
2 eggs, beaten
100 g/4 oz plain 85% or 100% wholewheat flour
½ teaspoon salt
½ teaspoon freshly grated nutmeg
½ teaspoon ground ginger
1½ teaspoons mixed spice
50 g/2 oz ground almonds
75 g/3 oz finely grated carrot
100 g/4 oz currants
100 g/4 oz raisins
100 g/4 oz sultanas
100 g/4 oz chopped candied peel
50 g/2 oz blanched almonds, chopped
100 g/4 oz fresh wholewheat breadcrumbs
grated rind and juice of 1 lemon
1 tablespoon treacle
about 4 tablespoons water or water and rum mixed
butter for greasing
TO FLAME
4 tablespoons brandy
TO SERVE
holly sprigs
Brandy Butter (below)

1 Grease a 1.2-litre/2-pint pudding basin and have ready a saucepan which is large enough to hold the pudding basin.

2 Cream together the butter or vegan margarine and the sugar, until light and fluffy, then whisk in the beaten egg, a little at a time.
3 Sift the flour, salt and spices into the bowl on top of the creamed mixture.
4 Add the remaining ingredients with just enough of the water or water and rum to make a soft mixture which will fall heavily from the spoon when you shake it. Mix well.
5 Spoon the mixture into the prepared pudding basin, cover with a piece of pleated greased greaseproof paper and then a piece of foil, and tie down securely with string.
6 Put the basin into the saucepan and pour in enough boiling water to come halfway up the sides of the basin.
7 Bring to the boil, then cover the pan and steam gently for 4 hours. Check the water level and top up with boiling water.
8 Remove the pudding from the pan and allow to cool, then store in a cool, dry place. Steam the pudding again for 3 hours before serving, then remove the paper and foil and turn the pudding out on to a warmed serving plate. Flame with brandy, decorate with holly and serve with brandy butter.

BRANDY BUTTER

SERVES 6

100 g/4 oz unsalted butter
100 g/4 oz soft light brown sugar
2 tablespoons brandy
TO DECORATE
holly leaves

1 Cream the butter and sugar together until light, pale and fluffy, then gradually beat in the brandy.
2 Transfer the mixture to a serving dish and chill until required. Decorate with holly to serve.

V

MINCE PIES

V

This mincemeat is unusual in that it contains no sugar or fat; the dried fruits provide the sweetness. It tastes delicious, but doesn't store in the same way as ordinary mincemeat because of the lack of sugar. This recipe makes 12 mince pies, with enough mincemeat left over for 2 further batches. The mincemeat will keep for up to a week in a covered bowl in the fridge. Uncooked mince pies freeze excellently; put them into the tin, freeze, then carefully remove them from the tin and store in a polythene container until required. Replace the mince pies in the tin for baking. (They can be baked from frozen, allowing a few extra minutes.)

MAKES 12

Top to bottom: Double-crust Blackcurrant Pie (p. 295); Country Apple Pie (p. 294); Mince Pies

1 quantity Basic Shortcrust Pastry (p. 260)
butter or vegan margarine for greasing
TO FINISH
caster sugar
FOR THE MINCEMEAT
100 g / 4 oz currants
100 g / 4 oz raisins
100 g / 4 oz sultanas
100 g / 4 oz cooking dates, chopped
50 g / 2 oz candied peel, chopped
50 g / 2 oz glacé cherries, quartered
50 g / 2 oz flaked almonds
4 tablespoons brandy or whisky
½ teaspoon each ground ginger, mixed spice, freshly grated nutmeg
1 ripe banana, peeled and mashed

1 To make the mincemeat, put the dried fruit, peel, cherries and almonds into a bowl. Sprinkle with the brandy or whisky and the spices. Stir, then leave to stand for 1–2 hours, stirring from time to time. Add the banana and mix well.
2 Preheat the oven to 200 C/400 F/Gas Mark 6. Grease a 12-hole bun tin.
3 Roll the pastry out thinly. Using 2 cutters, cut out 12 × 8-cm/3-inch circles and 12 × 6-cm/2½-inch circles.
4 Press the larger circles gently into each section of the bun tin, then put a heaped teaspoon of mincemeat into each and cover with the smaller pastry circles.
5 Press down at the edges and make a steam-hole in the top of each pie. Bake for 10 minutes, until lightly browned.
6 Cool in the tin, then transfer to a wire rack. Serve the pies warm, sprinkled with a little sugar.

WAFFLES

Waffles are nourishing and make an excellent breakfast, supper or snack at any time. They're particularly popular, in my experience, with children and teenagers. You need a waffle iron to make them.

MAKES 6

250 g/9 oz plain 85% or 100% wholewheat flour
3 teaspoons baking powder
½ teaspoon salt
3 eggs, separated
450 ml/15 fl oz milk
50 g/2 oz butter, melted
3 tablespoons caster sugar

1 Heat the waffle iron according to the manufacturer's instructions.
2 Put the flour, baking powder and salt into a mixing bowl. Add the egg yolks, milk and melted butter. Mix well to make a smooth batter.
3 Whisk the egg whites until stiff but not dry, then add the sugar and whisk again until glossy.
4 Fold the egg white mixture into the batter.
5 Spread ½ cup batter in the hot waffle iron. Bake for 2–3 minutes, until golden. (If it sticks, cook for a minute longer.)
6 Serve hot, with butter and honey or golden or maple syrup. Or serve the waffles with a jam sauce or cream or ice cream and fresh fruit.

STEAMED PUDDING

Everybody's favourite homely pudding, wonderful to keep out the chill on a winter's day.

SERVES 4

4 tablespoons jam or golden syrup
100 g/4 oz self-raising 85% wholewheat flour
1 teaspoon baking powder
100 g/4 oz soft butter
100 g/4 oz sugar
2 eggs
extra butter for greasing

1 Grease a medium pudding basin with butter and put the jam or golden syrup into the base.
2 Put the flour, baking powder, butter, sugar and eggs into a large mixing bowl and beat together for 1–2 minutes until the mixture is thick, smooth and looks slightly glossy.

3 Spoon the mixture into the bowl on top of the jam or syrup. Cover the basin with a piece of pleated greased greaseproof paper and then with foil. Tie down securely. Stand the basin in a saucepan and pour in boiling water to come halfway up the sides of the basin.
4 Bring to the boil, then simmer for 1½ hours. Check the water level and top up with boiling water if necessary.
5 Remove the paper and foil, run a palette knife around the sides of the pudding and turn it out on to a warmed plate. Serve hot.

Sweet Pancakes

Pancakes are delicious served simply with warmed maple syrup, honey or golden syrup. They are, however, marvellously adaptable, since both the batter and the fillings are infinitely variable.

For chocolate pancakes, replace 2 teaspoons of the flour with 2 teaspoons of cocoa powder and add a teaspoon of vanilla extract or 1 tablespoon rum; serve with warmed black cherry preserve and whipped cream.

For nutty-tasting buckwheat pancakes, replace 25–50 g/1–2 oz of the flour with buckwheat flour. These are good with strongly flavoured fillings, either sweet or savoury.

For orange pancakes, add grated orange rind and 1 tablespoon Cointreau or Grand Marnier to the batter; try these with pineapple, peaches or apricots.

Fill pancakes with sliced ripe peaches or nectarines.

For spicy pancakes, add ½ teaspoon cinnamon or ginger to the batter; try filling these with toning fruits, such as apples with cinnamon, pears with ginger.

Waffle Irons

Most automatic waffle irons have a thermostat showing when they are hot enough to add the batter. If yours does not, put a teaspoon water into the iron: it is ready when the steaming stops. Since the batter contains fat, you do not need to grease a waffle iron. If the waffle sticks, simply cook for a minute longer. You shouldn't have any trouble with sticking after the first one.

PANCAKES

Pancakes can be thin and lacy, so that you can almost see through them – these are the elegant French crepes – or they can be thick and filling – cheap and comforting homely food. The thick variety were the favourite after-college snack of one of my daughters and her friends who seemed to arrive at our door on motor bikes in droves. It was then that I really learnt to make pancakes – fast!

MAKES 12–14

100 g / 4 oz plain 85% wholewheat flour
½ teaspoon salt
2 eggs
150 ml / 5 fl oz milk
150 ml / 5 fl oz water
1–2 tablespoons melted butter or sunflower oil
oil or melted butter for frying
TO SERVE
caster sugar
4 lemons

1 Put all the ingredients into a blender or food processor and whizz until smooth. Or put the flour and salt into a mixing bowl, mix in the eggs, then gradually beat in the milk and water and melted butter.
2 Brush the inside of a small non-stick frying pan with oil or melted butter. Set the frying pan over a high heat until a drop of water flicked into it sizzles immediately.
3 Remove the pan from the heat, pour in 1½–2 tablespoons of batter for thin pancakes, more for thick ones, tipping the frying pan as you pour it in, so that the batter runs all over the bottom of the frying pan.
4 Immediately return the pan to the heat and cook the pancake for about 30 seconds, until it is set on top and golden-brown underneath, then flip the pancake over, using your fingers and a small palette knife, and cook the other side until golden-brown.
5 Serve immediately, or stack the pancakes on a plate and keep them warm until all are ready. Re-grease the frying pan as necessary. Serve sprinkled with sugar, with the lemons cut in half to squeeze over.

Crepes Suzette

Variation
CREPES SUZETTE
The favourite pudding of my daughter Katy. Make the pancakes as described. Heat 100 g / 4 oz butter, 150 g / 5 oz caster sugar, the grated rind and juice of 3 medium oranges and the grated rind and juice of 1 lemon in a shallow flameproof oven-to-table casserole or good-looking frying pan. When the mixture is melted, remove from the heat and dip in the pancakes on both sides, one by one, folding them in half and then in half again to make triangles. When each pancake is done push it to the side of the frying pan. When they're all done, leave them in the frying pan until you're ready to eat, then reheat gently. When all the pancakes are heated through, turn the heat up high for 1 minute to make the sauce really hot, then flame it in the pan with 4 tablespoons warmed brandy.

Greasing a Pancake Pan

A pastry brush – bristle, not nylon, which melts in the heat – is ideal for greasing a pancake pan.

V # RASPBERRY COULIS V

A delicious sauce for serving with fruit salads, over ice cream or poached fruits.

SERVES 4

350 g/12 oz fresh raspberries, washed, or frozen raspberries, thawed
6 teaspoons water
6 teaspoons caster sugar

Left to right: Skimmed Milk Topping (p. 301); Sabayon Sauce (p. 301); Raspberry Coulis

1 Blend the raspberries in a blender or food processor with the water and sugar. Sieve, then turn into a saucepan, bring to the boil and boil for 1 minute, to make the sauce clear and glossy.
2 Cool and refrigerate until needed.

Variation
BLACKBERRY COULIS
Make exactly as described, using blackberries instead of raspberries.

Chocolate Fondue

Hot chocolate sauce makes a delicious sweet fondue, a special-occasion pudding that children and students love. Serve surrounded by prepared fresh fruit for dipping; pieces of apple, apricot, pineapple, peach – whatever is available. Some marshmallows, soft peppermints and pieces of Turkish delight are also good for dipping, (though not as healthy!).

V # HOT CHOCOLATE SAUCE V

This sauce is delicious over meringues, profiteroles or ice cream.

SERVES 4

100 g/4 oz plain chocolate, broken into pieces
150 ml/5 fl oz single or non-dairy cream

1 Put the chocolate and cream into a small saucepan.
2 Heat gently until the chocolate has melted. Stir well, then serve.

POURING EGG CUSTARD

Delicate in flavour and texture, this sauce is well worth making, although it does need a little care, because it separates if it gets too hot. Making it in a double saucepan – or a bowl set over a pan of simmering water helps to avoid this problem.

SERVES 4–6

300 ml/10 fl oz milk
1 tablespoon caster sugar
1 vanilla pod
2 egg yolks

1 Put the milk into a medium saucepan with the sugar and vanilla pod and bring to the boil. Immediately remove the saucepan from the heat. Remove the vanilla pod (which can be thoroughly rinsed, then dried and kept for re-use).
2 Meanwhile mix the egg yolks together in a bowl. Pour on the scalded milk, stirring, then return the mixture to the pan.
3 Stir over a gentle heat until the mixture thickens enough to coat the back of the spoon. Do not let the custard get too hot or it will curdle. Pour into a clean bowl until ready to use.

Tips for Making Egg Custard

To make life easier for yourself when making an egg custard, a teaspoon of cornflour can be mixed in with the egg yolks to stabilize the mixture and prevent it from curdling if it does get too hot.

To prevent a skin from forming on top of egg custard, sprinkle the top with a thin layer of caster sugar and whisk in just before serving.

SABAYON SAUCE

SERVES 4

50 g/2 oz caster sugar
4 tablespoons water
2 egg yolks
4 tablespoons sweet white wine or sherry
a little lemon juice (optional)
150 ml/5 fl oz whipping cream, whipped,
(optional)

1 Put the sugar and water into a small pan and heat until syrupy.
2 Mix the egg yolks in a bowl. Add the hot syrup to the egg yolks in a thin stream and whisk well until thick and pale, then add the wine and a little lemon juice, if liked. Fold in the cream, if used.

Using Sweet Sauces

A sweet sauce can add the finishing touch to a pudding, transforming a simple dish like home-made ice cream into something special.

Try raspberry coulis with vanilla ice cream; blackberry coulis with apple ice cream; or a coulis made from blackberries or blackcurrants with chocolate ice cream.

For a pretty effect, pour a pool of coulis on to an individual serving plate, top with poached fruit or ice cream, then pour circles of cream on top of the coulis. Make a 'feather' pattern in the circles of cream by drawing a cocktail stick through them, in lines like spokes of a wheel, first towards the centre, then, with the next one, from the centre to the outside.

Sweet sauces are excellent with fresh or cooked fruit; try chocolate sauce, raspberry coulis or sabayon sauce with poached pears; or pouring egg custard with thin circles of juicy tangerines or satsumas (and flavour the custard with some of the grated rind).

SKIMMED MILK TOPPING

This is a whipped, low-calorie, low-fat topping. It's useful on top of fruit salads or as a filling for a cake you're going to eat the same day. You need an electric whisk to make this and you must use skimmed milk powder from the health shop, and not a milk-substitute powder nor granules.

SERVES 4–6

40 g/1½ oz skimmed milk powder
150 ml/5 fl oz ice-cold water
2 tablespoons lemon juice
½ teaspoon vanilla extract
1–2 tablespoons caster sugar

1 Put the skimmed milk powder and water into a bowl or the bowl of a food processor and whisk electrically for 4–5 minutes, until the mixture is thick and forms soft peaks.
2 Add the lemon juice and whisk again until the mixture forms stiff peaks.
3 Carefully fold in the vanilla extract and sugar. Use the topping within a few hours of making it.

Cakes

This chapter contains a medley of favourite cakes, ranging from homely Rock Cakes (p. 308), Parkin (p. 308) and easy All-in-One Sponge (p. 304) to classics such as Carrot Cake (p. 306), Madeira Cake (p. 307), Dundee Cake (p. 311) and Rich Fruit Cake (p. 312), and some sheer indulgences like Meringues (p. 314), Éclairs (p. 314) and the most wonderful chocolate cake of all, Chocolate Roulade (p. 305). At the end of the chapter are some favourite fillings and icings. Amongst the recipes are a number which do not contain eggs or milk, for vegans or people allergic to dairy produce.

Making Assorted Fancy Cakes

Whisked sponge cake, baked in a Swiss roll tin as described under Swiss Roll, can be cut up to make 12–16 tiny cakes. You can either cover the top of the cake with glacé icing (p. 315) before cutting into pieces, or cut the cake into different shapes, using a sharp knife and pastry cutters, then ice and decorate the shapes individually. If you're doing the cakes individually, there is plenty of scope for different colours and flavours; coffee icing decorated with chocolate or walnuts; chocolate icing with chocolate curls; vanilla icing with crystallized rose or violet petals; lemon icing with angelica and minosa balls; orange icing with small pieces of jellied orange segments. If the cake is very 'crumbly', before putting on the icing or butter icing, dip the pieces of cake in a glaze made by boiling 225 g/8 oz sieved apricot jam with 3 tablespoons water for a few minutes, until syrupy.

WHISKED SPONGE CAKE

The lightest sponge of all and comparatively low in calories, because it does not contain fat.

MAKES ONE 20-cm/8-inch CAKE

4 eggs
100 g/4 oz caster sugar
100 g/4 oz plain unbleached white flour
a pinch of salt
butter for greasing
FOR THE FILLING
75 g/3 oz jam
TO FINISH
caster sugar

1 Grease two 20-cm/8-inch sandwich tins and line the base of each with a circle of greased greaseproof paper.
2 Put the eggs and sugar into a mixing bowl and whisk electrically for about 5 minutes until the mixture is very pale, has doubled in bulk and leaves a ribbon trail on surface when whisk is lifted.
3 Alternatively, put the eggs and sugar into a bowl fitted over a saucepan of gently simmering water (make sure that the bowl does not touch the water) and whisk until the same stage is reached. Allow to cool, whisking occasionally.
4 Preheat the oven to 180C/350F/Gas Mark 4.
5 Sift the flour with the salt gently on top of the egg mixture. Then, using a metal spoon, fold it in gently but thoroughly.

6 Pour into the cake tins. Bake for 30–35 minutes, or until the cakes are shrunk from the sides of the tins and spring back when touched lightly in the centre.
7 Cool in the tins for 2–3 minutes, then turn out on to a wire rack and carefully strip off the lining paper.
8 When the cakes are cool, sandwich with the jam and dredge with sugar.

Variations
SWISS ROLL
Use the same mixture, but bake it in a 33 × 23-cm/13 × 9-inch Swiss roll tin, lined with greased greaseproof paper, for 10–12 minutes, until golden-brown and firm to a light touch. Turn out on to a piece of greaseproof paper sprinkled with caster sugar. Spread with 100 g/4 oz warmed jam and roll up quickly, using the paper to help. Cool on a wire rack.

GENOESE SPONGE
This slightly richer whisked sponge is made in exactly the same way, except that 50 g/2 oz of very soft (but not melted) butter is added. Pour this around the edge of the bowl after folding in the flour, then carefully fold into mixture.

V VEGAN CHOCOLATE SPONGE CAKE V

MAKES ONE 20–22-cm/8–8½-inch ROUND CAKE

300 g/10 oz self-raising 85% wholewheat
flour
50 g/2 oz cocoa powder
3 teaspoons baking powder
250 g/9 oz vanilla sugar or caster sugar with
1½ teaspoons vanilla extract
9 tablespoons sunflower oil
350 ml/12 fl oz water
vegan margarine for greasing
TO DECORATE
1 quantity Chocolate Fudge Icing (p. 316) or
Chocolate Buttercream (p. 316)
coarsely grated chocolate
icing sugar

1 Preheat the oven to 170 C/325 F/Gas Mark 3.
2 Grease two 20–22-cm/8–8½-inch sandwich tins and line the base of each with a circle of greased greaseproof paper.
3 Sift the flour, cocoa and baking powder into a bowl. Add the sugar, vanilla, if used, oil and water. Mix well to a batter-like consistency.
4 Pour the mixture into the prepared tins and bake for about 40 minutes, until the cakes spring back to a light touch in the centre.
5 Turn the cakes out on to a wire rack and strip off the lining paper. Leave to cool completely.
6 Sandwich the cakes together with half the fudge icing or buttercream and coat the top with the rest. Decorate with grated chocolate and icing sugar.

Variation

VEGAN LEMON CAKE

Use 350 g/12 oz flour and omit the cocoa. Replace 2 tablespoons of the water with 2 tablespoons lemon juice, and add the grated rind of 1 lemon. Sandwich and top with lemon buttercream or fudge icing and decorate with mimosa balls and leaves cut from angelica.

Raising Agents

BAKING POWDER Consists of a mixture of bicarbonate of soda and cream of tartar in a base of flour. Low-sodium gluten-free baking powder, made from potassium carbonate and potato flour, is also available.

CREAM OF TARTAR A white powder with a slightly sour flavour, cream of tartar is an ingredient in baking powder and can also be used in soft drinks. If you need to make up a baking powder, the proportions are three parts cream of tartar to one part bicarbonate of soda, and they should be added separately to the mixture.

BICARBONATE OF SODA This white powder is one of the ingredients of baking powder and, because of its effervescent qualities, can also be used as a raising agent on its own. It is usually dissolved in a little acid liquid, such as buttermilk or milk and vinegar, then mixed quickly with the dry ingredients just before baking.

Vegan Chocolate Sponge Cake; Vegan
Lemon Cake

ALL-IN-ONE SPONGE CAKE

This is a sponge which you can whizz up in no time at all.

MAKES ONE 20-cm/8-inch CAKE

DECORATING A SPONGE CAKE

Applying a coating of nuts to the edge of a sponge cake

Decorating the top

Making a feather pattern

175 g/6 oz self-raising 85% brown flour
1½ teaspoons baking powder
175 g/6 oz soft light brown sugar
175 g/6 oz butter, softened
3 eggs
extra butter for greasing
FOR THE FILLING AND TOPPING
4 tablespoons warmed jam, preferably reduced-sugar type
a little caster sugar

1 Preheat the oven to 170C/325F/Gas Mark 3. Grease two 20-cm/8-inch sandwich tins and line the base of each with a circle of greased greaseproof paper.
2 Sift the flour with the baking powder into a mixing bowl and add the sugar, butter and eggs.
3 Beat with a wooden spoon for 2 minutes, or in an electric mixer for about 1 minute, until the mixture is smooth, thick and glossy.
4 Spoon the mixture into the prepared tins and level the tops.
5 Bake, without opening the oven door, for 30 minutes, until the cakes spring back to a light touch in the centre.
6 Leave the cakes in the tins to cool for 1 minute, then turn them out on to a wire rack and carefully remove the lining paper, then leave the cakes to cool completely.
7 Sandwich the cakes together with the warmed jam and sprinkle the top with caster sugar.

Variations
VICTORIA SANDWICH CAKE
For this traditional version, omit the baking powder. Cream the butter and sugar together until light and fluffy, then gradually add the beaten eggs, beating well after each addition. Fold in the flour in 2 batches. Bake at a slightly higher temperature, 190C/375F/Gas Mark 5, for about 30 minutes.

COFFEE AND WALNUT SPONGE CAKE
Dissolve 3 teaspoons strong good-quality instant coffee in a little boiling water. Add to the rest of the ingredients, together with 50 g/2 oz walnut pieces. Sandwich together and coat with a double quantity of Coffee Buttercream (p. 315) and coat the sides of the cake with 50 g/2 oz chopped walnuts.

CHOCOLATE SPONGE CAKE
Replace 25 g/1 oz of the flour with 25 g/1 oz cocoa powder; or, for a rich, gooey cake, add 225 g/8 oz melted plain chocolate to the ingredients and bake for a little longer. Sandwich together with redcurrant, cherry or raspberry jam. Coat the top and sides with 7-Minute Frosting (p. 317) or Chocolate Buttercream (p. 316), then coat the sides with chopped toasted hazelnuts, and the top with a generous amount of coarsely grated chocolate or chocolate curls. Dust with icing sugar.

LEMON SPONGE CAKE
Add the grated rind of 1 lemon to the mixture. Sandwich together with Lemon Curd (p. 341) and dust with icing sugar.

ICED SPONGE FINGERS
Use 100 g/4 oz each flour, sugar and butter. Bake for 30 minutes in a shallow 28 × 18-cm/11 × 7-inch tin, lined with greased greaseproof paper. Ice with Glacé Icing (p. 315) and cut into 16–20 fingers. Decorate with chopped nuts or glacé cherries.

FRUIT AND ALMOND FINGERS
Make up a half quantity of mixture. Add 100 g/4 oz mixed dried fruit or chopped dates and sprinkle 25–50 g/1–2 oz flaked almonds on top before baking. This does not need icing.

CHOCOLATE ROULADE

This needs to be eaten with a fork, and makes an excellent dessert.

SERVES 6–8

5 eggs, separated
175 g / 6 oz soft light brown sugar
3 tablespoons hot water
175 g / 6 oz plain chocolate, melted
icing sugar, sifted
butter for greasing
FOR THE FILLING
200 g / 7 oz can unsweetened chestnut purée
300 ml / 10 fl oz whipping cream
sugar to taste
a few marrons glacés

1 Preheat the oven to 200 C/400 F/Gas Mark 6. Grease a 25 × 35-cm / 10 × 14-inch Swiss roll tin and line with greased greaseproof paper.
2 Put the egg yolks into a bowl with the sugar and whisk until thick and pale.
3 Stir the hot water into the melted chocolate, then gently mix this into the egg yolk mixture. Whisk the egg whites until stiff, then fold into the mixture.
4 Pour the mixture into the tin, spreading it out to the edges. Bake for 15 minutes. Remove from the oven and leave to cool in the tin for 10 minutes, then cover with a damp tea-towel and leave for a further 10 minutes.
5 Have ready a piece of greaseproof paper sprinkled with icing sugar. Remove the cloth and turn the roulade out on to the piece of greaseproof paper. Carefully strip off the lining paper and leave to cool completely.
6 To prepare the filling, beat the chestnut purée until soft then add half the cream and whisk until thick. Sweeten to taste.
7 Trim the edges of the roulade and spread with the chestnut cream. Then carefully roll the roulade up from one long end, using the paper to help.
8 Whip the remaining cream and spoon or pipe on top of the roulade. Decorate with the marrons glacés and sprinkle with icing sugar. This roulade will keep well in the fridge for several hours, and also freezes well.

Variation
CHOCOLATE ROULADE WITH ROSEBUDS
Make the chocolate mixture as described. Fill with 300 ml / 10 fl oz whipping cream, and decorate the plate with fresh pink rosebuds. Lovely for a summer birthday!

Freezing Chocolate Roulade

Chocolate roulade freezes excellently; make it completely, open-freeze, then, when solid, wrap carefully. To use, unwrap and place on a serving dish to thaw, allowing 2–3 hours.

All-in-one Sponge Cake (p. 304); Chocolate Roulade

CARROT CAKE

This cake is easy to make, but is best done by hand, rather than in a food processor, which chops up the nuts and fruit too much, spoiling the texture. Properly made, it's delicious, with a moist texture and spicy flavour. Carrot cake is particularly good for serving at picnics and barbecues, but pack carefully and supply forks and paper napkins.

MAKES ONE 23-cm/9-inch CAKE

Madeira Cake (p. 307); Carob Brownies (p. 307)

175 ml/6 fl oz sunflower oil
250 g/9 oz soft light brown sugar
2 large eggs
1 teaspoon vanilla extract
175 g/6 oz cold puréed carrot
150 g/5 oz canned pineapple chunks, drained
   and roughly chopped
75 g/3 oz walnuts, roughly chopped
75 g/3 oz unsweetened desiccated coconut
200 g/7 oz plain 85% wholewheat flour
½ teaspoon salt
1 teaspoon ground cinnamon
1 teaspoon baking powder
butter for greasing
TO DECORATE
1 quantity Cream Cheese Frosting (p. 316)
a few walnuts

1 Preheat the oven to 180 c/350 f/Gas Mark 4. Grease two 23-cm/9-inch sandwich tins and line the base of each with greased greaseproof paper.
2 Put the oil into a large mixing bowl and add the sugar. Mix well, until there are no lumpy bits of sugar.
3 Beat in the eggs, then add the vanilla, carrot purée, pineapple, walnuts and coconut.
4 Mix lightly, then sift in the flour, salt, cinnamon and baking powder. Mix together quickly but gently.
5 Spoon the mixture into the prepared tins and level the tops. Bake for 30 minutes, or until a warmed skewer inserted into the centre comes out clean.
6 Turn out on to a wire rack, and leave to cool for 10 minutes, then strip off the lining papers.
7 When the cakes are completely cold, sandwich them together with half the cream cheese frosting. Spread the rest on top. Decorate with walnuts.

MADEIRA CAKE

I like this best made with unbleached white flour, because this allows the flavours to come through, though I have made it successfully too with both brown and wholewheat flours.

MAKES ONE 20-cm/8-inch CAKE

175 g/6 oz plain flour
175 g/6 oz self-raising flour
250 g/9 oz butter
250 g/9 oz caster sugar with 1½ teaspoons
  vanilla extract
4 large eggs, beaten
2–3 tablespoons milk (optional)
extra butter for greasing
TO DECORATE
2–3 thin slices citron peel

1 Preheat the oven to 180 C/350 F/Gas Mark 4. Grease a 20-cm/8-inch round cake tin and line with greased greaseproof paper.
2 Sift the flours together on to a piece of greaseproof paper.
3 Cream the butter with the sugar until light, pale and fluffy, then add the eggs, a little at a time, beating well each time.
4 Add the vanilla extract, then fold in the flour, adding a little milk if necessary to make a soft, dropping consistency.
5 Spoon the mixture into the prepared cake tin. Bake for 20 minutes, then carefully lay the citron peel on top of the cake and bake for a further 1¼ hours, or until a warmed skewer inserted into the centre of the cake comes out clean.
6 Turn out on to a wire rack and cool.

Serving Madeira Cake

Madeira cake makes, I think, a very pleasant accompaniment to a fruit salad or creamy fool; it is particularly good with Pashka (p. 288). Serve in thin slices.

Or, for a quick and easy pudding, serve with some lightly stewed fruit, such as blackcurrants, and some cream or thick yogurt.

LINING A ROUND CAKE TIN

CAROB BROWNIES

Sweet and gooey, these brownies have a crisp, cracked top and a wonderful flavour. Definitely my favourite recipe using carob.

MAKES 12–16

100 g/4 oz butter
50 g/2 oz carob bar (not the sugarless type),
  broken up
2 eggs
225 g/8 oz soft light brown sugar
50 g/2 oz plain 85% wholewheat flour,
  sifted
½ teaspoon vanilla extract
50 g/2 oz walnuts or pecans, chopped
extra butter for greasing
TO FINISH
icing sugar, sifted

1 Preheat the oven to 180 C/350 F/Gas Mark 4. Line a 20-cm/8-inch square shallow tin with greaseproof paper and

grease the paper well with butter.
2 Heat the butter and carob bar together in a small saucepan until melted. Cool.
3 Whisk the eggs with the sugar until thick and pale – this takes 10 minutes with an electric whisk.
4 Fold the melted mixture into the whisked eggs, then the flour, vanilla and walnuts or pecans.
5 Pour the mixture into the prepared tin. Bake for 40–45 minutes, or until the centre is set. Don't over-bake – the inside should be gooey.
6 Cool in the tin, then dredge with icing sugar, cut into fingers and remove from the lining paper.

PARKIN

This parkin keeps well and gets stickier the longer it's kept. Wrap in foil to store.

MAKES 12–16 SLICES

Syrups for Sweetening

GOLDEN SYRUP Refined version of molasses (below) but lacking the nutrients

HONEY The sweetening preferred by natural health experts, though others argue that it is just another form of sugar (but lower in calories); many different flavours available

MALT EXTRACT Syrup obtained from malted cereal grains, especially barley

MAPLE SYRUP Smoky-tasting sap of maple trees; be sure to buy the genuine article, not 'maple-flavoured syrup'

MIRIN A sweet brown liquid made from rice; has been used in Japan for centuries. Boil for 1 minute before using

MOLASSES Dark, treacly syrup left behind when sugar is refined; rich in iron, calcium and B vitamins

TREACLE A blend of refined syrup and molasses

100 g / 4 oz plain 100% wholewheat flour
2 teaspoons baking powder
2 teaspoons ground ginger
100 g / 4 oz medium oatmeal
4 tablespoons real barbados sugar
100 g / 4 oz black treacle
100 g / 4 oz golden syrup
100 g / 4 oz butter or vegan margarine
175 ml / 6 fl oz milk or soya milk
extra butter or margarine for greasing

LINING A SQUARE CAKE TIN

1 Preheat the oven to 180 C / 350 F / Gas Mark 4. Line a 20-cm / 8-inch square cake tin with greased greaseproof paper.
2 Sift the flour with the baking powder and ginger into a bowl. Add the bran from the sieve and the oatmeal.
3 Heat the sugar, treacle, golden syrup and butter or vegan margarine gently in a saucepan until melted. Cool until you can comfortably put your hand against the pan, then stir in the milk or soya milk.
4 Add the melted mixture to the dry ingredients. Mix thoroughly, then pour the mixture into the prepared cake tin. Bake for 50–60 minutes, until the parkin feels firm on top.
5 Remove the parkin from the tin and put on a wire tray to cool, then cut into slices and carefully remove from the lining paper.

ROCK CAKES

Easy to make, spicy and delicious eaten while still warm.

MAKES 10

225 g / 8 oz self-raising 85% or 100% wholewheat flour
1/2 teaspoon mixed spice
100 g / 4 oz butter
75 g / 3 oz demerara sugar
100 g / 4 oz mixed dried fruit
1 egg, beaten with 1 tablespoon milk
extra butter for greasing

1 Preheat the oven to 200 C / 400 F / Gas Mark 6.
2 Sift the flour with the spice into a mixing bowl, add the bran from the sieve, if you're using 100% wholewheat flour, then rub in the butter with your fingertips until the mixture looks like fine breadcrumbs.
3 Add two-thirds of the sugar, the fruit and the egg and milk mixture, and mix lightly, so that the mixture just holds together.
4 Spoon heaps of the mixture on to a greased baking sheet, leaving a little room around each for spreading, then sprinkle with the rest of the sugar.
5 Bake for about 15 minutes, until lightly browned. Remove with a fish slice, as these rock cakes are fragile while still warm, and cool on a wire rack.

Variation
VEGAN ROCK CAKES
Use vegan margarine instead of butter, add 1 teaspoon baking powder to the flour and use 4 tablespoons soya milk instead of the milk and egg.

Opposite page, clockwise: Vegan Fruit Cake (p. 310); Rock Cakes; Quick Buns (p. 310); Parkin

QUICK BUNS

These colourful buns make an excellent tea time treat for children.

MAKES 18

*175 g/6 oz self-raising 85% or 100%
    wholewheat flour*
100 g/4 oz butter, softened
100 g/4 oz soft light brown or caster sugar
2 eggs
TO DECORATE
*Glacé Icing (p. 315), made with 100 g/4 oz
    icing sugar*
*chopped nuts, or a few chocolate dots and
    sliced glacé cherries*

1 Preheat the oven to 190C/375F/Gas Mark 5.
2 Sift the flour into a mixing bowl and add the bran from the sieve, if you're using 100% wholewheat flour.
3 Add the butter, sugar and eggs and beat well with a wooden spoon or with an electric mixer, until all the ingredients are well-blended and the mixture is thick and slightly glossy-looking.
4 Drop a heaped teaspoon of mixture into 18 paper cases. Stand the cases in a deep bun tin, or on a baking sheet.
5 Bake for 15–20 minutes until the cakes have risen and feel firm to a light touch.
6 Cool on a wire rack, then ice and decorate as you like.

Types of Tea

The natural partner for a piece of cake is a good cup of tea! Many types are available; for instance:

ASSAM Has a strong flavour and is often blended with other teas

CEYLON Good quality tea with a delicate flavour

DARJEELING Fine flavoured tea from the Himalayan foothills

EARL GREY Tea flavoured with oil of bergamot, originally formulated by the second Earl Grey; best without milk

ENGLISH BREAKFAST Generally a blend of Ceylon and Assam teas

GUNPOWDER One of the Chinese green teas with a sharp flavour

JASMINE My favourite; China tea mixed with jasmine flowers, to be taken without milk

KEEMUM The best China tea, with a delicate flavour and fragrance. Can be taken with or without milk

LAPSANG SOUCHONG A black China tea with a large leaf and a distinctive smoked flavour

V # VEGAN FRUIT CAKE V

This eggless cake is best fresh, but will keep for 7–10 days in a tin.

MAKES ONE 20-cm/8-inch ROUND CAKE

350 g/12 oz plain 100% wholewheat flour
1 teaspoon mixed spice
175 g/6 oz vegan margarine
175 g/6 oz real barbados sugar
225 g/8 oz mixed dried fruit
50 g/2 oz mixed peel
50 g/2 oz glacé cherries, rinsed and halved
grated rind of 1 orange
2 tablespoons ground almonds
25 g/1 oz blanched almonds, chopped
125 ml/4 fl oz soya milk or water
2 tablespoons vinegar
¾ teaspoon bicarbonate of soda
extra vegan margarine for greasing

1 Preheat the oven to 150C/300F/Gas Mark 2. Grease a 20-cm/8-inch cake tin and line with a double layer of greased greaseproof paper.
2 Sift the flour with the mixed spice into a mixing bowl, adding the bran from the sieve, too.
3 Rub the margarine into the flour with your fingertips until the mixture looks like fine breadcrumbs, then stir in the sugar, dried fruit, mixed peel, cherries, orange rind, ground and blanched almonds.
4 Warm half the soya milk or water in a small saucepan and add the vinegar. Dissolve the bicarbonate of soda in the rest of the soya milk or water, then combine the two mixtures.
5 Stir this mixture into the dry ingredients, stirring well so that everything is combined.
6 Spoon the mixture into the prepared tin. Bake for 2–2½ hours, or until a skewer inserted into the centre of the cake comes out clean.
7 Leave the cake in the tin to cool, then remove and strip off the lining paper. Transfer to a wire rack to allow the cake to cool completely.

Dundee Cake

DUNDEE CAKE

This cake is good made with unbleached white or
85% wholewheat flour.

MAKES ONE 20-cm/8-inch ROUND CAKE

225 g/8 oz butter
225 g/8 oz soft light brown sugar
4 large eggs, beaten
350 g/12 oz plain flour
1–2 tablespoons milk
175 g/6 oz sultanas
175 g/6 oz currants
175 g/6 oz raisins
75 g/3 oz candied peel, chopped
75 g/3 oz glacé cherries, halved
50 g/2 oz ground almonds
grated rind of 1 orange or lemon
75 g/3 oz blanched almonds, split
extra butter for greasing

1 Preheat the oven to 170 C/325 F/Gas
Mark 3. Grease a 20-cm/8-inch round
cake tin and line with a double thickness
of greased greaseproof paper.
2 Cream the butter and sugar in a bowl
until light and fluffy, then add the eggs, a
tablespoon at a time, beating well after
each addition.
3 Sift the flour in on top of the butter

mixture, then fold it in gently.
4 If the mixture seems stiff, add a little
milk; it should drop heavily from the
spoon when you bang it against the side
of the bowl.
5 Gently stir in all the other ingredients
except the split almonds.
6 Turn the mixture into the prepared
cake tin. Arrange the split almonds
lightly on top.
7 Bake for about 2½ hours, or until a
warmed skewer inserted into the centre
of the cake comes out clean. Cool the
cake in the tin, then turn out on to a wire
rack, strip off the lining paper and leave
to cool completely.

Variation

SUGARLESS DUNDEE CAKE
Replace the sugar with 225 g/8 oz cooking dates, stewed in 150 ml/5 fl oz water
for about 10 minutes until soft, then
beaten to a purée. Cool, then use in place
of the sugar.

Cake-making Tips

The most critical part of making
cakes by the traditional creaming
method is the creaming of the butter
and sugar, which should be done
really thoroughly, until they are
light, pale and fluffy. The beaten
egg, which needs to be at room
temperature, should be added very
gradually, a tablespoon at a time,
with thorough beating after each
addition, so that the mixture doesn't
curdle.

If the worst happens and it does
curdle, however, don't despair. Add
a little flour, then continue to add the
egg and flour alternately. The
texture of the cake will not be so
light and crumbly, but it will still
taste good.

If the top of a cake seems to be
browning too quickly, cover it with
a folded piece of greaseproof paper,
with a hole cut in it, as described for
the Rich Fruit Cake (p. 312).

Don't open the oven door when a
cake is cooking until nearly the end
of the cooking time, or the cake will
probably sink in the middle. There's
a delicate chemical reaction taking
place which is upset by a blast of
cold air!

Rich Fruit Cake

Alternative Christmas Cake Decorations

Almond paste can be used on its own, attractively fluted around the top of the cake (as you'd flute a pie), and perhaps lightly scored in a criss-cross pattern with a knife. Arrange a candle and holly or marzipan fruit around the centre and tie a toning ribbon around the outside, or try a jewel-bright topping of crystallized fruits and brazil nuts, halved pecans and whole cashew nuts or blanched almonds. Stick these to the top of the cake in an attractive pattern with warmed clear honey; brush over with more warmed honey to glaze. For a sparkling finish, brush the whole cake over with clear honey then sprinkle with preserving sugar or coloured coffee sugar crystals and little silver balls.

Sieved apricot jam is often used to stick the almond paste on a rich fruit cake, but redcurrant jelly is easier, as no sieving has to be done.

COVERING FRUIT CAKE WITH ALMOND PASTE

RICH FRUIT CAKE

This is a rich, moist fruit cake, and the 20-cm/8-inch size is excellent for Christmas or special birthdays or celebrations. It can also be made as a wedding cake: for the quantities for different sized tins, see opposite.

MAKES ONE 20-cm/8-inch CAKE

250 g/9 oz currants
250 g/9 oz sultanas
175 g/6 oz raisins
50 g/2 oz cherries
100 g/4 oz whole candied peel
250 g/9 oz plain 85% or 100% wholewheat
*   flour*
1 teaspoon baking powder
½ teaspoon salt
½ teaspoon mixed spice
¼ teaspoon freshly grated nutmeg
250 g/9 oz butter
250 g/9 oz soft light brown sugar
4 eggs, lightly beaten
grated rind of 1 orange
grated rind of 1 lemon
75 g/3 oz ground almonds
75 g/3 oz chopped blanched almonds
3 tablespoons sherry
2 tablespoons brandy
extra butter for greasing
TO DECORATE
1 quantity Almond Paste (p. 317)
1 quantity Royal Icing (p. 317)
red ribbon, Christmas cake decorations

1 Make sure that the dried fruit is clean; wash it if necessary in warm water, dry with kitchen paper and spread it out on trays lined with kitchen paper, to dry.
2 Wash the cherries to remove the syrup, then dry and cut into quarters. Chop the candied peel.
3 Sift the flour with the baking powder, salt, mixed spice and nutmeg. Set aside.
4 Preheat the oven to 140 C/275 F/Gas Mark 1. Grease a 20-cm/8-inch round cake tin and line with a double thickness of greased greaseproof paper.
5 Cream the butter with the sugar thoroughly, until very light and fluffy, then add the eggs, a tablespoon at a time, beating well between each addition.
6 Fold in the sifted flour mixture, then stir in the fruit, orange and lemon rinds, ground and chopped almonds and the sherry.
7 Spoon the mixture into the cake tin, hollowing out the centre slightly.
8 Tie a band of brown paper around the outside of the tin and place a folded piece

of greaseproof paper, with a 2.5-cm/ 1-inch diameter circle cut in the middle, over the top of the brown paper, to prevent the top and sides of the cake browning before the inside is done.

9 Bake on a low shelf for 4½–5 hours. Do not open the oven door until the cake has been baking for at least 4 hours.

10 The cake is done when a skewer inserted into the centre comes out clean. Allow it to cool in the tin, then prick the top all over with a skewer and pour 2 tablespoons brandy over it.

11 Wrap the cake in a double thickness of greaseproof paper and store in an airtight tin until needed. It will keep well for 2–3 months and mature; prick the top and sprinkle a little more brandy over it occasionally during this time if you wish.

12 A week before you want to ice the cake, trim it if necessary to level it, then brush with melted redcurrant jelly.

13 Roll out two-thirds of the almond paste and cut into 2 pieces to cover the sides of the cake; press them into position.

14 Roll the remaining almond paste into a circle to cover the top; press down and trim. Leave the cake in a dry, airy place for 3–7 days.

15 Put all the icing on top of the cake and roll it backwards and forwards a few times with a palette knife to remove any air bubbles.

16 Spread the icing over the top and sides of the cake. Finally use the blade of the palette knife to flick the icing up into peaks. Arrange decorations on the cake and leave for at least 24 hours to set, then tie a ribbon round the cake.

Simnel Cake

For this traditional Easter cake, put half the rich fruit cake mixture into the tin, then top with a 5 mm–1-cm/ ¼–½-inch thick circle of almond paste the same size as the tin. Spoon the rest of the mixture on top and bake as usual. Cool, then stick another circle of almond paste on top of the cake and a circle of 11 balls of almond paste (representing the Apostles minus Judas) around the edge. Pop the cake under a moderate grill just to brown the almond paste. Decorate with ribbon, and flowers and Easter chicks, if you like.

Quantities for rich fruit cakes in various tin sizes

Round tin sizes	15 cm	6 in	18 cm	7 in	20 cm	8 in	23 cm	9 in	25 cm	10 in	30 cm	12 in
Square tin sizes	13 cm	5 in	15 cm	6 in	18 cm	7 in	20 cm	8 in	23 cm	9 in	28 cm	11 in
Depth of cake	6 cm	2½ in	8 cm	3 in	8 cm	3 in	8 cm	3 in	9 cm	3½ in	9 cm	3½ in
	g	oz	g	oz	g	oz	g	oz	g	oz	g	oz
currants	150	5	200	7	250	9	350	12	450	1 lb	750	1 lb 10 oz
sultanas	150	5	200	7	250	9	350	12	450	1 lb	750	1 lb 10 oz
raisins	150	5	150	5	175	6	225	8	350	12	500	1 lb 2 oz
cherries	25	1	25	1	50	2	50	2	75	3	100	4
whole candied peel	75	3	100	4	150	5	175	6	250	9	400	14
butter	150	5	200	7	250	9	350	12	450	1 lb	750	1 lb 10 oz
soft brown sugar	150	5	200	7	250	9	350	12	450	1 lb	750	1 lb 10 oz
plain flour	150	5	200	7	250	9	350	12	450	1 lb	750	1 lb 10 oz
baking powder	½ tsp		½ tsp		1 tsp		1 tsp		2 tsp		2 tsp	
salt	pinch		pinch		½ tsp		⅔ tsp		1 tsp		1 tsp	
spice	⅓ tsp		½ tsp		1 tsp		1 tsp		2 tsp		2 tsp	
freshly grated nutmeg	pinch		pinch		¼ tsp		½ tsp		1 tsp		1 tsp	
eggs, lightly beaten	2		3		4		5		7		10	
grated rind of lemon	¼		½		1		1 large		2–3		2 or 3	
grated rind of orange	¼		½		1		1 large		2–3		2 or 3	
ground almonds	25	1	50	2	75	3	75	3	150	5	175	6
chopped blanched almonds	25	1	50	2	75	3	75	3	150	5	175	6
sherry	1 tbs		2 tbs		3 tbs		3 tbs		5 tbs		6 tbs	
brandy	1 tbs		1½ tbs		2 tbs		2 tbs		3 to 4 tbs		4 tbs	
almonds to make paste	225	8	350	12	450	1 lb	500	1 lb 4 oz	800	1 lb 12 oz	1.1 kg	2½ lb
icing sugar for royal icing	450	1 lb	700	1½ lb	900	2 lb	1.1 kg	2½ lb	1.6 kg	3½ lb	2.25 kg	5 lb

MERINGUES

MAKES 6 WHOLE MERINGUES

2 egg whites
a pinch of cream of tartar
100 g / 4 oz caster sugar or real demerara sugar
300 ml / 10 fl oz double cream

1 Preheat the oven to 150C/300F/Gas Mark 2. Line a baking sheet with non-stick baking parchment.
2 Put the egg whites into a clean, grease-free bowl with the cream of tartar and whisk until stiff and dry. You should be able to turn the bowl upside down without the egg white falling out.
3 Next whisk in half the sugar. When this has been absorbed, whisk in the remaining sugar, until the meringue is very stiff and glossy.
4 Drop spoonfuls of the mixture on to the prepared baking sheet, making 12 meringues in all.
5 Put the meringues into the oven, then turn down to 110C/200F/Gas Mark ¼. Bake the meringues for 1½–2 hours, until dried out.

6 Turn the oven off and leave the meringues to cool in the oven. Remove the meringues from the lining paper with a palette knife.
7 Whip the cream and use this to sandwich the meringues together in pairs. Serve as soon as possible.

Variations
HAZELNUT MERINGUES
Fold 50 g/2 oz roasted, skinned and finely ground hazelnuts into the meringues after the sugar has been added. These are delicious sandwiched with cream, as described, and served as a dessert, with Hot Chocolate Sauce (p. 300).

MINIATURE MERINGUES
Make as described, but drop heaped teaspoons of mixture on to the baking sheet; or use a piping bag fitted with a 1-cm/½-inch shell nozzle to make tiny meringues. Bake for 1½–2 hours. Sandwich together in pairs as described.

Using Broken Meringues

Crush the meringues even more so that they are in bite-sized pieces, then fold them into whipped cream. Or, to make a wonderful pudding, crush a whole batch of meringues, fold into 300 ml/10 fl oz lightly-whipped whipping cream, then gently mix in a purée made from 450 g/1 lb blackcurrants, cooked, sweetened and sieved, to give a ripple effect. Cover and keep in the freezer until required. A useful pudding to have in the freezer as it can be served without thawing.

Piping Tip

Many people feel nervous about using a piping bag because they hardly get any practice. The way to become an expert is to have to hand a plastic piping bag, fitted with a star nozzle, and every time you're serving cream or have some butter icing over, have some fun piping it (and let eager children try, too!). Or even make up a batch of butter icing and keep practising with it. It's surprising how quickly you can get the knack, and once you have, it's satisfying to be able to give a cake a professional look quickly and easily.

ÉCLAIRS

MAKES 8

1 quantity Choux Pastry (p. 271)
300 ml / 10 fl oz whipping cream, whipped
100 g / 4 oz chocolate, melted

1 Preheat the oven to 200C/400F/Gas Mark 6.
2 Grease a baking sheet then moisten it under the cold tap.
3 Pipe or spoon the choux pastry mixture on to the baking sheet to make strips about 10 cm/4 inches long and 2.5 cm/1 inch wide.
4 Bake for about 35 minutes, until crisp and golden.
5 Make a slit in the side of each éclair, then cool on a wire rack.

6 Just before serving, fill the éclairs with whipped cream, piping it into the slit in the side of each éclair, then carefully dip each top into the melted chocolate and leave for a few minutes to set.

Variation
PROFITEROLES
Pipe or spoon the choux pastry into small balls, about the size of walnuts. Bake for 15–20 minutes, slit and cool. Fill each with cream, then pile up in a pyramid shape on a flat serving dish or cake stand and pour some Hot Chocolate Sauce (p. 300) over the top. Serve the rest of the sauce in a jug.

V

GLACÉ ICING

V

TO TOP A 20–23-cm/8–9 inch ROUND CAKE

175 g/6 oz icing sugar
1–2 tablespoons water

1 Sift the icing sugar into a mixing bowl and beat in the water a little at a time. Continue beating in until you have a thick mixture.
2 Use the icing immediately to ice one large cake or 18 small buns.

V

SIMPLE BUTTERCREAM

V

TO TOP AND FILL, OR COAT, A 20-cm/8-inch ROUND CAKE

Meringues and Hazelnut Meringues (p. 314)

100 g/4 oz butter or vegan margarine
200 g/7 oz icing sugar
1–2 tablespoons hot water

1 Beat the butter or vegan margarine in a mixing bowl until creamy, then sift in the icing sugar and beat again until light.
2 Add enough hot water to loosen the mixture a little, beating well.

Variations

CHOCOLATE BUTTERCREAM
Melt 50 g/2 oz plain chocolate, or dissolve 1–2 tablespoons cocoa powder in hot water; beat into the mixture.

COFFEE BUTTERCREAM
Dissolve 2 teaspoons good-quality strong instant coffee (continental or espresso type) in a little hot water; beat into the mixture.

VANILLA BUTTERCREAM
Add a few drops of vanilla extract.

LEMON OR ORANGE
BUTTERCREAM
Add 1 teaspoon grated orange or lemon rind to the mixture, and replace 1 tablespoon of the water with orange or lemon juice.

REDUCED SUGAR
BUTTERCREAM
Replace 50 g/2 oz of the icing sugar with skim milk powder. Beat well.

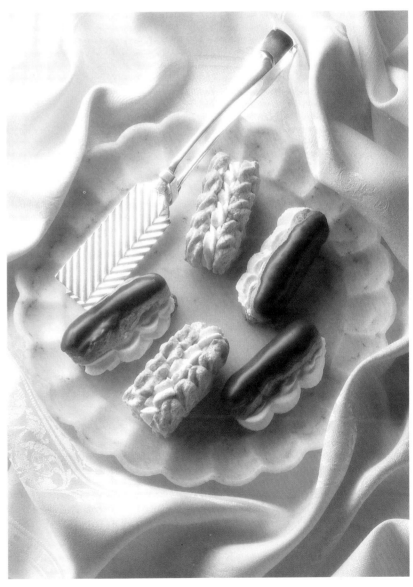

FRENCH BUTTERCREAM

This is light and delicately flavoured, worth the extra effort involved, although it isn't difficult to make.

TO TOP AND FILL, OR COAT, A 20-cm/8-inch ROUND CAKE

2 egg yolks
50 g/2 oz vanilla sugar, or caster sugar and a
  few drops of vanilla extract
120 ml/4 fl oz milk
250 g/9 oz unsalted butter

1 Whisk the egg yolks with half the vanilla sugar or caster sugar until the mixture is pale and light.
2 Heat the milk with the rest of the sugar in a heavy-based saucepan, then pour on to the egg yolks. Return to the pan and stir until the mixture coats the back of the spoon.
3 Remove from the heat and allow to cool, then strain.

4 Beat the butter until light and fluffy, then gradually beat in the custard mixture a little at a time, and the vanilla extract if used.

Variations
COFFEE BUTTERCREAM
Make as described, adding 2 teaspoons good-quality strong instant coffee (continental or espresso type) to the hot milk and stirring until dissolved. Omit the vanilla.

CHOCOLATE BUTTERCREAM
Melt 50 g/2 oz plain chocolate and add to the butter with the custard.

CREAM CHEESE FROSTING

TO TOP AND FILL, OR COAT, A 23-cm/9-inch ROUND CAKE

225 g/8 oz cream cheese
50 g/2 oz butter, softened
50 g/2 oz soft light brown sugar
a few drops of vanilla extract

1 Put all the ingredients into a mixing bowl.
2 Beat well until thoroughly blended, light and fluffy.

V # FUDGE ICING V

The flavouring of fudge icing can be varied as suggested for Simple Buttercream (p. 315).

TO TOP AND FILL, OR COAT, A 20–23-cm/8–9-inch ROUND CAKE

50 g/2 oz butter or vegan margarine
3 tablespoons water
250 g/9 oz icing sugar
a few drops of vanilla extract

1 Heat the butter or vegan margarine and water in a saucepan until melted. Remove from the heat and sift in the icing sugar.
2 Add the vanilla and beat well. The icing will thicken up as it cools.

FONDANT ICING

TO COAT A 20–23-cm/8–9-inch ROUND CAKE

450 g / 1 lb icing sugar
¼ teaspoon cream of tartar
1 egg white

1 Sift the icing sugar with the cream of tartar into a mixing bowl.

2 Whisk the egg white lightly, just to break it up, then gradually stir it into the icing sugar mixture, to give a firm but pliable consistency.
3 Roll the icing out on a surface dusted with icing sugar.

Cake Decorations

Fondant icing is easy to use because you simply roll it out. Decorations can be cut out with pastry cutters; children's pastry-making sets have some interesting shapes.

ALMOND PASTE

TO COAT A 20–23-cm/8–9-inch ROUND CAKE

450 g / 1 lb ground almonds
450 g / 1 lb soft light brown or caster sugar
1 teaspoon lemon juice
a few drops of almond essence
2 eggs, beaten

1 Mix all the ingredients together in a mixing bowl to give a pliable consistency. Do not over-work the mixture or it may become oily.
2 Use immediately, or keep wrapped in clingfilm.

Crystallized Violets and Rose Petals

A pretty, fragrant garnish for ice cream, cheesecake, sorbet or a special cake. Wash the violets or rose petals gently, shake dry. Beat an egg white until frothy, then dip the rose petals or violets first into this then into caster sugar, to coat thoroughly. Spread out on baking sheets lined with non-stick baking parchment and bake in a very cool oven (lowest setting) until dry and crisp. Cool completely on wire racks, then store in an airtight tin.

ROYAL ICING

TO COAT A 20-cm/8-inch ROUND CAKE

4 egg whites
900 g / 2 lb icing sugar, sifted
1 tablespoon lemon juice
2 tablespoons glycerine

1 Whisk the egg whites until frothy, then gradually whisk in all the other ingredients.
2 Whisk until the mixture thickens and stands in peaks. Use immediately.

7-MINUTE FROSTING

This icing sets crisp on the outside with a soft, marshmallowy texture inside.

TO COAT A 23-cm/9-inch ROUND CAKE

2 large egg whites
350 g / 12 oz caster sugar
4 tablespoons water
¼ teaspoon salt
¼ teaspoon cream of tartar

1 Put all the ingredients into a mixing bowl and whisk until foamy.
2 Set the bowl over a saucepan of simmering water (making sure that the bowl does not touch the water) and whisk until the mixture stands in soft peaks – about 7 minutes. Use immediately.

MENU

Christmas Dinner

SERVES 8

Avocado on a Raspberry Coulis
148

Brazil Nut Roast en Croûte
236

Vegetarian Gravy
172

Cranberry Sauce
174

Bread Sauce
175

Julienne of Carrots
184

Brussels Sprouts

Christmas Pudding with Brandy Butter
296

All the traditional Christmas flavours – apart from the turkey, of course – are present in this dinner, and the Brazil Nut Roast en Croûte makes a handsome centre-piece. This can be made well in advance and kept in the fridge for a day or two, or frozen for up to 4 weeks. The pudding, of course, can also be made several weeks beforehand and kept in a cool, dry place. The Cranberry Sauce and Vegetarian Gravy can be made the day before. The Raspberry Coulis for the first course can be made the day before, too, but the dish needs to be assembled not more than an hour before you want to eat it. Garnish it with holly berries, but remove them before serving.

The nut and herb flavours in the roast need a firm wine to stand up to them, such as a Châteauneuf-du-Pape; or, if you prefer a white, choose a sturdy medium-dry one.

Biscuits

Biscuits are easy and rewarding to make and delightful for when you want to offer something light with a cup of tea or coffee, or for giving a crisp texture to a smooth pudding such as a fruit fool or ice cream. Biscuits also make appealing gifts, packed in pretty boxes or jars, decorated with coloured ribbons, fabric or paper flowers and tissue paper. There are many different types, ranging from the quick tray bakes, such as Flapjacks, Easy Shortbread and Date Fingers, in which the mixture goes straight into the tin and is cut up after it is cooked, to the more fiddly but delicious Brandysnaps (p. 324) and Almond Tuiles (p. 325).

Freezing Biscuits

Biscuits freeze excellently; cool them thoroughly, then spread them out on a tray and freeze until solid. Pack in a rigid container.

Biscuits do not take long to thaw; put them in a single layer on a wire rack and leave at room temperature for 30–60 minutes.

V ## FLAPJACKS V

One of the quickest recipes ever, flapjacks keep well in an airtight tin.

MAKES 12–16

175 g/6 oz butter or vegan margarine
175 g/6 oz real barbados sugar
2 tablespoons golden syrup
225 g/8 oz rolled oats

1 Preheat the oven to 190 c/375 f/Gas Mark 5.
2 Grease an 18 × 28-cm/7 × 11-inch Swiss roll tin.
3 Melt the butter or vegan margarine, sugar and syrup gently in a saucepan. Remove from the heat and mix in the oats.
4 Spread the mixture into the tin and press down evenly with the back of the spoon. Bake for 20–30 minutes, until brown all over.
5 Mark into fingers while still hot, then leave in the tin until cold. The flapjacks become firm as they cool.

V ## EASY SHORTBREAD V

MAKES 12 PIECES

175 g/6 oz butter or vegan margarine
75 g/3 oz soft light brown sugar
250 g/9 oz plain 85% wholewheat flour

1 Preheat the oven to 150 c/300 f/Gas Mark 2.
2 Beat the butter or vegan margarine with the sugar until blended, then add the flour and mix together to form a dough.
3 Knead the dough on a floured surface, then press into a 20-cm/8-inch flan tin and prick the top all over with a fork.
Bake for 1¼–1½ hours until set and just beginning to turn golden.
4 Mark the shortbread into sections with a sharp knife, then leave to cool completely in the tin.

Variation
SHORTBREAD BISCUITS
Make the mixture as described, then roll it out about 3 mm/⅛ inch thick. Cut into circles, place on a baking sheet and bake for about 30 minutes.

ICEBOX COOKIES

MAKES ABOUT 80

100 g / 4 oz butter
200 g / 7 oz vanilla sugar, or caster sugar and
  ½ teaspoon vanilla extract
1 large egg
225 g / 8 oz plain 85% wholewheat flour
2 teaspoons baking powder
a pinch of salt

1 Cream the butter with the sugar and vanilla extract if used.
2 Beat in the egg, then sift the flour with the baking powder and salt on top. Mix well, to make a dough.
3 Turn the dough on to a lightly floured surface and form into a sausage about 5 cm / 2 inches in diameter. Wrap in clingfilm and chill for several hours.
4 When you're ready to bake the biscuits, preheat the oven to 190 C / 375 F / Gas Mark 5.
5 Using a sharp knife, cut 3-mm / ⅛-inch slices from the cookie roll and place on baking sheets, leaving room for spreading.
6 Bake for 8–10 minutes, until the cookies are just turning brown at the edges. Remove from the oven and transfer to a wire rack to cool completely.

Icebox Cookies Tip

This dough will keep in the icebox of the refrigerator for up to 2 weeks, ready for you to cut thin slices off it for baking whenever you want fresh biscuits.

V   DATE FINGERS   V

MAKES 12–16

225 g / 8 oz dates (not sugar-rolled), chopped
150 ml / 5 fl oz water
225 g / 8 oz self-raising 85% or 100%
  wholewheat flour
½ teaspoon salt
100 g / 4 oz butter or vegan margarine
3 tablespoons cold water, to mix

1 Preheat the oven to 200 C / 400 F / Gas Mark 6.
2 Put the dates into a saucepan with the water and cook gently for 5 minutes until soft and the liquid is absorbed.
3 Mash the dates, carefully discarding any hard pieces of stem or stone. Cool.
4 Put the flour into a mixing bowl with the salt. Rub in the fat with your fingertips until the mixture looks like fine breadcrumbs.
5 Add the 3 tablespoons water, then press the mixture together to make a dough. Roll out half to fit an 18 × 28-cm / 7 × 11-inch Swiss roll tin.
6 Spread the date mixture on top of the pastry. Roll out the rest of the pastry to fit the top, press into position and trim the edges.
7 Prick the pastry all over with a fork. Bake for 30 minutes, until firm and lightly browned.
8 Cool for 30 minutes in the tin, then cut into fingers, ease out of the tin and place on a wire rack to cool completely.

Date Fingers

V   # OATCAKES   V

These are thin, crisp oatcakes, based on the recipe given in one of my favourite books, *Don't Mix Foods which Fight*, by Doris Grant and Jean Joice. Make sure the oatmeal smells and tastes really fresh.

MAKES 16

Serving Idea for Biscuits

Home-made biscuits look wonderful served in a shallow basket; have at least two varieties and pile them up generously. Presented like this, biscuits can be served as a quick and easy pudding.

Storing Biscuits

Store biscuits in an airtight tin to keep them fresh and crisp.

½ teaspoon salt
1 teaspoon unsalted butter or vegan margarine
120 ml / 4 fl oz boiling water
150 g / 5 oz medium oatmeal
flour for rolling out

1 Preheat the oven to 180 C / 350 F / Gas Mark 4.
2 Stir the salt and butter or vegan margarine into the boiling water, then add to the oatmeal in a bowl. Mix well, then leave for 2–3 minutes to allow the oatmeal to swell.
3 Turn the oat mixture on to a floured board and knead lightly.

4 Divide into 2 pieces. Roll each piece into a circle about 10 cm / 4 inches in diameter, then cut each circle into 8 triangles.
5 Roll each triangle as thinly as possible, rolling from cut edge to cut edge (not from the outer edge to the point) to make a good wedge shape.
6 Using a fish slice, transfer the oatcakes to a baking sheet and bake for 20–25 minutes, carefully turning them over halfway through the cooking time, until the oatcakes are pale golden, crisp and curled at the edges.
7 Transfer to a wire rack and leave to cool completely.

CRUNCHY PEANUT COOKIES

These cookies are quick to make and very popular, especially with children. They freeze well and thaw rapidly.

MAKES ABOUT 36

Choosing Peanut Butter

Look for a variety which does not contain emulsifiers and other additives. It may have a layer of oil on top (because of the lack of emulsifiers), but this is normal; just stir the peanut butter before using it.

65 g / 2½ oz butter or vegan margarine
65 g / 2½ oz soft light brown sugar
65 g / 2½ oz vanilla sugar, or caster sugar and a few drops of vanilla extract
1 egg
50 g / 2 oz crunchy peanut butter
100 g / 4 oz plain 85% wholewheat flour
1 teaspoon baking powder
½ teaspoon salt
50 g / 2 oz chopped roasted peanuts (if salted, omit the ½ teaspoon salt)

1 Preheat the oven to 180 C / 350 F / Gas Mark 4.
2 Cream the butter or vegan margarine with the sugars and vanilla, if used, then add the egg and peanut butter, and beat again until light.
3 Sift in the flour with the baking

powder and salt and mix in. Add the peanuts and mix again, until thoroughly combined.
4 Roll teaspoons of the mixture into small balls, then place on a greased baking sheet, allowing plenty of room for spreading, and flatten them slightly.
5 Bake for 12–15 minutes. Cool slightly, then transfer to a wire rack to cool completely.

Variation
CHOCOLATE OR CAROB CHIP COOKIES
For this delicious variation, leave out the peanut butter and peanuts. Stir in 100 g / 4 oz chocolate or carob chips and 25 g / 1 oz chopped skinned hazelnuts after adding the flour.

CRUNCHY ORANGE BISCUITS

MAKES 20–24

100 g/4 oz butter
75 g/3 oz soft light brown sugar
1 egg
grated rind of 1 orange
100 g/4 oz self-raising 81% or 85%
  wholewheat flour
crushed wheatflakes, cornflakes or flaked
  almonds for coating
extra butter for greasing

1 Preheat the oven to 180C/350F/Gas Mark 4.
2 Grease one or two large baking sheets.

3 Cream the butter with the sugar, then beat in the egg and grated orange rind. Add the flour and mix until the ingredients are combined.
4 Roll heaped teaspoons of the mixture in crushed wheatflakes, cornflakes or flaked almonds.
5 Place the little balls on the baking sheets, allowing a little space for spreading, and flatten them slightly.
6 Bake for 15 minutes, until golden-brown. Transfer to a wire rack to cool completely.

*Left to right: Oatcakes (p. 322);
Crunchy Peanut Cookies (p. 322);
Crunchy Orange Biscuits; Gingersnaps
(p. 325)*

V   # CRUMBLY ALMOND BISCUITS   V

The best biscuits of all, in the opinion of my 8-year-old daughter, Claire. They are excellent for serving with tea or coffee, or with ice creams, fools and fruit salads.

MAKES 40

125 g/4½ oz butter or vegan margarine
65 g/2½ oz vanilla sugar or caster sugar and
  a few drops of vanilla extract
115 g/4½ oz plain 85% wholewheat flour
¼ teaspoon salt
25 g/1 oz flaked almonds, crushed
15 g/½ oz flaked almonds
extra butter for greasing

1 Preheat the oven to 170C/325F/Gas Mark 3.
2 Cream the butter or vegan margarine

with the sugar until light and fluffy.
3 Sift the flour with the salt into the bowl, then stir this into the creamed mixture, with the crushed almonds.
4 Roll teaspoonfuls into small balls, then place on a greased baking sheet, allowing plenty of room for spreading. Flatten the biscuits with the prongs of a fork. Decorate with flaked almonds.
5 Bake for 25 minutes, until golden. Cool slightly, then transfer to a wire rack to cool completely.

V # BRANDYSNAPS V

A delicious treat on their own, and also an excellent
accompaniment to a creamy pudding or fruit salad, brandysnaps
are easy to make if you use non-stick baking parchment and don't
try to roll them up too soon.

MAKES 20

Serving Ideas for Biscuits

Brandysnaps, filled with cream, make a luxurious accompaniment to a simple fruit salad, for a special meal.

Serve fruit salad, ice cream, sorbet or fool in a thin, crisp 'cup' made from an almond tuile.

If you haven't time to make a pudding or just want to serve something light, arrange several types of home-made biscuits in a pretty basket and offer with coffee or with little bowls of chilled strained Greek yogurt.

50 g / 2 oz butter or vegan margarine
100 g / 4 oz caster sugar
50 g / 2 oz golden syrup
50 g / 2 oz plain 85% wholewheat flour, sifted
½ teaspoon ground ginger
½ teaspoon grated lemon rind
a little oil
FOR THE FILLING (OPTIONAL)
150 ml / 5 fl oz double or non-dairy cream, whipped, with 1–2 tablespoons brandy (optional)

1 Preheat the oven to 180 C / 350 F / Gas Mark 4.
2 Melt the butter or vegan margarine, sugar and syrup gently in a small saucepan.
3 Remove from the heat and stir in the flour, ginger and lemon rind. Cool.
4 Line a large baking sheet with non-stick baking parchment.

5 Drop 2 heaped teaspoons of the mixture on to the baking sheet, placing them well apart, then flatten them slightly. Bake for 7–8 minutes, until evenly browned.
6 Cool on the tray for 3–4 minutes, until you can comfortably pick up the brandysnaps. Quickly roll them up, by wrapping them round the oiled handle of a wooden spoon. Slide them off on to a wire rack. If the brandysnaps harden before you manage to roll them up, pop them back into the oven for a minute or two to soften up.
7 Make the rest of the brandysnaps in the same way; the same non-stick baking parchment can be used for the whole batch.
8 Serve the brandysnaps plain, or fill the ends with whipped cream, with the brandy added if liked, using a teaspoon or a piping bag fitted with a shell nozzle.

Brandysnaps

GINGERSNAPS

These ever-popular ginger biscuits are easy to make, crisp and delicious. They keep well either in the freezer or in a tin.

MAKES 36

50 g/2 oz butter
100 g/4 oz caster sugar
40 g/1½ oz golden syrup
1 tablespoon beaten egg
175 g/6 oz self-raising 85% wholewheat flour
1 teaspoon bicarbonate of soda
1 teaspoon ground ginger
extra butter for greasing

1 Preheat the oven to 180C/350F/Gas Mark 4.

2 Cream the butter with the sugar and syrup, then add the egg and beat again until light.
3 Sift in the wholewheat flour, bicarbonate of soda and ground ginger, then mix to a dough.
4 Divide the dough into 36 small pieces, roll each into a ball and place well apart on greased baking sheets.
5 Bake for 12–15 minutes. Cool slightly, then transfer to a wire rack to cool completely.

Gingersnap Dessert Log

Gingersnaps can be made into a delicious dessert log. Sandwich the biscuits together with whipped double cream, to make a log shape. Cover with more cream and decorate with chopped crystallized ginger. Chill for 3–4 hours to allow the biscuits to soften in the cream and for the flavours to blend.

ALMOND TUILES

These thin, crisp biscuits make an ideal accompaniment to ice creams and light, fruity desserts. They can also be made larger, to make edible petal cases for holding ice cream.

MAKES 16

2 egg whites
100 g/4 oz vanilla sugar, or caster sugar and ½ teaspoon vanilla extract
50 g/2 oz plain 85% wholewheat flour
50 g/2 oz butter, melted
50 g/2 oz flaked almonds

1 Preheat the oven to 190C/375F/Gas Mark 5.
2 Line a large baking sheet with non-stick baking parchment.
3 Whisk the egg whites until frothy, then whisk in the sugar. Gently mix in the flour, butter and almonds.
4 Spread the mixture on the prepared baking sheet, making circles about 10 cm/4 inches across. Bake for 7–8 minutes, until flecked with golden-brown.
5 Allow the biscuits to stand for a second or two, then immediately lift them off the baking sheet with a spatula and place over the rim of a large empty bowl or over a stick balanced over 2 cans, so that they harden into a curved tuile shape.

6 Make the rest of the tuiles in the same way, re-using the paper. When the biscuits are cool, put into an airtight tin.

Variations
CIGARETTES RUSSES
Make as described, but omit the almonds. As you take the biscuits off the baking tray, roll them tightly round a greased wooden spoon handle. Cool slightly, then ease the rolled biscuits off the handle and place on a wire rack.

FLOWER CUPS FOR HOLDING ICE CREAM
To make these, draw 15-cm/6-inch circles on non-stick baking parchment and spread the uncooked mixture into these. Bake for about 10–15 minutes. As you take the biscuits off the baking sheet, put them over a lightly oiled upturned tumbler, pressing them down with your hands to make a cup shape and pulling the edges out slightly to give a petal effect.

Biscuit-making Tips

Make the biscuits the same size and thickness so that they take the same amount of time to cook.

Use a flat baking tin or sheet to enable the heat of the oven to reach the sides of the biscuits.

Cooking sticky biscuits like brandysnaps on a tin lined with non-stick paper makes it easy to lift them off when they are done.

Leave space around the biscuits to allow them to spread during cooking. Some biscuits, such as brandysnaps, spread considerably.

Let the biscuits cool for a few minutes on the tin before removing with a spatula and placing on a wire rack to cool.

Biscuits which are to be rolled or shaped after baking, such as brandysnaps and almond tuiles, need to cool on the baking sheet until they are firm enough to lift but still pliable. Once you've made the first batch, you soon recognize this stage. If the biscuits harden too much, they will soften again if you pop them back into the oven for a minute or two.

Bread and Scones

Nothing ensures your reputation as a good cook more quickly than making your own bread, and there is something particularly satisfying about being able to offer friends and family your own home-baked bread. Yet making bread from a simple recipe is no more difficult than making a cake. This chapter contains my favourite recipes for yeast breads together with a selection of non-yeasted breads and scones, which are also easy to bake and make a pleasant change. If you like bread, it's worth making a bigger batch of the Quick and Easy Wholewheat Bread (p. 328); simply double or treble all the ingredients.

Quick and Easy Wholewheat Bread (p. 328)

Making Tea and Herb Tea

The method for making tea is the same, whether you are using herb or flower tea, or traditional tea leaves. Warm the pot and, if you like normally strong tea, put in a teaspoon of tea for each person and, if it's for more than three people, an extra spoon for the pot. If, like me, you like weak tea without milk, use less tea. I use just 1 teaspoon to the pot; it's a question of personal taste. Bring a kettle of fresh cold water to the boil, then pour this on to the tea. Leave to infuse for 2–3 minutes for China or herb tea, 4–5 minutes for Indian tea, then strain into cups. Add milk or slices of lemon as required. For herb teas, try adding a little cinnamon or a dash of fragrant honey.

Herb Teas

Many different herb teas are available; buy in small quantities and experiment until you find the ones that you like. Try serving scones, muffins and teabreads with herb teas instead of ordinary tea. Individual herb teas have healing properties:

PEPPERMINT Helps digestive upsets

COMFREY Has cleansing properties

CAMOMILE Calming and sleep-inducing

LEMON VERBENA and LEMON GRASS Perks you up, good as a tonic

GOLDENROD A natural diuretic, helps get rid of excess fluid

LIME BLOSSOM Helps you relax

EASY WHOLEWHEAT SCONES

Serve with butter and clear honey, or with jam and cream.

MAKES 10

225 g/8 oz 100% brown flour
2 teaspoons baking powder
50 g/2 oz butter
25 g/1 oz sugar
1 egg, whisked and made up to 150 ml/5 fl oz with milk

1 Preheat the oven to 220 C/425 F/Gas Mark 7.
2 Sift the flour with the baking powder into a mixing bowl, then add the butter and rub in with your fingertips. Mix in the sugar. Add the egg and milk and mix to a soft but not sticky dough.
3 Turn the dough out on to a floured board and knead lightly, then press out to a depth of at least 1 cm/½ inch.
4 Cut the scones out with a 5-cm/2-inch round cutter and place them on a floured baking sheet.
5 Bake for 12–15 minutes, until the scones are golden-brown and the sides spring back when lightly pressed. Cool on a wire rack, or serve immediately.

Variations
VEGAN SCONES
Use 150 ml/5 fl oz soya milk instead of the egg and milk, and 75 g/3 oz vegan margarine instead of the butter, for extra richness.

CHEESE SCONES
These are delicious to eat warm from the oven, for a quick lunch or supper. They're good buttered, with a little salad, and some fresh, firm tomatoes and crisp celery sticks. Omit the sugar. Add ½ teaspoon mustard powder and 40 g/1½ oz grated cheese to the mixture. Sprinkle another 40 g/1½ oz grated cheese on top of the scones before baking.

RAISIN SCONES
Add 50–100 g/2–4 oz raisins to the mixture. ½ teaspoon mixed spice or cinnamon is also a pleasant addition.

LIGHT BROWN SCONES
Replace the flour with 85% flour, or half wholewheat and half plain unbleached flour.

CRANBERRY SCONES
For this Christmas version, add 100 g/4 oz cooked sweetened cranberries to the mixture and a good pinch of ground cloves. Cook as above.

Clockwise from top: Wholewheat
Banana Teabread (p. 330); Bran,
Honey and Sultana Muffins; Easy
Wholewheat Scones (p. 326)

V — BRAN, HONEY AND SULTANA
MUFFINS
— V

These healthy muffins are quick and easy to make and are delicious
served warm from the oven. You can use raisins instead of sultanas
or a mixture of both, if preferred.

MAKES 12

75 g/3 oz plain 100% wholewheat flour
25 g/1 oz bran
3 teaspoons baking powder
a pinch of salt
75 g/3 oz sultanas
50 g/2 oz clear honey
4 tablespoons sunflower oil
100 ml/3–4 fl oz water
a little extra oil for greasing

1 Preheat the oven to 180 C/350 F/Gas
Mark 4. Grease a 12-section bun tin.

2 Put the flour and bran into a mixing
bowl with the baking powder, salt and
sultanas. Add the honey, sunflower oil
and water.
3 Mix well to make a batter-like consistency.
4 Spoon the mixture into the bun tin,
dividing the mixture equally among the
sections.
5 Bake for 15–20 minutes, until the
muffins are risen and feel firm to a light
touch. Serve warm.

Making Coffee

The traditional way to make coffee
is to put coarse grounds into a pot,
pour on almost boiling water, cover,
leave to infuse for 4 minutes, then
strain into cups. Allow 50 g/2 oz
coffee to 600 ml/1 pint water.

My favourite ways of making coffee
are the filter method, pouring
almost boiling water on to finely
ground coffee in a filter and letting it
drip through into a jug; and in a
cafetière, where you put
medium-ground coffee into the
cafetière, pour on the water, leave to
infuse for 4 minutes, then push the
plunger down into the coffee,
pushing the coffee grounds to the
bottom of the pot.

V QUICK AND EASY WHOLEWHEAT V BREAD

This bread can be made in a variety of shapes.

MAKES ONE 450-g/1-lb LOAF

SHAPING BREAD DOUGH IN A LOAF TIN

1 Press out the dough so that its width is the same as the length of the tin

2 Form the dough into a loose roll

3 Place the roll of dough into the tin, seam-side down

4 Push the dough down well into the corners and sides of the tin, to encourage it to form a dome-shaped loaf

325 ml/8–10 fl oz tepid water
1 teaspoon sugar
2 teaspoons dried yeast
450 g/1 lb 100% wholewheat flour or
    350 g/12 oz wholewheat flour and
    100 g/4 oz unbleached white flour
2 teaspoons salt
butter or oil for greasing
TOPPING
sesame seeds
rolled oats
poppy seeds
crack wheat or
wholewheat flour

1 Put half the water into a measuring jug with half the sugar and the yeast; mix, then leave for 5–10 minutes to froth.
2 Grease a 450-g/1-lb loaf tin generously.
3 Put the flour into a bowl with the remaining sugar and the salt and make a well in the centre.
4 Pour in the frothed-up yeast, add the rest of the water and mix to a dough.
5 Turn out on to a clean work surface and knead for 10 minutes, until the dough is smooth, supple and silky.
6 Flatten the dough into a rectangle and gently roll it up to fit the tin. Put the roll into the tin with the fold underneath. Push it down into the sides and corners to give a nice domed shape to the loaf.
7 Cover with a clean tea-towel wrung out in hot water and put in a warm place for about 30 minutes to rise.
8 Preheat the oven to 180 C/350 F/Gas Mark 4.
9 When the dough has doubled in size and come right up out of the tin, sprinkle with any of topping ingredients and bake for 40–45 minutes.
10 Turn out of the tin. It should sound hollow, when you bang it on the base. Cool on a wire rack.

Variations

HERB AND ONION BREAD
Add 1 small finely chopped onion and ½ teaspoon each of oregano (or dill) and rosemary. Serve this bread warm.

THE GRANT LOAF
For this extra speedy variation, increase the water to 350 ml/12 fl oz to make a soft mixture. Don't knead; divide the mixture into two, shape the pieces as described and put each into a greased 450-g/1-lb tin. Leave to rise until the sides of the loaves are about 5 mm/¼ inch from the top of the tins. Bake for 30 minutes at 200 C/400 F/Gas Mark 6.

QUICK WHOLEWHEAT ROLLS
Rub 50 g/2 oz butter or vegan margarine into the flour, then use 150 ml/5 fl oz each of milk (or soya milk) and water to make the dough. Knead for 5 minutes, then put the dough into a clean, lightly oiled bowl, cover and leave in a warm place for about 1 hour, until doubled in bulk. Shape into 8–10 rolls, or rounds, plaits, knots, tricorns or miniature cottage loaves, and place well apart on a floured baking sheet. Cover and leave in a warm place for 15–20 minutes, until well risen. Bake for 15–20 minutes at 220 C/425 F/Gas Mark 7.

HOT CROSS BUNS
Make the dough as described for quick rolls. After the first rising, knead into the dough ½ teaspoon each of mixed spice, cinnamon and grated nutmeg, 75 g/3 oz currants, 50 g/2 oz chopped mixed peel and 25 g/1 oz sugar. Form into rolls, cut crosses out of 75 g/3 oz shortcrust pastry and place on top. Bake for 20 minutes. Heat 25 g/1 oz caster sugar in 2 tablespoons milk until dissolved; brush over the buns.

Guide to Bread Rising Times

Place	First rising times	Second rising times	Place	First rising times	Second rising times
In a warm place, 23 C/74 F, e.g. an airing cupboard, by a pilot light, near a radiator	45–60 mins	30 mins	In a refrigerator (brush with oil and cover bowl with clingfilm to prevent hard crust forming; leave at room temperature for 15 minutes before baking)	up to 24 hrs	up to 12 hrs
At room temperature, 18–21 C/65–70 F	1½–2 hrs	40–50 mins			
In a cool room or larder	8–12 hrs	2–3 hrs			

Proving Bread Dough

Bread will 'prove' or rise slowly in the refrigerator. Brush it with oil and cover with polythene. Leave for 12 hours. Let the bread stand at room temperature for 30 minutes before baking, while the oven heats up, to allow it to 'come to'.

POPPYSEED PLAIT

This is an attractive bread with a delicate flavour and a golden crust coated with poppy seeds.

MAKES 1 LARGE PLAIT

25 g/1 oz fresh yeast or 15 g/½ oz dried yeast plus ½ teaspoon sugar
450 ml/15 fl oz warm milk
700 g/1½ lb strong plain unbleached white flour
1½ teaspoons salt
1½ teaspoons sugar
50 g/2 oz butter
TO GLAZE
1 small egg, beaten
poppy seeds

1 Blend the yeast into the milk; for dried yeast, add the sugar, too, and leave for 10–15 minutes until frothy.
2 Put the flour, salt and sugar into a large mixing bowl and rub in the butter with the fingertips. Add the frothed-up yeast liquid and mix to a dough.
3 Knead for 10 minutes, put into a bowl, cover with polythene and leave until doubled in bulk – 1 hour in a warm place.
4 Knock back the dough, knead briefly, then make a plait: divide the dough into 3 equal pieces, roll each into a sausage about 30 cm/12 inches long, fat in the middle and tapering at the ends. Start plaiting from the centre, finishing the ends of the plait off in a neat point.
5 Place on a greased baking sheet, cover and leave to prove for 30 minutes, until puffy. Preheat the oven to 230 C/450 F/ Gas Mark 8.
6 Brush the plait with beaten egg, sprinkle with poppy seeds and bake for about 35 minutes. Cool on a wire rack.

Variations

VEGAN POPPYSEED PLAIT
Use soya milk instead of dairy milk and vegan margarine instead of butter. Brush the loaf with soya milk instead of egg.

SWEDISH TEA RING
Make the dough as described and let it rise in the bowl. Instead of making a plait, roll out to a rectangle 23 × 30 cm/ 9 × 12 inches. Brush with melted butter, then roll up like a Swiss roll, and join the ends to make a ring. Place on a baking sheet and using kitchen scissors make diagonal slashes 2.5 cm/1 inch apart. Pull open the cut sections. Leave to prove for 30 minutes, then bake at 190 C/375 F/Gas Mark 5 for 30–35 minutes. Decorate with icing, glacé cherries and almonds.

SHAPING POPPYSEED PLAIT

WHOLEWHEAT BANANA TEA BREAD

Serve this tea bread sliced and buttered.

MAKES ONE 450-g/1-lb LOAF

Clockwise from top right: Jasmine Tea; Camomile Tea; Peppermint Tea

50 g/2 oz butter
50 g/2 oz real barbados sugar
75 g/3 oz golden syrup or clear honey
225 g/8 oz self-raising 100% wholewheat
   flour
50 g/2 oz walnuts, chopped
2 ripe bananas, peeled and mashed
1 egg, beaten
extra butter for greasing

1 Preheat the oven to 180 C/350 F/Gas Mark 4. Grease a 450-g/1-lb loaf tin and line with a strip of greased greaseproof paper to cover the base of the tin and extend up the narrow sides.
2 Heat the butter, sugar and golden syrup or honey gently in a small saucepan until melted. Set aside to cool until you can comfortably put your hand against the saucepan: stand the pan in a bowl of cold water if you're in a hurry.

3 Put the flour into a mixing bowl with the chopped walnuts and mashed bananas. Add the cooled melted mixture and the egg. Mix well.
4 Spoon the mixture into the prepared tin. Bake for 40 minutes, or until a warmed skewer inserted into the centre of the loaf comes out clean.
5 Turn out on to a wire rack to cool. Strip off the lining paper.

Variations

VEGAN BANANA TEA BREAD
Use vegan margarine and 1 extra teaspoon baking powder. Replace the egg with 2 tablespoons soya milk.

DATE AND WALNUT LOAF
Make as described, using 100 g/4 oz chopped cooking dates and 2–3 tablespoons milk, instead of the bananas.

SODA BREAD

Soda bread needs to be eaten the day it is made, although it makes good toast the next day. I like it particularly with clear honey.

MAKES ONE 450-g/1-lb LOAF

Measuring Golden Syrup or Honey

If you can set your scales, place your mixing bowl or saucepan on the scale, set to zero, and pour in the golden syrup or honey until you have the right weight.

Or put the jar of honey or tin of golden syrup on the scales and remove it from the jar until the scales show you've taken out the quantity you need. Use a heated spoon to remove the honey or syrup from the jar, and flour the inside of your scale pan if you wish to transfer the honey or syrup to another container.

450 g/1 lb plain wholewheat and unbleached
   white flour mixed, or plain wheatmeal or
   scofa flour
1 teaspoon salt
2 teaspoons bicarbonate of soda
25 g/1 oz butter, softened
300 ml/10 fl oz buttermilk, sour milk, or
   milk warmed with 1 tablespoon vinegar to
   sour it

1 Preheat the oven to 220 C/425 F/Gas Mark 7. Flour a baking sheet.
2 Sift the flour, salt and bicarbonate of soda into a mixing bowl. Add the butter

and rub in with the fingertips until the mixture resembles fine breadcrumbs.
3 Make a well in the centre and pour in the milk, then gradually mix together to make a dough.
4 Turn the dough on to a floured board and knead it lightly, then form it into a round loaf.
5 Put the loaf on the prepared baking sheet and cut a cross shape in the top, using a sharp knife.
6 Bake the loaf for 30–35 minutes until it has risen and is golden-brown and crusty. Cool on a wire rack.

V   # CHAPATTIS   V

These round unleavened breads make an excellent accompaniment to curry or a lentil soup. Brush with a little melted butter or ghee before serving, if you like.

MAKES 12

250 g/9 oz plain 100% wholewheat flour
1½ teaspoons vegetable oil or ghee
1 teaspoon salt
about 150 ml/5 fl oz cold water

1 Put the flour into a mixing bowl with the oil or ghee, salt and water and mix to a soft dough.
2 Turn the dough out on a floured surface and knead for 5 minutes. Cover the dough with a damp cloth and leave for 2–3 hours, then knead again for a few minutes.
3 Divide the dough into 12 equal pieces. Form each into a ball, then roll out to a circle 15–20 cm/6–8 inches in diameter.
4 Fry the chapattis on both sides in an ungreased frying pan until set and lightly flecked with brown.
5 Pile the chapattis up on a plate as they're cooked, covering with a piece of foil to prevent them from drying out.

Ghee

A cooking fat which is much used in Indian cookery. To make ghee, melt 100–225 g/4–8 oz unsalted butter slowly in a saucepan, then cook it very gently for 30–45 minutes, until the sediment at the bottom of the pan has become a golden-brown. Strain the butter through a sieve lined with surgical gauze. Ghee can also be bought from supermarkets and Indian shops, and vegetable oil ghee is available.

Left to right: Quick Wholewheat Rolls (p. 328); Soda Bread (p. 330); Quick and Easy Wholewheat Bread (p. 328)

Sandwiches and Quick Snacks

Popular with everyone and the most practical of foods, sandwiches are also infinitely variable. They can be wafer-thin and delicate, enclosing a small amount of piquant filling, or rolled around some delicacy such as an asparagus spear, or rolled and sliced to make pinwheels, for serving at a formal occasion, with drinks or elegant cups of tea. Or sandwiches can be filling and easygoing for eating with friends round the kitchen table.

Bread for Sandwiches

The bread for sandwiches can be soft and light or crusty; any shade ranging from white to black, through various shades of brown, with or without added grains or flavourings. The bread can be a slicing loaf, cut either downwards or across; it can be a pitta pocket, French stick, slightly hollowed out and packed with filling, then cut into lengths for feeding a crowd; or it can be a soft or crusty roll, bap or scone.

Toasted Sandwich Fillings

Cheese, perhaps with tomato, pickle or thinly sliced onion is probably the best-known and most popular filling, but there are many other possibilities. The filling should be moist, but not so runny that it runs out. Aubergine Dip (p. 145), Mushroom and Herb Terrine (p. 146), Hummus (p. 144) or Guacamole (p. 144) are also good, as are red kidney beans, perhaps mashed with some tomato or tomato sauce. Cooked cauliflower florets mashed with mayonnaise and grated nutmeg, and creamy coleslaw also make good fillings, and, for perfection, cooked asparagus with lemony mayonnaise.

Toasted Sandwiches without a Toaster

If you haven't got a sandwich toaster, toast two pieces of bread on one side, spread with the filling, grill until heated through, then sandwich them together.

V PINWHEEL SANDWICHES V

Easy to make and attractive for a children's party or as part of a canapés selection. Prepare them in advance as they need chilling in the fridge.

MAKES ABOUT 50

100 g/4 oz soft butter or vegan margarine
2 tablespoons finely chopped parsley
2 tablespoons very finely chopped sweet red pepper
½ large sliced wholewheat loaf
TO GARNISH
thyme sprigs

1 Blend half the butter or vegan margarine with the parsley; in a separate bowl, blend the remaining half of the butter or vegan margarine with the chopped red pepper.
2 Cut the crusts off the bread and flatten each slice with a rolling pin.
3 Spread half the slices quite generously with the parsley butter and half with the red pepper butter.
4 Roll up the slices like a Swiss roll, from a long end.
5 Chill for 30–60 minutes, then slice thinly into rounds with a sharp knife and arrange on a plate to reveal the pinwheel effect.
6 Garnish with thyme sprigs.

V CLUB SANDWICH V

A chunky club sandwich with layers of toasted bread and different fillings turns a sandwich into a complete meal.

SERVES 1

3 slices wholewheat bread, toasted
butter or vegan margarine
a little wholegrain mustard
2 lettuce leaves
1 small tomato, sliced
a little Mayonnaise (p. 155), (optional)
1 slice Cashew Nut Roast (p. 230)
1 tablespoon sweet chutney or pickle
TO FINISH
4 stuffed olives

1 Spread one piece of toast with a little butter or vegan margarine and mustard and arrange the lettuce leaves, tomato slices and mustard or mayonnaise on top.
2 Spread another piece of toast on both sides with butter or vegan margarine, then top with the nut roast and chutney. Place on top of the other toast.
3 Spread the remaining piece of toast with butter or vegan margarine and place, spread-side down, on top.
4 Press down. Cut the sandwich into quarters.
5 Spear each quarter with a cocktail stick and decorate with a stuffed olive.

V TOASTED AVOCADO SANDWICH

SERVES 1

½ ripe avocado pear, peeled and stoned
1 spring onion, finely chopped
1–2 teaspoons lemon juice
salt and freshly ground black pepper
2 slices wholewheat bread
butter or vegan margarine for spreading

1 Heat a sandwich toaster.
2 Mash the avocado with the spring onion, lemon juice, salt and pepper.
3 Butter the bread on one side. Spread the unbuttered sides with the avocado mixture and sandwich together.
4 Toast for 4–5 minutes, until crisp and golden-brown. Serve immediately.

V OPEN SANDWICHES

SERVES 4

8 slices wholewheat or rye bread
butter or vegan margarine for spreading
8 radiccio leaves
½ endive
½ quantity Pink Potato Salad (p. 166)
1 × 425-g/15-oz can artichoke hearts, drained and sliced
8 radishes, sliced
8 dill sprigs, or a few chopped chives

1 Spread the bread lightly with butter or vegan margarine, then place on a flat serving dish.
2 Put one radiccio leaf and a sprig of endive on each piece of bread.
3 Top the radiccio with some Pink Potato Salad, artichoke heart slices, radish slices and dill or chives, making an attractive arrangement.

Open Sandwich Toppings

☐ Radiccio, Guacamole (p. 144) or mashed avocado, pink peppercorns
☐ Lettuce, scrambled egg, asparagus spears, parsley
☐ Watercress, sliced Lentil Loaf (p. 213), cranberry mayonnaise or mango chutney
☐ Lettuce, Hummus (p. 144), paprika, black olives and a drizzling of olive oil
☐ Lettuce, curd cheese, sliced ripe pear, halved black grapes
☐ Lettuce, slices of cheese and tomato, chopped parsley, stuffed green olives
☐ Watercress, coarsely grated carrot, mayonnaise, sliced tomato, Black Olive Pâté (p. 258)

Left to right: Open Sandwiches; Pinwheel Sandwiches (p. 332) and Asparagus Rolls (p. 334); Sandwich Gâteau (p. 335)

V FILLED PITTA V
POCKET

SERVES 1

1 wholewheat pitta bread
2 lettuce leaves, shredded
1 tomato, sliced
¼ quantity Continental Lentil and Walnut
   Salad (p. 158)

1 Slit the pitta bread at the top and ease it open, to make a pocket for the filling.
2 Fill the pitta bread with the lettuce, tomato and lentil salad.

V FILLED FRENCH V
BREAD

SERVES 4

2 wholewheat French sticks
butter, vegan margarine, mustard or
   mayonnaise
1 lettuce, washed and shredded
225 g/8 oz tomatoes, sliced
100 g/4 oz beansprouts
1 onion, peeled and sliced
1 × 425-g/15-oz can red kidney beans,
   drained
salt and freshly ground black pepper

1 Make a slit down the side of each French stick and scoop out a little of the crumb.
2 Spread the inside of each French loaf thinly with butter, vegan margarine, mustard or mayonnaise.
3 Fill each loaf with the vegetables and beans, and season with salt and pepper.
4 Press the slits together, wrap the loaves tightly in foil and chill until required, then cut each in half.

*French Bread, Tacos
and Pitta Bread Fillings*

Build these up into glorious colourful extravaganzas with your choice of:

☐ Shredded crisp lettuce, sliced tomato, spring onion, cucumber
☐ Cubes of cold nut or lentil loaf
☐ Sliced, grated or diced cheese
☐ Wedges of hardboiled egg
☐ Favourite Coleslaw (p. 161)
☐ Sliced red or green pepper, avocado pear, cooked asparagus tips or artichoke hearts
☐ Grated carrot, cauliflower, cooked or raw button mushrooms, sliced or whole
☐ Mayonnaise, Guacamole (p. 144), Sweet Pepper Dressing (p. 156)
☐ Juicy black olives, chopped fresh herbs, walnuts or pecans

Elegant Sandwich Fillings

☐ Scrambled egg with asparagus tips
☐ Duxelles or mushroom pâté
☐ Cream cheese or curd cheese with chopped herbs or chopped nuts
☐ Yeast extract or a thin spreading of light miso and wafer-thin cucumber slices
☐ Ripe avocado mashed with a little vinaigrette
☐ Finely grated cheese blended with cream, milk or curd cheese
☐ Herb butters (p. 118)
☐ Hummus (p. 144) with a little Black Olive Pâté (p. 258)

QUICK
BREAD PIZZA

SERVES 4

1 round or oval wholewheat loaf, about
   450 g/1 lb
olive oil
2 large onions, peeled and sliced
2 garlic cloves, crushed
1 × 425-g/15-oz can chopped tomatoes
oregano
salt and freshly ground black pepper
100 g/4 oz cheese, grated
8 black olives

1 Preheat the oven to 220 C/425 F/Gas Mark 7. Cut the loaf in half horizontally and scoop out some of the crumbs. Brush inside and outside the halved loaf with oil and place on a baking sheet.
2 Fry the onions in a tablespoon of oil for 10 minutes, then add the garlic and fry for a further minute or two.
3 Remove from heat and add tomatoes and a little oregano, salt and pepper.
4 Spoon the mixture on to the bread halves and sprinkle with grated cheese.
5 Bake for 15 minutes, then put on the olives and bake for a further 5–10 minutes. Serve hot.

V ASPARAGUS V
ROLLS

A pleasant tea-time or drinks'
party nibble.

MAKES ABOUT 40

½ sliced large wholewheat loaf
butter or vegan margarine
1 × 225-g/8-oz packet frozen asparagus
   spears, cooked and drained, or
   1 × 350-g/12-oz can asparagus spears,
   drained

1 Cut the crusts off the bread, then flatten each slice with a rolling pin.
2 Spread the slices thinly with butter or

vegan margarine, then wrap each piece of bread round an asparagus spear, cutting off any spare bread, so that the edges meet but do not overlap.

3 Cut each roll into 2 or 3 pieces so that they are a manageable size for eating.

4 Cover with clingfilm and keep in a cool place until needed.

CHEESE ON TOAST

SERVES 1

1–2 slices wholewheat bread
75–100 g / 3–4 oz cheese, grated
1–2 tablespoons milk
freshly ground black pepper

1 Heat the grill to high. Toast the bread on one side.

2 Blend the cheese to a paste with the milk, and season with pepper.

3 Spread the cheese mixture on the untoasted side of the bread and grill until puffed up and golden-brown. Serve immediately.

MOZZARELLA IN CARROZZA

SERVES 2

1 Mozzarella cheese
4 slices bread, crusts removed
2 eggs
oil for shallow frying

1 Cut the cheese into thin slices and arrange on 2 of the slices of bread. Top with the remaining slices.

2 Beat the eggs, then strain them into a shallow dish.

3 Put the sandwiches in the egg, leaving them to soak it up, and turning them over once.

4 Shallow-fry the sandwiches on both sides in a little oil, until golden-brown and crisp. Drain on kitchen paper and serve immediately.

SANDWICH GÂTEAU

This savoury gâteau looks attractive on a party table, when sliced to reveal the coloured layers.

SERVES 8

100 g / 4 oz soft butter
1 tablespoon finely chopped parsley
1 tablespoon finely chopped red pepper
2 hardboiled eggs, finely chopped
1–2 tablespoons Mayonnaise (p. 155)
salt and freshly ground black pepper
10 slices wholewheat bread
¼ quantity Hummus (p. 144)
450 g / 1 lb curd cheese
TO GARNISH
whole chives
thin radish slices
endive

1 Beat the butter, divide into equal portions. Beat the parsley into one half and the pepper into the other half.

2 Mix the eggs with mayonnaise to bind; season with salt and pepper.

3 Cut the crusts off the bread. Place 2 slices side by side on a serving platter and spread with the parsley butter.

4 Put 2 more slices on top, spread with the red pepper butter. Continue in this way with the rest of the bread, using the hummus and egg mayonnaise, building up the layers to make a gâteau shape. Finish with a layer of bread.

5 Spread the curd cheese over the top and sides of the gâteau. Arrange whole chives in a lattice pattern over the top of the gâteau. Halve the radish slices and arrange between the chives and around the edge of the gâteau. Arrange endive around the base of the gâteau. Chill for 1 hour in the fridge before serving.

School Lunch Box
Sandwich Fillings

Children have their own definite ideas about these – one of my daughters would only ever eat plain yeast extract sandwiches – and they generally like their sandwiches to look as much like everyone else's as possible. Here are some ideas:

☐ Yeast extract, miso, salad cream, peanut butter, sesame spread, curd or cream cheese with cucumber, lettuce, beansprouts, tomato or grated carrot

☐ Curd or cream cheese with finely chopped nuts or dates

☐ Mashed cooked red kidney beans with salad

☐ Chopped hardboiled egg mixed with salad cream or milk, or scrambled egg, with cress

☐ Grated carrot mixed with mayonnaise and chopped herbs or raisins

☐ Sliced or grated cheese with lettuce, tomato or cucumber

☐ Sliced banana, with or without peanut butter or sesame spread

☐ Honey and finely ground nuts

Iced Tea

Make the tea as described, then strain and chill. Serve with crushed ice and a slice of lemon and a sprig of mint or lemon balm, if liked. Iced herb teas make a specially good summer drink. For a fruity flavour, try Leslie Kenton's tip of adding a sliced peach to the tea before chilling.

Iced Coffee

Make coffee by the filter method, then chill. Serve in tall glasses with ice. Top with a spoonful of whipped cream, if liked, and hand sugar separately

MENU
Children's Tea

SERVES 4–6

Little Basket of Crudités
143

Yogurt and Herb Dressing
156

Potato and Cheese Layer
200

Fresh Tomato Sauce
170

Peas

Chocolate Ice Cream with Crumbly
Almond Biscuits
280 and 323

This is a substantial meal for children arriving home from school ravenous, and features dishes which in my experience are always popular. The Potato and Cheese Layer is easy to make but allow time for it to cook. It is served with Tomato Sauce, Crudités and Yogurt and Herb Dressing – many children will eat vegetables raw that they wouldn't eat cooked!

I've never quite been able to understand why children like the Chocolate Ice Cream so much, but they always do, and as it's a low-fat, low-sugar one, I'm not arguing! A Crumbly Almond Biscuit goes well with it, or you could serve some slices of fresh fruit. To drink, whatever is your child's favourite healthy drink of the moment; sparkling apple or grape juice is usually popular, or apple juice concentrate (p. 340), diluted with water or soda water.

Preserves and Chutneys

Home-made jams, jellies, preserves and chutneys add a delightful touch of luxury to a meal, yet are both easy and satisfying to make. If you're lucky enough to have fruit trees and bushes, a cheap source of fruit is readily available; but even if you have to buy them, at the peak of their seasons fruit and vegetables are likely to be inexpensive. Delicious with home-made bread and scones, jams and jellies also make excellent fillings and toppings. Chutneys and pickles, with their piquant, sweet and sour flavour, are excellent with cold nut and lentil roasts and burgers.

Preserving Pan

You need a preserving pan, or an extra large saucepan or saucepan part of a pressure-cooker, because the mixture needs plenty of room. Because of this, it's best not to make too much at a time. If you're using a microwave – which is a very clean way to make preserves – it's best to make in even smaller quantities (see recipe) and to use a large bowl.

Preparing Jam Jars

Wash jam jars thoroughly and sterilize them by drying them off in a cool oven, 140 C/275 F/Gas Mark 1. Fill the jars while they are still warm.

Covers for Jam Jars

Use cellophane covers for jam and plastic clip-on or Porasan covers for chutney. Wipe the jars after filling while still warm, but stick on the labels when the jars have cooled.

Sugar for Preserves

Granulated sugar is the cheapest and just as good as the more expensive preserving sugars (which give a particularly clear jelly) for normal use. Real brown sugar can be used, and gives a dark colour and mellow flavour to chutney and marmalade, but is not successful in jam, in my opinion. Whatever kind of sugar you use, make sure it is completely dissolved before the jam is boiled, or it may not set properly.

ROSE PETAL JAM

Use petals from unsprayed roses which have not been growing near a busy road. Cut away the white triangle at the base of each petal.

MAKES 900 g/2 lb

150 g/5 oz scented rose petals, washed and trimmed
750 ml/1¼ pints water
185 ml/6 fl oz lemon juice
600 g/1¼ lb sugar
5 tablespoons commercial pectin
3 tablespoons rose water

1 Put the petals, water, lemon juice and sugar into a large saucepan and heat gently until the sugar has dissolved.
2 Bring to the boil, then cover and simmer gently for 30 minutes.
3 Add the pectin and rose water, stir well, then boil hard for 5 minutes.
4 Test for a set (p. 339); if the jam is not ready, test again in 2 minutes, and keep testing until a set is reached.
5 Cool slightly, then pour into warmed sterilized jars (left). Cover, seal and label when completely cold.

PLUM JAM

Do not use any bruised or over-ripe plums for making jam as they will not give a good set and could cause the jam to ferment.

MAKES 2.25 kg/5 lb

1.4 kg/3 lb plums
450 ml/15 fl oz water
1.4 kg/3 lb sugar
a knob of butter

1 Wash the plums, then put them into a preserving pan with the water and simmer for about 30 minutes, until the fruit is soft.
2 Remove the pan from the heat and stir in the sugar. Stir well until the sugar has completely dissolved.
3 Bring to the boil, then boil hard for 10–15 minutes, stirring often.
4 Test for a set (p. 339) then, when this point is reached, stir in the butter.
5 Using a slotted spoon, remove the plum stones from the top of the jam.
6 Let the jam stand for 15 minutes to settle, then pour it into warmed, sterilized jars (left). Cover, seal and label when completely cold.

Variations

DAMSON JAM
Use the same recipe but you'll only need 1–1.1 kg/2½ lb of fruit. Test for a set after 7–10 minutes.

BLACKCURRANT JAM

Use 900 g / 2 lb blackcurrants, 900 ml / 1½ pints water and 1.4 kg / 3 lb sugar. Simmer the blackcurrants for 45 minutes, until the skins are really tender, before adding the sugar.

GOOSEBERRY JAM

Use 1.4 kg / 3 lb gooseberries, 600 ml / 1 pint water and 1.4 kg / 3 lb sugar. Cook the gooseberries in the water for 30 minutes, until soft.

STRAWBERRY JAM

MAKES 2.25 kg/5 lb

1.8 kg / 4 lb small, slightly under-ripe strawberries, hulled and wiped
1.6 kg / 3½ lb sugar
3 tablespoons fresh lemon juice
a small knob of butter

1 Put the strawberries into an enamel or stainless steel preserving pan with the sugar and leave for an hour or so, or overnight if convenient.
2 Add the lemon juice and heat slowly, over a very low heat, until the sugar has dissolved.
3 Return to the heat, bring to the boil and boil rapidly for 7–8 minutes, then remove from the heat and test for a set (see right).
4 If the jam isn't ready, return to the heat and test again in 2–3 minutes' time. Keep on testing until a set is reached.
5 Remove from the heat and stir in the butter.
6 Let the jam stand for 30 minutes, for the fruit to settle, then stir gently and pour into warmed, sterilized jars (p. 338). Cover, seal and label when cold.

Variation

RASPBERRY JAM

Make this in the same way, omitting the lemon juice, and using 1.8 kg / 4 lb raspberries and 1.8 kg / 4 lb sugar. After adding the sugar, boil the jam for about 30 minutes. Test for a set, then add the butter. Cover, seal and label when cold.

V MICROWAVE V
STRAWBERRY JAM

MAKES 700 g/1½ lb

450 g / 1 lb strawberries, washed and hulled
4 tablespoons fresh lemon juice
350 g / 12 oz caster sugar

1 Put the strawberries into a 2.4-litre/ 4-pint bowl with the lemon juice. Cook, uncovered, on full power for 5–6 minutes, until the strawberries are soft.
2 Add the sugar, stirring until dissolved.
3 Return the bowl to the oven and cook on full power for 20 minutes, stirring at the end of every 5 minutes.
4 Test for a set (see right); if the jam has not yet reached setting point, return the bowl to the oven for a further 1½ minutes, then test again. Continue this process until the jam sets.
5 Leave the jam to cool until tepid, then pour it into warmed, sterilized jars (p. 338).
6 Cover, seal and label when cold.

Testing for a Set

Setting point is reached when the jam or jelly reaches 104 C / 220 F on a sugar thermometer, or when a teaspoon of the mixture put on to a chilled saucer, and chilled for a few minutes in the freezing compartment of the fridge, wrinkles at the edges and does not run together again when you run your finger through it. It's important to take the pan off the heat while you test for a set, to avoid overcooking.

De-scumming Jam

Stirring in a knob of butter after setting point is reached helps disperse the surface scum on jam.

Clockwise from top right: Rose Petal Jam (p. 338); Lemon Curd (p. 341); Strawberry Jam; Mary's Marmalade (p. 341)

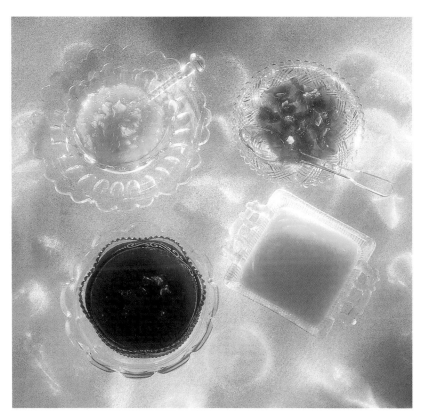

Fruit–Sugar Proportions in Jam

For fruits rich in pectin and acid, such as cooking apples, red and blackcurrants and gooseberries, the proportions are 600–700 g/ 1¼–1½ lb sugar to each 450 g/1 lb of fruit. For fruits with a moderate amount of pectin and acid, such as blackberries, loganberries and raspberries, allow 450 g/1 lb sugar to 450 g/1 lb fruit.

Fruit–Sugar Proportions in Jelly

Basic proportions are 450 g/1 lb sugar to each 600 ml/1 pint fruit juice.

Sugarless Jam and Jelly

I'm indebted to Jackie Applebee, of the Wholefood Cookery School, for this information on making sugarless jams and jellies, and for the sugarless jam recipes included in this book. The basic proportions are 450–700 g/1–1½ lb fruit to 225 g/8 oz concentrated apple juice weighed in a polythene container. You cook the fruit in just enough water to prevent sticking (soft fruits such as raspberries and strawberries can be puréed in a blender or food processor and heated gently without water), then add the apple juice concentrate and boil until a set is reached. Make this jam in small quantities and store in the refrigerator.

Apple Juice Concentrate

Concentrated apple juice can be bought at health shops. As well as its use in preserves, and, well diluted, as a drink, concentrated apple juice makes a healthy sugar replacement in cakes, puddings and other sweet treats.

V SUGAR-FREE V
MIXED BERRY JAM

Although this delicious, fruity jam should be made in small quantities and kept in the refrigerator, it can be made from frozen berries throughout the year.

MAKES 700 g/1½ lb

225 g/8 oz strawberries, hulled
225 g/8 oz blackberries
225 g/8 oz gooseberries, topped and tailed
225 g/8 oz apple juice concentrate, weighed in a polythene container

1 Wash the berries, then purée half of them in a blender or food processor and place in a large saucepan with the rest of the fruit.
2 Simmer gently until the fruit is cooked.
3 Add the apple juice concentrate and boil for 15 minutes, then test for a set (p. 339). If this is not achieved, continue to boil, testing frequently, until setting point.
4 Remove from the heat and cool slightly, then pour into warmed, sterilized jars (p. 338). Cover, seal and label when cold.
5 Store in a cool place for up to 4 weeks, or in the refrigerator.

V V CRAB APPLE V
JELLY

A delightful, sharp-tasting jelly, good with nut roasts.

MAKES 900 g–1.4 kg/2–3 lb

1.8 kg/4 lb crab apples
1.2 litres/2 pints water
1.8–2.25 kg/4–5 lb sugar

1 Wash the fruit, then cut away any damaged parts, and cut any large fruits into halves or quarters, so that they are all about the same size.
2 Put the crab apples into a saucepan with the water and boil gently until the fruit is soft and pulpy.
3 Have ready a large nylon sieve lined with some muslin or chemist's gauze and set over a large bowl.
4 Tip the apple mixture into the sieve and leave overnight to drip through.
5 Measure the liquid and put it into a saucepan with 450 g/1 lb sugar for every 600 ml/1 pint.
6 Heat gently, stirring, until the sugar has dissolved, then bring to the boil.
7 Boil for 10–15 minutes. Test for a set (p. 339) and when this point is reached, remove from the heat and pour into warmed, sterilized jars (p. 338). Cover, seal and label when cold.

Pectin Content of Fruits and Vegetables

*high in acid

High	Medium	Low
*Cooking and crab apples	Under-ripe apricots	Cherries
*Cranberries	*Bilberries	Elderberries
*Currants, black, red and white	Blackberries	Japonica
*Damsons	*Greengages	Marrows
*Gooseberries (should be under-ripe)	*Loganberries	Medlars
*Grapefruit	*Mulberries	Peaches (dried ones are best)
*Lemons	Nectarines	
*Limes		
*Oranges		
Plums, if under-ripe,* especially yellow ones	Ripe plums	
	*Under-ripe raspberries	Rhubarb
Quinces	*Sloes	Under-ripe strawberries

LEMON CURD

Tangy and delicious, and very easy to make.

MAKES 450 g/1 lb

75 g/3 oz butter
grated rind and juice of 2 large, well-scrubbed lemons
225 g/8 oz caster sugar
3 eggs, beaten

1 Put all the ingredients into the top of a double saucepan or a heatproof bowl set over a saucepan of boiling water, making sure the base of the bowl does not touch the water.
2 Stir until the sugar has dissolved, then continue to cook gently for about 20 minutes, stirring often, until the curd thickens.
3 Strain into jars. Cover, seal and label when cold, then store in a cool, dry place.

V   MARY'S   V
MARMALADE

This recipe, which was given to me by a friend who is an expert marmalade-maker, makes a light marmalade with a tangy flavour. It's easy to make with a blender or food processor.

MAKES ABOUT 4.5 kg/10 lb

12 Seville oranges
1 sweet orange
2 small lemons
2 litres/3½ pints water
2.25 kg/5 lb sugar
a knob of butter

1 Scrub the oranges and lemons well, then quarter them and remove the pips.
2 Put the pips into a piece of muslin and tie loosely with string.
3 Purée the oranges and lemons with the water in a blender or food processor. Put into a bowl with the bag of pips; leave overnight.

4 Next day, transfer mixture to a pan and simmer, uncovered, for 2 hours.
5 Put the puréed orange and lemon mixture into a large saucepan or preserving pan, strain in the pip liquid and bring to the boil. Add the sugar and cook, stirring often, until setting point is reached (p. 339).
6 Remove from the heat and stir in the butter. Cool slightly, then pour into warmed, sterilized jars (p. 338). Cover, seal and label when cold.

V   PRESSURE   V
COOKER
MARMALADE

Pressure cooking cuts out messy preparation.

MAKES 3.1 kg/7 lb

12 Seville oranges
2 lemons
2.7 litres/4½ pints cold water
2.7–3.1 kg/6–7 lb sugar
a knob of butter

1 Scrub the oranges and lemons, then put them into a pressure cooker with 1.2 litres/2 pints of the water. Cook at 6.75 kg/15 lb pressure for 25 minutes, or until the oranges are completely soft.
2 Drain juice into a non-metal bowl.
3 When the fruit is cool enough to handle, scoop the insides of the fruit away from the skin, using a teaspoon.
4 Sieve the pulp and add the purée to the bowl of juice.
5 Cut the peel into shreds and add this to the bowl, with the remaining water. Cover and leave overnight.
6 Next day, measure the mixture into a preserving pan. Bring to boil, then add 450 g/1 lb sugar for every 600 ml/1 pint.
7 Heat gently until the sugar has dissolved, then bring to the boil and boil until setting point is reached (p. 339).
8 Remove from heat and stir in butter. Leave to settle for 15 minutes, then pour into warmed, sterilized jars (p. 338). Cover, seal and label when cold.

Potting Jam

Put circles of waxed paper on top of the jam immediately you pour it into the jars, when it is still very hot, or wait until it is completely cold. Putting the circles on warm jam may cause condensation and encourage mould.

Making Reduced-sugar Jams and Jellies

The sugar in standard recipes can be reduced by 20 per cent without affecting the set. This jam will not keep for more than about a month in a cool place, or 6–8 weeks in a refrigerator.

A few sprigs of sweet cicely cooked with acid fruit counteracts the sharpness so that less sugar is needed.

Sugar-free Marmalade

Use 450 ml/15 fl oz freshly squeezed orange juice (ready-squeezed orange juice is not suitable) and the thinly pared rind of 1 orange and 1 lemon, well scrubbed. Make as for Sugar-free Mixed Berry Jam (p. 340), boiling the mixture until the rind is soft before adding the apple juice concentrate.

Pectin

Pectin is a carbohydrate found in the cell walls of plants. It is important for the setting of jams and jellies. The pectin content of fruits varies (p. 340). Pectin can be bought and is useful for making preserves from ingredients with a low pectin content, such as rose petals, in Rose Petal Jam (p. 338). It is widely available in liquid form from supermarkets.

SWEET SPICED APRICOT CHUTNEY

This is a sweet, spicy chutney, rather like mango chutney. It can be made with peaches or plums instead of apricots.

MAKES 1.8–2 kg/4–4½ lb

1.8 kg/4 lb fresh apricots or 700 g/1½ lb dried apricots, soaked in water overnight, then drained
2 small cooking apples, peeled, cored and chopped
100 g/4 oz raisins
600 ml/1 pint distilled vinegar
350 g/12 oz granulated or demerara sugar
1 tablespoon ground ginger
3 garlic cloves, crushed
1 teaspoon freshly grated nutmeg
¼ teaspoon cayenne pepper
1 teaspoon salt

1 Put all the ingredients into a large saucepan or preserving pan.
2 Bring to the boil, then cook gently, uncovered, stirring occasionally, for about 1½ hours, until the mixture is thick and no excess liquid appears when it is parted with the spoon.
3 Spoon the mixture into warmed, sterilized jars (p. 338) and cover immediately with airtight, vinegar-proof tops. Label when cold. Store in a cool, dry place.

APPLE CHUTNEY

An easy chutney to make, with a deliciously spicy flavour.

MAKES ABOUT 2.7 kg/6 lb

1.4 kg/3 lb cooking apples, peeled, cored and diced
1.4 kg/3 lb onions, peeled and chopped
450 g/1 lb sultanas
700 g/1½ lb soft dark brown sugar
600 ml/1 pint malt vinegar
25 g/1 oz ground ginger
25 g/1 oz salt
½ teaspoon cayenne pepper

Basic Chutney-making

To make chutney, you cook together a mixture of chopped fruits and vegetables, including onions and dried fruit such as raisins or chopped dates, with vinegar, sugar and spices. The chutney should be simmered gently, uncovered, for 1–3 hours, until nearly all the vinegar has disappeared and when you part the mixture with a spoon the channel does not immediately fill with liquid. The chutney will thicken up more as it cools.

The covers for chutney and pickles are important as the vinegar may corrode metal, and will evaporate through paper coverings. So use plastic caps or synthetic covering material, or line metal covers with vinegar-proof paper.

Pieces cut from a wide (10 cm/4 inch) bandage, or some surgical gauze, from the chemist, can be used for tying up the pickling spices. Secure with string then loop this round the handle of the pan, for easy removal.

Chutneys vary a good deal in spiciness, fruitiness and the balance of sweet and sour. So it's a good idea to make up a new recipe in a small quantity, to try. But remember most chutneys, pickles and relishes need at least 6–8 weeks to mature before you can judge their true flavour.

1 Put all the ingredients into a preserving pan and bring to the boil.
2 Reduce the heat and simmer gently, uncovered, for about 1½–2 hours, stirring occasionally, until the mixture is very thick and no excess liquid appears when it is parted with a wooden spoon.
3 Spoon the mixture into warmed, sterilized jars (p. 338) and cover immediately with airtight covers (snap-on plastic covers are ideal – avoid metal which the vinegar may corrode). Label when cold.
4 This chutney improves with keeping, stored in a cool, dry place.

BREAD AND BUTTER PICKLES

Delicious on bread and butter, and very easy to make.

MAKES ABOUT 1.8 kg/4 lb

900 g/2 lb cucumber, washed and sliced
2 large onions, peeled and sliced
1 large green pepper, de-seeded and chopped
50 g/2 oz salt
450 ml/15 fl oz white wine vinegar or cider vinegar
350 g/12 oz soft light brown sugar
½ teaspoon ground turmeric
½ teaspoon ground cloves
2 teaspoons mustard seed
½ teaspoon celery seed

1 Put the cucumber into a bowl with the onion and pepper. Sprinkle with the salt, mix well, and leave for at least 3 hours.
2 Rinse the vegetables thoroughly under the cold tap. Drain well and put into a large saucepan with the vinegar.
3 Bring to the boil and simmer for about 20 minutes until vegetables are tender.
4 Add the sugar and spices to the pan and heat gently until the sugar has dissolved.
5 Bring to the boil, then remove from the heat, pour into a bowl, cover and leave until cold.
6 Spoon the mixture into warmed, sterilized jars (p. 338) and immediately cover with airtight, vinegar-proof tops. Label when cold and store in a cool, dry place.

V PRESERVED V
KUMQUATS

This is an attractive way to use baby kumquat oranges. They are delicious spooned over ice cream, or served as they are, chilled, with some whipped cream and a scattering of almonds. Packed into pretty jars, they make good presents, and keep well for up to 6 months.

MAKES 2 × 600-ml/1-pint JARS

700 g / 1½ lb kumquats
450 g / 1 lb granulated sugar
600 ml / 1 pint water
6 tablespoons brandy

1 Scrub the kumquats, then prick them all over with a fine skewer.
2 Put the sugar and water into a saucepan and heat gently until the sugar has dissolved, then bring to the boil.
3 Add the kumquats, cover and cook gently for about 15 minutes, or until they are very tender and almost transparent.
4 Using a slotted spoon, take the kumquats out of the syrup and place in warmed, sterilized jars (p. 338).
5 Add the brandy, then pour in enough of the cooking syrup to cover the kumquats. Cover, seal and label when cold, then store in a cool, dry place.

V SPICED ORANGE V
SLICES

These spicy orange slices are good with cold nut or lentil roasts.

MAKES ABOUT 4.5 kg/10 lb

12 thin-skinned oranges
1.1 kg / 2½ lb soft light brown sugar
600 ml / 1 pint white wine vinegar or cider vinegar
12 whole cloves
5 cm / 4 inches cinnamon stick
½ teaspoon ground mace or 6–8 mace blades

1 Scrub and dry the oranges. Slice them about 3 mm / ⅛ inch thick; remove the pips.
2 Put the orange slices into a large saucepan and cover with cold water. Bring to the boil and simmer gently, covered, until the orange skin is just tender – about 20–30 minutes.
3 Put the remaining ingredients into another large saucepan and heat gently until the sugar has dissolved, then boil for 3 minutes.
4 Using a slotted spoon, remove the orange slices from the pan and add to the vinegar mixture.
5 Add enough of the orange cooking liquid to cover the orange slices, then simmer them gently until tender but not disintegrated – 35–45 minutes.
6 Remove from the heat and leave the oranges in the syrup for 24 hours.
7 Remove the orange slices with a slotted spoon and place in warmed, sterilized jars (p. 338), filling them no more than half full.
8 Bring the syrup to boiling point, then boil for a few minutes to reduce slightly.
9 Cool for 15 minutes, then pour the syrup into the jars, filling them to the top. Cover immediately with airtight, vinegar-proof tops. Label the jars when cold. Store them in a cool, dry place for 4 weeks before using.

Left to right: Preserved Kumquats; Bread and Butter Pickles (p. 342); Sweet Spiced Apricot Chutney (p. 342); Spiced Orange Slices

Spiced Vinegar

This is used for some chutneys and pickles. Tie 15 g / ½ oz each of blade mace, cinnamon stick, allspice and cloves, and a few peppercorns, in a piece of muslin. Put into a saucepan with 2.4 litres / 4 pints vinegar and 1 tablespoon salt. Bring to the boil, then cover and simmer for 5 minutes. Strain and use immediately, or cool, bottle and store. For sweet pickles, add sugar to the vinegar, allowing 450 g / 1 lb to 600 ml / 1 pint, and add a few strips of lemon rind. For pickled pears poach 900 g / 2 lb peeled cooking pears (whole if small, halved or quartered if larger) in spiced vinegar with 450 g / 1 lb soft brown sugar, for 30–40 minutes. Bottle and keep for 6 weeks before using.

Sweets

Making sweets is frivolous but fun, and, as with puddings, I'm all for the occasional indulgence. The sweets in this section are the ones I find most popular and easy to make, without the need for any special equipment. Home-made sweets make a delightful treat; they can be served as petits fours at the end of a meal and they also make attractive gifts and bazaar items. If you're giving them away, it's worth making them look extra good, in bonbon cases, jars and pretty boxes, or in cones made of coloured light-weight card or twists of coloured cellophane, with decorations of hearts, flowers and ribbons. . . .

Healthy Sweet Ideas for Children

Dried fruits make natural sweets; add a mixture of sun-dried raisins, dates and apricots in a twist of clingfilm to a child's lunch box. For children over 6, replace the stone in dates with a whole almond or small brazil nut. For younger children, replace the stone with a paste of ground almonds and honey.

Coat peeled banana chunks first in clear honey, then in carob powder and chopped nuts. Freeze until firm. Eat as frozen sweets, or insert sticks before freezing and eat as lollies.

Cleaning a Toffee Pan

To clean a sticky toffee pan, fill the pan with water and bring to the boil. The toffee will melt and can be poured away with the water.

Sweets for Gifts

Home-made sweets make delightful gifts, but presentation makes all the difference. Pack sweets or biscuits in pretty jars, small baskets lined with a doily and covered with clingfilm, pretty boxes you've saved, a twist of scrunchy cellophane. Decorate with coloured ribbon, small fabric flowers, coloured labels.

V FRUIT SNACK BITES

A healthy sweet that contains no added sugar. In my experience children like these as long as they don't have them too often!

MAKES 64

350 g/12 oz mixed dried fruit, such as dates, apricots, peaches and raisins
100 g/4 oz brazil nuts
100 g/4 oz desiccated coconut (unsweetened)
grated rind of 1 orange or lemon
1–2 tablespoons fresh orange juice
a little extra desiccated coconut for coating

1 Put the dried fruit and brazil nuts into a food processor and whizz until finely chopped. Or chop the dried fruits very finely by hand, grind the nuts and mix together.
2 Add the 100 g/4 oz desiccated coconut, grated citrus rind and enough orange juice to make the mixture stick together, and process again, or mix the ingredients very well by hand.
3 Put the desiccated coconut into a shallow bowl Roll the dried fruit mixture into small balls and toss in the coconut until they are thoroughly coated.
4 Place on trays and chill the fruit snack bites in the fridge for 1–2 hours, until they have firmed up.

V V CAROB, CASHEW V AND HONEY SWEETS

Another healthy sweet that children like in moderation. These sweets are rich and nourishing: a little goes a long way.

MAKES 21 PIECES

100 g/4 oz cashew nuts
1 tablespoon carob powder
a few drops of vanilla extract
1 tablespoon thick honey

1 Put the cashew nuts, carob and vanilla into a food processor and whizz to a powder. Or grind the nuts finely, then put into a bowl with the carob and vanilla.
2 Add the honey and process the mixture again (or mix by hand) until it forms a stiff paste.
3 Put the mixture into a 20-cm/8-inch square tin and press it out so that it is 1 cm/½ inch thick (it will fill only about a third of the tin).
4 Chill in the refrigerator until firm, then cut into squares.

Variation
CAROB, BRAZIL NUT AND HONEY SWEETS

Use brazil nuts instead of the cashew nuts, if preferred, and make the sweets as described above.

V TREACLE TOFFEE V

MAKES ABOUT 600 g/1¼ lb

175 g/6 oz demerara sugar
75 g/3 oz butter or vegan margarine
250 g/9 oz treacle
3 tablespoons water
¼ teaspoon cream of tartar
extra butter for greasing

1 Grease a 20-cm/8-inch square tin, then line with non-stick baking parchment.
2 Put the sugar, butter or vegan margarine, treacle and water into a heavy-based saucepan. Heat gently until the sugar has dissolved, then bring to the boil, remove from the heat and add the cream of tartar.
3 Return the pan to the heat and boil until the mixture reaches 119–122 C/ 246–252 F, the hard ball stage (see right), stirring from time to time.
4 Pour the mixture into the prepared tin. Leave until nearly set, then mark into squares.
5 When the toffee is completely cold and set, turn it out of the tin and break into squares.

CHOCOLATE RUM TRUFFLES

MAKES 36

225 g/8 oz plain chocolate
300 ml/10 fl oz double cream
2 tablespoons rum
cocoa powder for coating

1 Break the chocolate into pieces and put into a heavy-based saucepan with the cream.
2 Heat very gently until the chocolate has melted, then remove from the heat, transfer to a bowl and cool.
3 Add the rum, then beat until pale and thick. Chill in the refrigerator until firm enough to handle.
4 Sprinkle some cocoa on a plate, then put heaped teaspoons of the mixture on to this and sprinkle with more cocoa.

5 Roll each piece of mixture in cocoa, to make a truffle, and place in a bonbon case or on a small serving dish.
6 Chill until ready to serve.

CREAMY FUDGE

I've tried many fudge recipes, and this one I always find the best.

MAKES ABOUT 1 kg/2¼ lb

100 g/4 oz butter
1 × 425-g/15-oz can condensed milk
450 g/1 lb caster sugar

1 Line a 20-cm/8-inch square tin with non-stick baking parchment.
2 Put the butter, milk and sugar into a large, heavy-based saucepan.
3 Heat gently, stirring, over a low heat, until the sugar has dissolved.
4 Raise the heat and boil for 5 minutes, stirring all the time, until the mixture starts to come away from the sides of the pan.
5 Pour the mixture into the tin. Leave to cool at room temperature.
6 Just before the fudge is cold, mark the fudge into squares. Cut into squares with a sharp knife when it is completely cold.

Sugar Boiling Stages

A cooking thermometer is useful for sweet-making, but not essential, because the mixture behaves quite distinctively at different temperatures:

Thread (120 C/225 F): a little of the mixture forms a short thread when placed between finger and thumb and pulled apart

Soft ball (135 C/240 F): a little of the syrup put into a cup of cold water forms a small soft ball

Hard ball (140 C/255 F): a little of the mixture forms a hard ball when dropped into a cup of cold water

Crack (150 C/280 F): a drop of the syrup put into cold water becomes brittle

Caramel (160 C/312 F): the syrup turns a dark brown colour

When testing the sugar syrup, remove it from the heat to prevent further cooking.

Creamy Fudge; Fruit Snack Bites (p. 344); Chocolate Rum Truffles; Carob, Cashew and Honey Sweets (p. 344)

Index